Trees and Shrubs of the Trans-Pecos and Adjacent Areas

Trees and Shrubs of the Trans-Pecos and Adjacent Areas

A. MICHAEL POWELL

Mike Powell

University of Texas Press
AUSTIN

Second University of Texas Press paperback printing, 2004

Requests for permission to reproduce material from this work should be sent to
Permissions, University of Texas Press, Box 7819, Austin, TX 78713-7819.

♾The paper used in this publication meets the minimum requirements of
American National Standard for Information Sciences
Permanence of Paper for Printed Library Materials, ANSI Z39.48-1984.

Library of Congress Cataloging-in-Publication Data

Powell, A. Michael.
    Trees and shrubs of the Trans-Pecos and adjacent areas / A. Michael Powell.—
  1st University of Texas Press ed.
       p.   cm.
    Includes bibliographical references (p.   ) and index.
     ISBN 978-0-292-76573-3
      1. Trees—Texas—Identification.   2. Shrubs—Texas—Identification.
    3. Trees—Trans-Pecos (Tex. and N.M.)—Identification.   4. Shrubs—Trans-
  Pecos (Tex. and N.M.)—Identification.   I. Title.
  QK188.P72   1998
  582.16'09764'9—dc21   97-13155

To my parents, Welma and Everett

Contents

Preface to the
Revised Edition

T his revised edition of *Trees and Shrubs of Trans-Pecos Texas*, now titled *Trees and Shrubs of the Trans-Pecos and Adjacent Areas*, represents a significant revision of the first edition published in 1988. It includes taxonomic or nomenclatural changes in 62 (about 30%) of the genera treated in the book, and it also includes new distributional or taxonomic information in 60 (about 29%) of the genera. The taxonomic arrangements and nomenclature in *A Synonymized Checklist of the Vascular Flora of the United States, Canada, and Greenland*, 2d ed. (1994), by John T. Kartesz, were followed consistently, but not exclusively, in making changes at the family, genus, species, and subspecies levels. Information from pertinent taxonomic revisions published since the Kartesz work also has been included in the second edition of *Trees and Shrubs*. In addition, there are relevant changes in keys to the genera and species.

The key to the families has been changed very little even though it was adapted from a much-maligned key to the families in the *Manual of the Vascular Plants of Texas* (1970) by D. S. Correll and M. C. Johnston. For those who will use the family key, I believe that it will work well for *Trees and Shrubs*. There is a change in the preferred use in the names of certain families treated in the revision: Fabaceae (Leguminosae); Buddlejaceae (Loganiaceae); Lamiaceae (Labiatae); Grossulariaceae and Hydrangeaceae (Saxifragaceae); Capparaceae (Koeberliniaceae); and Brassicaceae (Cruciferae). There are numerous name changes at the genus level. The blackberry or dewberry genus *Rubus* has been added to the woody flora of the Trans-Pecos, with possibly as many as three species that still require additional taxonomic evaluation.

The first edition of *Trees and Shrubs* was subtitled *Including Big Bend and Guadalupe Mountains National Parks*, and was published by the Big Bend Natural History Association (BBNHA). The BBNHA has a background of supporting, promoting, and even publishing works that are relevant to the natural history of Big Bend National Park and the Big Bend region of Trans-Pecos Texas. The acknowledgments section, virtually unchanged from the first edition, reveals my continuing gratitude to BBNHA for publishing *Trees and Shrubs*. Now that all copies of the original printing have been sold, I am once again grateful to BBNHA, this time for initiating dialogue with the University of Texas Press regarding a second printing or revised edition; I am also grateful to Shannon Davies of the University of Texas Press for encouraging a revision of *Trees and Shrubs* that was "as thorough as necessary," rather than a simple second printing. As a matter of some personal redemption, as the author and sole editor of the first edition, I have been waiting meekly for an opportunity to correct errors that should have been removed in page proofs of the first edition.

ABOUT THE REGION

Trans-Pecos Texas is the only part of the state where mountain and desert habitats are found. The region is characterized by diverse vegetation and there are many plant species in the Trans-Pecos that are not found elsewhere in the state. Along with grasses, woody plants are prominent in the vegetation of Trans-Pecos Texas. The major mountain ranges are dominated by woodland vegetation comprised mostly of small trees. The Chihuahuan Desert habitats at lower elevations and in arid mountains are characterized by shrubs. Even the expansive grasslands of mountain basins and plateaus are surrounded by and subject to invasion by shrubs.

ABOUT THE TEXT AND FORMAT

In *Trees and Shrubs* an attempt was made to include all of the native and naturalized woody plant species that are known to occur in the Trans-Pecos region, and some introduced woody species. Also included are the larger semisucculent plants such as yuccas and agaves, many in-between species with woody basal stems and herbaceous tops, and even "miniature shrubs," perhaps less than 10 cm high, exemplified by the rock-dwelling species of *Perityle* and *Polygala*.

Trees and Shrubs was originally designed to be usable by non-scientists as well as scientists in identifying the woody plant species of the region concerned. Reviews of the first edition and personal feedback from individuals who have used it suggest that this somewhat elusive objective was substantially realized. Plant species identification aids include rather non-technical keys and descriptions that can be used along with illustrations and photographs. Distributional information is presented for each species, including specific localities for most taxa. Most of the locality data were obtained from extensive collections housed in the herbarium at Sul Ross State University. The uses of certain woody plant species to humans and their value to other animals are considered.

The *Manual of the Vascular Plants of Texas* (1970) by D. S. Correll and M. C. Johnston influenced and facilitated the first edition of *Trees and Shrubs*, which was designed to be used along with the *Manual*, the only complete flora of Texas. The original format is retained in this revision. The *Manual*, still available in reprint, remains an invaluable taxonomic resource, although various workers are now involved in updating and revising the flora of Texas. Some keys and descriptions in *Trees and Shrubs* are adapted from the *Manual*. The vegetational areas of Texas (referred to in distributions), the arrangements of families, and most of the abbreviations of geographic names follow those of the *Manual*. The authors of taxa and the abbreviations of authors' names follow those in the Kartesz *Synonymized Checklist*. Geographic directions (N, E, S, W) are in caps and capitalized abbreviations for states are those of the U.S. Postal Service. The selected glossary is intended to be helpful in using the simplified descriptions and keys to classes, families, genera, and species. Descriptions of species have been omitted, since the essence of this type of information leading to the identification of species can be inferred from key characters, illustrations, distributions, and comparative traits discussed with the species. For genera with only one species treated, the description may characterize both the genus and species. The common names follow those in the USDA-SCS standardized list (November 1974), those in the *Manual*, and those from various other sources. Complete synonymy is not included, but the partial list of synonyms, taken largely from the Kartesz *Synonymized Checklist*, should be useful in recognizing recent name changes.

Metric system measurements are used in keys and descriptions. The millimeter units are more accurate in smaller scale measurements, and rulers in millimeter and centimeter units are readily available. The English system is used for elevations and distances because those measurements are most easily followed by a majority of southwesterners and because maps and road signs usually have elevations and distances in feet and miles.

Trees and Shrubs may be useful to visitors who observe the woody plants of the national parks, state parks, state lands, wildlife managements areas, and other accessible sites in or near Trans-Pecos Texas. Some of the following areas are accessible only by organized tour or permit. Plant collecting on federal and state land is prohibited without a specific permit. The following list is arranged geographically by county from west to east:

National Parks and Historic Sites.
Culberson Co.: Guadalupe Mountains. *Jeff Davis Co.*: Fort Davis National Historic Site. *Brewster Co.*: Big Bend.

State Parks.
El Paso Co.: Franklin Mountains; Hueco Tanks. *Presidio Co.:* Fort Leaton; Big Bend Ranch. *Jeff Davis Co.:* Davis Mountains/Indian Lodge. *Reeves Co.:* Balmorhea. *Ward Co.:* Monahans Sand Hills. *Val Verde Co.:* Seminole Canyon; Devils River. *Crockett Co.:* Fort Lancaster.

State Wildlife Management Areas.
Hudspeth Co.: Sierra Diablo. *Presidio Co.:* Ocotillo Unit of La Paloma. *Brewster Co.:* Elephant Mountain; Black Gap.

Acknowledgments

I am grateful to several individuals who contributed taxonomic and other information to the text: Robert P. Adams provided the treatment of *Juniperus*; William R. Anderson supplied direction about the Malpighiaceae; Dana K. Bailey kindly offered much information about *Pinus*; Meredith Lane contributed the treatments of *Gutierrezia* and *Gymnosperma*; C. H. Muller generously revised and edited the treatment of *Quercus*; Del Weins helped with the mistletoes (*Phoradendron*); Richard D. Worthington provided much information particularly about the plants of El Paso County; Neville Haynes verified the localities of *Pistacia texana*; Allan Zimmerman helped with the identification of some *Opuntia* taxa.

Special appreciation is extended to Marshall C. Johnston and Jim Henrickson who reviewed the manuscript for the first edition. I am grateful to these outstanding floristic botanists for allowing the use of much unpublished taxonomic information prepared for the *Chihuahuan Desert Flora*. Jim Henrickson also was most generous in offering the use of the line drawings included here even before he was ready to use them in his own floristic works for which they were prepared.

Personal gratitude is extended to James F. Scudday who patiently shared his knowledge with me during the past 22 years we have been colleagues at Sul Ross State University. Professor Scudday has studied and enjoyed the Trans-Pecos for over 40 years and is perhaps the person who is best informed about the biology of the entire region.

Helpful cooperation and services were provided by others including Bonnie M. Pattillo, Carol Sigmund-Ross, and Rena Gallego who typed and assisted in editing the manuscript during its final stages. Karen Green Bennack typed most of the manuscript in its early stages. I am grateful to Emily J. Lott and Julia O. Larke whose editing expertise and botanical knowledge were graciously lent to this "bush book." Shirley Ridout Powell, my wife, also helped with typing and has been my constant and supportive field companion during many years of hiking in the mountains and desert.

The information about State and National champion trees in Big Bend National Park was provided by James E. Liles, former Chief Ranger at the Park. Since 1940 The American Forestry Association has been recording National champion trees. The big trees are listed in the "Register of Big Trees" in the journal *American Forests*, with their champion status based upon points derived from height, crown spread, and circumference of the trunk. Jim Liles searched for and recorded the 11 National champion or cochampion trees listed for Big Bend National Park in the November, 1984 issue (vol. 90) of *American Forests*. In the Park Jim has also found several trees that are regarded as State champions.

Members of the Board of Directors of the Big Bend Natural History Association (BBNHA) believed in the potential of my unpublished manuscript, and they recommended support for its publication. I am deeply grateful for their sponsorship, and I particularly thank John Pearson of the BBNHA for his professional and friendly management of affairs dealing with the publication of this work.

Much of the locality data would not have been available without the extensive collections (in the Sul Ross Herbarium) by Barton H. Warnock. A collective but special thanks is offered to the many ranchers who allowed access to their properties for the purpose of studying and collecting woody plants. Harry Gordon, Sammy Marshall, and Alan Brenner provided assistance with certain photographs. Leo Ofenstein expedited publication by giving his time and computer expertise. The illustrations are mostly those of Bobbi Angell; some illustrations are by Julia Larke, Felicia Bond, and Francis Runyon. My lasting appreciation goes to Professor B. L. Turner for being my major advisor and for consistently recharging my enthusiasm.

Permission to use certain illustrations has been provided by the following botanical journals: *Aniscanthus puberulus* and *A. linearis* by *Brittonia* (34: 173; 1982); *Carlowrightia texana*, *C. torreyana*, and *C. mexicana* by *Madroño* (26: 28–29; 1979); *Leucophyllum frutescens*, *L. minus*, and *L. candidum* by *Sida* (11: 135, 151; 1985).

Those I wish to acknowledge for contributions made to the revision are: Roger Corzine, who edited the printed first edition; Linda Hedges and Lee Greer, who helped in securing taxonomic literature; Linda also tracked down information about high temperatures in Presidio, Texas, with the help of Rod Trevizo and John Lee; Sharon Yarborough, my colleague in the herbarium, whose review of the Trans-Pecos species of *Philadelphus* helped to improve the revised treatment of that genus; and Richard D. Worthington, who has been generous in sharing the results of his floristic work, mostly in El Paso County, but also elsewhere in the Trans-Pecos. Some of his locality records are included in the text without specific citation of the sources of documentation, which were as follows: *An Annotated Checklist of the Native and Naturalized Flora of*

El Paso County, Texas (1989), R. D. Worthington; *Biota of the Franklin Mountains, Part II, Flora* (1995), R. D. Worthington (a report to Texas Parks and Wildlife Department); and *Comments on Plant Species Added to the Flora of Texas from El Paso County with More Additions* (unpublished manuscript), R. D. Worthington.

Trees and Shrubs of the Trans-Pecos and Adjacent Areas

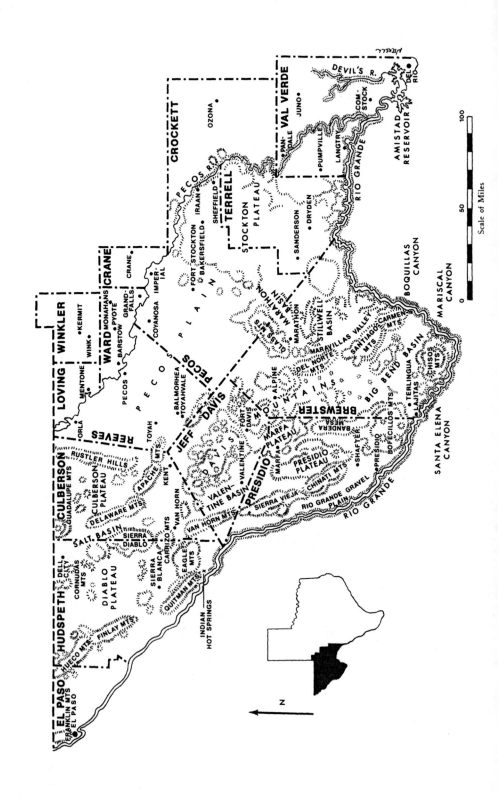

Scale of Miles

100

50

0

Introduction

Trans-Pecos Texas is the region of the Pecos River in the extreme western part of the state (Fig. 1). New Mexico borders to the north and the Rio Grande separates Texas from Mexico to the south. There are nine relatively large counties (El Paso, Hudspeth, Culberson, Reeves, Jeff Davis, Presidio, Brewster, Pecos, and Terrell) completely within the Trans-Pecos. Brewster County is larger than the state of Connecticut. Val Verde County to the southeast is partially in the region. Counties bordering the Pecos River to the east (Loving, Winkler, Ward, Crane, Upton, and Crockett), adjacent southern New Mexico, and adjacent Mexico are considered to be associated with the Trans-Pecos in this floristic account of woody plants. There are about 20,500,000 acres, about 32,000 square miles, in the Trans-Pecos, an area roughly equal to the state of Maine (Schmidly, 1977).

Most of the Trans-Pecos is under private ownership in the form of relatively large ranches. Cattle ranching is emphasized in most areas, particularly where there are abundant desert grasslands. Sheep and goats are still favored on a few ranches, located mostly on the Stockton Plateau, but in most areas predators and poisonous weeds have forced ranchers to stop raising these animals. There are few cultivated areas, these being centered around El Paso, Valentine, Van Horn, Pecos, Balmorhea, Presidio, and Fort Stockton. These all depend upon irrigation water either from wells or a diminishing river flow. In 1979 a vast new farming area was plowed in the grassland near Valentine, where irrigation water is supplied from deep wells. There are two national parks, Guadalupe Mountains National Park in northern Culberson County, and Big Bend National Park in southern Brewster County.

PHYSIOGRAPHY AND CLIMATE

Most of the Trans-Pecos is physiographically diverse and different from the rest of Texas mainly because of the numerous mountain systems and low, arid basins (Fig. 1). The lowest elevation in the Trans-Pecos is about 1,000 ft. at the mouth of the Pecos River. Elevations increase steadily up the Rio Grande to 1,360 ft. at the mouth of San Francisco Canyon on the Brewster-Terrell county line, 1,650 ft. at Reagan Canyon, and about 1,800 ft. at the head of Boquillas Canyon. The highest elevation in the Trans-Pecos is 8,749 ft. at Guadalupe Peak. Elevations of other peaks in the Guadalupe Mountains include the following: Bush (8,631 ft.), Shumard (8,615 ft.), Bartlett (8,508 ft.), Hunter (8,368 ft.), and El Capitan (8,085 ft.). Other major peaks in the Trans-Pecos include Mt. Livermore (8,382 ft.) in the Davis Mountains, Emory Peak (7,835 ft.) in the Chisos Mountains, and Chinati Peak (7,730 ft.) in the Chinati Mountains. In all there are 90 peaks that are a mile or more above sea level. The elevations of some major towns are: El Paso, 3,762 ft.; Sierra Blanca, 4,512 ft.; Van Horn, 4,010 ft.; Pecos, 2,580 ft.; Fort Davis, 5,000 ft.; Marfa, 4,688 ft.; Alpine, 4,481 ft.; Presidio, 2,594 ft.; Fort Stockton, 3,050 ft.; Sanderson, 2,775 ft.

The mountains are composed of either igneous or sedimentary (mostly limestones) substrates and in some formations both substrates are present. In El Paso County the Franklin Mountains are predominantly limestone. In Hudspeth County the Hueco and southern Quitman Mountains and Sierra Diablo are limestone, while the Northern Quitman and Eagle mountains are composed of igneous rocks. In Culberson County the Guadalupe, Delaware, and Apache mountains are limestone. The Van Horn Mountains are composed of igneous rocks as are the Davis Mountains that dominate Jeff Davis County and northern Brewster County. Igneous mountains, the Sierra Vieja, Chinati, and Bofecillos, also dominate Presidio County. In Brewster County, the Glass, Del Norte, Santiago, and Dead Horse mountains are limestone, while the magnificent Chisos Mountains are of igneous origin. The Edwards Plateau of central Texas extends west across the Pecos River in Terrell County and parts of Pecos, Brewster, and Val Verde counties where it is also known as the Stockton Plateau. The Stockton Plateau is a highly dissected array of limestone-capped mesas and deep canyons at about 2,000–3,200 ft. that extend north to Ft. Stockton and west to the Glass Mountains and Marathon Basin. Erosional outwash materials have in some areas accumulated to form high basins between the mountains. Alluvial fans or bajadas (alluvial slopes formed by rushing water) are deposited characteristically at the bases of desert mountains. In overall profile the Trans-Pecos can be pictured as extensive lower elevation flats, slopes, dunes, basins, hills, and ridges surrounding the higher, islandlike mountains, plateaus, and basins.

The soils are variable in texture and profile. In general the soils are basic. Salt lakes and alkali flats in poorly drained areas are located throughout the region, most conspicuously in northern Hudspeth and Culberson counties and near the Pecos River in Reeves and Pecos counties. Extensive or localized gypsum substrates are scattered throughout the region, perhaps best exemplified by gypsum plains of the Castile Formation south of the Guadalupe Mountains in northern Culberson and Reeves counties. Deep clay, sand, and gravel deposits predominate in certain areas.

The general climate of the Trans-Pecos may be characterized as arid. It is cool and dry during the winter and hot and dry during the summer. The average annual precipitation is about 12 in. with most of the rainfall coming in the form of thundershowers in July, August, and early September. Annual precipitation generally decreases from east to west and increases with elevation. El Paso annually records less than 8 in. of precipitation while Presidio averages 8.5 in., Alpine 15.5 in., and up to about 20 in. are usual in the higher elevations. In Big Bend National Park annual records furnished by Jim Liles show less than 10 in. at Rio Grande Village (1,850 ft.), about 13 in. at Panther Junction (3,800 ft.), and almost 19 in. in the Chisos Basin (5,400 ft.). Average midsummer high temperatures range from about 85 to 95°F, depending largely upon elevation, to 100°F in Presidio, where the highest official temperature is 122°F (125°F reported). Average mid-winter low temperatures are from 27° to 32°F, with a record low temperature of −10°F in Ft. Davis.

VEGETATION

Ten Vegetational Areas are recognized for Texas (Gould, 1962; Correll and Johnston, 1970), one of them being the Trans-Pecos, Mountains and Basins. The Trans-Pecos Vegetational Area is more a geographic distinction than a vegetative one because there is extreme diversity of habitats and vegetation in the region. The Edwards (Stockton) Plateau Vegetational Area extends across the Pecos River into the southeastern Trans-Pecos according to Gould (1962), thus adding to the plant diversity of the Trans-Pecos as a geographic region.

Perhaps the unique vegetative aspect of the Trans-Pecos is the Chihuahuan Desert, the largest desert in North America. About one-third of the Chihuahuan Desert, and its only representation in the United States, is in the Trans-Pecos and parts of southern New Mexico and southeastern Arizona. Two-thirds of the Chihuahuan Desert is in Mexico. In the Trans-Pecos essentially all of the lower elevational vegetation is more or less part of the northern Chihuahuan Desert flora. The Desert vegetation is most characteristic in southern Brewster County surrounding the Chisos Mountains, and it extends in northerly directions intermixing with other vegetation types where physiographic (mostly erosional) and climatic factors allow encroachment of desert plants. The author often has been asked to define, in his opinion, what are the precise boundaries of the Chihuahuan Desert in Trans-Pecos Texas. There are of course no precise topographic features that contain the Desert but its boundaries can be defined generally on the basis of characteristic vegetation or indicator plant species such as Lechuguilla (*Agave lechuguilla*), Creosotebush (*Larrea tridentata*), Tarbush (*Flourensia cernua*), Ocotillo (*Fouquieria splendens*), sotol (*Dasylirion* spp.), yucca (*Yucca* spp.), and certain other shrubs (*Parthe-*

nium spp.; *Acacia* spp.; *Mimosa* spp.). The mountains of the Trans-Pecos "rise up out of the desert," so to speak, and certain desert plants extend up the slopes and canyons as far as growth factors will permit, perhaps to 6500 ft. or more on some southern slopes. The elevational boundary of the Desert flora as a whole, depending upon slope exposures and other factors, is approximately 4500 ft. There is no clear boundary of the Chihuahuan Desert in the southeastern Trans-Pecos where desert plants intermix with Edwards Plateau vegetation on eroded rangelands to the vicinity of Langtry in Val Verde County. Desert plants have slowly encroached upon grasslands of the Trans-Pecos as over-grazed ranges permitted soil erosion and the establishment of new habitats suitable for desert species. Van Devender and Spaulding (1979) have presented paleoecological data, plant fossils from ancient packrat middens, that the Chihuahuan Desert achieved much of its present northerly distribution less than 8000 years ago when the climate started to become arid. Precise boundaries of the northern Chihuahuan Desert are difficult to define partly because the Desert is still growing. Schmidt (1979; 1985) provides a rather precise delineation of the whole Chihuahuan Desert based upon climatic data. An excellent synopsis of the Chihuahuan Desert is available in Key (1980).

Another unique aspect of the Trans-Pecos vegetation is the higher mountain flora. The Davis Mountains in the central Trans-Pecos are reported to be the southern end of the Rocky Mountains, while the Glass Mountains in the central Trans-Pecos may be the end of the Appalachian range. Present floristic surveys suggest phytogeographic connections between certain mountains of the Trans-Pecos and the southern Rocky Mountains of New Mexico, the mountains of southeastern Arizona, the Sierra Madre Occidental of Mexico, and the Del Carmen-Sierra Madre Oriental of Mexico.

Although the flora of the Trans-Pecos is diverse and complex, at least five general vegetation types may be recognized:

Chihuahuan Desert Scrub. At lower elevations (Fig. 2) where annual precipitation ranges from seven to nearly 12 in. about half of the Trans-Pecos is dominated by various shrub species and semi-succulents such as Lechuguilla, sotol (*Dasylirion* spp.), and yucca (*Yucca* spp.). Paleoecological and contemporary ecological data suggest that the desert scrub has gained its present distribution to a large extent through invasion of eroded grassland. Creosotebush (*Larrea tridentata*) is a prominent element of the desert scrub (Fig. 3), occurring with mixed shrubs or in some areas forming extensive, almost pure stands. Present evidence suggests that Creosotebush dispersed from South America (Argentina) to the Chihuahuan Desert region, probably in Mexico, from whence it spread to the western Sonoran and Mohave deserts. Other common shrub species include Catclaw Mimosa (*Mimosa aculeaticarpa* var. *biunicifera*), acacias (*Acacia constricta, A. neovernicosa,* and *A. greggii*), Mariola (*Parthenium in-*

Fig. 2. Chihuahuan Desert scrub, sotol (*Dasylirion leiophyllum*) featured in foreground, Big Bend National Park, Del Carmen Mountains in background (photo by Harry Gordon).

Fig. 3. Chihuahuan Desert scrub, Lechuguilla prominent, Chisos Mountains in background.

Fig. 4. Gypsum exposure near Pecos.

canum), Honey Mesquite (*Prosopis glandulosa*), Fourwing Saltbush (*Atriplex canescens*), Tarbush (*Flourensia cernua*), Javelinabush (*Condalia ericoides*), Skeletonleaf Goldeneye (*Viguiera stenoloba*), Allthorn (*Koeberlinia spinosa*), and Ocotillo (*Fouquieria splendens*). Among the common grasses are gramas (*Bouteloua ramosa, B. gracilis, B. curtipendula*, and *B. eriopoda*), threeawns (*Atristida* spp.), tridens (*Tridens* spp.), and Fluffgrass (*Dasyochloa pulchella*).

Within the Chihuahuan Desert scrub there are several kinds of plant associations that may be recognized (even as distinct vegetation types), these usually being associated with specific soil types or substrates. Saline habitats exhibit characteristic halophytic vegetation (Henrickson, 1977), including Fourwing Saltbush, Alkali Sacaton (*Sporobolus airoides*), Winged Sesuvium (*Sesuvium verrucosum*), Frankenia (*Frankenia jamesii*), Pickleweed (*Allenrolfea occidentalis*), Seepweed (*Suaeda* spp.), and Saltgrass (*Distichlis spicata*). Fourwing Saltbush is also a widespread species in various habitats. Crusty gypsum exposures are scattered throughout the Trans-Pecos (Fig. 4), often near the saline habitats, and characteristic assemblages of plants are restricted to these areas, for example *Tiquilia hispidissima, Gaillardia multiceps*, Gypgrass (*Sporobolus nealleyi*), *Selinocarpus* spp., and *Anulocaulis* spp. (Powell and Turner, 1977). Gypsum endemic species are also found in the gypseous clays which occur near Terlingua in southern Brewster County and from southern Hudspeth County southeast near the Rio Grande to Presidio County. Deep sandy soils are found in parts of El Paso and Hudspeth counties where Honey Mesquite, Broom Psorothamnus (*Psorothamnus scoparius*), and Sand Sagebrush (*Artemisia filifolia*) are common. Extensive deep sand and dunes are also found adjacent to the Trans-Pecos in Ward, Winkler, Crane, and other counties where Havard Oak (*Quercus havardii*), Honey Mesquite, Plains Yucca (*Yucca campestris*), and Sand Sagebrush are prominent plants.

Limestone and igneous-rock habitats are widespread throughout the Chihuahuan Desert scrub and these support several characteristic plant associations including Sotol-Lechuguilla on rocky limestone hills, and Sotol-grassland on igneous-rock slopes. The Stockton Plateau is a limestone area that might be categorized as a vegetative entity because of its somewhat distinct plant associations (Schmidly, 1977). The highly eroded area is characterized by rolling tablelands, caprocked mesas, steep canyons, low rocky hills, and shallow valleys. The vegetation is a mixture of Chihuahuan Desert scrub and grassland with Creosotebush, Lotebush (*Ziziphus obtusifolia*), Texas Persimmon (*Diospyros texana*), Guayacan (*Guaiacum angustifolium*), Lechuguilla, and Texas Sotol (*Dasylirion texanum*) constituting some of the important scrub plants. Important grasses include several gramas, Chino Grama (*Bouteloua ramosa*), Red Grama (*B. trifida*), Black Grama, and Sideoats Grama, several threeawns (*Aristida* spp.), and tridens (*Tridens* spp.). Either Red Berry Juniper (*Juniperus pinchotii*) or Ash Juniper (*J. ashei*) may be found on the mesas with Mohr Shin Oak (*Q. mohriana*) and Vasey Shin Oak (*Q. pungens* var. *vaseyana*).

Grassland. Desert grassland areas, some of them extensive, are widespread throughout the Trans-Pecos, and they are best developed at 3500–5200 ft. on plateaus, rolling hills, and basins where the soils are relatively deep and fertile and annual precipitation is 10 to 18 in. Much of the original grassland in the Trans-Pecos is now covered by desert scrub vegetation, or is severely invaded by a mixture of desert scrub species. The invasion of desert scrub into grassland began or was enhanced when livestock were introduced to the Trans-Pecos and when subsequent over-grazing, soil erosion, and periodic droughts allowed the opportunistic desert plants to become established. Encroachment of desert scrub has proceeded most successfully in marginal grassland areas at lower elevations, but many scrub species, e.g., Catclaw Mimosa, Cane Cholla (*Opuntia imbricata*), prickly pear (*Opuntia* spp.), Honey Mesquite, Soaptree Yucca (*Yucca elata*), Spanish Dagger (*Y. torreyi*), sacahuiste (*Nolina* spp.), sotol, and broomweeds (*Gutierrezia* spp.) can be found scattered throughout most grassland areas at any elevation.

Perhaps the best remaining grassland area in the Trans-Pecos is the "highland grassland" (Fig. 5) of the Davis Mountains near Valentine, Marfa, Alpine, and Fort Davis. Blue Grama (*Bouteloua gracilis*) is the dominant species but several other gramas and many other grasses are interspersed. Other grassland areas with relatively good cover or grassland remnants are associated with most every mountain range or large plateau in the Trans-Pecos. Blue Grama still

Fig. 5. Basin or "highland" grassland near Marfa, Mt. Livermore in the background.

dominates in most areas but soil conditions and other factors promote various dominant species such as other gramas, Tobosa Grass (*Hilaria mutica*), threeawns, needlegrass (*Stipa* spp.), bluestems (*Bothriochloa* spp.; *Schizachyrium* spp.), Burrograss (*Scleropogon brevifolius*), and tridens. Extensive tobosa flats occur particularly in lower elevation grassland basins where run-off water tends to accumulate. About 268 species of grasses are known to occur in the Trans-Pecos.

Oak-Juniper-Pinyon Woodland. In the major mountain systems of the Trans-Pecos, where annual precipitation exceeds 15 in., a woodland association (Fig. 6) begins characteristically at middle elevation slopes and valleys, intergrading with upper grassland, and extending to upper mountain slopes and valleys. About 8000 years ago woodland extended across much of the Trans-Pecos (Wells, 1966; Van Devender and Spaulding, 1979). At present dense woodland usually is found on north slopes, east slopes, in valleys, and on some mesas while south and west slopes typically support rather open woodland with scattered trees. The lowest woodland association in the Davis Mountains is usually oak-juniper at about 4400–5500 ft. The dominant oaks are Gray Oak (*Quercus grisea*) and Emory Oak (*Q. emoryi*). The dominant juniper species are Rose-fruited Juniper (*Juniperus coahuilensis*) and Red Berry Juniper. A pinyon-juniper association occurs potentially at an even lower elevation, 3200–

Fig. 6. Oak-juniper-pine woodland, Green Gulch, Big Bend National Park.

5000 ft., in the limestone southeast portion of the Trans-Pecos from Altuda Peak, the Glass Mountains, and the Del Norte Mountains southeastward along the western edge of the Stockton Plateau. Here the dominant juniper is Red Berry Juniper and the pine is Papershell Pinyon (*Pinus remota*).

A pinyon-juniper-oak association occurs on upper mountain slopes and valleys, about 5500–7500 ft. Alligator Juniper (*Juniperus deppeana*) replaces the other junipers at higher elevations. At higher elevations in the Davis Mountains the pine species is Mexican Pinyon Pine (*Pinus cembroides*), while in the Guadalupe Mountains and Sierra Diablo the pine is Colorado Pinyon (*P. edulis*). The dominant oaks are Silverleaf Oak (*Quercus hypoleucoides*), Gray Oak, and Emory Oak. Various grasses, including needlegrass (*Stipa* spp.), Pinyon Rice Grass (*Piptochaetium fimbriatum*), Bulb Panicum (*Panicum bulbosum*), and muhlys (*Muhlenbergia* spp.) are found beneath the trees and in open areas. Chisos Red Oak (*Q. gravesii*), Texas Madrone (*Arbutus xalapensis*), and Bigtooth Maple (*Acer grandidentatum*) are locally common especially in moist canyons.

Conifer Forest. At the highest elevations of the Guadalupe, Davis (Mt. Livermore), and Chisos mountains there are remnants of a coniferous forest mixed with oaks (Fig. 7). The pine-oak forest also has been referred to as a montane woodland (Schmidly, 1977). The trees are thought to be relictual of the wide-

Fig. 7. Relic forest in Pine Canyon, Chisos Mountains (photo by Harry Gordon).

spread coniferous forest in western North America, although there are some phytogeographical differences between the three mountain ranges. Character- istic forest trees are Ponderosa Pine (*Pinus ponderosa*), *Pinus arizonica*, South- western White Pine (*P. strobiformis*), Douglas-Fir (*Pseudotsuga menziesii*), Quaking Aspen (*Populus tremuloides*), and Chinkapin Oak (*Quercus muehlen- bergii*). In the Chisos Mountains, Arizona Cypress (*Cupressus arizonica*) is also present. Douglas-Fir is not known to occur in the Davis Mountains, but it is present in both the Guadalupe and Chisos mountains. In the Chisos Moun- tains *Pinus arizonica* var. *stormiae* is found in place of Ponderosa Pine. Quak- ing Aspen is more common in the Guadalupe Mountains than in the Davis and Chisos mountains where the plant is known only from one or a few small populations in each range. Other characteristic plants of the conifer forest are Birchleaf Buckthorn (*Rhamnus betulifolia*), snowberry (*Symphoricarpos* spp.), and needlegrass (*Stipa* spp.). Ponderosa Pine and *P. arizonica* are not restricted to the highest elevations but may also occur on north and east slopes and in protected canyons at intermediate elevations.

Riparian Communities. Riparian vegetation (Fig. 8) occurs along the only two major rivers of the Trans-Pecos, the Pecos and Rio Grande, along ephem- eral streams such as Limpia Creek and Alamito Creek, and along the many watercourses (canyons, arroyos, draws) that carry runoff from the mountains.

Fig. 8. Riparian vegetation along the Rio Grande near Presidio (photo by Harry Gordon).

The banks of some stock tanks and small lakes also support riparian vegetation. The introduced salt cedar (*Tamarix* spp.) is thick along the Pecos River and is choking out the upper half of the River. Honey Mesquite and Desertwillow (*Chilopsis linearis*) are also common trees along the Pecos River. Parts of the Rio Grande, particularly between El Paso and Presidio, are also choked with salt cedar. Screwbean (*Prosopis pubescens*), Honey Mesquite, Rio Grande Cottonwood (*Populus deltoides* ssp. *wislizeni*), willows (*Salix gooddingii* and *S. exigua*), Desertwillow, and two cane grasses, Common Reed (*Phragmites australis* and Giantreed (*Arundo doxax*) also prevail along the Rio Grande. The introduced small tree or shrub species *Elaeagnus angustifolia* L., Russian Olive (Elaeagnaceae), is reported to have become established in recent years along the Rio Grande in El Paso County. This potentially troublesome species has either moved down the Rio Grande from New Mexico, where already it is reported to be a problem along the river, or it has escaped from cultivation in El Paso. In the mountain areas riparian vegetation may be comprised of many different trees including oaks, cottonwoods (*Populus* spp.), willows (*Salix* spp.), Little Walnut (*Juglans microcarpa*), Texas Madrone, Bigtooth Maple, Velvet Ash (*Fraxinus velutina*), Netleaf Hackberry (*Celtis laevigata* var. *reticulata*), and Seepwillow Baccharis (*Baccharis salicifolia*).

In the Stockton Plateau area well-defined riparian vegetarian marks even dry arroyos, where Little Walnut is a prominent species. Along Independence

Creek in Terrell County, where water is usually present, Netleaf Hackberry and Plateau Oak (*Quercus fusiformis*) are common.

Number of Woody Species in the Trans-Pecos. The present work includes keys and descriptions for 447 species of woody plants in 203 genera and 70 families. At least 29 of these species are endemic to the Trans-Pecos and about 210 woody species are found in Texas only in the Trans-Pecos. Additional species, either woody or herbaceous, are briefly mentioned or discussed in connection with the trees and shrubs native to the Trans-Pecos.

The family with the most woody species represented in the Trans-Pecos is the Asteraceae with 70 species in 44 genera. Fabaceae is next in representation with 43 woody species in 21 genera, while Rosaceae has 20 species in 11 genera, Fagaceae has 21 species in one genus, Agavaceae has 21 species in five genera, and Grossulariaceae and Hydgrangeaceae together have 15 species in four genera.

Illustrations. Most of the illustrations include a branch of the tree or shrub and one or more enlargements of diagnostic characters (e.g., leaf, pubescence, flower, fruit). Sizes of the drawings are not included on the figures or in the legends, but they may be inferred from measurements given in keys and descriptions.

Key to the Classes and Subclasses

1. Plants without true flowers, producing seeds exposed in "cones," those with woody scales as in pines, fleshy, berrylike cones in junipers, or cones with only a few thin scales as in *Ephedra*   **Class I. *Gymnospermae*, p. 13**

1. Plants with flowers, producing seeds enclosed in ovaries
    Class II. *Angiospermae*, p. 14

   2 (1). Main veins of leaves parallel; flower parts, sepals, petals, and other parts usually in 3's or multiples of 3; seed leaf (cotyledon) 1 in embryo; root system fibrous; stems with vascular bundles scattered, no annual rings of wood   **Subclass A. *Monocotyledonae*, p. 14**

   2. Main veins of leaves branching from a midrib, forming a network; flower parts usually in 4's, or 5's, less often in 2's, 3's, or 6's; seed leaves 2 in embryo; root system fibrous or not; stems with vascular tissue in a cylinder, with a cambium forming a new cylinder each season   **Subclass B. *Dicotyledonae*, p. 14**

CLASS I. GYMNOSPERMAE   CONEBEARING PLANTS

1. Leaves reduced, scalelike and deciduous, opposite or in whorls of 3 at the nodes, stems jointed; seeds in smallish thin-scaled cones
    3. *Ephedraceae*, p. 38

1. Leaves needlelike, or scalelike and closely overlapping, evergreen; stems not jointed; seeds in woody cones or berrylike cones (2)

   2 (1). Leaves scalelike, pointed, short, overlapping; cones round and woody or rounded and fleshy at maturity   **1. *Cupressaceae*, p. 23**

   2. Leaves needlelike in clusters of 2–5, sheathed at the base; cones elongate, dry and woody when mature   **2. *Pinaceae*, p. 30**

CLASS II. ANGIOSPERMAE FLOWERING PLANTS

SUBCLASS A. MONOCOTYLEDONAE MONOCOTS

1. Plants grayish from a partial cover of scurfy scales, our species with an *Agave*-like habit   **4. *Bromeliaceae*, p. 42**

1. Plants not grayish from a cover of scurfy scales, but perhaps with *Agave* or *Yucca* habit   **5. *Agavaceae*, p. 44**

SUBCLASS B. DICOTYLEDONAE DICOTS

1. Stems fleshy and succulent, leafless, with clusters of spines (areoles); plants cactuslike   **45. *Cactaceae*, p. 277**

1. Stems and plants otherwise (2)
   2 (1). Corollas tubular, cup or saucershaped, resulting from all petals fused at edges, at least near the base (3)
   2. Corollas otherwise, petals free from one another, not fused, at least not all of them and not at the edges, or petals absent (30)
      3 (2). Ovary inferior or partly so; flower parts arising from top, middle, or sides of ovary (4)
      3. Ovary superior or partly so; flower parts arising from beneath or around the ovary (floral tube) (6)
         4 (3). Flowers small, arranged in heads surrounded by a tight series of bracts forming an involucre; anthers coalescent in corollas; fruit an achene usually crowned by a pappus of scales or bristles; style branches 2   **70. *Asteraceae*, p. 387**
         4. Flowers perhaps aggregated in heads but not in involucrate heads; anthers free; fruit a capsule, berry, or drupe; style branches usually 1 (5)
            5 (4). Stipules present (these often leaflike); fruit a capsule   **68. *Rubiaceae*, p. 375**
            5. Stipules absent; fruit a berry or drupe   **69. *Caprifoliaceae*, p. 378**
            6 (3). Plants vinelike with alternate leaves; fruit a cluster of grapes   **37. *Vitaceae*, p. 256**
            6. Plants and fruit otherwise (7)
               7 (6). Stigma of pistil very large; very young ovary 2-lobed, styles fused to form one (8)
               7. Stigma of pistil not usually large; ovary entire, or if 2-lobed then styles not fused, or if so then the one style attached at base of ovary (9)
                  8 (7). Sap not milky; stigmas free from anthers and corolla, or anthers loosely coherent with stigma   **57. *Apocynaceae*, p. 322**
                  8. Sap milky; very large stigma fused with anthers and corolla to form a "crown"   **58. *Asclepiadaceae*, p. 327**

9 (7). Leaves pinnately twice-compound   **23. Fabaceae, p. 158**
9. Leaves simple, pinnately once-compound, or palmate (10)
  10 (9). Plants with strong spines on sometimes leafless, wandlike stems, the leaves appearing soon after rains; flowers in apical clusters, tubular, reddish   **42. Fouquieriaceae, p. 273**
  10. Plants without spines on wandlike stems (11)
    11 (10). Filaments fused to form a tube that encloses the style
        38. Malvaceae, p. 259
    11. Filaments not fused to form tube (12)
      12 (11). Stamens 5–18, usually 2–3 times as many as petals or corolla lobes (13)
      12. Stamens 2–5 (rarely 6), as many as or fewer than petals or corolla lobes (17)
        13 (12). Stamens 10, petals or corolla lobes 5; flowers bisexual, radially symmetrical (14)
        13. Stamens and petal or corolla lobe numbers different; flowers bisexual and bilaterally symmetrical or unisexual (15)
          14 (13). Leaves leathery, more or less ovate, essentially glabrous; fruit berrylike or drupelike; anthers with hornlike appendages   **50. Ericaceae, p. 300**
          14. Leaves thin, somewhat roundish, with stellate hairs, fruit dry; anthers without appendages   **54. Styracaceae, p. 308**
          15 (13). Petals usually 3; flowers bisexual, bilaterally symmetrical   **30. Polygalaceae, p. 217**
          15. Petals or corolla lobes 4–7; flowers unisexual, not bilaterally symmetrical (16)
            16 (15). Large shrubs or small trees; leaves entire; fruits fleshy, persimmonlike   **53. Ebenaceae, p. 306**
            16. Smaller shrubs; leaves often lobed; fruits dry, capsules usually with 2–3 seeds (carpels usually 3, rarely 2)   **31. Euphorbiaceae, p. 219**
          17 (12). Petals 5, hooded (umbrellalike), bases very slender   **39. Sterculiaceae, p. 265**
          17. Petals otherwise (18)
            18 (17). Leaves opposite; stipules present, sometimes reduced to stipular lines at the nodes   **56. Buddlejaceae, p. 318**
            18. Leaves opposite or alternate; stipules absent, even stipular lines (19)
              19 (18). Stamens 2 or 4, fewer than the 5 corolla lobes (20)
              19. Stamens 5 when corolla lobes 5, stamens 4 when corolla lobes 4 (25)

20 (19). Leaves opposite; fruit either breaking into 1-seeded parts (schizo-carp) or else (a drupe) fleshy and 1-seeded (capsule or samara in *Oleaceae*) (21)

20. Leaves opposite or alternate; fruit a capsule or winged (23)

    21 (20). Flowers strongly bilaterally symmetrical; style bifed at apex; fruit splitting into 4, 1-seeded parts   **63. *Lamiaceae*, p. 341**

    21. Flowers not bilaterally symmetrical, or only weakly so; style not bifed, or inconspicuously so; fruit a schizocarp, a twin capsule, a samara, or a drupe (22)

        22 (21). Fruit fleshy with one seed (*Forestiera*), a twin capsule with 2–4 seeds in each cell (*Menodora*), or a samara with an elongated wing (*Fraxinus*); trees or shrubs   **55. *Oleaceae*, p. 309**

        22. Fruit splitting into 1-seeded parts or fleshy with 2 seeds; shrubs only   **62. *Verbenaceae*, p. 335**

    23 (20). Seeds flattened, winged, with or without a tuft of hair at one or both ends   **66. *Bignoniaceae*, p. 362**

    23. Seeds flattened or not, but without wings (24)

        24 (23). Capsule elastically opening with 2 valves recurving from a central column, the seeds forcefully ejected when fruit opens; corolla lobes in bud usually rolled up longitudinally   **67. *Acanthaceae*, p. 365**

        24. Capsule not elastically opening and not recurving, the seeds not ejected; corolla lobes in bud usually overlapping   **65. *Scrophulariaceae*, p. 357**

    25 (19). Each flower with one seed maturing (26)

    25. Each flower with 2 or more seeds maturing (27)

        26 (25). Plants weak shrubs, perhaps herbaceous above, unarmed; flowers perfect; fruit dry (a circumscissile, globose capsule)   **51. *Plumbaginaceae*, p. 303**

        26. Plants strong shrubs or small trees, with strong thorns; flowers unisexual; fruit fleshy (a 1-seeded drupe)   **52. *Sapotaceae*, p. 305**

        27 (25). Ovary 3-celled; styles usually 3-branched at apex; sepals united by transparent tissues   **59. *Polemoniaceae*, p. 328**

        27. Ovary 2–4-celled, rarely 1-celled; styles 2-lobed or entire; sepals not united by transparent tissue (28)

            28 (27). Fruit dry, deeply lobed (a schizocarp), breaking into 2–4, 1-seeded parts   **61. *Boraginaceae*, p. 332**

            28. Fruit a berry or capsule (29)

29 (28). Flowers small, crowded into terminal clusters; stigma bifed; fruit a capsule **60. *Hydrophyllaceae*, p. 330**

29. Flowers usually rather large, solitary or in loose clusters; stigma entire, sometimes shallowly 2-lobed; fruit a berry or capsule **64. *Solanaceae*, p. 350**

30 (2). Plants parasites on stems of trees or strong shrubs **12. *Viscaceae*, p. 102**

30. Plants not parasitic (31)

31 (30). Corolla absent, flowers either with whole parianth absent or with only one series of parianth parts, either sepals or "tepals," these perhaps corollalike (32)

31. Corolla present, each flower with both sepals and petals, or when flowers unisexual, petals may be absent from female flowers (48)

32 (31). Sepals fused, at least at the base (above the receptacle if ovary superior, above the floral cup if flower perigynous, or above the ovary if ovary inferior) (33)

32. Sepals separate to their bases, or absent (34)

33 (32). Calyx membranous or scalelike **15. *Amaranthaceae*, p. 119**

33. Calyx usually corollalike **16. *Nyctaginaceae*, p. 122**

34 (32). Fruit nutlike (a drupe in *Garrya*) including acorns, walnuts, and pecans; ovary entirely inferior (as seen by scales, sepals, or stamens at top of ovary) (35)

34. Fruit usually otherwise; ovary superior or at least half-superior (38)

35 (34). Fruit (nut) an acorn subtended by a cupule (acorn cup) of fused bracts **9. *Fagaceae*, p. 76**

35. Fruit (nut) not an acorn nor subtended by a cupule (36)

36 (35). Leaves compound; fruit a walnut or pecan **7. *Juglandaceae*, p. 71**

36. Leaves simple; fruit nutlets in conelike clusters, or a drupe (37)

37 (36). Leaves usually with toothed margins; stipules present; fruit nutlets in clusters **8. *Betulaceae*, p. 74**

37. Leaves usually with smooth margins; stipules absent; fruit a drupe **49. *Garryaceae*, p. 298**

38 (34). Shrubs, with straight or curved thorns (rarely unarmed); fruits fleshy; (see also *Maclura* of the Moraceae) (39)

38. Trees or shrubs, unarmed, or if with few thorns (as in *Maclura*, Moraceae) the fruit an aggregate of achenes (40)

39 (38). Thorns usually paired, short, perhaps curved; fruit orange; styles 2 (*Celtis pallida*)   **10. Ulmaceae, p. 96**

39. Thorns single (rarely branched), straight, fruit black, red, or white, rarely orange; styles usually not 2   **36. Rhamnaceae, p. 245**

    40 (38). Embryo surrounding endosperm spirally coiled; fruit an indehiscent nutlet; petals absent, perianth usually not petallike
                                                  14. Chenopodiaceae, p. 109

    40. Embryo and characters otherwise (41)

        41 (40). Plants subshrubs, herbaceous above; fruit achenelike, angled or winged   **13. Polygonaceae, p. 107**

        41. Plants woody shrubs or trees; fruit otherwise (42)

            42 (41). Stems with curved (roselike) prickles (*Zanthoxylum*)
                                                  26. Rutaceae, p. 204

            42. Stems (plants) without curved prickles (43)

                43 (42). Leaves opposite; fruit a 2-winged samara
                                                34. Aceraceae, p. 242

                43. Leaves alternate; fruit otherwise (44)

                    44 (43). Flowers with prominent floral cup; fruit an achene, enclosed by mature floral cup; style long, persistent; featherlike   **22. Rosaceae, p. 140**

                    44. Flowers without prominent floral cups or long, persistent, featherlike styles (45)

                        45 (44). Leaves pinnately compound (*Pistacia*)
                                          32. Anacardiaceae, p. 231

                      45. Leaves simple (46)

                          46 (45). Seeds numerous, each with a basal tuft of hairs   **6. Salicaceae, p. 60**

                        46. Seeds usually 1 or a few, without a tuft of hairs (47)

                            47 (46). Sap usually milky; flowers unisexual, closely aggregated, the entire cluster of female flowers maturing as an aggregate fruit (syncarp)   **11. Moraceae, p. 100**

                            47. Sap not milky; flowers perfect or unisexual, each female or perfect flower maturing separately as a circular samara or a roundish drupe   **10. Ulmaceae, p. 96**

                            48 (31). Ovary inferior or essentially so (49)

                            48. Ovary superior or essentially so (in *Rhamnaceae* and *Celastraceae* the disk may adhere somewhat to the ovary) (55)

49 (48). Herbage with stinging hairs; fruit a 1-seeded achene

44. *Loasaceae*, p. 276

49. Herbage usually without stinging hairs; fruit otherwise (50)

50 (49). Fruit a pome (applelike but small), or of other types (follicle, achene, drupe)   **22. *Rosaceae*, p. 140**

50. Fruit not a pome, or if appearing like one then the seeds numerous (51)

51 (50). Fruit a drupe (blackish or dark purple with 1–2 seeds)

49. *Garryaceae*, p. 298

51. Fruit a berry or capsule (52)

52 (51). Leaves compound   **48. *Araliaceae*, p. 296**

52. Leaves simple (perhaps deeply lobed) (53)

53 (52). Top of ovary usually obscured by long floral tube; stamens (usually 8) twice as many as petals; fruit a capsule

47. *Onagraceae*, p. 295

53. Top of ovary visible (except in *Ribes*), stamens and perianth attached on rim of floral cup; stamens 4, 5, 12, or numerous; fruit a berry or capsule (54)

54 (53). Leaves alternate, palmately lobed; fruit a berry

19. *Grossulariaceae*, p. 128

54. Leaves opposite, entire, rarely toothed; fruit a capsule

20. *Hydrangeaceae*, p. 131

55 (48). Stamens with filaments united in one or two groups, or fused with the pistil, the anthers separate or united (56)

55. Stamens with filaments separate, or else fused into more than two groups (60)

56 (55). Pistil one, simple; stigma one (57)

56. Pistil one, compound; stigmas usually 2 or more (58)

57 (56). Flowers with 3 upper petals purplish or reddish, fused at their slender bases, and 2 lower petals separate, these usually greenish, glandlike; fruit a nearly globose pod armed with straight prickles

24. *Krameriaceae*, p. 197

57. Flowers otherwise, but often bilateral with 5 petals, and variable characteristics of the family; fruit otherwise (usually a legume)

23. *Fabaceae*, p. 158

58 (56). Flowers strongly bilaterally symmetrical; carpels usually 2; stamens with filaments united in 1 or 2 groups

30. *Polygalaceae*, p. 217

58. Flowers essentially radially symmetrical; carpels more than 2; filaments united in 1 group (59)

59 (58). Leaves simple; stamens (forming filament tube) numerous
38. Malvaceae, p. 259

59. Leaves bipinnately compound; stamens forming filament tube (about 10)
28. Meliaceae, p. 213

60 (55). Fertile stamens exactly as many as sepals and alternate with them and/or as many as petals and opposite them (61)

60. Fertile stamens either more numerous than petals or sepals, or if the same number then opposite the sepals and alternate with the petals (62)

61 (60). Leaves with spiny margins; anther valves lifting like trap-doors; petals conspicuous, 6 or 9, bright yellow
17. Berberidaceae, p. 124

61. Leaves without spiny margins; anthers opening by longitudinal slits; petals small, usually 4–5, whitish or greenish-yellow
36. Rhamnaceae, p. 245

62 (60). Fruit a specialized capsule (silique or silicle), divided into 2 cells by a thin partition, at maturity the 2 valves separating from persistent partition, starting at the base, and falling
18. Brassicaceae, p. 127

62. Fruit otherwise (63)

63 (62). All-thorny shrubs; stems green, leafless; sepals and petals 4; stamens 8; fruit a small berry, tan to black when ripe
43. Capparaceae, p. 275

63. Plants and characters otherwise (64)

64 (63). Herbage with aromatic oil glands present, these detectable with the naked eye, under a lens, and by a smell in fresh material
26. Rutaceae, p. 204

64. Herbage usually without aromatic oil glands (65)

65 (64). Petals and stamens inserted on the rim of or well into a floral cup (66)

65. Petals and stamens free, inserted below the ovary, not in or on a floral cup, except perhaps slightly so in some *Sapindaceae* and *Celastraceae* (67)

66 (65). Flowers usually 5-merous; stamens 10–40, inserted near rim of floral cup near petal insertion; stipules present
22. Rosaceae, p. 140

66. Flowers 4–7-merous; stamens 4–numerous, inserted deep into floral tube, petal insertion near the floral cup rim between calyx teeth; stipules absent or minute
46. Lythraceae, p. 294

67 (65). Trees or shrubs (Salt Cedar) often grayish overall; leaves numerous, ca. 1 mm long, alternate, scalelike or cylindrical; flowers pink or white, very small but often collectively showy in elongated clusters

41. *Tamaricaceae,* p. 270

67. Plants and characters otherwise (68)

68 (67). Plants woody at base, somewhat vinelike; leaves opposite, simple, with stipules, petals with slender, stalklike bases; sepals usually with 2 dorsal glands   **29.** *Malpighiaceae,* p. 214

68. Plants and characters otherwise (69)

69 (68). Shrubs with thorny to very thorny (all-thornlike) branches; leaves simple, alternate, small (to 2.5 cm long) or absent; ovary deeply lobed, the lobes mostly separating at maturity, developing into reddish, drupelike structures (*Castela, Holacantha*)

27. *Simaroubaceae,* p. 210

69. Plants and characters otherwise (70)

70 (69). Fruit usually fleshy, not opening at maturity (71)

70. Fruit usually dry and opening at maturity (72)

71 (70). Fruit a colorless or yellowish berry with one rather large, dark seed (*Sapindus*)   **35.** *Sapindaceae,* **p. 243**

71. Fruit usually a reddish drupe (somewhat flattened, hairy, resinous)   **32.** *Anacardiaceae,* **p. 231**

72 (70). Leaves opposite or in fascicles (72)

72. Leaves alternate (74)

73 (72). Leaves compound; stamens 10

25. *Zygophyllaceae,* **p. 201**

73. Leaves simple; stamens 6   **40.** *Frankeniaceae,* **p. 269**

74 (72). Leaves compound (76)

74. Leaves simple (75)

75 (74). Fruit a capsule, drupe, or achene

33. *Celastraceae,* **p. 238**

75. Fruit a follicle, ca. 5 mm long

21. *Crossosomataceae,* **p. 138**

76 (74). Trees (often large) with odd-pinnately compound leaves and 13–41 leaflets; fruit samaralike (*Ailanthus*)

27. *Simaroubaceae,* **p. 210**

76. Trees or shrubs with odd-pinnately compound leaves and 3–7 leaflets; fruit a 3-lobed pod 3.5–5 cm. wide, 1 large seed in each cell (*Ungnadia*)

35. *Sapindaceae,* **p. 243**

Descriptive Flora

1. CUPRESSACEAE BARTL. CYPRESS FAMILY

Evergreen trees or shrubs, monoecious or dioecious. Leaves overlapping, scalelike or awlshaped, usually closely appressed to branchlets, cones small, woody or fleshy; seeds winged or merely angled.

About 20 genera and 130 species of this family occur in both hemispheres.

KEY TO THE GENERA

1. Mature seed cones woody and persistent, with several obscurely winged seeds under each of 6–8 flattened and separating scales **1. Cupressus.**
1. Mature seed cones berrylike and not long persistent, with 1 or 2 nonwinged seeds under each of the few fleshy scales which remain coalesced
2. Juniperus.

1. CUPRESSUS L.

Tree 10 m or more tall; bark on small trunks smooth, shedding in scales, inner bark reddish, bark on larger trunks thick and rough, often peeling. Leaves ca. 2 mm long, pointed. Cones roundish 2–2.5 cm wide, woody, with 6–8 persistent scales, these flattened with a point in the middle; seeds ca. 2 mm long.

A genus of about 15 species found in both hemispheres, with a single species found in the Trans-Pecos.

1. **Cupressus arizonica** Greene. ARIZONA CYPRESS. Fig. 9. [*Cupressus arizonica* var. *bonita* Lemm. and C. *glabra* Sudw.]. The only native occurrence of Arizona Cypress in Texas is in the higher canyons of the Chisos Mts. in Brewster Co. where a State champion tree 112 ft. tall is found in Boot Canyon. It is more abundant in SW NM, S AZ, and also occurs in CA; also in Son., Chih., Coah., and Dgo., Mex.

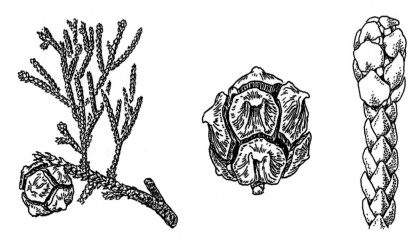

Fig. 9. *Cupressus arizonica* (Arizona Cypress)

These monoecious trees occasionally reach 25–35 m tall, but usually are less than half that size. These trees have been widely planted as ornamentals and windbreaks in Trans-Pecos Texas. In this region the trees are prized ornamentals because they are fast-growing aromatic evergreens that do well under arid conditions, even at low elevations, as long as they receive periodic watering during dry spells.

2. JUNIPERUS L.

Evergreen trees or shrubs, usually dioecious, sometimes monoecious, with short trunks and shredded, furrowed, or checkered bark and soft, usually reddish wood; distal branches (whips) erect or drooping. Leaves either scale-like and appressed or awlshaped, sometimes jointed at the base. Cones small, berrylike, with 1 to several seeds.

There are about 60 species of junipers widely dispersed over the Northern Hemisphere. In the Trans-Pecos, junipers are most common at moderate elevations in rocky or poor soils, commonly associated with oaks and pinyon, but much more abundant than oak or pine in many localities. It is not unusual to find individual color variation within the juniper species, with a few bluish-gray, glaucous trees amongst those with more typical green foliage. The stems and trunks of junipers have been used extensively as fence posts and firewood. Succulent berries are eaten by many birds and ground animals. The fibrous bark of many species was used by Indians to make mats, saddles, and other items. The seeds of certain species have been used as beads. Junipers, especially *Juniperus ashei* in Texas, are noted for producing troublesome allergenic pollen in the winter.

KEY TO THE SPECIES

1. Female cones 1 (–2)-seeded, 4–8 mm wide, red, copper, red-brown, rose, blue, bluish-black at maturity, cones juicy and pulpy, not fibrous to woody.
   2. Leaf margins smooth (at 40 ×); cones 1–2-seeded, dark bluish-black with bloom; branches erect to weeping; upper branches (12–20 mm wide) reddish under peeling bark; glands on whip leaves narrow (3–10 times as long as wide); cones mature in 2 years   **1. *J. scopulorum.***
   2. Leaf margins finely denticulate; cones 1 (rarely 2)-seeded, copper, red, reddish-brown, pink or rose; upper branches without red under peeling bark; cones mature in 1 year.
      3. Mature cones copper, red, pink, or rose colored; some whip leaves with conspicuous white crystalline exudate.
         4. Cones rose to pink or pinkish-blue with bloom; whip leaves glaucous on adaxial surface (easily seen by looking directly toward a terminal whip); plants tend toward a stronger central axis than *Juniperus pinchotii*   **2. *J. coahuilensis.***
         4. Cones copper, red to red-brown, without bloom; whip leaves not glaucous on ventral surface; plants tend to branch at the base with limbs ascending   **3. *J. pinchotii.***
      3. Mature cones blue, brownish blue, bluish-black; glands of whip leaves, if ruptured, without white crystalline exudate.
         5. Whip leaves with a conspicuous, hemispherical gland (often 2–3 times as long as wide) conspicuous on brown whip leaves; whip leaf glands less than ½ length of leaf sheath, plants with strong central axis and one main trunk-stem unless damaged; cones blue not brownish beneath the bloom   **4. *J. ashei.***
         5. Whip leaves with an elongated, flat (or slightly raised) gland 4–10 times as long as wide; whip leaf gland continuing over ¾ or more of length of whip leaf sheath (flat part of leaf appressed to stem), plants often branched at base; cones with brownish to reddish cast beneath the bloom   **5. *J. monosperma.***
1. Female cone 2–13-seeded, (sometimes 1 in *Juniperus deppeana*) 9–20 mm wide, fibrous to woody, reddish-brown at maturity, but appearing somewhat bluish with bloom on old specimens.
      6. Cones (2–)3–5(–6)-seeded; leaf margins finely denticulate (at 40 ×); bark in square to rectangular plates (except in *Juniperus deppeana* var. *sperryi* which has furrowed bark); branchlets erect

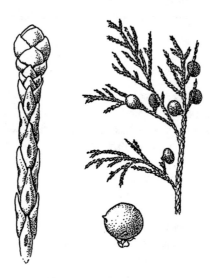

Fig. 10. *Juniperus scopulorum*
(Rocky Mountain Juniper)

not drooping (except in *J. deppeana* var. *sperryi*); whip leaves mostly on the extreme tips of branchlets; scale leaves with tips rounded to acute.

7. Bark checkered in square to rectangular plates, branches erect   **6. *J. deppeana.***

7. Bark in strips or furrowed, branches drooping but not in long whips as in *J. flaccida*   **6a. *J. deppeana* var. *sperryi.***

6. Cones 6–13-seeded; leaf markings irregularly toothed (at 40 ×) almost appearing smooth; bark in strips or furrowed; foliage drooping; whip leaves on extreme tips of branchlets and extending back several inches along the branchlets; scale leaves with sharply pointed tips (mostly acuminate)   **7. *J. flaccida.***

1. Juniperus scopulorum Sarg. ROCKY MOUNTAIN JUNIPER.   Fig. 10.   In the Trans-Pecos, known only in the Guadalupe Mts.; in TX also in Palo Duro Canyon, in the northern Plains Country; widespread (Adams, 1975) in the W U.S., NM, AZ, CO, UT, NV, OR, ID, MT, WA, and in NE, ND, B.C., and Alberta, Can.; also a few isolated sites in Serranias del Burro, Coah. and the Sierra Madre Occidental, Chih., Son., Mex.

According to Correll and Johnston (1970), this species is closely allied to *Juniperus virginiana*, of more northeastern distribution, and even though the two species can be delimited by several technical features in allopatric populations, they are difficult to distinguish when growing together. The cones of *J. scopulorum* are smallish, bright blue, and require two years to reach maturity. The species is easily distinguished from the more troublesome taxa, e.g., *J. pinchotii* and *J. coahuilensis*, of the Trans-Pecos. In the Guadalupe Mountains a form of *J. scopulorum* with drooping leaves occurs as scattered trees in Dog Canyon and Upper Pine Spring Canyon (Northington and Burgess, 1979).

2. **Juniperus coahuilensis** (Martinez) Gaussen *ex* R. P. Adams. ROSE-FRUITED JUNIPER. [*Juniperus erythrocarpa* Cory var. *coahuilensis* Martinez]. The common juniper in *Bouteloua* grasslands around Alpine, and S and SW of Alpine on the grasslands; Chisos Mts., Quitman Mts., Hueco Tanks, Franklin Mts.; W of the Rio Grande in SW NM, and S AZ below the Mogollon Rim; grasslands of Chih. and Coah., S to Dgo.; NE Son.; in grassland foothills of Sierra Madre Oriental, Coah., N.L., S.L.P., Zac., perhaps N of Pachuco in Hgo., Mex.

The Rose-fruited Juniper is closely related to and apparently intergrades with *Juniperus pinchotii* with which it overlaps in distribution in the SW part of the Trans-Pecos (Adams and Zanoni, 1979). A possible hybrid swarm of the two species exists in the Basin of the Chisos Mountains (Adams and Kistler, 1991). Also *J. coahuilensis* is similar in morphology (not cone color) to *J. monosperma* which occurs in the Guadalupe Mountains and northward. Adams (1975) believes that the complexity in Trans-Pecos and Mexican junipers is a result of back and forth movements of populations during Pleistocene glaciation periods (and perhaps earlier also) resulting in rapid evolution of specialized adaptations as empty niches appeared, and intergradations of different genomes that were brought into contact by the movement. Recent work by Adams (1993; 1994) is pertinent to this and other Trans-Pecos species of *Juniperus*.

3. **Juniperus pinchotti** Sudw. RED BERRY JUNIPER, PINCHOT JUNIPER. Fig. 11. [*Juniperus texensis* Van Melle, *J. monosperma* var. *pinchotii* (Sudw.) Van Melle]. The most common juniper in the Trans-Pecos, commonly in highly eroded, rocky areas, mostly Marathon and NE, but throughout the Trans-Pecos, except in El Paso Co. and the NE bordering Ward and Winkler counties; also in gypseous and other soils from the E Trans-Pecos NE to the Plains Country, and SE to central TX where it overlaps with *J. ashei*; also in the Guadalupe Mts., SE NM and W OK; Coah., Sierra del Carmen, Serranias del Burro, Mex.

According to Correll and Johnston (1970), this species sprouts rapidly from cut or burned stumps. The stems are used for fence posts, but are not as durable in the soil as are posts cut from *Juniperus ashei*.

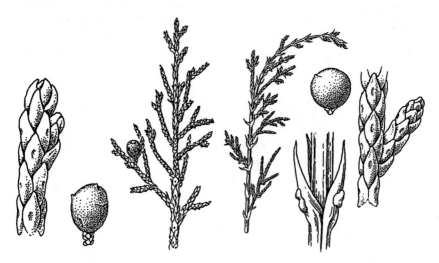

Fig. 11. *Juniperus pinchotii* (Red Berry Juniper)   Fig. 12. *Juniperus ashei* (Ash Juniper)

4. Juniperus ashei Buchh. ASH JUNIPER, MOUNTAIN CEDAR, POST CEDAR, ROCK CEDAR. Fig. 12. [*Juniperus mexicana* Spreng., *J. savinoides* (H.B.K.) Nees (not Griseb.) *Sabina sabinoides* (H.B.K.) Small]. Of peripheral Trans-Pecos distribution, in Terrell, Val Verde, and Crockett counties, with one small outlier population reported in Maravillas Canyon, Brewser Co. (Adams, 1977); distributionally centered on the Edwards Plateau, also extending NE to Dallas Co., N to Nolan, Taylor, and Stephens Co., and S to Zavala Co.; also S MO, N AK; Sierra del Carmen, Serranias del Burro, Coah., La Encantada Mts., Mex.

In the broad central and NW TX area, this species is the main source of the extensively used cedar posts, especially valuable because of their durability in the soil.

5. Juniperus monosperma (Engelm.) Sarg. ONE-SEEDED JUNIPER. Fig. 13. [*Juniperus monosperma* var. *gymnocarpa* (Lemm.) Rehd., *J. gymnocarpa* (Lemm.) Cory, *J. mexicana* var. *monosperma* (Engelm.) Cory]. Rocky slopes and various eroded areas in the Guadalupe Mts. Culberson Co.; NE of Van Horn on gypsum; NW of Van Horn in Sierra Diablo, Apache Mts., and gypsum plains in vicinity; perhaps near Toyahvale in Reeves Co.; also in the N Plains Country of TX; extreme W OK, NM, S CO, where it may reach its maximum size of about 17 m; possibly N Mex.

The One-seeded Juniper is closely related and morphologically similar to

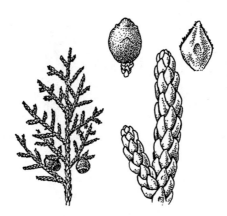

Fig. 13. *Juniperus monosperma*
(One-seeded Juniper)

Juniperus coahuilensis except in cone color (see key). Cone size is 4–7 mm in *J. monosperma* and 7–8.5 mm in *J. ashei.* Gland characters (in key) are most reliable in distinguishing these species.

6. **Juniperus deppeana** Steud. var. **deppeana.** ALLIGATOR JUNIPER. Fig. 14. [*Juniperus deppeana* var. *pachyphloea* (Torr.) Martinez, *J. pachyphloea* Torr.]. Abundant, usually in oak zones, in the main mts. of the Trans-Pecos, Guadalupe, Davis, and Chisos; reported also from the Sierra Vieja, Eagle Mts., and Chinati Peak; also in NM and AZ; Chih., Son., Zac., Pue., Mex.

This species is easily recognized by its checkered bark, resembling the plates on an alligator's back. The trees are usually taller and with longer, thicker trunks than other Trans-Pecos junipers. The largest Alligator Juniper recorded in Big Bend National Park is 33 ft. high with a 25 ft. crown spread and a girth of nearly 8 ft.

6a. **Juniperus deppeana** var. **sperryi** Correll.   An unusual and extremely rare juniper, with only 3 or 4 plants known in the Davis Mountains and possibly the Guadalupe Mountains, distinguished from *Juniperus deppeana* by bark that is furrowed and peels in strips as opposed to the checkered bark of typical junipers. Also the plants have flaccid, drooping branchlets much like those of *J. flaccida.* The var. *sperryi* is tentatively recognized here even though the author is inclined to agree with Adams (1973) who reduced the taxon

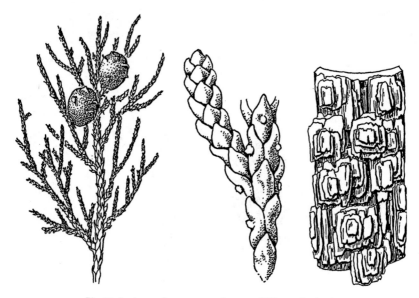

Fig. 14. *Juniperus deppeana* var. *deppeana* (Alligator Juniper)

to a mere form of the species. Adams investigated the possibility that the drooping branchlets might reflect ancient hybridization between *J. deppeana* and *J. flaccida*, but did not find any evidence to support the idea. Instead, the drooping effect probably has resulted from a rare and unusual gene combination. Occasional trees with drooping branches have been observed by the author in other junipers and in ornamental Arizona Cypress.

7. Juniperus flaccida Schlecht.   WEEPING JUNIPER, DROOPING JUNIPER Fig. 15.   Mostly a Mexican species of Chih., Son. and southward; in the U.S. found only in the Chisos Mts. where it is common on the intermediate and upper rocky slopes; most common juniper in Mex.

The conspicuous drooping branchlets give the impression that the whole tree is wilting. The glaucous dark-reddish berries have 4–12 pinkish seeds. The National champion Weeping Juniper occurs in Juniper Canyon in the Chisos Mountains with the measurements 55 ft. high, 35 ft. crown spread, and 8.5 ft. girth.

2. PINACEAE LINDL.   PINE FAMILY

Evergreen trees or shrubs, resinous, monoecious, with whorled branches. Leaves usually needlelike, solitary or clustered in fascicles of 2–5. Male cones

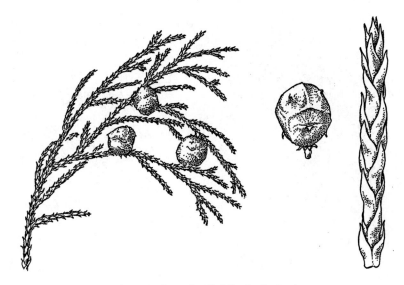

Fig. 15. *Juniperus flaccida* (Weeping Juniper)

with spirally arranged scales, 2 pollen sacs per scale, female cones becoming woody at maturity after 1–3 years. Seeds with or without wings, cotyledons several.

A family of 10 genera and about 250 species occurring over most of the Northern Hemisphere. These plants are of tremendous economic importance, accounting for most of our timber and pulpwood, and for many other things such as naval stores, fence posts, and firewood. The Trans-Pecos Douglas-Fir and pine species occur primarily near the higher peaks and in deep canyons of the Guadalupe, Davis, or Chisos mountains, the southernmost extension of the Rocky Mountain chain.

KEY TO THE GENERA

1. Leaves solitary at nodes, or seemingly 2-ranked, not subtended by scalelike sheaths; cones maturing in 1 year   **1. *Pseudotsuga.***
1. Leaves in bundles of 2–5 at nodes, with scaly, basal sheaths; cones maturing in 2–3 years   **2. *Pinus.***

1. PSEUDOTSUGA CARR.

Evergreen tree to 50 m high, trunk straight; bark furrowed. Leaves lasting 6–8 years, linear, arranged on all sides of twigs or in 2 rows, 1.5–3 cm long,

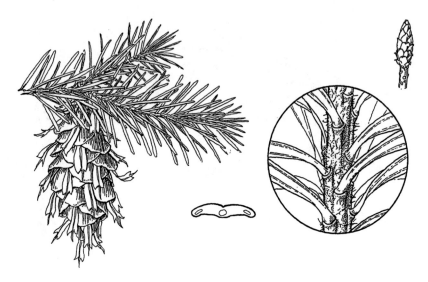

Fig. 16. *Pseudotsuga menziesii* (Douglas-Fir)

flat, slightly grooved rounded at the tip; leaf scar rounded. Cones 4–7 cm long, scales thin, rounded, bracts 3-pointed, longer than the scales; seeds brown with whitish spots.

1. **Pseudotsuga menziesii** (Mirb.) Franco. DOUGLAS-FIR. Fig. 16. [*Pseudotsuga douglasii* (Lindl.) Carr.; *P. taxifolia* (Lamb.) Britt.; *P. mucronata* (Raf.) Sudw.]. Rather common in upper canyons and slopes of the Guadalupe Mts., scattered in the upper Chisos Mts. 6000–8000 ft.; strangely absent from the Davis Mts., although this range is of intermediate distribution, and suitable habitats seemingly exist on high slopes of Mt. Livermore; throughout much of the mountainous W U.S. and well into W Can., and N Mex.

Douglas-Fir is often rated as the most important timber tree in the United States, having the largest total stand of any timber species. The trees are straight and tall, commonly reaching a height of more than 50 m. The leaves are linear, flat, usually spreading on all sides of the twigs, or sometimes in 2 rows. The cones are easily recognized by thin bluntish scales, and 3-pointed bracts projecting beyond the scales.

The Rocky Mountains and Trans-Pecos trees are usually referred to as *Pseudotsuga menziesii* var. **glauca** (Beissn.) Franco, in that they differ from the West Coast variety by more compact habit, palish blue-green leaves which are shorter, and cones only about 5 cm long (instead of 7 cm). Douglas-Fir frequently occurs in association with Ponderosa Pine, a tree that is abundant in the Davis Mountains. The State champion Douglas-Fir occurs in Boot Canyon of the Chisos Mountains in Big Bend National Park, with a height of 72 ft.

2. PINUS L. PINE

Evergreen trees (rarely shrubs); bark thin and scaly, furrowed, or layered. Leaves needlelike, in clusters of 2–5, rarely solitary, persistent for 2–8 years subtended by a basal, membranous sheath. Male cones clustered near twig apexes, at base of season's growth, of merely firm tissue at maturity, not long persistent in spring; female cones borne at twig apexes or in pairs, maturing and becoming woody the 2nd year (rarely the 3rd), the cone scales spreading and shedding seeds at maturity, or remaining closed with cones persistent for many years; seeds usually obovoid, with fairly hard coats, with or without membranous wings. Cotyledons 3–15 or more.

A genus of about 100 species distributed over much of the Northern Hemisphere, with many timber species known for their economic value in lumber, paper pulp, and naval stores. The Trans-Pecos species, occurring mostly at higher elevations, do not occur in dense stands except in limited areas, and thus have not been subjected to extensive timbering.

KEY TO THE SPECIES

1. Mature trees 20 m or more tall; leaves 3–5 per cluster; white and yellow pines.
    2. Leaves 5 in a bundle; bundle sheaths falling early; cones exceeding 12 cm long   **1. *P. strobiformis.***
    2. Leaves usually 3 in a bundle (rarely 2, 4, or 5); bundle sheaths persistent; cones 5–10 cm long.
        3. Leaves on same tree mainly in 3's and 2's; prickles on female cones stout, persistent, 1.5–2 mm long   **2. *P. ponderosa.***
        3. Leaves on same tree mainly in 5's, 4's, and 3's; prickles fine often deciduous, ca. 1 mm long   **3. *P. arizonica* var. *stormiae.***
1. Mature trees seldom more than 10–15 m tall, usually shorter; leaves 2–3 per cluster; pinyon pines.
    4. Leaves usually stout and somewhat curved, semicircular in cross section, whitish lines on outer rounded surface; Culberson Co.   **4. *P. edulis.***
    4. Leaves usually slender and rather straight (rarely somewhat stout and curved), often triangular in cross section; S-cen. Trans-Pecos.
        5. Crown conical; fascicle bases (scales) recurved in near complete curl or more; first-year fascicle sheaths and scales rich chestnut; elevations of 5000 ft. or more, usually in Davis Mts.   **5. *P. cembroides.***

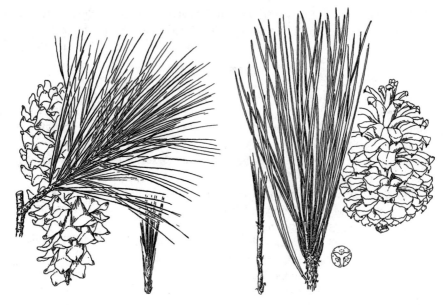

Fig. 17. *Pinus strobiformis*   Fig. 18. *Pinus ponderosa* (Ponderosa Pine)
(Southwestern White Pine)

5. Crown rounded; fascicle bases (scales) merely reflexed or recurved by about one-half or less; first-year fascicle sheaths and scales pale, sand-colored; widespread in SE Trans-Pecos, mostly below 5000 ft.   **6. *P. remota.***

1. Pinus strobiformis Engelm. SOUTHWESTERN WHITE PINE, PINO ENANO. Fig. 17. [*Pinus flexilis* James; *P. flexilis* var. *reflexa* Engelm.; *P. reflexa* (Engelm.) Engelm.]. Scattered or in small stands, higher elevations and deep canyons. Culberson Co., Guadalupe Mts. Jeff Davis Co., Davis Mts., Mt. Livermore and vicinity (especially Madera Canyon). 5000–8200 ft. Not known from the Chisos Mts. Easily distinguished from the other, more common tall pine, *P. ponderosa,* by smooth whitish-grey bark, and 5-bundled leaves, 4–9 cm long; also Coah., Mex.

2. Pinus ponderosa P. & C. Laws. PONDEROSA PINE, WESTERN YELLOW PINE. Fig. 18. [*Pinus brachyptera* Engelm.]. Common tall pine (about 60–80 ft.) at higher elevations and deep canyons. Culberson Co., Guadalupe Mts. Jeff Davis Co., Davis Mts. According to Dana K. Bailey (pers. comm.), genuine *Pinus ponderosa* occurs in the Guadalupe and Davis Mts., but the large pines in the Chisos Mts. long held to be ponderosas are actually *P. arizonica* var. *stormiae* Martinez. Our ponderosa is referable to *P. ponderosa* var. **scopulorum** Engelm. which continues W to S CA and N to Rocky Mts., cen. MT; Son.; Chih., Mex.; *P. ponderosa* var. *ponderosa* occurs from CA N into B.C., Can.

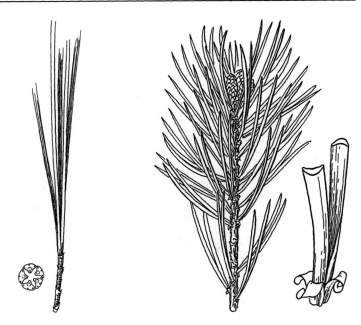

Fig. 19. *Pinus arizonica* var. *stormiae*   Fig. 20. *Pinus edulis* (Colorado Pinyon)

Ponderosa Pine is an important timber tree in the western United States, and is perhaps the most widespread pine in North America. Ponderosa stands in the Trans-Pecos are not dense enough even for limited timbering. In the 1880's a sawmill was built in the Davis Mountains (upper Limpia Canyon, also known locally as Sawmill Canyon) to provide lumber for the cavalry post at Ft. Davis.

3. **Pinus arizonica** var. **stormiae** Martinez.   Fig. 19.   Brewster Co., Chisos Mts., Pine Canyon; Crown Mt., N slope; Boot Canyon, S slopes. This primarily Mexican species (Coah., Tam., N.L.) occurs in the United States only in the Chisos Mts. (Bailey, pers. comm.). According to Bailey the var. *stormiae* may be distinct enough to deserve species status. In the Chisos Mountains *P. arizonica* is most common in Pine Canyon, where the National champion tree was recorded by Jim Liles to be 105 ft. high, with a 48 ft. crown spread, and 9 ft. girth. Few plants occur at the other sites. Kral (1993) seemingly recognizes (my inference) the ponderosa-like pine in the Chisos Mountains as *P. ponderosa* var. *scopulorum*.

4. **Pinus edulis** Engelm. PINYON, NUT PINE, COLORADO PINYON, NEW MEXICO PINYON PINE. Fig. 20. [*Pinus cembroides* var. *edulis* (Engelm.) Voss]. Culberson Co. common on slopes of the Guadalupe Mts.; Sierra Diablo, rim of Victorio Canyon and elsewhere; locally frequent N through NM to CO

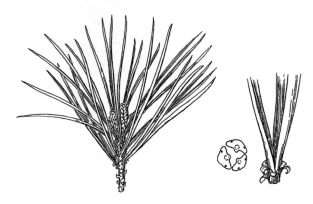

Fig. 21. *Pinus cembroides* (Mexican Pinyon)

and W to UT and AZ; also in N Mex., and localized in SE CA, SW WY, and NW OK.

The edible seeds (pinyon nuts) of *Pinus edulis,* the State tree of New Mexico, are gathered from native stands, especially in New Mexico, and sold in stores, at roadsides, and shipped to the eastern cities. Smaller trees of *P. edulis* have been confused with *P. cembroides,* in that some plants of both species have short trunks with compact, globose, spreading crowns and 2–3-fascicled leaves, 2.5–4.5 cm long. More typically the crowns of *P. edulis* are somewhat globose, while those of *P. cembroides* are conical. In addition to the key characters above, *P. edulis* is usually 12–17 m tall, has cones 3.5–5 cm long, and seeds usually soft-shelled, while *P. cembroides* seldom exceeds 10 m, with cones 2.5–4 cm long, and hard-shelled seeds. The seeds of *P. remota* are thin-shelled. All three taxa are basically delimited by their distributions. It has been observed that *P. edulis* is frequently parasitized (in West Dog Canyon, Guadalupe Mountains; Warnock, 1977), by the forking Dwarf Mistletoe *Arceuthobium divaricatum.* Occasional parasites of the same species are found on *P. cembroides* in the Davis Mountains. In the Trans-Pecos Dwarf Mistletoe parasites have not been found on pines distributed south of the Davis Mountains.

5. **Pinus cembroides** Zucc. MEXICAN PINYON PINE, PINYON, PINO PIÑONERO. Fig. 21. Slopes, mesas, and in higher canyons, mostly igneous substrates. Jeff Davis Co., Davis Mts.; Haystack Mt. Brewster Co., Mt. Ord;

Fig. 22. *Pinus remota* (Papershell Pinyon)

Altuda Mt.; Elephant Mt.; Chisos Mts.; Dead Horse Mts.; NE Rosillos Mts. Presidio Co., Sierra Vieja, upper Musgrave Canyon. 4700–7000 ft. Major distribution in N Mex.

The Trans-Pecos plants are *Pinus cembroides* var. **cembroides** which does not occur in the United States except in Texas (Bailey, pers. comm.). Mexican Pinyon seeds are hard-shelled thus not easy to eat, although they are tasty. *Pinus cembroides* in the Trans-Pecos is a higher elevation taxon, usually occurring at 5000 ft. or more (or low as 4700 ft. in the Chisos Mountains). The National champion of this species, 46 ft. tall, 44 ft. crown spread, 9.2 ft. girth, is found on the north slope of Mt. Emory in Big Bend National Park. Kral (1993) treated *P. remota* as a synonym of *P. cembroides*, citing the intergradation of reported distinguishing characters (see *P. remota*). My current observations suggest that *P. remota* and *P. cembroides* are distinct taxa, usually recognizable in the field by broader, rounded crowns in *P. remota* and rather conical crowns in *P. cembroides*.

6. Pinus remota (Little) Bailey & Hawksworth. PAPERSHELL PINYON. Fig. 22. *P. cembroides* Zucc. var. *remota* Little. Scattered and often isolated populations, mostly limestone substrates. Hudspeth Co., Eagle Mts., S end below highest peaks. Brewster Co., Mt. Ord; Altuda Mt.; Glass Mts.; Sierra Madera; Cienega Mt.; Cathedral Mt.; 19 mi E Marathon; Pine Mt., 8 mi SE Santiago Peak; Shely Ranch, near San Francisco Canyon; reported from E side

Dead Horse Mts., and ½ mi NW Sue Peaks, Big Bend National Park. Pecos Co., Sierra Madera. Val Verde Co.; between Del Rio and Loma Alta. 2500–5000 ft. Also W-cen. Edwards Plateau, centered around Rocksprings; Coah., N.L., N Chih., Mex.

Pinus remota, previously referred to as *P. cembroides* var. *remota* and thought to be restricted to the Edwards Plateau, is now considered to be the most widespread pinyon in the Trans-Pecos. It is a lower elevation taxon, usually occurring at less than 5000 ft. in the Trans-Pecos region. Bailey and Hawksworth (1979) have concluded that *P. remota* and *P. cembroides* occur together without hybridization in a few localities (e.g., Altuda Mt.; Mt. Ord) at an intermediate elevation of about 5000 ft. Additional characters for distinguishing *P. remota* are that its mature cones are relatively fragile and have sharp-pointed scales, and the frequent presence of more than two resin ducts per needle. Two resin ducts per needle are typical of *P. cembroides* and *P. edulis.* Also, according to Bailey (pers. comm.) the cones of *P. remota* are borne on stalks 5–8 mm long, and in mature, dry cones the apophyses (exposed portions of cone scale) are ochre to reddish-brown, the umbos (convex area of scale) are recessed and much less than half width of the apophysis. The cones of *P. cembroides* are borne on stalks 2–5 mm long, and in mature, dry cones the apophyses are reddish-brown and wrinkled, the umbos protuberant and about half the width of the apophysis.

The isolated nature of the pinyon colonies and the work of Wells (1966) and Van Devender et al. (1978), with fossil packrat middens suggest that *Pinus remota* and *P. cembroides* were more widespread and perhaps continuous in the west Texas area during the Pleistocene. The pinyon species, including *P. edulis,* are among the most drought-resistant pines, usually growing in association with junipers.

3. EPHEDRACEAE DUM. EPHEDRA FAMILY

Bushy or viny dioecious shrubs, stems green, yellow-green or blue-green, almost naked, jointed, opposite or whorled. Leaves tiny, usually in scalelike sheaths at conspicuous nodes, opposite or whorled, the sheaths persistent or deciduous. Female cones of 1 or 2 ovules enclosed in a vaselike perianth, hardening at maturity; male cones with fused stamens in a calyxlike perianth; both male and female cones produced in the spring.

A family with one genus of about 40 species, geologically old, and distributed in the arid regions of the Northern Hemisphere in North America, northern Africa, and Asia.

1. EPHEDRA L. MORMON TEA, MEXICAN TEA

Shrubs; stems jointed, green. Leaves scalelike at the nodes.
A Chinese species, *Ephedra sinica*, produces the alkaloid ephedrine which has been known for its medicinal value (for colds and hay fever) since 2737 B.C. In North America these desert shrubs are widely distributed throughout the southwestern United States and northern Mexico. American Mexicans and Indians have used decoctions of roots and stems, especially of *E. antisyphilitica*, to treat syphilis. Dried stems are used to boil or steep a flavorful and refreshing hot tea or cooling beverage. *Ephedra* seeds have been used to make a bitter bread. The plants are browsed by deer and cattle, the latter usually when other food is scarce. Seeds are eaten by quail. Another species of *Ephedra*, *E. intermixta* Cutler, other than those treated below, has been reported from the Franklin Mountains near El Paso.

KEY TO THE SPECIES

1. Leaves in 3's at each node; scales of cones in 3's.
    2. Leaves 2–5 mm long, with obtuse or acute tips   **1. E. torreyana.**
    2. Leaves 5–13 mm long with tips awnlike   **2. E. trifurca.**
1. Leaves in 2's at nodes; scales of cones in 2's.
    3. Leaf bases persistent, swollen, brown to blackish; plants bright green or yellowish.
        4. Female cones on long, naked peduncles; seeds paired   **3. E. coryi.**
        4. Female cones sessile, or on short, scaly peduncles; seeds solitary, rarely paired   **4. E. nevadensis var. aspera.**
    3. Leaf bases not long-persistent, not swollen, grayish or with a brown or tan line encircling the stem; plants dull green or grayish-green.
        5. Shrubs vinelike, climbing or trailing; stems without narrow bands below the leaves; cones on naked peduncles to 2 cm long, seeds in pairs; anthers stipitate   **5. E. pedunculata.**
        5. Shrubs erect or spreading; stems with narrow pale orange to brown bands below the leaves; cones sessile or on short peduncles, seeds solitary (rarely two); anthers essentially sessile   **6. E. antisyphilitica.**

1. Ephedra torreyana S. Wats. TORREY EPHEDRA, MORMON TEA. Rocky hills and slopes, especially in gypsum and saline habitats. El Paso, Hudspeth, Culberson, Reeves, Ward, and Brewster counties; also in the Panhandle, and with isolated populations in gypsum around salt lakes in Howard Co.; widely distributed from TX to W CO, and to N AZ and NV.

Wendt (1993) has recognized two varieties of *Ephedra torreyana* in the Trans-Pecos: *E. torreyana* Wats. var. **torreyana**, which occurs in the northern Trans-Pecos from El Paso County east in Hudspeth, Culberson, Reeves, Ward,

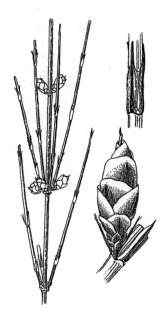

Fig. 23. *Ephedra trifurca* (Longleaf Ephedra)

and Winkler counties, also in the Texas Panhandle, and northwest through New Mexico to Colorado, Utah, Arizona, and Nevada; and *E. torreyana* var. **powelliorum** Wendt, which occurs in southern Brewster County in Big Bend National Park, 6.9 mi north of Panther Junction and in Tornillo Flats, and adjacent Chihuahua, Mexico. The var. *torreyana* is distinguished by seeds mostly 2–3 (rarely 1) per cone, seed surface rough with minute papillae, and anthers mostly 6–7(–4–8) per male cone, while the var. *powelliorum* has seeds mostly 1 (rarely 2) per cone, seed surface smooth except wrinkled at the base, and anthers mostly 3–5(–2–7) per male cone. *Ephedra torreyana* may hybridize with other species of the genus (Wendt, 1993).

2. **Ephedra trifurca** Torr. *ex* S. Wats. LONGLEAF EPHEDRA, CANATILLA. Fig. 23. Widely distributed in all counties of the Trans-Pecos in various desert habitats, less common in Terrell and Val Verde counties; NE to Ward and Loving counties; also in S NM, W to CA, and adjacent Mex.

The persistent spinose leaves of main stems and spinose terminal buds of yellowed branches are readily distinguishable traits of this species.

3. **Ephedra coryi** E. L. Reed. CORY EPHEDRA. Of peripheral Trans-Pecos distribution, Winkler, Loving, Ward counties (near Kermit, Wink, Mentone, Monahans); chiefly in the rocky hills of the Edwards Plateau, or sandy areas and prairies of the south Plains country; also in SE NM.

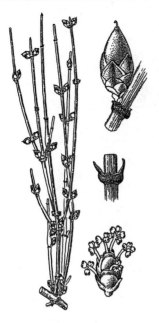

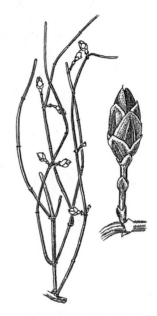

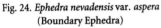

Fig. 24. *Ephedra nevadensis* var. *aspera*   Fig. 25. *Ephedra pedunculata* (Vine Jointfir)
(Boundary Ephedra)

4. Ephedra nevadensis S. Wats. var. **aspera.** (Engelm. *ex* S. Wats.) L. Benson. BOUNDARY EPHEDRA, POPOTILLO.   Fig. 24.   [*Ephedra reedii* Cory; *E. aspera* Engelm.]. Rocky hills and various desert habitats throughout the Trans-Pecos, on the W edge of the Edwards Plateau, with disjunct occurrences in Webb Co. of the Rio Grande Plains; widespread in the SW U.S. and N Mex.
This species is distinguished from the similar *Ephedra coryi* by its stems which are rough to the touch (although some plants are smooth), one-seeded female cone, and leaves which are connate most of their length; also, *E. coryi*, which may have slightly rough stems, is of more northern and eastern distribution. A tea made from stems of *E. nevadensis* var. *aspera* is used in the vicinity of Marfa as a treatment for arthritis.

5. Ephedra pedunculata Engelm. *ex* S. Wats.   VINE JOINTFIR, COMIDA DE BIBORA.   Fig. 25.   Of peripheral Trans-Pecos distribution (Val Verde, Crockett counties) in the W Edwards Plateau, N to Howard Co. and E of the Pecos River S to Hidalgo Co. in the Rio Grande Plains, all the way S to S.L.P., Mex.
This species is distinctive in its clambering vinelike habit.

6. Ephedra antisyphilitica Berl. *ex* C. A. Mey.   VINE EPHEDRA, CLAPWEED, POPOTE, CANATILLA.   Fig. 26.   [Including var. *brachycarpa* Cory, *E. texana*

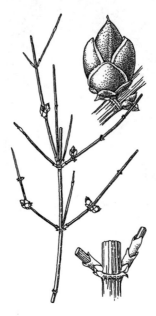

Fig. 26. *Ephedra antisyphilitica* (Vine Ephedra)

E. L. Reed]. Seemingly isolated in central and S Trans-Pecos, from Sanderson to Rankin to Del Rio (Warnock, 1970). Val Verde, Terrell, Pecos, Brewster (SR campus; Glass Mts. 20 mi E of Alpine) counties; also widely distributed in various habitats throughout most of the Rio Grande Plains, Edwards Plateau, and S Panhandle; and in SW OK; NE Mex.

A tea made from stems of this species has been used (unsuccessfully) in the treatment of syphilis, hence its name. Other species also have been widely used for the same purpose in the practice of folk medicine. The best traits for distinguishing *Ephedra antisyphilitica* are the slender pale-orange to tannish stem bands, found just below the leaves, and the reddish, fleshy-succulent female cones.

MONOCOTYLEDONAE

4. BROMELIACEAE JUSS.   PINEAPPLE FAMILY

Herbs or rarely shrublike, in the many epiphytic species roots serving merely as holdfasts. Leaves simple, arranged in spirals, usually basal, sheathed below, usually with peltate scales, margins smooth, toothed, or spined. Flowers usually in elongate clusters; usually with prominent bracts; flowers perfect or unisexual (and dioecious); perianth with obvious calyx and corolla, sepals and petals separate or fused; stamens 6, in 2 series; style 3-lobed; ovary superior, 3-celled; placentae axile. Fruit a capsule or berrylike and pulpy; seeds naked, winged or plumose.

A family of about 2000 species in about 45 genera, the largest family of seed plants almost completely native to the New World. A single genus, *Pitcairnia* L'Her., occurs in Africa. Prominent members of the family include the Pineapple, *Ananas comosus* (L.) Merrill, the famous epiphytic Spanishmoss, *Tillandsia usneoides* L., and epiphytic Small Ballmoss, *Tillandsia recurvata* L. Two genera are native to Texas, both with members in the Trans-Pecos.

1. HECHTIA KL.

Succulents, dimorphic, with the habit of *Agave lechuguilla* or short-stemmed yuccas. Leaves in dense basal rosettes, usually recurving, pointed, the margins coarsely spine-toothed, covered with scurfy scales at least on upper side. Flowers of male and female individuals loosely arranged at the apex of a scapose stalk, this usually sheathed above; flowers small, unisexual (one sex usually vestigial); sepals and petals free; anthers ovate; ovary superior, glabrous or scaly. Fruit a dehiscent capsule, ovate or nearly so; seeds oblong, numerous, narrowly winged or nearly naked.

A genus of above 50 species, mostly Mexican but distributed from Nicaragua to Texas. Two species occur in Texas, one in the Trans-Pecos.

1. Hechtia texensis S. Wats. TEXAS FALSEAGAVE. Fig. 27. [*Hechtia scariosa* L.B. Sm.]. Locally abundant rocky limestone mesas, ridges and slopes. Brewster Co., northern Lower Canyons of the Rio Grande; Dead Horse Mts., near Frog Tank, near McKinney Springs; Cave Hill, Stairstep Mt., Maravillas Canyon; Sierra Quemada, Dominguez Spring; above Boquillas; above Glenn Springs; near Reed Plateau and Black Mesa between Terlingua and Lajitas. Presidio Co. Bofecillos Mts. 1800–3700 ft.; Feb–May; NE Mex.

The Texas Falseagave is perhaps more common in southern Brewster County than once was believed. The plants often grow with and resemble Lechuguilla in succulent clusters to one meter across. The scurfy leaves, lighter in color, are distinctive from Lechuguilla, and in the fall usually turn reddish. The distribution of *H. texensis* is localized and spotty.

Hechtia glomerata Zucc. (Guapilla) has been reported from one collection in Presidio County, hill over Fresno Creek, ca. 2 mi southwest of Buenas Suerte, 2800 ft., 15 Apr 1949, although this record seems out of place with known localities of *H. glomerata* in Starr and Zapata counties of South Texas. The present treatment follows Burt-Utley and Utley (1987) in recognizing but one species for the area.

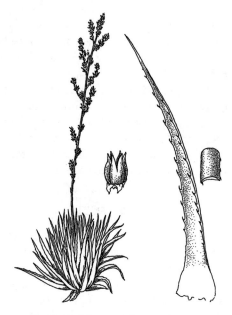

Fig. 27. *Hechtia texensis* (Texas Falseagave)

5. AGAVACEAE ENDL.   AGAVE FAMILY

Perennials, often ponderous with thick stems at least at the base, often tree-like, with fibrous roots. Leaves often in basal rosettes or in rosettes at the apexes of exposed stems, these thick, succulent, fleshy, or hard, or thin narrow, and tough, often-sharp-pointed, with or without marginal spines. Flowers in clusters, usually bisexual, if unisexual male and female may be on separate plants; perianth of 2 petallike (tepals) whorls, each in 3 parts, united into a short or long tube; stamens 6; ovary superior or inferior (*Agave*), carpels 3; style 1, slender. Fruit a capsule or berry.

A family of about 600 species in 18 genera distributed in the tropics, subtropics, and arid regions, with many species of notable horticultural and economic value. In organizing this family Hutchinson (1934) extracted members of the classical Liliaceae Juss. and Amaryllidaceae St.-Hil. and produced a seemingly natural alliance which might better be placed in the Agavaceae (Benson and Darrow, 1981; Cronquist, 1981). Most members of the Agavaceae, e.g., the yuccas, agaves, sotols, and sacahuistes, have in common rather bizarre habits in that the desert or semidesert plants develop spectacular rosettes of leaves from thick, mostly subterranean stem bases, which produce slender, upright flowering stalks. *Yucca, Agave,* and *Hesperaloe* and other genera of this group are also manifestly allied by a peculiar karyotype of 5 large and 25 small chromosomes. *Nolina* and *Dasylirion* lack this distinctive karyotype. In the Trans-Pecos only the yuccas (most species) develop conspicuous trunks or stems and thus have a treelike aspect. Members of the Agavaceae are the primary fiber plants of the Trans-Pecos.

KEY TO THE GENERA

1. Ovary superior.
   2. Leaf margins without prickles, sometimes minutely saw-toothed, horny, or filiferous (fibrous, sometimes peeling margins).
      3. Flowers white, cream, greenish-white, often pinkish-tinged.
         4. Leaves thick or thin, daggerlike, spine-tipped in most Trans-Pecos species   **1. Yucca.**
         4. Leaves grasslike, flexible, not spine-tipped   **2. Nolina.**
      3. Flowers pinkish-red   **4. Hesperaloe.**
   2. Leaf margins with prominent curved prickles   **3. Dasylirion.**
1. Ovary inferior   **5. Agave.**

1. YUCCA L.   SPANISH BAYONET, DAGGERS, BEARGRASS

Plants with simple or branching trunks (stems), with corky bark, fibrous and sometimes covered with withered leaves, or trunkless or nearly so with leaves clumped at ground level. Leaves in terminal rosettes, thick and stout or thin and flexible, usually widest near the middle, often concave on upper side, with fibrous or horny margins, spine-tipped. Inflorescence of racemes or panicles; flowers cream-white to greenish-white, with 3 outer sepals and 3 inner petals of similar appearance; stamens 6; stigmas 3. Fruit either dry or fleshy at maturity, and dehiscent or indehiscent, with numerous black seeds.

Yuccas flower mostly in the spring (April–May) or early summer (June–July), occasionally earlier or later. Supposedly these were very important plants to the Indians of the southwest (Kearney & Peebles, 1951). Roots and stems were used as a soap, and as a laxative. Leaf fibers, noticeable along the leaf margins of many species, were used to make cloth and rope from which many articles such as mats, baskets, and sandals were prepared. Flower buds and young flower stalks were eaten raw or cooked. Fruits were eaten raw or cooked, as were the seeds, or both were ground into meal. The pollination spectrum in our local yucca species is not totally understood, but in general yuccas are presumably pollinated by a specific moth (Dodd and Linhart, 1994). The Yucca Moth (*Tegeticula*) flies at dusk to a flower where she climbs stamens to collect pollen and pack the pollen in a large ball-like mass under her neck. She then visits another flower where she inserts her ovipositer directly through the ovary wall and deposits 20–30 eggs, one at a time, each directly into an ovule. She then climbs to the stigma of the same flower and spreads the pollen, thus ensuring pollination, subsequent fertilization, and developing seeds that provide nourishment for the moth larvae. Each larva ultimately destroys the seed in which it grows, but there are many undamaged seeds in left in the yucca capsule.

KEY TO THE SPECIES

1. Leaves thick and stout; fruit fleshy, indehiscent, pendent.
  2. Trunks or branches short or leaves clumped at ground level
                                                                    1. *Y. baccata.*
  2. Trunks obvious, usually tall.
    3. Pistils 40 mm long or less; plants usually of moderate size, usually not much exceeding 2 m high   **2. *Y. torreyi.***
    3. Pistils 45 mm long or longer; plants usually large, often exceeding 2.5 m high   **3. *Y. faxoniana.***
1. Leaves mostly thin (2–4 mm thick) and narrow; fruit dry or barely fleshy, dehiscent, not pendent.
    4. Leaf margins horny, saw-toothed or smooth   **4. *Y. thompsoniana.***
    4. Leaf margins with loose, peeling fibers.
      5. Plants with prominent trunks, usually exceeding 1 m in height
                                        5. *Y. elata.*
      5. Plants trunkless or with short stems.
        6. Leaves ca. 7 mm wide above the base; deep sand and dunes of northern Trans-Pecos   **6. *Y. campestris.***
        6. Leaves usually exceeding 8 mm wide above the base; brushlands of southeastern Trans-Pecos   **7. *Y. constricta.***

  1. Yucca baccata Torr. DATIL YUCCA, BANANA YUCCA. Fig. 28. Common in rocky soils from the south side of the Guadalupe Mts. in Culberson Co. to the Franklin Mts. in El Paso Co., E to W Edwards Plateau, in juniper and oak woodlands, grasslands, or rocky mountain slopes. 2500–7000 ft; Apr–Jun. Widespread in SW U.S., W to CA and adjacent Mex.

  This species reportedly hybridizes with *Yucca torreyi.* Datil Yucca is particularly notable for its edible, large bananalike fruits often exceeding 20 cm long.

  2. Yucca torreyi Shafer. SPANISH DAGGER, TORREY YUCCA. Fig. 29. [*Yucca baccata* Torr. var. *macrocarpa* Torr.; *Y. crassifolia* Engelm.; *Y. macrocarpa* (Torr.) Cov.]. Scattered to common on mesas, hills, and slopes in desert scrub or grassland; throughout the Trans-Pecos to El Paso Co. Feb–May. E and SE to the Edwards Plateau and upper Rio Grande Plains; also NM; northern Mex.

  According to Correll and Johnston (1970), some forms of the Spanish Dagger have bluish-green, glaucous leaves while commonly they are yellowish-green. *Yucca torreyi* is closely related to *Y. treculeana* Carr. of the brushland in

Fig. 28. *Yucca baccata* (Datil Yucca),
plant with fruits.

Fig. 29. *Yucca torreyi* (Spanish Dagger),
plant with flowers.

south-central Texas and northern Mex., and perhaps should be combined with
that species. *Yucca torreyi* and *Y. elata* are the most common yuccas of the
Trans-Pecos.

3. Yucca faxoniana (Trel.) Sarg. FAXON YUCCA, SPANISH BAYONET.
Fig. 30. [*Yucca carnerosana* (Trel.) McKelvey]. Scattered but locally common
in high desert plateaus, rim rock areas, and mountain slopes in Jeff Davis, Pre-
sidio, Culberson, and Hudspeth counties, especially near and below the Sierra
Vieja rim and 1 mi N Indian Hot Springs, to Sierra Blanca, to the Sierra Diablo
Mts. and Guadalupe Mts. Brewster Co., rocky slopes and flats, at Dagger Flat
between the Chisos and Dead Horse mountains, and scattered in the northern
Dead Horse Mts., Big Bend National Park. 2700–6700 ft. Mar–Jul. Also
Coah., S.L.P., Zac., Chih., Mex.

Faxon Yucca reportedly hybridizes with *Yucca torreyi*. Plants of *Y. faxoniana*
are the largest yuccas of the Trans-Pecos, in some areas reaching about 9 m
high with massive trunks more than 0.5 m in diameter. Locally these plants are
often referred to as "giant" yuccas. They have been widely transplanted as ornamentals, and visitors to the Trans-Pecos area will see them along highways
and on the Sul Ross State University campus. The giant yucca of southern
Brewster County has long been known as *Y. carnerosana* (Spanish Dagger), but
it is here regarded as synonymous with *Y. faxoniana*.

Fig. 30. *Yucca faxoniana* (Faxon Yucca)

Fig. 31. *Yucca thompsoniana*
(Thompson Yucca)

4. Yucca thompsoniana Trel. BEAKED YUCCA, THOMPSON YUCCA. Fig. 31. [*Yucca rostrata* Engelm.]. Abundant in canyons and mountain slopes, mostly in extreme SE Brewster Co., common in the Black Gap Refuge; also common or scattered in limestone substrates, Brewster, Pecos, Terrell, and Val Verde counties; also Crockett Co. Mar–Apr. More widespread in Coah. and Chih., Mex.

This species is easily identified by its horny and saw-toothed or smooth leaf margins and conspicuously beaked fruits. Mature plants of the Black Gap populations, previously known as *Yucca rostrata* (Beaked Yucca), are 3–3.5 m high, characteristically larger and with longer leaves than the more northern and eastern populations (1–2 m high) classically referred to as *Yucca thompsoniana*. The Thompson Yucca has been one of the most commercially exploited species of the Trans-Pecos, the plants having been dug by the thousands and sold in many parts of south-central U.S. *Yucca thompsoniana*, particularly the larger plants, is perhaps the most handsome yucca of the Trans-Pecos. This species reportedly hybridizes with *Y. reverchonii*.

5. Yucca elata (Engelm.) Engelm. SOAPTREE YUCCA, PALMELLA, SOAPWEED. Fig. 32. Widespread in the Trans-Pecos, in grasslands, desert hills, gypsum soils, mostly above 4000 ft., but does occur at lower altitudes in Big Bend Park. May–Jul. Common SW yucca, from TX to cen. NM and AZ; also Coah., Chih., and Son., Mex.

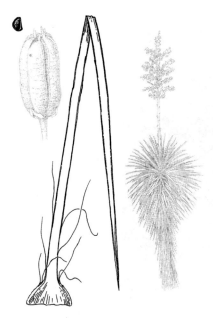

Fig. 32. *Yucca elata* (Soaptree Yucca)

Fig. 33. *Yucca campestris* (Plains Yucca),
plant with fruits.

According to Kearney and Peebles (1951) the stems of some plants reach a height of nearly 30 ft. The Soaptree Yucca receives its name from the detergent nature of its crushed stems and its roots (amole) which have been used to make shampoo and soap. During drought periods southwestern ranchers have used the leaves, sometimes mixed with other food, to feed livestock. Supposedly, cattle seek out young flowering stalks, thus on stocked ranges only the taller plants may produce flowers. The plants are known to sprout from roots, and may reproduce almost entirely by vegetative means except in the most favorable years (Smith and Ludwig, 1976).

6. **Yucca campestris** McKelvey. PLAINS YUCCA. Fig. 33. Of peripheral Trans-Pecos distribution, mostly in Ward, Crane, Winkler, Loving, and Ector counties, in the sand dune areas; also reported in sand, El Paso Co., 10 mi E El Paso. Apr–Jun. Also in Midland and Howard counties, TX.

The stemless Plains Yucca is a conspicuous element of the deep sands in Ward Co. and surrounding counties. It is reported that this species could have originated from hybridization between *Yucca elata* and *Y. constricta*.

7. **Yucca constricta** Buckl. BUCKLEY YUCCA. Fig. 34. Of peripheral Trans-Pecos distribution, mostly to the southeast in rocky limestone habitats and bushlands; known in Crockett Co. near Ozona. Apr–Jun. Distributionally centered in S and cen. TX; also in NE Mex.

This essentially trunkless species is not common in the Trans-Pecos.

Fig. 34. *Yucca constricta* (Buckley Yucca),
plants with flower buds.

2. NOLINA MICHX.

Plants with a subterranean woody caudex, resembling large, coarse grasses, or an unbranched above ground stem, and resembling yucca. Leaves linear, elongated, numerous and clustered, flat or channeled on upper surfaces, the margins finely toothed or smooth. Inflorescence a compound racemose panicle on a short stem, with numerous flowers, either bisexual, staminate, or pistillate; sepals and petals 6, white or greenish, thin, not more than 4 mm long; stamens 6, usually abortive, filaments shorter than perianth. Fruit a capsule, more or less inflated, with 3 thin-walled compartments, bursting irregularly; seeds roundish, swollen, brown to blackish.

Reportedly there are about 30 species native to the southern United States and Mexico. All of the Trans-Pecos species resemble large, coarse grasses in habit, while in Arizona and other southwestern states one species, *Nolina bigelovii* (Torr.) S. Wats., has a yuccalike trunk. Indians used fibers from the long leaves of many species for weaving baskets and mats, or used the entire leaves for these purposes. Sheep and goats eat young flower stalks but rarely eat the leaves, and the plants are reputed to be poisonous to these animals under certain conditions. The taxonomy, ecology, and precise distributions of the Trans-Pecos species are in need of further study.

KEY TO THE SPECIES

1. Leaf margins minutely and regularly sawtoothed   **1. *N. erumpens.***

1. Leaf margins smooth or essentially so, if toothed, then the small teeth few and far apart.
  2. Flowering parts purple-tinged; main flower stalk and branchlets slender and flexible; leaves semiterete   **2. *N. micrantha.***
  2. Flower parts not purple-tinged, or rarely so; main flower stalk and branchlets thick and rigid; leaves flat or concavo-convex.
    3. Leaves about 5 mm wide in lower half, flat or channeled on upper surfaces   **3. *N. arenicola.***
    3. Leaves 2–4 mm wide in lower half, channeled on upper surfaces toward bases, more triangular toward apexes   **4. *N. texana.***

1. **Nolina erumpens** (Torr.) S. Wats. FOOTHILL NOLINA, BEARGRASS. Fig. 35. Various rocky igneous and limestone soils, rocky hills and grasslands, Hudspeth, Culberson, Presidio, Jeff Davis, Brewster, and Terrell counties. 2100–7500 ft. Also in N Mex.

2. **Nolina micrantha** I. M. Johnst. Fig. 36. Limestone habitats. Culberson County, Guadalupe Mts. 4000–6500 ft. Also Chih. and Coah., Mex. According to Burgess and Northington (1981) this is the common species in the Guadalupe Mountains.

3. **Nolina arenicola** Correll. SAND SACAHUISTE. Fig. 37. Reported in deep sand, endemic in Culberson Co., 18 mi E of Van Horn and probably elsewhere. At least some plants produce purple-tinged inflorescences.

4. **Nolina texana** S. Wats. var. **texana.** TEXAS SACAHUISTE, BUNCHGRASS. Fig. 38. [*Nolina texana* var. *compacta* (Trel.) I. M. Johnst.; *N. affinis* Trel.]. Hills, slopes, grasslands, brushlands, various habitats, El Paso Co., Franklin Mts., E throughout most of the Trans-Pecos from the upper Rio Grande plains to cen.-TX, and in Garza Co. in the South Plains; also in N Mex.

3. DASYLIRION ZUCC. SOTOL

Plants dioecious, close to the ground with the stem mostly or completely subterranean. Leaves numerous, linear, flattened, striate, with prominent hooked teeth on the margins, the leaf bases spoonlike. Flowers unisexual, numerous and in compact racemes, overall forming a slender compound panicle toward the end of the long flower stalk; sepals and petals ca. 2 mm long, thin and whitish; stamens exserted and longer than the perianth. Fruit 3-winged and triangular, leathery and indehiscent; seeds solitary, obtusely triangular.

There are about 20 sotol species native to the southwestern United States

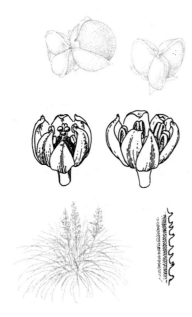

Fig. 35. *Nolina erumpens* (Foothill Nolina)

Fig. 36. *Nolina micrantha*, plant with panicles
of whitish flowers.

Fig. 37. *Nolina arenicola* (Sand Sacahuiste),
habit of species near Van Horn.

Fig. 38. *Nolina texana* (Texas Sacahuiste),
habit of species in grassland.

and northern Mexico. Flowering occurs in the spring or early summer. The long flower stalks have been used extensively in the southern Trans-Pecos and elsewhere, especially Mexico, to construct temporary shelters, porch and house roofs, corrals, and other structures. The spongy pith inside the basal trunks contains a lot of starch, and this material is roasted, fermented, and distilled to make a liquor known as "sotol." The sugary trunks and leaf bases also have been used to feed cattle during droughts. The headlike trunks, including the leaf bases, can also be roasted or boiled and eaten by man. Indians roasted and ate the young flower stalks and they used the narrow, tough leaves to fashion baskets, mats, coarse ropes, and other items (Benson and Darrow, 1954). The unusual spoonlike leaf bases are used in artificial floral arrangements. Sotols are easily grown from seed and the plants are desirable ornamentals. Further study is needed to help clarify the taxonomy, ecology, and precise distributions of the Trans-Pecos species.

KEY TO THE SPECIES

1. Curved teeth of leaves directed forward.
  2. Leaves rather bluish, glaucous, to 2–4 cm wide at the base; mature fruits narrowly obcordate, 4–8 mm wide, deeply notched at apex

    1. D. wheeleri.
  2. Leaves light green, 0.8–1 cm wide at the base; mature fruits broadly elliptic, 3–5 mm wide, shallowly notched at apex   **2. D. texanum.**
1. Curved teeth of leaves directed basally, or teeth straight and spreading laterally.
  3. Marginal teeth rather stout, mostly recurved; fruit broadly elliptic; leaves mostly 12–25 (–20) mm wide   **3. D. leiophyllum.**
  3. Marginal teeth slender, mostly straight, or with some curved forward or backward; fruit obovate-elliptic; leaves mostly 12–15 mm wide

    4. D. heteracanthum.

1. **Dasylirion wheeleri** S. Wats.   WHEELER SOTOL.   Common on slopes and hills of limestone or granite, El Paso Co., Franklin Mts. Hudspeth Co., Hueco Mts., northern Quitman Mts. 4000–4800 ft. Organ Mts. of NM across to S AZ; N Chih., Mex.

2. **Dasylirion texanum** Scheele.   TEXAS SOTOL.   Fig. 39.   Mostly in rocky limestone habitats, southeastern Trans-Pecos. Terrell Co. and Val Verde Co.; possibly in the novaculite hills near Marathon, Brewster Co.; common on the Edwards Plateau; also adjacent Mex.

3. **Dasylirion leiophyllum** Engelm. *ex* Trel.   SMOOTH SOTOL, DESERT CANDLE.   The most common species of the Trans-Pecos, hills and grasslands. Hudspeth, Culberson, Jeff Davis, Presidio, Brewster, and Pecos counties. 2200–6500 ft. Also in NM; Chih., Mex.

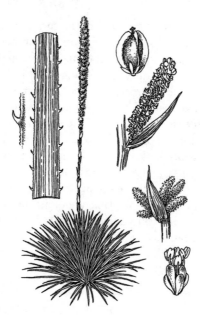

Fig. 39. *Dasylirion texanum* (Texas Sotol)

4. Dasylirion heteracanthum I. M. Johnst.   SOTOL.   Rocky slopes and desert grasslands, reported to occur in S Brewster and Presidio counties; adjacent Mex.

4. HESPERALOE ENGELM.

Coarse semisucculent with habit of *Agave* and *Yucca*, stem very short. Leaves clustered at the base, linear, to 120 cm long, usually shorter, ca. 2.5 cm wide, ridged on the back, the margins with peeling threads. Flowers loosely arranged on few branches at the apex of a flowering stem 1–2.5 m high; petals pinkish red, corolla tubular to broadly so to 3.5 mm long; stamens shorter than corolla, anthers 2 mm long; style slender, extended above corolla. Fruit a capsule, ca. 3 cm long, ovoid, 3-celled; seeds black, flattened, ca. 8 mm wide.

A genus of two species, occurring in Mexico and Texas. One species is native to Texas.

1. Hesperaloe parviflora (Torr.) Coult.   RED HESPERALOE, REDFLOWERED YUCCA.   Fig. 40.   Infrequent to rare, limestone hills and arroyos, often in crevices of rocks, growing with Lechuguilla and often beneath shrubs. Val Verde Co., 12 mi E of Langtry; J. Skiles ranch, near rim of the Pecos River Canyon, ca. 10 mi N of hwy. 90; 2 mi N of Devils crossing. 1800 ft.; Mar–Jul.

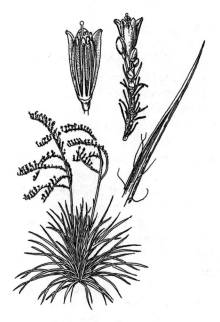

Fig. 40. *Hesperaloe parviflora* (Red Hesperaloe)

10 mi NW Del Rio; SW of Comstock near Rio Grande; mostly central TX, Collin, Haskell, Mills, San Saba counties, where relatively uncommon on rocky slopes and in mesquite thickets; also Mex.

This semisucculent plant with its rosy-red flowers is an attractive addition to cactus gardens and can be found planted as an ornamental in Alpine and other towns of the Trans-Pecos. The second species of the genus, *Hesperaloe funifera* (Koch) Trel., a native of Coahuila, Mexico, has been found once in the vicinity of the Devils River (Johnston, 1990), and is also prized as an ornamental.

5. AGAVE L. CENTURY PLANT, MAGUEY

Plants with evergreen, succulent leaves forming basal rosettes, often forming colonies from underground sprouts. Leaves large, margins with or without prickles, tipped with a hard spine. Flower stalks formed once after 8–20 years, relatively tall and large at maturity, bearing numerous flowers in spikes, racemes, or in panicles with umbellate flower-clusters; flowers greenish to yellow or pinkish, with 6 perianth segments forming a floral tube; ovary inferior, 3-celled, green, succulent. Fruit a brown capsule, often cylindrical, 3-celled, dehiscent, with flattened, black seeds in 2 rows in each cell.

The genus *Agave* with about 250 species is native to the tropical and subtropical Americas. A large number of the species occur in Mexico. Many agaves are valued for food and fiber, and as ornamentals, and they are cultivated in more than 40 tropical and subtropical countries. Eleven species are reported for Texas. Agave is included by some authors in the Amaryllidaceae. A definitive treatment of the agaves of North America is available (Gentry, 1982).

The large agaves are among the most spectacular desert plants of the southwestern United States and Mexico. The big long-lasting succulent leaves easily draw the attention of those who appreciate plants, but the agaves perhaps are best noted for the tall, attractive flowering stalks that appear once in the life of each plant. The name century plant, properly applied to any of the large agaves, originated from the erroneous belief that each plant lives for 100 years before it produces a flowering stalk during the last year of its life. Actually the age of flowering is variable, from eight to 20 (except reportedly 3–4 years in *Agave lechuguilla*), after which a plant does produce one rapidly growing flower stalk and die, seemingly exhausting all of its resources.

One of the most famous uses of agaves, especially in Mexico, is the production of alcoholic beverages known as pulque, mescal, and tequila. A sugary juice, which is the source of pulque, is obtained from the starchy central stems (crowns or heads) of certain large Mexican Maguey agaves. In order to obtain the juice for making pulque, a deep hole (juice basin) is made in the center of the crown of mature plants by cutting out the terminal leaf bud, allowing the green, yellowish, or whitish sap to exude into the cavity. The juice is collected from the plants and transported to a central locality where it is allowed to undergo fermentation, a brewing process, yielding pulque. Pulque has been described as the national drink of Mexico. Mescal and tequila are distilled products of mash made from the starchy crown. Tequila has become especially well-known for its use in making "margaritas," a favorite cocktail drink.

Agaves are cultivated extensively in Mexico and Central America for the production of fibers known as sisal hemp and henequen. Indians of the southwestern United States also used the native species for fibers, and as sources of food, medicine, drink, and soap (Castetter, et al., 1938). The sweet food, mescal, was prepared from the crowns of several of the larger *Agave* species, such as *A. parryi* Engelm., by removing the leaves and baking the crowns or heads ("cabezas") in pits lined with hot stones. Heat converts the starches to sugars. The Mescalero Apache derived their name from the extensive use of mescal as food, but other Indians, including the Chiricahua Apache, also ate mescal. Indians prepared a highly intoxicating drink, also known as mescal, from roasted crowns which were cut into pieces, pounded to a soft pulp, and allowed to ferment. Certain smaller *Agave* species, known commonly as amoles, were the source of a soapy substance (containing sapogenin) obtained from their stems. Many other uses of agaves are discussed by Gentry (1972; 1982). Other than the *Agave* species listed below, R. Worthington (pers. comm.) has reported *A. palmeri* Engelm. to be of rare occurrence in the Franklin Mts., El Paso Co.

KEY TO THE SPECIES

1. Plants relatively small; inflorescence cylindrical, a spike or raceme; flower tube shallow and open.
    2. Leaves light-green to yellowish, 2–4 cm wide above base, lower surfaces, if fresh, checked with green lines; marginal teeth directed downward
                                                                1. *A. lechuguilla.*
    2. Leaves dark green to bluish-green, 5–7 cm wide above base, lower surfaces not checked with green lines; marginal teeth directed upward
                                                                2. *A. glomeruliflora.*
1. Plants of medium or large size; inflorescence a slender to broad panicle with flowers arranged in clusters; flower tube deep, cylindrical (except perhaps in *Agave gracilipes*).
    3. Leaves 40–70 cm long, 15–20 cm wide above base; panicles large and broad with lateral branches horizontal to mostly declined
                                                                3. *A. havardiana.*
    3. Leaves smaller, 18–45 cm long, 5–12 cm wide above base; panicles smaller, narrower, the lateral branches ascending or horizontal, not declined.
        4. Rosettes small and compact; flowers small with rather shallow, open tubes, the tepals 2.5–4 times as long as tube; flowering in fall
                                                                4. *A. gracilipes.*
        4. Rosettes large and compact or small and open; flowers large with deep tubes, the tepals only 1–2 times as long as tube; flowering in spring   **5. *A. neomexicana.***

    1. Agave lechuguilla Torr. LECHUGUILLA. Fig. 41.   Perhaps the most widely distributed of all agaves, on rocky slopes throughout the Chihuahuan Desert in Trans-Pecos TX, S NM, and N Mex, S to Hgo. *Agave lechuguilla* is almost restricted to and is considered an indicator species of the boundaries of the Chihuahuan Desert.

    The flowering stalk with purplish or yellowish flowers may reach 5 m tall. The plants reproduce largely by rhizomelike offshoots, which are eaten by deer and javelina (Warnock, 1970). Lechuguilla is the source of hard fibers, known as "istle," used for rope, twine, and other materials. Lechuguilla is poisonous to livestock but is seldom eaten except in times of stress. The toxic principle is saponin. The specific epithet "*lechuguilla*," long misspelled "*lecheguilla*," was corrected by Gentry (1982).

    2. Agave glomeruliflora (Engelm.) Berger. CHISOS AGAVE. [*Agave heteracantha* var. *glomeruliflora* Engelm.; *A. lechuguilla* f. *glomeruliflora* (Engelm.) Trel.; *A. chisosensis* C. H. Mull.]. Grassland slopes, scattered in several mountain ranges. Culberson Co., 6 mi NE of Nickel Creek Camp on Boger Canyon, E slope of Guadalupe Mts.; near Kent. Hudspeth Co., N of Allamoore. Brew-

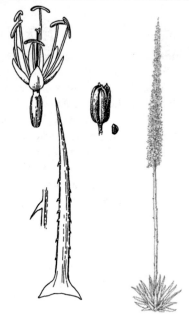
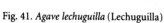

Fig. 41. *Agave lechuguilla* (Lechuguilla)

Fig. 42. *Agave havardiana* (Havard Agave),
Chisos Mountains, Big Bend National Park
(photo by Harry Gordon).

ster Co., Glass Mts., Gilliland Flat; Chisos Mts., Basin area. 2000–5000 ft.;
Jun–Oct. Mex., Coahuila, Sierra del Carmen, Sierra de la Madera.

This agave is suspected to be of hybrid origin, perhaps resulting from a cross
between *Agave lechuguilla* and *A. gracilipes, A. neomexicana,* or *A. havardiana*
in different portions of its range (Gentry, 1982). *Agave glomeruliflora* is similar
to *A. gracilipes* but the former species has leaves to 55 cm long, and the corneous margin is continuous from the base to the terminal spine, while the leaves
of *A. gracilipes* are less than 30 cm long and the terminal spine extends along
the margin only to about the middle of the blade (Burgess, 1979).

3. Agave havardiana Trel.   HAVARD AGAVE.   Fig. 42.   Rocky and grassy
slopes. Culberson Co., Guadalupe Mts., one collection near mouth of Mc-
Kittrick Canyon, Gentry (1982). Jeff Davis Co., mountains near Ft. Davis.
Brewster Co., common in the Glass Mts., and the Chisos Mts. Pecos Co., Ma-
dera Mts. Presidio Co., Chinati Mts.; 4000–6500 ft.; June–Oct. Mex., Chih.,
Coah.

The large agaves in the Glass Mountains, Brewster Co., and in the Davis
Mountains have been identified as *Agave havardiana* (Gentry, 1982). *Agave
neomexicana* (Warnock, 1977) does not occur in the Davis and Glass mountains according to Gentry (1982). Havard Agave is distinguished by its deep

Fig. 43. *Agave gracilipes* (Slimfooted Agave),
habit of species in Guadalupe Mountains

flower tubes and relatively short tepals and by the broad-based leaves with reflexed teeth.

4. Agave gracilipes Trel. SLIMFOOTED AGAVE. Fig. 43. El Paso-Hudspeth counties, Franklin Mts., Hueco Mts.; Sierra Diablo, 12 mi N of Allamoore; Culberson Co., Mex., Chih. The *Agave gracilipes* reported to occur in the Glass Mts., Brewster Co. (Warnock, 1977) is *A. glomeruliflora* according to Gentry (1982).

Agave gracilipes may hybridize with *A. lechuguilla* at a locality north of Allamoore in Hudspeth County and at other sites in the northern Trans-Pecos. Burgess (1979) considers *A. gracilipes* to be a product of hybridization between *A. neomexicana* and *A. lechuguilla*, and Gentry (1982) also discusses this possibility. *Agave gracilipes* is the smallest agave in the Trans-Pecos, although some forms of *A. neomexicana* are also quite small. In fact, these two species are similar vegetatively, but can be distinguished by the floral characters included in the key. Also, in *A. gracilipes* the panicle is usually slender with lateral branches ascending, while the broader panicle of *A. neomexicana* has lateral branches.

5. Agave neomexicana Woot. & Standl. NEWMEXICO AGAVE. Fig. 44. Rocky slopes and grasslands. El Paso Co., Franklin Mts., S of South Mt. Cul-

Fig. 44. *Agave neomexicana* (New Mexico Agave), habit of species in Guadalupe Mountains.

berson Co., Guadalupe Mts., E slopes. 5000–7000 ft.; Apr–Jun. More common in S NM (Gentry, 1982); Mex., Coah.

Previous reports of *Agave parryi* Engelm. (Parry Agave) in the Guadalupe Mts. are considered by Gentry (1982) to be in error. Plants in the Guadalupes thought to be *A. parryi* are actually larger plants of *A. neomexicana. Agave parryi* is considered by Gentry (1982) to be confined to areas west of the Rio Grande, while Ullrich (1992) recognized *A. neomexicana* as a subspecies of *A. parryi: A. parryi* subsp. *neomexicana* (Woot. & Standl.) Ullrich.

DICOTYLEDONAE

6. SALICACEAE MIRB. WILLOW AND COTTONWOOD FAMILY

Trees or shrubs, with bark bitter, deeply grooved or checkered, wood light-colored and soft. Leaves alternate, simple and with stipules, narrowly linear or lanceshaped to broadly heartshaped, margins entire or toothed. Flowers unisexual, with male and female flowers in catkins (aments) and on separate plants (dioecious), sepals and petals absent, each flower subtended by a small scale; stamens 2 to numerous; anthers yellow. Fruit a capsule, 1-celled, but formed from 2–4 carpels; seeds small, numerous, with tufts of long, comose hairs.

In the arid Trans-Pecos, willows and cottonwoods are found where water is close to the surface, beside rivers or ephemeral streams, in mountain canyons, or close to water holes and seeps. Willows are easily distinguished by their narrow leaves, while cottonwoods have broader lanceolate, triangular, or heart-shaped leaves. The characteristic catkins of flowers appear in early spring before or at the same time as the leaves.

KEY TO THE GENERA

1. Leaves narrowly lanceolate or linear; buds with one scale, not resinous; flowers without a subtending disc; floral bracts somewhat persistent; stamens 2–8 in each flower; fruits elongated   **1. Salix.**
1. Leaves broadly lanceolate or about as broad as long; buds with several resinous scales; flowers borne on a cuplike or shallow disc; floral bracts early deciduous; stamens 6–60 in each flower; fruits nearly round or conical
                                                                2. Populus.

1. SALIX L.   WILLOW, SAUZ

Small shrubs or trees up to 12 m in our species; bud scales single. Leaves usually with stipules, blades linear, lanceolate, oblong, or elliptic, glabrous to hairy, lower surfaces green or glacous, margins entire or toothed. Catkins (aments) directed upwards, not pendulous, 1–10 cm long, slender; flower scales somewhat persistent, usually hairy, entire or irregularly toothed. Flowers without a disc; stamens 2–8; style 1; stigmas 2, entire or double. Fruits elongated, lanceolate to nearly oval, glabrous or hairy, at maturity with 2 recurving valves; seeds small, 0.8–1.2 mm long, numerous, with basal tufts of fine hairs; seeds dispersed by wind.

Willows are common throughout the Northern Hemisphere, with most of the ca. 300 species occurring in temperate and arctic regions, and with a few species in the tropical Americas and Southern Hemisphere. Although willows often are abundant along the banks of desert streams, relatively few species occur in the arid regions. The following key and discussion is adapted from a treatment (for the *Chihuahuan Desert Flora*) kindly provided by M. C. Johnston.

KEY TO THE SPECIES

1. Twigs greatly elongated and "weeping"; leaf blades linear-lanceolate and sickleshaped; trees to 12 m tall   **1. S. babylonica.**
1. Twigs not elongated, or only moderately so, and not weeping, perhaps

slightly drooping; leaf blades, linear, lanceolate, or otherwise; shrubs or trees to 10 m tall.
2. Usually trees 4–10 m high; leaf blades pendulous; stamens 3–8 per flower.
   3. Leaf blades glaucescent on lower surfaces, the lower surfaces noticeably paler than upper surfaces   **2. S. amygdaloides.**
   3. Leaf blades with lower and upper surfaces nearly of uniform color.
      4. Branchlets (and often leaves) with a yellowish cast   **3. S. gooddingii.**
      4. Branchlets rather dark   **4. S. nigra.**
2. Usually shrubs or small trees to 5 m high; blades often spreading or ascending, rarely drooping; stamens 2 per flower.
   5. Leaf blades usually linear, less often linear-lanceolate, with stomates about the same number on both surfaces; flowers more or less spreading on catkin axis.
      6. Catkins short, male catkins usually 5–13 mm long and ca. 8 mm wide, female catkins few-flowered, at most 2 cm long and 1.2 cm wide in fruit   **5. S. taxifolia.**
      6. Catkins averaging longer   **6. S. exigua.**
   5. Leaf blades linear-lanceolate to linear-oblanceolate, with stomates absent or very few on upper surfaces; flowers appressed
      7. S. lasiolepis.

   1. **Salix babylonica** L. WEEPING WILLOW. Fig. 45. This striking species, a native of north China, is planted as an ornamental in the yards of many Trans-Pecos towns, as it is in other parts of America, mostly at elevations below 3500 ft., and in Europe. It is not known to grow wild as an escaped cultivar in the Trans-Pecos, although its twigs sprout readily under favorable conditions.

   2. **Salix amygdaloides** Anderss. PEACHLEAF WILLOW. Fig. 45, 46. [*Salix amygdaliodes* var. *wrightii* (Anderss.) Schneider]. Along streams and other water sources, especially the Rio Grande. El Paso Co., near El Paso and elsewhere. Hudspeth Co., Fort Quitman. Scattered elsewhere in the western Trans-Pecos. 2900 ft. S NM, W to AZ and NV, N from KY to Can; probably in extreme N Chih., Mex.

Salix amygdaloides, *S. gooddingii*, and *S. nigra* are closely related taxa commonly referred to as the black willows. The black willows are usually fairly large trees (arboreal) with drooping leaves that are usually 0.8 cm or more wide and usually with prominent petioles more or less 0.5 cm long. The three species are not easily distinguished morphologically, but *S. amygdaloides* supposedly differs in its firmer leaves with smooth, pale undersurfaces and little evident vein-reticulum. The black willows differ markedly in their known Trans-Pecos distributions. *Salix amygdaloides* is scattered in distribution, being most common near the Rio Grande in El Paso and Hudspeth counties. *Salix nigra* is restricted

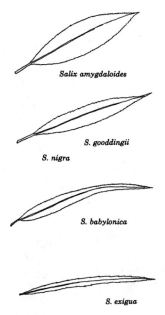

Salix amygdaloides

S. gooddingii

S. nigra

S. babylonica

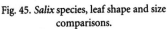

S. exigua

Fig. 45. *Salix* species, leaf shape and size comparisons.

Fig. 46. *Salix amygdaloides* (Peachleaf Willow)

to the extreme southeastern Trans-Pecos while *S. gooddingii* is by far the most common and most widely distributed willow in the region.

Another willow, *Salix bonplandiana* Kunth., somewhat like the Peachleaf Willow has been tentatively identified by M. C. Johnston (pers. comm.) to occur in the Trans-Pecos. The tentative identification is based upon a recent sterile collection from Tinaja Prieta Canyon, Chinati Mts., Presidio Co., which differs from the Peachleaf Willow in its leaves not glaucous underneath but with both surfaces of the same color, somates absent from the upper surfaces, and reddish petioles. *Salix bonplandiana* is widespread in the dry highlands of Mexico and north to Arizona, New Mexico, California, Nevada, and Utah, with its closest known distribution near Chihuahua City, Mexico, about 120 miles to the southwest. Confirmation of the occurrence of this species in the Trans-Pecos must await the collection of more complete material from the Chinati Mts.

3. **Salix gooddingii** Ball. GOODDING WILLOW. Fig. 45, 47. [*Salix gooddingii* var. *variabilis* Ball]. Widespread along watercourses and near springs, the most common willow in the Trans-Pecos, El Paso Co., E to Val Verde Co. (Mile Canyon near Langtry); also Winkler and Ward counties. 2000–4600 ft. W to CA; Baja CA, S to Sin. and Coah., Mex.

Salix gooddingii is weakly distinguished from *S. nigra*, supposedly differing

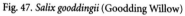

Fig. 47. *Salix gooddingii* (Goodding Willow)   Fig. 48. *Salix taxifolia* (Yewleaf Willow)

only in the yellowish coloration of its leaves and twigs, the paler bark, and the slightly greater number of hairs on young twigs and leaves. However, almost any large, drooping-leaved willow in the Trans-Pecos will be *S. gooddingii*. According to Jim Liles the State champion of this species is located near the Alamito Creek bridge below Presidio.

4. Salix nigra Marsh. BLACK WILLOW. Fig. 45. [*Salix nigra* var. *lindheimeri* Schneider]. Near water sources. Val Verde Co., Amistad Reservoir; also Scurry Co., near Snyder and along the shore, Lake J. B. Thomas. 1000–2600 ft. E to Dallas Co. and S to the Guadalupe River; N to MN, E to FL; N. L., Coah. (Cuatro Cienegas basin; near Monclova), and Tam., Mex.

The Black Willow occurs only on the eastern periphery of the Trans-Pecos. It differs from the closely related *Salix gooddingii* in the dark coloration of its twigs, leaves, and bark.

5. Salix taxifolia Kunth. YEWLEAF WILLOW. Fig. 48. [*Salix taxifolia* var. *limitanea* I.M. Johnston; not *S. microphylla* Schldl. & Cham., see Argus and McJannet, 1992]. Along permanent and ephemeral streams and near springs. Jeff Davis Co., Limpia Canyon, 12 mi N Ft. Davis; Limpia Creek near Ft. Davis; Wild Rose Pass; Musquiz Creek; Horse Thief Canyon, Kokernot Ranch. Presidio Co., Cibolo Creek near Shafter; near Cieniquita. Brewster Co.,

Fig. 49. *Salix exigua* (Coyote Willow)

Calamity Creek, 22 mi S Alpine. 3900–4500 ft. Also NM and S AZ; in Baja CA, Coah., Chih., and Son., and southward, Mex.

The species and common names refer to the crowded, small, yewlike leaves. *Salix taxifolia* and *S. exigua* are exceedingly closely related taxa of the section *Longifoliae* Andersson. These plants are usually shrubs or small trees with ascending, relatively narrow leaves that are sessile or with very short petioles. The group is further distinguished by very small catkins, usually in clusters of two or three at the ends of the branchlets. Some workers consider *S. taxifolia* and *S. exigua* to be conspecific, but these entities seem to be somewhat distinct geographically and ecologically in the Trans-Pecos, with *S. taxifolia* being relatively confined to mid-elevations in igneous-rock mountains while *S. exigua* is found at lower elevations especially near the Rio Grande and often in limestone substrates.

The Yewleaf Willow reportedly serves as good browse for livestock. Indians have used a brew from the bark as a remedy for malaria.

6. Salix exigua Nutt. COYOTE WILLOW. Fig. 45, 49. [*Salix exigua* var. *stenophylla* (Rydb.) Schneid.; *S. exigua* var. *nevadensis* (S. Wats.) Schneid.; *S. interior* Rowlee; *S. interior* var. *pedicellata* (Anderss.) Ball; *S. interior* var. *angustissima* (Anderss.) Dayton]. Near water sources. El Paso Co., near El Paso; 3 mi E Fabens. Hudspeth Co., 4 mi E Ft. Hancock. Presidio Co., ZH Canyon,

Fig. 50. *Salix lasiolepis* (Arroyo Willow)

Sierra Vieja; Chinati Mts., S side; Rio Grande 10 mi SE Redford; Rio Grande between Redford and Presidio; Panther Canyon, near Big Hill and Rio Grande. Brewster Co., farm near Boquillas; 02 Ranch, Sid Place, Green Valley. Terrell Co. 1800–3900 ft. W to Baja CA, Mex., N to Can. Coah., N Dgo., Mex.

Salix exigua and *S. interior* (Sandbar Willow) were long considered by some workers to be closely related but distinct. Cronquist (1964) treats *S. interior* as a subspecies of *S. exigua*, while other workers have regarded *S. interior* as completely synonymous with *S. exigua*, as is reflected here.

7. **Salix lasiolepis** Benth. ARROYO WILLOW. Fig. 50. [*Salix lasiolepis* var. *bracelinae* Ball]. Watercourses in wooded, mountain canyons. Culberson Co., Guadalupe Mts., S McKittrick Canyon. Jeff Davis Co., Mt. Livermore, lower Merrill Canyon, H.O. Canyon; Limpia Canyon, near Ft. Davis and 12 mi N; backside of Timber Mt.; Fern Canyon, Mitre Peak Girl Scout Camp. Presidio Co., Sierra Vieja, canyons above Ft. Holland; Chinati Mts., Tigner Canyon. Brewster Co., Chisos Mts. 4200–5500 ft.; Mar–Jul. W to Baja CA, N to WA, ID, and UT; N Chih., NW and SE Coah., N.L., and Dgo., Mex.

The Arroyo Willow is easily recognized by its lanceolate or oblanceolate petiolate leaves (6–18 mm wide) that are persistently and densely canescent-pubescent underneath with antrorse, silky white hairs. The plants may be trees or shrubs, usually with many trunks. Reports of *Salix irrorata* Anderss. from near El Paso are believed by M. C. Johnston (pers. comm.) to be based upon specimens of *S. lasiolepis*.

2. POPULUS L. COTTONWOOD, ALAMO, POPLAR

Large trees, 15–30 m high, with fissured bark; mature buds covered by several overlapping scales, usually sealed with resin. Leaves with early-falling stipules, alternate, usually broad and variable in shape, deltoid, deltoid-ovate, cordate-ovate, rhombic, or lanceolate, margins entire to variously toothed or wavy, often glandular, apexes usually attenuated; leaf scars with 3 bundle scars, deltoid to elliptic in shape. Catkins of male and female flowers on separate trees (dioecious), borne singly stalked and pendulous, appearing before leaves in spring; flowers without a perianth, borne on a shallow or cuplike disc; single floral bracts with irregularly cut or slashed margins; stamens 6–60, anthers purplish or yellowish-red; styles short, with 2–4 stigmas, these large and dilated or divided into narrow lobes. Fruit a 2–4 valved dehiscent capsule, usually maturing before the leaves; capsule brown, globose, ellipsoid-conic, or ovoid; seeds numerous, small, with basal tufts of long hairs, the hairs sweeping forward and enveloping the seed; seeds dispersed by wind.

In Trans-Pecos Texas the recent past or present availability of water along water courses is marked by the presence of cottonwoods, even along the numerous desert streams that are dry for most of the year. A solitary cottonwood tree or small grove along a desert stream frequently marks the location of a spring, a seep, or an underground pool of water. The Spanish word for cottonwood, "alamo" inspired the name of Alamito Creek in Presidio Co., south of Marfa, because of the trees which line the banks of this now mostly dry desert stream. Also the famous Alamo of San Antonio supposedly received its name from a grove of cottonwoods that grew near the structure.

Cottonwoods are fast growing trees with large attractive canopies of leaves, they are easily propagated from cuttings, and thus they are widely planted as ornamentals and shade trees. About 40 species of *Populus* are native to the Northern Hemisphere.

Eckenwalder (1977) points out that existing herbarium collections of cottonwoods are generally insufficient for thorough taxonomic and distributional work. A major reason is that three separate collection times are required to gather adequate material; early spring (Feb–Apr) for male and female flowering material; late spring (May–Jun) for fruiting material; and later summer (Aug–Oct) for winter buds, before mature leaves drop in the autumn.

KEY TO THE SPECIES

1. Trees with closely ascending branches and columnar crowns; leaf petioles laterally compressed especially just below the blades; introduced ornamentals   **1. *P. nigra.***
1. Trees with broad or cylindrical crowns; leaf petioles laterally compressed or nearly round; native trees.
    2. Leaf blades more than three times as long as wide; petioles rarely exceeding 1.5 cm long   **5. *P. angustifolia.***

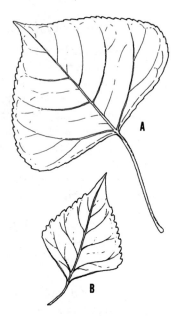

Fig. 51. A) *Populus nigra* (Black Cottonwood);
B) *P. freemontii* subsp. *mesetae*
(Arizona Cottonwood)

2. Leaf blades mostly about as wide as long, or slightly longer; petioles usually exceeding 2.5 cm long.
  3. Leaf blades nearly round to broadly ovate; found only in high
  mountains   **2. *P. tremuloides.***
  3. Leaf blades diamond or trowelshaped to broadly deltoid; found along
  streams and other water sources at lower elevations.
    4. Leaf blades diamond or trowelshaped, usually cuneate at the base,
    attenuate at the apex; twigs and petioles often pubescent; floral disc
    in fruit deeply cupshaped, 5–9 mm wide
                                   3. *P. fremontii* subsp. *mesetae.*
    4. Leaf blades broadly deltoid to deltoid-ovate, cordate or truncate at
    the base, abruptly pointed at the apex; twigs and petioles glabrous;
    floral disc in fruit flat to shallowly cupshaped, 1–4 mm wide
                                   4. *P. deltoides* subsp. *wislizeni.*

  1. Populus nigra L. BLACK COTTONWOOD, SAUCE. Fig. 51. This species is native to Europe and Asia, but is widely planted as an ornamental in the
United States. The sterile horticultural form, var. *italica* Muenchh., widely
known as "Lombardy poplar," often escapes cultivation and becomes natural-

Fig. 52. A) *Populus tremuloides* (Quaking
Aspen); B) *P. angustifolia* (Narrowleaf
Cottonwood); C) *P.* × *acuminata*

ized because it is easily propagated by sprouts. In the Trans-Pecos this tree is easily distinguished from other cottonwoods by its columnlike crown.

2. Populus tremuloides Michx. QUAKING ASPEN, ALAMO TEMBLON. Fig. 52. In canyons and on talus slopes, above 7000 ft. Culberson Co., Guadalupe Mts., 2.5 km E of Bush Mt.; head of South McKittrick Canyon. Jeff Davis Co., Mt. Livermore, Davis Mts., head of Madera Canyon; Pine Mt., at summit. Brewster Co., Emory Peak of the Chisos Mts., NE and SW sides. Although Quaking Aspen is restricted in the Trans-Pecos, it is perhaps the most widely distributed tree in North America, occurring throughout most of the United States, except for the SE, and in most of Can. and AK. In the Western States it is most common in and near the mountains, and in N Mex., it occurs only in the high mountains.

The common name of this tree is taken from the collective "quaking" movement of the leaves which may be caused even by a mild breeze. In autumn the leaves turn a beautiful yellow or orange-yellow (about 1 November in Big Bend National Park), an aspect which has accounted for wide cultivation of the species (but not in the Trans-Pecos). In nature it spreads readily from root sprouts or by seeds and may quickly cover forested areas which have been denuded by man or by fire. In the Trans-Pecos Quaking Aspen appears to be a montane relic surviving by clonal (asexual) reproduction. Early pioneers used the bark of Quaking Aspen as a remedy for fevers and as a treatment for scurvy (Vines, 1960). The State champion of this species was recorded under the summit of Emory Peak in Big Bend National Park, with measurements 32 ft. tall, 24 ft. crown spread, and 4 ft. girth.

3. **Populus fremontii** S. Wats. subsp. **mesetae** Eckenw.   ARIZONA COTTONWOOD, CHOPO.   Fig. 51.   [*Populus mexicana* auct. non Wesmael, Sarg.; *P. arizonica* auct. non Sarg., I. M. Johnst.]. Along rivers and desert streams in canyons and valleys, and near water tanks and springs, in the southwestern Trans-Pecos. Presidio Co., Pinto Canyon; on Rio Grande, 3–4 mi E Redford; Fresno Creek, 12 mi W Terlingua; 5 mi N Ruidosa; San Estaban Canyon, Alamito Creek. Brewster Co., Big Bend Park, Rio Grande; Nine-Point Mesa; Rosillas Mts. Jeff Davis Co., Fern Canyon; 18 mi N Alpine. 2600–4800 ft. From W TX to SE AZ; also S on the Central Plateau to the Valley of Mexico.

This species is common throughout much of the Chihuahuan Desert region and the arid Mexican plateau region (Eckenwalder, 1977). These cottonwoods become large trees, 6–20 m high, and historically have been widely planted in towns and elsewhere. The State champion of this species, 60 ft. high, 60 ft. crown spread, 12.8 ft. girth, is recorded by Jim Liles at Red Ass Spring in Big Bend National Park.

4. **Populus deltoides** Bartr. subsp. **wislizeni** (S. Wats.) Eckenw.   RIO GRANDE COTTONWOOD, ALAMILLO.   Fig. 53.   [*Populus fremontii* var. *wislizeni* S. Wats.; *P. wislizeni* (S. Wats.) Sarg.]. Deep alluvial soils, banks of rivers, streams, and in irrigation canals in valleys and canyons. El Paso Co., near Rio Grande. Hudspeth Co., near Rio Grande. Culberson Co., foothills of Guadalupe Mts., 12 mi SW Texline; Presidio Co., near Ruidosa; near Shafter; Pinto Canyon; San Estaban Canyon; Jeff Davis Co. and N Brewster Co. 2800–5100 ft.; Mar–Jul. NW W to UT, CO; N Mex.

In the Trans-Pecos *Populus deltoides* subsp. *wislizeni* is a prominent large tree (to 25 m) of the Rio Grande drainage area from near Presidio northward. The taxon also occurs in the Davis Mountains area where Eckenwalder (1977) postulates local hybridization to occur between subsp. *wislizeni* and *P. fremontii* subsp. *mesetae*. Rio Grande Cottonwood has been planted as a shade tree in Big Bend National Park near Panther Junction and Chilicotal Springs. Cottonwoods are reported to hybridize readily, accounting for some of the confusing morphological variation in certain localities.

5. **Populus angustifolia** James.   NARROWLEAF COTTONWOOD.   Fig. 52. Reported to occur along streams and near springs above 3000 ft., rare in the Trans-Pecos. Tentatively identified from Brewster Co., Big Bend Park, Santa Elena Crossing below Castolon, Boquillas Crossing, Rio Grande Village, Chilicotal Springs, and McKinney Springs. Reported from Culberson Co., Dela-

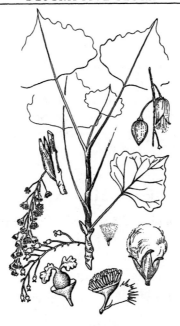

Fig. 53. *Populus deltoides* subsp. *wislizeni*
(Rio Grande Cottonwood).

ware Creek. Mar–Jun. Widespread from NM to WA, and in S Sask., and Alberta, Can.; N. Coah. and NW Chih., Mex.

The leaves of this cottonwood resemble those of willows, being long and lanceolate or ovate-lanceolate. Mature trees may reach 20 m high. Two other cottonwoods reported by Correll and Johnston (1970) to occur in the Trans-Pecos are *Populus acuminata* Rydb. and *P. hinckleyana* Correll. It is now believed that these are hybrids, with *P.* × *acuminata* (Fig. 52) resulting from hybridization between *P. deltoides* subsp. *wislizeni* and *P. angustifolia*, and with *P.* × *hinckleyana* resulting from hybridization between *P. fremontii* subsp. *mesetae* and *P. angustifolia*. Populations of *P.* × *acuminata* were once more common along the Rio Grande and even along Terlingua Creek and Roughrun Creek, but in most places the plants were removed by miners.

7. JUNGLANDACEAE KUNTH   WALNUT FAMILY

Trees or large shrubs. Leaves alternate, odd pinnately compound, without stipules; leaflets opposite, lanceolate to ovate, usually dotted with glands underneath. Flowers unisexual, with male flowers in catkins, female flowers solitary or in small clusters; male flowers without sepals but subtended by a bract and 2 bractlets; female flowers with a bract, 2–3 bractlets, and 4 sepals fused with the ovary; pistils 2, ovary inferior with sepals appearing at top; stigmas 2, feathery. Fruit a walnut or pecan (a dry drupe), with a rather thick, fleshy and tough husk (involucre and calyx) that dries to cover a nutshell (mature carpels); seeds, 2–4 lobed, convoluted.

Many species of this rather small family, about seven genera and 50 species, produce edible nuts, including the widely cultivated pecans and the Persian or "English" black walnuts. Walnut wood is extremely desirable for making furniture, musical instruments, cabinets, and other items, and is used for posts and fuel.

KEY TO THE GENERA

1. Fruit with persistent husk, and furrowed shell; catkins (male) sessile, singular, on last years growth; stamens 8–40; pith of branchlets separating into thin layers   1. *Juglans.*

1. Fruit husk splitting into valves, the shell smooth or slightly wrinkled; catkins (male) stalked, in groups of 3, on new growth; stamens 3–8; pith of branchlets not layered   2. *Carya.*

1. JUGLANS L.   WALNUT, NOGAL

Trees or shrubs, bark furrowed and scaly. Leaves odd pinnate with many, opposite, lanceolate leaflets in our species, the margins toothed. Flowers formed in spring, greenish; male catkins separate but close, near apexes, drooping, on year-old growth, appearing before the leaves; stamens 8–40; female flowers singular or clustered at ends of branches; sepals 4; style short, with 2(–3) elongated style branches with inner, fringed, stigmatic surfaces. Fruit a walnut with a tough, fleshy, indehiscent husk, and an irregularly furrowed nutshell.

There are about 20 species of *Juglans* occurring in both hemispheres. The Trans-Pecos species rarely occur in pure stands, but are usually scattered in the bottoms of canyons and along streams and other watercourses that descend into otherwise drier surroundings.

KEY TO THE SPECIES

1. Leaflets of pinnate leaves usually 15 or fewer, these (7–)9–15(–17) mm wide, with prominently toothed margins; fruit at least 2.5 cm wide   1. *J. major.*

1. Leaflets of pinnate leaves more than 15, these (7–)8–13(–16) mm wide, with finely toothed or nearly smooth margins; fruit usually 2.0 cm or less wide   2. *J. microcarpa.*

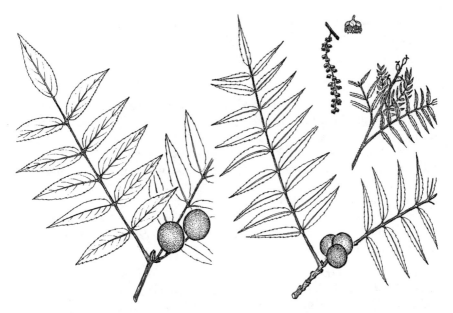

Fig. 54. *Juglans major* (Arizona Walnut)   Fig. 55. *Juglans microcarpa* (Little Walnut)

1. **Juglans major** (Torr.) Heller. ARIZONA WALNUT, NOGAL SILVESTRE. Fig. 54. Scattered in canyons and along watercourses in the eastern Trans-Pecos. Culberson Co., Guadalupe Mts. Brewster Co., old Sam Nail Ranch, Big Bend Park. Jeff Davis Co., Timber Mt. Presidio Co., Chinati Mts., Wildhorse Canyon near Shely ranch house; also on the adjacent Edwards Plateau; from SW NM to central AZ and to CO; Son., Chih., Dgo., Mex.

This plant forms trees to about 15 m high, with durable wood that is valued for fence posts, and to some extent for furniture. Normally the trees produce an abundance of fruits every two to three years, and these contain small, edible kernels which were eaten by Indians.

2. **Juglans microcarpa** Berl. LITTLE WALNUT, RIVER WALNUT, TEXAS BLACK WALNUT. Fig. 55. [*Juglans rupestris* Engelm. *ex* Torr.]. Scattered along streams and gullies, mostly in valleys at intermediate elevations. Culberson Co., Guadalupe Mts. Jeff Davis, Presidio, Brewster, Pecos, Terrell counties; also S and E in TX to near the Colorado River; also from SE NM to W OK; N Mex.

The wood is used in making furniture, cabinets, paneling and other materials. This species and *Juglans major* may hybridize where their ranges overlap.

Juglans microcarpa var. **stewartii** (I. M. Johnst.) W. Manning, occurs in the Chisos Mts. (Correll and Johnston, 1970), and also in Canyon Indio Felipe of the

Hechiceros Mts. in Coah., Mex. The var. *stewartii* is distinguished by its slightly larger fruits (21–25 mm wide) and broader leaflets, 15–23(–31) mm wide.

2. CARYA NUTT.   HICKORY, PECAN.

Trees with hard, very resilient wood; bark furrowed. Leaves pinnate; leaflets 5–25, often glandular-dotted, with one terminal leaflet. Flowers formed in spring on new growth, male catkins in groups of 3 below, and female flowers above the leaves; stamens 3–8; female flowers in clusters of 2–10; true calyx none, but with bract and usually 3 bractlets sepallike in flower; stigmas 2, short, sessile, often divided. Fruit with a 4-parted husk that splits and falls away at maturity, revealing a smooth nutshell; nut 2–4-celled.

A genus of about 15 species mostly in eastern North America and eastern Asia, with nine species occurring in Texas. Species of *Carya* are introduced but not native to the Trans-Pecos.

1. Carya illinoinensis (Wang.) K. Koch.   PECAN, NOGAL MORADO. [*Carya pecan* (Marsh.) Engl. & Graebn.; *Hicoria pecan* (Marsh.) Britt.]. Mostly along steams and rich bottomlands in central and NW TX where the plants are native; N to IN and IA, E to AL. Pecans, the State of Tree of Texas, are planted in yards throughout the Trans-Pecos.

Pecans are the largest of all the hickories, some reaching 50 m high with massive trunks. Pecans are widely cultivated throughout the southern United States and in northeastern Mexico. In some areas orchards have been established to take advantage of the commercial value of the pecans. Well over 100 horticultural varieties, many resulting from artificial hybridizations, have been developed in an attempt to improve the size and shape of the nuts, the thickness of their shells, the quality of the kernels, and the ability of the trees to thrive and produce in various habitats.

8. BETULACEAE S. F. GRAY   BIRCH OR HAZELNUT FAMILY

Trees or shrubs. Leaves alternate, simple, with stipules, blades pinnately veined, veins straight, leaves and stipules deciduous. Flowers male and in catkins, or female in spikes, clusters, or scaly catkins, on same plants (monoecious); perianth bractlike, minute, or absent; male catkins drooping or spreading; stamens 2 to many; ovary inferior, 2-celled, each with 2 ovules; styles 2. Fruit a nutlet, with 1 cell and 1 seed, with or without a leaflike involucre.

A small family of 4–6 genera and about 140 species, chiefly restricted to the Northern Hemisphere and known for their hard wood. Best known members include the birches (*Betula*), a source of hard wood lumber, the alders (*Alnus*), a source of charcoal, and the hazelnuts (*Corylus*), a source of edible nuts.

1. OSTRYA SCOP. HOPHORNBEAM, IRONWOOD

Tall or smallish trees, usually with slender, round trunks and branches; wood very hard; bark furrowed, somewhat flaky, brownish. Leaves ovate to elliptic, less than 5 cm long, in bud open and concave. Flowers production in spring before or with the leaves; male catkins in groups of 1–3 on previous year's branches; female catkins solitary, loose, borne at tips of new growth; female flowers with adherent calyx crowning a 2-celled, 2-ovuled ovary, with 2 linear stigmas, enclosed by bract and bractlets. Fruit with a compressed, ovoid to ellipsoid or obovoid, bladderlike involucre, formed from bract and bractlets, with stiff hairs at the base, or more or less hairy throughout, especially the tip, loosely imbricated to form a hoplike (conelike) cluster; nutlet smooth or ribbed, much smaller than inflated involucre.

Of the 10 species of *Ostrya*, all are of the Northern Hemisphere, two occur in Texas, and two of these are found in the Trans-Pecos mountains.

KEY TO THE SPECIES

1. Leaf blades roundish-ovate to ovate-elliptic; stalked glands present especially on leaf petioles and small branches **1. O. knowltonii.**

1. Leaf blades elliptic to elliptic-lanceolate; stalked glands not present
2. O. virginiana var. chisosensis.

1. Ostrya knowltonii Cov. BAILEY HOPHORNBEAM. Fig. 56. [*Ostrya baileyi* Rose]. In the canyons and on slopes of the Guadalupe Mts., Culberson Co., mostly in the pinyon belt at 5000–8300 ft. Mar–May. Also in SE NM, W to AZ, and N to SE UT.

These small trees, to about 12 m high, are also distinguished by leaf margins which are sharply double-toothed, male catkins 2–3 cm long, bracts of male flowers with small glandular hairs on the margins, and short-tipped apexes of the male bracts. The *Ostrya knowltonii* of Arizona does not have glands.

2. Ostrya virginiana (Mill.) K. Koch var. **chisosensis** (Correll) Henrickson. BIG BEND HOPHORNBEAM. Fig. 56. [*Ostrya chisosensis* Correll]. Known only from higher elevations in the Chisos Mts., Brewster Co., N side of Emory Peak; Crown Mt.; above Boot Springs, May–Jun.

Other than the traits listed in the key above, identifying characters of this species include leaf margins which are finely double-toothed, male catkins 3.5–4 cm long, bracts of male flowers with rather coarsely fringed margins, and apexes tipped with a sharp point at least 1 mm long. Jim Liles recorded the National champion of this species, 32 ft. high, 24 ft. crown spread, 2.3 ft. girth, from the north slope of Emory Peak in Big Bend National Park. *Ostrya*

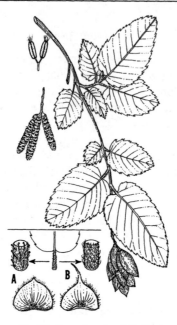

Fig. 56. *Ostrya knowltonii* (Bailey
Hophornbeam); A) *O. knowltonii*;
B) *O. virginiana* var. *chisosensis*

virginiana var. *virginiana* occurs in Texas east of the Trans-Pecos and in the
eastern United States.

9. FAGACEAE DUM.   BEECH FAMILY

Trees or shrubs; monoecious. Leaves deciduous or evergreen, alternate,
simple; stipules deciduous. Flowers unisexual; male flowers in spikelike (aments or catkins) or beadlike clusters; female flowers solitary or in loose clusters;
ovary inferior, 3–7-celled, ovules 1–2 in each cell, but usually only one
develops; styles 3. Fruit a nut (or acorn), 1-celled, 1-seeded, completely or
partly enveloped by a cupule, which becomes hardened, and perhaps bristly or
spiny.

A family of eight genera and about 900 species, nearly worldwide in distribution but concentrated in the Northern Hemisphere. The family is of considerable economic importance for the lumber produced by species of Oak
(*Quercus*), Beech (*Fagus*), and Chestnut (*Castanea*). Cork of commerce is obtained from the bark of *Quercus suber*. Insect galls of various oak species are
the source of tannic acid. Three genera of the Beech Family, *Quercus*, *Fagus*,
and *Castanea*, are represented in Texas.

1. QUERCUS L. OAK

Trees or shrubs; monoecious. Leaves alternate, simple, usually with petioles, the margins smooth, toothed, or lobed; veins pinnate. Flowers unisexual; male flowers in elongate catkins, without petals; calyx of 5 lobes, joined and cuplike, enclosing 5–10 stamens; female flowers 1–several in loose catkins; sepals 6, joined to form a tube; ovary 3-celled; styles 3. Fruit an acorn (nut), 1-celled, 1-seeded, the seed in a shell, and seated in a cup that partially or completely envelops the acorn.

A genus of about 500 species in the Northern Hemisphere. About 250 species occur in the New World, with a distributional center in Mexico, and extending south to Columbia, South America, and north to Canada. About 45 species are known to occur in Texas, and at least 21 species are found in the Trans-Pecos. Hybridization occurs between numerous oak species, thus often blurring species boundaries and sometimes making identifications difficult. The identification of "pure" species is emphasized in the treatment of Trans-Pecos oaks that follows, although discussion of morphological variations and influences of hybridization is included. Different oak species reveal elevational displacement in the Trans-Pecos mountains. Gambel Oak usually occupies the uppermost zone. Oak acorns are eaten by numerous bird and mammal species. The acorns of certain species are eaten by humans. Deer and other animals may browse the leaves of many species.

A fossil record of *Quercus toumeyi* Sarg. has been reported from Hueco Tanks State Park (Van Devender and Riskind, 1979). *Quercus toumeyi*, a shrub or small tree of SW NM, SE AZ, and N Mex., has been known from Texas by one previously undetermined collection in 1958 (*I. M. Johnston 1924*) from the rim of an igneous ledge, Franklin Mountains, E of Canutillo, El Paso Co., according to C. H. Muller (pers. comm.). Richard D. Worthington has collected specimens from the NW slope of the North Franklin Mountains, El Paso Co., that are said by Muller to be "heavily introgressed" with *Q. toumeyi*, and Worthington has collected specimens identified as *Q. toumeyi* from 0.5 mi NE of the top of the North Franklin Mountains at 6600 ft. Muller also reports that he has seen *Q. toumeyi* from the Quitman Mountains. The status of *Q. toumeyi* in the Trans-Pecos requires further evaluation. Muller suggests that two other oak species, *Q. deliquescens* C. H. Mull. and *Q. chihuahuensis* Trel. of Mexico, may occur rarely in the Trans-Pecos in the mountains along the Rio Grande. In fact, *Q. chihuahuensis* has been reported to occur in the Eagle and Quitman mountains, where it is introgressed by *Q. grisea*. Specimens of two trees of the eastern oak, *Q. sinuata* Walt. var. *sinuata* (Bastard Oak), were collected by the author in 1985 at Buttrill Spring, North Rosillos Mountains, Brewster County. The plants probably were introduced by early residents.

KEY TO THE SPECIES

1. Bark rather soft, gray, and scaly (perhaps black and deeply furrowed in *Quercus fusiformis*); leaves (if toothed) only mucronate-tipped or rounded, rarely spinose and never aristate-tipped; stigmas abruptly dilated on short styles; fruit annual; cup scales usually prominently thickened basally and loosely appressed apically; acorns with the shell glabrous on the inner surface; abortive ovules basal (White Oaks).
2. Leaves slightly obovate, elliptic-oblong, or ovate, 2.5–6 cm long, 1.2–2 cm wide, bluish-green and shiny above, paler underneath, apices rounded to acute, rarely emarginate, margins entire, somewhat undulate, or with small teeth   **1. *Q. oblongifolia.***
2. Leaves otherwise.
   3. Leaves glabrous beneath or nearly so at maturity.
      4. Leaves very small, markedly crisped and spinose-toothed, completely glabrous and glaucous   **2. *Q. hinckleyi.***
      4. Leaves over 2 cm long, not spinose-toothed.
         5. Leaves bluish-green above, green beneath at maturity, the petioles waxy.
            6. Leaves 5–10 cm long or more, the veins very prominent beneath; petioles more than 5 mm long   **3. *Q. laceyi.***
            6. Leaves 1–3 cm long, the veins not very prominent beneath, petioles less than 5 mm long   **4. *Q. depressipes.***
         5. Leaves with a glaucous bloom beneath at maturity (usually obovate, evenly repand, usually acute)   **5. *Q. muehlenbergii.***
   3. Leaves pubescent beneath at maturity (sometimes minutely so).
      7. Leaves deeply lobed   **6. *Q. gambelii.***
      7. Leaves shallowly lobed, toothed, or entire.
         8. Leaves glaucous and glabrous above, noticeably fulvous-puberulent beneath, the margins heavily cartilaginous, the teeth strongly mucronate or even spinose 7. *Q. turbinella.*
         8. Leaves various but not as above.
            9. Leaves prominently reticulate beneath, the veins impressed above.
               10. Leaves not over twice as long as broad, the broadly rounded apex abruptly mucronately several-toothed; fruit borne on prominent peduncles **8. *Q. rugosa.***
               10. Leaves twice as long as broad or more, the apex acute to obtuse or entire to toothed but not abruptly mucronate; fruit subsessile or short-stalked
                                        9. *Q. arizonica.*
            9. Leaves not markedly reticulate beneath, the veins not strikingly impressed above.

11. Leaves toothed, undulately crisped, the stellate pubescence very harsh to the touch **10a. Q. pungens.**

11. Leaves variously toothed or entire but not undulate-crisped, or if so the pubescence not harsh to the touch.

    12. Leaves very small and thick, coarsely revolute, densely woolly-tomentose beneath **11. Q. intricata.**

    12. Leaves small or moderate-sized, not coarsely revolute, if tomentose beneath not strikingly woolly.

        13. Leaves spreading-pubescent beneath.

            14. Leaves dark-green above, white-tomentose beneath.

                15. Leaves oblong, uniformly white-tomentose beneath; acorn cups ca. 1.5 cm broad or rarely broader **12. Q. mohriana.**

                15. Leaves ovate to oblong, the veins visible through the white tomentum beneath; acorn cups usually more than 1.5 cm broad **13. Q. havardii.**

            14. Leaves usually similar in coloration above and beneath, at least not strikingly dissimilar; variously entire to toothed but not lobed **14. Q. grisea.**

        13. Leaves pubescent beneath with tightly appressed minute stellate hairs, often appearing glabrous and glaucous to the naked eye.

            16. Leaves green beneath even with minute pubescence; usually shrubs with flaking bark.

                17. Leaves oblong, usually coarsely 3–5 toothed **10b. Q. pungens var. vaseyana.**

                17. Leaves ovate-elliptic, margins undulate to serrate or entire **21. Q. carmenensis.**

            16. Leaves creamy-canescent beneath with dense appressed stellate hairs; usually trees, with bark black or dark gray, hard and deeply furrowed) **15. Q. fusiformis.**

1. Bark rather hard, black and furrowed but scarcely scaly; leaves (if toothed) aristate-tipped, never round-lobed or if so these aristate from the veins; stigmas gradually or rarely abruptly dilated, on long styles; fruit biennial or annual; cup scales scarcely thickened basally (or if so the leaf characters definitely as here described) and usually tightly appressed apically; acorns with the shell tomentose on the inner surface; abortive ovules usually apical (Black Oaks).

                18. Leaves densely white-tomentose beneath, the veins impressed above and the margins revolute **16. Q. hypoleucoides.**

                18. Leaves variously pubescent or glabrous but not as above.

Fig. 57. *Quercus oblongifolia* (Mexican Blue Oak)

19. Fruit annual; leaves commonly glabrous below except for a tuft of stellate hairs on each side of the base of the midrib   **17. *Q. emoryi.***
19. Fruit biennial; leaves variously pubescent or glabrous but not as above.
    20. Leaves at most only coarsely toothed, 4 or 5 times longer than broad, narrowly lanceolate   **18. *Q. graciliformis.***
    20. Leaves definitely lobed, at most only 2 or 3 times longer than broad, broadly lanceolate to ovate.
        21. Terminal leaf lobe elongate, oblong, truncate apically with usually 2 lateral teeth   **19. *Q. gravesii.***
        21. Terminal leaf lobe scarcely more prominent than the lateral lobes or distinctly obscure, variously acute or rounded but not oblong
                20. *Q. tardifolia.*

    1. Quercus oblongifolia Torr.   MEXICAN BLUE OAK.   Fig. 57.   Mountain canyons, exceedingly rare. Hudspeth Co., N Quitman Mts. Presidio Co., Bofecillos Mts., above Charro Canyon and the waterfall; Chinati Mts. 4000–5000 ft. Also, SW NM, AZ; Son., Chih., and Coah., Mex.
    This rare species possibly occurs in desert mountains of the southern Trans-Pecos other than those listed above. Trees of this deciduous species may reach a height of about 10 m.

Fig. 58. *Quercus hinckleyi* (Hinckley Oak)   Fig. 59. *Quercus laceyi* (Lacey Oak)

2. Quercus hinckleyi C. H. Mull.   HINCKLEY OAK.   Fig. 58.   Rocky lime-stone slopes, endemic. Presidio Co., NW of Solitario Peak, in the Solitario, Glen Rose limestone, associated with Lechuguilla; vicinity of Shafter. 3500–4500 ft.

This remarkable endemic species was first collected and once known only from the Solitario. Recently it has been discovered in at least two sites near Shafter. The plants are intricately branched, evergreen shrubs to 1 m high, forming coarse thickets or growing singly, and with smallish, markedly spines-cent leaves. Leaves and acorns of the Hinckley Oak were found in a fossil pack-rat midden (about 15,000 years old) in a small cave ca. 7 km south of Shafter (Van Devender, Freeman, and Worthington, 1978). Fossil leaves of the Hinck-ley Oak also have been found in a packrat midden in the Dead Horse Moun-tains (Van Devender, pers. comm.). It is possible that living plants persist in the rugged and little botanized Dead Horse Mountains.

3. Quercus laceyi Small.   LACEY OAK.   Fig. 59.   [*Quercus glaucoides auct. non.* Mart. & Gal.]. Limestone hills, arroyos, and canyons. Brewster Co., E rim of Solitario. Terrell Co., upper Big Canyon, ca. 30 mi N of Sanderson toward Sheffield. 2800 ft. Mostly restricted to the Edwards Plateau in TX; also NE Mex., Tam., N.L., S.L.P., Coah., and throughout central and S Mex.

Plants of this species form shrubs or moderate-sized trees, 3–8 m high. The oblong to obovate leaves of this deciduous oak reach 12 cm long and 6 cm

Fig. 60. *Quercus depressipes*
(Mexican Dwarf Oak)

wide, but are usually much smaller, and the margins usually are strongly wavy or with few shallow lobes. Nixon and Muller (1992) have clarified the status of *Q. laceyi* in Texas and have determined that *Q. glaucoides* Mart. & Gal., with which *Q. laceyi* has been included as synonymous in recent literature, is a Mexican species.

4. Quercus depressipes Trel. MEXICAN DWARF OAK. Fig. 60. Openly wooded grasslands at high elevations in the Davis Mts. Jeff Davis Co., near the summit of Mt. Livermore; reported from near Mt. Locke; ca. 8000 ft. Also Chih. and Dgo., Mex.

Plants of this species are subevergreen low shrubs to ca. 1 m tall, either growing singly or forming dense thickets by stolons. The smallish leathery leaves are oblong to elliptic, to 3 cm long and 1.2 cm wide.

5. Quercus muehlenbergii Engelm. CHINKAPIN OAK. Fig. 61. [*Quercus prinoides* sensu Coult., not Willd.; *Q. prinus* sensu Coult., not L.; *Q. brayi* Small]. Usually protected slopes and canyons of the higher mountains. Culberson Co., Guadalupe Mts., common in most canyons, to the top. Jeff Davis Co., Davis Mts., Timber Mt., Little Aguja Canyon, Limpia Canyon, Wild Rose Pass, Madera Canyon of Mt. Livermore. Brewster Co., Chisos Mts., Maple or Pulliam Canyon. 5000–8000 ft. Elsewhere mostly in calcareous upland forests; to NE and central TX; east to the Atlantic; N to WI; W into S NM; also N Mex.

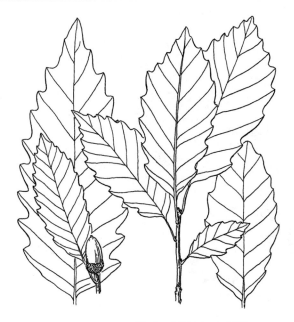

Fig. 61. *Quercus muehlenbergii* (Chinkapin Oak)

This is one of the most attractive oaks of the Trans-Pecos. The plants are deciduous moderate-sized to large trees, 5–16 m high, with large leaves, usually obovate in outline with strongly undulating margins. Jim Liles measured a Chinkapin Oak 65 ft. high in Maple Canyon of the Chisos Mountains in Big Bend National Park. The Chinkapin Oak is valuable for its wood, and it sprouts from the stump. It is relatively free of insects and disease. *Quercus muehlenbergii* is similar to *Q. prinus* L. (Chestnut Oak) of east Texas and the southeastern U.S.

6. Quercus gambelii Nutt. GAMBEL OAK. Fig. 62. [*Quercus novomexicana* (A. DC.) Rydb.; *Q. undulata* Torr.; *Q. fendleri* Liebm.; *Q. obtusifolia* (A. DC.) Rydb.]. Slopes, valleys and canyons, higher elevations. El Paso Co., 0.5 mi NE of top of North Franklin Mts. Culberson Co., Guadalupe Mts., Pine Top Mt., in the Bowl, and at the head of South McKittrick Canyon. Presidio Co., N face Chinati Peak. Jeff Davis Co., Davis Mts., upper Madera Canyon; Mt. Livermore; N side of Mt. Livermore; NW slopes Sawtooth Mt.; N slopes Haystack Mt. Brewster Co., Mt. Ord, igneous soil; Chisos Mts., upper slopes Casa Grande; Lost Mine Peak. Jul–Sept.; 5000–8300 ft. Also N to CO and UT; N Mex., Chih. and Coah.

The Gambel Oak is variable in habit, being either shrubs 1–2 m high, often forming dense thickets, small trees, or rather large trees to 17 m high. The

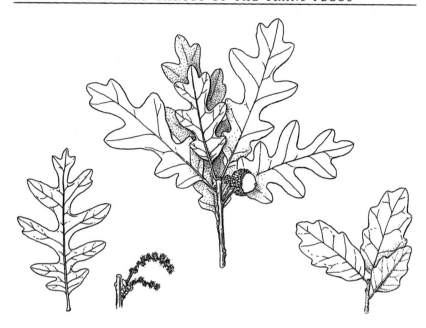

Fig. 62. *Quercus gambelii* (Gambel Oak)

species possibly hybridizes with *Quercus mohriana* at the summit of the Pine Top Mt., and elsewhere in the Guadalupe Mountains and with other species in the region (e.g., *Q. grisea, Q. pungens, Q. turbinella, Q. muehlenbergii*) forming a multitude of shrubby, shallowly lobed narrow-leafed forms variously known as *Q. undulata* (Wavyleaf Oak), *Q. fendleri*, or *Q.* × *pauciloba* Rydb. (pro sp.). The acorns of *Q. gambelii* and *Q. emoryi* are perhaps the most edible of any species in our area.

7. Quercus turbinella Greene. SCRUB LIVE OAK, SCRUB OAK. Fig. 63. Rocky limestone slopes and canyons, desertic mountains. El Paso Co., Franklin Mts., W slopes, Tom Mays Park, McKelligan Canyon, E slopes N of reservation, 8 mi NE of El Paso. Hudspeth Co., Quitman Mts.; Eagle Mts.; sandstone and metamorphic stone, road to Allamoore, Reed Hill, ca. 15 mi NE Sierra Blanca. Brewster Co, 9 mi SE Alpine. 4000–5200 ft. W to UT and S CA; Baja CA, Mex.

Plants of this species are rigid shrubs or small trees to 4 m high and evergreen or subevergreen. In the Franklin Mountains, it is the common shrub oak or "low shrub-tree" in the arroyos and canyon bottoms. The leaves are leathery, elliptic to ovate, to 4 cm long and 2 cm wide, 3–5 toothed or lobed, with each tooth spinose-tipped. The leaf margins are cartilaginously thickened, not revolute, flat or slightly crisped-undulate. The upper leaf surfaces are lustrous or rather dull, rather glaucous or bluish-green, glabrous or very sparsely and

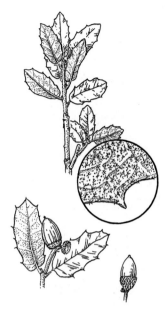

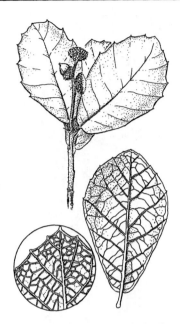

Fig. 63. *Quercus turbinella* (Scrub Live Oak)   Fig. 64. *Quercus rugosa* (Netleaf Oak)

minutely stellate-pubescent. The lower surfaces are dull, usually glaucous, minutely simple-or stellate-puberulent, the puberulence often glandular and usually yellow or reddish overall, a character not shown by other species of the Trans-Pecos.

8. Quercus rugosa Nee. NETLEAF OAK. Fig. 64. [*Quercus reticulata* H.&B.; *Q. diversicolor* Trel.]. Wooded slopes and canyons, relatively high elevations. Jeff Davis Co., Davis Mts., upper Merrill Canyon of Mt. Livermore. Brewster Co., Chisos Mts., upper Boot Canyon, between Boot Springs and the South Rim; upper Pinnacles trail. 6000–7000 ft. W to AZ and CA; Baja, CA to S Mex.; Coah., Sierra del Carmen.

Plants of the Netleaf Oak are usually medium-sized trees (to 12 m), or they may be shrubs. The species is evergreen, subevergreen, or perhaps deciduous and is easily recognized by its large leaves that are usually obovate to elliptic, to 10 cm long, 7 cm wide, thick and hard, the margins entire or toothed on the rounded apices, somewhat revolute, thickened, the whole blade somewhat concave or flat and with a brownish tomentum underneath. Some of the specimens in the Chisos Mountains seem to be hybridized with *Quercus grisea* and intermediate in venation and pubescence. Spellenberg (1995) has documented hybridization in Mexico between *Q. rugosa* and *Q. depressipes*. In Boot Canyon of the Chisos Mountains Liles recorded the National champion Netleaf Oak to be 38 ft. tall, with a 36 ft. crown spread and 7.1 ft. girth.

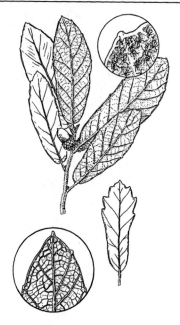

Fig. 65. *Quercus arizonica*
(Arizona White Oak)

Fig. 66. *Quercus pungens* var. *pungens*
(Sandpaper Oak)

9. Quercus arizonica Sarg.   ARIZONA WHITE OAK.   Fig. 65.   [*Quercus endemica* C.H. Mull.]. Rocky slopes and arroyos of desertic mountains and wooded areas at higher elevations. El Paso Co., Franklin Mts., E slopes, 8 mi NE of El Paso; Hueco Tanks, near rock wall dam. Hudspeth Co., Quitman Mts.; Eagle Mts.; Sierra Diablo. Culberson Co., Guadalupe Mts. Brewster Co., Chisos Mts. 4000–5000 ft. W to AZ; also N Mex.

The Arizona White Oak is a small or medium-sized tree, 2–12 m high. The leaves are evergreen or subevergreen, narrowly obovate or oblanceolate to elliptic or oblong, to 8 cm long, 3 cm wide, the margins entire or coarsely toothed. The population at Hueco Tanks, and possibly also in the Guadalupe Mountains, is hybridized with *Quercus mohriana* and exhibits very pubescent foliage. According to Richard Worthington, *Q. arizonica* is the common oak at Hueco Tanks. Reportedly the population at Hueco Tanks is introgressed by *Q. chihuahuensis*.

10a. Quercus pungens Liebm. var. **pungens.**   SANDPAPER OAK, SCRUB OAK.   Fig. 66.   [*Quercus undulata* var. *pungens* (Liebm.) Engelm.; *Q. undulata* Sperry]. Rocky limestone slopes and canyons mostly of desertic mountains; one of the more widespread species of the Trans-Pecos. El Paso Co., Franklin Mts., head of McKelligan Canyon. Hudspeth Co., Sierra Diablo, Victorio Canyon; Quitman Mts. Culberson Co., Guadalupe Mts. Presidio Co.,

Fig. 67. *Quercus pungens* var. *vaseyana*
(Vasey Shin Oak)

Chinati Mts. Brewster Co., Dead Horse Mts., Heath Canyon, Big Brushy Canyon; Packsaddle Mt. 3500–6000 ft. S through Mex., Coah. to Zac.

Plants of this evergreen to subevergreen species in the Trans-Pecos are usually low shrubs, often forming thickets, less often they are medium-sized trees. The Sandpaper Oak takes its name from its lead surfaces that are sandpaperlike to the touch, the distinctive character of this species. The leaves are thick, hard and stiff, elliptic to oblong, to 9 cm long and 4 cm wide but usually much smaller, the margins coarsely toothed, undulately crisped, and always mucronate-tipped. The upper surfaces are lustrous, with minute, sparse, stiff-spreading-stellate hairs, and the lower surfaces canescent, densely pubescent with two types of hairs, sericeous, appressed simple or stellate hairs covering the surface and scattered stiff-spreading-stellate hairs (rarely nearly glabrous on both surfaces).

10b. Quercus pungens var. **vaseyana** (Buckl.) C. H. Mull. VASEY SHIN OAK. Fig. 67. [*Quercus vaseyana* Buckl., *Q. undulata* var. *vaseyana* (Buckl.) Rydb.; *Q. sillae* Trel.]. Rocky limestone substrates, sometimes igneous; a widespread species throughout much of the Trans-Pecos, often in desertic mountains. Hudspeth Co., Hueco Mts.; Quitman Mts.; Eagle Mts.; Sierra Diablo. Culberson Co., Guadalupe Mts., Sierra Diablo; Apache Mts. Presidio Co., Chinati Mts.; Sierra Vieja; Solitario. Brewster Co.; Chisos Mts.; Del Norte Mts.;

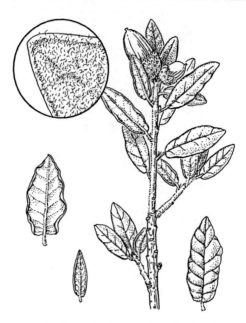

Fig. 68. *Quercus intricata* (Coahuila Scrub Oak)

Glass Mts.; Packsaddle; Dead Horse Mts. Pecos Co., 5 mi W of Sheffield. Terrell Co., Sanderson to Sheffield, Independence Creek canyon; 29 mi N Dryden; Pecos River. Val Verde Co., near Langtry, Mile Canyon, 18 mi N Langtry; mouth of Pecos River; Rio Grande Canyon; Devils River Canyon. 2100–8000 ft. Also W-cen. TX; also NE Mex.

The Vasey Shin Oak is frequently seen as a low shrub 1–2 m high, or less often as a small tree to 4 m (rarely 15 m) high, and is evergreen to subevergreen. The leaves of this variety are usually oblong, usually 3–5-toothed or lobed on each margin, the teeth mucronate-tipped, the upper surfaces dark green and lustrous, glabrous or nearly so, and the lower surfaces more pubescent with appressed stellate hairs, but also somewhat lustrous green, with conspicuous veins (except in the more easterly populations, the intermediates with *Quercus pungens* var. *pungens* are more numerous than the typical Vasey Oak). The National co-champion Vasey Shin Oak, 45 ft. high, 40 ft. crown spread, 3.75 ft. girth, is recorded in Cattail Canyon of Big Bend National Park.

11. Quercus intricata Trel.   COAHUILA SCRUB OAK.   Fig. 68.   Rocky or woody slopes of mountains. Hudspeth Co., Eagle Mts. Brewster Co., Chisos Mts., upper Cattail Canyon bottom; trail to Cattail Canyon; Laguna Meadow; above Boot Springs to South Rim; summit of Lost Pine Trail. 5000–7500 ft. S through Mex., Coah., Chih., N.L. to Zac.

The Coahuila Scrub Oak is a characteristic species of the Coahuila, Mexico chaparral (Vines, 1960), but is rare in Texas. The plants are evergreen, intri-

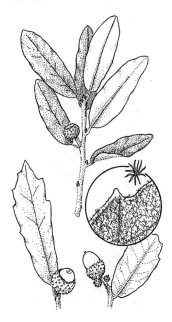

Fig. 69. *Quercus mohriana* (Mohr Shin Oak)

cately branched low shrubs, 1-2 m high, usually forming thickets. The leaves are thick and hard, small (1-2.5 cm long; 0.5-1.3 cm wide), ovate to oblong, the margins coarsely revolute, entire or few-toothed, upper surfaces rather lustrous, sparsely stellate, lower surfaces felty.

12. Quercus mohriana Buckl. *ex* Rydb. MOHR SHIN OAK, SCRUB OAK. Fig. 69. Predominantly limestone habitats, slopes and canyons of mostly desertic hills and mountains at lower to moderate elevations. Hudspeth Co., Sierra Diablo, Victorio Canyon; Quitman Mts., Culberson Co., Sierra Diablo; Guadalupe Mts. Jeff Davis Co., Davis Mts. State Park; marly limestone hills, N part of county. Presidio Co., N rim of the Solitario; San Estaban Canyon, S of Marfa. Brewster Co., Glass Mts.; Sierra Madera; 40-45 mi SE Ft. Stockton. Pecos Co., 30 mi E Ft. Stockton. Terrell Co., 10-15 mi, 30 mi N of Dryden. 2200-6500 ft. N to the Plains Country; Coah., Mex.

This is one of the most widespread oaks of the Trans-Pecos, evidently frequently hybridizing with *Quercus grisea* where they come in contact. Supposedly *Q. mohriana* occurs mostly (but not entirely) on limestone and *Q. grisea* occurs predominantly in igneous habitats, but also in limestone. Hybrids are sometimes formed where limestone and igneous substrates come in contact, at least on Mt. Ord. Hybrids between *Q. mohriana* and *Q. grisea* also are reported at the following sites: Eagle Mts., Hudspeth Co.; San Estaban Canyon, Presidio Co.; Old Blue, Glass Mts., and Iron Mt., Brewster Co.

Mohr Shin Oak is a shrub or small tree 1-7 m high with evergreen or

Fig. 70. *Quercus havardii* (Havard Oak)

deciduous leaves. The leaves are leathery, oblong or elliptic, to 8 cm long, 3.5 cm wide, usually smaller, the margins entire or undulately toothed, the upper surfaces sparsely stellate, dark green, lustrous, and the lower surfaces densely gray- or white-tomentose. The species is distinguished by its characteristic bicolored leaf pubescence.

13. Quercus havardii Rydb.   HAVARD OAK, SHIN OAK, SHINNERY OAK. Fig. 70.   In deep to shallow sand, rarely in gypsum, in the counties on the NE border of the Trans-Pecos. Loving Co. Ward Co. Crane Co. Winkler Co. Andrews Co. Plants found almost everywhere there is deep sand. 2300–3400 ft. Sandy plains of southern Panhandle, into SE NM; also N to E OK; W to NE AZ and SE UT.

The Havard Oak usually is a shrub (spreading by rhizomes) from less than 1 m to 2 m high, but its hybrids with *Quercus stellata* Wang. occasionally form small trees to 4 m high. The deciduous leaves are thick, variable in shape, with toothed or lobed margins, lustrous upper surfaces, and grayish or yellowish, felty lower surfaces. The acorn cups are very broad (to 2.5 cm). Havard Oak is reported to cause some poisoning of livestock, but it is generally a valuable cover and food plant for wildlife. *Quercus havardii* reportedly hybridizes with *Q. stellata* and with *Q. mohriana*.

14. Quercus grisea Liebm.   GRAY OAK.   Fig. 71.   [*Quercus oblongifolia* Coult., not Torr.].   Igneous or dolomitic substrates, foothills, slopes, and can-

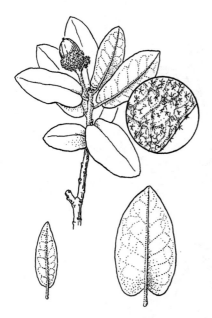

Fig. 71. *Quercus grisea* (Gray Oak)   Fig. 72. *Quercus fusiformis* (Plateau Oak)

yons, one of the most common species in the Trans-Pecos. Hudspeth Co., Sierra Diablo; Eagle Mts. Culberson Co., Guadalupe Mts. Jeff Davis Co., Davis Mts. Presidio Co., Chinati Mts.; Sierra Vieja; Solitario; Elephant Mt.; Brewster Co., vicinity of Alpine S to the Chisos Mts. 3400–7800 ft. Also NM and AZ; Chih. and Coah., Mex.

The Gray Oak in the Trans-Pecos is usually seen as a medium-sized tree (to 17 m) but the plants may also be shrubby. The deciduous or perhaps subevergreen plants have leaves that are leathery, grayish, rather ovate, the upper surfaces dull-green, and the lower surfaces felty. The Gray Oak is known to hybridize with a number of other oak species, and may hybridize with *Quercus intricata* (near Boot Spring Canyon, Chisos Mts.) and *Q. pungens* var. *vaseyana* (Nine-Point Mesa, Brewster Co.). The National co-champion Gray Oak, 50 ft. tall, 48 ft. crown spread, 6.2 ft. girth, was found by Liles in Boot Canyon of the Chisos Mountains in Big Bend National Park.

15. Quercus fusiformis Small. PLATEAU OAK. Fig. 72. [*Quercus virginiana* var. *fusiformis* (Small) Sarg. and var. *macrophylla* Sarg.; *Q. oleoides* var. *quaterna* C. H. Mull. (type only); *Q. virginiana* (juvenile) C. H. Mull.]. Limestone canyons, near streams. Terrell Co., Independence Creek Canyon, and headers of the canyon, ca. 2 mi below the Sheffield-Dryden highway to the Pecos River. Val Verde Co., Pecos River, near the mouth; Devils River. 1200–2500 ft. Also to S TX; Coah.; N.L., and Tam., Mex.

Fig. 73. *Quercus hypoleucoides* (Silverleaf Oak)

Plants of this evergreen species form large shrubs in canyon headers, or large trees with rough black bark and spreading crowns in deep soil along streams. The Plateau Oak resembles the Live Oak (*Quercus virginiana*) of E and S TX.

16. Quercus hypoleucoides A. Camus.   SILVERLEAF OAK, WHITELEAF OAK. Fig. 73.   [*Quercus confertifolia* Torr., not H.&B.; *Q. hypoleuca* Engelm., not Gand.]. Higher slopes, plateaus, and canyons. Jeff Davis Co., Davis Mts.; Timber Mt.; Forbidden Mt.; Mt. Livermore. 4500–7500 ft. Also Sierra Del Carmen, Coah., and the Sierra Madre, Chih., Mex.

The Silverleaf Oak is usually a small to medium-sized, subevergreen tree with coarsely furrowed hard black bark when growing in moist areas such as in drainages. In certain areas, however, such as upper and top slopes or plateaus of Timber Mountain, the plants are shrublike (1–2 m high), forming dense chaparral-thickets of considerable extent. The leaves of this species are leathery, lanceolate, to ca. 10 cm long, 1.5–3 cm wide, the margins typically entire and strongly revolute, with bluish-green upper surfaces and densely canescent-tomentose (whitish) lower surfaces.

Quercus hypoleucoides is known to hybridize with *Q. gravesii* in moist canyons at ca. 8000 ft., in the Davis Mts. The hybrids were once regarded as the distinct species *Q. livermorensis* C. H. Mull.

Fig. 74. *Quercus emoryi* (Emory Oak)   Fig. 75. *Quercus emoryi* × *Q. gravesii*
                                                    (= *Q. robusta*)

17. Quercus emoryi Torr. EMORY OAK. Fig. 74. Mountains and canyons of igneous origin, a common species usually above 5000 ft. Presidio Co., Sierra Vieja (in the Trans-Pecos not reported to occur W of the Sierra Vieja); Elephant Mt. Jeff Davis Co., Davis Mts. Brewster Co., vicinity of Alpine S to Chisos Mts. 4400–6000 ft. W to AZ; Chih., Son., Mex.

Emory Oaks are small to large trees that are subevergreen and with roughly furrowed black bark, reaching 20 m in favorable localities. The leaves are usually oblong to ovate or hastate, 3–6 cm long, 1–2.5 cm wide, the margins entire or strongly toothed, these aristate-tipped. The acorns of this species are often used for food, especially by Indians. Numerous bird species, including quail, and small mammals also eat the acorns. The plants are heavily browsed by mule deer. Measurements of the State champion Emory Oak, recorded by Liles in upper Oak Canyon of Big Bend National Park, are 45 ft. tall, 66 ft. crown spread, and 9.1 ft. girth.

Emory Oak is known to hybridize with certain sympatric species. *Quercus emoryi* × *Q. graciliformis* hybrids, occurring on igneous slopes at 4000–6000 ft. elevations in the Chisos Mountains, were previously recognized as *Q. tharpii* C. H. Mull. Hybrids between *Q. emoryi* × *Q. gravesii* (Fig. 75), previously recognized as *Q. robusta* C. H. Mull., occur in moist wooded canyons (Oak Canyon) in the Chisos Mountains, with both parents. After additional study *Q. robusta* might again receive the status of distinct species.

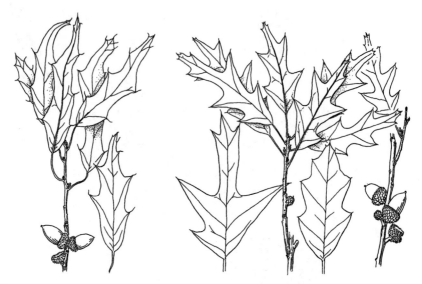

Fig. 76. *Quercus graciliformis* (Chisos Oak)   Fig. 77. *Quercus gravesii* (Graves Oak)

18. Quercus graciliformis C. H. Mull.   CHISOS OAK.   Fig. 76.   [*Quercus graciliformis* var. *parvilobata* C. H. Mull.; *Q. graciliformis* f. *parvilobata* C. H. Mull.; *Q. canbyi* Cory & Parks, not Trel.]. Rocky canyons, intermediate elevations, usually associated with a high water table, known only from the Chisos Mts., Brewster Co.; mid to upper Blue Creek Canyon; upper Juniper Spring; old Nail Place; endemic.

Plants of *Quercus graciliformis* are small, subevergreen trees to 8 m (rarely 20 m) tall, with hard, furrowed, gray bark. The species name is taken after the slender, arching, graceful branches and pendent leaves. The leaves are rather thin, narrowly lanceolate, 8–10 cm long, 2–3 cm wide, aristate apically, usually unequally 8–10 toothed or lobed, these aristate. A form (*parvilobata*) with lanceolate leaves and entire margins does occur. Fruit maturation requires two years. It is possible that some plants in the populations of *Q. graciliformis* are instead *Q. emoryi* × *Q. graciliformis* (synonym, *Q. tharpii*). Recent information (K. Nixon, pers. comm.) indicates that *Q. graciliformis* is a valid species restricted to the Chisos Mts., and that it is closely related to *Q. canbyi* Trel. of northeastern Mexico. Fruit maturation in *Q. canbyi* requires one year (K. Nixon, pers. comm.). The National champion Chisos Oak in Blue Creek Canyon was found by Liles to be 66 ft. high with a girth of 5.4 ft.

19. Quercus gravesii Sudw.   GRAVES OAK, CHISOS RED OAK.   Fig. 77. [*Quercus texana* Sarg., not Buckl., *Q. stellipila* (Sarg.) Parks; *Q. chesosensis*

Fig. 78. *Quercus tardifolia* (Lateleaf Oak)

(Sarg.) C. H. Mull.]. Mountains, canyons, and arroyos, igneous and limestone substrates, rather common in Davis, Glass, and Chisos Mts. Presidio Co., Sierra Vieja. Jeff Davis Co., Davis Mts., Timber Mt. to Mt. Livermore. Brewster Co., vicinity of Alpine, S to the Chisos Mts. Pecos Co., Sierra Madera. Val Verde Co., Hidden Trail Canyon. off Rio Grande below Seminole Canyon. 1200–7600 ft. Also common in mts. of Coah. Mex.

The small or large trees of Graves Oak may reach 14 m high, with roughly furrowed, hard black bark. The leaves are deciduous, scarlet in autumn, rather thin in texture, to 14 cm long, 12 cm wide, usually with 2–3 lobes on each side with deep rounded sinuses, the lobes few-toothed and aristate-tipped. The National co-champion was discovered by Liles in Panther Canyon, Chisos Mountains, Big Bend National Park, with measurements 42 ft. tall, 40 ft. crown spread, and 12.8 ft. girth.

It is somewhat surprising to find Graves Oak, normally a species of moderately high elevations (above 4000–5000 ft.) in Hidden Trail Canyon at about 1200 ft. in Val Verde Co. There, plants grow with the rare American Pistachio (*Pistacia texana*).

20. Quercus tardifolia C. H. Mull. LATELEAF OAK. Fig. 78. Along arroyos and canyons, in woodlands at about 7000 ft., endemic in the Chisos Mts., Brewster Co. This is a rare species. Only two colonies or clones have been discovered, between Boot Spring and the South Rim along upper Boot

Fig. 79. *Quercus carmenensis* (Delcarmen Oak)

Canyon. Also Mex., Coah., Sierra del Carmen, one colony near Schott Tower (El Pico).

The plants of Lateleaf Oak are small, erect, evergreen trees with short branches and furrowed bark. The leaves appear late in the year, the new ones about the first of July, covered by a dense tomentum. The leaves are 5–9 cm long, 2.5–5.5 mm wide, with 3–4 aristate-tipped lobes on each side. The upper surfaces are a dull bluish-green, and the lower surfaces are detachably stellate-tomentose. *Quercus tardifolia* may prove to be a hybrid, *Q. gravesii* Sudw. × *Q. coahuilensis* Nixon & C. H. Mull. (Nixon and Muller, 1993).

21. Quercus carmenensis C. H. Mull.   DELCARMEN OAK.   Fig. 79.   High wooded ridge. Brewster Co., Chisos Mts., Casa Grande, ca. 7300 ft., just below the SE bluffs. Collected by the author, Sept. 1982, a new record for the United States. Otherwise known from Coah., Mex., Sierra del Carmen.

The one plant seen was a shrub, 0.5 high, with leaves ovate-elliptic, evenly and minutely stellate, the upper surfaces lustrous and perhaps glabrous. More information should be sought about this oak in the Chisos Mountains.

10. ULMACEAE MIRB.   ELM FAMILY

Trees or shrubs. Leaves alternate, 2-ranked, blades ovate or elliptic, usually asymmetrical at the bases, the margins usually toothed, rarely entire, pinnately veined. Flowers unisexual, with male and female flowers on same plant (monoecious), some flowers bisexual, sepals 4 or 5, rarely more or less, usually somewhat united greenish-yellow; petals none; stamens the same as or twice as many as the sepals; ovary superior, 1-celled, with 1 ovule; styles 2. Fruit a nut, a flattened, winged structure (samara), or roundish and berrylike (drupe).

Members of the Elm family occur in both hemispheres, represented by more than 200 species and about 15 genera. Three genera occur in Texas. Some authors segregate *Celtis* and related genera as a separate family (Celtidaceae).

KEY TO THE GENERA

1. Leaf blades doubly toothed; fruit winged, flat   1. *Ulmus.*
1. Leaf blades entire or toothed; fruit globose, berrylike   2. *Celtis.*

1. ULMUS L.   ELM

Trees, usually deciduous, rarely semievergreen. Leaves usually in 2 rows, short petioled, bases usually asymmetrical, margins mostly doubly toothed, with 7 or more pairs of straight, prominent veins. Flowers bisexual, produced in spring before leaves, or in fall in axils of leaves; calyx bellshaped, 4–9 lobed; stamens 4–9, with long, slender filaments. Fruit 1-celled and 1-seeded, a flattened nutlet girdled by a membranous wing, maturing in a few weeks.

A genus of about 45 species in the Northern Hemisphere, some of them widely planted as ornamentals. Five species occur in Texas.

1. Ulmus pumila L.   SIBERIAN ELM, CHINESE ELM.   Fig. 80.   Cultivated as an ornamental in most Trans-Pecos towns, where it often escapes and becomes a pest along canals, streams, and other water sources; also is extensively cultivated in the United States; a native of Siberia, Mongolia, and north China. The American Elm (*Ulmus americana*) is planted in a few towns. There are no native elms in the Trans-Pecos, or in the southwestern deserts.

2. CELTIS L.   HACKBERRY, SUGARBERRY

Trees or shrubs; bark usually grayish, smooth, often with protruding, corky knobs. Leaves deciduous (in our species), with longish petioles, blades entire or toothed, 3-nerved at the bases. Flowers small, appearing with leaves on new growth, staminate (calyx and stamens) produced in clusters first and thus at base of branches, pistillate (calyx and pistil) produced later and solitary above in axils of leaves; calyx 5-lobed; stamens 5–6. Fruit a drupe (berrylike), roundish or nearly oval, with a single smooth or sculptured seed surrounded by thin, sweet pulp and a firm outer coat, maturing in the fall and persisting.

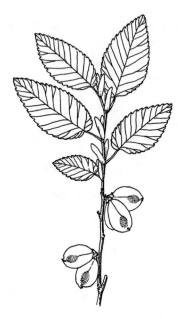

Fig. 80. *Ulmus pumila* (Chinese Elm)

About 80 hackberry species, some commonly planted as ornamentals, are known in the Northern Hemisphere and in the tropics. Six species occur in Texas. The Trans-Pecos hackberries are distinguished from other trees and shrubs in that they have simple, ovate or elliptic leaves, lack flower petals, and have yellow, orange, or reddish berrylike fruits. One of the species, the Netleaf Hackberry, always occurs along watercourses, canyons, and other areas of constant water supply, while the Spiny Hackberry commonly occurs away from water on desert hills and brushlands.

KEY TO THE SPECIES

1. Shrubs 1–2(–3) m high; branches with spines in pairs   **1. *C. pallida.***
1. Trees (or large shrubs) 4–14 m or more high; branches without spines.
  2. Smaller trees, usually to 6–8 m high; leaves 3–7 cm long, usually ovate and obtuse, apex acute or perhaps acuminate; margins entire or serrate above the middle; upper surface shining, very scabrous, strongly reticulate-veined, lower surface pale or yellowish   **2. *C. laevigata* var. *reticulata.***
  2. Larger trees, usually to 7–14 or more m tall; leaves 4–19 cm long, usually lanceolate to elliptic- or ovate-lanceolate, apex usually long-acuminate and curving, margins entire to somewhat serrate; both surfaces pale green with prominent veins; not so scabrous   **3. *C. laevigata* var. *laevigata.***

Fig. 81. *Celtis pallida* (Spiny Hackberry)

Fig. 82. *Celtis laevigata* var. *reticulata* (Netleaf Hackberry)

1. Celtis pallida Torr. SPINY HACKBERRY, GRANJENO. Fig. 81. [*Celtis spinosa* Spreng. var. *pallida* (Torr.) M. C. Johnst.]. Hills, brushlands, washes, not restricted to water sources, throughout much of the Trans-Pecos, especially in S Brewster, S Presidio, Terrell, and Val Verde counties; also in S TX; to S AZ; N Mex.

Other than the key characters above, *Celtis pallida* is distinguished by numerous spreading and whitish branches, toothed leaf blades to 3 cm long, 2 cm wide, and yellow, orange, or red ovoid fruit about 6 mm long. The dense semievergreen shrubs provide cover for quail and other birds, and the fruits are eaten by many birds and mammals.

2. Celtis laevigata Willd. var. **reticulata** (Torr.) L. Benson. NETLEAF HACKBERRY, PALO BLANCO. Fig. 82. [*Celtis reticulata* Torr.]. Along water courses, in canyons, near tanks and ponds, hillsides and many other habitats, usually but not always close to water sources, throughout the Trans-Pecos, widespread to OK, CO, W to WA and CA; N Mex.

This species is also characterized by gray bark, slightly flattened branches, leaf blades 3–5 cm long, 1.5–5.4 cm wide, rough or smooth to touch, with margins smooth or somewhat toothed toward the apexes, and round fruit that is reddish or reddish-black, 8–9 mm in diameter, and often beaked. The fruits were eaten by Indians, and are preferred by numerous birds and mammals.

3. Celtis laevigata Willd. var. **laevigata**   SUGAR HACKBERRY.   [*Celtis laevigata* var. *anomala* Sarg.]. Various soil types along drainages and other moist areas. 2700–4500 ft. Jeff Davis Co. and N Brewster Co. (Simpson, 1988). Pecos Co., old road from Fort Stockton to Alpine (J. M. Carpenter, pers. comm.). Val Verde Co.; throughout much of TX; much of E and central U.S. NE Mex.

Sugar Hackberry trees reach 20 m high or more in eastern Texas, but are probably not so tall in the arid Trans-Pecos. Like other hackberries, the fruits provide valuable food for wildlife.

11. MORACEAE LINK   MULBERRY FAMILY

Trees or shrubs, monoecious or dioecious, with milky sap. Leaves deciduous, usually alternate, entire, toothed, or lobed. Flowers unisexual, without petals, small, usually in catkins or heads, or inside of or attached to a receptacle; male flowers with 2–6 sepals (or more); stamens same number as sepals; female flowers with 4 united (or partially so) sepals; stigmas 1–2; ovary superior or inferior, with 1 cell and 1 ovule. Fruit small, an achene or drupe, enclosed by the fleshy sepals, often the achenes clustered to form an aggregate fruit.

Most members of the Mulberry family, about 1000 species and 40 genera, are tropical in distribution. Only four genera and six species occur in Texas, of which only one, *Morus*, is native to the Trans-Pecos.

Ficus carica L., the Common Fig or Higuera, is widely cultivated in the Trans-Pecos, as it is in much of the southern and eastern United States and other parts of the world. There are about 800 species of *Ficus* in tropical and subtropical regions of both hemispheres. The Common Fig, a native of western Asia, has been cultivated since ancient times for its fruit and also for various medicinal purposes which include the laxative action of ripe figs and the antihelmintic activity of the latex.

Maclura pomifera (Raf.) Schneid. (Fig. 83), commonly known as Osage Orange or Bois d'Arc, occurs in fields, fence rows, and waste places in OK, MO, AR, LA, and E TX. The plants, once widely grown as windbreaks and hedgerows because of their tendency to form thickets, have escaped cultivation throughout the southern United States. Osage Orange is rarely planted as windbreaks and yard trees in the Trans-Pecos, and has infrequently escaped cultivation here probably because of insufficient moisture. Curiously the plant has been collected in the Left Hand Shutup of the Solitario in Presidio Co. Plants also are known from 2 mi N of Ft. Davis in Limpia Canyon (Jeff Davis Co.), near Doubtful Canyon (Brewster Co.), and near Ft. Stockton (Pecos Co.). The male or female trees grow to 20 m high with roundish crowns, have prominent, stout spines on the stems, milky sap, bright green and lustrous leaves which turn yellow and are deciduous in the fall, and have large, orange-

Fig. 83. *Maclura pomifera* (Osage Orange)

like but conspicuously wrinkled fruits. Osage Orange is also known as Bow Wood, the French translation of Bois d'Arc which refers to use of the wood by Oklahoma Indians to make bows. It has been suggested that nomadic Indians of the Oklahoma region planted Bois d'Arc in suitable localities throughout their territories to assure a ready supply of the wood. According to a few residents of Alpine, the fruits serve as a cockroach and insect repellent if placed about the house in cabinets and other strategic spots.

1. MORUS L.   MULBERRY, MORAL

Trees or shrubs usually with scaly bark and imbricated buds. Leaves deciduous, entire, toothed, or lobed. Flowers unisexual, both male and female flowers in drooping catkins; sepals 4, united; petals absent; stamens 4; stigmas 2. Fruit an aggregate, overall ovoid to cylindric, resembling a blackberry, whitish to black, edible; each separate achene ovoid, flattened, and enclosed by the succulent calyx.

There are three mulberry species in Texas, two of them native, and one species occurs in the Trans-Pecos. In the Northern Hemisphere about 12 species occur in temperate and subtropical zones. Mulberries are frequently cultivated as ornamentals, and for their sweet fruit, the latter aspect often bemoaned by those who have crushed the fruits underfoot as they have walked along paths lined by the trees. They are grown also for their leaves which are

Fig. 84. *Morus microphylla*
(Mountain Mulberry)

the primary food of silkworms. The hard wood of some species is used to build furniture, boats, and other objects.

1. Morus microphylla Buckl.   MOUNTAIN MULBERRY, TEXAS MULBERRY. Fig. 84.   Most commonly found on limestone hills, slopes, and canyons, but also in igneous-rock soils, scattered and usually infrequent in moist canyon systems of mountains throughout the Trans-Pecos; in TX also E approximately to the Colorado River; in NM and AZ, Chih. and Dgo., Mex.

The Mountain Mulberry, a shrub or scrubby tree to about 7 m, is distinguished by leaves which are rough on both surfaces. The Indians of New Mexico, Arizona, and Texas supposedly grew this tree and used the wood to make bows. Indians also ate the fruit, although it is rather dry and small compared to other mulberries. Quail, dove, and many other birds eat the fruit, and deer may browse the branches.

12. VISCACEAE MIQ.   MISTLETOE FAMILY

Aerial parasites, small shrubs or herbaceous, on stems of evergreen or deciduous trees and shrubs; hairy or glabrous; monoecious or dioecious; stems evergreen usually much-branched and brittle, and with swollen and jointed nodes. Leaves evergreen or scalelike, opposite, simple, margins smooth. Flowers solitary or in clusters, unisexual, small (ca. 2 mm long), corolla absent, but with 2–4 perianth parts; male flowers with stamens same number as perianth parts and attached opposite them; female flowers with inferior ovary, ovary 1-celled. Fruit berrylike, usually sticky.

A family of about eight genera and 350 species, essentially worldwide in distribution but concentrated in tropical and subtropical areas. Until recently the Viscaceae were treated as a subfamily of the Loranthaceae, but the group is now accorded family status. Only two genera of the Mistletoe Family occur in the mainland United States. *Phoradendron tomentosum* is the mistletoe of Christmas time popularity. The parasitic species of *Arceuthobium* and *Phoradendron* included below are not necessarily woody plants, but they do exist as attached associates of trees.

KEY TO THE GENERA

1. Parasites on pines; plants leafless, yellow-green to orange, usually less than 20 cm tall; stems usually angled; female flowers usually with 2 perianth parts; fruit greenish or purplish **1. *Arceuthobium.***
1. Parasites on Junipers, Arizona Cypress, Oaks, and other angiosperms; plants with or without foliaceous leaves, green, usually more than 20 cm tall; stems roundish; female flowers usually with 3 perianth parts; fruit white or pinkish **2. *Phoradendron.***

1. ARCEUTHOBIUM BIEB.   DWARF MISTLETOE

Shrubs or herbs, parasites on conifers; plants dioecious, glabrous; stems usually angled, greenish-yellow to orange or reddish and black. Leaves reduced, minute, opposite, scalelike. Flowers small, 2–3 mm wide; male flowers 3–4-merous; anthers sessile, 1-celled, circular, one at the base of each perianth segment; female flowers 2-merous, perianth segments fused to ovary; style 1; ovary 1-celled. Fruit a berry, oval, greenish or purplish, with a transverse median line, borne on a stalk, reflexed, flattened, opening explosively; seeds 1, sticky, bicolored.

A genus of about 28 species distributed primarily in the western United States and Mexico. Three species occur in Texas and in the Trans-Pecos. A Texas species not included below, *Arceuthobium douglasii* Engelm., a parasite of Douglas-Fir (*Pseudotsuga*) with tiny plants (to 3 cm long, stems 1 mm wide at base) scattered along stems of the host plant, is known from the West Bowl, Guadalupe Mountains, Culberson County.

KEY TO THE SPECIES

1. Plants greenish-yellow to brownish; basal shoots less than 3 mm in diameter; parasite on pinyon pines **1. *A. divaricatum.***

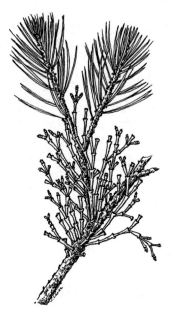

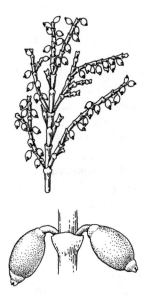

Fig. 85. *Arceuthobium divaricatum*
(Forking Dwarf Mistletoe), on pine.

Fig. 86. *Arceuthobium vaginatum*
(Pine Dwarf Mistletoe)

1. Plants orangish; basal shoots more than 3 mm in diameter; parasite on Ponderosa Pine   **2. A. vaginatum subsp. cryptopodum.**

1. Arceuthobium divaricatum Engelm. FORKING DWARF MISTLETOE. Fig. 85.   Parasitic on *Pinus edulis* in West Dog Canyon, Guadalupe Mts., Culberson Co. (Warnock, 1977); on *P. edulis* 20 mi N Allamoore, W side Sierra Diablo (Hawksworth, pers. comm.); and on *Pinus cembroides* var. *cembroides* in the Davis Mts., Jeff Davis Co. 4800–6500 ft.; Aug–Sep. Also NM W to CA, N to CO and UT; Baja CA, Mex.

This species has not been found on *Pinus remota*, or in any Trans-Pecos populations of *P. cembroides* except in the Davis Mts. proper. It is likely that susceptibility or immunity to *Arceuthobium divaricatum* is an indication of genetic difference between pine populations.

2. Arceuthobium vaginatum (Willd.) J. Presl. subsp. **cryptopodum** (Engelm.) Hawksworth & Wiens. PINE DWARF MISTLETOE. Fig. 86. [*Arceuthobium cryptopodum* Engelm.]. Parasitic on *Pinus ponderosa* in the Guadalupe Mts. (Culberson Co.) and in the Davis Mts. (Jeff Davis Co.). 6200–8000 ft.; May–Jun. Also NM W to CA, N to CO and UT; Son., Chih., Coah., Mex., including the Sierra del Carmen.

Recently Bailey (pers. comm.) has determined that *Pinus ponderosa* does not occur in the Chisos Mountains, but that the large pine there is *P. arizonica* var. *stormiae*. Possibly this explains the absence of *Arceuthobium vaginatum* subsp. *cryptopodum* in the Chisos Mountains. Additional subspecies of *A. vaginatum* occur in Mexico.

2. PHORADENDRON NUTT. MISTLETOE

Shrubs, parasites on woody plants, mostly trees; plants dioecious (our species), glabrous or pubescent. Leaves opposite, evergreen, well developed or reduced to scales. Flowers recessed in the rachis, small (to 2 mm wide); perianth segments usually 3-merous (rarely 2–4), triangular, scalelike; male flowers with anthers sessile, 2-celled; female flowers with perianth segments attached to ovary; style 1; ovary 1-celled. Fruit a drupe, fleshy, mucilaginous, white or pinkish, sessile, erect; seed 1.

A genus of about 250 species, mainly in the New World tropics. Five species are reported for Texas and the Trans-Pecos.

KEY TO THE SPECIES

1. Parasites on juniper and cypress; leaves reduced to scales or well-developed and narrow, usually less than 2.5 cm long or 0.5 cm wide; internodes usually less than 2 cm long.
   2. Leaves reduced to scales   **1. *P. juniperinum.***
   2. Leaves well-developed   **2. *P. hawksworthii.***
1. Parasites on dicotyledons (oak, mesquite, etc.); leaves well-developed and broad usually more than 2.5 cm long and 1 cm wide; internodes usually more than 2 cm long.
   3. Parasites almost entirely on *Quercus*; plants with a light, frosty pubescence, often with splotches of dense pubescence thus giving really frosty appearance, short-canescent with starshaped hairs; fruit with a ring of hairs at summit; flowering Jul–Sep   **3. *P. villosum* subsp. *coryae.***
   3. Parasites on *Celtis, Fraxinus, Populus, Prosopis, Acacia, Juglans, Quercus*, etc.; plants glabrous or with short-tomentose pubescence, hairs possibly stellate; fruit glabrous; flowering Nov–May.
      4. Plants short-tomentose, at least on young shoots, first internode, often elsewhere   **4. *P. tomentosum.***
      4. Plants glabrous   **5. *P. macrophyllum* subsp. *cockerellii.***

1. **Phoradendrum juniperinum** Engelm. JUNIPER MISTLETOE. Fig. 87. Parasitic on *Juniperus* and on *Cupressus* (Chisos Mts.). Hudspeth Co., Sierra Diablo, Victorio Canyon. Culberson Co., Guadalupe Mts. Jeff Davis Co., Davis Mts., Mt. Livermore, Madera Canyon and vicinity. Presidio Co., Chinati Mts. Brewster Co., Chisos Mts. 4000–6700 ft.; Jul–Sep. Also NW to CO, UT, and OR; Chih., Mex. Also reported on *Pinus strobiformis* on Mt. Livermore, al-

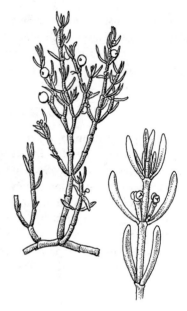

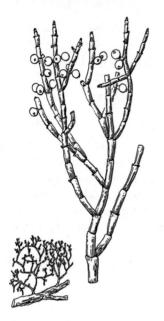

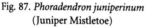

Fig. 87. *Phoradendron juniperinum*
(Juniper Mistletoe)

Fig. 88. *Phoradendron hawksworthii*
(Rough Mistletoe)

though Hawksworth reports (pers. comm.) that the mistletoe on *P. strobiformis* "should be" *Arceuthobium apachecum* Hawksworth & Wiens.

2. **Phoradendron hawksworthii** (Wiens) Wiens. ROUGH MISTLETOE. Fig. 88. [*Phoradendron bolleanum* (Seem.) Eichler subsp. *hawksworthii* Wiens]. Parasitic on *Juniperus*. Mountains of Trans-Pecos, reported in El Paso, Brewster, Presidio, Pecos, and Terrell counties. 4500–5700 ft.; Jul–Sep. Another taxon, subsp. *densum* (Trel.) Wiens with flattened leaves 2 mm or more wide, and 6 or more flowers per segment on the staminate inflorescence, occurs in the Sierra del Carmen of Coahuila, Mexico, and may occur in the adjacent Trans-Pecos.

3. **Phoradendron villosum** (Nutt.) Nutt. subsp. **coryae** (Trel.) Wiens. OAK MISTLETOE. Fig. 89. [*Phoradendron coryae* Trel.; *P. havardianum* Trel.]. Parasitic on *Quercus* species. El Paso Co., Franklin Mts.; Hueco Tanks. Culberson Co., Guadalupe Mts.; Sierra Diablo. Jeff Davis Co., Davis Mts. Presidio Co., Sierra Vieja; Chinati Mts.; Bofecillos Mts. Brewster Co., vicinity of Alpine S to Chisos Mts. and Dead Horse Mts. 3500–7000 ft.; Jul–Sep. Also NM and AZ; Chih., Coah., Mex.

This is one of the most common mistletoes in the Trans-Pecos, along with *Phoradendron tomentosum*. There are two reports of *P. villosum* on mesquite, both in southern Brewster County, Black Gap Refuge.

Fig. 89. *Phoradendron villosum*
(Oak Mistletoe)

4. Phoradendron tomentosum (DC.) Engelm *ex* A. Gray. CHRISTMAS MISTLETOE, INJERTO. [*Phoradendron "flavescens"* of many authors; *P. serotinum* var. *pubescens* (Engelm.) M. C. Johnst.]. Common throughout much of the Trans-Pecos (and elsewhere), parasitic on a number of woody dicotyledons, including: *Celtis, Populus, Prosopis, Acacia, Quercus, Juglans, Salix*, etc. 1100–5700 ft.; Nov–Mar. Common throughout TX, N to KS, E to AR and LA; also N Mex.

5. Phoradendron macrophyllum (Engelm.) Cockerell subsp. **cockerellii** (Trel.) Wiens. BIGLEAF MISTLETOE. [*Phoradendron tomentosum* subsp. *macrophyllum* (Engelm.) Wiens]. Mainly parasitic on *Populus, Fraxinus*, and *Prosopis*. Along and near the Rio Grande from El Paso Co. to Presidio Co. (including mouth of Alamito Creek below Presidio, Cibolo Creek near Shafter, Pinto Canyon). 2500–3500 ft.; Dec–Mar. W to CA; Baja CA, Son., Chih., Coah., Mex. This species resembles *P. tomentosum* but is completely glabrous.

13. POLYGONACEAE JUSS.   KNOTWEED FAMILY

Herbs, subshrubs, shrubs, or vines, with or without obvious leafy stems. Leaves alternate, rarely opposite or whorled, usually with petioles, blades usually entire, rarely toothed or lobed; stipules long or short, sheathing the stems (not in *Eriogonum*). Flowers bisexual or unisexual, small, in racemes, solitary, or in clusters and surrounded by involucres; sepals 2–6, often whitish or pinkish, petal-like, sometimes with wings or keels; petals absent; stamens 2–9; ovary superior, 1–celled, usually 3–angled, sometimes lens-shaped; styles usually surrounded by persistent calyx at maturity; seed 1, with much endosperm.

Only four of the approximately 30 genera of this widespread family occur in the Trans-Pecos; *Eriogonum, Rumex, Polygonum*, and *Persicaria*. Among the Trans-Pecos species of *Eriogonum*, there are several that are considered to be subshrubs, but otherwise members of the Polygonaceae in this region are essentially herbaceous.

1. ERIOGONUM MICHX.   WILDBUCKWHEAT.

Herbaceous annuals or biennials, subshrubs, or shrubs; plants scapose, with basal leaves, or with leafy stems. Leaves alternate, entire, without stipules. Flowers small, usually in clusters, each cluster subtended by a bellshaped involucre of bracts; petallike sepals in 2 whorls of threes, white, yellow, red, or purple; stamens 9. 3-angled achenes winged in some species, smooth or hairy.

A large genus of about 225 species, concentrated in western North America. About 19 species occur in the Trans-Pecos including *Eriogonum hieracifolium, E. hemipterum, E. jamesii, E. tenellum, E. havardii, E. wrightii*, and *E. suffruticosum* with compact woody bases or short, slender woody stems.

Two species, *Eriogonum wrightii* and *E. suffruticosum*, most closely approach a shrubby habit and are included below.

KEY TO THE SPECIES

1. Leaves covered with dense, wooly hairs; perianth white; calyx segments similar; widespread species   **1. E. wrightii.**
1. Leaves covered with fine silky hairs; perianth white or yellowish with reddish midribs; calyx segments dissimilar; endemic to the Trans-Pecos
                                                                      1. E. suffruticosum.

1. Eriogonum wrightii Torr. *ex* Benth.   WRIGHT WILDBUCKWHEAT.   Fig. 90.   Scattered and infrequent or locally abundant, rocky slopes in the mountains at lower to moderate elevations, El Paso Co. E to Brewster Co.; Jul–Sep. Also W to AZ; N Mex. Also identified by leaves crowded on lower half of plants, with leaf blades oblanceolate to elliptic, with the margins entire or with small rounded teeth, and fruits 2.5–3 mm long.

2. Eriogonum suffruticosum S. Wats.   Fig. 91.   An endemic on rocky limestone hills and associated clay hills and flats, S Brewster and Presidio coun-

Fig. 90. *Eriogonum wrightii*
(Wright Wildbuckwheat)

Fig. 91. *Eriogonum suffruticosum*

ties, from about 4 mi S of Alpine to near Agua Fria and to Terlingua and Lajitas
to the S, and to near Santiago Peak to the E. Mar–May. A low gnarly shrub
also identified by leaves tufted at branch ends, elliptic leaf blades with the leaf
margins rolled toward the undersides, and by fruits 3–3.5 mm long. This species was thought to be rare until recent field studies have shown it to be rather
widespread and locally common mostly in southern Brewster County.

14. CHENOPODIACEAE VENT. GOOSEFOOT FAMILY

Herbs (predominantly), subshrubs or shrubs, often weedy, glabrous or
hairy, often with scurfy white scales; stems rather succulent, sometimes appearing jointed. Leaves alternate or opposite, with or without petioles; blades
simple, flat, with entire, toothed, or lobed margins, or roundish and succulent,
sometimes reduced, scalelike. Flowers small and inconspicuous, perfect, unisexual, or both kinds on same plant, various inflorescence types; sepals usually
5; petals none; stamens usually 5, rarely 1–4; ovary superior, with 1 cell and
1 ovule; styles or stigmas usually 2, rarely 3–5, persistent. Fruit 1-seeded, ovary
wall inflated or attached to seed coat; embryo curved or spiraled.

A worldwide family of about 100 genera and 1400 species. In the Trans-
Pecos region many members are characteristic of alkaline habitats. Also, there

are many herbaceous, weedy species that occur in various soil types and in waste places, especially in towns, along roadsides, and other disturbed habitats. Best known examples of the southwest are Russian Thistle or Tumbleweed, Goosefoot, *Kochia*, and *Bassia*. Some members of the Goosefoot Family are garden vegetables, including the familiar spinach, beets, and chard. Many species of this family are quickly recognizable by the scurfy, white-scale aspect of the leaves and stems, especially in mature plants.

KEY TO THE GENERA

1. Jointed stems, scalelike leaves, and bracts subtending flowers alternate, the bracts peltate; flowers in dense, cylindric spikes   **1. *Allenrolfea.***
1. Stems not jointed, leaves well developed, bracts otherwise; flowers clustered in headlike glomerules or solitary in axils.
    2. Leaves flattened or with margins rolled underneath (revolute); flowers usually unisexual.
        3. Leaves flattened, margins entire, toothed, or lobed; bracts of fruit without hairs   **2. *Atriplex.***
        3. Leaves linear to lanceolate with margins strongly rolled underneath; bracts of fruit with long whitish hairs (turning reddish-tan on dried plants), ca. 5 mm long   **3. *Krascheninnikovia.***
    2. Leaves linear-round, relatively small; flowers mostly perfect, clustered or solitary in upper axils   **4. *Suaeda.***

1. ALLENROLFEA O. KTZE.   PICKLEWEED

Shrubs 3–15 dm tall, with green, glabrous, succulent, alternate branches with swollen joints 2–10 mm long. Leaves alternate, reduced to triangular scales. Flowers bisexual, subtended by fleshy, peltate bracts, in numerous, dense cylindrical spikes; sepals 4 or 5, somewhat united, fleshy; stamens 1 or 2; stigmas 2 or 3. Fruit ovoid, flattened, utricles enclosed by swollen sepals, pericarp membranous; seed smooth, oblong, reddish-brown.

   1. Allenrolfea occidentalis (S. Wats.) O. Ktze.   PICKLEWEED.   Fig. 92. [*Allenrolfea mexicana* Lundell]. In alkaline flats, margins of salt lakes, near saline streams such as the upper Pecos River, in Pecos, Reeves, Culberson, Hudspeth, and El Paso counties; also in saline soils throughout the SW U.S. to OR; Baja CA, Son., Chih., Coah., Mex. There are three species of *Allenrolfea*, with two native to Argentina.

   The pickleweed, sometimes called Iodine Bush because its crushed stems yield an iodinelike sap, is characteristic of strongly saline soils, usually with subsurface water. In fact, the plant should be considered as an indicator of alkalinity. Pickleweed provides little forage for livestock but may be eaten

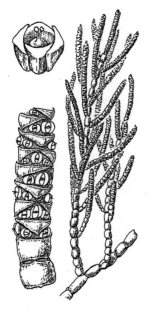

Fig. 92. *Allenrolfea occidentalis* (Pickleweed)

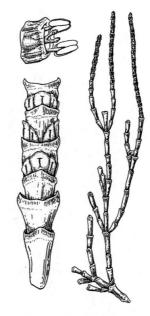

Fig. 93. *Salicornia utahensis*

in harsh times. The plants resemble members of the genus *Salicornia*, a well-known sand and salt-marsh herb especially common near sea coasts. In the Trans-Pecos *S. utahensis* (Fig. 93) is an uncommon herbaceous subshrub in the Salt Flat of Hudspeth County, and in saline habitats near the Pecos River. *Salicornia* has opposite stems, scalelike leaves and bracts, with the bracts united below the flowers that are sunken in stem cavities.

2. ATRIPLEX L.   SALTBUSH

Shrubs up to 1 m or more high, or smaller annual or perennial herbs, usually with scale-covered stems. Leaves with or without petioles, alternate or opposite, the margins entire, toothed or lobed. Flowers unisexual, single or clustered, in spikes or panicles, or axillary; male and female flowers on separate or same plants; male flowers without bracts, with 3–5 united sepals; stamens 3–5; female flowers each subtended by 2 swollen, glabrous bracts which are united or separate and enclose the fruit; ovary ovoid or roundish; stigmas 2. Fruit a utricle with a thin pericarp, and one free seed.

The southwestern and desert species of *Atriplex* occur mostly in saline or alkaline soils. In all there are about 200 species of the genus in temperate and subtropical regions. Many species provide nutritious forage plants, and the pollen of some species causes hay fever. The Indians ate part of some species, including leaves, young shoots, and fruits.

Fig. 94. *Atriplex semibaccata*
(Australian Saltbush)

KEY TO THE SPECIES

1. Male and female flowers on same plant; fruiting bracts fleshy, red and thick
$\qquad$ **1. A. semibaccata.**
1. Male and female flowers on separate plants, or with unisexual and bisexual flowers on same plant.
   2. Fruiting bracts longitudinally 4-winged $\qquad$ **2. A. canescens.**
   2. Fruiting bracts not longitudinally 4-winged.
      3. Leaf blades entire.
         4. Compact shrub to 60 cm high; stems woody throughout, thorny
$\qquad$ **3. A. confertifolia.**
         4. Perennial herb to 50 cm (rarely taller); stems woody below, rarely nearly throughout, herbaceous above, without spines **4. A. obovata.**
      3. Leaf blades toothed (dentate); fruiting bracts with long, spinelike tubercules
$\qquad$ **5. A. acanthocarpa.**

   1. Atriplex semibaccata R. Br.   AUSTRALIAN SALTBUSH.   Fig. 94.   A naturalized species, native of Australia and Tasmania. El Paso Co., saline-sandy flats, and along irrigation canals. Pecos Co., in and near Ft. Stockton. Reeves Co., in Pecos. 2500–4400 ft. Also NM, AZ, CA, and UT.

   This species, a herbaceous perennial from a woody taproot, was introduced as a forage plant because it supposedly is high in protein and well adapted to

Fig. 95. *Atriplex canescens* (Fourwing Saltbush)

the saline, alkaline, and dry soils (where few other plants survive) prevalent in the desert southwest. Its leaf blades are oblong or obovate-oblong, shallow toothed, with glabrous upper surfaces and white-scurfy lower surfaces.

2. **Atriplex canescens** (Pursh) Nutt. FOURWING SALTBUSH. Fig. 95. Common in alkaline flats, hills, slopes, grasslands, mesas throughout much of the Trans-Pecos; Apr–Oct; the most widely distributed *Atriplex* in the U.S., in various soil types, mostly desertic, including saline or alkaline, from sea level to 7000 ft., TX and OK, W to CA, N to Can. Coah., and S.L.P., Mex.

The Fourwing Saltbush is easily distinguished by its habitat usually in saline areas, 4-winged fruits, and linear, oblong, or spatulashaped gray-scurfy leaves which become glabrous. The foliage is highly nutritious to cattle, sheep, and goats, and the plants are valuable forage especially in the saline grasslands where few other plants grow. The plants develop extensive root systems, are highly drought resistant, and are thus useful in erosion control. The fruits are eaten by birds, notably scaled quail, and numerous small mammals. Indians of the southwest were known to grind the seeds into a "baking powder" for use in making bread. According to Sanderson and Stutz (1994), the Chihuahuan Desert *Atripex canescens* is var. **angustifolia** (Torr.) S. Wats.

3. **Atriplex confertifolia** (Torr. & Frem.) S. Wats. SPINY SALTBUSH, SHADSCALE. Alkaline basins, flats, hills, bluffs, reported to occur in extreme

Fig. 96. *Atriplex obovata*
(Obovateleaf Saltbush)

western Trans-Pecos, possibly in El Paso Co. Also in the Panhandle; widespread in eroded desert, alkaline soils, from TX and NM W to CA and OR, N to WY and ND; Chih., Mex. I have not seen specimens of this species from the Trans-Pecos, and Jim Henrickson (pers. comm., 1981) reports that he has not seen specimens of the taxon from the Chihuahuan Desert Region.

The plants are roundish, compact shrubs with spiny stems and twigs, ovate to elliptic leaves with grayish-green scurfy surfaces. Spiny Saltbush is good browse for sheep, goats, and mule deer when abundant enough, but not for cattle because of the spiny branches, especially when leaves fall during the winter. The fruits are eaten by several types of birds. This species is best known as Shadscale in northern Arizona and in the Great Basin desert where it may occur in nearly pure stands in alkaline soils.

4. **Atriplex obovata** Moq. OBOVATELEAF SALTBUSH. Fig. 96. [*Atriplex greggii* S. Wats.]. Dryish saline or alkaline soils and gypseous clays. El Paso Co. Hudspeth Co., between Finley and McNary; Presidio Co., between Ruidosa and Presidio. Brewster Co., vicinity of Terlingua, in Big Bend Park, N to Packsaddle Mt. Also in dry soils, probably mostly alkaline, S NM, AZ, and W and S-cen. CO; Chih., Zac., Mex.

This species is at most merely a subshrub, or herbaceous perennial, with white surfaces and permanent scurf on the obovate leaf blades, and it is not

Fig. 97. *Atriplex acanthocarpa*
(Tubercled Saltbush)

known to be an important desert forage plant as are some other species of the genus.

5. **Atriplex acanthocarpa** (Torr.) S. Wats.   TUBERCLED SALTBUSH.   Fig. 97.   Alkaline soils and gypseous clays. El Paso Co., Franklin Mts., scenic drive above El Paso. Hudspeth Co., 6 mi W of Ft. Hancock. Presidio Co., above Candelaria. Brewster Co., 5 mi W of the Chisos Mts.; near Terlingua; near Terlingua Creek on 02 Ranch. 2300–4400 ft.; summer–fall. Also in S NM, Graham Co., AZ; Chih., N.L., S.L.P., Mex.; reportedly planted in alkaline soils as ornamentals and cover.

The most conspicuous feature of this evergreen shrub with toothed leaf blades is the prominent flattened tubercles, to 8 mm long, on the spongy fruiting bracts. Tubercled Saltbush is evidently not an important browse plant. The Trans-Pecos taxon is *Atriplex acanthocarpa* subsp. **acanthocarpa,** which extends from adjacent Chihuahua and Coahuila, Mexico, to southwest New Mexico and southeast Arizona (Henrickson, 1988).

3. **KRASCHENINNIKOVIA** GULDENSTAEDT   WINTER FAT

Subshrub, 2–10 cm high, stems erect or spreading, covered with minute starshaped and simple hairs. Leaves alternate and clustered, the blades narrow,

Fig. 98. *Krascheninnikovia lanata*
(Common Winter Fat)

sessile or with short petioles, covered with starshaped hairs, the margins rolled underneath. Inflorescence an elongated panicle, covered with long hairs (whitish in nature); flower axillary in clusters or spikes; male and female flowers on separate plants, sometimes on same plant; male flowers with 4 hairy sepals; stamens 4; female flowers without sepals but enclosed by 2 bracts with long white hairs, forming beaked tube enclosing the fruit (utricle); styles 2.

There are about eight species of *Krascheninnikovia* in both the Old and New World.

1. **Krascheninnikovia lanata** (Pursh) Guldenstaedt. COMMON WINTER FAT. Fig. 98. [*Ceratoides lanata* (Pursh) J. T. Howell; *Ceratoides lanata* var. *subspinosa* (Rydb.) J. T. Howell; *Eurotia lanata* (Pursh) Moq.; *E. lanata* var. *subspinosa* (Rydb.) Kearn. & Peeb.]. Desert soils, usually somewhat alkaline. El Paso Co., 17 mi E of El Paso. Hudspeth Co., vicinity of Hueco Tanks; just W of Van Horn; from near Sierra Blanca to 40 mi N; Sierra Diablo, Victorio Canyon and Bat Cave Draw. Culberson Co., near Van Horn, and in the Guadalupe Mts. Jeff Davis Co., near Point-of-Rocks. Presidio Co., at Elephant Mt.; also in the Creosotebush and sagebrush deserts, and oak woodlands. 2000–8000 ft. N to WA, Sask., Can., and W to CA; and N Mex., S to S.L.P.

Common Winter Fat is drought resistant and is valuable as winter forage for livestock (especially sheep) and game. In some areas of the Great Basin, Common Winter Fat occurs in nearly pure stands over thousands of acres, remaining succulent during the winter months. Indians used a brew from the leaves for treating fever, and used a powder from the roots for treating burns.

4. SUAEDA FORSK. *ex* SCOP. SEEPWEED, SEA BLITE

Smallish shrubs or herbs. Leaves fleshy, alternate, relatively small, narrow, somewhat cylindrical. Flowers bisexual or plants with unisexual and bisexual flowers in axillary clusters or solitary on upper stems; sepals 5, barely winged or keeled; stamens 5; ovary 1-celled; styles usually 2. Fruit (utricle) somewhat flattened, enclosed by the sepals; seed with coiled embryo and little or no endosperm.

Most of the more than 100 annual or perennial species occur along sea coasts and in other saline habitats throughout the world. The Trans-Pecos species are all shrubs or herbs, and occur in saline soils, especially those in the vicinity of old salt lakes. They are of only emergency forage value.

The herbaceous annual, *Suaeda mexicana* (Standl.) Standl., occurs in saline-gypseous habitats throughout the Chihuahuan Desert in Mexico although previous reports (Powell, 1988; Worthington, 1989) that this species also occurs in the Trans-Pecos or any place else in the United States have not been verified through recent studies (H. J. Schenk, pers. comm.). The rather tall annual herbs have pale-green, glabrous stems which are 3–12 dm long, branched mostly at the base and nearly erect, long pointed leaves, 1.2–2.5 cm long, and brownish-red seeds 0.8 mm in diameter.

KEY TO THE SPECIES

1. Leaves densely hairy, becoming glabrate with age
   1. *S. suffrutescens* var. *suffrutescens.*
1. Leaves glabrous, green, glaucous.
   2. Leaves 3–13 mm long, subcylindrical, obtuse to acute
      2. *S. suffrutescens* var. *detonsa.*
   2. Leaves 5–30 mm long, linear, flattened   3. *S. moquinii.*

1. **Suaeda suffrutescens** S. Wats. var. **suffrutescens** DESERT SEEPWEED. Fig. 99. [*Dondia suffrutescens* (S. Wats.) Heller]. Alkaline gypseous bolsons and flats to 5000 ft., El Paso (in town), Hudspeth (Ft. Quitman), Culberson (common in Salt Basin), Presidio (Porvenir), Reeves (Pecos to Barstow), Pecos (Ft. Stockton), Brewster (Santa Elena Canyon, Lajitas), and Jeff Davis (Chispa) counties. Also in NW TX, (Crane Co., Ward Co.) and W through NM to AZ, N to OK; Chih., Coah., Mex.

This taxon with stems less than 1 m frequently is identifiable by its tendency

Fig. 99. *Suaeda suffrutescens* var. *suffrutescens*
(Desert Seepweed)

to form moundlike shrubs 12–15 dm across. It is the most common seepweed in the Trans-Pecos. In New Mexico this species is commonly known as Yerba de Burro. Southwestern Indians cooked and ate the young leaves, applied dried leaves to sores, and made a pinole flour from the seeds. Recent studies (W. R. Ferren and H. J. Schenk, 1996, pers. comm.) suggest that the woody seepweeds of the Trans-Pecos belong to a single, wide-ranging, morphologically variable species. If so, *Suaeda suffrutescens* would be brought in synonymy under *S. moquinii.*

2. **Suaeda suffrutescens** var. **detonsa** I. M. Johnst. [*Suaeda nigrescens* I. M. Johnst.; *S. nigrescens* var. *glabra* I. M. Johnst.; *S. duripes* I. M. Johnst.]. Saline gypseous soils. Hudspeth Co., near Ft. Quitmàn and Rio Grande; Brewster Co., Hot Springs near mouth of Tornillo Creek. Also Gonzales Co., of S TX and Andrews Co. of lower Plains; also NM, along Rio Grande and Pecos valleys; Coah., S.L.P., Chih., Zac., Mex.

The type specimen is from 3 mi W of Cuatro Cienegas, Coah., Mex. According to Hopkins and Blackwell (1977), *Suaeda nigrescens* and *S. nigrescens* var. *glabra* may eventually be separated as distinct; *S. moquinii* is close morphologically to *S. suffrutescens* var. *detonsa. Suaeda duripes* is listed by Hopkins and Blackwell (1977) as probably synonymous with var. *detonsa;* the taxon was known only from the type collection, and probably is endemic to Reeves and Pecos counties, thus extending the range of var. *detonsa.*

Fig. 100. *Suaeda moquinii* (Alkali Seepweed)

3. Suaeda moquinii (Torr.) Greene.   ALKALI SEEPWEED, QUELITE SALADO.
Fig. 100.   [*Suaeda torreyana* S. Wats.]. Alkaline soils and marshes. Pecos Co.
and probably elsewhere in the Trans-Pecos. Also in Oldham, Gonzales, and
Cameron counties; widespread W through NM to NV and CA, N to OR, WY,
and ND; Can.; Chih. and Sin., Mex.

The younger leaves of this species were used by Indians in the same manner
as were those of Desert Seepweed.

15. AMARANTHACEAE JUSS.   AMARANTH FAMILY

Annual or perennial herbs and subshrubs, many weedy species. Leaves opposite or alternate, sessile or with petioles; stipules absent. Flowers having
either stamens or pistils, or unisexual and bisexual flowers on same plant; flowers solitary or in clusters, or arranged in spikes or racemes, with membranous
bracts subtending each flower or cluster; perianth of 2–5 separate, membranous tepals, or rarely 1, or absent; corolla absent; stamens 2–5, usually fused,
opposite the tepals; ovary superior, 1-celled; styles 1–2 or absent. Fruit (utricle) membranous, indehiscent or dehiscent (circumscissle or irregular); seeds
smooth and shining, erect or inverted, lensshaped, oblong, or nearly round;
embryo ringlike.

This relatively large family with about 850 species and 65 genera is mostly tropical in distribution, but also many weedy species are cosmopolitan. Most species are herbaceous. Only three shrubby or subshrubby members are represented in the Trans-Pecos.

KEY TO THE GENERA

1. Stems and leaves pubescent; ovules 1; anthers 2-celled.
   2. Leaves opposite; plants densely grayish-pubescent with branched hairs; flowers mostly perfect, in small glomerules   **1. Tidestromia.**
   2. Leaves alternate; plants densely silky-pubescent, or leaves glabrate with age; flowers mostly unisexual, arranged in panicles   **2. Iresine.**
1. Stems glabrous, leaves green and glabrous or sparsely pubescent beneath; ovules 2; anthers 4-celled   **3. Celosia.**

1.   TIDESTROMIA STANDL.

Annual or perennial, erect or prostrate herbs, or subshrubs with stems woody at the base, stems with branched hairs. Leaves opposite and with petioles, the blades rather broad, or many shapes, with entire margins. Flowers perfect, very small, arranged in clusters (glomerules) in leaf axils, with subtending leaves becoming hard in involucrelike form around the glomerules; perianth with 3 wider outer segments and 2 narrower inner parts, these membranelike; stamens 5 with filaments basally fused; ovary roundish, style short, stigma enlarged; ovule 1. Fruit (utricle) indehiscent, glabrous, slightly flattened.

A genus of about 7 species in the southwestern United States and Mexico. Three species occur in Texas, one of them subshrubby, and all are found in the Trans-Pecos.

1. Tidestromia suffruticosa (Torr.) Standl.   SHRUBBY TIDESTROMIA. Fig. 101.   In gypseous clays and shales, and in rocky limestone soils; Brewster Co., 45–75 mi S of Alpine; Hot Springs and Boquillas Canyon in Big Bend Park; Goat Mt.; Buckhill Mt.; road to Tesnus; probably in S Presidio Co. 2000–3800 ft.; Jun–Sep. S. NM; Mex.

2. IRESINE POIR.

Erect shrubs, 2–10 cm tall, branches very slender, densely silky pubescent, rigid, often spinescent when older. Leaves mostly alternate and with short petioles; blades thickish ovate, ovate-lanceolate, or somewhat oblong, 0.7–2.5 cm long, 3–9 mm wide, sparsely silky or glabrate on upper surface, densely silky beneath or glabrate when older. Panicles usually dense, 2–15 cm long; spikelets

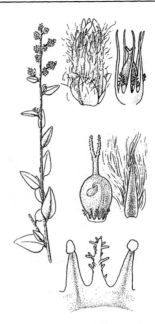

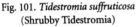

Fig. 101. *Tidestromia suffruticosa*
(Shrubby Tidestromia)

Fig. 102. *Iresine leptoclada*

with few flowers and short; perianth round, with 5 distinct parts; male and female flowers on separate or the same plant, flowers occasionally perfect; male flowers with short, pubescent bractlets; tepals densely hairy, 2 mm long; stamens fused, forming a cup, with 5 filaments as long as the tepals; staminodia very short, fringed; female flowers with hairy, roundish bractlets almost as long as the tepals; tepals 1.5 mm long, with hairs; style very short, stigmas elongated. Fruit (utricle) slightly flattened, membraneous; seed 1 mm wide.

A genus of about 80 species in North and South America. Henrickson and Sundberg (1986) recently provided evidence that *Dicraurus leptocladus* should be merged with *Iresine*.

1. **Iresine leptoclada** (Hook. f.) Henrickson & Sundberg.   Fig. 102.   [*Dicraurus leptocladus* Hook. f.]. Rocky habitats exposed to sun, southern Trans-Pecos. Brewster Co., Chisos Mts.; Rosillos Mts.; Sierra Quemada; 02 Ranch; Packsaddle Mt.; 24 mi S of Marathon; Doubtful Canyon. Presidio Co., 1 mi W of Solitario Peak; 4 mi S of Shafter; Pinto Canyon. Pecos Co. 3000–5800 ft.; Jul–Dec. Also NE Mex.

Iresine leptoclada is a weak-stemmed shrub that often grows within and receives support from other shrubs. The stems usually are slender and grayish in color.

3. CELOSIA L.

Herbs and shrubs with erect or lax stems. Leaves alternate, with petioles, blades entire or lobed. Flowers perfect, arranged in spikes or glomerules; perianth of 5 membranous tepals; stamens 5, fused at the base; ovary essentially glabrous; style usually short, stigmas expanded. Fruit (utricle) concealed by the tepals, thin, membranous, usually opening around the middle; seeds usually 2, lensshaped, lustrous.

About 60 species of *Celosia* occur in temperate and tropical zones, with only one representative in the Trans-Pecos.

1. **Celosia palmeri** S. Wats.   Reported to be in rocky and woodland mountains of the Trans-Pecos. Also in NE Mex.

16. NYCTAGINACEAE JUSS. FOUR-O'CLOCK FAMILY

Herbs, shrubs, or trees; stems erect, trailing, or climbing, pubescent or glabrous, sometimes with spines, the nodes often swollen. Leaves usually opposite, less often alternate or whorled, with or without petioles, stipules absent; blades entire, toothed, or lobed. Flowers bisexual or unisexual, usually regular and arranged in clusters, or solitary; flowers usually subtended by green or brightly colored calyxlike involucres; perianth inferior, leaflike or corollalike, enclosing the fruit, the perianth tube short or long, blunt, toothed, or lobed; stamens 1 to many, filaments usually united basally; anthers exserted or not, opening by lateral slits; ovary 1-celled, inside the perianth tube; style short or long, slender; stigmas simple and expanded or variously modified. Fruit an anthocarp (fruit united with base of the perianth tube), the outer tube leathery, fleshy, or hardened, ribbed, toothed, or winged, often sticky, the inner utricle thin or leathery, indehiscent and fused with outer tube; seed coat clear.

Most of the nearly 300 species and 30 genera of this family occur in tropical and subtropical zones of the Americas. Thirteen genera (one of them introduced) occur in Texas, and 12 of these are found in the Trans-Pecos. Only one genus is included in the treatment below, but members with woody or slightly woody basal parts are represented in most Trans-Pecos genera. These include *Anulocaulis, Cyphomeris, Acleisanthes, Nyctaginia, Abronia, Boerhavia* (*B. linearifolia*), and *Mirabilis* (*M. multiflora*, a large herbaceous shrublike perennial). *Bougainvillea*, a genus of about 18 species native to South America, is a large woody vine which is widely cultivated in tropical and subtropical North America for its colorful corollalike bracts. Bougainvillea, also the common name, is grown outside in the warmer southern parts of the Trans-Pecos, such as in Presidio, and may be grown as an inside plant in cooler regions. *Commicarpus*, a vinelike plant, *Allionia*, a prostrate herb, and *Ammocodon*, are more herbaceous members of the Four O'Clock family in the Trans-Pecos.

Nyctaginaceae is heavily represented in gypseous soils of the Trans-Pecos, and several species are restricted to gypsum. Members of *Nyctaginia, Mirabilis, Acleisanthes, Abronia, Allionia,* and *Ammocodon* are found in gypseous habitats, while all species of *Anulocaulis* and *Selinocarpus* apparently are restricted to gypsum.

1. SELINOCARPUS GRAY   MOONPOD

Low shrubs or subshrubs with stems pubescent, much-branched, erect, or decumbent. Leaves with petioles, opposite and unequal; blades rather thick and fleshy, the margins entire or wavy. Flowers perfect, often cleistogamous, sessile or on short stalks, each subtended by 2–3 slender bracts; parianth tubular, the tube usually elongate and expanded distally into 5 lobes, the lobes folded; stamens 5–6; with slender filaments attached to the perianth tube, anthers in pairs; ovary oblong, style slender, stigma flat and smooth. Fruit (anthocarp) flattened, with 3–5 prominent, clear wings; seed coats attached to pericarp; seed with endosperm enclosed by cotyledons, embryo folded lengthwise.

A genus of about eight species, mostly restricted to gypseous soils in the southwestern United States and northern Mexico. All four Texas species occur in the Trans-Pecos.

KEY TO THE SPECIES

1. Leaf blades ovate to roundish; petioles 3 mm or longer.
  2. Plants erect, branches dense, tangled; upper leaves much smaller than lower leaves; anthocarps 9–10 cm long   **1. *S. parvifolius.***
  2. Plants erect or decumbent, much-branched but stems not densely tangled; upper leaves not reduced; anthocarps 6–7 mm long   **2. *S. diffusus.***
1. Leaf blades linear-oblong, lance-oblong, to oblong lanceolate; petioles to 3 mm long or absent.
  3. Leaf blades basically linear-oblong, 0.8–1.8 cm long, 1–3 mm wide; perianth 8–10 mm long; plants erect, 20–100 cm tall, with few slender woody stems above   **3. *S. angustifolius.***
  3. Leaf blades basically lanceolate, 1.2–8 cm long, 3–11 mm wide; perianth 3–4 cm long; plants erect or decumbent, 10–30 cm tall, densely leafy   **4. *S. lanceolatus.***

1. Selinocarpus parvifolius (Torr.) Standl. LITTLELEAF MOONPOD. Fig. 103. Endemic in gypseous clays, shales, and sands, S Trans-Pecos near the Rio Grande in Brewster, Presidio, and Hudspeth counties, probably also in Jeff Davis and Culberson counties along the Rio Grande. Also in the clays of adjacent Coah., Chih., Mex.

Fig. 103. *Selinocarpus parvifolius*
(Littleleaf Moonpod)

Fig. 104. *Selinocarpus diffusus*
(Spreading Moonpod)

2. Selinocarpus diffusus Gray. SPREADING MOONPOD. Fig. 104. In gypseous soils, also in limestone and sandy soils, usually rare and scattered. El Paso, Brewster, Reeves, and Pecos counties; E to Crane, Winkler, and Ector counties. Also in N-cen. TX, W to S UT and NV. This species reportedly occurs in soils that do not contain gypsum, but perhaps it does require special edaphic factors, judging by its spotty distribution.

3. Selinocarpus angustifolius Torr. NARROWLEAF MOONPOD. Fig. 105. Gypseous clays, gravel, and rocky hillsides, southern Trans-Pecos near the Rio Grande. Brewster (to N of Agua Fria) and Presidio counties; probably in Culberson and Jeff Davis counties near the Rio Grande. Also in SW NM; Coah., Mex.

4. Selinocarpus lanceolatus Woot. GYP MOONPOD. Fig. 106. Gypsum and gypsum-saline soils, especially common in vicinity of the salt flats, N Culberson, Hudspeth, and El Paso counties. Also in adjacent NM.

17. BERBERIDACEAE JUSS. BARBERRY FAMILY

Shrubs or herbs. Leaves alternate, compound; stipules sometimes present. Flowers bisexual; sepals and petals 6 (in 2 rows of 3), with petals separate;

Fig. 105. *Selinocarpus angustifolius*
(Narrowleaf Moonpod)

Fig. 106. *Selinocarpus lanceolatus*
(Gyp Moonpod)

stamens 6 (rarely 12), the outer opposite the petals, anthers opening by hinged pores with lid opening upwards, or on the sides; pistil 1, ovary superior, 1-celled. Fruit a 1- or few-seeded berry, or pod.

Only about nine genera but more than 600 species occur mainly in the northern temperate areas. Two genera occur in Texas. Members of this family are recognizable by their evergreen leaves that are often palmate or pinnate with sharp spines terminating the lobes and leaflets.

1. BERBERIS L. BARBERRY

Shrubs, evergreen; wood yellow. Leaves pinnate or palmately trifoliolate, rarely simple, the leaflets stiff and leathery, glabrous, prominently toothed or lobed, with these ending in very sharp spines. Flowers in racemes; sepals and petals both yellow and similar in appearance, petals concave with 2 glandular spots at the base; stamens 6, filaments sensitive to touch. Fruit a roundish berry, red, blue-black, or blue, often glaucous; seeds elliptic or angular.

A large genus with most of the near 500 species occurring in Asia, but with members also in Africa, Europe, and America. Four species are known to occur in Texas. A delicious jelly and wine can be made from ripe fruits of the Trans-Pecos species. Quail and other types of birds eat the berries. Quail also utilize the evergreen shrubs as winter cover. Indians prepared a yellow dye from stems

Fig. 107. *Berberis trifoliolata* (Agarito)

and roots of *Berberis trifoliolata* and *B. haematocarpa*. The evergreen shrubs have good ornamental potential.

KEY TO THE SPECIES

1. Leaves palmate with 3 sessile leaflets arising at petiole apex
                                                            1. *B. trifoliolata.*
1. Leaves pinnate with 5 or more leaflets along the rachis.
    2. Shrubby strong, erect, much-branched, to 2 m high; leaflets ovate to nearly lanceolate in outline, with usually 5–7 prominent, spine-tipped teeth; fruits red   **2. *B. haematocarpa.***
    2. Shrubs low, prostrate, or weakly ascending, usually less than 30 cm high; leaflets broadly ovate to ovate-elliptic, with 11–21 small teeth, rather weakly spine-tipped; fruits purple   **3. *B. repens.***

   1. Berberis trifoliolata Moric. AGARITO, CURRANT-OF-TEXAS. Fig. 107. [*Mahonia trifoliolata* (Moric.) *Fedde; Berberis trifoliolata* var. *glauca* (I. M. Johnst.) M. C. Johnst.]. Various habitats, from flat pastureland to rocky hillsides, throughout the Trans-Pecos. Also widespread S and SE to coastal S TX; E Pima Co., AZ, Luna Co., NM; N Mex.

   This is the most common *Berberis* species in the Trans-Pecos, and also the most common Barberry in Texas. The roots contain small amounts of berber-

Fig. 108. *Berberis haematocarpa*   Fig. 109. *Berberis repens* (Creeping Berberis)
(Red Berberis)

ine and other alkaloids, which has been used as a decoction in folk medicine as a treatment for toothache. These alkaloids actually have little medicinal value but in high concentrations can cause serious poisoning.

2. **Berberis haematocarpa** Woot. RED BERBERIS. Fig. 108. [*Mahonia haematocarpa* (Woot.) Fedde]. In the mountains of central Trans-Pecos, and higher desert grasslands and canyons. El Paso Co., Hueco Tanks. Culberson Co., Guadalupe Mts.; Sierra Diablo. Jeff Davis Co., Mt. Livermore. Brewster Co., Chisos Mts.; Cathedral Mt.; 10 mi S Alpine. Presidio Co., Paisano Pass. 4600–7200 ft. Also in NM and central AZ; N Mex. The species and common names are taken from the deep red berries.

3. **Berberis repens** Lindl. CREEPING BERBERIS. Fig. 109. [*Mahonia repens* (Lindl.) G. Don]. Protected or wooded canyons and hillsides and in pine forests, Guadalupe Mts., Culberson Co. 6500–8000 ft.; W through NM, AZ, to CA, N to WY and B.C., Can., 4500–10,000 ft.

18. BRASSICACEAE BURNETT   MUSTARD FAMILY

Rarely subshrubs, mostly herbs; sap usually pungent. Leaves usually alternate, simple or pinnate, margins smooth, toothed, to deeply lobed; stipules absent. Flowers yellow, white or lavender, usually clustered, rarely solitary, bisexual, mostly regular; sepals 4; petals 4 (rarely absent); stamens usually 6, in two whorls, 2 outside, 2 pairs inside longer; ovary superior, 2-celled. Fruit a silique or silicle (narrow or short capsule with many seeds, 2 valves splitting from base, revealing partition between), dry, many shapes, linear to roundish.

A family of about 375 genera and more than 3000 species, mostly distributed in temperate regions and high altitudes. The family is important for its food species of *Brassica* (turnips, cabbage, broccoli, cauliflower, rutabaga, Brussel sprouts, and kohlrabi) and *Raphanus* (radish). The condiment mustard is taken from *Brassica*; horseradish comes from *Armoracia*. Many Mustard species are grown as ornamentals. Many species have become weeds. At least 40 genera occur in Texas, nearly half of these also in the Trans-Pecos. The conserved name for the Mustard Family is Cruciferae.

1. STANLEYA NUTT.

Subshrub to 1 m high, branching stems from a woody base, glabrous. Leaves mostly broadly lanceolate to oblanceolate, rather thick in texture, glaucous, the margins usually smooth. Flowers yellow, in dense, elongated clusters; buds clubshaped; petals narrow; older anthers coiled. Silique linear, 2–4 cm long, nearly round; seeds oblong.

A genus of only six species in western North America.

1. **Stanleya pinnata** (Pursh) Britt. var. **integrifolia** (James *ex* Torr.) Roll. DESERT PRINCESPLUME.   Fig. 110.   [*Stanleya integrifolia* James *ex* Torr.] Perhaps restricted to seleniferous clay flats. Brewster Co., S of Agua Fria; 10 mi N Terlingua; 3 mi SE Hen Egg Mt. 3000–3500 ft.; Apr–May, rarely Jun–Jul. Also KS to WY and UT.

This species is rare in the Trans-Pecos, and very little is known specifically about its biology or edaphic requirements.

19. GROSSULARIACEAE DC.   CURRANT FAMILY

Shrubs or small trees, sometimes spiny. Leaves usually alternate, simple, sometimes deeply lobed; stipules absent or these spinose in some species. Flowers usually single or in racemes; perigynous to epigynous with a saucer-shaped-to-tubular hypanthium; the 5 sepals often forming a calyx tube; petals usually 5; stamens opposite the sepals; 2–3(–7) carpels united to form a compound ovary, the ovary superior to usually inferior. Fruit a capsule or berry.

A family of about 25 genera and less than 350 species of worldwide distribution. *Ribes* is the largest genus. Two genera occur in Texas, and one in the Trans-Pecos. The broader concept of the family, including herbaceous mem-

Fig. 110. *Stanleya pinnata*
(Desert Princesplume)

bers, is Saxigfragaceae Juss. The family is named after the genus *Grossularia* Mill., which is synomymous with *Ribes.*

1. RIBES L.   CURRANT, GOOSEBERRY

Shrubs, usually with long arching branches, with or without spines. Leaves alternate or seemingly in clusters, fanshaped, mostly palmately lobed, the lobes toothed. Flowers single, in clusters, or in short racemes; calyx 5-lobed, the tube fused to the ovary; corolla of 5 small petals arising in the calyx tube; stamens 5, alternate with petals on the calyx tube; ovary 1-celled. Fruit a berry, smooth or hairy, with shriveled remains of flower at the top.

About 150 species occur in colder and temperate zones of both hemispheres. Three of the five Texas species occur in the Trans-Pecos. The fruits of many species are eaten by birds and other wildlife, and have been used to make a tasty jelly. The plants also furnish good browse for deer and domestic animals. Several species are known to serve as alternate hosts for the destructive white pine blister rust, and thus extensive cultivation of the plants is not encouraged.

KEY TO THE SPECIES

1. Branchlets with spines; flower stalks not jointed   **1. *R. leptanthum.***
1. Branchlets without spines; flower stalks jointed.

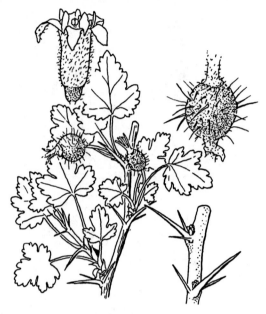

Fig. 111. *Ribes leptanthum* (Trumpet Currant)

2. Leaves, hypanthium, and sepals densely pubescent; flowers greenish white; anthers with a prominent cupshaped apical gland

2. *R. mescalerium.*

2. Leaves, hypanthium, and sepals glabrous or mostly so; flowers yellow; anthers perhaps with an apical callus only   3. *R. aureum.*

1. **Ribes leptanthum** Gray. TRUMPET CURRANT. Fig. 111. On and about rocky slopes and cliffs, up to about 8000 ft. Jeff Davis Co., Mt. Livermore. Culberson Co., Guadalupe Mts. Mar–May. N to NM and CO, W into AZ and UT.

2. **Ribes mescalerium** Cov. MESCALERO CURRANT. In Ponderosa Pine forests at higher altitudes, up to 8000 ft.; Guadalupe Mts., Culberson Co.; Jul–Sep. In the White Mts. and Sacramento Mts. of NM.

3. **Ribes aureum** Pursh. GOLDEN CURRANT. Fig. 112. In protected canyons, associated with the smaller mountains, up to about 6000 ft. Culberson Co. Brewster Co., Cathedral, Cienega, and Goat mountains. Presidio Co., Box Canyon, Sierra Vieja; near Shafter; Capote Mt.; in the canyon below San Estaban Lake; Chispa Mt.; Indian Cave Canyon, NE of Chinati Peak. Mar–Jun. Also in NM, AZ, CA, N to WA and MT, and adjacent Can. Three varieties of *Ribes aureum* are listed (in Kartesz, 1994).

Fig. 112. *Ribes aureum* (Golden Currant)

20. HYDRANGEACEAE DUM. HYDRANGIA FAMILY

Shrubs or small trees. Leaves usually opposite, simple, rarely toothed; stipules absent. Flowers in complex clusters, half to fully epigynous or hypogynous, perfect, regular; petals usually 4–5, distinct; stamens usually twice as many (or more) than petals; usually 3–5 or more carpels united to form a compound half inferior ovary. Fruit a septicidal or loculicidal capsule.

A family of about 17 genera and 170 species, widespread in the Northern Hemisphere, temperate and subtropical regions, with a few species in southeast Asia and Malaysia. Three genera occur in Texas, all of them also in the Trans-Pecos. Members of this family have been included by some workers in a broader Saxifragaceae. The three genera treated here are placed by some workers in Philadelphaceae (Mockorange Family).

KEY TO THE GENERA

1. Leaves elliptic in our species (relatively broad); stamens 15 or usually more
   1. *Philadelphus.*
1. Leaves linear or linear-elliptic (relatively narrow); stamens 12 or less.
   2. Petals narrowing to a slender base; capsules oval or conical, usually more than 8 mm long; stamen filaments with 2 narrow appendages parallel with anthers **2. *Fendlera.***

2. Petals not narrowed at base; capsules ellipsoid, 2–4 mm long; filaments without appendages   **3. Fendlerella.**

1. PHILADELPHUS L.   MOCKORANGE

Shrubs with many branches; bark peeling in scales or flakes. Leaves opposite, deciduous, usually entire, rarely toothed, usually slightly pubescent on upper surface, densely white-pubescent with appressed silky hairs on lower surface. Flowers usually single, less often in clusters, usually showy and fragrant; calyx with 4–5 lobes, glabrous or hairy, topshaped or nearly bellshaped, fused to ovary to form an hypanthium (floral cup); petals separate, white to whitish; stamens numerous, filaments awlshaped, anthers oblong; ovary partly inferior. Fruit a capsule, nearly round, topshaped, or ellipsoid.

About 50 mockorange species occur in both hemispheres, especially in temperate regions and in eastern Asia. Many species are planted as ornamentals. Eight of the 11 Texas species occur in the Trans-Pecos. The Trans-Pecos species of *Philadelphus* require further study in support of the work by Hu (1954–1956). In the treatment below many of the identifications are tentative.

KEY TO THE SPECIES

1. Axillary buds exposed and in leaf axils; flowers solitary; stamens 13–35; stigmas 4-notched, expanded or columnar; fruit topshaped or roundish, with persistent sepals at apex; seeds without appendages.
  2. Lower surface of leaves with woolly hairs mixed with straight stiff hairs, upper surface with stiff, appressed hairs; style 1–2 mm long
                1. P. serpyllifolius.
  2. Leaf surfaces with appressed, straight, stiff hairs; style 1 mm long.
    3. Leaves oblong-lanceolate, 2–5 mm wide; corolla somewhat starshaped, petals 2.5 mm wide; floral cup pubescent   **2. P. mearnsii.**
    3. Leaves ovate, 6–12 mm wide; corolla cross shaped, petals 4.5 mm wide; floral cup glabrous   **3. P. hitchcockianus.**
1. Axillary buds enclosed at ends of petioles; flowers one to several; stamens 25–75; stigmas slender; fruit ellipsoid, with persistent sepals below the apex; seeds with short or prominent appendages, lobed on the crown.
  4. Floral cup and sepals glabrous, or only sparsely hairy at the base
                4. P. microphyllus.
  4. Floral cup and sepals evenly pubescent.
    5. Leaves becoming glabrous or barely pubescent on upper surface; floral cup woolly   **5. P. argyrocalyx.**
    5. Leaves permanently pubescent with stiff and appressed or rather soft hairs on upper surface; floral cup prominently gray with dense, downy hairs, or slightly hairy.

Fig. 113. *Philadelphus serpyllifolius*
(Thymeleaf Mockorange)

6. Leaves with soft, appressed hairs on upper surface (hairs on lower surface, erect, long, dense)   **6. *P. crinitus.***
6. Leaves with straight, stiff, usually appressed hairs on upper surface.
    7. Surface of floral cup visible through scattered, soft hairs
                                                    7. *P. occidentalis.*
    7. Surface of floral cup thickly covered with hairs.
        8. Leaves 1–3 cm long, lanceolate to ovate-lanceolate; corolla somewhat bellshaped   **8. *P. palmeri.***
        8. Leaves 0.8–1.6 cm long, ovate to oblong-elliptic; corolla flat and circular   **9. *P. argenteus.***

1. Philadelphus serpyllifolius Gray. THYMELEAF MOCKORANGE. Fig. 113.   Presidio Co., Sierra Vieja, ZH Canyon. Jeff Davis Co., Davis Mts., Davis Mountains State Park; Wild Rose Pass; Big Aguja Canyon; Lower Madera Canyon; Timber Mt.; Forbidden Mt.; Million Dollar Canyon. Brewster Co., Glass Mts.; Del Norte Mts.; Cox Ranch. Apr–May. Also NM, W to CA and N to CO and NV; N Mex.

2. Philadelphus mearnsii Evans *ex* Koehne. MEARNS MOCKORANGE. Rare or uncommon. El Paso Co., reported in Franklin Mts. Brewster Co., Glass

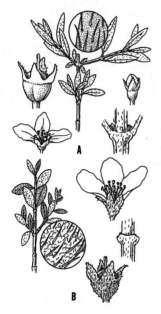

Fig. 114. A) *Philadelphus hitchcockianus*
(Hitchcock Mockorange);
B) *Philadelphus argenteus*

Fig. 115. *Philadelphus microphyllus*
(Littleleaf Mockorange)

Mts., Gilliland Canyon; Jail Canyon; Del Norte Mts., 12 mi NE Alpine. Jun–Jul. Also reported in Guadalupe Mts., Eddy Co., NM; N Mex.

3. Philadelphus hitchcockianus Hu.   HITCHCOCK MOCKORANGE Fig. 114.
Canyon walls and about boulders. El Paso Co., Franklin Mts. Culberson Co., Guadalupe Mts., South and North McKittrick canyons; Smith Springs. May–Jun. Also Coah., Mex.

4. Philadelphus microphyllus Gray.   LITTLELEAF MOCKORANGE.   Fig. 115. [Including subsp. *typicus* C. L. Hitchc.]. Higher slopes and canyons. El Paso Co., reported in Franklin Mts. Culberson Co., Guadalupe Mts., S McKittrick Canyon. Brewster Co., Chisos Mts.; Mt. Ord, E slopes. Jun–Oct. Also NM, AZ, NV, UT, CO.

5. Philadelphus argyrocalyx Woot.   SILVERCUP MOCKORANGE.   Jeff Davis Co., Mt. Livermore; closely related to *P. crinitus* and perhaps synonymous. Jun–Aug. S-cen. Mex.

6. Philadelphus crinitus (C. L. Hitchc.) Hu.   [*Philadelphus microphyllus* subsp. *crinitus* C. L. Hitchc.]. Canyons and talus slopes, usually higher elevations. Jeff Davis Co., Davis Mts. Mt. Livermore; Timber Mt. Jul–Aug. Also in AZ.

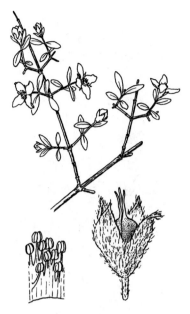

Fig. 116. *Philadelphus palmeri*
(Palmer Mockorange)

7. Philadelphus occidentalis A. Nels.   Steep slopes of canyons, reported to occur in El Paso Co., Franklin Mts. Culberson Co., Guadalupe Mts. Brewster Co., Chisos Mts., NE slopes Casa Grande; Cathedral Mt.; Mt. Ord. Jun–Aug. Also to CA and WY; N Mex.

8. Philadelphus palmeri Rydb.   PALMER MOCKORANGE.   Fig. 116.   Reported to occur in Culberson Co., Guadalupe Mts., South McKittrick Canyon. Jeff Davis Co., Mt. Livermore. Jul. Also in AZ; N Mex.

9. Philadelphus argenteus Rydb.   Fig. 114.   Steep upper slopes and canyons. Culberson Co., Guadalupe Mts., possibly Jeff Davis Co.; closely related to *P. palmeri*. Jul–Aug. Also W to CA, NV, UT, N to CO; N Mex.

2. FENDLERA ENGELM. & GRAY

Shrubs, somewhat evergreen or deciduous, branches intricate, striate. Leaves clustered or opposite, usually sessile, the margins entire. Flowers single or 2–3 in clusters; corolla white, sometimes red-tinged or streaked; floral cup bell-shaped, with 8 ribs; sepals 4; somewhat triangular, longer than floral cup; stamens 8, with flattened filaments, and with 2 narrow appendages at the top parallel with the anthers; ovary 4-celled, partly inferior; styles 4, pubescent.

Fig. 117. *Fendlera rupicola* (Cliff Fendlerbush)

Fruit (capsule) conical or ovoid, crustaceous, opening along the septa into 4 valves.

Four species occur in the central southwestern United States from Colorado and Utah southward into northern Mexico. The shrubs are occasionally planted as ornamentals, and in natural habitats are excellent browse for goats, sheep, and deer.

KEY TO THE SPECIES

1. Leaf blades 2 mm wide or more, narrowly lanceolate to ovate-oblong, the margins flat or slightly rolled under   **1. *F. rupicola.***
1. Leaf blades 1.5 mm wide or less, linear, the margins rolled under to the midrib   **2. *F. rigida.***

1. Fendlera rupicola Gray. CLIFF FENDLERBUSH. Fig. 117. Rocky ledges and steep slopes of cliffs and canyons, and among boulders both limestone and igneous soils. El Paso Co., Franklin Mts. Hudspeth Co., Quitman Mts.; Eagle Mts. Culberson Co., Guadalupe Mts.; Sierra Diablo; Apache Mts. Brewster Co., Altuda Point, Mt. Ord, Glass Mts., Elephant Mesa, Nine-Point Mesa, Goat Mt., Cienega Mt., Cathedral Mt. Jeff Davis Co., Davis Mts., Hay-

Fig. 118. *Fendlera rigida*
(Narrowleaf Fendlerbush)

stack Mt. Pecos Co., Sierra Madera. Presidio Co., Chinati Mts., Sierra Vieja. 4000–7000 ft.; Mar–Aug, rarely into Jul. Also NM, AZ, CO; N Mex.

According to Kartesz (1994) two varieties of *Fendlera rupicola* are recognized: var. **falcata** (Thornb.) Rehd., the common entity in the Trans-Pecos; and var. **wrightii** (Gray) Heller (*F. rupicola* Gray var. *wrightii* Gray) on the southeastern margin of the Trans-Pecos extending to the Edwards Plateau and northeastern Mexico.

2. **Fendlera rigida** I. M. Johnst. NARROWLEAF FENDLERBUSH. Fig. 118. Rare on rocky slopes. Brewster Co., Chisos Mts., on Crown Mt.; Agua Fria Mt.; Hen Egg Mt. Presidio Co., Solitario, where common. ca. 4500 ft.; Apr–May. Also in N Mex. According to M. C. Johnston the closely related *Fendlera linearis* Rehd. of N. L., Mexico has been reported erroneously to occur in the Trans-Pecos based upon specimens of *F. rigida*.

3. FENDLERELLA HELLER

Erect shrubs, stems many-branched, pubescent. Leaves opposite, to 2.5 cm long, to 4 mm wide, linear-lanceolate, linear to elliptic or oblanceolate, the margins smooth; with short petioles. Flowers small, in clusters, usually borne

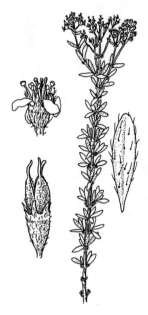

Fig. 119. *Fendlerella utahensis*
(Utah Fendlerella)

on peduncles raised above the leaves; sepals 5, fused to bottom half of capsule; petals 5, white or creamy, ca. 4 mm long, oblanceolate; stamens 4–12; styles 3. Fruit (capsules) 2–4 mm long, with 3 cells.

About three species of this genus occur in the southwestern United States and in Mexico.

1. Fendlerella utahensis (S. Wats.) Heller.   UTAH FENDLERELLA, YERBA DESIERTO. Fig. 119. [*Whipplea utahensis* S. Wats.]. Various rocky and mountainous limestone habitats. Culberson Co., Guadalupe Mts. 5000–7500 ft., the Bowl, McKittrick, West Dog, Smith, Upper Pine Spring, Lower Pipe Line canyons. Brewster Co., 4650–6300 ft., Altuda Mt.; N and NE slopes of Mt. Ord. Jun–Sep. Also in AZ, UT, S CA; Coah. and Chih., Mex. Plants of this species may reach 1 m high. Kartesz (1994) lists two varieties for this species.

21. CROSSOSOMATACEAE NUTT.   CROSSOSOMA FAMILY

Shrubs to 3 m high, or small and prostrate, deciduous, intricately branched, often spinescent. Leaves alternate, scattered or clustered, or opposite, glabrous or pubescent, the margins smooth or 3-lobed; stipules minute or absent. Flowers solitary, perfect, or unisexual, regular, cuplike with fleshy disk; sepal lobes

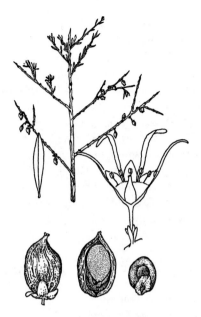

Fig. 120. *Glossopetalon spinescens* var.
spinescens (Spiny Greasebush)

usually 4–5; petals usually 4–5, white to purplish; stamens in 1–2 whorls, 15–50 or 4–5, anthers attached basally; carpels 1–9. Fruit an asymmetrical follicle, cylindric to ovoid; seeds 1 to many, shiny black or dark brown.

A family of three genera, *Crossosoma*, *Apacheria*, and *Glossopetalon*, distributed mostly in the western United States and northern Mexico.

1. GLOSSOPETALON A. GRAY GREASEBUSH

Shrubs to 1.5 m high; intricately branched, stems spinescent-tipped, slender, angled, greenish. Leaves alternate, deciduous, lanceolate to obovate with entire margins, 5–12 mm long, glabrous (in our species), with 2–4 parallel veins; minute stipules usually present. Flowers white, sepals and petals usually 5. Fruit a follicle, asymmetrical, ovoid, lined, ca. 5 mm long, opening ventrally.

A genus of eight species distributed mainly in the western United States. *Glossopetalon* was long misplaced in the Celastraceae before Thorne and Scogin (1978) recognized its relationship with the Crossosomataceae (Holmgren, 1988).

1. **Glossopetalon spinescens** Gray var. **spinescens.** SPINY GREASEBUSH. Fig. 120. [*Forsellesia spinescens* (Gray) Greene]. Infrequent, limestone habitats, usually in mountains and canyons. El Paso Co., Franklin Mts. Culberson

Co., Guadalupe Mts., McKittrick Canyon; Pup Canyon; Beach Mts. Presidio Co., Chinati Mts., Pinto Canyon. Brewster Co., Del Norte Mts.; Mt. Ord, Doubtful Canyon, 8 mi SE of Santiago Peak; Packsaddle Mt.; Rosillos Mts.; Dead Horse Mts., head of Heath Canyon; Glass Mts., Panther Canyon, Gilliland Peak, and Old Blue. 3500–6800 ft.; Mar–Jul. A widespread species, N to OK, W to AZ; N Chih., Coah., Mex.

This species, best recognized by its greenish, spinescent stems with small leaves and small white flowers, is browsed by sheep and deer. Two other greasebush species occur in Texas, *Glossopetalon planitierum* (Ensign) St. John of the Plains Country, and *Glossopetalon texense* (Ensign) St. John of restricted distribution on the Edwards Plateau. In fact the latter species from a chalk bluff on the Nueces River near Montell, Uvalde Co., and bluffs on the Devils River, Val Verde Co., may extend west of the Pecos River.

22. ROSACEAE JUSS. ROSE FAMILY

Trees, shrubs, or herbs. Leaves alternate, compound or simple; stipules usually present. Flowers mostly perfect and regular, with a floral cup; sepals usually 5, less often 3–8, sometimes subtended by a row of outer bractlets; petals 5, or as many as sepals, less often double the number, or absent; stamens usually numerous, arising near rim of floral cup; pistil one or many, separate or united, or fused to floral cup; ovules one or several per carpel. Fruit a follicle, pome, drupe, achene, or aggregate.

This family is well known for its contributions to mankind, perhaps best known are the rose and other ornamentals, and edible fruits such as peach, pear, apple, apricot, plum, cherry, strawberry, blackberry, raspberry, and almond. Members of this diverse family, more than 3000 species in about 100 genera, are found all over the world, but are most evident in North America, Europe, and Asia. Many species provide excellent forage for wildlife.

KEY TO THE GENERA

1. Plants low undershrubs less than 15 cm high, forming dense mats over limestone rock faces   **1. *Petrophyton.***
1. Plants erect or decumbent shrubs nearly 1 m high or taller, or trees.
 2. Fruit a plumlike, 1-seeded drupe   **8. *Prunus.***
 2. Fruit with more than one carpel, or if one carpel, fruit an achene.
  3. Ovary inferior, with adnate, usually fleshy, calyx tube; fruit an applelike pome.
   4. Stems armed with prominent woody spines; fruit hard **5. *Crataegus.***
   4. Stems unarmed; fruit berrylike.
    5. Leaves ca. 1.5 cm long or less; petals 2–4 mm long
                                                          3. *Malacomeles.*

5. Leaves ca. 3 cm long; petals ca. 7 mm long   **4. *Amelanchier.***
3. Ovary superior.
   6. Stems armed with prickles.
      7. Calyx tube fleshy at maturity, enclosing the achenes but not adenate, the pomelike rosehips crowned by persistent calyx lobes; corolla rose pink   **6. *Rosa.***
      7. Calyx tube not fleshy at maturity and enclosing the fruit; corolla white to pinkish   **7. *Rubus.***
   6. Stems without prickles.
      8. Fruits dehiscent capsules or follicles with 2 or more seeds.
         9. Leaves somewhat heartshaped; seeds not winged; shrub 1 m high or less   **2. *Physocarpus.***
         9. Leaves linear; seeds with a terminal wing; shrub 2–5m high   **9. *Vauquelinia.***
      8. Fruits 1-seeded achenes, these sometimes awned.
         10. Leaves pinnatifed or deeply lobed, or narrow and pointed.
            11. Bark exfoliating; achene tails purplish   **11. *Fallugia.***
            11. Bark not exfoliating; achene tails white   **12. *Purshia.***
         10. Leaves broad, margins toothed or cleft.
            12. Flowers numerous, in panicles; petals 5   **10. *Holodiscus.***
            12. Flowers solitary or in few-flowered groups; petals absent   **13. *Cercocarpus.***

1. PETROPHYTON RYDB.   ROCK-SPIRAEA

Low mat-forming undershrub, densely appressed to rock faces. Leaves persistent, crowded, spatulate, entire, densely pubescent, somewhat leathery, 0.5–1.2 cm long, rarely to 4 cm long, 2–4 mm wide. Flowering peduncles 3–10 cm high, with bractlike leaves; flowers perfect, in dense, spikelike racemes, 1–5 cm long; sepals 5, ca. 1.5 mm long; petals 5, white, 2–2.5 mm long; stamens ca. 20; pistils 3–5, pubescent below. Fruit a follicle, not inflated, ca. 2 mm long, opening along both sutures; seeds 2–4, linear.

A genus of about four species native to Western North America.

   1. **Petrophyton caespitosum** (Nutt.) Rydb.   TUFTED ROCKMAT.   Fig. 121. [*Eriogynia caespitosa* (Nutt.) S. Wats.; *Spiraea caespitosa* Nutt.]. In crevices of limestone bluffs, ledges, and rocks, usually in protected canyons, 4500–7500 ft. El Paso Co., Franklin Mts. Culberson Co., Guadalupe Mts., Sierra Diablo; Van Horn Mts. El Paso Co., Hueco Pass; Franklin Mts. Pecos Co., 25–40 mi S of Ft. Stockton. Brewster Co., N Del Norte Mts., Doubtful Canyon;

Fig. 121. *Petrophyton caespitosum*
(Tufted Rockmat)

Fig. 122. *Physocarpus monogynus*
(Mountain Ninebark)

Altuda Mt.; Packsaddle Mt.; Bissett Hills; Old Blue, Glass Mts.; Jul–Sep. Also 15 mi E of Leakey, Real Co.; Guadalupe Mts. and Big Hatchet Mts. of S NM, W to AZ and CA, N to MT and SD; also N Chih. and cen. Coah., Mex.

Two varieties of *Petrophyton caespitosum* are listed in Kartesz (1994). The spelling *Petrophytum* has been widely used in the literature.

2. PHYSOCARPUS MAXIM.

Shrubs, stems decumbent, 1 m high or less. Leaves alternate, 1–4 cm long, essentially glabrous, nearly round to kidneyshaped, palmately 3–5 lobed, margins toothed; petioles ca. 1.5 cm long. Flowers in terminal clusters; flower stalks 1–1.5 cm long; sepals 5, densely stellate-pubescent; petals 5, white, ca. 3 mm long; stamens 20–40, filaments arising from the disk at mouth of floral tube; pistils 2–3, basally joined; stigmas headlike. Fruit an inflated follicle, opening on both sides, 3–5 mm long, beaked; seeds usually 2, 1.5 mm or more long, pearshaped, shiny.

A genus of about 12 North American species, one occurs in Manchuria.

1. Physocarpus monogynus (Torr.) Coult.   MOUNTAIN NINEBARK.   Fig. 122.   High canyons and ledges. Culberson Co., Guadalupe Mts.; Apr–Jun.

Fig. 123. *Malacomeles denticulata*
(Toothed Serviceberry)

Widespread in the mountains of NM, W to AZ, N to WY and ND. This rare plant of the Trans-Pecos offers promise as an ornamental, its clusters of white flowers being the most attractive aspect.

3. MALACOMELES (DCNE.) ENGELM. SERVICEBERRY

Shrubs 1–2.5 m high; branches unarmed. Leaves persistent, leathery, glabrous and glossy above, tomentose beneath, elliptic to obovate or orbicular, the margins prominently denticulate. Flowers in clusters, malodorous; floral cup bellshaped, partially fused to ovary; sepals suborbicular, ca. 2 mm long; petals white, suborbicular, ca. 4 mm long. Fruit a berrylike pome, ellipsoid to subglobose, 6–8 mm wide, glabrous, reddish tinged, maturing purplish black.

A genus of two species of mostly Mexican distribution. Only *Malacomeles denticulata* extends into the United States (Jones, 1945) and then just into the southern Trans-Pecos. The genus name is derived from the Greek, *malakos*, soft, and *meles*, apple, supposedly in reference to the soft (and not bony) carpels.

1. **Malalcomeles denticulata** (Kunth) Engelm. TOOTHED SERVICEBERRY. Fig. 123. [*Amelanchier denticulata* (Kunth) Koch]. Limestone canyons,

slopes, rimrocks. Brewster Co., Glass Mts.; Dead Horse Mts., upper Heath Canyon; Rosillos Mts., Chisos Mts. Presidio Co., Sierra Vieja Rim; top of Pinto Canyon; N side Chinati Mts.; Solitario Peak and vicinity; Bofecillos Mts. Fruiting May. Also in Coah., Chih., Mex., S to Guat.

This species is distinguished from *Amelanchier utahensis* by smaller, shrubby habit, 1–3 m high, leaves with pubescent undersides and margins with sharp teeth, roundish sepals 1.5–2 mm long, and roundish petals ca. 4 mm long. The fruit is edible, and is sometimes eaten in Mexico where the plant is known as Membrillo, Madronillo, Cimarron, or Tlaxistle.

4. AMELANCHIER MEDIC. SERVICEBERRY

Shrubs or small trees to 5 m high; branches unarmed. Leaves deciduous, suborbicular to oval, pale green and tomentose, rounded to acute at the apex, 1–4 cm long, the margins crenate-serrate. Flowers in clusters, malodorous; sepals narrowly lanceolate; petals white, elliptic, ca. 7 mm long. Fruit a berry-like pome, 7–8 mm wide, yellow, reddish, maturing darker to bluish-black.

A genus of about 15 species widely distributed in the North Temperate region. Two species occur in Texas, one in the Trans-Pecos. The genus name is taken after the French name of a European species.

1. Amelanchier utahensis Koehne. UTAH SERVICEBERRY. Fig. 124. [*Amelanchier alnifolia* (Nutt.) Nutt. *ex* M. Roemer.]. Limestone slopes, canyons, rocks, frequently under conifers, higher elevations. Culberson Co., Guadalupe Mts. 5400–8000 ft.; North and South McKittrick canyons; Pine Springs Canyon; Signal Peak; West Dog Canyon; Fruiting Aug–Sep. Also in NM, and W and N to CA, WA, ID, MT.

This species is common in northwestern states, where it is good browse for domestic animals and deer. Plants have long been planted as ornamentals primarily because of the cluster of pink or white flowers that appear in the spring, and for the purplish fruit that matures in the fall. The fruit is edible, and was used by early travelers in the preparation of foods. Frontiersmen made a fruit-paste and mixed it into cornbread, basted it on jerked meat to make "pemican" and cooked the fruit in pies and puddings. Other common names are Pemican Bush, Shadbush, Western Juneberry, and Red Serviceberry.

5. CRATAEGUS L. HAWTHORN, RED HAW

Shrubs or small trees; branches thorny. Leaves simple, deciduous, the margins serrate or lobed; leaves on vegetative branchlets of different shapes from those on flowering branchlets. Flowers in clusters, or solitary; calyx tube with 5 lobes; petals usually 5; stamens usually 5–20; anthers white, yellow, or reddish; styles 1–5. Fruit a pome, with 1–5 nutlets.

Fig. 124. *Amelanchier utahensis*
(Utah Serviceberry)

A North American genus possibly with several hundred species, many of them poorly delimited and probably intergrading through hybridization. Thirty-three species are listed for Texas, most of them along rivers and creeks in southeastern parts of the state. Many hawthorns are grown as ornamentals, and many species produce edible fruit that has been widely used in jellies and other confections.

1. **Crataegus tracyi** Ashe *ex* Egglest. TRACY HAWTHORN, MOUNTAIN HAWTHORN. Fig. 125. [*Crataegus montivaga* Sarg.]. Principally along creeks in canyons, but also on protected slopes. Jeff Davis Co., Davis Mts.; Big Agua Canyon; Timber Mt.; Wild Rose Pass; Limpia Creek; Musquiz Canyon; Barillos Creek. Brewster Co., Paradise Canyon; Toronto Creek; Calamity Creek; Cienega Mt.; Cathedral Mt. Fruiting Sep–Oct. Also along streams on the Edwards Plateau.

These plants are recognizable in early spring as shrubs or small trees with prominant clusters of malodorous white flowers; also by spiny branches, glossy leaf upper surfaces, and later the fruits have persistent, lancelike sepals at the top. In the fall Tracy Hawthorn is recognizable by its reddish leaves and fruits. In Musquiz Canyon (Jeff Davis Co.) and elsewhere the plants grow among other trees and shrubs whose leaves do not turn red in the fall.

Fig. 125. *Crataegus tracyi* (Tracy Hawthorn)

6. ROSA L.   ROSE

Shrubs or subshrubs, upright or trailing; stems usually with prickles. Leaves alternate, usually compound; leaflets 3–15, with toothed margins. Flowers perfect, solitary or in clusters; sepals and petals usually 5; stamens numerous; ovaries numerous, in the floral tube; style fused or distinct; floral tube, the fleshy "hip" at maturity, contracted at the mouth and enlarged basally. Fruit an achene.

Most of the ca. 200 rose species are native in the Northern Hemisphere. Fourteen species occur in Texas.

KEY TO THE SPECIES

1. Leaflets 5–9, 1–3 cm long; receptacle (hip) smooth; petals pink, flowers 3 cm across; fruit roundish, ca. 8 mm wide   **1. *R. woodsii.***

1. Leaflets 3–5, 0.5–1 cm long; receptacle prickly-armed; petals rose-purple, flowers 3.5–6 cm across; fruit topshaped, 1–1.5 cm wide

2. *R. stellata* subsp. *mirifica.*

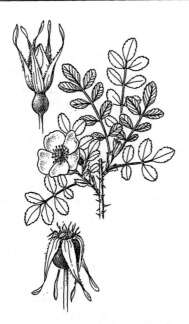

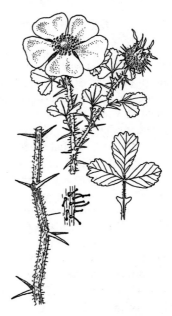

Fig. 126. *Rosa woodsii* (Woods Rose)

Fig. 127. *Rosa stellata* subsp. *mirifica* (Desert Rose)

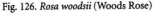

1. **Rosa woodsii** Lindl. WOODS ROSE. Fig. 126. [*Rosa woodsii* var. *fendleri* (Crep.) Rydb.]. Canyons and rocky slopes. Culberson Co., Guadalupe Mts. 5500–6000 ft., South McKittrick Canyon; near Turtle Rock, and elsewhere. Also reported by Vines (1960) to occur on NW slopes of Mt. Livermore, under aspens. Also reported by Barry Scobie of Ft. Davis as taken from Limpia Canyon (Wild Rose Pass) in Jeff Davis Co. in about 1935, a voucher specimen in SRSC supposedly taken from a transplant in Ft. Davis; one plant discovered in 1991 by K. Bryan and M. Lockwood, below Tobe Spring on Mt. Livermore; May–Jul. Also from N Mex. to NE and MO, NM, B.C. and Ont., Can.

Our taxon apparently is *Rosa woodsii* var. **woodsii.**

2. **Rosa stellata** Woot. subsp. **mirifica** (Greene) W. H. Lewis. DESERT ROSE, STAR ROSE. Fig. 127. [*Rosa mirifica* Greene]. According to Correll and Johnston (1970) our rose is the var. **erlansoniae** W. H. Lewis. Higher limestone slopes and canyons. Culberson Co., Guadalupe Mts. 5500–8000 ft. North and South McKittrick Canyons; West Dog Canyon; between the Bowl and Shumard Peak; Sierra Diablo, Wild Rose Canyon; igneous habitat, Eagle Mts., ca. 2000 ft. above Quitman Valley; reportedly a good browse plant. Also NM and AZ. Burgess and Northington (1981) further discuss *R. stellata* in the Guadalupe Mts.

7. RUBUS L.   DEWBERRY, BLACKBERRY, BRAMBLE

Shrubs or perennial herbs; stems with curved prickles (in our species). Leaves compound with 3–5 leaflets (in our species). Flowers perfect, corolla white to pinkish; sepals 5; petals 5; stamens numerous; pistils numerous, on an elongated receptacle. Fruit a group of drupelets, globose to oblong, black in some or all of our species.

A genus of perhaps 1000 taxa where taxonomic distinctions are complicated by hybridization, asexual reproduction, and polyploidy. The edible fruits are favored by wildlife. Three species of the Dewberry or Blackberry genus *Rubus* have been reported for the Trans-Pecos. Warnock (1970) reported *R. trivialis* Michx. (Southern Dewberry) to occur near the Rio Grande just below Langtry. Bonnie Amos listed *R. trivialis* and *R. persistens* Rydb. (Persistent Blackberry) in a 1991 checklist of plants for Big Bend National Park. *Rubus persistens* reportedly was found near Cattail Falls in the Chisos Mountains. A collection by Richard Worthington in 1993 from Presidio County, Bofecillos Mountains, was tentatively identified as *R. flagellaris* Willd. (Whiplash or Northern Dewberry). All of these collections represent significant range extensions (Correll and Johnston, 1970), and species identifications should be verified.

8. PRUNUS L.   PLUM, CHERRY, PEACH

Trees or shrubs; deciduous or evergreen; overlapping scales over winter buds. Leaves alternate, margins toothed, rarely entire; stipules present. Flowers perfect, in clusters or solitary; calyx 5-lobed; calyx tube usually expanded of various shapes, falling at maturity; petals 5, white, pink, or red; stamens numerous; pistil 1, style elongated. Fruit a drupe, usually with 1 seed.

A genus of over 400 species widely distributed in temperate zones, many of which have long been cultivated for their edible fruits or seeds, and for ornamental purposes, although kernels in the pits of some species (e.g., apricots) are poisonous. The fruits are a favorite food for wildlife. The wood of many tree species is valued for furniture, cabinets, and other such items.

KEY TO THE SPECIES

1. Trees to 10–15 m high, less often tallish shrubs; flowers in racemes.
2. Calyx lobes persistent; leaf margins mostly coarsely-toothed
                                                         1. *P. serotina.*
2. Calyx lobes falling at maturity; leaf margins mostly finely-toothed
                                                       2. *P. virginiana.*
1. Smallish shrubs to ca. 3 m high; flowers solitary or in umbels.
3. Leaves obovate, ovate, or ovate-lanceolate.
4. Leaves 0.7–2 cm long, obovate, toothed toward the apex; petioles less than 5 mm long; flowers sessile, usually solitary   **3. *P. havardii.***

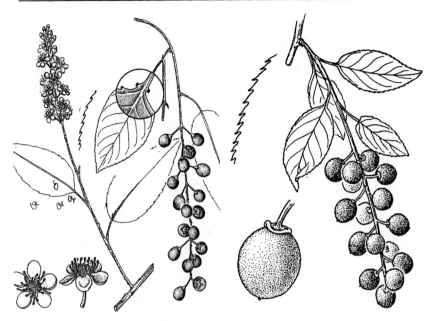

Fig. 128. *Prunus serotina* var. *virens*
(Southwestern Chokecherry)

Fig. 129. *Prunus virginiana*
(Common Chokecherry)

4. Leaves 3–5 cm long, ovate to ovate-lanceolate, margins finely
toothed from base to apex; petioles 5–10 mm long; flower stalks 8–
12 mm long, in 1–5-flowered umbels   **4.** *P. murrayana.*

3. Leaves oblong-elliptic, narrowed at the base   **5.** *P. minutiflora.*

1. Prunus serotina Ehrh. var. **virens** (Woot. & Standl.) McVaugh.
SOUTHWESTERN CHOKECHERRY, BLACK CHERRY. Fig. 128. [*Padus serotina*
(Ehrh.) Agardh.; *Prunus virens* (Woot. & Standl.) Shreve.]. Along streams, in
canyons, and other protected areas, widespread but infrequent. Culberson Co.,
South McKittrick Canyon; Smith Canyon; top of Guadalupes. Jeff Davis Co.,
Limpia Canyon; Mt. Livermore and vicinity; Mt. Locke; Timber Mt.; Point of
Rocks; Haystack Mt., Tippit Canyon. Brewster Co., Chisos Mts.; Panther Can-
yon; Ranger Canyon; Paradise Canyon; Mt. Ord; Old Blue, Glass Mts.; 6 mi
NW of Alpine. Presidio Co., lower slopes of Chinati Peak; Pinto Canyon; Sierra
Vieja. El Paso Co., boulders at Hueco Tanks. 4600–8000 ft.; fruiting Jun–Aug.
Also in NM and AZ; N Mex.; an isolated locality near the Bexar-Wilson Co.
line (designated as *P. parksii* Cory). Chokecherry furnishes good winter browse.
These plants have gray bark with horizontal linticel streaks. The western form
at Hueco Tanks in El Paso County is var. *rufula* (Woot. and Standl.) McVaugh.

2. Prunus virginiana L. COMMON CHOKECHERRY. Fig. 129. A widespread species in many habitats, mostly canyons, streams, bluffs. Culberson

Fig. 130. *Prunus havardii* (Havard Plum)

Co., Guadalupe Mts., summit of Bush Mt. Jeff Davis Co., W of Mt. Livermore. Brewster Co., Mt. Ord. Fruiting Jun–Aug. Also Panhandle and E TX; NM, N to KS and MO, E to GA, N to ME and Nfld., W to CA and B.C., Can.

This is one of the most widely cultivated chokecherries, with many vernacular names. The fruit is used in jams and jellies and the bark has been used in flavoring in cough syrup as is done with *Prunus serotina* and other species. Root sprouting may result in thicket formation, especially under cultivation, where the plants have been used ornamentally and to control erosion.

3. Prunus havardii (W. Wight) S. C. Mason. HAVARD PLUM. Fig. 130. [*Amygdalus havardii* W. Wight]. Mostly in limestone canyons, and on rocky slopes usually protected areas, also occasionally on igneous-rock slopes or novaculite hills; endemic to the Trans-Pecos. 2800–5800 ft. Brewster Co., Green Gulch, Window Trail, Pine Canyon, and perhaps most canyons of the Chisos Mts.; Del Norte Mts. SE of Santiago Peak; Packsaddle Mt.; S of Marathon; lower slopes Nine-Point Mesa, where specimens have atypical leaves. Presidio Co., 10 mi S of Marfa, on Casa Piedra Road; Solitario Peak area, to Fresno Creek; below and above Madrid Falls; Chinati Mts. N of old Ross Mine. Fruiting Jun–Jul.

These shrubby plants are highly localized in distribution but are not at all rare as was once believed by some workers.

Fig. 131. *Prunus minutiflora*
(Smallflower Peachbush)

4. Prunus murrayana E. J. Palm. MURRAY PLUM. Canyons and rocky slopes. Jeff Davis Co., Davis Mts.; head of Big Aguja Canyon; Limpia Canyon (Wild Rose Pass); near Ft. Davis; trail to Tricky Gap, Boy Scout Camp. Brewster Co., Doubtful Canyon, E of Mt. Ord; Elephant Mt. 4700–5500 ft. This endemic species remains rare and poorly known; available collections do not exhibit mature fruit.

5. Prunus minutiflora Engelm. SMALLFLOWER PEACHBUSH. Fig. 131. [*Amygdalus minutiflora* (Engelm.) W. Wight]. This species occurs mainly in limestone habitats on the Rio Grande Plains and Edwards Plateau, and probably extends rarely across the Pecos westward. One collection at SRSC appears to be *Prunus minutiflora*. Brewster Co., infrequent, among sandy basaltic rocks, NW slopes of Wildhorse Mt., W of Study Butte; also possibly in the Glass Mts.; supposedly reported from the Weyerts Ranch, 20 mi E of Alpine. These plants are low shrubs with rather zigzag branches, glabrous leaves that are entire or irregularly toothed, white flowers, and roundish fruit about 1 cm or more long.

9. VAUQUELINIA CORREA *ex* H.&B.

Shrubs or small trees, 3–5 m high, evergreen; bark of young twigs smooth, cracked on older branches. Leaves simple, blades linear, 5–10 cm long, leath-

Fig. 132. *Vauquelinia corymbosa* subsp.
angustifolia (Slimleaf Vauquelinia)

ery, dark green and shiny above, lighter green underneath, margins coarsely-toothed; petioles 1–2 cm long. Flowers perfect, in corymblike clusters; calyx tube short; sepals 5; petals 5, 4–5 mm long; stamens 15–25, arising at disk margins; styles 5, short. Fruit a 5-celled follicetum, densely hairy, becoming woody, ca. 6 mm long; seeds with a terminal wing.

Three species and 10 subspecies of this genus (Hess and Henrickson, 1987) are native to the southwestern United States and Mexico.

1. **Vauquelinia corymbosa** Humb. & Bonpl. subsp. **angustifolia** (Rydb.) Hess & Henrickson. SLIMLEAF VAUQUELINIA, GUAUYUL, PALO PRIETO. Fig. 132. [*Vauquelinia angustifolia* Rydb.]. Usually scattered and infrequent in canyons or on rocky slopes. Brewster Co., Chisos Mts., in the Basin and in Oak Canyon; Dead Horse Mts., above Roy's Peak. Presidio Co. 3 mi S of Shafter. 3800–6500 ft.; Jun–Aug. Also Coah., Chih., Mex.

In Mexico the wood and bark have been used in dyeing skins. These dense evergreens should be useful as ornamental screens.

10. HOLODISCUS (K. KOCH) MAXIM.

Smallish shrubs to 4 m high, branching at the base; young twigs hairy; bark peeling. Leaves simple, alternate, 1–10 cm long, ovate to roundish, margins

Fig. 133. *Holodiscus discolor* (Bush Rockspires)

prominently notched and toothed, base of blade often somewhat decurrent on petioles, upper surfaces green and essentially glabrous, lower surfaces slightly hairy to densely so. Flowers in prominent panicles to 20 cm long; calyx tubes small, saucerlike; sepals 5, ca. 1.5 mm long; petals 5, 1.5–2 mm long; stamens ca. 20, arising on a disk; pistils pubescent, 5, alternating with sepals. Fruit achenelike, small, 1-seeded, indehiscent, flattened, beaked.

A Western Hemisphere genus with about eight species.

1. Holodiscus discolor (Pursh) Maxim. BUSH ROCKSPIRES, RUSH ROCK-SPIRES. Fig. 133. [*Holodiscus dumosus* var. *australis* (Heller) Ley]. Canyons, rocky slopes, forested slopes. Culberson Co., Guadalupe Mts., South McKittrick Canyon; the Bowl; Signal Peak; and elsewhere at 6000–8000 ft. Jeff Davis Co., upper Madera Canyon of Mt. Livermore and SE of the peak; Sawtooth Mt., NW side. Brewster Co., N slopes of Cathedral Mt. at 5000 ft. and higher; Emory Peak of Chisos Mts. 5000–8000 ft.; Jun–Sep. Also NM N to WY, W to OR and CA; also Coah., Chih., Baja CA, Mex.

Some plants of the higher Guadalupe and Davis mountains, with larger thinner-textured leaves up to 10 cm, barely decurrent leaf bases, and not densely pubescent lower surfaces, are referable to *Holodiscus discolor*, while other Texas plants with smaller leaves and tomentose lower surfaces are of *H. dumosus* (Nutt. *ex* Hook.) Heller. Our observations basically confirm the

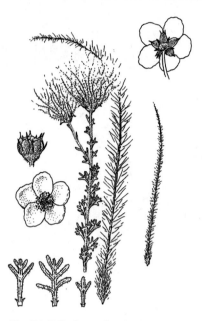

Fig. 134. *Fallugia paradoxa* (Apacheplume)

above, except that one collection from upper Madera Canyon of Mt. Livermore is somewhat intermediate in leaf size. Furthermore, in the Guadalupe Mts., the smaller-leafed *H. dumosus,* typically of lower altitudes, occurs at the same elevation as some *H. discolor* (ca. 7500 ft.), although evidently not together, and in South McKittrick Canyon, but probably at different elevations. These species require additional study in order to define more precisely their populational and ecological differences. For now only one Trans-Pecos species of *Holodiscus* is treated here.

11. FALLUGIA ENDL.

Shrubs to 2 m high, somewhat evergreen, bark peeling; slender branchlets whitish with very short, matted hairs. Leaves alternate, somewhat fascicled to 0.8–1.5 cm long, with 3–7 deep, narrow lobes. Flowers white, 2.5–3.5 cm wide and showy, 1–3 at branchlet ends; calyx tube cuplike, sepals 5, with 5 narrow, alternate bractlets; petals 5, spreading; stamens numerous; pistils many, arranged in a cone. Fruit an achene, each with a purplish feathery, persistent style 2–5 cm long.

A monotypic genus.

1. Fallugia paradoxa (D. Don) Endl. *ex* Torr.   APACHEPLUME.   Fig. 134. Common throughout the Trans-Pecos, especially along dry margins of streams,

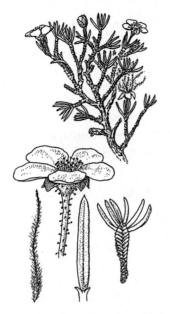

Fig. 135. *Purshia ericifolia* (Heath Cliffrose)

arroyos, and rocky slopes, in a variety of alluvial and gravel soils. May–Dec. Also the W Edwards Plateau; NW W to CA, N to CO and UT; Coah., Chih., and Dgo., Mex.

The common name was inspired by a resemblance of the feathery achene tails to an Apache headdress. The plant is occasionally cultivated for its attractive flowers and fruits.

12. PURSHIA DC. *ex* POIR.

Small evergreen shrubs to 1 m high, resembling Apacheplume, bark not peeling or only tardily so. Leaves alternate, usually fascicled, 4–6 mm long, linear and pointed, leathery, 3–5 lobed, dotted with glands. Flowers white or yellowish, solitary at ends of short stalks; calyx tube 3 mm long, sepals 5, 4 mm long, bractlets none; petals 5, spreading; stamens numerous, in 2 series; pistils ca. 8; styles elongate and densely hairy. Fruit a hairy achene, each tipped by a whitish, feathery tail (style), 1.5–2.5 mm long.

A genus of about five species in the southwestern United States and Mexico (Henrickson, 1986a).

1. **Purshia ericifolia** (Torr. *ex* A. Gray) Henrickson. HEATH CLIFF-ROSE. Fig. 135. [*Cowania ericifolia* Torr. *ex* A. Gray]. Rather dry limestone ridges, usually among rocks, and along cliffs, in mountains. Brewster Co.,

Dead Horse Mts. in Brushy Canyon and above Roy's Peak; near McKinney Springs; ca. .75 mi NE of Dagger Flats visitor area; Stairstep Mt.; southern Del Norte Mts.; E slopes Packsaddle Mt.; Christmas Mts.; 25–35 mi S of Marathon. Presidio Co., Solitario, west rim, north rim, and Solitario Peak vicinity. 2400–4600 ft.; Jul–Oct. Also adjacent Coah. and probably Chih., Mex.

These plants superficially resemble Apacheplume, but are readily distinguished by their narrow (heathlike), usually clustered leaves, instead of deeply lobed leaves of the more common Apacheplume. The species has long been known in our area as *Cowania ericifolia.*

13. CERCOCARPUS KUNTH   MOUNTAINMAHOGANY

Shrubs or small trees, 1–6 cm high; bark smooth on young branches. Leaves alternate, often fascicled, simple, 0.7–6 cm long, lanceolate to roundish, usually conspicuously veined and lighter green on lower surfaces, margins entire or toothed; stipules present. Flowers solitary or in small clusters, small and inconspicuous with yellowish sepals and no petals; calyx tube usually hairy; stamens numerous, attached in 2–3 rows to rim of calyx tube, anthers hairy; pistil 1, ovary superior. Fruit an achene, partially sheathed by calyx tube, the achenes marked by a plumose, twisted, persistent style, 2–8 cm long.

About 20 species of this genus, many of them noted as good browse, occur in the western United States and Mexico.

1. Cercocarpus montanus Raf.   TRUE MOUNTAINMAHOGANY.   Fig. 136. A variable species in the Trans-Pecos, also occurring throughout most of the W U.S. and N Mex. Mar–Jun. Following the work of previous authors, three varieties of *Cercocarpus montanus* are recognized for the Trans-Pecos. Some taxonomic revision of *Cercocarpus* appears warranted, however, perhaps including the recognition of the Trans-Pecos small-leafed entity, treated here as var. *paucidentatus*, as a distinct species. Mountain Mahogany is easily recognized by the long, twisting styles (tails) of the solitary fruit.

1a. Cercocarpus montanus var. paucidentatus (S. Wats.) F. L. Martin. SHAGGY MOUNTAINMAHOGANY.   Fig. 136.   [*Cercocarpus breviflorus* Gray]. Leaves usually less than 2 cm long; margins entire or with a few teeth at the apex; leaves and branchlets usually with appressed hairs, except for some plants with short, spreading hairs in Brewster Co. and Franklin Mts., El Paso Co. Brewster Co., common in upper Chisos Mts.; Mt. Ord and Doubtful Canyon; Altuda Mt.; Old Blue of Glass Mts.; Cienega Mt.; Haystack Mt. Jeff Davis Co., Sawtooth Mt.; Mt. Livermore; Timber Mt. Presidio Co., Sierra Vieja Peak, along the rimrock. Culberson Co., Guadalupe Mts., upper elevations,

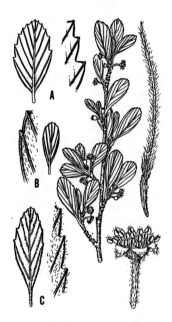

Fig. 136. *Cercocarpus montanus*
(Mountainmahogany); A) var. *glaber*, B) var.
paucidentatus, C) var. *argenteus*

McKittrick, Pine Springs, and Smith canyons. Hudspeth Co., Sierra Diablo, Victorio Canyon near Bat Cave; Eagle Mts., Panther Peak. El Paso Co., Franklin Mts. 4600–8000 ft.

1b. Cercocarpus montanus var. **glaber** (S. Wats.) F. L. Martin. SMOOTH MOUNTAINMAHOGANY. Fig. 136. [*Cercocarpus betuloides* Nutt.]. Leaves usually more than 2 cm long, margins toothed on upper half, essentially glabrous except for appressed hairs on the veins beneath. Brewster Co., common in the upper Chisos Mts.; Dead Horse Mts. Big Bushy Canyon and on top; Glass Mts., Old Blue, Leonard Mt., Gilliland Peak, Sibley Ranch; Mt. Ord; Cathedral Mt.; Cienega Mt.; Goat Mt. Presidio Co., Chinati Mts., upper Pinto Canyon. Pecos Co., Sierra Madera, 30 mi E of Ft. Stockton. 3400–7300 ft.

1c. Cercocarpus montanus var. **argenteus** (Rydb.) F. L. Martin. SILVER MOUNTAINMAHOGANY. Fig. 136. [*Cercocarpus argenteus* Rydb.]. Leaves usually more than 2 cm long, margins toothed on upper half, wooly pubescent beneath. Culberson Co., Guadalupe Mts., McKittrick Canyon, Pine Springs Canyon, Pine Top Mt. Hudspeth Co., Sierra Diablo, Victorio Canyon. 7500–8500 ft.

23. FABACEAE LINDL.   LEGUME FAMILY

Trees, shrubs, vines, or herbs. Leaves usually compound, rarely simple; usually with prominent and persistent stipules, leaflets often with minute stipules. Flowers in panicles, racemes, spikes, heads, or glomerules, rarely solitary, usually perfect, and complete, and perigynous, rarely hypogenous, bilaterally symmetrical and often markedly zygomorphic (especially Papilionoideae) or appearing radially symmetrical except for the pistil (in Mimosoideae); sepals 5 (rarely 4), usually at least partially fused but early separating into valves; petals 5, often appearing 4 by fusion of the lower 2 (keel in Papilionoideae); functional stamens 1 to numerous, separate or fused; pistil 1, superior; ovules 1 to numerous, attached in 2 alternate rows along margins or fused carpel. Fruit most commonly a legume (splitting lengthwise along dorsal "midrib" and ventral suture), or an indehiscent, dry pod (sometimes breaking into 1-seeded sealed units); seeds 1 to numerous, with large embryos, little or no endosperm, usually with a hard seed coat, requiring scarification for quick germination. Synonyms: Leguminosae, the conserved family name; Papilionaceae.

The Fabaceae are one of the largest and most extensively distributed plant families with over 14,200 species in more than 590 genera. They comprise one of the most important economic groups, including plants such as soybeans, beans, peas, clovers, alfalfa, and others. Many legumes are woody plants and these are extensively represented in the Trans-Pecos. There are also many herbaceous perennials with somewhat woody bases (e.g., *Indigofera, Dalea, Hoffmanseggia, Glycyrrhiza*) that are not included in this treatment. Three well-marked subfamilies of the Fabaceae are recognized, all of them at one time or another being previously treated as separate families. All three subfamilies include woody and herbaceous species.

KEY TO THE SUBFAMILIES

1. Leaves pinnately twice-compound; flowers small, arranged mostly in spikes, heads or tight racemes, radially symmetrical (except for the pistil); sepals fused almost their full length; petals 5, separate or coalescent, valvate in bud; stamens 4 to numerous, usually much longer than the petals
                                                        1. *Mimosoideae*.
1. Leaves pinnately once- or twice-compound, or simple; flowers often large and showy, weakly bilaterally symmetrical; sepals often parted to top of floral cup; petals 5, about equal in length, never valvate in bud, the uppermost petal internal in bud; stamens 5–10, shorter than the petals up to twice as long   **2. *Caesalpinioideae*.**
1. Leaves pinnately once-compound or simple (never pinnately twice-compound); flowers often showy and usually strongly bilaterally symmetrical; sepals fused forming a calyx tube beyond the floral cup; petals usually sepa-

rate, imbricate in bud, with the uppermost petal (banner) external, the 2 lateral petals (wings) with narrow, petiolelike bases, and the 2 lower petals formed into a boatshaped structure (keel); stamens 10 or fewer, the filaments of all or some usually fused. In some genera the wings (*Amorpha*) or the keel (*Amorpha, Eysenhardtia*, etc.) may be absent   **3. Papilionoideae.**

1. SUBFAMILY MIMOSOIDEAE   MIMOSA SUBFAMILY

This is the smallest subfamily of Fabaceae with over 2000 species in about 40 genera. Many of the shrub and tree species are good browse for domestic and game animals, and some (such as *Acacia*) are important in the Trans-Pecos as sources of pollen for honey. The herbaceous species of this family are of little agronomic value.

KEY TO THE GENERA

1. Stamens more than 10 or numerous.
  2. Plants unarmed, even stipules membranous; flower heads rather loose, each with 2–15 flowers; stamens usually about 20   **1. Calliandra.**
  2. Plants spinescent or prickly; flower heads congested, each with 10–15 or many flowers; stamens 20–100   **2. Acacia.**
1. Stamens 10 or fewer per flower.
  3. Plants unarmed, without spines.
    4. Plants trees 2–14 m tall   **3. Leucaena.**
    4. Plants decumbent or ascending shrubs, up to 0.5 m high
    5. Desmanthus.
  3. Plants armed, with spines.
    5. Plants armed with recurved prickles   **4. Mimosa.**
    5. Plants armed with straight spines, solitary or paired   **6. Prosopis.**

2. SUBFAMILY CAESALPINIOIDEAE   SENNA SUBFAMILY

This subfamily includes about 2200 species positioned in about 150 genera, and mostly of tropical or subtropical distribution. The flowers of this group are usually yellow or whitish, only rarely being pinkish or reddish. The species are considered to be of little forage value, but several tree and shrub species provide valuable timber and other commercial products such as senna and copal. Many species are grown as ornamentals.

KEY TO THE GENERA

1. Leaves simple, heartshaped to somewhat kidneyshaped   **7. Cercis.**
1. Leaves compound, with 2 or more leaflets.

2. Leaves pinnately once-compound   8. *Senna.*
2. Leaves pinnately twice-compound.
  3. Trees or shrubs; armed with spines or thorns.
    4. Pinnae of mature leaves 10 cm or longer, feathery; pods usually 5–10 cm long   9. *Parkinsonia.*
    4. Pinnae 8 cm long or less; pods 2–6 cm long   10. *Cercidium.*
  3. Shrubs (rarely small trees); unarmed; in some species with orange (dried black) sessile glands on lower leaflet surfaces   11. *Caesalpinia.*

3. SUBFAMILY PAPILIONOIDEAE   BEAN SUBFAMILY

This is the largest subfamily of the Fabaceae with over 10,000 species in about 400 genera, distributed throughout the world. The plants may be trees, shrubs, herbs, or twining vines and are usually without spines. Members of this subfamily, including beans and alfalfa, are of tremendous economic importance, perhaps second only to the grass family in this regard.

KEY TO THE GENERA

1. Leaves simple, blades linear to obovate   21. *Alhagi.*
1. Leaves compound (except usually simple in *Psorothamnus*).
  2. Plants conspicuously armed.
    3. Bushy, herbaceous plants to 1 m high, with numerous, pale-green stems; spinescent stipules light in color   19. *Peteria.*
    3. Shrubs or trees to 10 m high, with darkish stems; spines large and dark in color; fruit densely hispid   20. *Robinia.*
  2. Plants unarmed or with only inconspicuous spinescent stipules.
    4. Leaves gland-dotted (especially as seen with lens on under-surfaces).
      5. Leaflets 6–30 mm wide; flowers with only 1 petal (the banner) present   14. *Amorpha.*
      5. Leaflets 1–5 mm wide; flowers with 4–5 petals.
        6. Flowers white (rarely purplish); rachis of mature leaves 3–9 cm long; fruit much longer than calyx   15. *Eysenhardtia.*
        6. Flowers purplish or reddish (rarely white); rachis of mature leaves 0.5–2.5 cm longer than the calyx.
          7. Plants broomlike, seemingly almost leafless; leaves simple or some of them 3-foliate; stems with retrorse hairs
                          16. *Psorothamnus.*
          7. Plants variously branched, with leaves; leaves compound; stem hairs otherwise   17. *Dalea.*
    4. Leaves not gland-dotted.
      8. Leaves featherlike, leaflets less than 2 mm wide
                          18. *Brongniartia.*

8. Leaves not feathery, leaflets 4 mm wide or wider.
    9. Flowers bluish-purple (rarely white); filaments free
        above the floral cup   **12. Sophora.**
    9. Flowers yellow (or with reddish hues); 9 of the 10 fila-
        ments fused   **13. Genistidium.**

1. CALLIANDRA BENTH.

Small, low shrubs or rhizomatous perennial herbs, usually less than 30 cm high, rarely taller, unarmed with membranous stipules. Leaves pinnately twice-compound, with 1 to few pinnae and many small leaflets. Flowers small, whitish to pink, clustered into heads with 2–15 flowers; stamens usually ca. 20, the filaments fused basally to form a tube. Fruit a flattened legume, persistent, 3–8 cm long, tapered toward the base, elastically dehiscent; seeds 1–6, small, flattish; valves of legumes persistent and recurved after dehiscence. *Anneslia* Salisb.

About 130 species distributed mostly in warm regions of the Americas. Five species occur in Texas, four of these in the Trans-Pecos.

KEY TO THE SPECIES

1. Stamens maroon-pink   **1. C. coulteri.**
1. Stamens whitish   **2. C. conferta.**

1. **Calliandra coulteri** S. Wats.   Fig. 137.   Known in Texas from a single locality. Presidio Co., south Chinati Mts., Tinaja Prieta Canyon, north wall, near the mouth, above the rock dam; several low shrubs in crevices of the canyon wall. This new state record was collected by the author and Emily Lott. Otherwise known from Mex., Coah., Sierra Hechiceros, according to information provided by M. C. Johnston, and elsewhere in Mex.

The species in flower is easily distinguished from any other Texas *Calliandra* by its relatively long, deep-pink stamens.

2. **Calliandra conferta** Benth.   FALSEMESQUITE, CALLIANDRA.   Fig. 138. Mostly rocky limestone soils. Brewster Co., lower Chisos Mts.; Ward Spring; Burro Spring; near Terlingua; Buckhill Mts.; 20 mi NE of Alpine. Presidio Co., 25 mi SE Marfa near Alamito Creek; near Shafter. Terrell Co., near Sanderson. Val Verde Co., widespread from Langtry to the Pecos and Devils Rivers and Loma Alta. 2700–4500 ft.; spring–fall. Locally abundant, caliche and limestone, S parts of the Edwards Plateau; Rio Grande Plains; rare to Travis Co.; also in Coah., N.L. and Tam., Mex.

Calliandra conferta, usually a low, gnarly shrublet after browsing, has been confused with *C. eriophylla* Benth. (Fig. 138) of NM, AZ, and NW Mex. Trans-

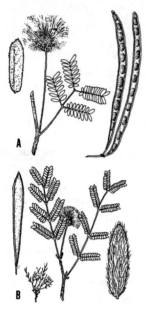

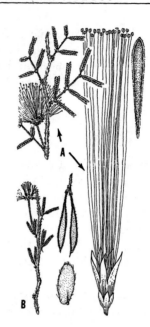

Fig. 137. A) *Calliandra coulteri*;
B) *C. humilis*

Fig. 138. A) *Calliandra eriophylla*, with flower;
B) C. *conferta* (Falsemesquite)

Pecos populations of *C. conferta* have longer peduncles than is typical of the species elsewhere, and may be deserving of varietal status (Turner, 1959; Isely, 1972, 1973). Another falsemesquite, *C. humilis* Benth. (Fig. 137), an herbaceous species with a woody base, occurs in the Trans-Pecos.

2. ACACIA MILL. ACACIA

Trees, shrubs, shrublets or rarely suffrutescent herbs armed with long or short stipular spines, or recurved prickles, or unarmed. Leaves pinnately twice-compound, pinnae 1 to several pairs, leaflets usually numerous. Flowers small, white to yellow, many-flowered in globose heads or spikes, often fragrant; stamens numerous (20–100) per flower, separate to the base. Fruit a legume, mostly linear, thin- or thick-walled, perhaps inflated, promptly dehiscent or seemingly indehiscent. [*Vachellia* Wight & Arn.; *Poponax* Raf.; *Acaciopsis* Britt. & Rose; *Acaciella* Britt. & Rose; *Senegalia* Raf.]

Acacia is a large genus with about 600 species widely distributed in warm regions of both hemispheres, being especially common in Australia where about 300 species occur. The genus name *Acacia* means a hard, sharp point, in reference to the prominent spines of some species. Many species, including those of the Trans-Pecos are of value as browse plants, and some, especially

Guajillo and Mescat Acacia, are noted as excellent honey plants. Eight of the 10 Texas species of *Acacia* occur in the Trans-Pecos. All the species flower in the spring, and occasionally in the summer following dry periods and rain, except for *A. angustissima* which usually flowers in the summer.

KEY TO THE SPECIES
Adapted from Turner (1959).

1. Inflorescence of spikes, 2–6 times as long as wide, when flowers open.
   2. Legume rather woody, 7 mm wide or less; spines usually long, straight, paired at each node; flowers bright yellow   **5. *A. rigidula.***
   2. Legume fleshy, 12 mm wide or more; spines recurved or absent, below the stipules, not paired at the nodes; flowers creamy-white.
      3. Leaflets mostly 3–6 mm long; mature pods somewhat leathery, often twisting; seeds circular   **6a. *A. greggii.***
      3. Leaflets mostly 5–12 mm long; pods thickly papery, not twisting; seeds narrowly obovoid to ovoid   **6b. *A. greggii* var. *wrightii.***
1. Inflorescence of globose heads or short spikes, one and one-half times as long as wide or less, when flowers open.
   4. Stipules spinose, straight, usually long (rarely much reduced or absent); flowers yellow.
      5. Bracts borne at top of main flower stalk; pods inflated (peanut-like)   **1. *A. farnesiana.***
      5. Bracts borne near middle of main flower stalk; pods otherwise.
         6. Pinnae 4–7 pairs   **2. *A. constricta.***
         6. Pinnae 1–2 (3) pairs.
            7. Leaflets ovate, flattened, barely alternate, spaced 0.8 mm apart or less; legume not conspicuously black-glandular   **3. *A. neovernicosa.***
            7. Leaflets linear, almost filiform, alternate, spaced 1 mm or more apart; legume conspicuously brown or black glandular-dotted   **4. *A. schottii.***
   4. Stipules not spinose; prickles recurved, not paired at the nodes, or prickles absent.
      8. Shrubs or trees, usually 1 m tall or more; flowers yellow or whitish; petiolar gland present.
         9. Leaflets 4–15 pairs; pinnae 1–4 (5) pairs.
            10. Leaflets 3 mm long or less; flowers yellow   **2. *A. constricta.***
            10. Leaflets 3–10 mm long; flowers creamy white   **7. *A. roemeriana.***
         9. Leaflets numerous (30–50 pairs); pinnae 3–many pairs; flowers creamy white   **8. *A. berlandieri.***

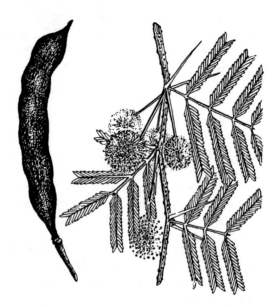

Fig. 139. *Acacia farnesiana* (Huisache)

8. Low suffrutescent plants, mostly less than 1 m tall; flowers creamy white, on short stalks; petiolar gland absent
9. *A. angustissima.*

1. Acacia farnesiana (L.) Willd.   HUISACHE, SWEET ACACIA.   Fig. 139. [*Vachellia farnesiana* (L.) Wight & Arn.]. Sandy or rocky limestone soil, infrequent in Brewster Co., near the Rio Grande, Boquillas and east in the corner of Big Bend National Park. Terrell Co., 10 mi E of Sanderson. Isely (1973) recognized *A. smallii*, or *A. minuta* (M. E. Jones) Beauchamp, in place of *A. farnesiana*, the name long used for the Trans-Pecos Huisache. Clarke (et al., 1989) restored the name *A. farnesiana* for the Trans-Pecos populations, and for this most widespread species of *Acacia* which is pantropical in distribution. Also S TX E to FL; disjunct in AZ and CA; throughout most of Mex.

Widely cultivated in Texas, in the Old World, and in many tropical countries. The fragrant oils of this species were once used in many "French" perfumes. The wood is valued for posts and various woodwork. Huisache is considered to be good forage, and one of the best honey plants where it grows abundantly, especially in more arid regions. The bark and fruit have been used for inkmaking, dying, and tanning. Glue from the pods has been used to mend pottery. A Huisache tree of near National champion status, 48 ft. tall, 60 ft. crown spread, 6.1 ft. girth, is reported by Liles to occur near Rio Grande Village in Big Bend National Park.

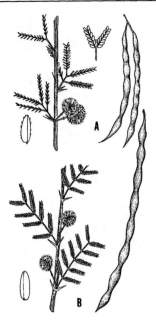

Fig. 140. A) *Acacia neovernicosa* (Viscid
Acacia); B) *A. constricta* (Mescat Acacia)

2. Acacia constricta Benth. MESCAT ACACIA, LARGANCILLO, WHITETHORN
ACACIA. Fig. 140. [*Acaciopsis constricta* (Gray) Britt. & Rose]. A widespread
species in the Trans-Pecos, occurring probably in all the counties, in various
desertic habitats, mostly along the Rio Grande drainage and W of the Pecos
River. 1500–6500 ft. Also Plains Country to NE of Trans-Pecos, and in Howard Co., rare in S TX in dry areas near the Rio Grande (Starr and Zapata counties); S NM, AZ; also, N Mex., S to S.L.P. and Pue.

This species is reported to hybridize to some extent with the closely related *Acacia neovernicosa*, but *A. constricta* is supposedly isolated by flowering
1–2 weeks earlier where the two species occur together. Two varieties of
A. constricta, var. *constricta* and var. *paucispina* Woot. & Standl., are listed in
Kartesz (1994). Mescat Acacia is occasionally browsed by game animals and
cattle, although the sharp spines make it unpalatable for larger animals. Quail
eat the seeds extensively in areas where the plants are abundant. This is one of
the favored honey plants of the southern Trans-Pecos. Indians of Arizona and
New Mexico reportedly made "pinole" out of the legumes.

3. Acacia neovernicosa Isely. VISCID ACACIA. Fig. 140. [*Acacia vernicosa* Standl.; *Acacia constricta* var. *vernicosa* (Standl.) L. Benson]. Gravelly and
rocky hillsides, throughout the desert portions of the Trans-Pecos from El Paso
to Val Verde counties; abundant in the Bofecillos Mts. of Presidio Co. NM and
AZ; N Mex.

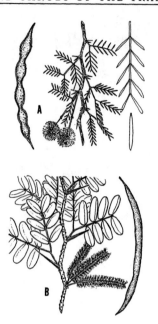

Fig. 141. A) *Acacia schottii* (Schott Acacia); B)
A. rigidula (Blackbrush Acacia)

This species is closely related and morphologically similar to *Acacia constricta*. Both species have somewhat sticky and vernicose (varnished) leaves, and are best distinguished by the number of leaflets as indicated in the key.

4. Acacia schottii Torr. SCHOTT ACACIA. Fig. 141. [*Acaciopsis schottii* (Torr.) Britt. & Rose]. Locally common in gypseous clay soils, and possibly rocky limestone. Brewster Co., Boquillas area; Packsaddle Mt.; Hen Egg Mt.; Agua Fria Mt.; Terlingua Creek near Study Butte; near Lajitas. 2300–4000 ft. Also adjacent Chih., Mex.

Label data indicate that this species grows in limestone soil, although the author has observed the plants only in cretaceous clay soils with which the distribution of Schott Acacia is correlated in southern Brewster County, and doubtless adjacent Presidio County. *Acacia schottii* apparently hybridizes with *A. neovernicosa* and *A. constricta*. In limestone habitats the plants resembling *A. schottii* possibly are hybrids, mostly with *A. neovernicosa*.

5. Acacia rigidula Benth. BLACKBRUSH ACACIA, CHAPARRO PRIETO. Fig. 141. [*Acacia amentacea* DC.]. Rare in rocky limestone areas of the Trans-Pecos, near the Rio Grande. Brewster Co., Mariscal Mt. Terrell Co., mouth of San Francisco Canyon; Val Verde Co., common on limestone hillsides and in canyons, near Langtry, Pecos River, Devils River, Loma Alta. 1100–1800 ft.

Fig. 142. A) *Acacia greggii* var. *greggii* (Catclaw Acacia); B) *A. roemeriana* (Roemer Acacia)

Abundant in the Rio Grande Plains and south Texas in general; N Mex. to S.L.P. and Tam.

The rigid branches and long, stiff spines cause many flat tires in Val Verde Co. and southeastward where the plants are abundant. Except for the vicious spines, Blackbrush Acacia could be recommended for wider cultivation as a honey plant and for erosion control. This species has been studied recently by Lee et al. (1989).

6a. Acacia greggii Gray. var. **greggii** CATCLAW ACACIA. Fig. 142. [*Senegalia greggii* (Gray) Britt. & Rose; *Acacia greggii* var. *arizonica* Isely]. Widespread and locally abundant throughout the Trans-Pecos, in the major and minor mountains, in canyons, and in brushy areas, in various soil types including gypsum. 1000–5000 ft. Also NE to Taylor and Coleman counties; Rio Grande Plains; NM N to CO, W to CA also N Mex. as far west as Baja CA.

Catclaw thickets offer shelter for wildlife, and the seeds are eaten by quail. As with many other acacias, this is an excellent honey plant. Indians made "pinole" mush or cakes from the legumes. The lac insect, *Tachardia lacca*, is known to feed on the sap of Catclaw Acacia and to exude a resinous lac (refined into shellac of commerce), but probably not in commercial quantities.

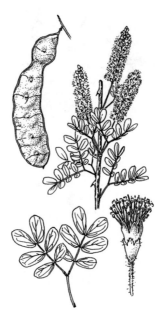

Fig. 143. *Acacia greggii* var. *wrightii*
(Wright Acacia)

6b. Acacia greggii var. **wrightii** Benth.   WRIGHT ACACIA, CATCLAW, UNA
DE GATO.   Fig. 143.   [*Senegalia wrightii* (Benth.) Britt. & Rose; *Acacia wrightii* Benth.]. Rare in the Trans-Pecos, occurring in Terrell Co., Pecos Co., and nearby Crane Co.; Apr–Aug. Replacing *A. greggii* var. *greggii* to the east on the Edwards Plateau where it is locally frequent in brushlands, arroyos, and in canyons (even as a tree around Brackettville); also S to the Rio Grande Plains, and with outliers N to Shackelford Co.; also N Mex.

Wright Acacia deserves wider use as an ornamental and honey plant.

7. Acacia roemeriana Scheele.   ROEMER ACACIA, CATCLAW.   Fig. 142.
[*Senegalia roemeriana* (Scheele) Britt. & Rose; *Acacia malacophylla* Benth]. Widespread in the SE Trans-Pecos, in the desertic mountains and Chisos Mts., in canyons and brushlands, and at Davis Mts. State Park. 1050–4600 ft. Infrequent across the Edwards Plateau and N to Jones Co., S to Maverick Co., E to Travis Co.; S NM near Carlsbad; N Mex.

Roemer Acacia forms trees to 10 ft. or more in some woodland and canyon areas. It has value as an ornamental, as honey plant, and as browse for deer. *Acacia malacophylla*, once treated as a weak species, is now considered to be only a pubescent form of *A. roemeriana*. The fruit pods of Roemer Acacia are flatter and do not twist as much as do those of the similar species, *A. greggii*.

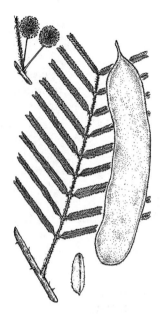

Fig. 144. *Acacia berlandieri* (Guajillo)   Fig. 145. *Acacia angustissima* (Fern Acacia)

8. Acacia berlandieri Benth.   GUAJILLO, BERLANDIER ACACIA.   Fig. 144.
[*Senegalia berlandieri* (Benth.) Britt. & Rose; *Acacia emoryana* Benth.]. Extending into the Trans-Pecos, but uncommon in limestone areas near the Rio
Grande. Brewster Co., Reagan Canyon; Burro Falls W of Chisos Mts.; mouth
of San Francisco Creek. Terrell Co., vicinity of Sanderson and Dryden. Becoming common in Val Verde Co., and continuing as a dominant low shrub in
brushy vegetation from near Langtry to Laredo. 1000–3000 ft. Also abundant
on limestone ridges and caliche cuestas in the Rio Grande Plains, becoming
rare in deeper soils of the Rio Grande Valley and delta; also S Edwards Plateau;
N Mex. from Coah., S and E to Qro. and Ver.

Guajillo is a famous honey plant where it grows in abundance, and a desirable ornamental, especially as a hedge, because of its low growth, fernlike
leaves, and globose white flowers. The plants can be propagated by seeds or by
seedlings that come up at the base of older plants. *Acacia* × *emoryana*, described from a collection with elongated rather than round heads, was found
by Johnston (1974) to result from sporadic hybridization between *Acacia berlandieri* and *A. greggii.*

9. Acacia angustissima (Mill.) Ktze.   FERN ACACIA, PRAIRIE ACACIA.
Fig. 145.   [*Acacia texensis* T.&G.]. Locally common in the grasslands and

nearby mountains at elevations of 3200–6500 ft. in Brewster, Jeff Davis, Presidio, Pecos, Culberson, Hudspeth (Eagle Mts.), and El Paso counties. Lower elevations S and E of the Trans-Pecos; also N Mex.

The taxonomy here follows Isely (1973) in recognizing two varieties for the poorly understood grassland, shrublet acacias which colonize by woody rhizomes. 1) *Acacia angustissima* (Mill.) Ktze. var. **chisosiana** Isely: contorted subshrub with sparsely hairy leaves, petiole and leaf axis together 0.8–2 (–3) cm long, pinnae (1 or)2–4 pairs, leaflets 6–10 per pinna, 4–8 (–10) flowered heads; desert mountains and slopes, S Brewster and Presidio counties; Jun–Aug. 3500–5000 ft. Also Coah. and Chih., Mex. 2) *A. angustissima* var. **texensis** (T.&G.) Isely: a suffrutescent herb with small leaves, petioles, and leaf axes together mostly 2.5–4 cm long, pinnae (3 or)4–6 pairs, leaflets 9–15 pairs per pinna, largely intercalary inflorescences, and 4–6-flowered heads; rocky habitats or sand, various substrates, S TX, Trans-Pecos, SW NM and SE AZ, overlapping with var. *chisosiana* in the Trans-Pecos. Five varieties of *A. angustissima* are listed in Kartesz (1994).

3. LEUCAENA BENTH. LEADTREE

Trees or shrubs, 2–13 m tall; stems brittle, unarmed. Leaves pinnately twice-compound, 8–30 cm long; pinnae 2–25 pairs, leaflets numerous; petiole gland on upper side. Flowers in globose heads, 1–2 cm across, white or yellow; stamens 10, separate. Fruit a legume, long-linear, flat, usually narrow, valves dehiscent, remaining intact; seeds 10 or more, obovate, brown.

A genus of about 20 species mostly distributed in tropical and subtropical North America, South America, and Polynesia. Three species occur in Texas, and except for *Leucaena retusa*, are frequently planted as ornamentals.

1. **Leucaena retusa** Gray. LITTLELEAF LEADTREE. Fig. 146. [*Caudoleucaena retusa* (Gray) Britt. & Rose]. Scattered trees or less often shrubs, in rocky limestone or igneous canyons or arroyos. Jeff Davis Co., Limpia Canyon, Wild Rose Pass; near Mt. Locke and Madera Springs; Merrill Canyon, SW foothills of Mt. Livermore; Musquiz Canyon. Brewster Co., Paradise Canyon and elsewhere near Alpine; Green Gulch, Chisos Mts.; Dagger Flats; near Sue Peaks, Dead Horse Mts.; Reagan Canyon; Hell's Half Acre near San Francisco Creek. Val Verde Co.; near Langtry E to the Pecos River and Devils River. 1200–5500 ft.; Apr–Jun. Dry canyons, W edge of the Edwards Plateau; Guadalupe Mts. and probably elsewhere, S NM; Coah., Mex.

These attractive small trees with bright yellow flower-balls have not been extensively cultivated, but are desirable ornamentals. The plants reportedly are excellent browse for cattle and deer.

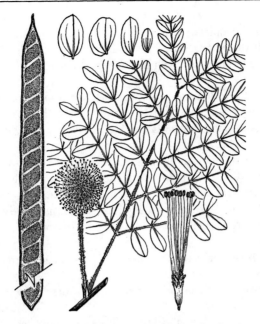

Fig. 146. *Leucaena retusa* (Littleleaf Leadtree)

4. MIMOSA L. MIMOSA, CATCLAW

Shrubs, trees, or lianes, rarely perennial herbs, usually heavily armed with recurved prickles. Leaves pinnately twice-compound; pinnae 1–14 pairs, leaflets usually small and numerous; stipules small, not spinescent. Flowers in globose heads, rarely short spikes, white or pink (in our species), to reddish; stamens 8–10, usually colored, separate, anthers without glands. Fruit an elongated, flattened legume; margins separate from valves at dehiscence, the margins rather persistent; valves often break transversely into 1-seeded sections.

A large tropical and subtropical genus of about 479 species (Barneby, 1991), mostly of the New World, with a few species also in Africa and Asia. About nine species occur in Texas, seven native to the Trans-Pecos. The genus name *Mimosa* is from the Spanish word *mimoso*, meaning sensitive (Barneby, 1991), which refers to a sensitive movement of the leaflets in some species.

KEY TO THE SPECIES

1. Flower heads spikelike, cylindric; leaves, at least some of them, with 8–14 pairs of pinnae   **1. *M. dysocarpa.***
1. Flower heads globose; leaves with 1–8 pairs of pinnae.
   2. Leaves, at least some of them, with 4–8 pairs of pinnae; valves of legume straight, separating entirely from the margin at maturity.

3. Leaflets very small, not more than 1.5 mm long; prickles conical, not much flattened near base, only slightly recurved; pods with short hairs, with straight prickles along the margin; branches flexuous
               4. M. warnockii.
3. Leaflets 2 mm long or more; prickles not conical, flattened near the base, usually recurved; pods essentially without hairs, the margins with or without short recurved prickles; branches straight to somewhat flexuous
 4. Prickles of long-shoots usually 2, at both sides of petiole on ribs lead-ing to stipules; corolla pubescent; pinnae 3–9 pairs, leaflets 7–14 pairs; pod usually curved **5. M. aculeaticarpa var. biuncifera.**
 4. Prickles of long-shoots usually 1, inserted immediately below petiole; corolla glabrous; pinnae 1–4, leaflets 7 pairs or less; pod usually straight   **6. M. texana.**
2. Leaves with 1–3 pairs of pinnae; pod valves remaining intact or breaking into joints.
 5. Valves of pod densely covered with short yellow prickles; leaflets densely silky   **2. M. emoryana.**
 5. Valves of the pod glabrous or essentially so; leaflets glabrous to sparsely pubescent.
  6. Leaves with 1–2 pairs of pinnae; leaflets 2(3) pairs per pinna; petals united more than half their length **7. M. turneri.**
  6. Leaves with 1–3 pairs of pinnae; leaflets 3–8 pairs per pinna; petals united only at base, free beyond calyx tube
             3. M. borealis.

 1. Mimosa dysocarpa Benth. VELVETPOD MIMOSA. Fig. 147. [*Mimosa dysocarpa* var. *wrightii* (Gray) Kearn. & Peeb.]. Brushy hillsides, in the Davis Mts. area, locally abundant. Jeff Davis Co., Davis Mts. State Park; Mt. Locke; vicinity of Bloys Campground; Fern Canyon. Brewster Co., Goat, Cienega, Cathedral, Paisano mountains. Presidio Co., Elephant Mt. 5000–6500 ft.; Jun–Jul. NM and AZ; N Mex., S to Dgo.
 Velvetpod Mimosa is an attractive plant with its pinkish-purple flower spikes, and it is occasionally browsed by livestock.

 2. Mimosa emoryana Benth. EMORY MIMOSA. Fig. 147. Rocky lime-stone or igneous habitats, locally common in southern desertic mountains. Brewster Co., Packsaddle Mt.; Reed Plateau and vicinity W of Terlingua; lower Chisos Mts. and vicinity. Presidio Co., foothills of the Chinati Mts.; Pinto Canyon; near Shafter; Alamito Creek 25 mi S of Marfa. 2700–4500 ft. May–Aug; also in adjacent Chih., and in Dgo., Mex.
 Emory Mimosa is a small shrub that is most easily recognized by its fruits with rather dense, yellowish spines covering the valve surfaces, and pubescent

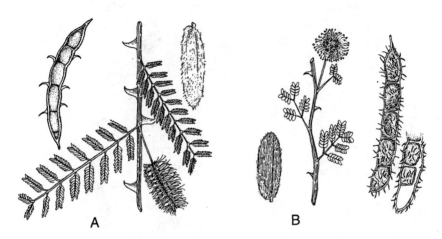

Fig. 147. A) *Mimosa dysocarpa* (Velvetpod Mimosa); B) *M. emoryana* (Emory Mimosa)

foliage. The flowers are in pinkish globes. The Trans-Pecos entity is var. **emoryana** (Barneby, 1991).

3. Mimosa borealis Gray. FRAGRANT MIMOSA. Fig. 148. [*Mimosa fragrans* Gray]. One of the most widespread and common mimosas in the Trans-Pecos, found in most all the counties, perhaps exclusively in limestone areas, particularly amongst brushy vegetation. 1200–4600 ft.; Apr–Jul. Also common E on the Edwards Plateau to about Travis Co.; less common in the Plains Country; also NM, OK, KS, and CO.

Fragrant Mimosa is attractive when in full flower, with its pinkish globes, and could be used as ornamental. The plants are occasionally browsed by livestock. The more northerly distribution of this mimosa supposedly inspired the species name. In this species the corolla lobes are free to the base (Barneby, 1991).

4. Mimosa warnockii B. L. Turner. WARNOCK MIMOSA. Fig. 149. [*Mimosa flexuosa* Benth.; *Mimosopsis flexuosa* (Benth.) Britt. & Rose]. Locally common, usually in open grasslands and igneous alluvial flats. Jeff Davis Co.; 2 mi N of Marfa; Barrel Springs, near Bloys Campground; 7 mi W of Ft. Davis; near the Point of Rocks. 4500–5500 ft.; May–Aug. Also NM, AZ, and Son., Mex. according to Correll and Johnston (1970); only in the Trans-Pecos (Isely, 1973).

Warnock Mimosa is a low shrub about 1–2 ft. high and 2–4 ft. across, with markedly zigzag branches, and it is the only white-flowered mimosa of the

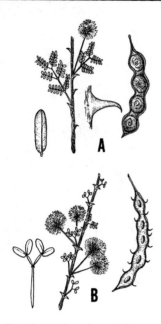

Fig. 148. A) *Mimosa borealis* (Fragrant Mimosa); B) *M. turneri*

Fig. 149. A) *Mimosa warnockii* (Warnock Mimosa); B) *M. aculeaticarpa* var. *biuncifera* (Catclaw Mimosa)

Trans-Pecos, although the flowers of *Mimosa aculeaticarpa* var. *biuncifera* are whitish to pinkish. This diploid species is closely related to the tetraploid *M. aculeaticarpa* var. *biuncifera*, and is regarded by Barneby and Isely (1986) and Barneby (1991) as a synonym of the latter taxon. I continue, for the present, to regard the localized population in Jeff Davis County as a distinct taxon because it appears to differ in habit and several other characters from the more widespread *M. aculeaticarpa* var. *biuncifera*.

5. **Mimosa aculeaticarpa** Ortega var. **biuncifera** (Benth.) Barneby. CAT-CLAW MIMOSA. Fig. 149. [*Mimosa lindheimeri* Gray; *M. biuncifera* var. *lindheimeri* (Gray) Robinson; *Mimosopsis lindheimeri* (Gray) Britt. & Rose]. Often forming dense thickets, limestone and igneous-rock habitats. 2000–5000 ft.; Apr–Sep. S NM and AZ; also N Mex. Legumes of this species may or may not have prominent prickles on the margins.

Barneby (1991) recognized several variants of *M. aculeaticarpa*, which is widespread in Mexico and the southwestern United States, including var. *biuncifera*, the most common *Mimosa* of the Trans-Pecos. This taxon has long been known in the region as *M. biuncifera* (Turner, 1959).

Dense thickets of *Mimosa aculeaticarpa* var. *biuncifera* furnish excellent quail cover and food throughout much of the Trans-Pecos. The plants are browsed by deer and livestock, and the flowers are a source of nectar for honey. Catclaw Mimosa is one of the most common and troublesome shrub invaders of desert grassland.

6. Mimosa texana (Gray) Small var. **texana.** TEXAS MIMOSA. Fig. 149, resembles *M. texana.* [*Mimosa texana* Small; *M. borealis* var.(?) *texana* Gray; *Mimosopsis wherryana* Britt. *in* Britt. and Rose]. Seemingly sympatric with the widespread *M. aculeaticarpa* var. *biuncifera,* in Hudspeth, Presidio, Brewster, Pecos, Terrell, Crockett, Val Verde, and perhaps other counties.

The status of *Mimosa texana* var. *texana* has been clarified by Barneby and Isely (1986) and Barneby (1991) who discuss additional distinguishing traits, distributions, and relationships of *M. texana, M. aculeaticarpa,* and other geographically proximal taxa of *Mimosa. Mimosa texana* was long confused with *M. aculeaticarpa* because of close similarity in superficial features.

7. Mimosa turneri Barneby. TURNER MIMOSA. Fig. 148. [*Mimosa zygophylla* auct. *non.* Benth.]. Limestone soils, localized and rather infrequent in S desert areas. Brewster Co., between Castolon and Smoky Creek; 3 mi SE of Hen Egg Mt.; flats N of Nine Point Mesa. Presidio Co., 21 mi above Lajitas. Hudspeth Co., Speck Ranch, NW side Eagle Mts; Quitman Mts. 2200–4000 ft.; Apr–Jun. Also Coah., N.L., Mex.

The status of this species has been clarified by Barneby (1986; 1991). Turner (1959) noted that the Trans-Pecos population he treated as *M. zygophylla* Gray was different from *M. zygophylla* as described in Mexico. Barneby (1986) recognized *M. zygophylla* as a Mexican species (Coah., Zac., N.L., S.L.P., Chih., Dgo.) closely related to *M. turneri* which has its major distribution in Trans-Pecos Texas. Barneby (1986; 1991) discussed the relationship of *M. turneri* and *M. zygophylla* to *M. borealis* and yet other species of northeastern Mexico. In *M. turneri* the globelike flower clusters are pinkish.

5. DESMANTHUS WILLD. BUNDLEFLOWER

Herbaceous or suffruticose perennials, rarely shrubs, with erect or spreading stems, 2–10 dm long, unarmed; roots often turnipshaped, rather woody. Leaves pinnately twice-compound, usually 2–10 cm long, with 2–10 pairs of pinnae, leaflets small, numerous. Flowers few to numerous in heads, usually white; sepals 5 separate; petals 5, separate; stamens 10 (or only 5, e.g., in *Desmanthus illinoensis*), free; some lower flowers in each head with sterile stamens. Fruit a legume, dry, flattened, 1–several seeded, promptly dehiscent. [*Acuan* Medic.].

A genus of about 24 species, occurring mostly in Mexico (14 species) and southern Texas (8 species), according to the recent monograph by Luckow (1993).

Fig. 150. A) *Desmanthus cooleyi* (Cooley
Bundleflower); B) *Prosopis glandulosa* var.
glandulosa (Honey Mesquite)

1. Desmanthus cooleyi (Eat.) Trel. COOLEY BUNDLEFLOWER. Fig. 150.
[*Acuan cooleyi* (Eat.) Britt. & Rose; *Desmanthus jamesii* T.&G.]. Widespread
and locally common, particularly in grasslands and mountains. Culberson,
Hudspeth, Presidio, Jeff Davis, Brewster, and Pecos counties. 4000–7000 ft.;
Jun–Aug. Also locally frequent in the Plains Country, N to NE, W to AZ; Mex.,
S to Dgo.

Five other species of this genus, *Desmanthus illinoensis* (Michx.) MacM. *ex*
B. L. Robins. & Fern. (Illinois Bundleflower), *D. velutinus* Scheele, *D. virgatus*
(L.) Willd., *D. glandulosus* (B. L. Turner) Luckow, and *D. obtusus* S. Wats. occur in the Trans-Pecos. All three species are woody-based perennials with herbaceous stems, although in some plants of *D. velutinus* the stems are woody
toward the base.

6. PROSOPIS L. MESQUITE

Shrubs or trees, usually armed with straight, stout spines, solitary or paired.
Leaves pinnately twice-compound; pinnae 1–several pairs; leaflets 4–30 per
pinna, usually linear and glabrous; petiolar gland present. Flowers in globose
heads or cylindric spikes, usually yellowish or creamy; sepals mostly fused;
petals 5, fused or not; stamens 10, anthers with a short gland at the apex, be-

Fig. 151. *Prosopis pubescens* (Screwbean)

tween the anther sacs. Fruit a straight, slightly curved (and rather long) or tightly coiled, indehiscent tough pod; seeds partitioned and embedded. [*Neltuma* Raf.; *Algarobia* Benth.; *Strombocarpa* Engelm. & Gray].

A genus of about 40 species occurring mostly in the warm and somewhat dry regions of the Americas, Africa, and Asia. Four species occur in Texas.

KEY TO THE SPECIES

1. Leaflets 4–8 pairs per pinna; fruit tightly coiled in a spiral   **1. *P. pubescens.***
1. Leaflets 10 to many pairs per pinna; fruit not coiled   **2. *P. glandulosa.***

1. Prosopis pubescens Benth. SCREWBEAN, TORNILLO. Fig. 151. Arroyos, washes, and larger tributaries and particularly the deltas along the Rio Grande, from El Paso Co. to SE Brewster Co., Tornillo Creek and near Glenn Springs in Big Bend Park; common in Presidio Co.; Reeves Co., Screw Bean Draw in gypsum, W of Orla; Ward Co., near Pecos River; spring (usually early May in Big Bend National Park), perhaps summer. Also SE of the Trans-Pecos along and near the Rio Grande to the upper Rio Grande Valley; W to CA; Mex.; adjacent to W TX and in Baja CA.

Powdered root bark of Screwbean mesquite was used by the Pima Indians

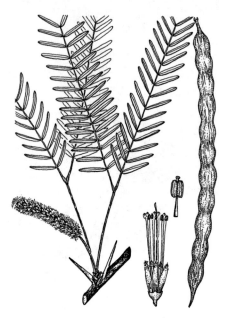

Fig. 152. *Prosopis glandulosa* var. *torreyana*
(Western Honey Mesquite)

of Arizona to treat wounds (Vines, 1960). Indians also ground the beans into a meal to make pinole bread or made a cool drink from the meal. A syrup was obtained by boiling the sweet beans. The durable wood is used for many purposes including fence posts, tool handles, and firewood. A National co-champion Screwbean mesquite, 30 ft. tall, 36 ft. crown spread, 3.25 ft. girth, was recorded by Liles to occur in Rio Grande Village, Big Bend National Park.

2. Prosopis glandulosa Torr.   HONEY MESQUITE.   Occupying many habitats, this is one of the most common plants in Texas. This species was long known erroneously as *Prosopis juliflora* or *P. chilensis*. Two varieties of *P. glandulosa* are recognized for Texas and the Trans-Pecos (Correll and Johnston, 1970; Isely, 1973).

2a. Prosopis glandulosa var. **torreyana** (L. Benson) M. C. Johnst.   WESTERN HONEY MESQUITE.   Fig. 152.   [*Prosopis juliflora* var. *torreyana* L. Benson; *P. odorata* Torr. & Frem.]. Leaflets 1–2.5 cm long; 5–8 times as long as broad; 5–20 pairs of leaflets per pinna; thorns often paired. This is the most widespread variety in the Trans-Pecos; flowering spring and later. Also across much of TX, the SW to CA, and N Mex.

2b. Prosopis glandulosa var. **glandulosa**   HONEY MESQUITE.   Fig. 150. [*Prosopis chilensis* (Molina) Stuntz var. *glandulosa* (Torr.) Standl.; *P. juliflora*

(Sw.) DC. var. *glandulosa* (Torr.) Cockerell]. Leaflets 2.5–6 cm long; 8–15 times as long as broad; 6–15 pairs of leaflets per pinna; thorns usually solitary. This variety is scattered and infrequent in the Trans-Pecos, but is common in much of Texas, including the Rio Grande Plains, and parts of N-cen. and SE regions of the state; Apr–May. Also in E NM, OK, and KS; also Tam., N.L., and Coah. of NE Mex.

According to historical records mesquite has always had a wide geographic range, although more or less restricted to arroyos, creeks, canyons, and otherwise rather narrow habitats. Mesquite has increased tremendously in abundance over the past 130 years, probably as a result of disturbed rangeland conditions. The species is easily disseminated by seeds, especially after they have passed through animal digestive tracts. New plants readily sprout from old stumps. The plants are notably hardy, with deep, drought-defying roots, and they are not easily damaged by insects or disease. Mesquite has many historical and contemporary economic uses. Indians made pinole bread from the pods which contain much sugar, and they made an intoxicating beverage by fermenting the meal. The gum that exudes from the bark was used to mend pottery, to make candy, and someday may be used as a substitute for gum arabic. The seeds are important wildlife food. The foliage and pods have constituted important livestock food, especially in drought years. The wood is used for many building purposes, fuel, and posts, and is hailed by some as the best wood for barbecuing meat. In Big Bend National Park the largest Western Honey Mesquite measured by Jim Liles was 42 ft. tall, with a 52 ft. crown spread, and 8 ft. girth.

7. CERCIS L. REDBUD

Small trees, rarely shrubby, deciduous, unarmed. Leaves simple, heart-shaped to somewhat kidneyshaped; stipules not persistent. Flowers appearing in early spring before the leaves, rose or pink-purplish, in clusters on last year's growth; corolla bilaterally symmetrical, petals 5; stamens 10, separate. Fruit a legume, oblong, flat, thin-walled, dark brown; seeds several to many.

A genus of about five species, distributed in temperate regions of North America, Europe, and Asia. Most of the species are widely used as ornamentals.

1. Cercis canadensis L. var. **mexicana** (Rose) M. Hopk. MEXICAN RED-BUD. Fig. 153. Brushy arroyos and canyons, limestone hillsides, mostly scattered trees. Central and S Brewster Co., Chisos Mts.; Dead Horse Mts.; Del Norte Mts.; eastward, prominently in Sanderson Canyon between Lemon Gap and Sanderson. Pecos, Terrell, and Val Verde counties; side canyons of the Lower Canyons of the Rio Grande. 2300–5000 ft.; Mar–Apr. Also Crockett Co. and slightly E on the Edwards Plateau; mts. of N Mex.

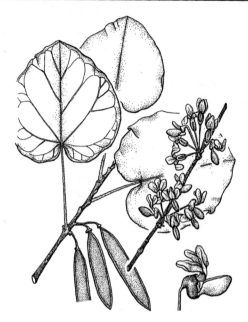

Fig. 153. *Cercis canadensis* var. *mexicana* (Mexican Redbud)

Three varieties of *Cercis canadensis* are recognized in Texas: 1) var. *canadensis,* the Eastern Redbud, of E and N-cen. TX, and throughout the E U.S. and part of Can. 2) var. *texensis* (S. Wats.) M. Hopk., the Texas Redbud, of the Edwards Plateau, E Plains Country, N-cen. TX, to OK and 3) var. *mexicana,* the Mexican Redbud, distinguished by cordate-reniform leaves that are deep green, shiny, and leathery, and wooly-pubescent petioles and young branchlets. Leaves of the Mexican and Texas Redbuds are the same, but in var. *texensis,* the petioles and branchlets are glabrous or nearly so. Leaves of var. *canadensis* are heartshaped in outline with acute tips, and thin, dull-green leaves.

In the Trans-Pecos redbuds are easily spotted near roadside (between Marathon and Sanderson) in early spring because of the attractive pinkish flowers that appear before the leaves. The early blooming is one of the most desirable ornamental aspects of this plant. The acid flowers may be pickled for use in salads or fried as is common in Mexico. The seeds and foliage furnish food for wildlife. A fluid extract from redbud bark, an active astringent, has been used in treating dysentery.

8. SENNA MILL.   SENNA

Herbaceous annuals or perennials, shrubs, or trees or woody vines, especially in the tropics. Leaves once pinnate, without an odd terminal leaflet, leaflets 2–20 (to 60); petiolar gland present or absent. Flowers yellow, rarely white,

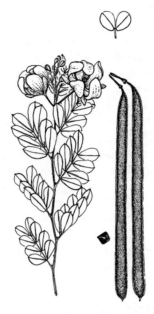

Fig. 154. *Senna wislizeni* (Wislizenus Senna)

in short or elongate clusters, rarely solitary; petals subequal or one larger; stamens 5–10, often unlike, some abortive. Fruit a flat, swollen, or round pod, somewhat woody, indehiscent or dehiscent; seeds few to many.

A large genus of about 400 species, mostly in tropical and subtropical regions of both hemispheres, with several species also occurring in the southwestern and eastern United States. Until recently most sennas were included in the genus *Cassia*. Eighteen species are found in Texas. Many tree species of the tropics are used for timber, and as shade trees on plantations. Various species are used for ornamentals, pharmaceuticals, and as soil conditioners. The raw seeds especially and perhaps whole plants of at least some species may be poisonous.

1. **Senna wislizeni** (Gray) Irwin & Barneby. WISLIZENUS SENNA. Fig. 154. [*Cassia wislizeni* Gray]. Mostly igneous soils, scattered in Chihuahuan Desert scrub. Presidio Co., Pinto Canyon; Chinati Mts.; above Capote Falls; Ruidosa; head of Colorado Canyon; Bofecillos Mts.; Casa Piedra road, 60 mi S of Marfa. Culberson Co., about 15 mi N of Indian Hot Springs. 3000–4000 ft.; May–Jul. SE AZ, S NM; also N Mex.

There are eight species of *Senna* in the Trans-Pecos. *Senna wislizeni* is the only true shrub, with plants 1.5–3 m high, and clusters of yellow flowers above dark stems with small leaflets. In other parts of Texas, *S. corymbosa* and *S. alata* are also shrubs, both introduced. The other six Trans-Pecos sennas are herbaceous perennials, some of them with woody roots. The largest of the Trans-Pecos herbs, *S. lindheimeriana* (Scheele) Irwin & Barneby (Lindheimer Senna), reaches 1–2 m tall, often with the bushy aspect of a shrub and has angulate stems and 5–8 pairs of leaflets with glands between most pairs. Four other Trans-Pecos sennas have 1 pair of leaflets: *S. pumilio* (Gray) Irwin & Barneby (Dwarf Senna), with solitary flowers and grasslike leaves; *S. roemeriana* (Scheele) Irwin & Barneby (Roemer Senna), with lanceolate leaflets, the most common senna in the Trans-Pecos; *S. bauhinioides* (Gray) Irwin & Barneby (Shrubby Senna), occasionally a subshrub with curved pods and leaflet hairs not more than 2 mm long; and *S. durangensis* (Rose) Irwin & Barneby (Durango Senna), with essentially straight pods, leaflet hairs 3–5 mm long, and distribution in lower Brewster and Presidio counties. *Senna orcuttii* (Britt. & Rose) Irwin & Barneby, endemic in the Del Norte Mts. to near Sanderson in lower Brewster Co., has terete stems, 4–6 pairs of leaflets with glands between only the lowest pair, and long slender pods.

9. PARKINSONIA L.   RETAMA, PALOVERDE

Trees to 10 m high, or shrubs; bark smooth, greenish; branches armed with sharp, slightly recurved spines. Leaves alternate feathery, pinnately twice-compound; petiole very short, whole leaf appearing as two once-compound leaves; pinnae 1–2 pairs, 10–50 cm long, rachis green, flattened ca. 2 mm wide; leaflets 2–4 mm long, numerous. Flowers bright yellow, in short clusters, often appearing solitary, slightly bilaterally symmetrical; sepals and petals 5. Fruit a linear pod, 3–10 cm long, very slightly flattened, somewhat swollen in places, deciduous; seeds few to several, arranged longitudinally in pod.

A genus with about 12–15 species, native in the tropical and subtropical Americas, and in semidesert parts of South America. Foliage, young stems, and pods are eaten by livestock and deer, particularly in times of stress. Another common name for *Parkinsonia* is Jerusalemthorn.

1. **Parkinsonia aculeata** L.   RETAMA.   Fig. 155.   Scattered and infrequent, mostly in sandy areas, southern Trans-Pecos. El Paso Co., Franklin Mts. Presidio Co., Cibolo Creek near Ft. Shafter; near Ruidosa; along the Rio Grande between Lajitas and Presidio. Val Verde Co., between the Pecos and Del Rio; planted as an ornamental especially near the Rio Grande. 1200–4300 ft.; spring–fall. Common and even weedy in S TX, Rio Grande Plains, especially in low areas, perhaps adventive; introduced possibly from S.A.; becoming established and naturalized along the Rio Grande in Presidio Co.; N at least to Williamson Co.; S NM, AZ; N Mex. Retama is subject to periodic freeze damage.

The closely related *Parkinsonia* and *Cercidium* have in the past been merged

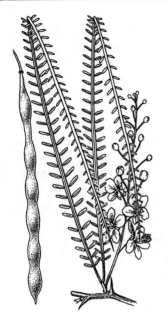

Fig. 155. *Parkinsonia aculeata* (Retama)   Fig. 156. *Cercidium texanum* (Texas Paloverde)

by some workers but maintained by others as separate genera. Lersten and Curtis (1995) have provided anatomical evidence for the separation of *Parkinsonia* and *Cercidium*.

10. CERCIDIUM TUL. RETAMA, PALOVERDE

Trees or shrubs, branches smooth, green, zigzag, with a short, straight spine at each node. Leaves alternate, twice pinnately-compound; pinnae 1–3 pairs, 1–4 cm long; leaflets few pairs, rather pale green, 4–6 mm long. Flowers bright yellow, in racemes 1–3 cm long, or appearing solitary; sepals and petals 5, the petals slightly unequal, slender at the base; stamens 10, separate, uniform. Fruit a flat legume, 1–6 cm long, oblong or linear, somewhat woody; seeds 1 to few.

A genus of about nine species in warmer regions of North and South America, most of the species being adapted to arid or semiarid habitats.

1. **Cercidium texanum** Gray. TEXAS PALOVERDE. Fig. 156. [*Parkinsonia texana* (Gray) S. Wats.]. Locally scattered, usually limestone areas. Val Verde Co., near the Pecos, Langtry, Comstock, and 10 mi N of Del Rio; reported from Brewster Co., Santa Elena crossing below Castolon; planted as an ornamental; more abundant in the semi-desert scrub SE to the Rio Grande Plains and to Starr Co.; spring–summer. Also Coah., N.L., Mex.

Cercidium texanum in Del Rio and vicinity is most commonly known as

Retama according to Jack Skiles of Langtry. This species is closely related to the Border Paloverde, *C. macrum* I. M. Johnst. The hard wood of Retama is used for fuel. Livestock and deer occasionally browse the young leaves and fruit.

11. CAESALPINIA L.

Trees, shrubs, or shrublets, unarmed. Leaves twice pinnate; pinnae 3–30; leaflets 2–10 pairs; stipules small. Flowers yellow or red, showy, in mostly elongate clusters, flower stalks 2–30 mm long; sepals and petals 5, uppermost petals dissimilar; stamens 10, filaments free, often elongate and reddish, hairy or glandular at the base. Fruit flattened, sickleshaped, dehiscent; seeds few to several. [*Erythrostemon* Kl.; *Poincianella* Britt. & Rose; *Pomaria* Cav.; *Schrammia* Britt. & Rose. Some authors include *Hoffmanseggia* in *Caesalpinia*].

A heterogeneous, worldwide genus with about 150 species, most abundant in warmer regions of the Americas. The smaller species resemble *Hoffmanseggia* Cav., a related genus of unarmed perennial herbs. Eleven species occur in Texas, four of these in the Trans-Pecos.

KEY TO THE SPECIES

1. Pinnae 14–30; leaflets glabrous, 7–10 pairs, without orange sessile glands on the lower surface; stamens (filaments) bright red   **1. *C. gilliesii.***
1. Pinnae 3–5; leaflets densely hairy, 2–3 pairs, with orange sessile glands (black on dried specimens); stamens yellowish?   **2. *C. parryi.***

1. Caesalpinia gilliesii (Hook.) Wallich *ex* D. Dietr.   BIRD-OF-PARADISE. Fig. 157. [*Poinciana gilliesii* Wallich]. Widely cultivated in yards and along highways; also an escape in towns and pastures of the Trans-Pecos. A native of Argentina; also in cen. TX, NM, AZ, FL; Mex.

A shrub or rarely small tree to 5 m high, and easily recognized by its yellow flowers with exceedingly long, red filaments of the stamens. The tannins produced by this species, and the seeds, reportedly are poisonous.

2. Caesalpinia parryi (Fisher) Eifert.   PARRY CAESALPINIA.   Fig. 158. [*Hoffmanseggia parryi* (Fisher) B. L. Turner]. Rocky limestone hills, among *Lechuguilla* and desert scrub. Southern Brewster Co., Dead Horse Mts., Heath Canyon, Big Brushy Canyon, Horse Canyon; near Glenn Springs E of the Chisos Mts.; Boquillas Canyon; 3 mi W of Terlingua. 1800–3800 ft. Also adjacent Mex.

Caesalpinia jamesii (T.&G.) Fisher, another Trans-Pecos species, is easily delimited from *C. parryi* as a perennial herb with woody base and 5–10 pairs of leaflets per pinna. Parry Caesalpinia is a small, mostly erect shrub, usually less than 0.5 m high, and with rather small yellow flowers.

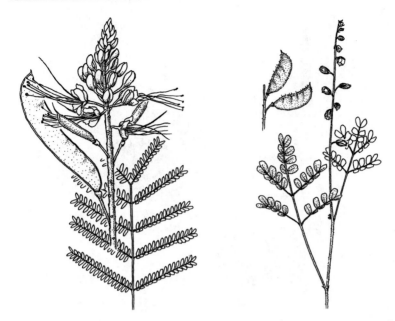

Fig. 157. *Caesalpinia gilliesii* (Bird-of-Paradise)   Fig. 158. *Caesalpinia parryi* (Parry Caesalpinia)

12. SOPHORA L.

Shrubs, trees, or perennial herbs, evergreen or deciduous, unarmed. Leaves once odd-pinnately compound; stipules small, deciduous. Flowers usually in dense, elongated racemes, terminal or axillary; sepals 5, united above the floral cup; corolla bluish-purple, rosy-pink, yellow, or white, strongly irregular; stamens 10, filaments separate above the floral cup. Fruit a woody or fleshy pod, usually indehiscent, elongated and somewhat cylindrical but constricted between the seeds; seeds 1 to several.

A genus of about 70 species distributed in warmer regions of the world. Five species occur in Texas, three of these in the Trans-Pecos, one of them a perennial herb, *Sophora nuttalliana* B. L. Turner.

KEY TO THE SPECIES

1. Leaflets glabrous above, 1.7 cm or more wide   **1. *S. secundiflora.***
1. Leaflets pubescent above, 0.5–1.5 cm wide
                                      2. *S. gypsophila* var. *guadalupensis.*

1. **Sophora secundiflora** (Ort.) Lag. *ex* DC. MESCALBEAN, TEXAS MOUNTAIN LAUREL, FRIJOLILLO. Fig. 159. Usually limestone soils, and usually scattered along bluffs, in canyons, and on slopes. Culberson Co., Guadalupe Mts. Brewster Co., in most mountain systems. Jeff Davis Co., Limpia Canyon;

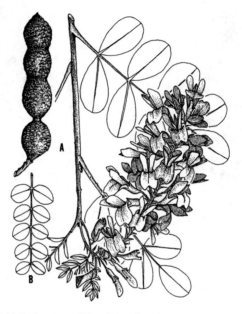

Fig. 159. A) *Sophora secundiflora* (Mescalbean); B) *S. gypsophila*, leaf only.

Musquiz Canyon. Presidio Co., Sierra Vieja. Pecos Co., Glass Mts.; between Ft. Stockton and Sanderson; near Iraan. Terrell Co., in the deep canyons. Val Verde Co., canyons of the Pecos and Rio Grande. 1000–5000 ft.; spring. Also scattered in brushy vegetation across the Edwards Plateau and the Rio Grande Plains; N to Travis Co. and Austin; isolated records from Cameron Co.; NM; N Mex., in the mts. S to S.L.P.

This species is variable in size with shrubs as small as about 1 m or slender trees up to 10 m high, especially in the deeper protected canyons. Mountain Laurel is a desirable ornamental because of its evergreen, lustrous foliage, and showy flowers. The red seeds or mescalbeans have very hard seed coats and were used by Indians as beads for necklace and other jewelry. Indians also exploited narcotic properties of the seeds, crushing them into a powder and mixing small amounts with beverage mescal to produce intoxication. Both seeds and flowers are reported to contain several alkaloids that are poisonous to humans and other animals.

2. **Sophora gypsophila** B. L. Turner & Powell var. **guadalupensis** B. L. Turner & Powell.   Fig. 159.   Limestone soils, Culberson Co., found only on NW slopes of the Guadalupe Mts., upper West Dog Canyon, at about 5000 ft. and on the S end of PX Flat. Plants of this species are often less than 1 m high, with silvery-pubescent foliage, elongated, slender pods, and smallish, some-what flattened seeds, and thus *Sophora gypsophila* is easily distinguished from

S. secundiflora. The var. *guadalupensis* was treated by Correll and Johnston (1970) as *S. formosa* Kearn. & Peeb. (= *S. arizonica* S. Wats.). *Sophora gypsophila* var. *gypsophila* is restricted to a small gypseous outcrop between Coyame and Chihuahua City, Mex. This species makes an attractive ornamental. *Sophora affinis* T.&G. (Texas Sophora or Eve's Necklace), another shrubby species with plants 2–5 m high occurs in limestone habitats of the Edwards Plateau near Kerrville, San Antonio, and Austin, and also near Dallas. The latter deciduous species is recognized by leaves with 13–17 leaflets, white to rosy-pink flowers, and black mature fruit pods.

13. GENISTIDIUM I. M. JOHNST.

Shrubs, usually less than 0.5 m tall, erect, unarmed, deciduous. Leaves alternate, pinnately 3-foliate; leaflets oblanceolate, 5–8 mm long, the terminal one largest, covered with small, appressed hairs; petioles 1–4 mm long; stipules awl-shaped, 1–1.5 mm long. Flowers yellow or reddish on short stalks, in axillary racemes; banner with a greenish eyespot; stamens 10, upper one free, 9 with fused filament. Fruit a flattened, dry dehiscent legume, 2–2.5 cm long, straight.

A monotypic genus with restricted distribution in the Chihuahuan Desert.

1. **Genistidium dumosum** I. M. Johnst. JOHNSTON GENISTIDIUM. Fig. 160. Dry limestone hills, and perhaps in clay soils, between Terlingua and Lajitas in southern Brewster Co., 3 mi W of Terlingua, Reed Plateau. A rare species known only from about 50 plants in Tex. 2700–3500 ft.; Jun–Sep. Described by I. M. Johnston from San Antonio de los Alamos in Coahuila, about 200 miles from the Texas locality, where it is said to be frequent along cliffs of volcanic tuff.

14. AMORPHA L. AMORPHA

Shrubs to ca. 3 m, or perennial herbs with woody bases, often rhizomatous, erect, and unarmed. Leaves alternate, deciduous, once-compound, odd-pinnate, usually more than 8 cm long, leaflets 7 or more, often gland-dotted, 0.4–3 cm wide; stipules slender, early falling; stipels present. Flowers in spike-like clusters; calyx 5-toothed, often gland-dotted; corolla reduced to one petal, the banner, purplish, bluish, or whitish; stamens 10, exserted, filaments, united only at the base. Fruit a gland-dotted pod, 4–8 mm long, indehiscent or tardily dehiscent; seeds 1–2.

A genus of about 20 species, characteristically of wet habitats in temperate North America. The species are of little economic significance.

1. **Amorpha fruticosa** L. BASTARD INDIGO. [*Amorpha occidentalis* Abrams; *A. fruticosa* var. *occidentalis* (Abrams) Kearn. & Peeb.]. Scattered near

Fig. 160. *Genistidium dumosum*
(Johnston Genistidium)

streams in the Trans-Pecos. Presidio Co., near the Rio Grande. Val Verde Co., near Dolan Falls, Devils River. 2200–2500 ft.; spring. A shrub 2–3 m tall with oval or oblong gland-dotted leaflets, and prominent, mostly solitary, purplish spikes of flowers with one petal. NM, AZ, CA, WY; also N Mex.

15. EYSENHARDTIA KUNTH   KIDNEYWOOD

Shrubs to 3.5 m high, much branched, usually unarmed, herbage and flowers gland-dotted and aromatic. Leaves alternate, deciduous, once-compound, odd-pinnate, 1–9 cm long; leaflets 13–47, 3–12 mm long, narrow; stipules short, awlshaped; stipels minute. Flowers white or purplish, in spikelike racemes 1–11 cm long; calyx irregularly lobed; corolla somewhat regular, petals 4–5 mm long; stamens 10, 9 partially fused, the uppermost one free. Fruit a small pod, 5–10 mm long, 1.6–2.5 mm wide, gland-dotted, mostly indehiscent, flattened, with only 1 mature seed.

A genus with about 12 species in the semidesert areas of North America from the southwestern United States to Guatemala. The species are not often grazed by cattle and otherwise are not of much economic value, although the name Kidneywood comes from the use of some Mexican species in the treatment of renal disorders.

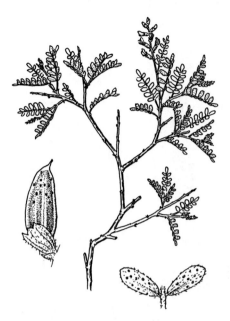

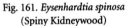

Fig. 161. *Eysenhardtia spinosa*
(Spiny Kidneywood)

Fig. 162. *Eysenhardtia texana*
(Texas Kidneywood)

KEY TO THE SPECIES

1. Leaflets 13–17, 3–4 mm long; leaves 1–3 cm long; shrub less than 1 m high; flowers white or purplish, racemes usually 3 cm or less   **1. *E. spinosa.***
1. Leaflets 15–47, 5–12 mm long; leaves 3–9 cm long; shrub 2–3 m high; flowers white, racemes 3–11 cm long   **2. *E. texana.***

   1. Eysenhardtia spinosa Engelm. SPINY KIDNEYWOOD. Fig. 161. A rare, small shrub, originally known in Texas only by a Hinckley collection from the west end of Capote Peak in Presidio Co., and recently reported also from a small population above the head of Pinto Canyon, and at the top of the Frenchman Hills south of Marfa, Presidio Co. (Warnock, 1977); first collected in Chih., Mex. 5000 ft.; Jul–Oct. The smallish shrubs are about two feet high, and not actually spiny as the species name would imply, but have rather stiff and sharp branches.

   2. Eysenhardtia texana Scheele. TEXAS KIDNEYWOOD, VARA DULCE. Fig. 162. [*Eysenhardtia angustifolia* Penn.]. A scattered to common shrub, usually in brushy vegetation and along arroyos in limestone regions. Brewster Co., Green Gulch in the Chisos Mts., at ca. 5000 ft.; widespread at lower elevations in the E Trans-Pecos; reported from Fern Canyon, Jeff Davis Co. Apr–

Fig. 163. *Psorothamnus scoparius*
(Broom Psorothamnus)

Nov. Extending E to Crockett, San Saba, and Bell counties; the type locality is at New Braunfels in Comal Co.; extending well into Mex.

Dyes have been extracted from the wood of *Eysenhardtia texana*. The wood is fluorescent in water. The plants are browsed by deer and livestock.

16. PSOROTHAMNUS RYDB.

Broomlike shrubs (in our species), to 1 m high, stems gray with short, retrorse, partly scalelike hairs, and with orange blister-glands. Leaves deciduous, 4–20 mm long, mostly simple, a few leaves perhaps with 3 leaflets, the terminal one much larger. Flowers in elongated clusters of 5–15; calyx 3.5–4.5 mm long, gray, the tube 2.2–3 mm long, with orange glands between ribs; petals deciduous, blue or blue-violet (rarely white); stamens 10. Fruit a slightly exserted pod, ca. 4 mm long. *Dalea* L.

A genus of several species segregated from the related *Dalea* (Barneby, 1977). One shrubby species occurs in Texas.

1. **Psorothamnus scoparius** (Gray) Rydb. BROOM PSOROTHAMNUS. Fig. 163. [*Dalea scoparia* Gray]. Dune areas mostly in sand, in hummocks, or in sandy river beds, common in El Paso Co., more scattered in Hudspeth

Co., down the Rio Grande to Ft. Hancock; and in the quartz sand and gypsum dunes 13 mi E of Dell City. 3700–4600 ft.; May–Sep. S NM and AZ; Chih. and Coah., Mex.

This species often occurs in dune habitats with mesquite and *Larrea*, helping to arrest the sand and form hummocks. The broomlike plants are almost leafless, truly leafless in the summer, and are distinguished by stems with retrorsely appressed hairs and speckled with orange glands, and many small clusters of blue flowers. The plants are drought resistant and could become a favorite ornamental in sandy soils.

17. DALEA L.   DALEA

Shrubs or herbs, perennial or annual, unarmed. Leaves alternate, once-compound, odd-pinnate, rarely palmately trifoliate; leaflets gland-dotted; stipules and stipels present, the stiples may be reduced to glands. Flowers in terminal racemes, spikes, or heads, colors various including yellows and purples; calyx cupped, gland-dotted, often ribbed; corolla papilionaceous, in a few species obscurely so, uppermost petal attached near rim of floral cup, other 4 petals of variable attachment, often from the base or side of the stamen tube; stamens 5–10, filaments united into a tube. Fruit a dry pod, dehiscent, slightly if at all flattened, mostly within the persistent calyx or slightly protruding; seeds 1–2. [*Parosela* Cav.; *Petalostemum* Michx.].

A genus with 250 to 300 species widely distributed in warmer regions of North and South America. Twenty-three species of *Dalea* occur in Texas, with about one-fourth of these being shrubs. Twenty *Dalea* species are known to occur in the Trans-Pecos, four of these being shrubby. The Daleas are of little economic importance although some of the shrubs, such as *D. formosa* and *D. frutescens*, are browsed by livestock.

KEY TO THE SPECIES

1. Foliage and branches green, glabrous.
  2. Calyx lobes as long as the tube or longer   **1. *D. formosa.***
  2. Calyx lobes much shorter than the tube   **2. *D. frutescens.***
1. Foliage and branches grayish with rather dense hairs.
  3. Plants straggling, the stems (along the ground with upturned tips) decumbent and rooting at the nodes; calyx lobes lanceolate, 1–3 mm long   **3. *D. greggii.***
  3. Plants with erect stems; calyx lobes triangular, 0.5–1 mm long
       4. *D. bicolor* var. *argyrea.*

1. Dalea formosa Torr.   FEATHER DALEA.   Fig. 164.   [*Parosela formosa* (Torr.) Vail]. Throughout the Trans-Pecos, particularly in rocky limestone soils, also in soils of igneous derivation. 2000–6500 ft.; Mar–Sep. E and S to

Fig. 164. *Dalea formosa* (Feather Dalea)   Fig. 165. *Dalea frutescens* (Black Dalea)

Taylor, Kimble, and Webb counties, N to the uppermost Panhandle in the Plains Country; OK, W to AZ; Son., Chih., Coah., Mex.

A low shrub up to 1 m high, attractive when in flower, and the plants may flower for several months. Feather Dalea, so-called because of the featherlike lobes of the calyx cup, is not widely used as an ornamental but might well serve in that manner. This is a host species of the tiny parasitic flowering plant, *Pilostyles thurberi*, appearing in some Trans-Pecos populations.

2. **Dalea frutescens** Gray.   BLACK DALEA.   Fig. 165.   [*Parosela frutescens* (Gray) Vail; *Dalea frutescens* var. *laxa* B. L. Turner]. Widespread in the Trans-Pecos, especially at moderate to higher elevations in the Davis Mts. and Chisos Mts., Brewster, Jeff Davis, Presidio, and Culberson (Guadalupe Mts.) counties; at somewhat lower elevations in Pecos, Terrell, and Val Verde counties. 2100–6800 ft.; Jul–Oct. E to cen. TX and NE TX, vicinity of Dallas Co., usually on dry limestone hills in brushy areas; SE OK, NM; Chih., Coah., Mex.

Black Dalea is a low, often spreading shrub up to 1 m high, but frequently exhibits a rather herbaceous aspect. Trans-Pecos populations frequently host *Pilostyles thurberi* on the lower stems.

3. **Dalea greggii** Gray.   GREGG DALEA.   Fig. 166.   [*Parosela greggii* (Gray) Heller]. Scattered in rocky limestone hills, SE Trans-Pecos. Brewster Co., Mt. Ord; Pena Colorado; Dead Horse Mts. Pecos Co., Glass Mts.; near Fort Stock-

Fig. 166. *Dalea greggii* (Gregg Dalea)

Fig. 167. *Dalea bicolor* var. *argyrea*
(Silver Dalea)

ton; Sierra Madera; near Longfellow. Terrell Co., 8 mi E of Dryden. 2000–4500 ft.; Mar–Aug. Also Chih., Coah., and much of N to S Mex.

Plants of this species are low grayish subshrubs with thick basal stems, the stems rooting at the nodes and often forming colonies to one meter or more across. Gregg Dalea with purplish flowers is easily distinguished from Silver Dalea, also with densely pubescent stems and foliage, in that the latter plants are erect.

4. **Dalea bicolor** Humb. & Bonpl. *ex* Willd. var. **argyrea** (Gray) Barneby. SILVER DALEA. Fig. 167. [*Parosela argyrea* (Gray) Heller; *Dalea argyrea* Gray]. Scattered, mostly on rocky limestone hills. Culberson Co., Guadalupe Mts. Presidio Co., foothills of the Chinati Mts., Doll Canyon, Wildhorse Canyon. Brewster Co., Marathon. Val Verde Co. 1500–5000 ft.; Jul–Sep. S NM: Chih., Coah., N.L., Mex. An erect shrub to 1 m high, reportedly poisonous to livestock (Turner, 1959). The flowers are yellow (banner) and purple.

18. BRONGNIARTIA KUNTH   BRONGNIART

Shrubs or woody based perennials, unarmed. Leaves alternate, once compound, odd-pinnate, glabrous, petiolate; stipules lanceolate; leaflets in *Brongniartia minutifolia*, linear, revolute, numerous, 2–5 mm long. Flowers solitary,

Fig. 168. *Brongniartia minutifolia*
(Littleleaf Brongniart)

stalks 6–15 mm long; calyx tube ca. 8 mm long; corolla yellow with a tinge of green in our species, purplish to cream colored elsewhere; banner nearly round, 8 mm long; stamens 10, filaments fused half their length. Fruit a dry, flattened pod, glabrous, dehiscent, 1.8–2.5 cm long.

A genus with about 30 species mostly in the drier parts of tropical America, of little or no economic importance.

1. Brongniartia minutifolia S. Wats.   LITTLELEAF BRONGNIART.   Fig. 168. Uncommon, known in the United States only from Brewster Co., Big Bend Park, arroyos, blackish sandy soil and perhaps also limestone soil, between the old Solis Ranch and Cow Heaven Mt., N around Mariscal Mt., S of Talley Mt.; between San Vicente and the Lindsey Mine; river road, from ca. 6 mi W of Boquillas hwy. to Solis turnoff; between Glenn Springs and San Vicente. 2300–3500 ft.; Jun–Aug. Also adjacent Chih., Mex.

An attractive shrub, more or less one meter high, with numerous, small leaflets and yellow-green flowers.

19. PETERIA GRAY   PETERIA

Herbaceous perennials, with slender, pale green, stiff, glabrous stems. Leaves (in *Peteria scoparia*) alternate, once-compound, odd-pinnate, 5–10 cm

Fig. 169. *Peteria scoparia* (Rush Peteria)

long; stipules spinescent, in pairs, 2–6 mm long; leaflets 9–15, usually falling in dry periods. Flowers in loose clusters; corolla 1.3–1.6 cm long, white (or blue); stamens 10, 9 of the filaments fused, upper one free. Fruit a linear legume, 3.5–6 cm long, 4–5 mm wide, dehiscent.

A genus of only four species, occurring in NV, UT, AZ, NM, and S to cen. Mex.

1. Peteria scoparia Gray.   RUSH PETERIA, CAMOTE DEL MONTE.   Fig. 169.
An infrequent species, usually in protected arroyos, lower mountain habitats. El Paso Co., Franklin Mts. Culberson Co., lower Pine Canyon. Presidio Co., 3 mi S and 5 mi E of Marfa; oak-capped hills at S end of Sierra Vieja. Jeff Davis Co., Scenic Loop near Bloys Encampment. Brewster Co. 4000–6000 ft.; Jul–Aug. NM, AZ.; Chih., Coah. (Sierra del Carmen), Mex.

The plant with slender, greenish stems is mostly herbaceous but often shrubby in aspect. The plants of Trans-Pecos Texas have whitish flowers with purplish and yellow tinges, although Don Kolle recently located in Jeff Davis Co. a small population with blue flowers. In species related to *Peteria scoparia* the roots are tuberous (meaning of the Spanish name), somewhat like sweet potatoes, and reportedly are edible. *Peteria scoparia* of the Trans-Pecos also forms tuberous roots but the palatability of these tubers is not known.

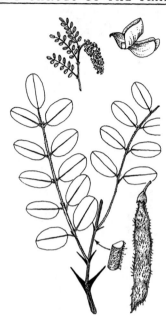

Fig. 170. *Robinia neomexicana*
(NewMexico Locust)

20. ROBINIA L. LOCUST

Trees to 10 m high or shrubs, often sprouting from the roots; usually armed with paired, spinescent stipules, these nearly straight and to 1 cm long. Leaves alternate 5–30 cm long, once compound, odd-pinnate, deciduous in fall; leaflets 7–19, elliptic or nearly so; stipels early falling. Flowers in axillary clusters, these short and pendulous; calyx bellshaped; corolla white to reddish; stamens 10, 9 with filaments fused and the upper one partially free. Fruit a dry, flattened legume, broadly linear, dehiscent; seeds few to several.

A genus of about 10 species in to the temperate regions of Mexico and the United States. Some species are widely cultivated outside native ranges.

1. Robinia neomexicana Gray. NEWMEXICO LOCUST. Fig. 170. Usually in limestone habitats along arroyos or streams, and high into the conifer zone, rare in the Trans-Pecos. El Paso Co., Franklin Mts. Hudspeth Co., Panther Peak, Eagle Mts. in igneous soil. Culberson Co., Guadalupe Mts., Pine Canyon; Pine Top Mt.; 1 mi W Pine Springs Station; South McKittrick Canyon; the Bowl. 5000–8000 ft.; spring. Also AZ and NM N to CO and UT and W to NV; Son., Mex.

Probably this is the only species of *Robinia* native to Texas. The Black Locust, *R. pseudoacacia* L., is widely cultivated in the Trans-Pecos and elsewhere in Texas. The Newmexico Locust is an infrequent or rare low shrub from less than one meter to nearly three meters high. The plants in Culberson Co. and the Eagle Mts. are of var. **neomexicana** (Kartesz, 1994). The plants are good browse for livestock, deer, and other wildlife. *Robinia neomexicana* has been cultivated for erosion control or other purposes. Correll & Johnston (1970) caution against the cultivation of *R. pseudoacacia*, as a weedy, root-sprouting nuisance, but the plants reportedly are high in protein and therefore nutritious browse for domesticated and wild animals, although bark, leaves and seeds may at times be poisonous.

21. ALHAGI GAGNEBIN CAMELTHORN

Shrubs to about 1 m high, much branched, thorny, glabrous, spreading by rhizomes. Leaves alternate, simple, small, linear to narrowly obovate. Flowers numerous in short racemes; calyx tube with 5 lobes; corolla purplish-pink. Fruit a flattened, indehiscent pod with 1 to several segments but these not separating at maturity.

A genus of three species native to desert areas of central and western Asia.

1. **Alhagi maurorum** Medik. CAMELTHORN. Fig. 171. [*Alhagi camelorum* Fisch.]. Along irrigation ditches, drainage canals, and often along salty streams in gypseous soils, recently established in the Trans-Pecos originally from Asia. El Paso Co. Culberson Co. Reeves Co., 5 mi W Pecos; Screw Bean Draw, 18 mi W of Orla. 2700 ft.; Jun–Aug. Desert parts of NM, AZ, CA. Reportedly an important browse plant in Asia, but here thought to be a potentially undesirable weed because its spreading rhizomes prevent easy eradication.

24. KRAMERIACEAE DUM. RATANY FAMILY

Low shrubs or perennial herbs; stems much-branched, often somewhat thornlike; herbage often grayish-pubescent. Leaves alternate, simple usually linear; petioles short or absent; stipules absent. Flowers purplish or reddish, solitary, sometimes clustered, bilaterally symmetrical; sepals 4 or 5 zygomorphic; petals unequal, the upper 3 largest, separate or partly united, with petiolelike bases, the 2 other petals smaller, reddish, pink, or orange, glandlike; ovary with 2 carpels; stamens 4. Fruit a roundish pod, indehiscent, armed with straight, sharp prickles; seed 1.

A family of one genus and 17 species (Simpson, 1989) distributed from the southern United States to Chile, with most species occurring in arid regions of Mexico. Traditionally *Krameria* has been treated as a member of Fabaceae,

Fig. 171. *Alhagi maurorum* (Camelthorn)

subfamily Caesalpinioideae, but modern information suggests that *Krameria* is not at all related to the legumes but is possibly closer to the Polygalaceae. The kramerias are not of much economic importance although the smaller shrubs are occasionally valuable browse plants. All species probably are hemiparasites rooted on mostly woody plants.

1. KRAMERIA L.   RATANY

Four species of the genus (characters of the family) occur in Texas and all of them are found in the Trans-Pecos. The key is adapted after Simpson (1989), who monographed the family.

KEY TO THE SPECIES

1. Perennial herb from a woody base; stems decumbent   **1. *K. lanceolata.***
1. Low shrubs or subshrubs; stems erect or ascending.
    2. Sepals reflexed; 3 petaloid petals narrowly oblanceolate, free to the base; 2 glandular petals orbicular to reniform, dorsal surfaces entirely covered with equal-sized round blisters; fruit spines bearing a whorl of amber-colored retrorse barbs near the tip   **4. *K. grayi.***
    2. Sepals not reflexed; 3 petaloid petals narrowed at the base and united basally; 2 glandular petals oblanceolate or cuneate, with blisters in vertical

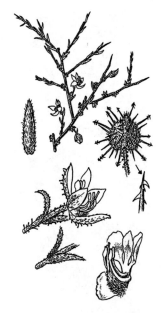

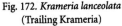

Fig. 172. *Krameria lanceolata*   Fig. 173. *Krameria erecta* (Range Krameria),
(Trailing Krameria)   glandular form

striations on upper or distal portion of dorsal surface; fruit spines with retrorse barbs scattered below the tip, or glabrous.

3. Leaves linear to linear-lanceolate, often with glandular trichomes
                                                              2. K. erecta.

3. Leaves much reduced, almost scalelike and in tufts, without glandular trichomes   **3. K. ramosissima.**

1. Krameria lanceolata Torr. TRAILING KRAMERIA. Fig. 172. In several books the name *Krameria secundiflora* has been used incorrectly for *K. lanceolata* Torr.; the most widespread *Krameria* in Texas, this species is abundant in the Trans-Pecos and the state except for the sandy, wet, dense pine forests of extreme E Texas. According to Turner (1959) populations of *K. lanceolata* along the Gulf Coast have more succulent leaves than is typical for the species in drier regions. In the field this species is easily recognized as the only herbaceous Texas species of *Krameria.*

2. Krameria erecta Willd. *ex* Schult. RANGE KRAMERIA. Fig. 173. [*Krameria glandulosa* Rose & Painter; *K. parvifolia* Benth.]. A low shrub, less than 1 m high, common in desert habitats in the Trans-Pecos, found in every county, 2800–5800 ft.; spring–fall. Also W to CA; Baja Calif., northern Mex.

 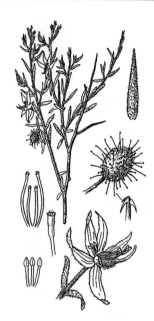

Fig. 174. *Krameria ramosissima* (Calderona)   Fig. 175. *Krameria grayi* (White Krameria)

Krameria erecta is closely related to *K. ramosissima*, which has a more southern distribution, reaching only the southeastern edge of the Trans-Pecos.

3. Krameria ramosissima (Gray) S. Wats. CALDERONA. Fig. 174. Locally abundant in rocky or gravelly limestone soils in the SE Trans-Pecos, but otherwise rare or missing in this region. Val Verde Co., 20 mi W of Del Rio; common in the vicinity of Del Rio, associated with *Cercidium texanum* and other low, spring shrubs. Brewster Co., one report from SE corner of county. Spring–fall. Also S mostly near the Rio Grande, to Hidalgo Co.; Coah., N.L., Tam., Mex.

4. Krameria grayi Rose & Painter. WHITE KRAMERIA, CHACATE. Fig. 175. Low shrub, less than 1 m high, common in desert habitats in the Trans-Pecos, all soil types, known or expected in every county. 1000–5000 ft.; spring–fall. W in NV, AZ, and CA; Baja Calif., northern Mex.

This species and *Krameria erecta* both occur commonly in desert scrub communities of the Trans-Pecos, *K. grayi* being readily distinguished in flower by its conspicuously reflexed sepals and triad of separate petals and two often orange glandlike petals inside the petaloid petals. White Krameria furnishes excellent browse. Indians extracted a reddish dye from the roots to stain baskets and other items. This dye has also been exploited commercially in the production of aniline stain. Indians used an extract of the herbage to treat sore eyes.

25. ZYGOPHYLLACEAE R. BR. CALTROP FAMILY

Shrubs, rarely small trees, annual or perennial herbs, prostrate to upright; stipules present. Leaves opposite or alternate (rarely clustered at nodes), once-compound, even-pinnate usually with opposite leaflets, rarely irregularly pinnatifid. Flowers perfect, regular, usually solitary, rarely clustered; sepals 4–5, separate; petals 4–5, separate; stamens 10–15, usually in 2 whorls; filaments bearing basal scales, separate or outer row fused at base to petals; disc usually apparent; ovary superior 2–5- or 10-lobed and -loculed; placentation axillary; single style usually persisting to form a beak on fruit. Fruit a capsule, lobed or winged, dehiscent or separating into 5–10 indehiscent seedlike carpels; seeds 1 to many per locule.

A family of about 250 species arranged in about 27 genera, widely distributed and with a number of relict genera found mostly in the warmer, arid regions. Six genera, three herbaceous (*Tribulus, Kallstroemia,* and *Peganum*) and three shrubby, occur in Texas and the Trans-Pecos region. One of the shrubs, *Zygophyllum fabogo* L., is a semisucculent that is introduced probably from the Mediterranean region, known in Texas from near El Paso.

KEY TO THE GENERA

1. Leaflets 2; flowers yellow; fruit a 5-lobed, roundish capsule, covered with whitish (to reddish) fuzz   **1. *Larrea.***
1. Leaflets 4–8 pairs; flowers bluish; fruit a 2-lobed, flat capsule, with very small, scattered hairs   **2. *Guaiacum.***

1. LARREA CAV. CREOSOTEBUSH

Shrubs to 3 m high, evergreen, with smell of creosote; nodes of ascending stems prominent. Leaves opposite, nearly sessile; leaflets 2, 5–10 mm long, fused basally, somewhat sickleshaped and leathery, glossy-green. Flowers solitary, bright yellow, ca. 2.5 cm wide; sepals and petals 2; stamens 10, filaments winged. Fruit a roundish capsule ca. 6 mm wide, 5-lobed, woolly with white to reddish hairs; 1 seed in each indehiscent carpel.

A genus of five species, four in the desert regions of South America and one in the southern deserts of North America.

1. **Larrea tridentata** (Sesse & Moc. *ex* DC.) Cov. CREOSOTEBUSH, GOBERNADORA. Fig. 176. [*Larrea mexicana* Moric.; *L. glutinosa* Engelm.; *L. divaricata* of Amer. authors, not Cav.; *L. divaricata* subsp. *tridentata* Felger & Lowe]. A very common and dominant plant especially in alluvial, hardpan soils of the Chihuahuan Desert in Trans-Pecos Texas; flowering in some places almost year-round. Also E to the W Edwards Plateau to Howard Co., S along the Rio Grande to Starr Co.; common throughout the arid regions of the SW U.S. and N Mex., Sonoran, and Mojave Deserts; S. in Mex. to Qro. and Hgo.

Fig. 176. *Larrea tridentata* (Creosotebush)

The North American Creosotebush has long been known as *Larrea tridentata*, but recent extensive studies have suggested that a South American entity *L. divaricata* Cav. dispersed to arid North America (probably the Chihuahuan Desert) from Argentina in Pliocene or Pleistocene times. If the bicontinental entities are conspecific, then the name *L. divaricata* has priority. Other members of the Zygophyllaceae, including the genus *Guaiacum*, also have bicentric distribution in the desert regions of North and South America. Populations of Creosotebush in the Chihuahuan Desert are reported to be diploid ($n = 13$) while those in the Sonoran and Mojave deserts are reported to be polyploid ($n = 26$; $n = 39$), suggesting that original dispersal in arid North America was from east to west. Some clones in the Mojave Desert are estimated to exceed 11,000 years old (Vasek, 1980).

Decoctions from the leaves and branches of Creosotebush have been used in folk medicine for treating various ailments including intestinal disorders, rheumatism, tuberculosis, venereal diseases, kidney and bladder troubles, and as an antiseptic for cuts and sores. According to Mrs. Jeff L. Smith (pers. comm.) strong decoctions are effective in healing difficult abrasions, and in toughening tender or thin skin. The plants are supposedly toxic to sheep, but are seldom browsed by cattle, probably because of a strong odor (especially after rains) and taste. Creosotebush foliage boiled to remove the offensive taste has been mixed with syrup and fed to cattle experimentally, supposedly with some success. The waxy covering of creosote leaves contains a relatively high

Fig. 177. *Guaiacum angustifolium* (Guayacan)

percentage of a powerful and valuable antioxidant substance (nordihydrogua-riaretic acid, NDGA) which might eventually be extracted in large quantities for industrial uses. The NDGA compound is being tested in Scandinavia as a potential treatment for cancer.

2. GUAIACUM L.

Shrubs or small trees to 6 m high, plants usually stout with many crooked branches; stipules persistent. Leaves opposite or bunched at the nodes, 1–3 cm long, pinnate, closed at night or half-folded under hot sun; leaflets 4–8 pairs, dark green and leathery, shiny, linear to linear-spatulate, 5–16 mm long, 2–3 mm wide. Flowers blue to purple, fragrant, 12–22 mm wide; sepals 5; petals 5, ca. 1 cm long; stamens 10. Fruit a flat, leathery capsule, 1–2 cm wide, usually with 2 (rarely 3–4) lobes, margins winged, beaked at the apex, dehiscent between the locules; seeds 1 in each locule, beanlike, shiny, usually bright red.

A genus of about four or five species in North America and South America. The genus name may be correctly spelled *Guajacum* (Kartesz, 1994).

1. **Guaiacum angustifolium** Engelm.   GUAYACAN, SOAPBUSH.   Fig. 177.
[*Porlieria angustifolia* (Engelm.) Gray.]. Arroyos and brushy areas, a rather

common shrub near the Rio Grande. Presidio Co. Brewster Co., as far N as Nine-Point Mesa and Goat Mt. Pecos Co., 30 mi E of Ft. Stockton. Terrell Co., 10 mi E of Dryden. Val Verde Co. 1600–4000 ft.; Mar–Sep. S along the Rio Grande valley, in the brush country to Cameron and Comal counties; also Chih., Coah., N.L., Tam., Mex.

One of the common names, Soapbush, is taken after the use of the root bark in Mexico as a source of soap. Root extracts are also used to treat various ailments such as venereal disease and rheumatism. The densely branched evergreen plants are reported to furnish good browse for livestock and wildlife, and good quail feed. In some areas the wood is used for posts and fuel. The change in generic names, *Porlieria* for *Guaiacum*, is explained by Porter (1974).

26. RUTACEAE JUSS.   CITRUS FAMILY

Shrubs or herbaceous perennials, rarely small trees, armed or unarmed. Leaves opposite or alternate, pinnately or palmately compound, or simple, with aromatic, translucent oil glands (these obscure in *Ptelea*); petioles and/or leaf axes often with winglike margins; stipules absent. Flowers perfect, dioecious, or with both unisexual and bisexual flowers on the same plant; sepals 4–5, often fused, less often absent or early falling; petals 3–5 (or more), usually overlapping, rarely absent; stamens usually twice (1–3 times) as many as petals; filaments separate or fused basally, if in 2 whorls then outer row opposite the petals; ovary superior, elevated on a disc, usually with 4–5 carpels weakly fused or only basally or apically fused and arranged around a central columella. Fruit a capsule, flattened and circular samara, follicle, or leathery-rind berry (hesperidium), or separating into seedlike carpels, or sometimes a samara, drupe, or winged berry; seeds usually with a bent embryo; much endosperm usually present.

A family of about 150 genera and more than 1000 species, widely distributed in tropical and temperate regions of both hemispheres, but most common in South America and Australia. Economically the family is especially known for the citrus fruits (grapefruit, orange, lemon, lime, etc.) of the genus *Citrus.*

KEY TO THE GENERA

1. Leaves opposite or mostly so; palmately compound   1. *Choisya.*
1. Leaves alternate; simple or compound.
   2. Subshrubs or perennial herbs, 30–80 cm high.
      3. Leaves pinnately or ternately compound; fruit 4–5 celled   2. *Ruta.*
      3. Leaves simple, linear; fruit 2-celled, with appearance of inflated Dutchman's Breeches   3. *Thamnosma.*
   2. Shrubs or small trees, usually exceeding 1 m high.

Fig. 178. *Choisya dumosa* (Mexican Orange)

4. Leaves trifoliolate; fruit flattened with a circular wing   **4. Ptelea.**
4. Leaves pinnately once-compound, with 5–11 leaflets; fruit dividing
into 1–5 folliclelike carpels   **5. Zanthoxylum.**

1. CHOISYA KUNTH   MEXICAN ORANGE

Rounded shrub, 1–2 m high or less, unarmed. Leaves opposite or sub-opposite, palmately compound; leaflets 3–10, linear, 1–5 cm long, leathery, with waxytoothed, glandtipped margins. Flowers perfect, in clusters; sepals 4–5, membranous; petals 4–5, white, ca. 1 cm long. Fruits lobed, gland-dotted separating at maturity into 3–5 leathery carpels; seeds usually single, black, 3–4 mm long, kidneyshaped.

A genus of few species distributed in the mountains of western North America. One species occurs in Texas.

1. Choisya dumosa (Torr.) Gray.   MEXICAN ORANGE, ZORRILLO.   Fig. 178. [Some authors have included this species under *Astrophyllum dumosum* Torr.]. Most commonly found in limestone habitats but also in igneous formations, mountain slopes and canyons. Culberson Co., Guadalupe Mts., North and South McKittrick Canyon; Pine Canyon; near Pine Springs; Delaware Mts. Brewster Co., NW slopes of Goat Mt.; S slopes of Cienega Mt.; vicinity of Alpine; Altuda Mt.; Glass Mts., Old Blue, Baldy Peak, W slopes, Gilliland Peak.

Fig. 179. *Ruta chalepensis* (Rue)

Pecos Co., N slopes, Sierra Madera; Allison Ranch, 38 mi S of Ft. Stockton. 3900–6500 ft.; spring–fall. Also NM; Chih., Coah., Mex.

Crushed leaves of Mexican Orange are very aromatic. This species should be considered for use as an ornamental. Supposedly the plants are seldom if at all browsed, but they are not known to be poisonous. Of three varieties of *Choisya dumosa*, ours is var. **dumosa**.

2. RUTA L.   RUE

Woody based highly aromatic, perennial herbs, less than 1 m high; unarmed; crushed leaves strongly malodorous. Leaves alternate, 2–3 pinnately or ternately divided, gland-dotted. Flowers perfect, in loose clusters; sepals persistent, 3–4 mm long; petals yellow or greenish, 5–9 mm long; disk 8–10-lobed, thick; stamens 8–10, in pairs. Fruit a capsule, 4–5-celled.

A genus of about 50 species, primarily in the Mediterranean region and Asia, with at least two widely distributed, weedy species in Texas and elsewhere.

1. Ruta chalepensis L.   RUE, RUDA.   Fig. 179.   In the Trans-Pecos one known collection, Presidio Co., near abandoned adobe huts on limestone hills 2 mi S of Shafter, near open mines 4400 ft., said by the collector to be

Fig. 180. *Thamnosma texana* (Texas Desertrue)

"probably cultivated." Rare on Edwards Plateau; native of N Africa; widely introduced.

3. THAMNOSMA TORR. & FREM. DUTCHMAN'S BREECHES.

Subshrubs or perennial herbs, usually less than 35 cm high; unarmed. Leaves alternate, simple, linear, gland-dotted and aromatic when crushed. Flowers perfect, purplish (with a yellowish center) west of the 100th meridian, canary-yellow east of the 100th meridian; sepals and petals 4; stamens 8. Fruit leathery, 2-lobed, 3–8 mm long, resembling inflated "dutchman's breeches."

A genus of about five species distributed mostly in arid North America, but also with one species in South Africa and one species in Socotra in the Gulf of Aden.

1. **Thamnosma texana** (Gray) Torr. TEXAS DESERTRUE, RUDA DEL MONTE. Fig. 180. The purple flowered form of the species, *Thamnosma texana* f. *purpurea* (Woot. & Standl.) Lundell has in the past been recognized as a distinct species (*Rutosma purpurea* Woot. & Standl.; *Thamnosma aldrichii* Tharp). Common but scattered mostly in the more desertic lowlands, plains, and mountains, in all counties of the Trans-Pecos. 2000–4650 ft.; spring–fall.

Fig. 181. *Ptelea trifoliata* (Skunkbush)

E to cen. TX, S to the Rio Grande Plains, N to S parts of the Plains Country; NM, AZ, CO; N Mex.

4. PTELEA L.   HOPTREE

Shrubs or small trees to 7 m high, mostly dioecious but also with bisexual flowers on some plants, unarmed, deciduous, unpleasantly aromatic; epidermal layer and bark light-colored. Leaves alternate, trifoliolate, the leaflets basically ovate but variable, 2–6 cm long. Flowers greenish-white, in loose, terminal clusters; sepals and petals 4–6, petals 4–6 mm long; stamens 4–6, alternate with petals, vestigial in pistillate flowers. Fruit flattened, circular, an indehiscent samara with a wing all around.

A genus of three species restricted to North America. One species, highly variable in many characters including leaf shape and size, and in fruit size, occurs in Texas.

1. Ptelea trifoliata L.   SKUNKBUSH, COMMON HOPTREE, WAFERASH, COLA DE ZORRILLO.   Fig. 181.   Locally common in several localities, variable in habitat and habit. El Paso Co., Franklin Mts.; Hueco Mts. Hudspeth Co., Reed Hill NE of Sierra Blanca. Culberson Co., Guadalupe Mts., Panther Peak of Eagle Mts. Jeff Davis Co., Mt. Livermore, Madera Canyon; Limpia Canyon;

Haystack Mt. Brewster Co., Chisos Mts.; Packsaddle Mt.; Mt. Ord; Ranger Canyon; Cathedral Mt. Presidio Co., Chinati Mts.; rim of the Sierra Vieja. Val Verde Co., 22 mi N of Comstock; Devils River; Amistad Dam.

In Correll and Johnston (1970) the Trans-Pecos populations of this highly variable species are treated as subsp. **angustifolia** (Benth.) Bailey var. **angustifolia** (Benth.) M. E. Jones. Fruits of this species allegedly were used as a substitute for hops in brewing beer.

5. ZANTHOXYLUM L. PRICKLYASH

Shrubs or trees, branches and even foliage armed with slightly curved prickles, dioecious or with both unisexual and bisexual flowers. Leaves alternate, once-compound; leaflet margins with blunt or acute teeth and glands in the marginal notches; flowers small, yellow-green, in clusters; sepals (if present), petals, and stamens 4–5, the latter alternate with petals, and only vestigial in pistillate flowers. Fruit a dry follicle 5–8 mm long, opening in two valves exposing 1 glossy-black seed. [*Fagara* L.; "Xanthoxylum" is an incorrect spelling of the genus name].

A genus of about 160 species distributed throughout tropical and subtropical regions. The bark, leaves, and fruit have long been used medicinally, especially in Latin America, for treatment of various ailments including toothaches, intestinal problems, and rheumatism.

KEY TO THE SPECIES

1. Leaflets 7–9, 0.6–1.2 cm long; short-hairy, marginal glands ca. 1 mm apart; sepals absent, petals 4   **1. Z. parvum.**
1. Leaflets 5–11, 1–4 cm long; glabrous, marginal glands 1–4 mm apart; sepals and petals 5   **2. Z. hirsutum.**

1. Zanthoxylum parvum Shinners SHINNERS' TICKLETONGUE. Fig. 182. Evidently a rare species with still nothing known about the staminate flowers and fruit. The type collection, *McVaugh 7890*, a shrub 1.5 m high, with pistillate flowers, was from Jeff Davis Co., Limpia Canyon near Wild Rose Pass, ca. 15 mi NE of Ft. Davis, under N-facing high cliffs, 10 Apr 1947. Another collection, *Warnock & Turner 8089*, was made in the Davis Mts. on the trail to Tricky Gap near the Boy Scout Camp, 5500 ft., 9 Aug 1948. The latter specimens were found in dense oak shinnery; endemic. 4000–5500 ft. Other known localities include: Jeff Davis Co., base of cliffs, N side of Timber Mt.; Pig Pen Canyon, Forbidden Mt.; 6000 ft.

2. Zanthoxylum hirsutum Buckl. TICKLETONGUE, TOOTHACHE TREE, PRICKLYASH. Fig. 182. [*Zanthoxylum clava-herculis* L. var. *fruticosum*

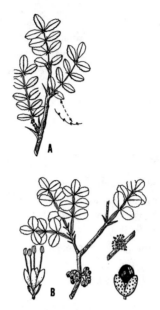

Fig. 182. A) *Zanthoxylum parvum*
(Shinners' Tickletongue); B) *Z. hirsutum*
(Tickletongue)

(Gray) S. Wats.]. Infrequent in limestone canyons. Brewster Co., upper reaches of Mexican Canyon, C. F. Cox ranch. Pecos Co., Richardson ranch near Iraan. Terrell Co., Independence Creek. Val Verde Co., 18 mi N of Langtry; frequent shrubs or rarely small trees, E in brushy areas of the Edwards Plateau, N-cen. TX, and lower parts of the Plains Country, S to sandy soils of the Rio Grande Plains. 1800–4000 ft.; spring. The Trans-Pecos collections of this species, if identified accurately, have essentially glabrous leaflets, but rather densely hairy petioles and rachis. Also AR, OK.

27. SIMAROUBACEAE DC.   QUASSIA FAMILY

Trees or spiny shrubs, usually dioecious, young branches somewhat hairy, bark usually bitter. Leaves alternate, pinnately compound, rarely simple, without glands, absent on mature branches in some species (*Holacantha*). Flowers unisexual or bisexual, clustered or in loose panicles; sepals and petals 3–8, or absent; stamen number equal or double the number of petals, with the outer series opposite, filaments separate often with basal scales. Fruit various but in our species (schizocarpous) the capsulelike fruit walls splitting into

1-seeded sections (mericarps), becoming samaralike (*Ailanthus*, 3–5 cm long), or drupelike.

A family of about 20 genera and 120 species widely distributed in both hemispheres. The bitter principle in the bark of most species is used to prepare various bitter substances. *Ailanthus altissima* (Mill.) Swingle (Tree-of-Heaven; Copal Tree) is a widely naturalized ornamental introduced from Asia, a tree to 20 m high, with long (to 65 cm) pinnate leaves and clusters of reddish, samaralike fruit. In Texas the highly allelopathic (Lawrence, 1991) Tree-of-Heaven is found mostly in eastern parts, but also is found in yards, alleyways, and waste places in Sanderson, Marfa, and probably in other towns of the Trans-Pecos. The highly phytotoxic compound, ailanthone, is concentrated in the stem and root bark of *A. altissima*, and has potential for development as a natural product herbicide (Heisey, 1996).

KEY TO THE GENERA

1. Low spinescent shrubs with well-developed leaves   **1. *Castela.***
1. Sprawling spinescent shrubs with leafless mature stems, or with leaves reduced to early-falling scales   **2. *Holacantha.***

1. CASTELA TURP. GOATBUSH

Low shrubs, to 2 m high, densely branched, the branchlets often ending in a spine and otherwise spinescent, young branches grayish white, the bark very bitter; plants mostly dioecious. Leaves rather spatulate, to 2.5 cm long but usually shorter, subsessile, somewhat leathery, upper surface shiny, lower surface grayish, the margins strongly rolled underneath. Flowers red, pink, or orange externally, yellowish inside, 3–4 mm long, solitary or clustered in the stem axils; sepals and petals 4–5; stamens 8–10, attached to a fleshy disk. Fruit at maturity spreading into 4 drupelike mericarps, these bright red and 6–10 mm long, roundish but slightly flattened.

A genus of about 13 species, mostly in the tropical Americas.

1. Castela erecta Turp. subsp. **texana** (T. & G.) Cronq. ALLTHORN GOATBUSH, AMARGOSO. Fig. 183. [*Castela texana* (T. & G.) Rose; *C. tortuosa* Liebm.]. Rocky limestone hills, in brushy areas. Val Verde Co., Shumla; vicinity of Langtry; near the mouth of Devils River. Terrell Co., Lozier Canyon, 23 mi E of Dryden. 1300–1800 ft.; Apr–May. E to Travis Co., S to Cameron Co.; Coah., S.L.P., Mex.

In Mexico extracts of the bark are used in folk remedies for various ailments including dysentery, fever, yellow jaundice, and skin disorders. The extract reportedly is effective in killing *Endamoeba histolytica*, the cause of amebic dysentery.

Fig. 183. *Castela erecta* subsp. *texana*
(Allthorn Goatbush)

2. HOLACANTHA GRAY   CRUCIFIXION THORN

Sprawling low shrubs usually less than 1 m high, with many, tangled, gray-green, leafless branches; dioecious; branchlets ending in rigid spines; younger stems with sparse to densely matted silky hairs; a single axillary bud at the base of branchlets. Leaves absent or scalelike and early falling. Flowers unisexual, in dense clusters; sepals 6, ca. 1 mm long; petals 6, ca. 4 mm long, fleshy; stamens ca. 12 or more. Fruit clustered, persistent for 1–2 years 8–9 mm long, acute and ridged, red, tan, or green, shiny and smooth; carpels 6.

A genus of two species, one of Trans-Pecos Texas and northern Mexico and the other, *Holacantha emoryi* A. Gray, restricted to Arizona and California.

1. Holacantha stewartii C. H. Muell.   CRUCIFIXION THORN.   Fig. 184. [*Castela stewartii* (C. H. Muell.) Moran & Felger]. Gravel and clay hills, flats, and arroyos. Brewster Co., mostly in Big Bend Park, Paint Gap Hills; Dagger Flat; 1 mi S of Government Springs; mesa 1.7 mi W of Sublett ranch; creosote flats between Glenn Springs and Lindsey Mine; Christmas Mts.; Solitario area; also in clay soil, top of Reed Plateau, W of Terlingua; Presidio Co., Eagle Canyon below Redford. 2300–4000 ft.; spring–summer. Mex., Coah., near Santa Elena, and other localities, Chih., and Zac., near Hacienda de Cedros.

The genus name *Holacantha* means "wholly thorn" in reference to the stiff, pointed branchlets of the plants, but this species is not to be confused with

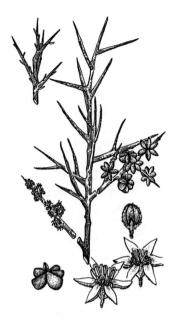

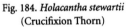

Fig. 184. *Holacantha stewartii*   Fig. 185. *Melia azedarach* (Chinaberry Tree)
(Crucifixion Thorn)

another "allthorn" genus, *Koeberlinia*, of another family, and with which it often associates. Further discussion of this species is given by Muller (1941). Van Devender et al. (1978) report abundant fossil evidence of this species in a packrat midden near Shafter in Presidio Co.

28. MELIACEAE JUSS.   MAHOGANY FAMILY

Trees or shrubs with hard, scented wood. Leaves usually compound and without stipules. Flowers with 8–10 stamens fused in a tube. Fruit a capsule or drupe.

A family of about 50 genera and more than 500 species, mostly in tropical regions. One species, a native of Asia, *Melia azedarach* L., the Chinaberry Tree (Fig. 185), occurs widely in the southern United States and Texas as an introduced cultivar and escapee. In the Trans-Pecos the Chinaberry Tree is grown as shade-ornamental in the yards of many towns. The Chinaberry Tree in our region reaches about 10 m high with bipinnate leaves 30 cm or more long, white to pale-lavender flowers, 1 cm long, and clusters of round, yellow fruits (drupes). Recently the fruits of the Chinaberry Tree have been shown to contain a powerful insecticide called azadirachtin. Reportedly both the fruit and bark are poisonous.

29. MALPIGHIACEAE JUSS.   MALPIGHIA FAMILY

Trees, shrubs, or vines, plants usually with one-celled hairs attached in the middle. Leaves opposite, often with petiole glands; blades with smooth or rough margins, or less often lobed. Flowers usually perfect, some usually self-fertilizing without opening (cleistogamous); sepals (usually with glands) and petals 5, the petals with slender bases; stamens 5–10, perhaps some sterile; styles 3, or reduced to 2 or 1. Fruit various, often lobed or winged, like a nut, capsule, or drupe, or dividing into 1–3 winged (samaralike) sections.

A family distributed mostly in the tropical and subtropical regions of North and South America, scattered in the Old World tropics, represented by about 60 genera and 1200 species. Four genera occur in Texas, three of these in the Trans-Pecos.

KEY TO THE GENERA

1. Stamens 5, only 2 with anthers; sepals (4 of the 5) with paired glands (in flowers with petals); style single, stout, stigma headlike; flower receptacle more or less pyramidal (in *Janusia*); fruit winged or a crested nutlet.
   2. Plants vinelike with twisted stems; fruit a 1–3-winged samara; flowers never cleistogamous   **1. *Janusia.***
   2. Plants low shrubs with straight stems; fruit a small, crested nutlet; some flowers cleistogamous   **2. *Aspicarpa.***
1. Stamens 10, all fertile; sepals without glands; styles 3, slender, pointed; flower receptacle flattened; fruit a capsule   **3. *Galphimia.***

1. JANUSIA JUSS.

Vinelike, stems slender, herbaceous to woody, somewhat climbing. Leaves opposite; petioles short; blades to 3.5 cm long, 7 mm wide, linear to lanceolate, with covering of appressed hairs, margins entire but with toothlike glands near the base. Flowers small, 2 on a peduncle, each of the 2 individual flower stalks subtended by a bract; sepals 5, petals 5, yellow and becoming reddish-brown with age, the petal margins wavy; flowers with petals (petaliferous), a glandular calyx, a single, stout style, stamens 5, only 2 with anthers; petals 4–6 mm long. Fruit of 1–3 samaras with veiny propellerlike wings; 9–12 mm long.

A genus of 12 species distributed from Argentina to the southwestern United States.

1. Janusia gracilis Gray.   SLENDER JANUSIA, PROPELLERBUSH.   Fig. 186. Widespread but infrequent, limestone, novaculite, igneous habitats, usually on rocky hillsides, a twining half-shrub often draped over another shrub. El Paso Co., Franklin Mts. Hudspeth Co., Beech and Eagle mountains. Presidio Co., Sierra Vieja, SE through the Chinati and Bofecillos mountains. Jeff Davis Co.,

Fig. 186. *Janusia gracilis* (Slender Janusia)

13 mi N of Alpine. Brewster Co., S half of county to the Rio Grande. Terrell Co., mouth of San Francisco Creek. 1800–4600 ft.; Apr–Oct. E to the Colorado River; W to S AZ; also N Mex. Easily recognized by the propellerlike yellow petals, but then this is also true in recognizing the other malpighs of the Trans-Pecos.

2. ASPICARPA RICH. ASPHEAD

Low shrubs, stems slender, erect or reclining. Leaves opposite, with short petioles or sessile, margins of the leaf blades entire. Flowers of 2 kinds; petaliferous flowers on short stalks usually in clusters, 4 of the 5 sepals with prominent glands, stamens 5, usually 2 with anthers, petals roundish, carrot-yellow, some perhaps with a reddish blotch in the center, carpels 3; cleistogamous flowers (not opening) sessile or on long stalks in the axils of lower leaves, calyx without glands. Fruit of petaliferous flowers usually with 3 nutlets, these ridged apically.

A genus of about 12 species distributed from Argentina to the southwestern United States. Three species occur in Texas.

KEY TO THE SPECIES

1. Leaves linear to linear-lanceolate, to 2.5 cm long, 6 mm wide; cleistogamous flowers sessile in leaf axils   **1. *A. hyssopifolia.***

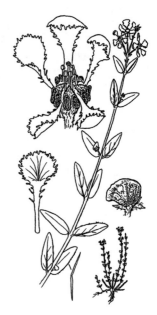

Fig. 187. *Aspicarpa hyssopifolia*   Fig. 188. *Aspicarpa longipes*

1. Leaves ovate, to 4.5 cm long, 1.5 mm wide; cleistogamous flowers on stalks, subtended by 2 leaflike bracts   **2. A. longipes.**

    1. Aspicarpa hyssopifolia Gray.   Fig. 187.   Rocky limestone hills, often among brush. Val Verde Co., Pecos River near the high bridge; Amistad Dam. Terrell Co., 6–9 mi E of Sanderson; 10 mi W of Dryden. Jeff Davis Co., one collection labeled Davis Mts. 1700–6000 ft.; May–Aug. E and S on the Edwards Plateau; also N Mex. Plants are erect shrubs to 30 cm high with numerous slender stems.

    2. Aspicarpa longipes Gray.   Fig. 188.   [*Aspicarpa humilis* (Benth.) Juss.]. Rocky igneous slopes of the mountains. Jeff Davis Co., 6 mi N of Ft. Davis; Merrill Canyon, Davis Mts.; Cox ranch 3 mi SW of Mt. Livermore; 3 mi N of Bloys Campground. 5200–5700 ft.; Jul–Sep. Also N Mex. Plants are more or less decumbent, with numerous stems ascending to about 30 cm high.

3. GALPHIMIA CAV.

    Shrub to 40 cm high, stems slender, mostly glabrous. Leaves opposite with or without petioles, linear to linear lanceolate, rarely oval, to 5.5 cm long, 1.3 cm wide. Flowers yellowish becoming reddish with age, in lax clusters,

Fig. 189. *Galphimia angustifolia*
(Narrowleafed Galphimia)

flower stalks ca. 6 mm long; sepal gland absent or present; petals to 7 mm long, entire or toothed. Fruit a roundish 3-lobed capsule, 3–4 mm long, carpels separating and dehiscent.

A genus of about 12 species centered in Mexico, with extensions into Central America and the West Indies.

1. **Galphimia angustifolia** Benth. NARROWLEAFED GALPHIMIA. Fig. 189. [*Thryallis angustifolia* (Benth.) O. Ktze.]. Rocky limestone hillsides, open or wooded. Val Verde Co., 35 mi N of Del Rio near Loma Alta; also Edwards Plateau; Apr–Oct. Also N Dgo., Coah., Cen. Amer. One species, *Galphimia brasiliensis*, is widespread in South America and is most closely related to *G. angustifolia*.

30. POLYGALACEAE R. BR. MILKWORT FAMILY

Herbaceous annuals or woody-based perennials (in the Trans-Pecos), elsewhere less often small trees or vinelike. Leaves alternate, less often opposite or whorled, simple, perhaps scalelike; without stipules or with small stipular glands. Flowers irregular, in elongated clusters; calyx irregular; sepals usually

5, lower 2 fused, or the sepals separate with inner two larger and somewhat petallike (overall resembling a pea flower); petals 5 but usually only 3 present; stamens 8 or less, filaments fused into a split sheath, basally united with petals, anthers opening usually by terminal pore; ovary superior, carpels usually 2. Fruit a capsule, less often a samara, nut, or drupe; seeds often hairy.

A family of 12 genera and about 800 species distributed over most of the world. Three genera occur in North America but only *Polygala* is found in Texas.

1. POLYGALA L. POLYGALA, MILKWORT

Herbaceous annuals or woody-based perennials, in Texas. Leaves simple, entire; petioles absent or short. Flowers in racemes, elevated or axillary; sepals 5, the 2 inner ones usually petallike; petals usually 3, 1 lower and keellike, usually with an apical beak or crest, 2 upper ones fused to the filament tube and perhaps also to the keellike petal; 2 lateral petals always minute, if present; stamens usually 8, filaments fused in a split sheath, anthers 1-celled at maturity, opening terminally; ovary 2-celled, with solitary ovules; stigma 2-lobed, often tufted. Fruit a compressed 2-celled capsule, often with winglike margins; seeds usually hairy.

A large genus of about 550 species distributed world-wide. About 25 species occur in Texas, with about 11 of these in the Trans-Pecos.

1. Polygala macradenia Gray. GLANDLEAF MILKWORT, PURPLE POLYGALA. Fig. 190. Mostly rockly limestone flats, slopes, mesas, and outcrops, also in igneous-derived soils and sand, probably in every county of the Trans-Pecos, most common in the S, more arid portions. 1500–4600 ft.; Apr–Oct. E on the W Edwards Plateau, N to the South Plains, and S to the Rio Grande Plains; also S NM and AZ; N Mex.

This is the only purple-flowered polygala of the Trans-Pecos with prominent glands on its leaves and fruit. *Polygala macradenia*, a low subshrub about 3–20 cm high, is the only polygala included here although it should be pointed out that most of the Trans-Pecos species are perennial with woody rootstocks and at least some slender woody stems at the base. One remarkable species, *P. rimulicola* Steyerm, endemic to the Guadalupe Mts., is only 1–5 cm high but has the aspect of a miniature shrub. *Polygala maravillasensis* Correll, a broomlike plant (to 40 cm high) with a woody base, is endemic and rare in and along the Lower Canyons of the Rio Grande between Maravillas Canyon and San Francisco Canyon. *Polygala nudata* Brandeg. is a small, shrubby perennial, often misidentified as *P. minutifolia* Rose *auct. non* according to T. Wendt (pers. comm.), that has been collected once in the Chinati Mts. (Presidio Co.) at lower elevations between Dead Horse and Pinto Canyons (*Butterwick 3807B*), only the fourth known U.S. locality for the species.

Fig. 190. *Polygala macradenia*
(Glandleaf Milkwort)

31. EUPHORBIACEAE JUSS. SPURGE FAMILY

Herbs or shrubs in the Trans-Pecos, also trees elsewhere, sometimes even fleshy and cactuslike; mostly monoecious; some genera with milky juice. Leaves mostly alternate, less often opposite, or whorled. Flowers unisexual, variable in inflorescence; petals may be present or absent; in pistillate flowers a lobate disc usually present; ovary superior, usually 3-celled, styles 3, in some genera (*Croton, Bernardia,* or *Jatropha*) less than 3 well-developed locules may be formed; ovules usually pendulous and axile in placentation, anatropous. Fruit usually a capsule, at maturity opening between the locules through the septa, usually from the columnlike central axis; seeds 1–2 per cell, emerging ventrally.

A large and diverse family with perhaps 250 genera and about 7500 species of near cosmopolitan distribution, but with more species concentrated in the tropics of both hemispheres. Twenty genera of Euphorbiaceae occur in Texas and about 11 genera in the Trans-Pecos. *Euphorbia* with over 1600 species worldwide is by far the largest genus of the family, and the largest in Texas. The Euphorbiaceae are of much economic importance, especially in tropical regions. Examples include: *Hevea braziliensis,* the Brazilian rubber tree, now widely planted in Africa, Malaysia, and elsewhere; *Manihot esculenta,* the source of cassava and tapioca (in South America and other lowland tropical areas) produced from its starchy, tuberous roots; important oils are produced from *Croton* spp. (croton oil), *Ricinus communis* (castor oil), and *Aleurites fordii* (tung oil), the latter being produced in the United States as well as elsewhere. Many members of the family are grown as ornamentals, with perhaps Poinsettia (*Euphorbia*) and Castorbean (*Ricinus*) being the most familiar examples in this region. Many species of the family are poisonous.

KEY TO THE GENERA

1. Plants densely clumped with numerous, essentially leafless, "waxy" cylindrical, stems, 20–100 cm long, 3–5 mm thick, erect, arising from horizontal, woody rhizomes   **1. *Euphorbia* (*antisyphilitica*).**
1. Plants otherwise.
  2. Stems wandlike, rubbery, fleshy, oozing clear or blood-red sap when broken (herbaceous in *J. macrorhiza*), 20–70 cm long; leaves clustered on short, lateral spur stems   **2. *Jatropha* (*dioica*).**
  2. Plants more conventional shrubs or subshrubs.
    3. Intricately branched shrubs, 25 cm to 2.5 m high.
      4. Leaf margins entire; plants mostly glabrous   **3. *Andrachne*.**
      4. Leaf margins with rounded teeth; herbage and fruit rather densely covered with forked or branched hairs   **4. *Bernardia*.**
    3. Shrubs or subshrubs 10–100 cm or more high, but not intricately branched or truly "shrubby" throughout.
      5. Plants mostly glabrous   **5. *Phyllanthus*.**
      5. Plants densely covered with stellate hairs or stalked, flat scales
                                                                    6. *Croton*.

1. EUPHORBIA L.   SPURGE

A huge genus of herbs, with milky juice, with only one species, *Euphorbia antisyphilitica*, treated here. Flowers in bisexual groups in cuplike involucres, usually with glands near the rim of the involucre, these often modified as "horns" or petallike appendages; staminate flowers few to many in each involucre, with one stamen; pistillate flower reduced, single in each involucre, often exserted; ovary 3-celled; styles 3 (each usually forked); seeds 2. [*Tithymalus* Trew; *Poinsettia* Grah.; *Agaloma* Raf.].

Members of this genus occur in temperate and tropical regions of the world. About 62 species of *Euphorbia* occur in Texas, with more than two-thirds of these in the Trans-Pecos.

1. **Euphorbia antisyphilitica** Zucc.   CANDELILLA.   Fig. 191.   Scattered or locally abundant, rocky or gravel slopes, ridges, and hills, usually limestone,

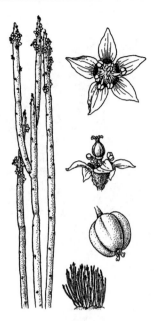

Fig. 191. *Euphorbia antisyphilitica*
(Candelilla)

lower desert parts of Hudspeth, Culberson, Jeff Davis, Presidio, Brewster, Terrell, and Val Verde counties, especially near the Rio Grande. 1100–3800 ft.;
spring–fall, after rains. S in Mex. to Hgo. and Qro.

The slender cylindrical stems of Candelilla produce a wax covering, theo-
retically as an adaptation to the hot desert environment, which for many years
has been the inspiration for smuggling operations from Mexico into Trans-
Pecos Texas. The Candelilla wax, one of the highest quality waxes known, is
extracted by boiling the stems in a vat of water and dilute acid, then floating
wax is simply scooped off and allowed to harden. Since the early 1900's mobile
"wax factories" have been operated on both sides of the Rio Grande in the
Chihuahuan Desert, occupying one place until most of the locally abundant
plants were destroyed, and then the operation was moved to another locality.
Candelilla is still relatively abundant in certain localities of the Trans-Pecos,
but in areas where wax camps operated, the populations are diminished. In
Coahuila, Mexico, Candelilla populations have been severely harvested. Plant
gathering procedures involve ripping up whole plants, but regeneration may
result in "many" years from underground rhizomes. Candelilla wax has many
uses including: chewing gum; shoe, floor, and car polish; ointments; soap; can-
dlemaking; phonograph records; sealing wax; insulation; lubricants; and
waterproofing. In Mexico the juices of this plant have been used to treat

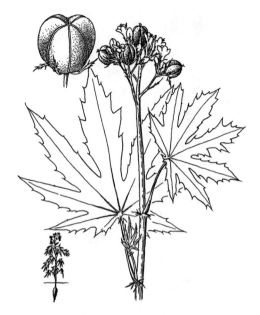

Fig. 192. *Jatropha macrorhiza*

venereal disease, an aspect that inspired the epithet *antisyphilitica*. An excellent historical and archeological account of Candelilla wax camps is presented by Tunnell (1981).

2. JATROPHA L.

Perennial herbs or (in our area) weak shrubs with wandlike, leathery stems, essentially glabrous. Leaves alternate or clustered. Flowers in loose clusters, sometimes single; staminate flowers with 5 fused sepals, 5 petals, and 5 glands opposite the sepals; stamens 7–10 in 2 close whorls; pistillate flowers with 5 partly fused sepals and petals, and 5 glands; ovary roundish with 1–3 cells; styles 1–3. Fruit a capsule.

A genus of about 200 mostly tropical species. Only 3 species occur in Texas. The most common Trans-Pecos species, *Jatropha dioica*, the easily recognizable Leatherstem, is atypical of the genus in habit. Another species, *J. macrorhiza* Benth., (Fig. 192), with herbaceous stems and large palmate leaves (15–20 cm long and wide), is known from one collection in the Trans-Pecos: Presidio Co., Brite Ranch near Valentine, 28 Jul 1938, *Hinckley 1101*. The latter species occurs in central Mexico and northwest Arizona.

Fig. 193. *Jatropha dioica* (Leatherstem);
A) var. *graminea*; B) var. *dioica*

1. Jatropha dioica Sesse *ex* Cerv. LEATHERSTEM, SANGRE DE DRAGO.
Two varieties of this species are recognized by Correll and Johnston (1970);
1a. *Jatropha dioica* var. **graminea** McVaugh (Fig. 193) is most widely distributed, occurring in the lower desert country of Culberson (also the Patterson
Hills), Jeff Davis, Presidio, and Brewster counties, especially near the Rio
Grande. 1800–4000 ft.; spring, early summer. Also N Mex. The var. *graminea*
is distinguished by its narrower and longer spatulate leaves (sometimes 2–3-
lobed), usually 1–4 mm wide or sometimes wider.

1b. Jatropha dioica var. **dioica.** Fig. 193. [*Mozinna spathulata* Ort. var.
sessiliflora Hook.]. Limestone hills and slopes. Val Verde Co., especially near
the Rio Grande, Pecos, and Devils rivers. The var. *dioica* typically has shorter,
broad-spatulate leaves 6–10 mm wide.

Leatherstem is a rather bizarre, easily recognizable plant with its sparingly
branched, arching brown stems with spatulate leaves clustered on short spur
branches. The plants are also characterized by rather long (about 1 m) orange-
colored rootstocks, fruits that are leathery, swollen, and beaked, with 1–
2 seeds, and an astringent, clear to yellowish sap in the stems that turns blood-
red upon exposure to air. Indians supposedly treated sore gums with the
astringent sap by rubbing with broken stems. The seeds of Leatherstem are

Fig. 194. *Andrachne arida*; F) female branch;
M) male branch

preferred by white-winged dove, at least in Presidio Co. According to Jack Skiles, the seeds of *Jatropha* occurring near Langtry have a taste very similar to pecans and are eaten by some people in that area, although the seeds of some (mostly tropical) *Jatropha* species reportedly are poisonous.

3. ANDRACHNE L.

Shrubs, intricately branched, less than 1 m high; dioecious. Leaves alternate, oval, 1–2 times as long as broad; stipules dark, 1–2 mm long. Flowers in small clusters or solitary; staminate flowers with 5 sepals and petals; stamens 5; ovary vestigial; pistillate flowers with 5 sepals and petals; ovary 3-celled. Fruit a capsule, 3–5 mm long; seeds ca. 3 mm long, wedgeshaped, 2 per cell.

A genus of about 15 species in warm regions of the world. The genus *Savia*, to which our species was first assigned, is weakly segregated from *Andrachne*.

1. **Andrachne arida** (Warnock & M. C. Johnst.) G. L. Webst.   Fig. 194. [*Savia arida* Warnock & M. C. Johnst.]. Rare low shrubs, rocky limestone slopes, canyons, and crevices. Brewster Co., Dead Horse Mts., mid W slopes, near Sue Peaks; above Roy's Peak; Black Gap, lower Maravillas Creek. Presidio Co., Solitario, NW of Solitario Peak, in Glen Rose limestone, 150–200 plants over 1 acre with Hinckley Oak. Jul–Oct. Also Coah., Mex.

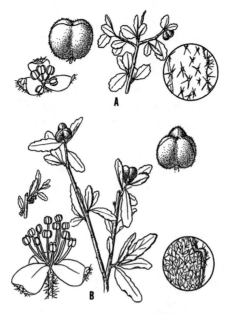

Fig. 195. A) *Bernarida obovata*
(Desert Myrtlecroton); B) *B. myricifolia*

This rare species is distinguished from *Andrachne phyllanthoides* (Nutt.) Coult., which occurs as far west as the Edwards Plateau, by its straight, grayish-white leafy twigs 5–10 cm long, oval leaf blades less than 1 cm long, pistillate flower stalks 3–4 mm long, and staminate flower stalks 2–3.2 mm long.

4. BERNARDIA MILL. BERNARDIA

Shrubs to 2.5 m high; dioecious; branches elongated 5–25 cm long, or short lateral spurs, the latter bearing flowers; leaves and capsules covered with branched hairs. Leaves alternate or clustered on the spur shoots; blades 0.7–3 cm long, margins with rounded teeth. Flowers in small clusters or solitary; staminate flowers with 3 greenish sepals; petals absent; stamens 3–18; pistillate flowers one per spur; sepals 4–5, minute; petals absent; ovary 2–3-celled; styles 2–3, forked or fringed. Fruit a capsule 6–8 mm long and slightly wider, dehiscent; seeds 5–6 mm long.

A genus of about 30 species in the Americas, and only two in Texas.

1. Bernardia obovata I. M. Johnst. DESERT MYRTLECROTON. Fig. 195. Widespread and locally common, in desert scrub, mostly in limestone habitats. Hudspeth, Culberson, Reeves, Jeff Davis, Presidio, Brewster, Pecos, Terrell, and

Val Verde counties. 990–4600 ft.; summer–fall. E to Crane Co.; N into NM; also Coah. and Chih., Mex.

A central and south Texas species, *Bernardia myricifolia* (Scheele) S. Wats., (Fig. 195), extends west to Val Verde Co. and into the Lower Canyons of the Rio Grande. *Bernardia obovata* is distinguished by its obovate leaves which are not so densely pubescent and are grayish-green (instead of dark green) when dry, usually less than 10 stamens, and usually 2-celled capsule with 1–2 seeds.

5. PHYLLANTHUS L. LEAFFLOWER

Herbs or shrubs (in our area) or trees; monoecious or dioecious. Leaves entire. Flowers usually in axils, single or in small clusters; sepals united; petals absent; staminate flowers with 3–6 stamens; pistillate flowers with 5–6 fused sepals; disk present; ovary 3-celled. Fruit a capsule, elastically dehiscent; seeds 2 per cell.

A large and variable genus of about 700 species, centered in tropical regions of the Old World. Seven species occur in Texas.

KEY TO THE SPECIES

1. Miniature subshrubs about 10 cm high, in rock crevices; leaves mostly less than 5 mm long; filaments of stamens fused into a column   1. *P. ericoides.*
1. Herbaceous perennial or somewhat woody at the base, in various habitats; leaves 5–10 mm long; filaments fused about halfway into a column
   2. *P. polygonoides.*

1. **Phyllanthus ericoides** Torr. HEATHER LEAFFLOWER. Fig. 196. A rare subshrub usually in crevices of limestone walls. Brewster Co., SE part of the county, Bullis Range. Terrell Co., mouth of San Francisco Canyon, and in 2–3 other side canyons of the Rio Grande, Lower Canyons (Reagan Canyon to Sanderson); about 2100 ft. Also one locality in Chih., and certainly in Coah., Mex.

2. **Phyllanthus polygonoides** Nutt. *ex* Spreng. KNOTWEED LEAFFLOWER. Fig. 197. Widespread and often common, various habitats, limestone and igneous, desert mountains and canyons up to moderate elevations, El Paso to Val Verde counties throughout the Trans-Pecos. 2100–6000 ft.; spring–fall. S to Rio Grande Plains, E to the Edwards Plateau, to OK, with outlying populations in MO and LA; N and cen. Mex.

6. CROTON L. CROTON

Shrubs or herbs (in our area) or trees. Characterized by scurfy appearance resulting from microscopic stellate (sea-urchinlike) hairs or stalked scales.

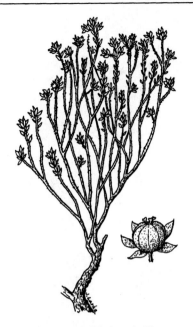

Fig. 196. *Phyllanthus ericoides*
(Heather Leafflower)

Fig. 197. *Phyllanthus polygonoides*
(Knotweed Leafflower)

Leaves alternate, with petioles, blades various in shape, margins toothed or entire. Flowers in terminal spikes or racemes, often with male and female flowers in same inflorescence; staminate flowers with 4–6 lobed calyx; petals absent or present; stamens 5–20; pistillate flowers with 5–9 lobed calyx; petals absent or present; ovary usually 3-celled; styles 3, each branched one or more times. Fruit a 3-celled capsule; seeds 3, 1 in each cell, resembling an engorged tick.

A variable genus of more than 600 species, mostly in tropical and subtropcial regions. Twenty species occur in Texas with about one-half of these found in the Trans-Pecos. Many species are reportedly toxic to livestock, and at least one species, *Croton ciliatoglandulifer* Ort. is noted for causing rashes of the skin and eyes when its glandular hairs are brought into contact. Most crotons are aromatic and many species exude sap from broken leaves or stems. Medicinal properties, most of them probably unfounded, have been attributed to many species, but *C. tiglium* L. is the source of croton oil, the well-known pharmaceutical. Seeds of the common crotons furnish abundant food for mourning doves and other birds.

KEY TO THE SPECIES

1. Styles (in at least some female flowers) branching to form at least 10
   stigmas   **1. *C. dioicus.***

Fig. 198. *Croton dioicus* (Grassland Croton)   Fig. 199. *Croton pottsii* (Leatherweed Croton)

1. Styles branching to form 6 stigmas.

  2. Petioles of lower leaves usually at least one-half as long as blades; perennial herbs   **2. *C. pottsii.***

  2. Petioles of most leaves less than one-third as long as blades; shrubs.

    3. Plants dioecious   **3. *C. sancti-lazari.***

    3. Plants monoecious (both male and female flowers in clusters).

      4. Leaf blades oblong, 2–4 times as long as broad   **4. *C. incanus.***

      4. Leaf blades tapering toward apex.

        5. Leaf blades ovate to ovate-lanceolate, the apexes attenuate and acute   **5. *C. fruticulosus.***

        5. Leaf blades somewhat roundish, or obovate to ovate, rather thick in texture, apexes bluntish   **6. *C. suaveolens.***

  1. Croton dioicus Cav. GRASSLAND CROTON. Fig. 198. [*Croton gracilis* H. B. K.; *C. neomexicanus* Muell.-Arg.]. One of the two most common crotons in the Trans-Pecos, occurring in various habitats, often abundantly, in every county. 1000–5800 ft.; summer–fall. E to cen. and N–cen. TX, N into NM; Mex. S to Oax. A perennial herb, often woody at the base, up to but usually less than 0.5 m high.

  2. Croton pottsii (Kl.) Muell.-Arg. LEATHERWEED CROTON. Fig. 199. One of the two most common crotons in the Trans-Pecos, occurring in various

Fig. 200. A) *Croton sancti-lazari*;
B) *C. fruticulosus* (Bush Croton)

desertic and grassland habitats in every county. 2000–6000 ft.; spring–fall. A
perennial herb, often woody at the base, up to 0.6 m high. Two varieties are
recognized:

2a. Croton pottsii var. **pottsii.** [*C. corymbulosus* Engelm.]. The most
common and widespread of the Leatherweed Croton varieties, easily distinguished by elongated, usually pointed leaves, more than 15 mm long. In all
counties of the Trans-Pecos, N to the S Plains Country, E infrequently to the
Edwards Plateau, rare S to the Rio Grande Plains; NW through S NM and AZ;
N Mex.

2b. Croton pottsii var. **thermophilus** (M. C. Johnst.) M. C. Johnst.
[*C. corymbulosus* var. *thermophilus* M. C. Johnst.]. Restricted to desertic southern Brewster Co., Dead Horse Mts.; Dagger Flats; Talley Mt.; Tornillo Creek;
Boquillas Canyon; distinguished by roundish leaves, less than 15 mm long; also
adjacent Coah., Mex.

3. Croton sancti-lazari Croizat. Fig. 200. [*Croton abruptus* M. C.
Johnst.]. Various desertic habitats. Pecos Co., N end of the Glass Mts. Brewster
Co., from about 10 mi S of Marathon to Packsaddle Mt. and Agua Fria. Presidio Co., the Solitario area. 3000–4600 ft.; spring–fall. Chih., Coah., Mex. A
definite shrub, 1–4 m high.

Fig. 201. *Croton incanus* (Torrey Croton)   Fig. 202. *Croton suaveolens* (Scented Croton)

4. Croton incanus Kunth. TORREY CROTON, VARA BLANCA. Fig. 201. [*Croton torreyanus* Muell.-Arg.]. Along and near the Rio Grande in limestone derived habitats, infrequent in the SE Trans-Pecos. Brewster Co., Boquillas Canyon. Terrell Co., San Francisco Canyon. Val Verde Co., Pecos and Devils rivers. 1000–2100 ft.; summer–fall. Rio Grande Plains to Hidalgo Co.; S NM; NE Mex. A shrub to about 2 m high, most easily distinguished by its oblong leaves.

5. Croton fruticulosus Engelm. *ex* Torr. BUSH CROTON, ENCINILLA, HIERBA LOCA. Fig. 200. The most widespread and common of the shrubby crotons in the Trans-Pecos, various limestone and igneous derived habitats. Hudspeth (Sierra Diablo), Culberson (Guadalupe and Beach Mts., near Kent), Presidio (near Marfa to the Solitario), Jeff Davis (in the mountain canyons), Brewster (near Alpine to the Dead Horse Mts.), Terrell and Val Verde counties. 1000–6000 ft.; summer–fall. E to the Edwards Plateau; less frequent on caliche ridges of the Rio Grande Plains; NM, AZ; N Mex. Shrubs to about 1 m or more high.

6. Croton suaveolens Torr. SCENTED CROTON. Fig. 202. Localized in the Trans-Pecos. Jeff Davis Co., igneous bluffs above Old Ft. Davis; Davis Mt. State Park; vicinity of Ft. Davis. Brewster Co., Packsaddle Mt. Val Verde Co. 3700–5200 ft.; summer–fall. Also Coah., Mex. Low shrubs usually less than 0.5 m high.

32. ANACARDIACEAE LINDL. SUMAC FAMILY

Trees, shrubs, or vines; a usually acrid resinous or milky juice in the bark and perhaps in the herbage. Leaves alternate, rarely opposite; pinnate, 3-foliate, or simple; persistent or deciduous. Flowers small, numerous, arranged in loose or tight clusters; usually perfect (rarely unisexual as in *Pistacia* and *Rhus*), sometimes with a receptacular disc; calyx and corollas usually 5, rarely 3–4; or absent; stamens as many or twice as many as petals; ovary with usually 3 but functionally 1 carpel; styles usually one. Fruit (in our species) a smallish sometimes nutlike drupe with a thin resinous or waxy coat.

A family of about 600 mostly tropical species in about 60 genera. A few genera are widespread in the United States. Only four genera, *Rhus*, *Cotinus*, *Schinus*, and *Pistacia*, occur in Texas. Poison Ivy (*Toxicodendron*) belongs with this family. The edible nuts (seeds) of Cashew (*Anacardium occidentale* L.) and Pistachio (*Pistacia vera* L.) are commercially important, as well as the fresh fruit of the Mango (*Mangifera indica* L.).

KEY TO THE GENERA

1. Flowers without sepals or petals   **1. *Pistacia.***
1. Flowers with sepals and petals.
   2. Fruit whitish to yellowish, glabrous or pubescent with simple, non-glandular hairs   **2. *Toxicodendron.***
   2. Fruit reddish, pubescent with simple and/or glandular hairs   **3. *Rhus.***

1. PISTACIA L. PISTACHIO

In our area usually small trees 4–7 m high, less often shrubs; dioecious; younger branches grayish and slightly hairy, becoming brownish and glabrous. Leaves odd-pinnately compound; leaflets to 21, basically sickleshaped and rather ovate with smooth margins, to 2 cm long and 1 cm wide, very slightly leathery and darker above. Flowers small, clustered in lateral spikes; sepals and petals none; stamens 5. Fruit a red, nutlike drupe, about 3.5 mm wide, with a thin waxy covering, becoming nearly black when dry.

A genus of about 10 species of the Mediterranean region, and several in America. The edible nut (seed), pistachio, comes from the Old World species *Pistacia vera* L.

1. **Pistacia texana** Swingle. TEXAS PISTACHE, MEXICAN PISTACHIO, LENTISCO. Fig. 203. [*Pistacia mexicana* Kunth]. Rocky limestone canyons, vicinity of the mouth of the Pecos River and Rio Grande. Val Verde Co., several localities inundated by Amistad Reservoir; known localities, lower side canyon

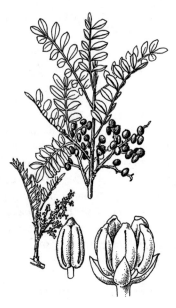

Fig. 203. *Pistacia texana* (Texas Pistache)

of the Pecos River canyon, between the high bridge and the Rio Grande; Hidden Trail Canyon, above Seminole Canyon, and other tributaries of the Rio Grande, both sides between the Pecos River confluence and Seminole Canyon. Also E to Bexar Co.; also adjacent Mex. where often common.

The Texas Pistachio has possibilities as a semievergreen ornamental with its attractive, rather dark leaves, and reddish new leaves in the spring. The fruits are not edible.

2. TOXICODENDRON MILL. POISONIVY, POISONOAK

Shrubs or woody vines, with poisonous emanation. Leaves alternate, deciduous, 3-palmate or odd pinnately compound, leaflets opposite. Flowers in loose clusters, sepals and petals 5, imbricate in bud, petals smaller in female flowers; ovary 1-celled; style terminal, stigma 3-parted. Fruit a drupe, roundish or flattened, whitish to yellowish, glabrous or pubescent with simple, nonglandular hairs; seeds bony, endocarp fused to seed coat.

About 15 species of eastern Asia, North America, and South America. In the Trans-Pecos Poisonivy is recognized by its three (rarely 5) leaflets which are green most of the year until the fall when they may turn scarlet or orange. The plants are dangerous when touched to the skin, and the fumes from burning plants can be dangerous.

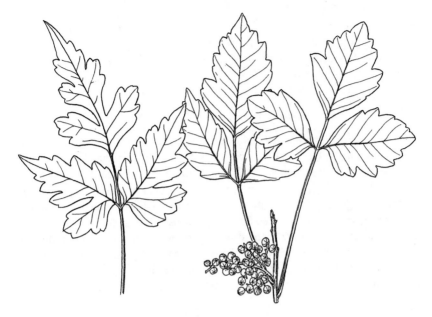

Fig. 204. *Toxicodendron radicans* (Poisonivy)

KEY TO THE SPECIES

1. Leaflets ovate to elliptic to elliptic-lanceolate; aerial roots present
   1. *T. radicans.*
1. Leaflets suborbicular or broadly ovate; aerial roots absent   2. *T. rydbergii.*

1. **Toxicodendron radicans** (L.) O. Ktze. POISONIVY. Fig. 204. [*Rhus radicans* L.]. Scattered and infrequent, protected canyons. Brewster Co., Chisos Mts., Oak Canyon, Cattail Canyon, Willow Canyon; N side of Talley Mt. in BBNP. Presidio Co., Cibolo Canyon; branches of Fresno Canyon (Arroyo Segundo and Mexican Canyon); 2100–5200 ft. Also Coah., Chih., Dgo., N.L., and Tam., Mex.

Nine (six in Kartesz, 1994) subspecies of *Toxicodendron radicans* are recognized (Gillis, 1971) throughout its wide range in the Old and New Worlds. The Trans-Pecos subspecies is *T. radicans* subsp. **eximium** (Greene) Gillis [*T. radicans* var. *eximium* (Greene) Barkl.; *T. eximium* Greene; *Rhus eximium* (Greene) Standl.].

2. **Toxicodendron rydbergii** (Small *ex* Rydb.) Greene. RYDBERG'S POISONIVY [*Rhus radicans* L. var. *rydbergii* (Small *ex* Rydb.) Rehd.; *R. toxicodendron* var. *vulgaris* Michx.]. Scattered and infrequent, protected canyons. Cul-

berson Co. South McKittrick Canyon. Jeff Davis Co., near mouth of Musquiz Canyon, 13 mi N of Alpine; Limpia Canyon; lower Madera Canyon. Lower canyons of Rio Grande. 1800–5400 ft. Widespread in N.A., but not known in Mex.

3. RHUS L. SUMAC, "SHUMAC"

Shrubs (in our area), small trees, or rarely vines. Leaves compound (in our species) or simple. Flowers unisexual and bisexual on the same plant, arranged in clusters; calyx lobes 4–6; petals present, usually whitish or pale yellow; stamens 5, on a disk; ovary 1-celled; styles 3. Fruit a smallish drupe, usually reddish-orange, pubescent with simple (often red-stained) and/or glandular hairs; seeds solitary, bony, often flattened, enclosed in scanty mesocarp.

Rhus is recognized to contain about 30 species in Europe, North America, Mexico, and Central America. The bark, leaves, and perhaps roots of many species contain considerable tannin. Many sumacs furnish excellent browse for deer, and the abundant fruits of most species are eaten by numerous bird species, including quail.

KEY TO THE SPECIES

1. Leaflets 13–19, linear-lanceolate, sickleshaped, to 5.5 cm long and 1.2 cm wide   1. R. lanceolata.
1. Leaflets otherwise.
    2. Plants evergreen shrubs or small trees; flowers usually appearing with the leaves; leaflets leathery.
        3. Leaflets 5–9, sparsely pubescent beneath, soft to the touch
                                                                                      2. R. virens.
        3. Leaflets 3–5, glabrous, not soft to the touch
                                                                      3. R. virens subsp. choriophylla.
    2. Plants mostly deciduous shrubs; flowers usually appearing before the leaves; leaflets not leathery.
        4. Leaflets 5–9, less than 2 cm long, 6 mm wide   4. R. microphylla.
        4. Leaflets 3, lateral ones 3.5–4.5 cm long, 1.7–3.5 cm wide
                                                                              5. R. trilobata.

1. **Rhus lanceolata** (Gray) Britt. LANCELEAF SUMAC. Fig. 205. [Rhus copallinum L. var. lanceolata Gray]. Usually infrequent, limestone or igneous habitats. Culberson Co., Guadalupe Mts., North and South McKittrick canyons; Smith Canyon; arroyos of the foothills. Jeff Davis Co., Goat Canyon of Mt. Livermore; Ft. Davis Canyon; Barrel Springs, near twin mountains; upper Fern Canyon, Girl Scout Camp. Brewster Co., Glass Mts., Jail Canyon and

Fig. 205. *Rhus lanceolata* (Lanceleaf Sumac)

Fig. 206. A) *Rhus virens* var. *virens* (Evergreen Sumac); B) *R. virens* var. *choriophylla* (Toughleaf Sumac)

elsewhere; Doubtful Canyon E of Mt. Ord and S in the Del Norte Mts. 4000–6500 ft. E to N-cen. TX; also NM.

Plants of this species are small trees or large shrubs to 10 m high, with dense clusters of white flowers and later red fruit, and leaflets that turn reddish-purple in the fall. The leaf rachis between the leaflets is slightly flattened or winged. The plants are attractive and should be tried as ornamentals in the Trans-Pecos. The acrid fruits of this species (and the closely related *Rhus copallinum* of more easterly distribution in Texas) were crushed in water by the Indians to make a palatable drink, and the leaves were mixed with tobacco and smoked.

2. **Rhus virens** Lindheimer *ex* Gray var. **virens.** EVERGREEN SUMAC, TO-BACCO SUMAC, LENTISCO. Fig. 206. [*Schmaltzia virens* (Lindh.) Small]. A common species in various broken-terrain habitats, in almost all mountains and canyons of the Trans-Pecos from El Paso Co. to Pecos and Val Verde counties. 2100–5000 ft. E on the Edwards Plateau; N Mex.

This species is easily recognized as a shrub or small tree to 3 m high with rather shiny, evergreen leaves that are short-pubescent and soft to the touch. The Comanche Indians supposedly sun-cured mature leaves and mixed them with tobacco for smoking. The acid red fruits of this species, like those of other sumacs, provide a refreshing drink when steeped in water. Reportedly the leaves have been used for asthma relief.

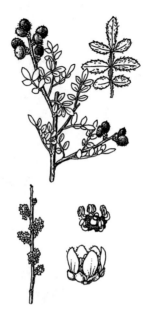

Fig. 207. *Rhus microphylla* (Littleleaf Sumac)

3. Rhus virens var. **choriophylla** (Woot. & Standl.) L. Benson. TOUGH-LEAF SUMAC. Fig. 206. [*Schmaltzia choriophylla* (Woot. & Standl.) Barkl.; *R. choriophylla* Woot. & Standl.]. Infrequent in El Paso Co., Franklin Mts., McKelligan Canyon and 8 mi N of El Paso, also supposedly occurring in hills of extreme W Edwards Plateau. W through NM to AZ; N Mex. This subspecies is distinguished by its glabrous leaves not soft to the touch and axillary inflorescences.

4. Rhus microphylla Engelm. *ex* Gray. LITTLELEAF SUMAC, DESERT SUMAC. Fig. 207. [*Schmaltzia microphylla* (Engelm.) Small]. A common species, various habitats from mountains to gypsum flats, but most common in broken desertic habitats, throughout the Trans-Pecos. El Paso Co. to Val Verde Co.; 1100–6400 ft. Also E to about the W three-fourths of TX; W to AZ; N Mex.

This much branched shrub, or rarely small tree to 5 m high, is easily rec-ognized by its 5–9 small leaflets, smaller than those of any other Trans-Pecos sumac. The whitish flowers of Littleleaf Sumac and the geographically related *Rhus trilobata* usually appear before the leaves. The abundant red fruits of Littleleaf Sumac are acid but edible, and have been used as flavoring in water drinks. Littleleaf Sumac probably furnishes important browse for Desert Mule Deer, and for various bird species including quail.

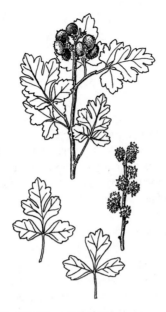

Fig. 208. *Rhus trilobata* (Fragrant Sumac)

5. Rhus trilobata Nutt.   FRAGRANT SUMAC, POLECATBUSH, SQUAWBUSH. Fig. 208.   [*Schmaltzia crenata* (Mill.) Greene]. A common scraggly to upright shrub to 2 m high, having much the same distribution as does *Rhus microphylla*, except that *R. trilobata* is somewhat more scattered and usually occurs at more moderate, slightly higher elevations. Two varieties are recognized in the Trans-Pecos.

5a. Rhus trilobata var. **trilobata**   [*R. aromatica* var. *flabelliformis* (Shinners) R. E. Brooks]; recognized by glabrous leaves, terminal leaflet blades cuneate-obovate or obtuse with a truncate tip, 1.5–2.5 cm long, 0.8–2 cm wide.

5b. Rhus trilobata var. **pilosissima** Engelm.   [*R. aromatica* Ait. var. *pilosissima* (Engelm.) W. A. Weber; *Schmaltzia trilobata* var. *pilosissima* (Engelm.) Barkl.]; recognized by leaflet blades rhombic-ovate, crenate-dentate near the blunt apex, entire near the base, and densely ferruginous-pubescent. Both varieties have overlapping distributions, often occurring on the same mountain.

Fragrant Sumac is conspicuous in the spring with its clusters of small yellowish flowers which open usually before leaves are produced. In the fall the leaves turn reddish or orange. The name Fragrant Sumac comes from the leaves which are aromatic, especially so when crushed. The species occurs throughout most of the United States and Mexico. The fruits are eaten by birds and steeped in water to make a cooling drink for man.

33. CELASTRACEAE R. BR.   STAFFTREE FAMILY

Shrubs, small trees, or woody vines. Leaves opposite or alternate, simple. Flowers regular, bisexual or unisexual, small and greenish, borne on jointed flower stalks; sepals and petals 4–5, overlapping in the bud; stamens 4–5 (rarely 10), borne on a disc that covers bottom of calyx and perhaps the ovary; ovules usually 2 in each locule; styles united. Fruit a capsule, drupe, or achene (in our species), 1–5-celled and separate from the calyx; seeds usually with a bright-colored, pulpy aril.

A family of more than 50 genera and about 850 species with worldwide distribution. The Stafftree Family is of slight economic importance. *Paxistima myrsinites* (Pursh) Raf. (Boxleaf) is known from one locality on the Edwards Plateau but is not included below, although its distribution (NM, AZ, and N Mex., N to Can.) suggests that it may eventually be found in the Trans-Pecos mountains. Also, the rare species, *Canotia wendtii* M. C. Johnst. may eventually be found in Trans-Pecos, the plant presently is known only from about 20 km NE of Coyame, Chihuahua, Mexico, not far west of Presidio and in a habitat similar to that of southern Presidio Co. (Johnston, 1975).

KEY TO THE GENERA

1. Climbing shrubs to ca. 15 m high; leaves 5–10 cm long; fruit a dehiscent capsule   **1. *Celastrus.***
1. Erect or spreading shrubs to 2.5 cm high; leaves to 2.5 cm long; fruit a follicle or indehiscent capsule.
   2. Plants glabrous; leaves basically wedgeshaped, at least some notched apically; flowers 4-merous; calyx not tubular; fruit 2-seeded, rather fleshy
                                                                                      2. *Schaefferia.*
   2. Plants with short, stiff hairs especially on leaves (except in some *Mortonia sempervirens*); leaves basically oval and pointed apically; flowers 5-merous; calyx tubular; fruit 1-seeded, dry   **3. *Mortonia.***

1. CELASTRUS L.   BITTERSWEET

Climbing and twining shrub; primary stem 2.5 cm thick. Leaves alternate, 5–10 cm long, blades basically ovate and pointed, margins fine-toothed. Flowers small, in loose clusters 3–8 cm long, greenish-white. Fruit a roundish capsule ca. 1 mm long, splitting into 3 parts, orangish; seeds elliptical ca. 6 mm long, covered with a crimson aril, 1–2 in each cell.

Fig. 209. *Celastrus scandens* (American Bittersweet)

A genus of about 30 species, centered in eastern Asia. Only one species occurs in Texas.

1. **Celastrus scandens** L. AMERICAN BITTERSWEET, CLIMBING BITTER-SWEET. Fig. 209. Rare in the Trans-Pecos. Culberson Co., McKittrick Canyon. Brewster Co., slopes of Mt. Ord. 6500 ft., among igneous boulders. Jeff Davis Co., Davis Mts., below Mt. Livermore in Elbow Canyon; Sawtooth Mt.; beneath oaks in Wild Rose Pass, Limpia Canyon, 4800 ft.; Apr – Jun. Across TX and SE U.S. to GA, N to Can. The root bark is said to have many medicinal uses (Vines, 1960). The seeds and maybe all plant parts reportedly are poisonous.

2. SCHAEFFERIA JACQ.

Shrubs, 1 – 2 m high; stems gray, much branched, rigid twigs somewhat spinescent; dioecious. Leaves alternate or clustered on very short spur branches, without petioles, 0.5 – 2.3 cm long, more or less wedgeshaped, many notched at the apex, somewhat leathery in texture, glabrous. Flowers small, single or in clusters, unisexual, male and female on separate plants; sepals 4, 0.5 mm long; petals 4, 3 mm long, greenish. Fruit a drupe, bright red and shiny, 3 – 5 mm long, 2.5 – 4 mm thick, roundish, slightly compressed.

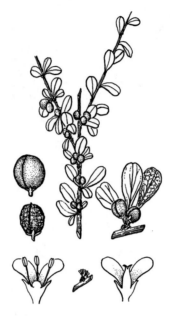

Fig. 210. *Schaefferia cuneifolia* (Desertyaupon)

A genus of about 16 species, occurring from the southern United States to the West Indies and South America.

1. **Schaefferia cuneifolia** Gray. DESERTYAUPON, CAPUL, PANALERO. Fig. 210. Localized, usually infrequent, rocky limestone slopes and canyons. Brewster Co., Reagan Canyon, 3 mi from the Rio Grande; near mouth of Pine Canyon, Big Bend Park. Terrell Co., mouth of San Francisco Creek; 8 mi N of Dryden. Val Verde Co., N of Langtry. South on the Rio Grande Plains and Valley; N Mex.

In Mexico roots of the Desertyaupon reportedly have been used to treat venereal disease. The species is easily recognized by its notched, cuneate leaves and bright red fruits.

3. MORTONIA GRAY

Shrubs to 2.5 m, erect; stems gray. Leaves alternate, crowded, usually oval, small (to 1.2 cm long) somewhat thick and leathery, margins entire, thickened or undercurled; stipules glandlike, early falling. Flowers white, small, in rather loose clusters; calyx tube 5-lobed; petals 5, fringed; stamens 5. Fruit an achene; seeds without an aril.

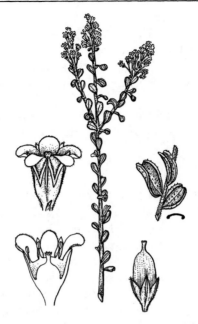

Fig. 211. *Mortonia sempervirens* subp. *scabrella*
(Rough Mortonia)

A genus of about eight species occurring in the southern United States and Mexico. Three species are found in Texas.

KEY TO THE SUBSPECIES

1. Leaves 5–10 mm long, 2.5–6 mm wide, covered with short, straight hairs; flowers numerous in rather loose clusters 2–4 cm long
   1. *M. sempervirens* subsp. *scabrella.*
1. Leaves 3–5 mm long, 1.5–2 mm wide, either essentially glabrous or with short hairs; flowers few in rather narrow clusters 1 cm long
   2. *M. sempervirens* subsp. *sempervirens.*

1. **Mortonia sempervirens** A. Gray. subsp. **scabrella** (A. Gray) Prigge. ROUGH MORTONIA.   Fig. 211.   [*Mortonia scabrella* A. Gray]. Locally frequent, rocky limestone (occasionally gypsum) ridges, slopes, and canyons. El Paso Co., Franklin Mts., McKelligan Canyon. Hudspeth Co., Quitman Mts.; Eagle Mts. Culberson Co., rather common in the Guadalupe Mts. Presidio Co., near Shafter; the Solitario; between Redford and Lajitas. 2200–6500 ft.; Feb–Sep. NM and AZ; also N Mex.

Rough Mortonia is easily recognized by erect, whitish stems with crowded oval leaves that are scabrous. The plant evidently is not palatable to deer or livestock.

2. Mortonia sempervirens A. Gray subsp. **sempervirens.** [*Mortonia sempervirens* A. Gray]. Rocky limestone bluffs and slopes. Pecos Co., N slopes of Sierra Madera. Brewster Co., Glass Mts., N side of Bissett Hill. Val Verde Co., bluffs at Langtry overlooking Rio Grande. 2000–4500 ft.; Apr–May. Probably in adjacent Mex.

This taxon is closely related and similar to subsp. *scabrella,* but distinguished by the key characters. The Sierra Madera plants have essentially glabrous leaves.

34. ACERACEAE JUSS.   MAPLE FAMILY

Trees and shrubs; sap watery and sweet; mainly dioecious but both male and female flowers may be on same plant. Leaves opposite, palmately lobed (in our species) or pinnately divided. Flowers small, regular; petals present or absent. Fruits a 2-celled, 2-winged samara (in *Acer*).

A family of 3 genera and about 200 species mostly of the North Temperate Zone; all but a few species belong to *Acer,* the maple genus. The family is important economically for maple syrup, sugar from the sap, and for maple lumber (mostly from *A. saccharum* of the northeastern U.S. and Canada). Many species are grown as ornamentals.

1. ACER L.   MAPLE

Trees (usually), with leaves turning yellow and reddish then abscising in the fall. Leaves 3–5 lobed (palmate) in our species. Flowers in small groups; calyx 5, colored; petals absent (in our species). Samara wings spreading and often rose-colored.

A genus of about 200 species distributed in the Northern Hemisphere. Five *Acer* species are represented in Texas. Only one maple occurs naturally in the Trans-Pecos, but *A. negundo* L., the Boxelder of eastern North America, has been transplanted at the Shely Ranch headquarters, near Pinto Canyon creek, Chinati Mts., Presidio Co.

1. Acer grandidentatum Nutt.   BIGTOOTH MAPLE, SUGAR MAPLE, PALO DE AZUCAR.   Fig. 212.   [*Acer saccharum* var. *grandidentatum* (Nutt.) Sudw.; *A. grandidentatum* var. *brachypterum* (Woot. & Standl.) E. J. Palm.]. Mountain canyons. Culberson Co., Guadalupe Mts., especially prominent in South McKittrick Canyon. Jeff Davis Co., many canyons of the Davis Mts., including Madera, Limpia, Big Ajuga, and Timber Mt. Brewster Co., 4 mi W of Alpine; Mt. Ord; Chisos Mts.; Glass Mts., upper Jail Canyon. Presidio Co., Sierra Vieja, Vieja Pass, Cottonwood Canyon, ZH Canyon. 4500–6500 ft.; Mar–Apr. Also in canyons of the Edwards Plateau; SE AZ, NM, N to WY and UT; Coah., Mex.

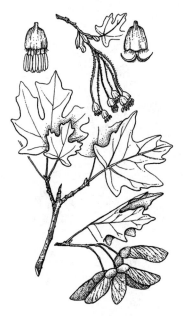

Fig. 212. *Acer grandidentatum*
(Bigtooth Maple)

The Bigtooth Maple in the Trans-Pecos is usually a small tree 3–6 m high, but may reach 15 m or more in other parts of the country. Jim Liles has measured the State champion tree, in Pine Canyon of Big Bend National Park, to be 60 ft. high, with a crown spread of 24 ft., and 4.2 ft. girth, but this is truly an exceptional size for the species in our area. The plants are easily identified by the leaves with 3–5 lobes, and fruit which is clearly 2-celled with one wing (15–25 cm long) attached to each cell. The Trans-Pecos entity probably is var. **grandidentatum**. Gehlbach and Gardner (1983) have studied the relationships of sugar maples in Texas and Oklahoma.

35. SAPINDACEAE JUSS. SOAPBERRY FAMILY

Trees, shrubs, or vines. Leaves alternate, pinnate (in our species) simple or palmate; stipules present or absent. Flowers small, unisexual, male and female on separate plants, or flowers perfect, borne in clusters, regular or irregular; sepals and petals 4–5, petals often with scaly or hair-tufted nectaries on inside; stamens 8–10, in 2 whorls, anthers 2-celled; ovary usually 3-celled. Fruit usually a berry or dehiscent capsule; seeds often arillate.

Fig. 213. *Sapindus saponaria* var. *drummondii*
(Western Soapberry)

A family of about 1500 species in about 140 genera, centered in tropical Asia and America, and of minor economic importance. Five genera occur in Texas.

KEY TO THE GENERA

1. Tree; flowers white, regular; leaves even-pinnate   **1. Sapindus.**
1. Shrub or small tree; flowers purplish-pink, irregular, leaves odd-pinnate
                                          2. Ungnadia.

1. SAPINDUS L. SOAPBERRY

Trees, usually less than 10 m high (in our species). Leaves pinnate; leaflets to 18, usually lanceolate and sickleshaped, to 3–10 cm long and 1–3 cm wide, sometimes less, strongly veined on upper surface. Flowers white, 4–5 mm wide, arranged in dense terminal clusters; sepals and petals usually with hairy margins; filaments of stamens with long hairs. Fruits round, ca. 13 mm across, with amber translucent flesh around the seed.

A genus of about 13 species, mostly in tropical Asia and America.

1. Sapindus saponaria L. var. **drummondii** (H.&A.) L. Benson. WESTERN SOAPBERRY, JABONCILLO. Fig. 213. [*Sapindus drummondii* H. & A.].

Mostly in canyons and along streams and arroyos, scattered but common in most counties of the Trans-Pecos. El Paso (Franklin Mts.), Hudspeth (Quitman Mts.), Culberson, Presidio, Jeff Davis, Brewster, Terrell, and Val Verde counties. 1100–6500 ft.; Mar–Jul. Scattered throughout most of TX, W to NM, N to KS, E to LA; also N Mex.

The fruit of this plant contains saponin which produces lather in water, and is used as soap in Mexico. Although saponin is poisonous, the fruit is also used as a treatment for fevers, rheumatism, and kidney problems. Western Soapberry is a desirable shade tree ornamental. When the plants are in bloom, often in early June in the Trans-Pecos, they are easily spotted from a distance by the white clusters of flowers.

2. UNGNADIA ENDL. MEXICANBUCKEYE

Shrubs or small trees, usually 3–6 m high; bark light gray. Leaves odd-pinnate; leaflets 3–7, ovate-lanceolate, to 12 cm long, 4 cm wide, hairy underneath when young, glabrate when mature, margins with rounded teeth. Flowers purplish-pink, in clusters, fragrant, usually appearing before the leaves; petals to 1 cm long; stamens 7–10, anthers cherry red. Fruit a woody, 3-lobed pod, 3.5–5 cm wide, pale green, turning light brown; seeds roundish, 1–1.5 cm across, shiny, dark brown to blackish.

1. **Ungnadia speciosa** Endl. MEXICANBUCKEYE, TEXAS BUCKEYE, MONILLA. Fig. 214. This is the only species in the genus. Usually scattered on mountain slopes and in canyons, across most of the Trans-Pecos. El Paso (Franklin Mts.), Hudspeth, (Eagle Mts.), Culberson, Presidio, Jeff Davis, Brewster, Pecos, Terrell, and Val Verde counties. 1000–6500 ft.; Mar–Jun. E in TX to Harris and Dallas counties; NM; adjacent Mex.

The sweet seeds of Mexicanbuckeye are reportedly poisonous, causing nausea and other abdominal discomfort. When in flower in the spring, the plants resemble redbuds from a distance, and should be favored ornamentals.

36. RHAMNACEAE JUSS. BUCKTHORN FAMILY

Shrubs (in our area), small trees, woody vines, or lianes; spinescent twigs in many species. Leaves alternate or opposite, simple; stipules minute, short-lived. Flowers bisexual, except unisexual in some *Rhamnus*, solitary or in clusters, small and inconspicuous, whitish or greenish, perigynous (floral parts borne around the ovary, stamens, corolla, and sepals on the floral tube), floral tube bellshaped; sepals and petals (if present) 4–5; 4–5 stamens borne opposite the petals; disc present in floral cup; style single; ovary 1–4-celled; ovules

Fig. 214. *Ungnadia speciosa* (Mexicanbuckeye)

1 per cell, attached basally. Fruit a drupe with 1–3 stones, or a capsule that splits into 1-seeded portions.

A family of about 900 species in more than 55 genera, nearly cosmopolitan in distribution. The larger genus is *Rhamnus* with about 100 species. Nine genera occur in Texas, and eight of these have members in the Trans-Pecos (Johnston, 1969).

KEY TO THE GENERA

1. Leaves opposite.
   2. Plants armed (stems green with opposite, thorntipped branchlets); fruit a capsule   **1. Adolphia.**
   2. Plants unarmed; fruit drupaceous   **8. Karwinskia.**
1. Leaves alternate, fasciculate, or opposite in *Ceanothus greggii* and *Sageretia*.
   3. Fruit a capsule, essentially dry at maturity.
      4. Remains of floral cup and disc adhering to base of the ovary at maturity and partaking of the more or less irregular dehiscence of the exo- and mesocarp   **2. Colubrina.**
      4. Floral cup and disc persistent on the pedicels at maturity, neatly separating from the parts of the fruit when they fall   **3. Ceanothus.**
   3. Fruit a drupe, with 1–3 stones.
      5. Fruit with 1 stone.

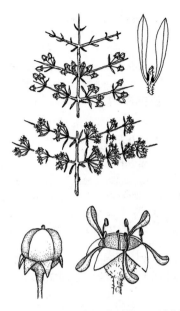

Fig. 215. *Adolphia infesta* (Texas Adolphia)

6. Petals present; disc thickened around ovary and partly hiding it
in early stages   **4. Ziziphus.**
6. Petals absent (except in *Condalia ericoides*); disc thin, if thickened at all then slightly near the rim of the floral cup
                                                                  5. Condalia.
5. Fruit with 2–3 stones.
7. Flowers arranged in terminal panicles; leaves opposite
                                                                  6. Sageretia.
7. Flowers arranged in few-flowered, axillary clusters; leaves
alternate   **7. Rhamnus.**

1. ADOLPHIA MEISN. JUNCO

Shrubs to 1 m; much branched with greenish, leafless, essentially glabrous, opposite thorntipped branchlets. Leaves essentially opposite, deciduous, small, linear. Flowers small, whitish, solitary or clustered in axils. Fruit at maturity a dry, 3-celled capsule; 1 seed in each cell. A genus of two species restricted to North America.

1. **Adolphia infesta** (Kunth) Meisn. TEXAS ADOLPHIA. Fig. 215. Scattered but relatively common, mountain slopes and foothills. Presidio, Jeff

Davis, Brewster, and Pecos counties. 4000–5700 ft.; spring–summer. S in Mex. to Oax.

Texas Adolphia is easily recognized by essentially leafless, greenish stems with opposite, thorntipped branchlets. The thorns are hard and sharp, in overall aspect resembling a small Allthorn (*Koeberlinia*). The roots have a smell much like anise or licorice, and possibly have medicinal properties.

2. COLUBRINA L. C. RICH. *ex* BRONGN. SNAKEWOOD

Shrubs (in our area) or small trees, unarmed. Leaves alternate, ovate, pubescent, usually with 3 main nerves, one in *Colubrina texensis*. Flowers greenish-yellow in axillary clusters; disc overfilling the floral cup and hiding ovary in early stages; ovary usually 3-celled. Fruit a hard capsule at maturity, dark brown or black, disc and floral cup adherent to lower third of fruit; dehiscence may be delayed 14 months.

A genus of about 30 species, 21 in the New World, one in Hawaii, and the rest in Madagascar and southeast Asia. Three species occur in Texas.

KEY TO THE SPECIES

1. Leaves usually 1.5–2.5 cm long   **1. *C. texensis.***
1. Leaves 3–8 cm long   **2. *C. stricta.***

1. **Colubrina texensis** (T.&G.) A. Gray. TEXAS COLUBRINA. Fig. 216. Locally common, rocky limestone hills and canyons. Terrell Co., from the mouth of San Francisco Canyon to near Dryden. Val Verde Co. 1000–2800 ft.; late spring to early summer. S on the Rio Grande Plains, to N-cen. TX and the S part of the Plains Country.

Plants in the Trans-Pecos are of var. **texensis.** Texas Colubrina is a rounded shrub, 1–2 m (or less) high, with zig-zaggish branches, the young branchlets often fuzzy, and with ovate, toothed leaves.

2. **Colubrina stricta** Engelm. *ex* M. C. Johnst. El Paso Co., Hueco Mts., Hueco Tanks State Park, SW side of North Mt.; flowering in May, a few plants in one population. This species is seemingly rare and spotty in distribution, otherwise known in Texas from Comal Co., Edwards Plateau (Correll and Johnston, 1970), and not collected in Texas since 1851 before the plants reported (as *Colubrina greggii* S. Wats.) by Van Devender and Riskind (1979); also known from one locality each in N.L. and Coah., Mex.

3. CEANOTHUS L.

Shrubs, armed or unarmed. Leaves opposite or alternate, usually toothed. Flowers white, in showy clusters. Fruit a 3-lobed capsule, disc and cup persistent as a subtriangular pedestal after fruit abscission.

Fig. 216. *Colubrina texensis* (Texas Colubrina)   Fig. 217. *Ceanothus greggii* (Desert Ceanothus)

A genus of about 55 species distributed in North America and Central America. Four species occur in Texas. Some Mexican and Californian species have been cultivated.

KEY TO THE SPECIES

1. Leaves and branches opposite; unarmed **1. C. greggii.**
1. Leaves alternate; at least some branchlets thorntipped **2. C. fendleri.**

1. Ceanothus greggii Gray. DESERT CEANOTHUS. Fig. 217. Mountains and canyons. El Paso Co., Franklin Mts. Culberson Co., Guadalupe Mts.; Sierra Diablo, Victorio Canyon. Brewster Co., Del Norte Mts., 8 mi W Santiago Peak; Chisos Mts., upper Cattail Canyon. Pecos Co., Glass Mts.; Sierra Madera. 3500–8000 ft.; spring. Also S NM; S to Oax., Mex.

A low shrub, 1–2 m high with intricate, short rigid branches and small, oblongish, leathery leaves with conspicuous white patches between the veins underneath. Reportedly excellent deer and elk browse (in the Guadalupe and Glass Mts.). Potentially a good hedge plant. Kartesz (1994) lists three subspecies of *Ceanothus greggii*.

2. Ceanothus fendleri Gray. FENDLER CEANOTHUS. Fig. 218. Reported from high elevations in the Trans-Pecos. Jeff Davis Co., upper Limpia Canyon (Sawmill Canyon), Davis Mts.; summer. Also N to SD and CO; Chih. and Coah., Mex.

A low spreading shrub usually not more than 1 m high, (but reaching 2 m

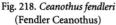

Fig. 218. *Ceanothus fendleri*
(Fendler Ceanothus)

Fig. 219. *Ziziphus obtusifolia* (Lotebush)

high and 3 m wide in Limpia Canyon) with at least some of the branchlets thorntipped, the branches often bluish-gray or glaucous, and the small leaves with close glandular teeth. Attractive to bees when in flower.

4. ZIZIPHUS MILL.

Shrubs or small trees, armed, nearly glabrous. Leaves alternate, ovate to linear, petioled. Flowers small, greenish, in axillary clusters; floral cup nearly filled with disc, around but not adherent to ovary; petals present, early falling. Fruit a round, elongated, or compressed drupe, dark purple, with 1 stone.

A genus of about 150 species in warmer regions of the New World and Old World. Two species occur in Texas, but one, *Ziziphus zizyphus* (L.) Karst. (*Z. jujuba* Mill.), Jujube, is a naturalized cultivar from the Old World, in the Trans-Pecos known from the towns of Ysleta, El Paso Co, and Alpine, Brewster Co.

1. **Ziziphus obtusifolia** (Hook. *ex* T.&G.) Gray. LOTEBUSH, GUMDROP TREE, CLEPE. Fig. 219. [*Condalia lycioides* (Gray) Weberb.]. Locally abundant, present in every county of the Trans-Pecos, our most common member of the Rhamnaceae. 1000–5500 ft.; summer. Also common elsewhere in TX except the E and higher parts of the Plains Country; NM, AZ; S in Mex. to S.L.P. and Ver.

This common shrub is densely branched and leafy, to 3–4 m high, with branches light gray and covered with a waxlike bloom, thorntipped branchlets, and variable leaves, from ovate to linear, often toothed on the upper half. The Trans-Pecos plants belong to var. obtusifolia. The drupes of Lotebush are eaten by birds and small mammals.

5. CONDALIA CAV.

Shrubs or small trees; armed with branchlets ending in thorns. Leaves alternate, often clustered on short spur-shoots; blades linear, obovate, or spatulate, entire. Flowers single or in small clusters at the spurs; disc absent or slightly present near rim of floral cup. Fruit a drupe, roundish.

A genus of 18 species in the Americas, five of which occur in Texas.

KEY TO THE SPECIES

1. Leaves linear, 2–13 mm long, ca. 1 mm wide; petals present **1. C. ericoides.**
1. Leaves not linear; petals absent.
  2. Leaves small, spatulate, usually 3–6 mm long, 1–2.6 mm wide; undersurface veins slightly prominent, occupying at least 30 percent of blade surface **2. C. warnockii.**
  2. Leaves larger, obovate, usually 5–8 mm long, 2.3–4 mm wide; undersurface veins inconspicuous, occupying much less than 30 percent of surface **3. C. viridis.**

1. **Condalia ericoides** (Gray) M. C. Johnst. JAVELINABUSH, TECOMBLATE. Fig. 220. [*Microrhamnus ericoides* Gray]. Widespread and locally common, variable but usually desertic habitats, in all counties of the Trans-Pecos. 2000–6000 ft.; spring–summer. Elsewhere in TX, to W part of Edwards Plateau, infrequent in the Plains Country; AZ, NM; N Mex.

Javelinabush is a low, spinescent shrub, usually less than 1 m high, or occasionally taller. The plants are intricately branched with 2–9 linear, fascicled leaves, yellowish petals, and fruit beaked, elongated, and reddish- or purplish-black when mature.

2. **Condalia warnockii** M. C. Johnst. WARNOCK CONDALIA. Fig. 221. Locally common, otherwise scattered in somewhat desertic habitats. El Paso Co., Franklin Mts., McKelligan Canyon. Hudspeth Co., Quitman Mts. Culberson Co., Guadalupe Mts. Jeff Davis Co., Leoncita Springs, Kokernot Ranch. Brewster Co., 20 mi E Alpine; 02 Ranch. Pecos Co., University Mesa; 30 mi E of Ft. Stockton. 2800–4600; summer. to W part of Edwards Plateau (and Crane Co.), to S part of Plains Country; NM; Chih., Coah., Zac., Mex.

The Trans-Pecos plants belong to var. **warnockii**, with another variety (var. *kearneyana* M. C. Johnst.) occurring in Arizona and in Sonora, Mexico.

Fig. 220. *Condalia ericoides* (Javelinabush)   Fig. 221. *Condalia warnockii*
(Warnock Condalia)

3. Condalia viridis I. M. Johnst.   GREEN CONDALIA.   Fig. 222.   [*Condalia viridis* var. *reedii* Cory]. Locally common, in dry limestone slopes, El Paso Co., Franklin Mts. Presidio Co., near Solitario Peak. Brewster Co., hills above Hot Springs. Pecos Co., 30 mi E Ft. Stockton. Terrell Co., 21 mi N Dryden. Val Verde Co., 10–12 mi N Del Rio. 1000–4500 ft.; summer. Edwards Plateau SE to Kinney and Uvalde counties; also Coah., N.L., and S.L.P., Mex.

Another *Condalia* species, *C. hookeri* M. C. Johnst. var. *hookeri*, distinguished by leaves 15–30 mm long, reportedly extends into Val Verde Co. from the Rio Grande Plains and southern Edwards Plateau, but this plant evidently does not occur in the Trans-Pecos proper.

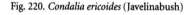

6. SAGERETIA BRONGN.

Low shrub. Leaves essentially opposite, small, shiny, with tiny points at the apex. Flowers small, white, borne in terminal clusters. Fruit an indehiscent drupe, black and juicy at maturity, with 3 stones.

A genus of perhaps 30 species, most of them from China, with two in North America, and one in Mexico and South America, and others in certain warm regions of the Old World.

1. Sageretia wrightii S. Wats.   WRIGHT SAGERETIA.   Fig. 223.   Reportedly on arid slopes in the Trans-Pecos. Jeff Davis Co., Davis Mts. Presi-

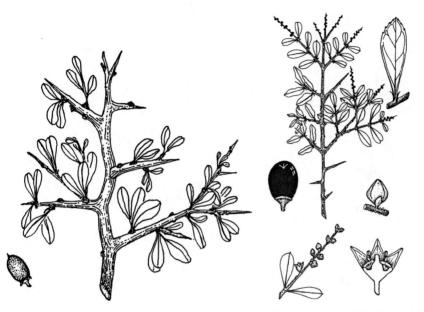

Fig. 222. *Condalia viridis* (Green Condalia)   Fig. 223. *Sageretia wrightii* (Wright Sageretia)

dio Co., Sierra Vieja, Capote Falls Canyon; S slope of Box Canyon, just SW of old army post, Espy Miller ranch; Chinati Mts. 4000–5000 ft.; Jul–Aug. Also NM, AZ; Chih., and Coah., Mex.

7. RHAMNUS L. BUCKTHORN

Shrubs or small trees; unarmed. Leaves alternate, not lobed, essentially glabrous, margins minutely toothed. Flowers bisexual or unisexual, greenish, solitary or in small clusters; floral cup and disk, small, free from ovary. Fruit a black and juicy drupe at maturity, with 2–3 stones.

A genus of about 100 species in tropical and temperate zones. The powerful cathartic drug, cascara sagrada, is obtained from some species of *Rhamnus*. The fruit and bark of many *Rhamnus* species reportedly are poisonous.

KEY TO THE SPECIES

1. Leaves numerous, usually 1.5–3.0 cm long, narrowly elliptic; flowers mostly unisexual, solitary in axils; shrubs to 1–3 m high   **1. *R. serrata.***
1. Leaves usually more than 5 cm long; ovate-elliptic; flowers bisexual, in axils on stalks in small clusters; shrubs or small trees to 6 m high
     2. *R. betulifolia.*

Fig. 224. *Rhamnus serrata*

Fig. 225. *Rhamnus betulifolia*
(Birchleaf Buckthorn)

1. Rhamnus serrata H. & B. *ex* Schult.   Fig. 224.   [*Rhamnus fasciculata* Greene; *R. smithii* subsp. *fasciculata* (Greene) Wolf]. Infrequent or rare, mountain slopes and canyons. Culberson Co., Guadalupe Mts., near west Bowl; S McKittrick Canyon. Jeff Davis Co., Davis Mts., high Goat Canyon of Mt. Livermore; upper NW slopes of Sawtooth Mts.; Haystack Mt. Brewster Co., N side of Cathadral Mt.; Chisos Mts., upper Cattail Canyon, and above Boot Spring. 5300–6000 ft.; Jul–Aug. Also in S-cen. NM; S through the cen. portions of Mex. to Chis.

The leaves of the specimens from the Guadalupe Mountains are smaller and thinner in texture than are those of the Davis Mountains population.

2. Rhamnus betulifolia Greene.   BIRCHLEAF BUCKTHORN.   Fig. 225. [*Rhamnus californica* Eschs. var. *betulifolia* (Greene) Trel.; *R. purshiana* DC. var. *betulifolia* (Greene) Cory.; *Frangula betulifolia* (Greene) Grub]. Infrequent, upper slopes and moist canyons. Culberson Co., Guadalupe Mts., from South McKittrick Canyon to the top. Jeff Davis Co., Davis Mts., upper Madera Canyon of Mt. Livermore; upper Rose Canyon; mid Little Aguja Canyon; mid NW slopes, Sawtooth Mt. Presidio Co., Chinati Mt., Upper Horse Creek Canyon on NE side. Brewster Co., Chisos Mts., above Boot Spring; Pulliam Bluff; upper Pine Canyon. 5000–8000 ft.; spring–early summer. NM; SE AZ; Coah., Mex.

The Trans-Pecos species of *Rhamnus* are easily distinguished by leaf shape

Fig. 226. *Karwinskia humboldtiana* (Coyotillo)

and size. Some authors segregate *R. betulifolia* in the genus *Frangula* Mill. (Kartesz, 1994).

8. KARWINSKIA ZUCC.

Shrubs, 1–2 m high, unarmed, glabrous. Leaves opposite, 3–8 cm long, oblong or elliptic, the margins entire or barely toothed, parallel veins underneath usually with prominent dark streaks. Flowers in small clusters, petals present. Fruit a round, fleshy drupe, blackish when ripe.

A genus of 12 species distributed in the West Indies, Mexico, Central America, and Columbia. One species is found in Texas.

1. Karwinskia humboldtiana (Schult.) Zucc. COYOTILLO. Fig. 226. Infrequent or locally abundant, plains, hills, canyons, arroyos, in the limestone country. Brewster Co., Boquillas Canyon; head of Reagan Canyon. Terrell Co., mouth of San Francisco Canyon. Val Verde Co., widespread throughout, especially from Langtry to Juno to Del Rio. 950–2500 ft.; summer–fall. Rio Grande Plains N to S part of SE TX and Edwards Plateau; Mex. S to Oax.

The fruit of Coyotillo reportedly is very toxic to sheep and other vertebrates including humans. Actually, the flesh of the fruit is sweet and may not be poisonous, but the stones supposedly contain a vertebrate neurotoxin.

37. VITACEAE JUSS. GRAPE FAMILY

Mostly climbing woody vines or shrubs, some herbaceous; tendrils opposite the leaves or on peduncles. Leaves essentially alternate, simple, palmately 3–7 lobed, or compound. Flowers small, in clusters opposite the leaves, unisexual or perfect (on same plant); petals 4–5, greenish; calyx very small; stamens few, opposite petals; style short or absent, stigma capitate or lobed. Fruit (grape) a berry, 2-celled; seeds 1–4, bony.

About 11 genera and 700 species widely distributed in tropical, subtropical, and temperate regions. The largest genus of the family is *Cissus* L., with about 300, mostly tropical species, one of which, *C. incisa* Des Moul., is widespread in the Trans-Pecos. *Cissus incisa* (Ivy Treebine) is recognized by its herbaceous habit with a tuberous, perhaps somewhat woody base, climbing tendrils, fleshy trifoliate leaves, and maladorous bruised tissue. Some species of *Cissus* are grown as house plants. Vitaceae is best known for the wine grape (*Vitis vinifera* L.) and other similar species that are grown for their edible fruit, and for wine and raisins obtained from the fruit. Certain species of *Parthenocissus* Planch. (Boston Ivy, Virginia Creeper) have long been used as ornamental vines to cover rock or brick walls.

KEY TO THE GENERA

1. Leaves simple; bark shredding; pith brownish; seeds pear-shaped   1. *Vitis.*
1. Leaflets 3–7; bark tight; pith white; seeds 3-angled   2. *Parthenocissus.*

1. VITIS L. GRAPE

Viny shrubs, climbing by tendrils, deciduous. Leaves simple, mostly heart-shaped, usually lobed, margins toothed. Flower clusters opposite a leaf; 5 minute sepals and 5 coherent petals, falling together; ovary 2-celled, above a disk of 5 glands alternate with stamens. Fruit a berry (grape); seeds 2–4, pearshaped and beaked, with 2 ventral grooves.

A genus of about 60 species, mainly in temperate regions of the Northern Hemisphere.

1. Vitis arizonica Engelm. CANYON GRAPE, PARRA DEL MONTE. Fig. 227.

[*Vitis arizonica* var. *glabra* Munson; *V. treleasei* Munson *ex* Bailey]. Widespread in mountain canyons and protected habitats, climbing on boulders, trees, and shrubs. El Paso Co., Franklin Mts. Culberson Co., McKittrick Canyon, Guadalupe Mts.; Victorio Canyon, Sierra Diablo. Jeff Davis Co., Madera Canyon and elsewhere near Mt. Livermore; Canyons near Timber Mt.; Limpia Canyon.

Fig. 227. *Vitis arizonica* (Canyon Grape)

Presidio Co., Vieja Pass, Capote Canyon, Sierra Vieja; Pinto Canyon and else-where near Chinati Peak. Brewster Co., canyons of mountains, including Ele-phant, Cathedral, Ranger, Nine-Point, Chisos, Glass. Val Verde Co., near Pumpville. 2500–6500 ft. Flowering in spring; fruiting Aug–Oct. Also NM, AZ; N Mex.

Correll and Johnston (1970) report *V. acerifolia* Raf. (Bush Grape) and *V. riparia* Michx. (Riverbank Grape) to occur in the Trans-Pecos. In October 1988, S. and P. McClinton collected what appears to be *V. acerifolia* Raf. 3.5 mi north of Ruidosa (Presidio County). Other species such as *V. rupestris* Scheele of the Edwards Plateau also have been reported to occur in the Trans-Pecos. Collections I have seen suggest that *V. arizonica* is widespread in the Trans-Pecos and might be the only species to occur in the region, except perhaps for *V. acerifolia* and taxa of the Edwards Plateau that might exist in canyons of extreme eastern Trans-Pecos, and *V. riparia* that is reported in the Lower Can-yons of the Rio Grande.

2. PARTHENOCISSUS PLANCH. VIRGINIA CREEPER

Woody vines, usually climbing by tendrils. Leaves palmate; leaflets 3–7, margins coarsely toothed. Flowers unisexual or bisexual; disk absent. Fruit a purple berry with thin flesh; seeds 1–4.

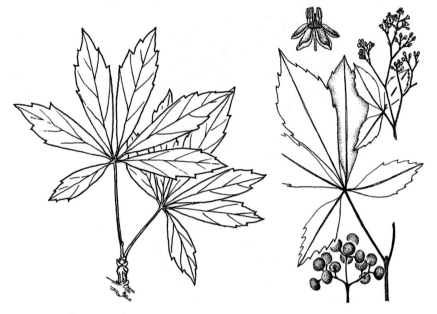

Fig. 228. *Parthenocissus heptaphylla*
(Sevenleaf Creeper)

Fig. 229. *Parthenocissus vitacea*
(Thicket Creeper)

KEY TO THE SPECIES

1. Leaflets mostly 7, 3–5 cm long   **1. *P. heptaphylla.***
1. Leaflets 3–6, 5–12 cm long   **2. *P. vitacea.***

1. **Parthenocissus heptaphylla** (Buckl.) Britt. *ex* Small. SEVENLEAF CREEPER. Fig. 228. [*Ampelopsis heptaphylla* Buckl.; *Parthenocissus texana* Rehd.; *Psedera heptaphylla* (Buckl.) Rehd.]. In rocky canyons and in sandy soils, climbing mostly over small trees, previously endemic on the Edwards Plateau, but collected in Pecos Co., head of a canyon on the Longfellow Ranch, by G. Garner, Oct., 1977.

The leaflets of this species turn an attractive reddish or orange in the fall, and thus the plant should be considered for cultivation. The species name is taken after the characteristic leaflet number.

2. **Parthenocissus vitacea** (Knerr.) Hitchc. THICKET CREEPER. Fig. 229. A rare species in the Trans-Pecos. Culberson Co., Guadalupe Mts. Jeff Davis Co., at the base of high cliffs, N slope, Mt. Livermore; Little Aguja Canyon; lower Madera Canyon. Brewster Co., Mt. Ord; lower canyons of the Rio Grande. 500–7000 ft.; spring. N to WY, MT, and Can.

This species closely resembles *Parthenocissus quinqueflora* (Virginia Creeper) and like the latter plant is widely used ornamentally for covering walls, arbors, and shrubbery. Its leaves turn red or yellow in the fall.

38. MALVACEAE JUSS. MALLOW FAMILY

Usually herbs or shrubs, rarely trees; often with stellate hairs, or the hairs simple or forked, sap more or less mucilaginous. Leaves alternate, simple, with stipules. Flowers perfect and regular; a calyx-like secondary involucre often subtending calyx; sepals and petals 5; petals rolled up longitudinally; stamens numerous, filaments fused forming a tube, anthers 1-celled, kidneyshaped; pollen spiny, large; ovary superior, carpels 1-celled, usually more than 3; style usually branched. Fruit a capsule, opening between partitions, usually carpels separating at maturity; seeds often pubescent, with long tufts in some species (e.g., cotton).

A family of world-wide distribution, with about 75 genera and over 1000 species, well represented in the American tropics. Many mallows are of economic value (e.g., cotton fibers, oil, meal from the seeds of *Gossypium* L. spp.; okra fruits from *Abelmoschus esculentus* (L.) Moench and certain species of *Althaea* L. (Hollyhock), *Callirhoe* Nutt., *Hibiscus* L., *Malva* L., and *Abutilon* Mill. and other genera are planted as ornamentals. Marshmallows are made from root sap of *Althaea officinalis* L., a European species. About 22 genera occur in Texas, some introduced through cultivation.

In the Trans-Pecos 13 genera of the Mallow family are known. Four of these genera are treated below as shrubs or subshrubs. At least six other genera are represented in the Trans-Pecos by one or more perennial species that may exhibit somewhat woody bases: *Sphaeralcea* St.-Hil. spp.; *Herrisantia crispa* (L.) Briz.; *Abutilon wrightii* Gray and *A. incanum* (Link) Sweet; *Sida* L. spp.; *Allowissadula holosericea* (Scheele) Bates; and *Gossypium hirsutum* L. (occasionally escaping from cultivated fields).

KEY TO THE GENERA

1. Styles (10) twice the number of carpels (5); flowers rose-colored
   1. Pavonia.
1. Styles same number as carpels, or styles not branched; flower color cyanic or yellow.
   2. Fruit a slightly elongated capsule, dehiscing longitudinally, seeds several in each cell **2. Hibiscus.**

Fig. 230. *Pavonia lasiopetala* (Wright Pavonia)

2. Fruit a flattened capsule (schizocarp), splitting into one-seeded portions.
  3. Secondary involucral bracts (involucel) present; flowers (in our spe-
    cies) yellow   **3. Malvastrum.**
  3. Secondary involucre absent; flowers violet or blue   **4. Batesimalva.**

1. PAVONIA CAV.

Slender shrub, to 1.5 m high. Leaves alternate, with petioles, somewhat heartshaped, 2.5–7.5 cm long, margins toothed, rarely shallowlobed. Flowers solitary in axils; secondary bracts 5–8, linear and longer than calyx; petals 5, rose; styles 10, carpels 5.

There are about 200 species of this genus, most of them in tropical and subtropical regions. One species occurs in Texas.

    1. Pavonia lasiopetala Scheele. WRIGHT PAVONIA. Fig. 230. [*Pavonia wrightii* Gray]. Seemingly rare in the E Trans-Pecos, known from 20 mi E of Dryden, Terrell Co., 2050 ft., flowering in April. More abundant in woodlands on rocky terrain of the Edwards Plateau and Rio Grande Plains; also Coah., N.L., Dgo., Mex.

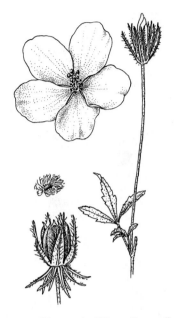

Fig. 231. *Hibiscus coulteri* (Desert Rosemallow)

2. HIBISCUS L. ROSEMALLOW

Perennial herbs or low shrubs (our species). Leaves deeply lobed, or with margins merely toothed. Flowers solitary, petals showy; secondary bracts present. Fruit an elongated (loculicidal) capsule; carpels 5; seeds several in each cell.

There are about 300 species of this genus, most of them in tropical and subtropical regions. Eleven species occur in Texas, three of them in the Trans-Pecos.

KEY TO THE SPECIES

1. Leaves, at least upper ones, deeply lobed (usually 3-cleft); flowers usually yellow, perhaps whitish or purple-tinged   **1. H. coulteri.**
1. Leaves roundish, ovate, to somewhat oblong, margins merely toothed; flowers lavender to purplish   **2. H. denudatus.**

1. Hibiscus coulteri Harv. *ex* Gray. DESERT ROSEMALLOW. Fig. 231. A rather common low subshrub, usually in desert hills and mountains. Hudspeth Co. (Eagle Mts.) E through the middle and S Trans-Pecos to Val Verde Co.; 1500–4600 ft.; Apr–Sep. NM, AZ; adjacent Mex.

Desert rosemallow is easily recognized by its deeply 3-cleft upper leaves with the narrow lobes coarsely toothed, and yellow flowers.

Fig. 232. *Hibiscus denudatus*
(Paleface Rosemallow)

2. Hibiscus denudatus Benth.   PALEFACE ROSEMALLOW.   Fig. 232.   [Including *Hibiscus denudatus* var. *involucellatus* Gray]. A rather common low shrub, usually in desert hills and mountains, sympatric with *H. coulteri* in the Trans-Pecos, but with a wider distribution than the latter species elsewhere. El Paso Co. across the southern Trans-Pecos to Brewster Co. 2000–4600 ft.; Mar–Oct; W through NM and AZ to CA; N Mex.

This species is easily recognized by its usually ovate grayish leaves, with a dense covering of stellate hairs, and purplish flowers. Plants with characters intermediate between *Hibiscus coulteri* and *H. denudatus* have been collected on the west slopes of the Eagle Mountains in Hudspeth County, suggesting hybridization in this area where both parents also are known to occur.

A third species of *Hibiscus*, *H. martianus* Zucc., extends into the eastern Trans-Pecos at the mouth of the Pecos River and westward at a few stations including Independence Creek in Terrell County and near the headquarters in Black Gap Game Refuge in southeastern Brewster County. This species, known as Heartleaf Hibiscus, is a strong herbaceous plant from a woody base, less than 1 m high with rather large, heartshaped leaves, and large, beautiful crimson flowers. The plant would make an attractive ornamental.

Fig. 233. *Malvastrum coromandelianum*
(Threelobe Falsemallow)

3. MALVASTRUM   GRAY

Shrubs or herbs, perennial or annual. Leaves roundish, ovate to lanceolate, the margins sharply toothed (in our species) to deeply lobed. Flowers purple or yellow (in our species), in axils of the stems, or terminal; secondary involucre present. Fruit a schizocarp, with 8–12 carpels in our species, the carpels hairy and beaked on top.

A genus of less than 15 species, these mostly of the American tropics and subtropics. Three species occur in Texas.

1. Malvastrum coromandelianum (L.) Gke.   THREELOBE FALSEMALLOW. Fig. 233.   [*Malva coromandeliana* L.]. Rare in the Trans-Pecos, known from Jeff Davis Co., near the mouth of the Musquiz Canyon, about 12 mi N of Alpine. 4600 ft.; Sep. Once common in the Devils River bed near Del Rio, Val Verde Co. (*Warnock W*855); this is a weedy species of the American tropics; it is found in S TX, to the Edwards Plateau, flowering year round. This plant is herbaceous throughout much of its range but specimens and label data from one collection (*Warnock W*855) suggest that it is occasionally shrubby.

Fig. 234. *Batesimalva violacea*

4. BATESIMALVA FRYXELL

Shrubs to 2 m high, erect and slender; stems with short dense hairs, and longer spreading hairs. Leaves 6–9 cm long, lanceolate to broadly so and long-pointed, green above, pale-pubescent underneath, margins with rounded teeth. Flowers blue or violet, in axils; petals ca. 8 mm long; fruit a schizocarp with 9 carpels. [*Gaya* H.B.K.].

A small genus of northern Mexico, barely reaching into the United States (Fryxell, 1975).

1. Batesimalva violacea (Rose) Fryxell.   Fig. 234.   [*Gaya violacea* Rose.]. In Texas known from among boulders below the "Window" near the "pour-off falls," Oak Canyon, and moist area at lower-most Window Trail from the Basin, W side of the Chisos Mts., Brewster Co.; Oct–Nov. Also Coah. and N.L., Mex.

Although rare in Texas this species is somewhat more common in Mexico. The Texas plants are small, bending shrubs to 1.4 m high with blue flowers, evidently restricted to moist, shady habitats in deep canyons.

39. STERCULIACEAE BARTL. CACAO FAMILY

Trees, shrubs, or herbs. Leaves alternate, simple, margins smooth or toothed, rarely deeply lobed, usually with stellate hairs, stipulate. Flowers usually perfect, regular or irregular, less often unisexual, small or large, mostly axillary; calyx usually with 5 sepals united; petals 5 or absent, separate or united, hypogynous; stamens fused into a tube, at least basally, 5 fertile, 5 infertile, anthers 2–3-celled; ovary superior. Fruit (capsule) usually 5-celled, leathery or rarely fleshy, dehiscent or indehiscent; seeds with much endosperm.

A mostly tropical family of more than 700 species in about 60 genera. One well known member of the family, *Theobroma cacao* L. of the American tropics, is the source of chocolate and cocoa produced from fermented seeds (beans). Species of several genera (including *Firmiana*, *Fremontodendron*, and *Cola*) are cultivated in southern regions of the United States. The Chinese Parasol tree, *Firmiana simplex* W. Wight, is grown in central and south Texas. Five genera of the Cacao family occur in Texas with three of these being represented in the Trans-Pecos.

KEY TO THE GENERA

1. Leaf blades usually much less than 3 cm long; petals hoodshaped **1. *Ayenia.***
1. Leaf blades exceeding 3 cm long; petals flat.
   2. Leaf blades roundish; capsule with dense pubescent processes; seeds many in each cell **2. *Hermannia.***
   2. Leaf blades ovate to lanceolate; capsule glabrate or with minute hairs; seeds usually 1 in each cell **3. *Melochia.***

1. AYENIA L.

Shrubs, subshrubs, or herbs. Leaves simple, toothed. Flowers reddish in our species, perfect, small, usually borne singly or in clusters on rather long, slender stalks; sepals and petals 5, the petals hoodshaped (together canopylike) and with slender bases, the top part attached to the stamen tube; stamens 5, alternating with sterile stamens, one anther in each cavity of stamen tube. Fruit a roundish capsule, with a warty or spiny surface, separating into 5 carpels each with one seed.

A genus of about 70 species distributed mostly in warm regions of the Americas. Four species occur in Texas.

KEY TO THE SPECIES

1. Blades of upper leaves lanceolate to linear, noticeably narrower than lower leaves **1. *A. filiformis.***

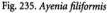

Fig. 235. *Ayenia filiformis*   Fig. 236. *Ayenia microphylla*

1. Blades of upper leaves smaller but mostly like lower leaves which are nearly round, ovate, or elliptic in outline.
  2. Lower surfaces of leaves (and stems) felty with dense covering of short, stellate hairs   **2. A. microphylla.**
  2. Lower surfaces of leaves with scattered or rather dense straight or few-branched hairs, rarely with scattered stellate hairs   **3. A. pilosa.**

  1. **Ayenia filiformis** S. Wats.   Fig. 235.   Mostly limestone but also igneous substrates, widely scattered in low mountains and canyons of the Trans-Pecos. El Paso Co., Franklin Mts., McKelligan Canyon and elsewhere. Presidio Co., Vieja Pass, Vieja Mts.; 6 mi N Candelaria; E side Chinati Mts., Oso Canyon; above Capote Falls, Cienega and Capote Mt.; between Redford and Lajitas; Panther Canyon near Big Hill, and elsewhere. Brewster Co., top Nine-Point Mesa; 2 mi W Study Butte; Big Bend Park, Onion Spring, Paint Gap Hills, head of Boquillas Canyon; Black Gap area, Maravillas Creek, Stairstep Mt. Terrell Co., mouth of San Francisco Canyon. 1900–4800 ft.; May–Dec. W to AZ; also N Mex.
  Plants of this species are subshrubs less than 1 m high.

  2. **Ayenia microphylla** Gray.   Fig. 236.   Mostly limestone substrates in dryish hills and canyons of the Trans-Pecos. El Paso Co., Franklin Mts. Hudspeth Co., Quitman Mts. Culberson Co., Guadalupe Mts.; Baylor Mts. Presidio

Fig. 237. *Ayenia pilosa* (Dwarf Ayenia)

Co., head of Pinto Canyon; W Chinati Peak; 2 mi S Shafter; 1 mi NE Solitario Peak; between Redford and Lajitas. Brewster Co., 20 mi NE Alpine; Packsaddle Mt.; many localities in Big Bend Park; Dead Horse Mts., Stairstep Mt. of Black Gap Refuge; Reagan Canyon. 1875–4400 ft.; flowering most of year. Also Crane Co., and on W Edwards Plateau; W to AZ; Chih. and Coah., Mex.

This species is similar to *Ayenia pilosa,* although *A. microphylla* is usually easily distinguished by its felty-stellate pubescence. Specimens intermediate in pubescence occur above Capote Falls (Presidio Co.), on Steamboat Mesa, and on lower slopes of Nine-Point Mesa. It is possible that *A. microphylla* and *A. pilosa* intergrade. The distributions of *A. microphylla* and *A. pilosa* are largely separate, while *A. microphylla* and *A. filiformis* have generally overlapping ranges.

3. **Ayenia pilosa** Cristobal. DWARF AYENIA. Fig. 237. [*Ayenia pusilla* L.]. Seemingly of somewhat restricted distribution in the Trans-Pecos, limestone and igneous substrates, rocky slopes, lower mountains. El Paso Co., Franklin Mts. Brewster Co., Sul Ross Hill E of Alpine; upper Big Brushy Canyon of Dead Horse Mts.; Chisos Mts. 3000–4900 ft.; flowering much of year. S and E to Rio Grande Plains and Edwards Plateau; W to NM; S to S.L.P. and Tam., Mex.

The petal blades of this species are notched at the apex, have an appendage on the upper part of the inner surface, and have two teeth on the lower part. These characters are absent in *Ayenia microphylla.*

Fig. 238. A) *Melochia pyramidata* (Anglepod
Melochia); B) *Hermannia texana*
(Texas Hermannia)

2. HERMANNIA L.

Plants (*Hermannia texana*) ca. 0.5 m high, with a dense covering of stellate
hairs; stems slender, herbaceous or somewhat woody below, from a woody
rootstock. Leaves roundish in outline, coarsely toothed. Flowers orange-yellow
to orange-red, axillary; petals 8–12 mm long, roundish. Fruit a roundish or
oblong capsule, covered with stiff hairlike processes to 3.5 mm long; opening
into 5 parts, several seeds in each cell.

A genus of perhaps 300 species found mostly in Africa. One species occurs
in Texas.

1. Hermannia texana Gray. TEXAS HERMANNIA. Fig. 238. Rare in
limestone canyons, E Trans-Pecos. Terrell Co., 20 mi N Dryden; Hicks ranch.
Val Verde Co., 5 mi W Comstock; Devils River N of Comstock. 1200–2200 ft.;
Jul–Nov. Also S to Gulf Coast in TX; adjacent Mex.

3. MELOCHIA L. BROOMWOOD

Shrubs or herbs, ours a slender shrub to 2 m high, and only lightly pubescent. Leaves ovate to lanceolate, blades to 3.5 cm long, toothed. Flowers small,
lavender, solitary or in axillary clusters; calyx 5-lobed; petals 5, ca. 7 mm long;

stamens 5, with filaments fused at base. Fruit a capsule, pyramidlike; carpels separating.

A genus of about 75 species, distributed in tropical and subtropical areas of both hemispheres. Three species occur in Texas.

1. **Melochia pyramidata** L. ANGLEPOD MELOCHIA. Fig. 238. Mostly in rocky limestone or sandy habitats, SE Trans-Pecos. Presidio Co., W. Chinati Peak. Brewster Co., Horse Canyon, Black Gap Refuge. Terrell Co., mouth of San Francisco Canyon. Val Verde Co., banks of Devils River, W of Del Rio. 1500–5600 ft.; Jun–Oct. Also S to the Gulf Coast in TX; Coah., Mex.; a widespread species in both hemispheres.

According to Correll and Johnston (1970) only *Melochia pyramidata* var. *pyramidata* occurs in Texas. The species name is taken after the pyramidlike fruit.

40. FRANKENIACEAE S.F. GRAY FRANKENIA FAMILY

Low shrubs or herbs, usually halophytic. Leaves opposite, mostly with very short petioles, the leaf pairs fused at base. Flowers perfect, solitary or in clusters; sepals 4–7, fused into a tube; petals 4–7, separate, each with a scalelike appendage extending down the narrow base; stamens usually 6; ovary superior, with 1 cell, style 2–4-branched; ovules parietal, with long funiculi. Fruit a capsule, enclosed by calyx; seeds 2 to several.

A family distributed mostly in the Mediterranean region, with about 80 species in three genera, and only one genus in Texas.

1. FRANKENIA L.

Small shrub (in our species), stems jointed, ca. 30 cm high, upper parts covered with short hairs. Leaves usually fascicled, with longer pairs, sessile, linear, 3–5 mm long, grooved dorsally, margins rolled backward. Flowers small, white; calyx tube ribbed, 4–5 mm long; petals 5, longer than calyx tube. Fruit linear and angled, ca. 5 mm long.

A genus of about 80 species, widely distributed in saline habitats. Only two species occur in Texas.

1. **Frankenia jamesii** Torr. *ex* Gray. FRANKENIA. Fig. 239. Margins of salt lakes, gypsum soil, rare. Hudspeth Co., near Salt Flat, gypsum soil, along hwy. 62. 4400 ft.; May–Aug. Also NM, AZ, CO, NV; N Mex.

This species is known only from the salt lake area (Salt Flat) of Culberson County, but possibly occurs elsewhere in saline-gypsum habitats of the Trans-Pecos. The low shrubs are easily recognized by leaf characters and the white petals.

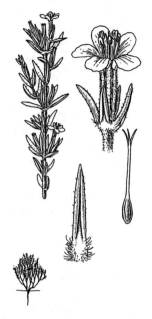

Fig. 239. *Frankenia jamesii* (Frankenia)

41. TAMARICACEAE LINK.   TAMARISK FAMILY

Trees or shrubs, often of saline habitats; branches slender. Leaves scalelike, appressed to stems, often overlapping. Flowers very small, regular, in elongated clusters (racemes); sepals and petals 4–5; petals arising from a fleshy, lobed disc; stamens 4–10; ovary superior, 1-celled; stigmas 2–5. Fruit a capsule; seeds hairy usually at one end.

An Old World family with about 100 species in four genera. Species of one genus have been introduced in Texas.

1. TAMARIX L.   SALT CEDAR, TAMARISK

Trees or shrubs, leaves and small branches deciduous. Leaves closely appressed, usually sheathing the stems. Flowers small with pink (or white) petals arising from under the disk. Fruit a capsule, opening into 3–5 valves; seeds numerous.

A genus of about 50 species, all native to the Old World. The Texas species have become naturalized in various waste places including salt flats, springs, and other saline habitats, especially streams. In the Trans-Pecos, salt cedars have become a critical nuisance most notably along the Rio Grande and Pecos River. Once thickly established along streams, salt cedars are extremely difficult to eradicate and may significantly choke the water source. In Big Bend Park an attempt is being made to eradicate salt cedar from around the historical springs in order to stimulate a return to natural conditions. These plants are often used as wind breaks or as ornamentals because of their spreading, feathery foliage, and dense clusters of pink flowers. The plants have some value in preventing the erosion of sandy-saline soils. Along the Rio Grande they serve as nesting sites for White-winged Dove.

KEY TO THE SPECIES
Adapted from B. R. Baum (1967).

1. Flowers with 4 sepals and 4 petals, usually 4 stamens, rarely more
   1. T. parviflora.
1. Flowers with 5 sepals and 4 petals, usually 5 stamens, rarely more.
   2. Leaves sheathing the stem; petals early falling (1 or 2 perhaps persistent)
      2. T. aphylla.
   2. Leaves not sheathing the stem; petals persistent.
      3. Filaments (of stamens) inserted between lobes of the floral disk (perhaps 2 of them) and (at least 3 of them) under the disk near the edge.
         4. Sepal margins essentially smooth; flowers of racemes on green branches with 1–2 filaments inserted between lobes of the disk
            3. T. chinensis.
         4. Sepal margins minutely toothed; all filaments of all flowers inserted under the disk near the edge   **4. T. ramosissima.**
      3. Filaments arising from disk lobes.
         5. Flower clusters mostly on branches of previous year
            5. T. africana.
         5. Flower cluster mostly on green branches of current year
            6. T. gallica.

1. **Tamarix parviflora** DC.   Fig. 240.   Uncommon, usually cultivated or escaped from cultivation, not usually in salty substrates. Brewster Co., Alpine. TX W to CA, NE to NC, N to Can.; native of lower Europe.

2. **Tamarix aphylla** (L.) Karsten.   ATHEL.   Fig. 241.   Uncommon near rather permanent watercourses. Brewster Co., Boquillas Canyon, along the Rio Grande, sandy banks. Presidio Co., near Presidio; near Ruidosa and Candelaria. 1825–2000 ft. TX, W to CA: native of N Afr., Middle East, lower Europe.

This species, native to the Middle East and North African deserts, is perhaps the easiest of all the salt cedars to recognize because of its sheathing leaves. The other salt cedars of the Trans-Pecos look much alike and could be part of one complex.

Fig. 240. A) *Tamarix ramosissima*; B) *T. parviflora*, flower with 4 stamens.

3. Tamarix chinensis Lour.　A rather common species, often cultivated or escaped, usually in non-salty habitats. El Paso, Culberson, Presidio, Brewster, Pecos, Crockett, Ward, Loving counties. W to CA, N to Can., NE to NC; native to China, Japan, and Mongolia. According to Horton (1977) *Tamarix chinensis* is the name that should be applied to a single widespread and variable species that has been naturalized in the western United States, and that the other names used here (*T. ramosissima, T. africana, T. gallica, T. parvifolia*) should be discarded at least for the western populations.

4. Tamarix ramosissima Ledeb.　Fig. 240.　Rather common in salty habitats. El Paso, Hudspeth, Culberson, Reeves, Presidio, and Brewster counties. TX, W to NV, N to Can., E to AR; native to Russia and Asia.

Tamarix ramosissima and *T. chinensis* reportedly are closely related, sometimes difficult to identify, and perhaps hybridize in mixed populations.

5. Tamarix africana Poir.　Of spotty distribution. Pecos Co., saline substrates, along the Pecos River near Imperial; 2680 ft. TX, W to CA; SC; native to Europe.

6. Tamarix gallica L.　Somewhat rare in TX and the U.S., once considered to be the most common species in the U.S.; TX, CA, GA, SC; native to Europe. A tree identified by Jim Liles as *T. gallica*, from the Rio Grande Village area of Big Bend National Park, is regarded as a National champion with a size of 64 ft. high, 66 ft. crown spread, and 10.6 ft. girth.

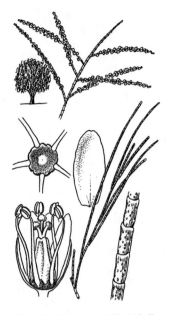

Fig. 241. *Tamarix aphylla* (Athel)

42. FOUQUIERIACEAE DC. OCOTILLO FAMILY

Spiny shrubs with wandlike branches, one species (*Fouquieria columnaris*) of Baja California with a large trunk and small branches; spines formed from petiole and midrib of first-season leaves. Leaves in clusters in axils of spines. Flowers prominent in terminal clusters; sepals and petals 5, the latter forming a tube; stamens 10–19, filaments thickened at base and attached to corolla tube. Fruit a capsule, 3–4-celled; seeds winged or angled with a hairy fringe. [*Idria* Kell.].

A monotypic family with 11 species, centered in Mexico, with one species in the southwestern United States. Another genus, *Idria*, the bizarre Boojum Tree of Baja California (one locality in Sonora), was recognized for the family until Henrickson (1972) decided that its one species, *I. columnaris* Kell., should be merged with *Fouquieria*.

1. FOUQUIERIA KUNTH OCOTILLO, CANDLEWOOD

Spiny shrubs with wandlike branches to 9 m long, and little or no trunk (in our species); stems covered with spines to 2 cm long. Leaves early falling, sessile in axils of spines, spatulate in shape and ca. 5 cm long. Flowers clustered at

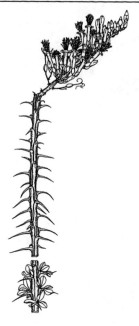

Fig. 242. *Fouquieria splendens* (Ocotillo)

stem tips, tubular corolla scarlet, to 15 mm long; stamens red, protruding. Fruit (capsule) to 15 mm long, 3-celled, persistent; seeds winged with whitish hairs.

1. **Fouquieria splendens** Engelm. OCOTILLO. Fig. 242. The most widely distributed species of the genus, various desert habitats throughout the Trans-Pecos; Mar–Jun. Also W to CA; N Mex.

Ocotillo is a characteristic species of the Chihuahuan Desert in Trans-Pecos Texas. The plant is easily recognized by its spiny wandlike branches which arise from the root crown, and clusters of scarlet flowers on the stem tips during the spring. Leaves are borne on the stems periodically during the year, always soon after rains. Leaves on Ocotillo stems are a reliable indication of recent rainfall. The leaves mature and may fall after a few weeks.

The stems of Ocotillo are cut and planted close together to make living fences or walls, especially in Mexico. The plant is an excellent ornamental in desert landscape themes and cactus gardens. Roots of the Ocotillo were powdered by Apache Indians and used to treat wounds. Indians sometimes ate the fruit and flowers. Resin and wax from the bark has been used to condition leather.

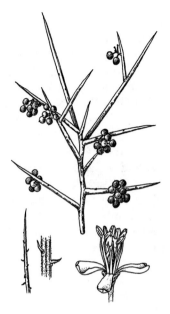

Fig. 243. *Koeberlinia spinosa* (Allthorn)

43. CAPPARACEAE JUSS. CAPER FAMILY

Shrubs, rarely herbs or small trees. Leaves usually alternate, simple or compound, reduced and scalelike in *Koeberlinia*; stipules small or absent. Flowers in clusters or solitary, usually perfect, hypogynous; sepals and petals usually 4; stamens usually 4, plus staminodea; ovary on a short stalk. Fruit usually on a stalk, often a berry, or dry and podlike; seeds curved. [*Koeberliniaceae* Engelm.]

A family of about 800 species in about 45 genera, widespread in tropical and subtropical zones, with a few species in temperate and arid climates. The largest genera are *Capparis* L. and *Cleome* L. *Koeberlinia* has been placed in the monotypic family Koeberliniaceae (Allthorn Family), where its anatomical relationship to Capparaceae has been studied by Gibson (1979).

1. KOEBERLINIA ZUCC. ALLTHORN, JUNCO

Plants usually roundish shrubs to 3 m high, less often small trees to 5 m high, with a short trunk; branches green, intricate, tipped with green spines. Berry tan to black and shiny when ripe, 3–4 mm across.

1. **Koeberlinia spinosa** Zucc. ALLTHORN. Fig. 243. Common in various desert habits throughout the Trans-Pecos, also scattered in the mountains. Mar–Oct. W to AZ; also N Mex.

This impenetrable thorny plant in the Trans-Pecos is usually referred to as Allthorn, but it is also known by some as Crucifixion Thorn, a common name more appropriately applied to the lookalike genus *Holacantha*. In southwestern Arizona, southeastern California, and adjacent Sonora, a separate variety, *Koeberlinia spinosa* var. *tenuispina* Kearn. & Peeb., with longer, more slender branches, bluish-green bark, (rather than yellowish-green) and longer flower parts has been recognized (Kearney and Peebles, 1951). Accordingly our plant is var. **spinosa**. In addition, Correll (in Correll and Johnston, 1970) has noted the existence of two different forms of *Koeberlinia* in Texas, the typical form found in the Trans-Pecos, and an atypical form with slender, spreading branches and branchlets found in south Texas.

Allthorns provide excellent cover for quail that may also eat the fruit. In times of drought, rodents and other small animals may browse the green thorns and branches. The Allthorn represents a good example of adaptation to desert conditions.

44. LOASACEAE DUM.   STICKLEAF FAMILY

Herbs (annual or perennial) or shrubs, usually covered with barbed, multicellular hairs, sometimes stinging. Leaves alternate or opposite; the margins smooth, toothed, or lobed. Flowers bisexual, regular; petals separate or fused, often with petallike staminodia alternating; stamens 5 to numerous, filaments slender or petallike; style 1; ovary inferior. Fruit a capsule, dry with many seeds, or an achene (one seed).

A family primarily of the New World, about 200 species in 14 genera of tropical and temperate America, and one genus (two species) in Africa. Three genera are represented in Texas and in the Trans-Pecos, only one of which can be considered as subshrubby.

1. CEVALLIA LAG.

Subshrub to 1 m high, with somewhat brittle stems arising from the base; stems and leaves covered with stinging hairs. Leaves essentially sessile, the margins wavy or lobed. Flowers numerous in headlike clusters, the heads on long stalks; sepals and petals opening in morning, similar in appearance, 5–8 mm long, covered with hairs, yellowish inside; stamens 5. Fruit dry, not opening, with one seed.

A genus with one species.

1. Cevallia sinuata Lag.   STINGING CEVALLIA, SHIRLEY'S NETTLE.   Fig. 244.   A common weed, roadside especially on rocky roadcuts, open areas, various rocky, gravel, or clay substrates, scattered in grassland habitats in lower

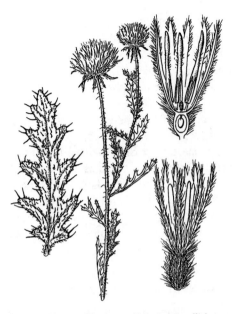

Fig. 244. *Cevallia sinuata* (Stinging Cevallia)

Davis Mts. Also on the lower High Plains, and in the W half of TX, W to SE AZ; N Mex., S to Zac.

The species name of this mild nettle is taken after its leaves with wavy margins. A common name recognizes Shirley Powell whose extensive cytological investigations revealed that two morphologically similar cytotypes ($n = 13, 7$) comprise the species. The $n = 13$ cytotype is most widespread and weedy, while populations with $n = 7$ are restricted to small areas east of Presidio, Texas, west of Ojinaga, Mexico, and a few other localities in north-central Mexico (Powell, et al., 1977).

45. CACTACEAE JUSS. CACTUS FAMILY

Plants with fleshy, succulent stems; the stems simple, clumped, or branched (and treelike), cylindrical, flattened, ribbed, or with tubercles (these fused into ribs or separate); often jointed; sap watery or milky. Leaves very small, usually absent in mature plants; axils (areoles) usually bearing spines; glochids (barbed hairs) present in *Opuntia*. Flowers solitary or in clusters, parts forming a floral tube, the scale leaves of floral tube grading upward into sepallike structures, and sepallike parts grading into petallike parts, these of various yellow or cyanic colors; ovary inferior, stamens numerous; style 1, stigmas separate; carpels 3–many. Fruit a berry, often bearing spines and glochids; seeds many.

A family of probably 1000–1500 species, distributed from Canada to southern South America, with one or more species in nearly every state of the United States (Benson, 1982). The center of distribution seems to be in the dry areas of Mexico, with numerous species extending to the south and north. Arizona and Texas are the most prominent cactus areas in the United States, with over 70 species and 130 taxa in each state. About 17 genera are found in Texas, and all but a few of these occur in the Trans-Pecos. More than 80 species (over 120 taxa) of Cactaceae occur in the Trans-Pecos, probably more species than in Arizona, but the large, spectacular cacti such as the Saguaro are absent from Texas. Cacti are extensively grown and sold as ornamentals. The fruit of many species are edible, particularly those of the large prickly pears (e.g., Indian Fig, Mexico) and the Strawberry Cactus in southern Trans-Pecos Texas. Only the larger cacti of the Trans-Pecos, particularly the shrublike prickly pears (*Opuntia* spp.) and chollas (*Opuntia* spp.) are included below. Benson (1982) and Weniger (1984) present treatments of Texas cacti.

1. OPUNTIA MILL. PRICKLY PEAR, CHOLLA

Stems of flattened or cylindroidal joints, not ribbed. Leaves absent on mature joints, short-lived on young joints, cylindroidal or awlshaped; spines often 1–10 per areole (absent in some species) whitish to nearly yellow, gray, brown, pink, red, or black; glochids barbed. Flowers borne near apexes of joints; flower tube above ovary very short, deciduous. Fruit fleshy or dry, with or without spines; seeds discoid.

A genus of many species in the Western Hemisphere, much in need of modern taxonomic study. The taxonomy of *Opuntia*, particularly the prickly pears, appears to be complicated by polyploidy, hybridization, and vegetative reproduction. More than 22 species of *Opuntia* occur in the Trans-Pecos, some of them with more than one variety. The cholla *O. spinosior* (Engelm.) Toumey, common in southwestern New Mexico and southern Arizona, recently has been reported but not confirmed to occur in southern Hudspeth County. Instead the cholla there, and perhaps in adjacent counties along and near the Rio Grande, may be undescribed. The low-growing prickly pear *O. cymochila* Engelm. & Bigel. has also been reported for the Trans-Pecos, but its distribution remains to be studied. Information provided by D. J. Pinkava (pers. comm.) was used in constructing the key to the prickly pears.

KEY TO THE SPECIES

1. Stem joints cylindroidal (chollas): glochids usually not prominent on above ground stems   **Subgenus 1. *Cylindropuntia.***

2. Plants shrubby; joints cylindroidal; spines slender, not papillose, with entire epidermis separating into a thin sheath; glochids usually small.
   3. Joints at plant apex 1.5 cm wide or more (at least some of them).
      4. Spines to 1–3 cm long; spine sheaths close fitting; flowers magenta
      1. *O. imbricata.*
      4. Spines to 3.8–5 cm long; spine sheaths loose; flowers yellowish green to brown
      2. *O. tunicata.*
   3. Joints at plant apex not more than 1.2 cm wide.
      5. Apical joints approaching 1 cm wide; flowers magenta; fruit reddish, tuberculate
      3. *O. kleiniae.*
      5. Apical joints less than 0.5 cm wide; flowers yellow; fruits bright red, not tuberculate
      4. *O. leptocaulis.*
2. Plants forming low mats; joints clavate to ovoid; spines flattened at least basally, cross papillose, with the epidermis separating and sheathlike only at the very apex; glochids large, strongly barbed.
   6. Stem joints ovoid to obovoid; spines mostly needlelike
   5. *O. grahamii.*
   6. Stem joints basically clubshaped; spines mostly flattened.
      7. Roots tuberous; spines 7–9 per areole; central spine absent
      6. *O. aggeria.*
      7. Roots fibrous; spines 8–16 per areole; central spine present.
         8. Stem joints 7–15 cm long; tubercles 3.5–5 cm long, 1–1.5 cm wide
         9. *O. emoryi.*
         8. Stem joints 4.5–7 cm long; tubercles 1.5–2 cm long, 0.5–0.8 cm wide.
            9. Older plants in dense mounds topped by bristling grayish-white spines; areole diameter 3–4 mm
            7. *O. densispina.*
            9. Older plants usually sprawling in mats; the spines yellow to reddish-brown; areole diameter 5–7 mm
            8. *O. schottii.*
1. Stem joints (pads) flattened (prickly pears): glochids usually prominent on above ground stems
Subgenus 2. *Opuntia.*
      10. Fruits dry, at first green or superficially reddish then tan at maturity, with barbed spines at least at the apical rim.
         11. Plants sprawling or prostrate, less than 30 cm high; spines tan, yellowish-brown to chalky white, not bright yellow; flowers yellow (perhaps pink), the centers not red   **10. *O. polyacantha.***
         11. Plants erect, more or less 90 cm high; spines yellow, often with red bases, aging brown to nearly black; flowers yellow with red centers
         20. *O. aureispina.*

10. Fruits fleshy or juicy, red to purple (rarely yellow or orange) at maturity, usually without spines (except in *O. spinosibacca*) and lacking an apical rim.

   12. Spines absent on pads, or at most vestigial.

      13. Pads purplish (at least near areoles)   **13. *O. macrocentra.***

      13. Pads green.

         14. Pad surfaces pubescent (under magnification); glochids deciduous, easily dislodged in the air (native)   **12. *O. rufida.***

         14. Pad surfaces glabrous; glochids not so easily dislodged (cultivars, perhaps escaped).

            15. Plants treelike, to 2–5 m high, with a trunk; pads (20–)40–60 cm long, 2–3 cm or more thick; glochids in a rim at apical margin of mid-pad areoles

                               11. *O. ficus-indica.*

            15. Plants shrubs, usually 1–2 m high, trunkless; pads to 25 cm long, ca. 1.5 cm thick; glochids subapical in mid-pad areoles, usually covered by cottony hairs

                               22. *O. ellisiana.*

   12. Spines present (spineless forms occasional in some species).

         16. Plants treelike, 2–5 m high, with a trunk; pads (20–)40–60 cm long, 2–3 cm or more thick; escape from cultivation   **11. *O. ficus-indica.***

         16. Plants not treelike, usually 1–2 m high (or less), rarely with a short main trunk; pads usually 20–30 cm long or less, usually 2 cm or less thick; native species.

            17. Spines all turned downward, except the longest one in a few areoles at top of pad, one lower spine longer than the others, red-brown at bases, tips yellow (turning black with age)   **14. *O. strigil.***

            17. Spines otherwise.

               18. Shrubs low, in prostrate clumps; pads 5–11 cm long, 3.5–7.5 cm wide; spines needlelike, white to gray, usually 1–3(–6) in upper areoles

                           18. *O. macrorhiza.*

               18. Shrubs erect to sprawling; pads 10–40 cm long; spines needlelike or flattened at bases, various colors, 1–12 per upper areole.

                  19. Areoles at mid-pad with glochids of irregular lengths (usually not in dense tufts), mostly to completely encircling areoles; flowers yellow, without red centers; fruit flesh reddish or purplish throughout.

20. Shrubs to 2.5 m high, erect (perhaps with a short trunk) or sprawling; spines chalky white to gray, yellow, or with red or reddish brown bases; widespread in the Trans-Pecos   17. *O. engelmannii.*
20. Shrubs to 1 m high, erect or somewhat sprawling; spines yellow, aging reddish-brown or darker; Chisos Mts.   21. *O. chisosensis.*
19. Areoles at mid-pad with glochids of equal length (usually in dense tufts), or gradually shorter from apex to base of areole, in an apical crescent only partly encircling the areole; flowers yellow, with red centers; fruit flesh greenish, perhaps purplish.
    21. Areoles at mid-pad prominently obovate, with a brushy tuft of large glochids in an apical crescent; spines, the divergent ones, nearly black to dark red with clearly marked yellow tips, other (deflexed) spines whitish; flowers yellow, without red centers
                                                  19. *O. atrispina.*
    21. Areoles at mid-pad elliptic to narrowly obovate, with glochids of various lengths; divergent spines without yellow tips, or if so, tips not clearly marked, deflexed spines present or absent; flowers with red centers or not.
        22. Pads purplish at least near the areoles   13. *O. macrocentra.*
        22. Pads green to yellow-green.
            23. Shrubs usually less than .75 m tall, trunkless; fruits not spiny, red to purplish, fleshy; widespread in Trans-Pecos
                                      15. *O. phaeacantha.*
            23. Shrubs to 1.5 m tall, perhaps with a short trunk; fruits somewhat spiny toward the top, drying at maturity; restricted S of Chisos Mts.   16. *O. spinosibacca.*

1. **Opuntia imbricata** (Haw.) DC. CANE CHOLLA, TREE CHOLLA. Fig. 245. [*Opuntia arborescens* Engelm.]. Gravelly and sandy soils, desert and grassland, throughout the Trans-Pecos; 1800–6000 ft.; May–Jun. S TX, to AZ, NM, CO, KS, OK to cen. Mex.

Cane Cholla is one of the most widespread and prominent cacti. Mature plants reach 1–3 m high with branching stems, magenta flowers in late May and early June and yellow fruits that persist through the summer. Cane Cholla is a weedy pest often infesting rangeland after overgrazing. New plants sprout readily from joints that fall to the ground. Two varieties are recognized in the Trans-Pecos: var. **imbricata** (Cane Cholla) is the widespread entity; and var. **argentea** Anthony (Silverspine Cane Cholla) distinguished by silvery spines (Fig. 246) and other traits (Benson, 1982), apparently restricted to southern Brewster County in Big Bend National Park near Mariscal Mountain, and perhaps in adjacent Mexico.

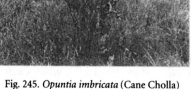

Fig. 245. *Opuntia imbricata* (Cane Cholla)   Fig. 246. *Opuntia imbricata* var. *argentea* (Silverspine Cane Cholla)

2. Opuntia tunicata (Lehm.) Link & Otto.   ICICLE CACTUS, TENCHOLOTE. Fig. 247.   Two varieties are recognized (Benson, 1982) in the Trans-Pecos. *Opuntia tunicata* var. **tunicata** (Icicle Cactus) is localized on the south and eastern slopes of the Glass Mountains, ca. 4500 ft., in Brewster and Pecos counties; S to Mex. and Chile. The most striking feature of the Icicle Cactus is caused by the copious spines with papery whitish-tan sheaths that glisten in the sun. *Opuntia tunicata* var. **davisii** (Engelm. & Bigel.) L. Benson (Davis Cholla) is widespread but scattered, mostly in grassland, 1800–4500 ft., in Brewster, Presidio, Jeff Davis, and Culberson counties; Jun–Jul. Also to cen. TX, N to OK and NM. Among other characters (Benson, 1982) var. *davisii* is recognized by its golden-tan spine sheaths. When the sun is right these plants are obvious, small golden shrubs conspicuous among other rangeland plants by their reflecting spine sheaths. In future treatments var. *davisii* likely will be regarded as a distinct species.

3. Opuntia kleiniae DC.   CANDLE CHOLLA, KLEIN CHOLLA.   Fig. 248. Alluvial basins, canyons, and rocky hillsides in the mountains, or gravel, sand, and silt in desert shrub, particularly along and near the Rio Grande. Hudspeth Co., between Ft. Hancock and Sierra Blanca. Culberson Co., near Pine Springs, Presidio Co., Chinati Mts. to near Lajitas. Jeff Davis Co., frequent in Musquiz Canyon, Limpia Canyon, and elsewhere. Brewster Co., scattered from near Alpine to Big Bend Park near the Rio Grande. May–Jun. S NM.

Fig. 247. *Opuntia tunicata* var. *tunicata*   Fig. 248. *Opuntia kleiniae* (Candle Cholla)
(Icicle Cactus)

Opuntia kleiniae is in need of taxonomic study. Candle Cholla plants in the Davis Mountains exhibit some differences from those found along the Rio Grande, and possibly more than one taxon exists in the Trans-Pecos.

4. **Opuntia leptocaulis** DC. CHRISTMAS CHOLLA, TASAJILLO, PENCIL CHOLLA. Fig. 249. Widespread and locally abundant throughout the Trans-Pecos, particularly in long abused habitats; May–Jun. Also S TX; W to AZ, N to NM and OK; N Mex.

The bright red fruits of Tasajillo are apparent in the late fall and winter when most of the desert shrubs have lost their foliage. The fruits are favored by quail and probably wild turkeys.

5. **Opuntia grahamii** Engelm. GRAHAM DOG CHOLLA. [*Opuntia schottii* Engelm. var. *grahamii* (Engelm.) L. Benson]. Desert habitats in various soil types, including sand, gravel, and clay. Presidio Co., above Candelaria. Brewster Co., widely scattered in lower middle part of county. 3000–3500 ft.; May–Jun; probably in adjacent Mex.

Benson (1982) recognized *Opuntia grahamii* as a variety of *O. schottii*, but Ralston and Hilsenbeck (1989; 1992) have redefined the *O. schottii* complex as comprising five distinct species, *O. grahamii*, *O. aggeria*, *O. densispina*, *O. schottii*, and *O. emoryi*. The ovoid stems of *O. grahamii* are the smallest (3.5–4.5 cm long) of any member of the complex, and the spines are mostly

Fig. 249. *Opuntia leptocaulis*   Fig. 250. *Opuntia aggeria*
(Christmas Cholla)   (Clumped Dog Cholla)

terete, as opposed to mostly flattened in other species of the complex. *Opuntia grahamii* is tetraploid ($2n = 44$). *Opuntia grahamii* is marginally sympatric with *O. schottii* in Big Bend National Park, but they do not intergrade (Ralston & Hilsenbeck, 1989). Key characters of the five club chollas included here were obtained largely from Ralston & Hilsenbeck (1989).

6. **Opuntia aggeria** Ralston & Hilsenbeck. CLUMPED DOG CHOLLA. Fig. 250. [*Opuntia grahamii* × *O. schottii* Anthony]. Various desert habitats along and near the Rio Grande in Brewster Co., in Big Bend National Park W to the Presidio-Brewster co. line, scattered in the lower middle part of Brewster Co. 2000–3500 ft.; Mar–Apr; to cen. Coah., Mex.

Opuntia aggeria is the predominant dog cholla in Big Bend National Park. It occurs sympatrically with *O. densispina*, and marginally so with *O. schottii* and possibly *O. grahamii*. *Opuntia aggeria* is the only diploid ($2n = 22$) of the otherwise tetraploid *O. schottii* complex (Ralston & Hilsenbeck, 1989). Both *O. aggeria* and *O. grahamii* have tuberous roots and lack central spines, while other members of the complex have fibrous roots and central spines.

7. **Opuntia densispina** Ralston & Hilsenbeck. DENSE DOG CHOLLA. Reportedly restricted to clay soil near the type locality in extreme southern Big Bend National Park near Solis, Brewster Co. 2000 ft. May–Jun; possibly adjacent Mex.

DESCRIPTIVE FLORA 285

Opuntia densispina is similar in appearance to *O. aggeria*, with which it is generally sympatric, but differs in chromosome number, clay habitat, and several morphological features (Ralston & Hilsenbeck, 1992), particularly the dense rounded mound habit of apparently older plants which accounts for a dense appearance of shining spine clusters. *Opuntia aggeria* also has a mounded habit, and whitish spines, but usually the mounds are somewhat flat. *Opuntia densispina* is most closely related to *O. schottii* and *O. emoryi* (Ralston & Hilsenbeck, 1992).

8. Opuntia schottii Engelm. SCHOTT DOG CHOLLA. Limestone hills and shallow alluvium, widespread and common in Val Verde Co., across Terrell Co., into lower cen. Brewster Co., where infrequent. 1000–3500 ft. Jun–Jul; also south TX near the Rio Grande (Zapata, Starr, and Cameron counties); outliers in cen. TX; adjacent Mex.

The major distribution of *Opuntia schottii*, recognized by Benson (1982) as *O. schottii* var. *schottii*, is in the southeastern Trans-Pecos in more mesic habitats near the Pecos River, and is increasingly abundant east of the Pecos River. Dog chollas in general, but particularly this taxon, are annoying to hikers because the spiny stem joints are easily detachable and cling to shoes and clothing.

9. Opuntia emoryi Engelm. DEVIL CHOLLA. [*Opuntia stanlyi* Engelm.]. Sand, loam, and gravel, known in the Trans-Pecos region only from near Candelaria and the Rio Grande, west-cen. Presidio Co. 3000 ft. May–Jun; probably adjacent Mex.

Plants of *Opuntia emoryi* form low, sprawling mats to 15 cm high, with the largest stem joints (7–15 cm) and tubercles (3.5–5 cm) of the *O. schottii* complex. The taxon appears to be related to a similar Arizona species, *O. stanlyi* var. *stanlyi*, with which it has been confused in the past (Benson, 1982; Pinkava and Parfitt, 1988).

10. Opuntia polyacantha Haw. PLAINS PRICKLY PEAR. Fig. 251 [*Opuntia missouriensis* DC.; *O. polyacantha* var. *rufispina* (Engelm. & Bigel. *ex* Engelm.) L. Benson; *O. polyacantha* var. *trichophora* (Engelm. & Bigel.) Coult.; *O. arenaria* Engelm.; *O. hystricina* Engelm.]. Sandy soils, alluvium, or rocky slopes, deserts and mountains, mostly in the northern Trans-Pecos, El Paso, Hudspeth, Culberson, Presidio (Chinati Peak), Brewster, and Jeff Davis counties; 3400–7000 ft.; May–Jun; one of the most widespread cacti, N into Canada and E to MO.

Parfitt (1991) submerged two varieties recognized by Benson (1982), *Opuntia polyacantha* var. *rufispina* and *O. polyacantha* var. *trichophora*, in *O. polyacantha* var. **polyacantha**. Parfitt treated *O. arenaria* (Sand Prickly Pear), long considered to be a rare but distinct species, as var. **arenaria** (Engelm.) Parfitt of *O. polyacantha*. The var. *arenaria* has the most slender ovary of the *O. poly-*

Fig. 251. *Opuntia polyacantha*
(Plains Prickly Pear)

Fig. 252. *Opuntia rufida* (Blind Prickly Pear)

acantha complex, being about three times as long as wide. Sand Prickly Pear occurs in El Paso and Hudspeth counties. *Opuntia polyacantha* var. *hystricina* (Engelm. & Bigel.) Parfitt has been reported to occur in Hudspeth County (Weedin, pers. comm.), but not listed for the Trans-Pecos by Parfitt (1991).

11. Opuntia ficus–indica (L.) Mill. INDIAN FIG PRICKLY PEAR. [*Opuntia megacantha* Salm-Dyck]. Cultivated as an ornamental and for its fruits, probably native to Mexico but grown in all warm countries, frequently escaping and becoming naturalized; cultivated in Presidio, Presidio County; reported from Brewster County at the Kokernot Ranch 7 mi NW of Alpine. Both spineless and spined forms occur. Reportedly hybridizes with native species in some areas of the Southwest, forming somewhat confusing prickly pear hybrid swarms (Benson, 1982).

12. Opuntia rufida Engelm. BLIND PRICKLY PEAR. Fig. 252. [*Opuntia rufida* var. *tortifolia* Anthony; *O. microdasys* var. *rufida* (Engelm.) K. Schum.]. Desert habitats, sand, gravel, rocky hillsides, relatively common in southern Presidio and Brewster counties, along and near the Rio Grande; 1800–3600 ft.; May–Jun. Adjacent Coah. and Chih., Mex.

Opuntia rufida is a fairly large blue-green prickly pear, to ca 1.5 m high and 2.5 m wide. Spines are absent but the joints have copious evenly spaced areoles in which numerous reddish glochids are borne. The glochids are loose and

Fig. 253. *Opuntia macrocentra*
(Purple Prickly Pear)

supposedly may fly into the air when the plants are shaken. The dislodged glochids may get into the eyes of animals and cause severe problems.

13. Opuntia macrocentra Engelm. PURPLE PRICKLY PEAR. Fig. 253. [*Opuntia violacea* Engelm.; *O. macrocentra* var. *minor* Anthony; *O. violacea* var. *macrocentra* (Engelm.) L. Benson; *O. violacea* var. *violacea*; *O. violacea* var. *castetteri*]. Various habitats in the desert, grasslands, and mountains of the Trans-Pecos; 2800–5200 ft.; May–Jun. Widely distributed in southern NM and AZ; also Son., Chih., Coah., Dgo., Mex.

This taxon was long known by the illegitimate name *Opuntia violacea*. Benson (1982) recognized four varieties of *O. violacea* to occur in the Trans-Pecos: var. *macrocentra* (Engelm.) L. Benson (Longspined Prickly Pear); var. *violacea* (Purple Prickly Pear); var. *santa-rita* (Griffiths & Hare) L. Benson (Purple Prickly Pear); and var. *castetteri* L. Benson. The correct name for this species is *O. macrocentra* (Pinkava and Parfitt, 1988; Ferguson, 1988). Recent studies (Pinkava, pers. comm.) have shown that three of the varieties listed above intergrade and are treated as synonyms with *O. macrocentra*. One of the varieties, var. *santa-rita*, is regarded by Pinkava (pers. comm.) as a distinct species, *O. santa-rita* (Griffiths & Hare) Rose, while Ferguson (1988) treats the taxon as a variety of *O. chlorotica* Engelm. & Bigel., var. *santa-rita* (Griffiths & Hare). *Opuntia santa-rita* has purple pads like *O. macrocentra*, but is distinguished by its spineless or few-spined pads where any spines, one per areole, more or less

Fig. 254. *Opuntia strigil* (Marblefruit Prickly Pear)

orangish in color, if present, are scattered in areoles of the upper pad margin. The plants of *O. santa-rita* also are treelike, with a short trunk, and have yellow flowers without red centers, while plants of *O. macrocentra* are shrubs that produce yellow flowers with red centers. There is some question about whether *O. santa-rita* occurs in the Trans-Pecos. Its primary distribution is in southeastern Arizona, Hidalgo County, New Mexico and in northern Sonora, Mexico, through Chihuahua into Durango. It has been reported in the Trans-Pecos by Weniger (1984), between Presidio and Big Bend National Park, and also in south-central Texas (Pinkava, pers. comm.). Previously the occasional spineless plants of *O. macrocentra* might have been interpreted as *O. santa-rita*. Ferguson (1988) points to the recognition of *O. macrocentra* var. *minor* Anthony in southern Presidio and Brewster counties, and another as yet unnamed variety of *O. macrocentra* from near El Paso, in Eddy County, New Mexico, and westward to Graham and Cochise counties in Arizona. Studies of the *O. macrocentra* complex are in progress.

14. Opuntia strigil Engelm. MARBLEFRUIT PRICKLY PEAR. Fig. 254. Limestone soils on rocky slopes and valleys, reported to occur in El Paso, Pecos, and Terrell counties, most common in the latter two; 3000–4500 ft.; May–Jun. Adjacent Crockett Co., and also Nolan Co., TX.

Opuntia strigil is a medium-sized prickly pear usually less than 1 m high, spines reddish-brown with yellow tips, 1–8 per areole, one longer than oth-

Fig. 255. *Opuntia phaeacantha* var. *phaeacantha* (Purplefruited Prickly Pear)

ers, all deflected downward. The var. *O. strigil* var. *flexospina* (Griffiths) L. Benson (Benson, 1982), of Webb County, Texas, has been realigned by Parfitt and Pinkava (1988) as a variety of *O. engelmannii.*

15. Opuntia phaeacantha Engelm.   PURPLEFRUITED PRICKLY PEAR.   Fig. 255.   Various habitats, desert, grassland, and mountains, probably the most widespread and common prickly pear in the desert southwest, at least according to the concept of Benson (1982); 2000–8000 ft.; May–Jun.

Reddish to purplish pigments may develop in the stems of *Opuntia phaeacantha* during cold and dry periods, but unlike in *O. violacea* the betacyanin pigments disappear in healthy plants with bluish-green stems during warm moist seasons. Benson (1982) recognizes 10 varieties of the complex species *O. phaeacantha*, these occurring in the general southwestern U.S. and Mexico. These varieties are geographically separated to some extent but some of them overlap in distribution. Hybridization reportedly occurs in some places where *O. phaeacantha* varieties come in contact with each other or with some other species of *Opuntia*, thus accounting for some past taxonomic confusion and to present complexity of the species. The *O. phaeacantha* complex has been under intensive study in recent years (Pinkava, pers. comm.; Parfitt & Pinkava, 1988; and others), and is still undergoing investigation.

Four varieties are recognized (Benson, 1982) to occur in the Trans-Pecos:

Fig. 256. *Opuntia spinosibacca*
(Spinyfruited Prickly Pear)

var. **major** Engelm. (Brownspined Prickly Pear) is perhaps the most abundant
prickly pear variety in the southwestern deserts, and it is widespread and common in the Trans-Pecos; spines usually 1–3, dark brown, to (3–)5.5–7 cm
long, 1–1.5 mm broad, located usually on the upper one-half, one-third, or
less of the broadly ovate or nearly orbiculate joints. The var. **phaeacantha**
(Purplefruited Prickly Pear) reportedly is somewhat rare in El Paso, Jeff Davis,
Brewster (Fig. 255), and Terrell counties; spines 3–5(–9) above, 1 or 2 below
per areole, usually whitish, to (3.8–)4.5–6.2 cm long, 0.7–1 mm broad, located on upper three-fourths or more of the ovate joints. Benson (1982) also
treated the var. *spinosibacca* (Anthony) L. Benson and the var. *discata* (Engelm.) L. Benson & Walkington as part of *O. phaeacantha*, but these two taxa
have been elevated by later workers as distinct species. *Opuntia phaeacantha*
var. *brunnea* Engelm., listed by Benson (1982) under var. *major*, is another
taxon that might be recognized as valid (Heil and Brack, 1988). At present we
continue to recognize var. *major* and var. *phaeacantha*, although additional
taxonomic changes are anticipated for *O. phaeacantha*.

16. **Opuntia spinosibacca** Anthony   SPINYFRUITED PRICKLY PEAR.   Fig.
256. [*Opuntia phaeacantha* Engelm. var. *spinosibacca* (Anthony) L. Benson].
Limestone hills and slopes. 1800–2800 ft.; Mar–Apr; apparently restricted in
occurrence between Mariscal Mt. and Boquillas Canyon, Brewster Co., Big
Bend National Park; probably adjacent Mex.

Fig. 257. *Opuntia engelmannii*
(Englemann's Prickly Pear)

Opuntia spinosibacca has spines 2–5 per areole, reddish to reddish-brown, to 7.5 cm long, 1 mm broad, located over most of the orbiculate pads, yellow green pads with a little purple near the areoles, and areoles raised on small mounds. The plants are erect shrubs to 1.5 m tall, sometimes with a short trunk, the flowers are yellow with red centers, and the spiny fruits are at first fleshy, then become dry and shrunken with age. Pinkava and Parfitt (1988) consider *O.* × *spinosibacca* to be of hybrid origin, with *O. phaeacantha* and *O. aureispina* as putative parents.

17. Opuntia engelmannii Salm-Dyck. ENGELMANN'S PRICKLY PEAR. Fig. 257. [*Opuntia phaeacantha* var. *discata* (Engelm.) L. Benson & Walking-ton; *O. dillei* Griffiths; *O. lindheimeri* Engelm.]. Widespread in various habitats, desert and mountains, one of the more common prickly pears in the Trans-Pecos, i.e., var. *engelmannii*; 2200–5000 ft.; May–Jun; south and cen. TX; E to LA, N to OK, W across NM and AZ to CA; Baja Calif. S to Zac. and S.L.P., Mex.

Traditionally *Opuntia lindheimeri* has been regarded as a distinct species (Benson, 1982), but Parfitt & Pinkava (1988) have realigned this taxon as a variety of *O. engelmannii*. Three varieties of *O. engelmannii* are recognized for the Trans-Pecos following Parfitt and Pinkava (1988). *Opuntia engelmannii* var. **engelmannii** (Engelmann's Prickly Pear) is widespread and common in the Trans-Pecos west to California and in northern Mexico. It is regarded as

Fig. 258. *Opuntia engelmannii* var. *linguiformis* (Cow's Tongue Prickly Pear)

one of the largest prickly pears in the southwest, with spines 1–4(–10) per areole, these white or ashy gray, and one or more of them directed downward, 2.5–5(–7) cm long, 1–1.5 mm broad, the spines in most areoles of the orbiculate to elliptic pads. The whitish spines are distinctive of var. *engelmannii*. *Opuntia engelmannii* var. *lindheimeri* (Engelm.) Parfitt & Pinkava (Texas Prickly Pear; Nopal Prickly Pear) is of limited occurrence in the Trans-Pecos, probably not advancing farther west than southern Brewster County, the Boquillas area in Big Bend National Park, but extending southeast, where it is common in south and central Texas, and in adjacent Mexico. Plants of var. *lindheimeri* form large shrubs 1–3.5 m high, with green, obovate to orbicular pads, and characteristic yellow spines, 1–6 per areole, usually in all but the lower areoles and 1.2–4(–5) cm long. The cultivated variety *O. engelmannii* var. **linguiformis** (Griffiths) Parfitt & Pinkava, commonly known as Cow's Tongue Prickly Pear (Fig. 258), is of scattered occurrence around dwellings in the Trans-Pecos, having been planted as an ornamental curiosity. The plants occasionally escape from cultivation. The most characteristic feature of var. *linguiformis* is the elongated pads, lanceolate to linear-lanceolate in shape, that may grow to 1 m long. Cow's Tongue Prickly Pear also has yellow spines. The variety is widespread to California and in Mexico. An undescribed prickly pear of Presidio County, possibly related to *O. engelmannii*, is under study by J. F. Weedin (Weedin and Powell, 1978).

Fig. 259. *Opuntia macrorhiza* var. *pottsii* (Potts Prickly Pear)

18. Opuntia macrorhiza Engelm. TUBEROUSROOTED PRICKLY PEAR. Mostly grassland habitats, the low cacti often partially hidden by grasses, found in most counties of the Trans-Pecos but concentrated in Brewster, Jeff Davis and northern Presidio counties in the basin grasslands; May–Jun; extremely widespread in the central U.S. in Great Plains Grassland and woodlands, N to MN, W to CA, E to AR and LA. This is a low clump-forming prickly pear, usually less than 30 cm high but perhaps spreading to more than 1 m wide; the main roots are usually tuberous; the mature joints are glaucous and bluish-green, orbiculate to ovate, 5–10 cm long, 5–7 cm broad, with spines 1–6 per areole, mostly flexed and in upper areoles, to 3–5.5 cm long, white or gray (rarely brownish or reddish brown).

It is not certain that *Opuntia macrorhiza* is the correct name for the taxon included here under that name. Two varieties of *O. macrorhiza* are reported for the Trans-Pecos (Benson, 1982): one is var. **macrorhiza** (Tuberousrooted Prickly Pear), found mostly in the grasslands from El Paso Co. east to Brewster Co.; flowers yellow, or centers reddish, joints 6–10 cm long, moderately glaucous, spines ca. 0.5 mm in diameter. In flowering season the var. **pottsii** (Salm-Dyck) L. Benson (Potts Prickly Pear) is strikingly distinguished by its red flowers when the small plants (Fig. 259) are not hidden by grasses; joints 5–6 cm long, markedly glaucous, (bluish), spines very slender, ca. 0.25 mm in diameter; the red-flowered Potts Prickly Pear is common in the disturbed grasslands in northern Brewster and Presidio counties and southern Jeff Davis County, but occurs in perhaps all the Trans-Pecos counties; also in adjacent NM and across to AZ, and scattered in the TX Panhandle. *Opuntia macrorhiza* var. *pottsii* probably should be given specific status.

19. Opuntia atrispina Griffiths. Reported to be of scattered occurrence, but probably not as widespread as suggested by Benson (1982); limestone hills and mesas, possibly restricted to SE Trans-Pecos in Terrell and Val Verde counties. 1500–2500 ft.; Apr–May; E to Taylor, Uvalde, and Bee counties, TX.

The sprawling dark green prickly pears are usually less than 0.6 m high with obovate to nearly orbiculate joints to 10(15) cm long and 7.5(10) cm broad, with needlelike spines mostly on the upper portion of joints, the spines black on the lower halves but yellow at the tips, mostly 4–7 per areole, and have pale yellow flowers.

20. Opuntia aureispina (Brack & Heil) Pinkava & Parfitt. [*Opuntia macrocentra* Engelm. var. *aureispina* Brack. & Heil]. Apparently restricted to the limestone hills near the Rio Grande, near Mariscal Mt. to Boquillas Canyon, Brewster Co., Big Bend National Park; 1700–2200 ft.; Mar–Apr; possibly adjacent Mex.

This diploid species with yellow spines, yellow flowers with red centers, and dry, tan, spiny fruits, was discovered by the author in 1985 and described by Heil and Brack (1988).

21. Opuntia chisosensis (Anthony) Ferguson. [*Opuntia lindheimeri* var. *chisosensis* Anthony]. Woodland slopes, Chisos Mts., Brewster Co., Big Bend National Park; 4500–6700 ft.; May–Jun; reported from the Sierra del Carmen, N Coah., Mex. (Ferguson, 1986).

In Texas this diploid species apparently is restricted to the Chisos Mountains. The plants are erect, to 1 m tall, with pads mostly orbicular, blue-green, spines 1–5 per areole, mostly yellow, rarely reddish, turning nearly black with age, flowers pale yellow, and fruits fleshy, reddish-purple, with a few yellow spines at the top. *Opuntia chisosensis* possibly is related to *O. aureispina*.

22. Opuntia ellisiana Griffiths. A cultivar, rarely escaping, at least in Alpine, Brewster Co., TX. 4500 ft.; May–Jun.

The plants are spreading shrubs to 2 m tall, with pads obovate to ovate, spines absent or vestigial, areoles with whitish hairs covering poorly developed glochids in early growth, flowers yellow, and fruit reddish-purple. Deer appear to relish *O. ellisiana* during dry periods.

46. LYTHRACEAE ST.-HIL.   LOOSESTRIFE FAMILY

Shrubs, small trees, or herbs. Leaves usually opposite or whorled, simple with smooth margins. Flowers usually regular, in clusters or solitary, sepals and petals 4–8, arranged in a floral tube; flower stalks usually with 2 bracts; petals (rarely absent) attached in the throat of floral tube between lobes, crumpled in bud; stamens often in 2 whorls, upper whorl attached to floral tube, usually opposite sepals, 4 to many in number, often of unequal length; ovary superior; style simple or absent, stigma headlike. Fruit a dry capsule, with 1–several cells.

A mostly tropical family with about 550 species in 25 genera. Many members are of ornamental value, most notably Crepe Myrtle (*Lagerstroemia indica* L.). Species of eight genera occur in Texas; two genera, *Lythrum* and *Nesaea*, are represented in the Trans-Pecos. *Lythrum californicum* T. & G. is a strong herbaceous perennial to one meter high, and often appears to have slender woody stems at the base.

1. NESAEA COMM. *ex* KUNTH

Shrubs or herbs, often vinelike; stems slender. Leaves deciduous, opposite, or with some alternate; stipules absent. Flowers solitary in leaf axils, on short stalks; calyx bellshaped, with hornlike projections between the lobes; petals 5–7, pink to purplish in our species and 6–7 mm long; stamens 10–18; style slender, prominent. Fruit a 4-celled capsule, opening by a small lid and then splitting (in *Nesaea longipes*).

A small genus of three species, occurring from Texas south to Argentina. Two species occur in Texas.

1. Nesaea longipes Gray. STALKFLOWER NESAEA. Fig. 260. [*Heimia longipes* (Gray) Cory.]. Near springs, seeps, and irrigation ditches, usually limestone habitats. Brewster Co., Big Bend Park, creek near Glenn Spring; near Fresno spring. Pecos Co., 7 mi W Fort Stockton; below Comanche Spring; Escondido Spring. 2600–3200 ft.; May–Aug. Also on the Edwards Plateau, an endemic species.

This plant is usually seen as a low subshrub with slender, sprawling and much branched stems to 1 m long, and pink flowers. It is relatively rare in the Trans-Pecos.

47. ONAGRACEAE JUSS. EVENING PRIMROSE FAMILY

Plants mostly herbs, some woody at base, rarely shrubs or trees. Leaves opposite or alternate, simple, margins smooth, toothed, or lobed. Flowers bisexual, usually regular, typically 4-merous (rarely 5–6-merous); with a short or distinct hypanthium; petals usually 4, separate, white, pink, purple, or yellow; stamens usually 4 or 8 (or as many or double the number of sepals); ovary inferior, usually 4-celled (rarely 2 or 5). Fruit usually a capsule, opening lengthwise, or nutlike and indehiscent.

Fig. 260. *Nesaea longipes* (Stalkflower Nesaea)

A world-wide family, most prominently distributed in temperate regions, particularly western North America; 650 species in about 20 genera. Species of seven genera occur in Texas, and six genera are represented in the Trans-Pecos. Most species are herbaceous, but in a few species such as *Calylophus hartwegii* (Benth.) Raven, *C. tubicula* (Gray) Raven, *Gaura macrocarpa* Rothr., and *G. boquillensis* Raven & Gregory, vigorous subshrubby plants are not uncommon. At the northeast margin of the Trans-Pecos in the sand hills, *Calylophus hartwegii* var. *maccartii* (Shinners) Towner and Raven is a prominent low shrub with showy flowers.

48. ARALIACEAE JUSS.   GINSENG FAMILY

Herbs, shrubs, or trees. Leaves usually alternate, usually palmately or pinnately compound. Flowers regular, bisexual or unisexual, arranged in umbellike clusters, usually 5(4)-merous; calyx small; petals separate, falling at maturity; stamens attached to disk inside calyx, alternate with petals; anthers opening longitudinally; ovary inferior, several-celled, with one ovule, styles several, or fused. Fruit a berry, 5-celled.

A family of about 70 genera and 700 species distributed primarily in the

Fig. 261. *Aralia racemosa*
(American Spikenard)

tropics. Only one genus is native to Texas, but the European English Ivy (*Hedera helix* L.) has been introduced in east Texas.

1. ARALIA L.

Plants perennial, in our species mostly herbaceous but with a shrubby aspect, to 2 m high, prickles absent; roots aromatic. Leaves pinnate, to 80 cm long with ovate leaflets to 18 cm long, margins prominently toothed. Flowers small, in umbellike clusters; petals 5; stamens 5. Fruit a dark purple berry, ca. 5 mm wide, with 5 seeds.

A genus of about 35 species in North America and in Asia. Two species occur in Texas.

1. Aralia racemosa L. AMERICAN SPIKENARD. Fig. 261. [*Aralia bicrenata* Woot. & Standl.]. In the Trans-Pecos known only from high elevations on Mt. Livermore, 7800 ft. or more. Jeff Davis Co. above upper spring, Madera Canyon, NE slopes of Mt. Livermore; base of the "dome," Mt. Livermore; 13–21 Sep. A widespread species from Can. S to GA and W to AZ.

The species is readily identified by its large, toothed leaflets of compound leaves, and small flowers in umbellike clusters. The Trans-Pecos entity is subsp. **bicrenata** (Woot. & Standl.) Welsh & Atwood. Roots and berries of related species have been used for medicine.

49. GARRYACEAE LINDL. SILKTASSEL BUSH FAMILY

Trees or shrubs. Leaves opposite (usually) or alternate, the margins without teeth; stipules absent. Flowers small, regular, bisexual or unisexual; sepals 4–5, calyx small; petals 4–5 (or absent); stamens 4–5 or double in two series; anthers opening toward inside; ovary inferior, 1–2 (–4)-celled; styles usually 1–2. Fruit usually a drupe (fleshy with one seed), less often a berry.

A family with a single genus of 18 species distributed in southwestern North America, Mexico, Guatemala, and the West Indies. Garryaceae is related to Cornaceae and has been placed with that family by some authors.

1. GARRYA DOUGL. *ex* LINDL. SILKTASSEL

Shrubs or small trees, evergreen, dioecious, branchlets 4-angled and opposite the leaves, petioles basally fused. Leaves leathery, usually ovate or elliptic in outline, less often nearly lanceolate. Flowers unisexual, in pendulous clusters; petals absent; staminate flowers on stalks; in clusters of 3; calyx 4-lobed; stamens 4; pistillate flowers sessile, solitary in axils; calyx 2-lobed or obscurely so; ovary 1-celled; styles 2. Fruit a drupe, dark blue in our species, dry or moderately juicy; bitter tasting; seeds 1–2.

Three taxa occur in Texas, all of them in the Trans-Pecos (Dahling, 1978).

KEY TO THE SPECIES

1. Mature leaves plane, essentially glabrous, perhaps rarely covered with upwardly appressed hairs; ovaries sparsely silky pubescent, becoming glabrous with age   **1. G. wrightii.**
1. Mature leaves markedly undulate or plane, densely covered with woolly hairs; ovaries glabrous   **2. G. ovata.**

1. Garrya wrightii Torr. WRIGHT SILKTASSEL. Fig. 262. Usually limestone but also volcanic soils, mountain and canyon habitats. El Paso Co., Franklin Mts.; Hueco Tanks. Hudspeth Co., Cornudus Mts., Sierra Tinaja Pinja, Black Mts.; Sierra Diablo, Victorio Canyon; N slopes Quitman Mts. Culberson Co., lower N slopes Beach Mts.; Apache Mts. Jeff Davis Co., Davis Mts., lower Madera Canyon; 15 mi S Kent; N slopes Timber Mt.; Little Aguja Canyon. Presidio Co., Sierra Vieja, Cottonwood Canyon, ZH Canyon, Vieja Pass. 4000–5500 ft.; May–Aug. W to SW NM and cen. and S AZ; also N Mex.

Fig. 262. *Garrya wrightii* (Wright Silktassel)

Plants of *Garrya wrightii* are shrubs 1–3 m high, with the mature leaves lighter green in color. The United States populations of *G. wrightii* are characterized by mature leaves that are more or less glabrous, but a few populations in Mexico may have upwardly appressed hairs on the leaves (Dahling, 1978). Wright Silktassel is good browse for cattle and deer.

2. Garrya ovata Benth. EGGLEAF SILKTASSEL. Dahling (1978) has recognized four subspecies of *Garrya ovata*, two of which occur in the Trans-Pecos.

1. Leaves strongly undulate   **2a.** *G. ovata* subsp. *goldmanii.*
1. Leaves mostly plane or slightly undulate   **2b.** *G. ovata* subsp. *lindheimeri.*

2a. Garrya ovata subsp. **goldmanii** (Woot. & Standl.) Dahling. Fig. 263. [*Garrya goldmanii* Woot. & Standl.]. Mountains and canyons, usually in shade. El Paso Co., Franklin Mts., near the top. Culberson Co., Guadalupe Mts., near Frijole, South McKittrick Canyon, Pine Springs Canyon, Smith Canyon; Eagle Mts., Panther Peak. Presidio Co., Sierra Vieja, Capote Mt.; Chinati Mts., Chinati Peak. Jeff Davis Co., Davis Mts., Mt. Livermore. Brewster Co., Ranger Canyon near Alpine; Goat Mt.; Cathedral Mt. 4000–8000 ft.; Mar–Apr. Also S NM; Chih. and Coah., Mex.

2b. Garrya ovata subsp. **lindheimeri** (Torr.) Dahling. Fig. 263. [*Garrya lindheimeri* Torr.]. Mountains and canyons, usually in shade. Brewster Co.,

Fig. 263. *Garrya ovata* (Eggleaf Silktassel; A) var. *lindheimeri*; B) var. *goldmanii*

Chisos Mts., Basin, Pulliam Bluff, Casa Grande, S slopes Lost Mine Peak, Chinese Wall, Laguna Meadow, Boot Spring, near S Rim, Blue Creek Canyon; Elephant Mt.; Glass Mts., Altuda Pass, Old Blue, Gap Tank. Val Verde Co. 2000–6600 ft.; Mar–Apr. Also Edwards Plateau in TX; Coah., N.L., Mex.

In the Trans-Pecos the best character for distinguishing subsp. *goldmanii* is the markedly undulate leaves, while the leaves of subsp. *lindheimeri* may be slightly undulate or plane. The leaves of subsp. *goldmanii* are usually densely woolly while those of subsp. *lindheimeri* may be sparsely pubescent or woolly underneath, but usually the leaves are sparsely pubescent on the upper surfaces. It is possible that the two subspecies intergrade in areas of sympatric occurrence in the Trans-Pecos.

50. ERICACEAE JUSS. HEATH FAMILY

Shrubs or trees, rarely vines or herbs, evergreens or deciduous. Leaves alternate, rarely opposite or whorled, often leathery, simple, margins smooth or toothed; stipules absent. Flowers usually in clusters, rarely singular, bisexual, regular or irregular; sepals 4–7, (5 in our species), fused or partially separate; petals 4–7 (5 in our species), separate or fused, commonly in a funnel or bell shape; stamens double the number of petals, arising from the base of a disc, anthers 2-celled, opening at apex; ovary superior or inferior (in *Vaccinium*); style one, stigma small. Fruit a capsule, drupe, or berry.

A family of about 3500 species in about 125 genera, almost worldwide in distribution, especially in acid soils of temperate regions of both hemispheres. The family is most important for its ornamentals, perhaps most notably rhododendrons and azaleas (*Rhododendron* L.). Commercial Blueberries (*Vaccinium* L. spp.) and Cranberries (*Vaccinium macrocarpon* Ait.) are members of Ericaceae. Briar pipes are made from knots of *Erica* L. species of the Mediterranean region. Eight genera of Ericaceae occur in Texas.

KEY TO THE GENERA

1. Shrubs; fruit brownish, 5–8 mm wide, drupelike, dryish, smooth, separable into 4–10 nutlets; cells of ovary with 1 ovule   **1. *Arctostaphylos.***
1. Trees (rarely shrubs); fruit reddish; 8–10 mm wide, berrylike, somewhat fleshy, surface papillose; cells of ovary with several ovules   **2. *Arbutus.***

1. ARCTOSTAPHYLOS ADANS. MANZANITA

Shrubs to 3 m high (usually less) usually forming thickets; bark smooth, red-brown, peeling; branchlets finely pubescent. Leaves alternate, leathery, dull green and rather shiny, with smooth margins, ovate to oblanceolate, to 3 cm long. Flowers in elongate clusters, small, nodding, corolla urnshaped, white or pinkish, ca. 7 mm long; stamens 10; ovary superior, glabrous. Fruit nearly round, brownish, drupelike, edible.

A genus of about 40 species, all but one of the New World. One species occurs in Texas.

1. **Arctostaphylos pungens** Kunth. POINTLEAF MANZANITA. Fig. 264. In Texas and the Trans-Pecos region known only from Jeff Davis Co., Tricky Gap area, top of the mountain, Boy Scout Ranch; 6000 ft.; Timber Mt. near NW crest, 6200 ft.; Mar–Apr. From TX W to CA, N to UT; also in Mex. S to Oax.

The Tricky Gap population of this evergreen species, said to be locally frequent in 1948, was reported to be decreasing (Warnock, 1977) as a result of browsing by goats. I visited the population in 1987 and found the plants to be numerous and thriving on several slopes and ridges in the area. A second Trans-Pecos population of *A. pungens* was discovered by Jack Brady in 1994 on Timber Mountain. Seeds identified as those of *Arctostaphylos* have been found by P. and S. McClinton in black bear scat in the Chisos Mountains. In regions where the Pointleaf Manzanita is abundant, the fruits are often used to make an excellent jelly. The fruit is eaten by many bird and mammal species, including Black Bear. In Mexico the leaves and fruits are used for medical purposes.

Fig. 264. *Arctostaphylos pungens*
(Pointleaf Manzanita)

2. ARBUTUS L.   MADRONE

Trees (in our species) 2–10 m high, rarely higher, rarely shrubby; evergreen bark pinkish to red brown, thin and peeling in sheets. Leaves alternate, leathery, basically ovate, to 10 cm long, usually shorter, the margins smooth or finely toothed. Flowers bisexual, in clusters, finely pubescent; calyx and corolla of 5 lobes, both whitish or pinkish, the corolla ca. 7 mm long and urnshaped; stamens 10; ovary superior. Fruit berrylike, nearly round, reddish, warty, edible.

A genus of about 20 species, distributed in the New World and Old World (Asia and Mediterranean region). Only one species occurs in Texas.

1. Arbutus xalapensis Kunth. TEXAS MADRONE, NAKED INDIAN. Fig. 265. [*Arbutus xalapensis* var. *texana* (Buckl.) Gray; *A. texana* Buckl.]. Wooded canyons and mountain slopes. Culberson Co., Guadalupe Mts., and drainages in foothills. Jeff Davis Co., widespread in the Davis Mts. Presidio Co., Sierra Vieja, upper Musgrave Canyon. Brewster Co., in most of the mountains from near Alpine south to the Chisos Mts. Pecos Co., Glass Mts. and foothills. 4000–7500 ft.; Feb–Apr. Also Edwards Plateau and South Plains; SE NM; Mex. S to Guat.

Exceptionally large trees with thick trunks are to be found in some areas,

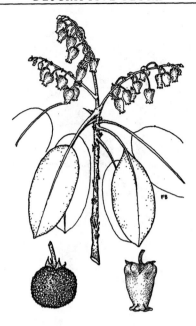

Fig. 265. *Arbutus xalapensis* (Texas Madrone)

particularly in arroyos of the southern foothills of the Guadalupe Mountains. The National champion recorded by Liles from the Chisos Mountains is 30 ft. tall with a 42 ft. crown spread and 9.3 ft. girth. The Texas Madrone is a much desired ornamental but the plants are difficult to transplant when taken from the wild. Madrones are easily grown from seed. The fruit is eaten by birds, and seeds are probably disseminated largely by birds. The plants are browsed heavily by goats. The wood is used for fuel, tool handles, and many other purposes, including charcoal for gunpowder (Vines, 1960). The bark and leaves are used occasionally as astringent medicines in Mexico.

51. PLUMBAGINACEAE JUSS. PLUMBAGO FAMILY

Perennial herbs or shrubs. Leaves alternate, often basal and rosettelike. Flowers bisexual, regular, usually arranged in tight, often slender, clusters; calyx tube inferior, ribbed, 4–5-toothed; corolla tubular or with 4–5, opposite petals, attached below ovary; anthers 2-celled, opening lengthwise; ovary superior, 1-celled, with 1 ovule; styles 5. Fruit small, inflated (utricle), an achene, or a capsule, often enclosed by calyx.

A family of about 500 species in 10 genera, these widely distributed especially in Asian and Mediterranean regions of the Old World, often preferring

Fig. 266. *Plumbago scandens*
(Climbing Plumbago)

semi-arid and saline habitats. Species of several genera are grown as ornamentals. Two genera, *Limonium* and *Plumbago*, are represented in Texas and in the Trans-Pecos.

1. PLUMBAGO L.   LEADWORT

Subshrub or perennial herb (in our species) with brittle branches woody at base; stems often vinelike. Leaves alternate, thin, glabrous, basically eggshaped to nearly lanceolate, to 10 cm long; petioles to 1 cm long. Flowers white, in slender, elongate clusters, 5–12 cm long; calyx tubular, 5-ribbed, 8–10 mm long, covered with glandular hairs; corolla tubular at base with spreading lobes; stamens 5. Fruit a linear, beaked capsule, ca. 7 mm long.

A genus of about 12 species distributed mostly in tropical and subtropical regions of the Old World and the Americas.

1. **Plumbago scandens** L.   CLIMBING PLUMBAGO.   Fig. 266. In the Trans-Pecos known only from one plant at one locality in Presidio Co., among gravel and boulders, floor of Palillos Canyon, S side of Chinati Mts., June, 1977. The presence of this species in the Trans-Pecos is somewhat enigmatic because other Texas localities for the taxon are in palm groves and wooded

areas of extreme S TX; the species is widespread in tropical America, also occurring in S FL, and S AZ. The leaves and roots of this plant are said to be poisonous if taken internally. Drugs to treat skin diseases are prepared from extracts of the plant which also may cause blisters. Other common names for *Plumbago scandens* are Hierba de Alacran and Pitillo.

Another Trans-Pecos representative of the Plumbago Family is *Limonium limbatum* Small (Sea Lavender), a coarse plant to 60 cm high with prominent, flattopped clusters of blue flowers. The latter species is especially abundant in saline waste areas near Pecos in Reeves Co.

52. SAPOTACEAE JUSS.   SAPODILLA FAMILY

Trees or shrubs, with milky sap; stems commonly spiny. Leaves usually alternate, with petioles, leathery, simple, the margins smooth; stipules usually absent. Flowers bisexual, small, usually in axillary clusters; calyx persistent; corolla short-tubular, attached below the superior ovary; fertile stamens opposite corolla lobes, sterile stamens also present in 1 or more rows; ovary 4–12-celled, a single ovule in each cell; style 1, pointed. Fruit a berry (or drupaceous); seed 1, large.

A family of about 800 species in 70 genera, most common in the Old World and American tropics. Several members of the family are of economic importance. For example, chicle for chewing gum is from *Manilkara zapota* (L.) van Royen, a tropical species that also produces edible fruits. One genus is represented in Texas.

1. SIDEROXYLON L.   IRONWOOD

Small trees or shrubs, usually with strong spines. Leaves usually clustered on short stalks, in our species usually oblanceolate to obovate, to 7 cm long and 2.5 cm wide. Flowers in clusters, usually whitish to yellowish; corolla lobes 5, each with 2 lateral appendages at base; sterile stamens petallike; ovary usually somewhat hairy. Fruit in our species roundish or somewhat elongated, purplish-black at maturity, 7–12 mm long, fleshy, edible; seed one.

A genus of about 60 mostly tropical species of the Western Hemisphere including *Bumelia* Sw. Three species and several subspecies occur in Texas.

1. Sideroxylon lanuginosum Michx.   WOOLLYBUCKET SIDEROXYLON. Fig. 267.   According to Correll and Johnston (1970) there are four varieties of this species in Texas. The taxonomy has been revised (Kartesz, 1994), and evidently one subspecies occurs in the Trans-Pecos; *Sideroxylon lanuginosum*

Fig. 267. *Sideroxylon lanuginosum*
(Woollybucket Sideroxylon)

subsp. **rigidum** (Gray) Pennington. [*Bumelia lanuginosa* var. *rigida* Gray; *B. lanuginosa* var. *texana* (Buckl.) Cronq.]. Rare or uncommon in limestone habitats (and perhaps on gypsum) along watercourses. Hudspeth Co., Sierra Diablo, head of Victorio Canyon. Brewster Co., Marathon Basin; Dog Canyon, Big Bend Park; between Longfellow and Reagan Canyon. Terrell Co., 20 mi S Longfellow; 21 mi N Dryden, and along Independence Creek; Pecos Co., 5 mi W Sheffield. Val Verde Co., near mouth of Pecos River. 1200–5500 ft.; Apr–Jul; E to cen. TX, N to SW OK, W to SE AZ; also N Mex.

The collection of subsp. *rigidum* from Hudspeth Co. is unusual in that the leaves are thin and not prominently veined. The Trans-Pecos bumelias are in need of additional study. The wood of *Sideroxylon lanuginosum* is very tough and has been used in making cabinets and tool handles. The mature fruit is edible to birds and man, but perhaps should not be eaten in quantity (Vines, 1960).

53. EBENACEAE GURKE   EBONY OR PERSIMMON FAMILY

Trees or shrubs, usually male and female flowers on separate plants. Leaves alternate, simple, margins smooth. Flowers usually unisexual, solitary in axils or in clusters; calyx persistent and increasing in size with fruit; corolla some-

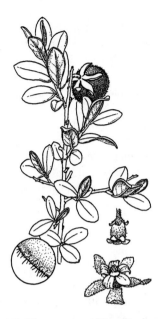

Fig. 268. *Diospyros texana* (Texas Persimmon)

what bellshaped; stamens 3 to many, attached at base of corolla; ovary 2–16-celled, ovules 1–2 in each cell. Fruit a berry; seeds several, large.

A family of three to five genera and about 450 species, mostly distributed in the Old World. The only species native to the United States are of *Diospyros*. The wood of *D. ebeneum* Konig (India and East Indies), Black Ebony, is valued for cabinet making. The fruits of *D. virginiana* L. (American Persimmon) and *D. kaki* L. (Japanese Persimmon) are valued commercially.

1. DIOSPYROS L. PERSIMMON

Shrubs or small trees (in our species). Leaves leathery, somewhat persistent. Flowers unisexual (rarely bisexual) in axils, male and female on separate plants; calyx 4–5-lobed; stamens usually 15–16. Fruit berrylike with 3–8 seeds (in our species). A genus of nearly 500 species, mostly of the Old World. Two species occur in Texas.

1. **Diospyros texana** Scheele. TEXAS PERSIMMON, MEXICAN PERSIMMON, CHAPOTE, BLACK PERSIMMON. Fig. 268. [*Brayodendron texanum* (Scheele) Small]. Widespread and rather common in certain localities of the SE Trans-

Pecos, mostly limestone but also igneous habitats, rocky slopes and arroyos, mostly semidesert areas. Brewster Co., common in the S part, Big Bend Park, Black Gap, N to Iron Mt. and Cienega Mt. Probably in SE Presidio Co. Rather widespread in S Pecos Co., and in Terrell Co., and Val Verde Co. 1100–5700 ft.; Feb–Jun. Also in TX E to Harris and Refugio counties; Coah., N.L. and Tam., Mex.

The Texas Persimmon is a shrub or small tree with persistent leaves, smooth reddish-gray, peeling bark, blackish and hard wood, white flowers, and fruit ca. 2 cm in diameter, black when ripe, and with juicy pulp that is rather sweet or insipid. The fruit is not as tasty as that of the Common Persimmon, but it is edible when ripe. The wood is used for engraving blocks, tools, and has been used to make art objects. In Mexico the black fruit juice is used to dye animal hides.

54. STYRACACEAE DUM. STORAX FAMILY

Small trees or shrubs, usually with stellate hairs. Leaves alternate, simple; stipules absent. Flowers bisexual, regular, usually in clusters; calyx 4–8-toothed, tubular, at least partially fused to ovary; petals 4–5, fused basally; stamens 8–12, in 1 whorl; anthers elongate; ovary (in *Styrax*) only partly inferior; style 1. Fruit a drupe or capsule, fleshy or dry.

A family of about 150 species in 10 genera, distributed in warm temperate regions of the New World and Old World. Certain species of *Halesia* Ellis *ex* L. and *Styrax* are valuable as ornamental shrubs and small trees. Benzoin, a resin used in medicines, is obtained from *Styrax benzoin* Dryand. Species of two genera occur in Texas.

1. STYRAX L. STORAX, SILVER BELLS

Shrubs (in our species) to 3 m high. Leaves deciduous, roundish but with an apical point, with stellate hairs and other fine white pubescence especially underneath. Flowers in clusters of 3–7, drooping, white, flower stalk with dense starlike hairs; calyx 5–7 lobed; petals 5, ca. 1.5 cm long; stamens 10. Fruit dry, usually 3-celled.

A genus of more than 130 species distributed in warm regions of North America and Eurasia. Four species are represented in Texas.

1. **Styrax youngiae** Cory. YOUNG'S SNOWBELL. Fig. 269.   In the Trans-Pecos known only from a single collection by Mary S. Young, 12 May 1914; a canyon in the Davis Mts., possibly close to Star Mt., 4000 ft. The species is

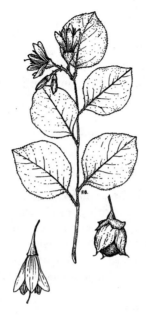

Fig. 269. *Styrax youngiae* (Young's Snowbell)

otherwise known from Mexico by a few collections from Coah. and N.L. (Gonsoulin, 1974). One recent collection was from Cañon de Diablo, Del Carmens, Coah. Young's Snowbell is closely related to *Styrax texanus* Cory of the Edwards Plateau. The plants are said to be favorite browse for goats.

55. OLEACEAE HOFFMSG. & LINK   OLIVE FAMILY

Trees, shrubs, or subherbaceous. Leaves usually opposite, simple to pinnatifid; stipules absent. Flowers bisexual or unisexual, regular; calyx usually 4-lobed (rarely 5–16-lobed or absent); petals fused, usually 4-lobed (rarely 6–12-lobed), or petals separate or absent; stamens usually 2 (rarely 3–5), attached to corolla alternate with lobes; anthers with cells back to back; ovary superior, 2-celled; ovules usually 2 in each cell; style 1 or absent; stigma 1–2. Fruit (in our species) a drupe, circumscissile capsule, or samara.

A family of about 30 genera and over 600 species distributed mostly in temperate and tropical regions in Asia and the East Indies. Economically the family is well known for the Olive (*Olea* L.), a source of food and oil, ash lumber from *Fraxinus* L., and numerous ornamentals including Jasmine (*Jasminum* L.), Lilac (*Syringa* L.), and Privet (*Ligustrum* L.). Five genera are represented in Texas, three of these with species native to the Trans-Pecos.

1. Plants small shrubs (or herbaceous perennials) more or less 0.5 m high; flowers showy, yellow; fruit a capsule   **1. Menodora.**
1. Plants rather large shrubs or trees, more than 1 m high; flowers not usually showy; fruit a drupe or capsule.
    2. Leaves simple; fruit a drupe   **2. Forestiera.**
    2. Leaves pinnately compound; fruit a samara   **3. Fraxinus.**

1. MENODORA BONPL. MENODORA

Small shrubs or perennial herbs. Leaves mostly alternate, simple, entire to deeply lobed. Flowers bisexual, usually in small clusters, rarely single, in upper leaf axils; sepals fused, with prominent, slender lobes, persistent; petals fused, short bellshaped to long-tubular, yellow (rarely whitish to light purplish); corolla lobes 5; stamens 2, attached to corolla; style slender, extending outward. Fruit a capsule, opening around the middle or not opening, found in pairs; seeds 2–4 in each cell.

A genus of perhaps 19 species, found mainly in the southwestern United States to South America. Three species occur in the Trans-Pecos (Turner, 1991). The two shrubby species have yellow flowers, while the one herbaceous taxon, *Menodora heterophylla* Moric. (with deeply lobed leaves) has flowers that are light yellow (drying whitish) to reddish-purple. The menodoras are reported to be of high forage value to livestock. Taxonomically the Trans-Pecos species are not well understood and require further study.

1. Corolla tube long, 2.5–5 cm, petals abruptly expanded at apex
                                         1. M. longiflora.
1. Corolla tube short, less than 0.7–1.6 cm, petals flaring   **2. M. scabra.**

1. Menodora longiflora Gray. SHOWY MENODORA. Fig. 270. [*Menodoropsis longiflora* Engelm.]. Rocky habitats, mostly mountains and canyons, most commonly on limestone, but also igneous soils; a rather common species. Hudspeth Co., Sierra Diablo. Culberson Co., Guadalupe Mts.; Apache Mts. Presidio Co. Jeff Davis Co., Little Aguja Canyon. Brewster Co. Terrell Co. Val Verde Co. 1100–6500 ft.; Jun–Sep. Also common on the Edwards Plateau; S NM; S to cen Mex.

The Showy Menodora is easily recognized by its rather long, tubular, yellow corollas. The leaves of this species are perhaps the largest of the Trans-Pecos menodoras, being to 5.5 cm long and to 10 mm wide. The species is worthy of cultivation.

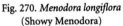

Fig. 270. *Menodora longiflora*
(Showy Menodora)

Fig. 271. *Menodora scabra* [*M. scoparia*]

2. Menodora scabra Gray. ROUGH MENODORA. Fig. 272. [*Menodora scabra* Engelm. var. *glabrescens* Gray; *M. scoparia* Engelm. *ex* Gray, Fig. 271; *M. scabra* var. *laevis* (Woot. & Standl.) Steyerm.; *M. scabra* var. *ramosissima* Steyerm.; *M. decemfida* (Gill. *ex* Hook. & Arn.) Gray var. *longifolia* Steyerm., Fig. 273]. Perhaps the most widespread menodora, occurring in various habitats, mostly limestone, throughout the region. 1500–5500 ft.; Mar–Nov; also E on the Edwards Plateau; W to CA; N to CO and UT; N Mex. S to Dgo.

This species is characterized by its low, clumped habit, pubescence rough to the touch, variable leaf shape and short corolla tube, usually 2.5–7(–16) mm long. The North American species of *Menodora* have been studied recently by Turner (1991), who combined several taxa previously recognized to occur in the Trans-Pecos (Correll and Johnston, 1970), with a broadened concept of *M. scabra*. Rough Menodora, like all members of the genus, is considered to be good forage for livestock and wildlife.

2. FORESTIERA POIR. FORESTIERA

Shrubs or small trees; branches often curved. Leaves opposite or nearly so, or crowded on short shoots (*Forestiera angustifolia*), blades simple, usually with minute, darkish depressions in the surface, margins smooth or toothed.

Fig. 272. *Menodora scabra* (Rough Menodora)   Fig. 273. *Menodora scabra* [*M. decemfida* var. *longifolia*]

Flowers bisexual or unisexual, small, in axillary clusters, male and female on separate plants; sepals very small; petals absent; male flowers of 4(5) stamens, and 4(5) minute sepals; female flowers of a stalked ovary, 4(5) functionless stamens, and 4(5) minute sepals. Fruit a drupe, slow developing, usually beaked by a persistent style, young fruits ribbed lengthwise before mature, becoming juicy just before maturity, in color at first purple, maturing to black, and with a whitish bloom; the stone of a series of longitudinal ribs, thin-walled.

A genus of about 15 species distributed in North America, Central America, and the West Indies. Some species provide excellent cover for wildlife, and the ripe fruits are eaten by various types of birds. Five species are represented in Texas.

KEY TO THE SPECIES

1. Leaf blades linear, rarely somewhat oblanceolate, margins smooth inrolled
                                                              1. F. angustifolia.
1. Leaf blades ovate, margins finely toothed.
    2. Older leaves with all or most veins raised above the leaf surface both above and below, forming a raised-reticulate pattern; mature leaves present at time of flowering   **3. F. reticulata.**
    2. Older leaves with only primary and sometimes secondary veins raised be-

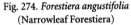

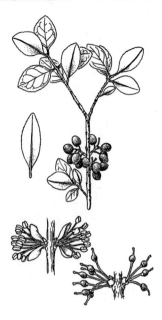

Fig. 274. *Forestiera angustifolia*
(Narrowleaf Forestiera)

Fig. 275. *Forestiera pubescens* (Elbowbush)

low, none raised conspicuously above; leaves absent or emerging at time
of flowering   **2. *F. pubescens*.**

1. Forestiera angustifolia Torr. NARROWLEAF FORESTIERA, DESERT OLIVE,
PANALERO. Fig. 274. [*Forestiera puberula* Eastw., *F. texana* Cory]. Widespread in the S Trans-Pecos, desertic hills, slopes, arroyos, and canyons. Hudspeth Co., Eagle Mts., NW side. Presidio Co., Chinati Mts. S to the Fresno
Canyon area. Brewster Co. widespread in S half of co., less common or rare
northward. Pecos Co. S half of co. Terrell Co., widespread. Val Verde Co. 1900–
3500 ft.; spring. Locally common on the Rio Grande Plains in S TX; widespread in NE Mex.

Leaves of this species are narrow (characteristically linear), 0.8–2 cm long,
0.2–0.3 cm wide, but plants with leaves to 3 cm long and 0.7 cm wide are not
uncommon. The leaves may be glabrous or pubescent. Flowers are bisexual
and usually appear in the spring before new leaves. Immature fruits of Narrowleaf Forestiera are usually dark purple, bananashaped, and beaked by the persistent style. The plants are reported to be excellent browse for livestock
and deer.

2. Forestiera pubescens Nutt. ELBOWBUSH, CRUZILLA. Fig. 275. [*Forestiera acuminata* (Michx.) Poir. var. *parviflora* Gray; *F. neomexicana* Gray;

Fig. 276. *Forestiera reticulata*
(Netleaf Forestiera)

F. sphaerocarpa Torr.; *F. pubescens* var. *glabrifolia* Shinners; *F. pubescens* var. *neomexicana* (Gray) Murr.]. Occurring in a disparity of habitats from saline flats to canyons of high mountains. El Paso Co., Franklin Mts. Hudspeth Co., Salt Flats W of Guadalupe Mts. Culberson Co., Guadalupe Mts., N McKittrick Canyon; upper Dog Canyon; shady canyon below the Bowl. Jeff Davis Co., Bloys Encampment; Mt. Livermore, Goat Canyon, Wood Canyon. Brewster Co., 10 mi S Alpine; N side Cathedral Mt.; Doubtful Canyon; Elephant Mesa; Chisos Mts. Presidio Co., N slopes Chinati Mts., Wildhorse Canyon. 3400–7800 ft.; spring; Crockett Co. to cen. TX; N to S UT and CO, W to NM and AZ; isolated populations in E U.S. in SC and N FL; N Coah. and Baja Calif., Mex.

The synonymous *Forestiera neomexicana* differs mostly in its glabrous inflorescences and leaves, while *F. pubescens* has pubescent inflorescences and leaves. The pubescence character is variable and the two forms occur together in some parts of the Trans-Pecos. The population in the Salt Flat of Hudspeth County may represent a separate taxon.

3. **Forestiera reticulata** Torr. NETLEAF FORESTIERA. Fig. 276. [*Forestiera racemosa* S. Wats.; *Gymnanthes texana* Standl.]. Uncommon and localized in canyons of limestone hills and plateaus. Terrell Co., 29 mi N Dryden. Val Verde Co., between Del Rio and Loma Alta. 2400–2600 ft.; Aug–Sep. Also

E on the Edwards Plateau (Uvalde, Real, Medina, Edwards, Bandera counties); NE Mex., Oax., S.L.P., N.L., Coah. in Sierra Del Carmen.

Leaves of this species are ovate, often tapering abruptly to a point, to 4 cm long, somewhat shiny, and with prominent veins. Little biological information is available regarding the Netleaf Forestiera.

3. FRAXINUS L. ASH

Trees, large or small, rarely shrubs; winter buds with 1–2 pairs of dark outer scales, the outer ones sometimes leaflike. Leaves opposite, pinnate, with a terminal leaflet. Flowers small, in clusters, unisexual, male and female on separate plants; calyx 4-lobed, or absent; corolla usually of 4 (2–6) petals, or absent; stamens 2; stigmas 2. Fruit a samara (or nutlet), usually with an elongated wing.

A Northern Hemisphere genus of about 70 species. Some species of larger trees are important for lumber, and many species are grown as ornamentals. Nine species are represented in Texas.

KEY TO THE SPECIES

1. Leaves 2.5–4 cm long; leaflets obovate to oblanceolate, to 3.5 cm long, rounded at apex; petiole and leaf rachis somewhat winged   1. *F. greggii.*
1. Leaves longer; leaflets of different shape and longer; petiole and leaf rachis not winged.
   2. Leaflets usually 7, ovate to lanceolate, 3.5–7 cm long, the apex usually long-attenuated and pointed; flowers with whitish, fragrant petals, in terminal clusters   **2. *F. cuspidata.***
   2. Leaflets usually 5, lanceolate, ovate, or elliptic (but variable), 2.5–7.5 cm long, the apex pointed; flowers in axillary clusters, corolla absent
                                                3. *F. velutina.*

   1. Fraxinus greggii Gray.   GREGG ASH, LITTLEAF ASH.   Fig. 277.   [*Fraxinus greggii* var. *nummularis* (Jones) C. H. Mull.]. Rocky hills, slopes, canyons, and arroyos, mostly limestone habitats. Culberson Co., Sierra Diablo, S fork of Victorio Canyon. Brewster Co., Chisos Mts.; Dog Canyon; Stairstep Mt.; Cave Hill. Terrell Co., near the Rio Grande. Val Verde Co., near the Rio Grande. 1200–6000 ft.; Mar–May. W to AZ.

Plants of this species are nearly evergreen shrubs (rarely small trees to 6 m high) with smallish leaflets that are rather leathery, dark green above, and remain attached with the leaves through winter until after flowering time. Flowers appear in axillary clusters before new leaves of the year are produced. Stems and trunks of Gregg Ash are used for firewood.

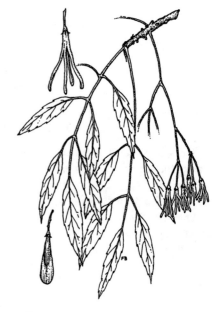

Fig. 277. *Fraxinus greggii* (Gregg Ash)   Fig. 278. *Fraxinus cuspidata* (Fragrant Ash)

2. Fraxinus cuspidata Torr.   FRAGRANT ASH, FLOWERING ASH.   Fig. 278.
Mountain slopes and canyons, igneous and limestone habitats. Hudspeth Co.,
N Hueco Mts.; N end of Quitman Mts. Culberson Co., Sierra Diablo, S fork of
Victorio Canyon; Hammer Handle Canyon, near Lobo. Brewster Co., Chisos
Mts.; Dead Horse Mts.; Rosillos Mts.; Del Norte Mts., 15 mi S Alpine to 35 mi
S; Mt. Ord; Nine-Point Mesa. Presidio Co., lower and upper slopes of Chinati
Peak; Cibolo Creek. Jeff Davis Co., Davis Mts. Resort, SE lower slopes of Mt.
Livermore. 2400–7000 ft.; early summer. W to AZ.

The Fragrant Ash is named after the pleasant smell of its whitish flowers.
This is the only ash of the Trans-Pecos with flower corollas. The plants are
usually shrubs, or less often small trees to 6 m high. One of its most distinctive
features is the leaflets with apexes long attenuated, a trait which inspired the
species name. Fragrant Ash is browsed by deer and livestock.

3. Fraxinus velutina Torr.   VELVET ASH, ARIZONA ASH.   Fig. 279.
[*Fraxinus velutina* var. *toumeyi* (Britt.) Rehd.; *F. velutina* var. *glabra* Rehd.].
Along streams and creeks, usually in protected canyons where there is almost
constant water. El Paso Co., Franklin Mts.; near Ysleta and the Rio Grande.
Culberson Co., Guadalupe Mts., and drainage creeks. Jeff Davis Co., Mt. Liv-
ermore; Limpia Canyon; Musquiz Canyon; Aguja Canyon. Presidio Co., Ca-
pote Falls Canyon, and above the falls; Chinati Mts., Cibolo Creek; Redford;
Fresno Canyon; Arroyo Segundo; Charro Canyon. Brewster Co., Iron Mt.; Ca-

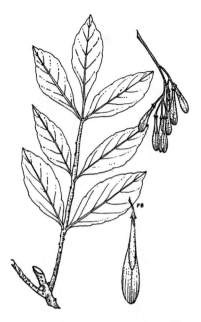

Fig. 279. *Fraxinus velutina* (Velvet Ash)

lamity Creek; Rio Grande Village, Big Bend National Park. Terrell Co., near mouth of San Francisco Canyon. Val Verde Co., Mile High Canyon, Langtry; mouth of Pecos River. 2000–6000 ft.; spring. N to UT; W to NV and CA; N Mex.

The flowers of Velvet Ash appear in axillary clusters before the leaves of the year. Plants of this species form trees to 12 m high with spreading branches and a rounded crown. The species name refers to a velvetlike covering of hairs on lower surfaces of the leaflets, at least in many specimens. Actually, *Fraxinus velutina* is reported to be extremely variable in leaflet size, shape, and pubescence, with many plants having glabrous leaflets. These glabrous forms are designated as var. *glabra* Rehd. In Velvet Ash the fruits occur in dense clusters and supposedly have wings equal to or shorter than the body. However, Trans-Pecos plants of this species are variable in fruit characters, with some plants exhibiting samaras with wings longer than the body.

Velvet Ash appears to be the common tree ash in the Trans-Pecos, although two other tree species, *Fraxinus papillosa* Lingelsh. (northern Chinati Mts.) and *F. texensis* (Gray) Sarg. (Brewster Co.), are reported to occur in this region (Miller, 1955; Henrickson, pers. comm.). Supposedly both *F. papillosa* and *F. texensis* are recognized by whitened leaves that are microscopically papillose underneath. *Fraxinus papillosa* has sessile or nearly sessile leaflets while *F. texensis* has leaflets with short petioles. Both of the latter taxa are close to *F. velutina* and are not clearly distinguished from this species, at least in the Trans-

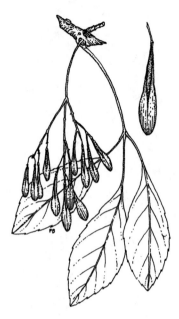

Fig. 280. *Fraxinus berlandieriana*
(Mexican Ash)

Pecos. Miller (1955) treats the Velvet Ash as a subspecies of *F. pennsylvanica* Marsh. (*F. pennsylvanica* subsp. *velutina* (Torr.) Miller). Still another tree ash, *F. berlandieriana* DC. (Mexican Ash), is known to occur on the Edwards Plateau and along the Devils River near the Trans-Pecos region, but as yet no plants of the latter species have been identified west of the Pecos River except in the lower canyons of the Rio Grande, perhaps as far west as eastern Boquillas Canyon (Fig. 280). Velvet Ash, a fast-growing tree, has been used extensively for ornamental purposes. Its wood is used to make ax handles and lumber used in wagons.

56. BUDDLEJACEAE WILHELM.   BUTTERFLYBUSH FAMILY

Herbs, shrubs, trees, or vines. Leaves opposite, entire, toothed, or lobed; stipules present. Flowers bisexual, regular; calyx 4–5-lobed or sepals separate; corolla with petals united in a tube, 4–5-lobed; stamens attached on floral tube, alternate with corolla lobes; ovary superior, 2-celled, not attached to calyx. Fruit a capsule or pod, usually dehiscent.

A family mostly of tropical and warm temperate regions of the Old World and the Americas, including nearly 150 species in about 10 genera. Many members of the family are grown as ornamentals, including some species of *Buddleja*, Butterflybush, the largest genus of the family. Traditionally, the Buddlejaceae has been placed in Loganiaceae Mart.

KEY TO THE GENERA

1. Corolla tube rather short and bellshaped with the lobes in a flat circle; anthers attached directly to corolla throat; leaves densely pubescent on both sides (in our species) **1. Buddleja.**
1. Corolla tube slender, the apical lobes abruptly forming a flat circle; anthers on filaments, these attached to middle of corolla tube; leaves essentially glabrous on top (or with scattered stellate hairs), whitish-pubescent below **2. Emorya.**

1. BUDDLEJA L. BUTTERFLYBUSH

Shrubs (in our area), with a dense covering of hairs. Leaves opposite, the margins usually with sharp or rounded teeth; with or without short petioles, these connected by stipules or by a transverse stipular line. Flowers in dense, rounded heads (in our species) or in racemes, 4-merous; calyx and corolla short-tubular and bellshaped, lobed; anthers essentially sessile in corolla throat. Fruit a roundish to ellipsoidal pod with 2 valves.

A genus of about 100 species, mostly of warmer regions of both hemispheres. Five species are represented in Texas.

KEY TO THE SPECIES

1. Leaves rather ovate or roundish, to 5 cm long, usually much shorter; flowers at maturity orange, arranged in roundish, headlike clusters (ca. 1 cm wide), on short stalks **1. B. marrubiifolia.**
1. Leaves rather narrow, oblong to linear, to 4.5 cm long, usually shorter; flowers at maturity yellowish, in roundish clusters in the axils of uppermost leaves **2. B. scordioides.**

1. Buddleja marrubiifolia Benth. WOOLLY BUTTERFLYBUSH. Fig. 281. Usually limestone habitats in desertic mountains, canyons, and arroyos. Presidio Co., 4 mi W of Shafter; 10 mi SE Redford; Panther Canyon near Big Hill. Brewster Co., Wildhorse Mt. near Study Butte; Dead Horse Mts., McKinney Springs; Packsaddle Mt.; Black Gap Refuge, Stairstep Mt., Heath Canyon, Maravillas Creek; near Dow Crossing. 1800–3800 ft.; Mar–Aug. Coah., Chih., Mex., S to S.L.P.; subsp. *occidentalis* Norm. occurs in W and cen. Chih.

This species is easily recognized by its flowers in "orange balls" (the corollas

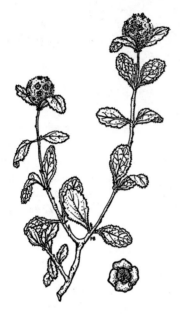

Fig. 281. *Buddleja marrubiifolia*
(Woolly Butterflybush)

Fig. 282. *Buddleja scordioides*
(Escobilla Butterflybush)

are yellow at anthesis) and oval leaves. The spreading shrubs grow to about 1.5 m high and are said to be fair browse for livestock. The plants are used medicinally in Mexico. An infusion of the flowers is used to color butter yellow.

2. Buddleja scordioides Kunth. ESCOBILLA BUTTERFLYBUSH. Fig. 282. Widespread in various habitats, limestone and igneous soils, throughout the Trans-Pecos. 2200–6500 ft.; Jun–Oct. Also E on the Edwards Plateau, N to NM; in Mex. S to Hgo. and Jal.

This aromatic shrub, to 3 m high but usually much shorter, is distinguished from the Woolly Butterflybush by its narrow leaves, and yellow flowers in axillary clusters (like beads on a string) at stem apexes. The plants are reported to be good browse for livestock. A tea made from the leaves is used to treat indigestion.

A third species of *Buddleja* (*B. racemosa* Torr.), the Wand Butterflybush, is endemic to the southern Edwards Plateau, and is known to occur just east of the Trans-Pecos area along the Devils River in Val Verde Co. It is possible that *B. racemosa* occurs somewhere in the eastern Trans-Pecos, in which case it can be recognized as a low shrub to 1 m high, with lax branches, leaves glabrous on the upper surfaces, and ball-like sessile clusters of cream-color flowers in beadlike arrangement (racemes) on leafless terminal peduncles.

Fig. 283. *Emorya suaveolens* (Emorybush)

2. EMORYA TORR.

Shrub to 2 m high, much-branched. Leaves opposite, blades to 5 cm long, basically eggshaped or somewhat triangular, the margins with a few teeth or lobes, upper surface green, usually with star-shaped hairs, lower surface whitish with dense hairs; petioles to 1 cm long. Flowers in apical clusters, 4-merous, fragrant; calyx ca. 1.5 cm long, tubular, with narrow lobes about half the length; corolla to 3.5 cm long, tubular, yellow and tipped with green; anthers extending from corolla tube on slender filaments; style long and slender, extending from the tube. Fruit a roundish or ellipsoid, 2-celled pod.

A monotypic genus extending barely into the United States from Mexico.

1. Emorya suaveolens Torr. EMORYBUSH. Fig. 283. In Texas and the U.S. presently known from one locality. Brewster Co., Black Gap Refuge, lower Maravillas Creek near Indian Cave, limestone, 2100 ft.; collected in flower and fruit, 17 Nov 1962, *T. Rogers* 256; collected originally from an imprecise locality, "canyons of the Rio Grande below Presidio," during the U.S.-Mexico boundary survey. Also Coah. and N.L., Mex., flowering Jul–Oct.

Little is known about this rare species. Perhaps it could be grown as an ornamental.

57. APOCYNACEAE JUSS.   DOGBANE FAMILY

Trees, shrubs, herbs, or vines, usually with milky sap. Leaves usually oppo-site, sometimes alternate or whorled, simple, entire; mostly without stipules. Flowers bisexual, regular, solitary or in clusters; sepals fused, 5-lobed, usually overlapping, often glandular within; petals 5, united below, tubular, funnel-form, or bellshaped, contorted in bud, the tube often appendaged within, 5-lobed; stamens 5, alternate with corolla lobes, anthers 4-celled, turned in-ward; ovary superior to nearly inferior, with two distinct carpels (or 2 ovaries of 1 carpel each); style 1, topped by a large stigma, variable in form. Fruit a follicle (in our species), elongated, opening only along the vented suture; seeds naked or with a tuft of hairs.

A family of about 2000 species in 200 genera, these most abundant in the tropics, but of cosmopolitan distribution. The family is related to Asclepiada-ceae, the Milkweed family. Members of *Nerium* L. (Oleander), *Vinca* L. (Peri-winkle), *Amsonia* Walt. (Amsonia), and other dogbanes are grown as orna-mentals in the United States and elsewhere. Vegetative parts and fruits of many dogbanes are poisonous when eaten. Seven genera of the family are repre-sented in Texas. Members of five genera occur in the Trans-Pecos, and three of these are treated below. In the Trans-Pecos the other two genera, *Apocynum* L. (3 spp.) and *Amsonia* (6 spp.), include species with vigorous herbaceous perennial habits. In *Amsonia* (Bluestar), some species, particularly *A. longiflora* Torr. (Fig. 284), exhibit stout woody bases and slender, somewhat woody stems. These species with pale bluish, tubular corollas produce herbaceous stems in early season growth, but the stems may present a tough or woody appearance at the base by year end.

KEY TO THE GENERA

1. Leaves alternate (opposite in some); corolla to about 1 cm long
                                                              1. Haplophyton.
1. Leaves opposite or in whorls; corolla 2.5–12.5 cm long.
    2. Low subshrub to 40 cm high; flowers 1–3 in number, not in clusters; native   **2. Telosiphonia.**
    2. Clumped shrubs or small tree, usually more than 1 m high (to 5 m high); flowers in clusters of few to numerous; introduced ornamental
                                                              3. Nerium.

1. HAPLOPHYTON A. DC.   COCKROACH PLANT

Shrubs (in our species) to 60 cm high; stems green, slender, much-branched. Leaves mostly alternate, 1.5–3.5(–5) cm long, 0.3–1.2 cm wide, lanceolate, with short hairs arising from pustules (rough to the touch). Flowers

Fig. 284. *Amsonia longiflora* (Bluestar)

bright yellow, solitary or paired in upper leaf axils; sepals 5, lobes linear, 3–5 mm long; corolla tubular, not appendaged within the 5 lobes, abruptly flaring, longer than the tube, directed leftward. Fruit a follicle, usually paired and upright, elongated, slender; seeds black, 6–8 mm long, with an apical tuft of white to charcoal gray hairs (coma yellowish in *H. cimicidum*), with vertical ridges broken by transverse grooves in *H. crooksii*.

A genus of two species of the western hemisphere (Williams, 1995). *Haplophyton cimicidum* A. DC. is restricted to Guatemala and southern Mexico.

1. Haplophyton crooksii (L. Benson) L. Benson. ARIZONA COCKROACH PLANT. Fig. 285. [*Haplophyton cimicidum* var. *crooksii* L. Benson]. Rocky slopes and canyons, limestone, igneous or sandstone soils. El Paso Co., Franklin Mts., Hudspeth Co., Davis Arroyo, Quitman Mts. Presidio Co., Capote Falls, in the canyon below and above the falls; mouth of Tinaja Prieta Canyon, Chinati Mts. Brewster Co., ledges near Tres Cuevas Mt. 2300–3500 ft. W to AZ; N Mex.

The generic description above is essentially that of *Haplophyton crooksii*. Like many members of the family, the Cockroach Plant produces poisonous substances, and its name comes from the reported use of leaf extracts, when mixed with syrup, as a cockroach poison. Extracts are also included in a sort of lotion which is then used to repel or kill fleas, ticks, mosquitoes, and flies.

Fig. 285. *Haplophyton crooksii*
(Arizona Cockroach Plant)

2. TELOSIPHONIA (WOODSON) HENR. ROCKTRUMPET

Subshrubs or suffrutescent herbs, perhaps rhizomatous. Leaves mostly opposite, sessile or short-petiolate; blades entire, or undulate-margined. Flowers usually single, rarely 2–3, usually at plant apex; sepals 5, linear-lanceolate, separate, herbaceous or petaloid, bearing scales on the inside base; corolla salverform, whitish, the tubes slender, long, abruptly expanded to a broader throat, the lobes 5, turned to the right; anthers 5, clustered at the massive stigma. Fruit of paired, terete, elongate follicles; seeds many, the apex with a tuft of hairs.

A genus of six species in North America (Henrickson, 1996). Three species occur in Texas and in the Trans-Pecos.

KEY TO THE SPECIES

1. Leaves to 6.5 cm long, to 4.5 cm wide, both surfaces felty pubescent; corollas 7–15 cm long, the slender tubes 3.5–9.5 cm long   **1. *T. macrosiphon.***
1. Leaves to 9 cm long, to 1–2 cm wide, both surfaces hairy to nearly glabrous, or the lower surface whitish woolly; corollas 4–7 cm long, the slender tubes 1–2.5 cm long.
    2. Leaves bicolored, green above, whitish woolly beneath, oblong to oblong-linear, 2–6(–9) cm long, 0.4–1(–2) cm wide, margins often undulate
                                    2. *T. hypoleuca.*

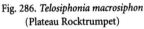

Fig. 286. *Telosiphonia macrosiphon*
(Plateau Rocktrumpet)

Fig. 287. *Telosiphonia hypoleuca*
(Bottomwhite Rocktrumpet)

2. Leaves green throughout, oblong-ovate to elliptic, 1.5–3 cm long, 0.7–
1.5 cm wide, margins entire   **3. *T. brachysiphon.***

1. Telosiphonia macrosiphon (Torr.) Henr. PLATEAU ROCKTRUMPET,
FLOR DE SAN JUAN. Fig. 286. [*Macrosiphonia macrosiphon* (Torr.) Heller].
Mostly in mountain and foothill areas, open or brushy rocky slopes, often in
desertic habitats, limestone and igneous soils, widely distributed in the Trans-
Pecos, from Hudspeth Co. (Eagle Mts.) and Culberson Co. (Apache Mts.) E to
S Reeves Co., and SE through Jeff Davis, Presidio, Brewster, and Pecos coun-
ties, to Terrell and Val Verde counties. 2300–6500 ft.; May–Sep. Also Edwards
Plateau in TX. N Mex.

   This subshrubby species is readily delimited from *T. hypoleuca*, which occupies some portions of the same range, by leaf shape and pubescence, and by
the longer corollas of *T. macrosiphon*. The corollas of both species are white
(or pinkish-tinged in *T. macrosiphon*); they tend to open after dark, when they
are sweetly aromatic, and reportedly they are hawkmoth pollinated.

   2. Telosiphonia hypoleuca (Benth.) Henr. BOTTOMWHITE ROCKTRUM-
PET, GUIRAMBO. Fig. 287. [*Macrosiphonia hypoleuca* (Benth.) Muell.-Arg.].
Open or wooded slopes, rocky igneous soil. Presidio Co., N slope Chinati Mts.
Jeff Davis Co., Mt. Locke, various exposures, including lower S slopes. Brewster

Co., upper Chisos Mts., near the Laguna. 4700–7000 ft.; Jul–Sep. Also W to Sonora and S to cen. Mex.

Plants of this species have woody bases with herbaceous stems. The specific epithet of *T. hypoleuca* is in reference to the lower leaf surface that is whitish, while the names *macrosiphonia* and *brachysiphon* allude, respectively, to long and short corollas. The rocktrumpet species would make handsome ornamentals.

3. **Telosiphonia brachysiphon** (Torr.) Henr. WESTERN ROCKTRUMPET. [*Macrosiphonia brachysiphon* (Torr.) Gray]. Collected by Richard Worthington in 1995 for the first time in Texas, granite outcrop, Franklin Mts., El Paso Co., 1.1 air miles NE of the top on Anthony's Nose. Previously known from SW NM, S AZ, and adjacent Mex.

Considerable additional information about *Telosiphonia*, particularly concerning taxonomic history, morphology, and pollination biology, is given by Henrickson (1996). In addition to its relatively short corollas, *T. brachysiphon* is distinguished by its thin leaves that are short or scarcely pubescent and green on both surfaces.

3. NERIUM L. OLEANDER

Shrubs or small trees; mostly glabrous. Leaves opposite or in whorls of 3–4, oblong-lanceolate, to 30 cm long, upper surface lustrous. Flowers showy, in clusters of few to many, variable in color, red, white, or pinkish-yellow, corolla funnelform, ca. 2 cm long, lobes 5. Fruit a follicle, in pairs, 0.5–1.5 cm long; seeds flattened, covered by short hairs, the apex tufted.

A genus of several Old World species, some of which have been introduced as ornamentals and widely naturalized in the United States. The common Oleander has become naturalized in many areas of Texas especially southeastern parts.

1. **Nerium oleander** L. COMMON OLEANDER, LAUREL ROSA. Cultivated as an ornamental in many towns of the Trans-Pecos, but seldom naturalized here even though its native habitat is in dry regions of the Mediterranean and the Orient. The leaves, flowers, and roots of *Nerium oleander* (and other oleanders) are extremely poisonous and can be fatal if eaten. It is reported that ingestion of one leaf may in some instances be sufficient to cause death in humans. Even the water in which flowers have been placed and smoke from burning plants are toxic. The plants are also poisonous to livestock. The poisonous principle is a glycoside known as oleandrin. In Europe Oleander has long been used as a rat poison.

58. ASCLEPIADACEAE R. BR. MILKWEED FAMILY

Perennial herbs, shrubs, or vines; with milky sap. Leaves, usually opposite or whorled, rarely alternate, simple. Flowers bisexual, regular, commonly in umbellike clusters, 5-merous; flower structure unusual; a crown, 5-lobed, usually present between corolla and stamens and is fused to one or both; stamens 5, attached to corolla tube, filaments usually fused in one column; anthers 2-celled, in New World species pollen grains in each anther sac fused into a saclike pollinium, the pollinia in pairs, each pollinium bearing a translator arm, and the arms joined by a glandlike body; pistil 1, carpels 2, usually of 2 distinct, superior ovaries, styles 2, but fused above into a 5-lobed, much-enlarged stigma. Fruit of 2 follicles (often 1 aborts); seeds many, flattened, with tufts of long silky hairs.

A family of about 2000 species in about 250 genera, primarily pantropical but with a few representatives in temperate regions. A few members of the family are grown as ornamentals, e.g., Carrion Flowers (*Stapelia* L. spp.), Butterfly Weed (*Asclepias tuberosa* L.), and Blood Flower (*A. curassavica* L.). A low quality "down" is made from silky hair of the seeds. Natural rubber can be obtained from the Rubber Vine [*Cryptostegia grandiflora* (Roxb. *ex* R. Br.) R. Br.]. The sap of *Matelea* Aubl. has been used as a poison for arrow tips. The repellent toxins (cyanogenic glycosides) of certain Monarch butterflies are taken from the sap of *Asclepias* L. sp. *Asclepias* is the largest North American genus. Five genera of the Milkweed family are represented in Texas and four of these are also found in the Trans-Pecos.

1. ASCLEPIAS L. MILKWEED, SILKWEED

Mostly herbaceous perennials, rarely subshrubs or annuals, stems not twining. Flowers usually in clusters, solitary in *Asclepias sperryi*; stamens surrounded by 5 fleshy appendages called hoods.

A genus of about 120 species distributed mostly in the Americas. About 36 species occur in Texas, and at least 13 of these are found in the Trans-Pecos. Several of the Trans-Pecos species, including the common roadside weed, *Asclepias latifolia* (Torr.) Raf., are relatively large and coarse in habit, but they are not woody.

1. Asclepias sperryi Woods. SPERRY MILKWEED. Fig. 288. Limestone substrates, rocky canyons and mountain slopes, usually growing with grasses. Brewster Co., Glass Mts., Altuda Point, Old Blue, Panther Canyon, Jail Canyon; Del Norte Mts., Mt. Ord, E side; Cienega Mt., E side where there is exposed limestone, and said to be in igneous soil there also. Pecos Co., Sierra Madera, NE side. 4200–6500 ft.; Apr–Oct. Also N Coah., Mex.

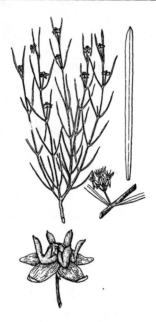

Fig. 288. *Asclepias sperryi* (Sperry Milkweed)

This low, wiry subshrub is recognized by its solitary flowers (rarely two) sharply deflexed stamenhoods, and narrow leaves that are 6–8 cm long and to 1 mm wide, glabrous, and with inrolled margins. Another species with similar habit, *Asclepias macrotis* Torr., often has its slender stems woody at the base.

59. POLEMONIACEAE JUSS.   PHLOX FAMILY

Annual, biennial, or perennial herbs, rarely subshrubs. Leaves alternate or opposite, often opposite below and alternate up the stems, simple or compound, margins smooth or toothed. Flowers usually in tightly clustered or loose arrangements, rarely solitary; bisexual, usually regular; sepals 5, forming a partly fused calyx; petals 5 rolled up longitudinally in bud, fused to form a tubular, bellshaped or flat and circular corolla; stamens 5, partly fused to corolla tube; ovary superior, carpels 3; style slender, branching into 3 stigmas. Fruit a capsule, opening between the partitions; seed usually many in each cell, to as few as one, sometimes sticky when wet.

A family of about 15 genera and about 300 species, mostly distributed in North America, with a majority of the species in the western United States. Garden flower ornamentals have been developed from some herbaceous members of the family, including species of *Phlox* L., *Polemoniurn* L., *Linanthus* Benth., and *Gilia* Ruiz & Pavon. Seven genera are represented in Texas, and members of all of these are found in the Trans-Pecos.

Fig. 289. *Ipomopsis wrightii*

1. IPOMOPSIS MICHX.

Herbaceous perennials, subshrubs, biennials, or annuals. Leaves alternate, entire to pinnate, the lobes with firm, sharp tips. Flowers solitary or in clusters, each flower usually subtended by a bract; calyx partly fused by thin membranes, the sepals sharptipped; corolla slender-tubular, white, lavender, pink, or red, in our species irregular or slightly so; stamens attached unevenly inside corolla tube. Seeds sticky when wet.

A genus of about 25 species concentrated in the southwestern United States. Ten species occur in Texas, with eight of these mostly herbaceous taxa being found in the Trans-Pecos. A few taxa including *Loeselia greggii* S. Wats are sometimes woody at the base. The two species treated below are subshrubby in habit.

KEY TO THE SPECIES

1. Plants to 0.5 m high; leaves linear, to 2.5 cm long; corolla lobes white to lavender   **1. *I. wrightii.***
1. Plants to 0.2 m high; leaves pinnate, to 1.5 cm long; corolla lobes pink or purple-blotched   **2. *I. havardii.***

1. **Ipomopsis wrightii** (Gray) Gould.   Fig. 289.   [*Gilia wrightii* Gray; *Navarretia wrightii* (Gray) O. Ktze.]. Sandy soil of low desert mesas. El Paso Co.,

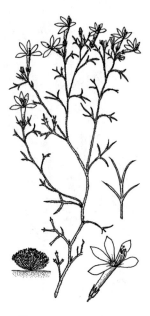

Fig. 290. *Ipomopsis havardii*

5 mi E Yselta. Hudspeth Co., 25 mi W Sierra Blanca. 4000 ft.; summer. Also CO and UT.

2. **Ipomopsis havardii** (Gray) V. Grant.   Fig. 290.   [*Loeselia havardii* Gray; *Gilia havardii* Gray; *Navarretia havardii* (Gray) O. Ktze.]. Slopes of desertic mountains and hills, endemic. Presidio Co., Little Cienega Mts. near Shafter; between Ruidosa and Presidio. Brewster Co., N end of Mariscal Mt.; near Johnson's Ranch on river road; 02 Ranch at Live Oak; 2500–4000 ft.; Mar–Oct. Also Chih., Mex.

60. HYDROPHYLLACEAE R. BR.   WATERLEAF FAMILY

Herbaceous annuals or perennials, less often shrubs, often hairy, glandular, or bristly. Leaves alternate or opposite, the margins smooth or pinnately divided. Flowers bisexual, regular, often arranged in helicoid cymes (coiled) or solitary; sepals 5, calyx deeply lobed; petals 5, corolla usually bellshaped, less often tubular or flat and circular; stamens borne on petals, alternate with corolla lobes, usually with a pair of scales on lower filaments; ovary superior (or half inferior in *Nama*), 1–2 celled, usually separate from calyx; styles 1–2; stigma headlike. Fruit a capsule, usually opening into 2–4 valves; seeds few to many.

Fig. 291. *Nama carnosum* (Gypnama)

A family of about 18 genera and about 300 species, occurring on all continents except Australia, but most abundant in western North America. Hydrophyllaceae is closely related to Boraginaceae. *Phacelia* Juss. is the largest genus with perhaps 200 species. Six genera of the Waterleaf Family occur in Texas, and three of these are represented in the Trans-Pecos.

1. NAMA L. NAMA

Plants mostly low annual or perennial herbs; pubescent. Leaves mostly alternate and entire. Flowers solitary or in clusters; sepals united basally; corolla white to purplish, tubular to bellshaped; stamens usually unequal in length and attachment in corolla tube; style solitary but shallow-bilobed at apex. Fruit an oval or roundish capsule, essentially unilocular; seeds numerous, minute.

A genus of about 50 species distributed mostly in northern Mexico and the southwestern United States, with a few species in South America, and one species in Hawaii. Twelve species occur in Texas, all but one of these also being found in the Trans-Pecos.

1. **Nama carnosum** (Woot.) C.L. Hitchc. GYPNAMA. Fig. 291. [*Nama stenophyllum* Gray *ex* Hemsl. var. *egenum* Macbr.]. Nearly pure gypsum or gypseous substrates. Hudspeth Co., Malone Hills W of Sierra Blanca. Culberson Co., between Orla and Texline, to 35 mi N Van Horn. 3500–4500 ft.; Jun–Oct. Also in gypsum habitats in S NM.

This white-flowered species is often seen as herbaceous with a thick, woody caudex, but it also becomes robust with stems woody at the base. It is regarded as a gypsum indicator species.

61. BORAGINACEAE JUSS.   BORAGE FAMILY

Herbs, shrubs, or trees, usually with bristly hairs. Leaves alternate, simple. Flowers bisexual, regular, arranged in scorpioid or helicoid cymes (coiled, un-coiling as flowers open) or solitary, usually with bracts subtending the flowers; sepals 5, somewhat irregular; corolla 5-lobed, tubular, bellshaped, or flat and circular, commonly with folds or saclike appendages in the throat; stamens 5, attached to corolla tube alternate with lobes; ovary superior, 2-celled, smooth or lobed; ovules usually 4 (2 in each cell); style 1, borne at fruit apex, between the lobes, or on receptacle elongated between the lobes; stigma headlike, less often bilobed or divided. Fruit of 4 nutlets or drupelike.

A family of about 2000 species in about 100 genera, widely distributed, with many representatives in North America. Family classifications are based largely upon fruit or nutlet characters. Some members are grown as ornamentals, including species of *Myosotis* L. (Forget-me-nots) and *Heliotropium* L. (Heliotrope). Seventeen genera are represented in Texas, with seven or eight of these also found in the Trans-Pecos. *Antiphytum heliotropioides* A. DC., a slender-stemmed shrub to 0.5 m high, is not treated below although this species of north-central Mexico has been questionably reported from near Marfa, Presidio County. I have seen no specimens that document its occurrence in the Trans-Pecos.

KEY TO THE GENERA

1. Style deeply cleft; in *Tiquilia greggii* older plants much-branched, compact, grayish, roundish shrubs, more or less 0.5 m high, with flowers pink to magenta and in dense round clusters at ends of leafy branches; calyx lobes plumose   **1. Tiquilia.**
1. Style usually short and enlarged-conic apically; shrubs or subshrubs 0.1–0.5 m high, not round and compact, pallid to grayish, flower clusters small-ish, somewhat scorpioid; calyx lobes not plumose   **2. Heliotropium.**

1. TIQUILIA PERS.

Herbs or shrubs. Leaves small and many, petioles present or absent. Flowers arranged along the stems or in clusters, commonly opening late in day; corolla small, tubular; style terminal, bilobed or cleft at apex. Fruit dry, in *Tiquilia greggii* elongated and wider near middle (2–2.5 mm long), by abortion 1-seeded instead of four.

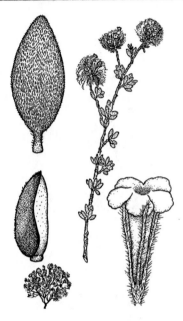

Fig. 292. *Tiquilia greggii* (Plume Tiquilia)

A genus of about 26 species of arid regions in North and South America, until recently (Richardson, 1976) recognized as *Coldenia* L. The latter genus is now considered as monotypic in the Old World. In North America, *Tiquilia* is centered in and around the Chihuahuan Desert region. All five Texas species are found in the Trans-Pecos.

1. **Tiquilia greggii** (T. & G.) Richards. PLUME TIQUILIA. Fig. 292. [*Ptilocalyx greggii* T. & G.; *Coldenia greggii* (T. & G.) Gray]. Common in limestone habitats of desertic mountains, slopes, and flats. El Paso Co., E throughout most of the Trans-Pecos. 2000–4200 ft.; Mar–Sep. Also NM; Mex., Chih., and Coah., S to N Dgo. and Zac.

This species is usually recognizable as rather low grayish densely branched and leafy globose shrubs with roundish clusters of pink flowers. When in full flower the plants are extremely attractive and should be considered for ornamental use especially in limestone substrates.

2. HELIOTROPIUM L. HELIOTROPE, TURNSOLE

Annual or perennial herbs or subshrubs. Leaves large to small, with or without petioles. Flowers white, yellow, or purple, usually in scorpioid clusters; anthers attached inside a usually pubescent corolla throat, filaments very short. Fruit dry, breaking into 2 or 4 parts.

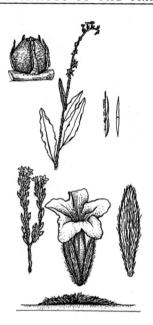

Fig. 293. *Heliotropium confertifolium*
(Leafy Heliotrope)

A genus of about 250 species, nearly world-wide, with preference to warm and arid regions. Fifteen species occur in Texas, with about half of these being represented in the Trans-Pecos.

KEY TO THE SPECIES

1. Plants prostrate, usually less than 10 cm high, the crowded stems with small, densely arranged leaves, herbage grayish-silvery; flowers white with a yellow throat   **1. *H. confertifolium.***
1. Plants upright, rather stiff and bushy, 10–50 cm high, with slender stems, the leaves linear and closely arranged, herbage gray-green; flowers greenish-yellow to cream   **2. *H. torreyi.***

1. **Heliotropium confertifolium** (Torr.) Torr. *ex* Gray. LEAFY HELIO-TROPE. Fig. 293. Desertic limestone habitats, usually upper Cretaceous in age and perhaps gypseous. Brewster Co., southern half. Pecos Co., W portion. Terrell Co., vicinity of Sanderson and Dryden to Rio Grande. Val Verde Co., from near Langtry to the Pecos River. 1300–4000 ft., Mar–Oct. Also S along and near the Rio Grande to the S tip of TX; N Mex.

Fig. 294. *Heliotropium torreyi*
(Torrey Heliotrope)

2. Heliotropium torreyi I. M. Johnst. TORREY HELIOTROPE. Fig. 294.
[*Heliotropium angustifolium* Torr.]. Limestone habitats, desertic mountains,
hills, and slopes. Southern Presidio Co. (Shafter; Solitario) and Brewster Co.,
SE across Pecos, Terrell, and Val Verde counties. 1100–4000 ft.; Apr–Nov. Also
the Edwards Plateau, S along and near the Rio Grande to Hidalgo Co.; N. Mex.
This species is supposedly good browse for sheep (Correll and Johnston,
1970).

62. VERBENACEAE ST.-HIL. VERBENA FAMILY

Herbs, shrubs, trees, or woody vines; stems mostly square. Leaves usually
opposite, mostly simple, less often compound, margins smooth, toothed, or
cleft; stipules absent. Flowers in terminal clusters of various arrangements, or
axillary and then often solitary; usually bisexual, irregular, rarely regular; sepals
fused to form a bellshaped to tubular calyx, 4–5 lobed (2–7 lobed); corolla
tubular or funnelform, usually with 4–5 lobes and somewhat 2-lipped; stamens usually 4(5) and in 2 pairs of unequal length, or reduced to 2, attached
in corolla tubes; ovary superior, usually 4-lobed, carpels 2 (4–5), 2–5-celled
or more by false partition, placentation axillary, usually with one ovule in each

apparent locule; style borne at top of ovary, slender, stigma lobes as many as carpels. Fruit usually dry (schizocarp), separating into 1-seeded portions, less often drupaceous, dry or fleshy, 2–4-celled, indehiscent, or dehiscent into 2(4–10) nutlets of 1–2 cells each.

A family of over 2500 species in more than 95 genera, mainly of tropical and subtropical distribution, but also widely distributed elsewhere except in Arctic and Antarctic regions. The Verbena family is closely related to the Mint family, Lamiaceae. Members of several genera are important ornamentals, including species of *Verbena* L., *Lantana* L., and *Vitex* L. Fourteen genera are represented in Texas, and seven genera occur in the Trans-Pecos.

KEY TO THE GENERA

1. Flowers (and fruits) arranged in headlike clusters.
  2. Calyx rim flat or only slightly toothed or lobed; fruit usually with a fleshy outer layer   **1. Lantana.**
  2. Calyx rim 2–4-toothed; fruit with a thin dry outer layer   **2. Lippia.**
1. Flowers (and fruits) arranged in elongated clusters or spikes.
  3. Flowers white; calyx very small, membranous; fruit not beaked
                                                                  3. Aloysia.
  3. Flowers lavender to purplish; calyx elongated, herbaceous; fruit beaked   **4. Bouchea.**

1. LANTANA L.   LANTANA

Herbs or shrubs, in our species to 2 m high or usually smaller, hairy. Leaves opposite, the margins toothed. Flowers clustered to form rather compact heads; calyx rather small, membranous; corolla red, yellow, orange, pink, or purplish, flaring at apex; stamens 4, in 2 pairs. Fruit drupelike, blue-black and somewhat fleshy to nearly dry, thin, and translucent.

A genus of about 160 species and numerous varieties centered in tropical and subtropical America. Nine species are found in Texas with only two or three of these extending into the Trans-Pecos. *Lantana camara* L. is a showy ornamental shrub that occasionally escapes cultivation in the Trans-Pecos. Reportedly the immature fruits of *L. camara* are toxic.

KEY TO THE SPECIES

1. Stems with recurved prickles, or unarmed, moderately hairy; corollas larger, orange-red or orange-yellow; leaf blades 3–5 cm wide   **1. L. urticoides.**
1. Stems unarmed, rather densely grayish-hairy especially on younger parts; corollas smaller, pink to purplish, often with a yellow spot in the tube; leaf blades 0.5–3.5 cm long, 0.5–1.5 cm wide   **2. L. achyranthifolia.**

Fig. 295. *Lantana achyranthifolia*
(Veinyleaf Lantana)

1. Lantana urticoides Hayek. COMMON LANTANA, TEXAS LANTANA, CALICO BUSH, HIERBA DE CRISTO. [*Lantana horrida* Kunth var. *latibracteata* Moldenke]. Limestone canyon country, extending across the Pecos River to near Langtry, Val Verde Co. 1100–2400 ft.; flowering much of the year. Also throughout most of TX; NM, AZ, CA; introduced and cultivated widely; also N Mex.

The species is a desirable ornamental because of its dense clusters of colorful flowers. In Mexico a decoction of the leaves is sometimes used to treat snake bites, and crushed leaves are applied to the wound. A decoction is also employed as a remedy for stomach ailments. In Mile Canyon near Langtry, Common Lantana was found growing at the mouth of an Indian cave suggesting that Indians might have used the plant. Common Lantana supposedly is toxic to cattle and sheep. The synonymous epithet *horrida* refers to the malodorous leaves (when crushed), although the armed stems also could have inspired the name. The alkaloid lantamine, an antipyretic, is found in this species.

2. Lantana achyranthifolia Desf. VEINYLEAF LANTANA, DESERT LANTANA, MEJORANA, HIERBA NEGRA. Fig. 295. [*Lantana macropoda* Torr.]. Mostly in rocky limestone habitats. Presidio Co., Sierra Vieja; Chinati Mts.; Solitario. Brewster Co., Chisos Mts. and vicinity; Agua Fria; Alpine. Pecos Co., Val Verde

Fig. 296. *Lippia graveolens* (Scented Lippia)

Co., vicinity of Langtry and SE. 1200–4600 ft.; Feb–Mar. S to the Rio Grande Valley and Rio Grande Plains, E to Houston Co.; also N Mex.

A form with white flowers occurs in Starr and Cameron counties, and in northern Mexico. The plant is aromatic and often is incorrectly considered to be a mint species.

2. LIPPIA L.   LIPPIA

Shrubs or subshrubs, aromatic. Leaves usually opposite, toothed. Flowers in our species arranged in clusters on slender stalks 1 cm or more long, these 4 to 6 per node, individual flowers small and sessile, borne in the axils of bractlets, these overall in 4 distinct series; corollas tubular, in our species yellow or whitish with a yellow spot. Fruit small, dry, enclosed by a small membranous calyx, separating into two parts at maturity.

A genus of about 200 species centered in tropical and subtropical America. Only two species occur in Texas.

1. **Lippia graveolens** Kunth. SCENTED LIPPIA, REDBRUSH LIPPIA. Fig. 296. [*Lippia berlandieri* Schauer; *Goniostachyum graveolens* (Kunth) Small]. Desert rocky limestone hills, mountains, slopes, and canyons. Brewster Co., 4 mi W Hot Springs, Big Bend Park; Dead Horse Mts.; several localities in

Black Gap Refuge. Terrell Co., mouth of San Francisco Canyon. Val Verde Co., vicinity of Langtry; near Pecos River. 1200–3200 ft.; Mar–Dec. S to Rio Grande Plains and Rio Grande Valley, NE to Austin Co.; NM; Mex. and C.A. This species is named after its strong aromatic scent. It is said to be good browse for deer.

3. ALOYSIA JUSS. BEEBRUSH

Shrubs, erect, much branched, sweet-aromatic. Leaves opposite, deciduous, the margins smooth or toothed. Flowers white, rather loosely arranged in elongate clusters (spikes or racemes); each flower subtended by a bractlet; calyx angular, 4-toothed, hairy; corolla tubular, 2-lipped. Fruit small, dry, splitting into 2 parts.

A genus of about 40 species distributed in the southwestern United States, Mexico, and southern South America, with one widely cultivated species introduced into the West Indies. Three species occur in Texas.

KEY TO THE SPECIES

1. Leaf blades linear, oblong-elliptic, to lanceolate, 0.4–2.8 cm long, 0.2–0.8 cm wide, the margins smooth or few-toothed   **1. A. gratissima.**
1. Leaf blades ovate to roundish, 0.3–1.8 cm long (rarely longer), 0.3–1.8 cm wide, the margins evenly toothed   **2. A. wrightii.**

1. Aloysia gratissima (Gill. & Hook.) Troncoso. WHITEBRUSH, COMMON BEEBRUSH. Fig. 297. [*Aloysia lycioides* Cham.; *Lippia lycioides* (Cham.) Steud.]. Grasslands, rocky slopes, arroyos, canyons, bluffs, throughout most of the Trans-Pecos. 1100–5000 ft.; Mar–Nov. Also throughout TX except Plains Country; NM; Mex.; S S.A.

This plant is famous in the Trans-Pecos and other areas as a source of Whitebrush honey. The leaves are said to be good browse for sheep, but the flowers supposedly are toxic to horses. The var. **schulziae** (Standl.) L. Benson differs in having broader, more hairy leaves with more prominent marginal teeth, and occurs in the Trans-Pecos (Val Verde Co., 1 mi W of Pecos River), S to Cameron Co.

2. Aloysia wrightii Heller *ex* Abrams. OREGANILLO. Fig. 298. [*Lippia wrightii* Gray]. Desert shrub, rocky slopes, mountains, canyons, and arroyos, throughout much of the Trans-Pecos, generally overlapping *Aloysia gratissima* in distribution. 2100–6500 ft.; Jun–Nov. Also S to Starr Co., and NE to Tom Green Co.; NM, AZ, NV, CA; N Mex.

This plant is a good source of honey and is said to be good browse for livestock.

Fig. 297. *Aloysia gratissima* (Whitebrush)   Fig. 298. *Aloysia wrightii* (Oreganillo)

4. BOUCHEA CHAM. BOUCHEA

Herbs or low shrubs usually less than 1 m in our species, hairy or glabrous. Leaves opposite or in threes, sessile, the margins entire or toothed. Flowers lavender to purplish, arranged in elongate clusters; each flower in the axil of a bractlet; calyx tubular, 5-ribbed, 5-toothed at apex; corolla tubular, flaring apically, 5 unequal lobes. Fruit dry, linear, beaked, enclosed by calyx, separating with 2 parts.

A genus of about 16 species distributed from the southern United States south to South America. Three species occur in Texas.

KEY TO THE SPECIES

1. Leaves linear to narrowly lanceolate, 0.8–4.5 cm long, 1.4–4 mm wide, essentially glabrous, thin in texture; stems ridged   **1. *B. linifolia.***
1. Leaves spatulate, 0.5–2.6 cm long, 2–6 mm wide, hairy, thick in texture; stems nearly cylindrical   **2. *B. spathulata.***

1. Bouchea linifolia Gray. GROOVESTEM BOUCHEA. Fig. 299. Desertic limestone habitats. Presidio Co., near Shafter; Tres Cuevos Mt. Pecos Co., ca. 30 mi S Fort Stockton toward Sanderson; between Big Canyon and Downie

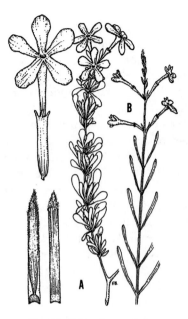

Fig. 299. A) *Bouchea spathulata*
(Spoonleaf Bouchea); B) *B. linifolia*
(Groovestem Bouchea)

Canyon. Terrell Co., 15 mi N Sanderson; upper Big Canyon. Val Verde Co., Del Rio and N toward Loma Alta. 1100–3800 ft.; Jul–Oct. SE to Sutton and Uvalde counties; Coah., Mex.

2. Bouchea spathulata Torr. SPOONLEAF BOUCHEA. Fig. 299. Desertic limestone habitats. Brewster Co., near top of Dead Horse Mts., head of Heath Canyon; along old Boquillas road opposite Alto Relex; E of Tornillo Creek; above Boquillas Canyon. 2200–3800 ft.; Jun–Oct. N Mex.

This rare species is easily distinguished by its crowded, spatulate leaves while *Bouchea linifolia* has flaxlike leaves.

63. LAMIACEAE LINDL. MINT FAMILY

Herbs, annual or perennial, sometimes shrubs; stems usually square in section; herbage aromatic. Leaves opposite or whorled, simple or compound; stipules absent. Flowers bisexual, usually irregular, in clusters of various arrangement or solitary; calyx usually somewhat 2-lipped, 5-toothed, the upper 3 teeth usually fused, the calyx tube usually ribbed and enlarging with fruit, corolla usually 5-lobed, usually 2-lipped, the 2 upper lobes often fused and erect, lower 3 lobes usually spreading, with central one dipperlike; stamens usually in 2 unequal pairs, less often 2, connective between anthers sometimes much developed; ovary superior, 4-lobed; style arising from central depression between the 4 lobes, or from near apex of ovary; style bifed, stigmas minute and at end of style branches. Fruit usually of 4 nutlets, within persistent calyx. The conserved family name is Labiatae Juss.

A large family of cosmopolitan distribution, with over 3200 species in about 200 genera. The center of distribution is in the Mediterranean region, but about 50 genera also occur in the United States. Typically plants of the Mint family produce aromatic "essential oils" that are responsible for much economic importance. Essential oils are taken from *Mentha* L. (Mint), *Rosemarinus* L. (Rosemary), *Salvia* L. (Sage), *Lavandula* L. (Lavender) and other members of the family. Among the culinary herbs, used for condiments or aroma, are *Ocimum* L. (Basil), *Thymus* L. (Thyme), *Hedeoma pulegioides* (L.) Pers. (Pennyroyal), and *Hyssopus* L. (Hyssop). Many species are cultivated as ornamentals. Thirty-one genera are represented in Texas, with at least 12 of these also occurring in the Trans-Pecos.

KEY TO THE GENERA

1. Calyx 2-lipped, in fruit markedly inflated and bladderlike   **1. Salazaria.**
1. Calyx with 5–10 teeth, or 2-lipped with 3 upper teeth and 2 lower teeth.
  2. Plants woolly pubescent especially on younger stems and underside of leaves; flowers whitish, in dense axillary clusters   **2. Marrubium.**
  2. Plants not woolly (but perhaps with short matted hairs); flowers otherwise.
    3. Corolla prominently 2-lipped, upper lip often helmetlike   **3. Salvia.**
    3. Corolla moderately 2-lipped, upper lip not helmetlike or curved.
      4. Plants shrubs to 1 m high; calyx with a dense covering of long, soft hairs; gypseous substrates   **4. Poliomintha.**
      4. Plants low subshrubs or herbs; calyx hairs short; mostly mountain habitats   **5. Hedeoma.**

1. SALAZARIA TORR.   BLADDERSAGE

Shrub to 2 m high, usually smaller, much branched, the smaller branches wiry, rather spinetipped. Leaves with very short petioles, the blades ovate-oblong, to 2.5 cm long, markedly reduced in size and becoming linear toward branch apexes. Flowers pink with a purple lip, each in the axil of a small leaf; calyx 2-lipped, 6–8 mm long, at maturity becoming inflated into a papery bladder 1.5–1.8 cm long; corolla 2-lipped, 1.2–1.8 mm long. Fruit 4-lobed, rough-surfaced.

Fig. 300. *Salazaria mexicana* (Bladdersage)

A genus of but one species, considered by some to be distinct from the Lamiaceae and to warrant recognition as the monotypic family Salazariaceae Barkley.

1. Salazaria mexicana Torr. BLADDERSAGE, PAPERBAGBUSH. Fig. 300. Desert slopes, washes, and flats often in sand, gravel, or clay. Brewster Co., Big Bend Park, Near Smoky Creek; between Smoky Creek and Castolon; near Alamo Spring; between Castolon and Santa Elena Canyon; top of Mesa de Anguila. Presidio Co., ca. 1.5 mi NE La Mota, 70 mi S Marfa. 2200–3100 ft.; May–Nov. W to CA and UT; Coah., Chih., Mex.

The most recognizable feature of this species, when fruit are present, is the inflated calyx that forms around the fruit, thus inspiring the vernacular names. The plant is said to be good browse for livestock.

2. MARRUBIUM L. COMMON HOREHOUND

Herbaceous perennial to 1 m high often with a woody base; aromatic; sap bitter; stems stout, ascending, white-woolly. Leaves ovate to nearly round, toothed, prominently veined, woolly but greenish above and whitish underneath. Flowers whitish, in dense axillary clusters along the upper stems; calyx tubular, 4–5 mm long, 10-toothed at apex; corolla 5–6 mm long, 2-lipped. Fruit oval, smooth, 2 mm long.

Fig. 301. *Marrubium vulgare*
(Common Horehound)

A genus of about 45 species distributed in the Old World. The one species in Texas is a native of Eurasia, but has become naturalized throughout much of North America.

1. Marrubium vulgare L.   COMMON HOREHOUND, MARRUBIUM.   Fig. 301. Widespread and weedy at roadside, in waste places, and disturbed areas; common about corrals and animal pens, also throughout TX and elsewhere.

This plant is so common and robust that it is included here even though it is not considered to be a shrub. Dried leaves and flowers are used to make medicine and as a flavoring. A delicious confection, horehound candy, is made from leaf extracts, and is sometimes sold in stores in the United States and Mexico. The candy and a leaf tea are used to treat sore throats and coughs. In large doses the tea or candy acts as a laxative, and it has been used to remove fly larvae from the nose. Powdered leaves are applied to skin sores. The bitter principle is marrubium.

3. SALVIA L.   SAGE

Shrubs or herbs, often aromatic. Leaves variable in shape. Flowers red, blue, purple in our species, usually showy, usually loosely arranged in elongated clusters; calyx 2-lipped, somewhat flattened; corolla strongly 2-lipped, the upper lip plane with an apical notch or helmetshaped; stamens 2, each with a single terminal anther sac; style usually extending from the corolla. Fruit smooth.

A genus of about 700 species with world-wide distribution, but centered in South America. In Texas 22 species are known, with at least 16 of these also being found in the Trans-Pecos. Most native salvias are to be recommended for ornamental use because of their attractive flowers and because they can be grown from seeds and cuttings. The seeds of *Salvia* (known to the Indians as Chia) are rich in protein and easily digested fats, and were heavily used by the Indians for food. Seeds were usually toasted and ground to make a flour that tripled in bulk when mixed with water, thus furnishing a nourishing and filling meal even in small quantities. Chia supposedly neutralizes alkaline water.

KEY TO THE SPECIES

1. Corolla red, at least 2.5 cm long; calyx 1–2 cm long.
    2. Plants to 2 m high; leaves deltoid-ovate, to 5 cm long, prominently toothed; corolla 4–5 cm long   **1. *S. regla.***
    2. Plants usually less than 1 m high; leaves obovate to elliptic, narrow at base, to 2.5 cm long, margins essentially smooth; corolla 2.5–3 cm long
                                                                      2. *S. greggii.*
1. Corolla lavender, blue, or purple, less than 1.5 cm long; calyx 1 cm long or less.
    3. Plants usually less than 0.5 m high; leaves oblong-elliptic to oval, 1–3 cm long; flowers loosely arranged in slender, naked racemes, corolla tube longer than the calyx; calyx lobes pointed   **3. *S. lycioides.***
    3. Plants usually exceeding 0.5 m high, to 2.5 m high; leaves deltoid or ovate, less often oblong-elliptic, 1–5 cm long; flowers tightly arranged in short dense racemes; corolla tube not longer than calyx; calyx lobes round, blunt, rarely pointed.
        4. Leaf blades broadly deltoid-ovate, 2–5 cm long; Franklin Mts
                                                                  4. *S. pinguifolia.*
        4. Leaf blades ovate-deltoid to oblong-elliptic, 1–4 cm long; Val Verde Co.   **5. *S. ballotiflora.***

1. **Salvia regla** Cav. MOUNTAIN SAGE, ROYAL SAGE. Fig. 302. Wooded slopes and canyons. Brewster Co., Chisos Mts. (Green Gulch; Pullliam, Pine, Boot, and Wade canyons; Lost Mine Peak; Casa Grande; Laguna; near Mt. Emory; and elsewhere). 4500–7000 ft.; Jun–Sept. Coah. to Oax., Mex.; type from Regla, Hgo.

This large, leafy shrub with its showy scarlet flowers is one of the most attractive plants in the Trans-Pecos. It is attractive as an ornamental.

Fig. 302. *Salvia regla* (Mountain Sage)   Fig. 303. *Salvia greggii* (Autumn Sage)

2. Salvia greggii Gray. AUTUMN SAGE. Fig. 303. Rocky habits, mostly in the mountain and canyon country. Presidio Co., Chinati Mts., 3 mi W Shafter; W side Solitario. Brewster Co., most mountain areas from Glass Mts. and Del Norte Mts. (Mt. Ord and Goat Mt.), S to the Dead Horse Mts. Pecos Co., Sierra Madera. Terrell Co., 17 mi W Sanderson. 2200–5800 ft.; Mar–May. Cen. and S TX; also Mex.

White and pink forms are known for this normally red-flowered species. The plant has great ornamental potential.

3. Salvia lycioides Gray. CANYON SAGE. Fig. 304. [*Salvia romosissima* Fern.]. Mountain canyons, slopes and ledges. El Paso Co., Franklin Mts. Culberson Co., Guadalupe Mts.; Sierra Diablo, Victorio Canyon. Presidio Co., above Capote Falls, Sierra Vieja. Brewster Co., Chisos Mts. 3500–8000 ft.; Apr–Oct. Also NM; Mex. This is a smallish blue-flowered shrub usually 40–50 cm high.

4. Salvia pinguifolia (Fern.) Woot. & Standl. ROCK SAGE. Fig. 305. Rocky limestone habitats. El Paso Co., Franklin Mts. (McKelligan Canyon; E lower slopes). Hudspeth Co., reported from "the little canyon at Cerro Alto." 4500–4650 ft.; Aug–Sep. Also W to AZ; N Mex.

This is a rare shrub to 1.5 m high with lavender-purple flowers. A larger-flowered taxon, *Salvia vinacea* Woot. & Standl., with the corolla tube 8.5–

Fig. 304. *Salvia lycioides* (Canyon Sage)   Fig. 305. *Salvia pinguifolia* (Rock Sage)

10 mm long and wine-colored calyces and corollas, also occurs in the Franklin Mountains (Peterson, pers. comm.). Corollas of *S. pinguifolia* are 5–8 mm long. The specific epithet *pinguifolia* means "greaseleaf," in reference to the texture of the leaves.

5. Salvia ballotiflora Benth. SHRUBBY BLUE SAGE, MEJORANA. Fig. 306. [*Salvia laxa* Benth.]. Rocky limestone canyons. Val Verde Co., Mile Canyon, Langtry; 1 mi N Langtry; mouth of the Pecos River; near the Pumpville turnoff (U.S. 90); between Del Rio and Loma Alta. 1200–2400 ft.; Jan–Oct. Edwards Plateau S to the coast; also Mex.

This shrub, to 2.5 m high, has bluish or purplish flowers. Its dried leaves are used for flavoring foods.

4. POLIOMINTHA GRAY ROSEMARYMINT

Grayish shrubs, ca. 0.5 m high. Leaves linear to linear-oblong, margins smooth. Flowers pink or purplish, clustered in axils of leaves near branch apexes; calyx tubular, with 13–15 longitudinal lines, 5-toothed; corolla tube equaling or longer than calyx, 2-lipped, upper lip erect, lower lip 3-notched; stamens 2.

A genus of about six species in Mexico and southwestern United States.

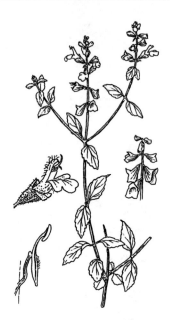

Fig. 306. *Salvia ballotiflora*
(Shrubby Blue Sage)

Fig. 307. *Poliomintha incana*
(Hoary Rosemarymint)

KEY TO THE SPECIES

1. Plants with a dense covering of short white hairs; leaves linear, sessile; calyx 6–7 mm long, fuzzy with long white hairs   **1. P. incana.**
1. Plants with short hairs, becoming glabrous with age; leaves linear-oblong (to roundish), with short petioles; calyx 4–5 mm long, with short hairs
2. P. glabrescens.

1. Poliomintha incana (Torr.) Gray. HOARY ROSEMARYMINT. Fig. 307. [*Hedeoma incana* Torr.]. Gypsum hills, flats, and sands. Culberson Co., gypsum hills and plains between Orla and Texline, including Rustler Hills. Hudspeth Co., white gypsum dunes, 13 mi E Dell City. El Paso Co., Hueco sand hills. 3600–5400 ft.; Apr–Jun. W to AZ and UT; also N Mex.

This aromatic shrub is attractive and should be considered for ornamental use in desert landscaping. Hopi Indians ate the leaves dry, fresh, or boiled. A refreshing tea can be made from the leaves. The flowers can be used for seasoning.

2. Poliomintha glabrescens Gray. LEAFY ROSEMARYMINT. Fig. 308. [*Hedeoma glabrescens* (Gray) Briq.]. Rocky limestone slopes and canyons. Presidio Co., Solitario Peak area. Brewster Co., McRae Canyon, 15 mi SE Alpine; S Housetop Mt. 2800–3800 ft.; Jun–Oct. Also NE Mex.

The plants are ca. 0.5 m high and pungent.

Fig. 308. *Poliomintha glabrescens* (Leafy Rosemarymint)

Fig. 309. *Hedeoma mollis* (Hairy Hedeoma)

5. HEDEOMA PERS. MOCK PENNYROYAL

Annual or perennial herbs, rarely subshrubs, often with a woody caudex; pubescence of simple hairs or branched hairs (in *Hedeoma mollis*). Leaves variable in shape and texture, usually less than 2 cm long. Flowers clustered in axils on upper stems; calyx tubular, 13-nerved, 2-lipped, the lower calyx teeth reflexed in *H. mollis*; corolla 2-lipped, lavender with maroon spots in *H. mollis*; stamens 4, lower pair fertile, upper pair sterile and reduced. Fruit lobes oblong, brown, covered with a bloom, sticky when wet.

A genus of about 37 species centered in the southwestern United States and adjacent Mexico. Nine species occur in Texas. Only one species is treated below even though several taxa, including *Hedeoma apiculata* W. S. Stewart, might be considered miniature shrubs with woody basal stems.

1. **Hedeoma mollis** Torr. HAIRY HEDEOMA. Fig. 309. [*Poliomintha mollis* (Torr.) Gray]. Mountain habitats among rocks, endemic. Presidio Co., Chinati Mts.; Sierra Vieja. Brewster Co., Lizard Mt. near Alpine; Sunny Glen; top of Packsaddle Mt.; Chisos Mts. 3500–5500 ft.; Jul–Nov.

This low, grayish subshrub, usually less than 0.5 m high, is evidently endemic to Trans-Pecos Texas. A strong woody caudex supports slender stems that are more or less woody at the base, depending upon the specimen. The grayish appearance comes from an even covering of short, branching hairs.

64. SOLANACEAE JUSS.
POTATO FAMILY, NIGHTSHADE FAMILY

Herbs, shrubs, or trees; stems with bicollateral vascular bundles. Leaves usually alternate or clustered, upper leaves may be opposite; blades entire to lobed or odd-pinnate. Flowers solitary or in clusters, perfect, regular or essentially so, 4–6-merous; calyx tubular, bellshaped, or flat-circular, usually 5-toothed; corolla tubular, bellshaped, or with most or part flat-circular, 5-lobed, the lobes usually folded fanlike in bud; stamens 5, attached alternate with corolla lobes; anthers opening by pores or slits; style 1; stigma usually 2-lobed; ovary superior, usually 2-celled. Fruit a berry (sometimes enclosed in inflated calyx) or capsule.

A family of about 85 genera and more than 2800 species of widespread distribution but primarily in tropical regions of the Western Hemisphere. Some members of the Solanaceae are well known because of their economic importance as food plants, e.g., *Lycopersicon* Mill. (tomato), *Solanum* L. spp. (Potato, Eggplant), *Capsicum* L. (Red Pepper), and *Physalis* L. sp. (Tomatillo or Strawberry Tomato). Some members of the family are famous drug plants, e.g., *Atropa* L. (Belladonna; atropine), *Hyoscyamus* L. (Henbane), and *Datura* L. (Stramonium); smoking tobacco comes from leaves of *Nicotiana tabacum* L. Species from many genera including *Petunia* Juss. are grown as ornamentals. Seventeen genera occur in Texas. Species of at least 11 genera are found in the Trans-Pecos. Three species of the infamous toxic plant *Datura* (Jimsonweed) occur in the Trans-Pecos. The large, rank, herbaceous plants may reach 1.5 m high.

KEY TO THE GENERA

1. Plants, shrubs or small trees to ca 4 m high; leaf blades leathery, glaucous, large, to 18 cm long; corolla long-tubular, yellow; along and near the Rio Grande   **1. Nicotiana.**
1. Plants, shrubs or subshrubs; leaf blades smaller; corolla flat and wheellike, bellshaped, or funnelform or tubular, purplish to whitish.
   2. Shrubs rank, branches tough, usually tapering into thorns; corolla bellshaped, tubular, or somewhat funnelform   **2. Lycium.**
   2. Shrubs or subshrubs with slender, brittle branches, thorns absent; corolla flat and wheellike or broadly bellshaped.
      3. Anthers bluish, opening longitudinally; corolla ca. 0.7 cm across; fruit hot to the taste   **3. Capsicum.**
      3. Anthers yellowish, opening terminally; corolla to 1.5 cm across; fruit not hot to taste   **4. Solanum.**

Fig. 310. *Nicotiana glauca* (Tree Tobacco)

1. NICOTIANA L. TOBACCO

Herbs annual or perennial, sometimes shrubs or small trees; usually with a strong smell and sticky. Leaves with or without petioles, the margins smooth, wavy, or the blades fiddleshaped. Flowers in clusters; calyx bellshaped to tubular, 5-toothed; corolla long-tubular to funnelform, perhaps expanded and 5-toothed at apex; stamens 5; stigma headlike. Fruit a capsule, oval to narrowly so, opening by 2–4 segments from apex; seeds many, very small.

A genus of about 60 species distributed in South America, the South Pacific, and Australia. Six species occur in Texas, perhaps three in the Trans-Pecos.

1. **Nicotiana glauca** Grah. TREE TOBACCO, TRONADORA. Fig. 310. In sand, silt, clay, or gravel, near streams or in disturbed areas such as roadsides. In the S Trans-Pecos, common along and near the Rio Grande, infrequent elsewhere, El Paso Co. to Val Verde Co. 1300–1400 ft.; flowering most months of the year. To extreme S TX; also W to CA, E to FL; Mex; W.I.; a native to Arg., S.A., naturalized in N.A.

This species, often a slender tree near the Rio Grande, is easily recognized by its rather large, glaucous leaves and clusters of long-tubular, yellow corollas. Tree Tobacco is reputed to have several medical uses when leaves or extractions are applied externally, but it is supposedly poisonous if taken internally.

2. LYCIUM L. WOLFBERRY

Shrubs, usually thorny. Leaves usually clustered, elongated, margins smooth. Flowers solitary or in small clusters, usually in axils on short or relatively long peduncles; calyx persistent with fruit, bellshaped, sometimes very small, 4–6-toothed; corolla bellshaped to tubular, 4–7-toothed; stamens 4–5; stigma headlike or 2-lobed. Fruit a berry, roundish or oval, fleshy or dry.

A genus of about 100 species centered in arid and semiarid regions of the New World. Chiang (1981) recognizes 21 species for North America. Six species occur in Texas, five of them in the Trans-Pecos. The species are browsed by livestock. The berries may be eaten raw or made into a sauce. The plants have been used for a multitude of medicinal purposes.

KEY TO THE SPECIES

1. Leaves densely covered with very short hairs.
  2. Leaves oblanceolate-obovate, 0.6–4 cm long, 0.2–1.1 cm wide, the short hairs with terminal glands; calyx 5–8 mm long, 5 teeth equal in length; corolla 0.7–1.3 cm long, greenish-white (tube perhaps pale lavender), lobes recurved; fruit hardened, 4–9 mm long, constricted below middle, glaucous, greenish to pale orange-yellow, 1–2 seeds per carpel
  1a. *L. puberulum* var. *puberulum.*
  2. Leaves linear-oblanceolate to narrowly spatulate, to 2 cm long, 0.2 cm wide, usually much smaller, without glands; calyx 1.5–3 mm long, somewhat 2-lipped; corolla 0.7–0.8 cm long, lavender fading to white, lobes spreading; fruit fleshy, 3–8 mm long, ovoid, not glaucous, red-orange; seeds 2–6–numerous
  2. *L. texanum.*
1. Leaves glabrous or finely pubescent.
  3. Leaves gray-glaucous; fruit hardened, (other characters of *L. puberulum* var. *puberulum* except leaves glabrous)
  1b. *L. puberulum* var. *berberioides.*
  3. Leaves green to green-glaucous; fruit juicy, seeds 1–2 seeds per carpel, few–numerous.
    4. Shrubs strongly armed with thorns; corolla usually more than 2 cm long; calyx teeth equal, more than 2 mm long, usually as long as tubular part of calyx
    3. *L. pallidum.*
    4. Shrubs with few thorns or unarmed; corolla less than 1.5 cm long; calyx teeth 2-lipped or irregularly cleft, usually less than 2 mm long, less than two-thirds as long as tubular part of calyx.
      5. Leaves pale green, somewhat succulent, usually spatulate, 1–3 cm long and 0.4–1 cm wide; corolla greenish-lavender or whitish, the teeth with a fringe of white hairs
      4. *L. torreyi.*
      5. Leaves dark green, thin, linear to nearly spatulate, 1–2.5 cm long and 0.1–0.6 cm wide; corolla white or pale lavender, the teeth not fringed
      5. *L. berlandieri.*

Fig. 311. *Lycium puberulum* var. *puberulum*
(Downy Wolfberry)

Fig. 312. *Lycium puberulum* var. *berberioides*
(Silvery Wolfberry)

1. **Lycium puberulum** Gray. DOWNY WOLFBERRY. Two varieties are recognized by Chiang (1981). **1a.** *Lycium puberulum* var. **puberulum.** (Fig. 311). Limestone or igneous soils, often among other shrubs in desert habitats. El Paso Co., near El Paso. Presidio Co., 10 mi S, 4 mi N Porvenir; S side Chinati Mts.; Pinto Canyon, Capote Falls area; 8 mi N Ruidosa; near Shafter; 0.4 mi E Lajitas. Hudspeth Co., 10 mi ESE McNary; 1 mi N Indian Hot Springs; Van Horn Mts.; 20 mi SE Sierra Blanca. 2300–3800 ft.; Mar–Apr. Chih., Coah., Dgo., Mex.

1b. Lycium puberulum var. **berberioides** (Correll) Chiang. Fig. 312. [*Lycium berberioides* Correll]. Scattered to locally common, gravel-clay hills and flats from near Aqua Fria and Santiago Peak S to Chisos Mts., endemic. Presidio Co., between Rincon Mt. and Fresno Creek, ca. 0.5 mi N of Smith house. Brewster Co., lower slopes of Chisos Mts., Chisos Pens, Chisos Mts.; locally common Study Butte to Panther Jnct.; 3–4 mi S Persimmon Gap; between Todd Hill and Burro Mesa; mouth of Juniper Canyon, Chisos Mts.; Sublett Ranch, Big Bend Park; lower slopes Crown Mt.; Christmas Mts.; Aqua Fria; S of Santiago Peak; 33 mi N Study Butte; N of Terlingua; Mar–Apr.

The var. *puberulum* has short-hairy leaves and calyces while the var. *berberioides* (Silvery Wolfberry) has glabrous (gray-glaucous) leaves and calyces (Chiang, 1981). The gray-glaucous foliage of var. *berberioides* (the foliage of

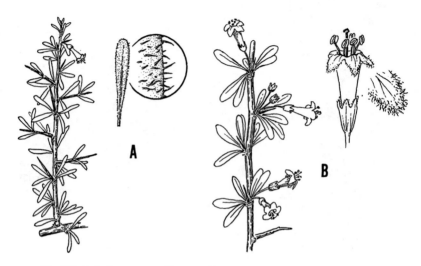

Fig. 313. A) *Lycium texanum* (Texas Wolfberry); B) *L. torreyi* (Torrey Wolfberry)

some plants is gray-green) gives the whole plant, excepting the chocolate stems, a gray aspect. Only *Lycium pallidum, L. torreyi*, and infrequently var. *puberulum* with gray-green foliage approach the color aspect of var. *berberioides*, and these taxa are not known to be sympatric in south Brewster County. *Lycium puberulum* is the only Trans-Pecos species with hardened fruit.

2. **Lycium texanum** Correll. TEXAS WOLFBERRY. Fig. 313. Rocky and sandy soils, shrubby desert plains and canyons. Hudspeth Co., Quitman Gap; base of Quitman Mts.; 10 mi E and 10 mi W Sierra Blanca. Culberson Co., 10 mi E Van Horn. Brewster Co., 39 mi S and 51 mi S Alpine. 3500–4600 ft.; Mar–Oct; endemic in the Trans-Pecos. This species is set apart from *Lycium puberulum* by its small, narrow leaves, non-glandular short-pubescence, floral differences, and fleshy red berry.

3. **Lycium pallidum** Miers. PALE WOLFBERRY. Fig. 314. Rocky slopes and canyons of hills and mountains, limestone and igneous habitats. El Paso Co., Franklin Mts.; 4 mi E Fabens. Hudspeth Co., 12 mi N Allamoore; N end Quitman Mts.; 4 mi E Ft. Hancock; 10 mi E Hueco Inn. Culberson Co., 7 mi NW Van Horn; Eagle Mts.; Beach Mts.; near Salt Flats. Presidio Co., upper Pinto Canyon and vicinity. Jeff Davis Co., Davis Mts. Brewster Co., 8 mi S Alpine. 4000–5200 ft.; Feb–May. N to S CO, W to S UT and AZ; also N Mex. The taxon in our area is *Lycium pallidum* var. **pallidum** with leaves glabrous

Fig. 314. *Lycium pallidum* (Pale Wolfberry)

Fig. 315. *Lycium berlandieri*
(Berlandier Wolfberry)

and glaucous (with a bloom), bark commonly reddish-purple (or chocolate), flowers 1.5–2.5 cm long, and juicy fruits with numerous seeds. Another variety, *L. pallidum* var. *oligospermum* Hitchc., occurs in the Mojave Desert. The berries of this rather common species are eaten by man as well as by wildlife species, especially birds. The armed hardy plants have long been grown as ornamentals, but on a limited scale. The Pale Wolfberry is recognizable by its pale, usually spatulate leaves, dark stems, and longest corolla of the Trans-Pecos species.

4. Lycium torreyi Gray. TORREY WOLFBERRY, AGRITO. Fig. 313. Flats, arroyos, canyons, along canals and near the Rio Grande, Pecos River, and other drainages, commonly in silty, sandy, or alluvial soils, often in alkali areas. Locally common throughout much of the southern Trans-Pecos. particularly along and near the Rio Grande, El Paso Co., E to Val Verde Co. 1600–4500 ft.; Apr–Oct. W through S NM to NV and CA; Mex. S to Hgo.

This species, recognizable by its grayish leaves (somewhat succulent) and stems, and densely hairy corolla lobes. The plants often form dense thickets, frequently in silt and saline habitats.

5. Lycium berlandieri Dun. BERLANDIER WOLFBERRY. Fig. 315. Rocky arid gravel hills, flats, arroyos, in various soil types including alkali and gypsum, locally common throughout much of the Trans-Pecos, El Paso Co., E to

Val Verde Co. 2100–4600 ft.; Feb–Oct. Also S to coastal and S TX; E NM; Mex., Tam. to Baja CA.

Four varieties of Berlandier Wolfberry are recognized by Chiang (1981), with two of these occurring in the Trans-Pecos. The var. **parviflorum** (Gray) Terracc. [var. *brevilobum* Hitchc.] is more common in the Trans-Pecos while var. **berlandieri** is more common in south Texas. The var. *parviflorum* is distributed from west Texas to NM, AZ, and to central N Mexico, and is distinguished from the var. *berlandieri* by its corolla lobes ca. ⅓ shorter. The var. *berlandieri* occurs in south and west Texas south to central Mexico, and is characterized by its corolla lobes short in relation to the length of the corolla tube, ⅙ to ¼ its length. Characteristically the nearly unarmed stems of *Lycium berlandieri* are less intricately branched and the plants less dense than any other *Lycium* of the Trans-Pecos.

3. CAPSICUM L. CAYENNE PEPPER

Shrub to 3 m high; branches slender, green, brittle, glabrous or essentially so. Leaf blades ovate to lanceolate, to 6 cm long, 3 cm wide. Flowers often in pairs; calyx small, toothed, cupshaped; corolla whitish, ca. 7 mm wide, covered with branched hairs; anthers bluish. Fruit oval or roundish, to ca. 1.5 cm long, red or yellowish, pungent.

A genus of about 50 species all native to the tropical and subtropical Americas.

1. Capsicum annuum L. var. **glabriusculum** (Dun.) Heiser & Pickersgill. CHILIPIQUIN, BIRD PEPPER, BUSH PEPPER. Fig. 316. [*Capsicum annuum* var. *minus* (Fing.) Shinners]. Planted in yards and gardens as an ornamental and as a perennial source of the very pungent berries that are used as a hot pepper flavoring in various dishes, and used medicinally as a powerful local stimulant. The plant evidently is not native in the arid Trans-Pecos, but does occur naturally on the Edwards Plateau and in S TX; W to AZ; E to S FL; throughout the tropical Americas; flowering any time of the year.

The most important active principle of *Capsicum* is an irritant substance called capsaicin. The extremely pungent berries of numerous varieties have many uses as medicines and flavoring agents (Vines, 1960). The berries are eaten by wild turkeys, throughout the year if plants are abundant. It is said by some that the berries serve to season the turkey meat, while others maintain that turkey meat is not edible after a diet of the pungent berries.

4. SOLANUM L. NIGHTSHADE

Trees, shrubs, or herbs. Leaves various, larger ones and smaller ones often together. Flowers usually on lateral stalks; calyx usually 5-toothed; corolla bell-

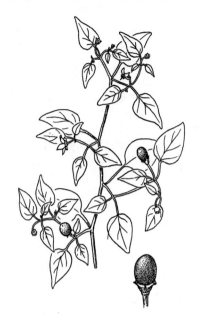

Fig. 316. *Capsicum annuum* var. *glabriusculum*
(Chilipiquin)

Fig. 317. *Solanum triquetrum*
(Texas Nightshade)

shaped or wheellike, 5-parted, plaited in bud; stamens extending from corolla but filaments short; anthers arranged around the style, opening by terminal pores. Fruit a berry, usually 2-celled.

A genus of perhaps 1800 species, morphologically diverse, mostly tropical in distribution. About 21 species occur in Texas, and 13 species are found in the Trans-Pecos.

1. **Solanum triquetrum** Cav. TEXAS NIGHTSHADE, HIERBA MORA. Fig. 317. Rocky slopes and canyons, usually limestone habitats. Presidio Co., Sierra Vieja, at Vieja Pass and ZH Canyon; N of the Solitario. Brewster Co., most of the mountains S of the Glass Mts. and Mt. Ord. Pecos Co., Glass Mts.; 40 mi SE Ft. Stockton. Terrell Co., vicinity of Sanderson and Dryden. Val Verde Co., Langtry; Comstock; Pecos River; Devils River. 1400–5800 ft.; flowering much of the year. Also cen. and S TX; N Mex.

65. SCROPHULARIACEAE JUSS. FIGWORT FAMILY

Mostly herbs, less often shrubs, rarely small trees. Leaves usually alternate or opposite, various in shape. Flowers arranged in clusters (racemes or panicles) perfect; calyx of 4–5 sepals, these separate or fused; corolla more or less irregular, 2-lipped to nearly regular, with a short or prominent tube, lobes 4–5, overlapping in bud; stamens commonly 4, sometimes 2 or 5, of unequal lengths, attached to corolla tube; style 1, stigma entire or 2-lobed. Fruit a 2-celled capsule; seeds usually many.

A family of about 190 genera and more than 4000 species of worldwide distribution. Some of the larger genera represented in the United States include *Penstemon* Schmid., *Pedicularis* L., *Castilleja* Mutis., *Mimulus* L., and *Veronica* L. Economically members of the family are valued mostly as garden ornamentals, including *Antirrhinum* L. (snapdragons). *Digitalis* L. (Foxglove) is well-known as a drug plant. In Texas 31 genera are represented. Members of at least 11 genera are found in the Trans-Pecos.

KEY TO THE GENERA

1. Plants strong shrubs 0.5–2.5 m high; leaves alternate, whitish-gray, covered with branched hairs; all 4 filaments with anthers   **1. Leucophyllum.**
1. Plants strongly woody mostly at the base, 15–100 cm high; leaves opposite, green, glabrous or with simple hairs; the posterior fifth filament lacking an anther   **2. Penstemon.**

1. LEUCOPHYLLUM BONPL. CENIZA

Shrubs, stems much-branched, blackish, brownish, or whitish pubescent with woolly branched hairs. Leaves alternate, mostly obovate to broadly spatulate, covered with whitish branched hairs. Flowers pinkish-purple to deep purple, rarely white, single or short stalks in leaf axils; calyx 5-toothed; corolla broadly funnelform, 5-lobed; stamens 4. Fruit a dehiscent capsule.

A genus of 13 species found in Texas, extreme southern New Mexico, and Mexico. All 13 species are distributed in Mexico while three of them extend into the Trans-Pecos (Flyr, 1970). There is considerable evidence that *Leucophyllum* belongs in the Myoporaceae Brown. Plants of this genus appear to flower only after significant rainfall, even those under cultivation. Most cenizas are extraordinarily attractive when in full bloom, and thus are desirable ornamentals. All three Texas species are found in the Trans-Pecos.

KEY TO THE SPECIES

1. Leaves gray-greenish, elliptic-obovate, to 2.5 cm long, midrib prominent; corolla purple to a pinkish-purple, the throat 1–1.5 cm long, somewhat expanded, lower lobes hairy inside   **1. L. frutescens.**
1. Leaves silver-gray, oval to spatulate, less than 2 cm long, midribs obscure; corolla violet, the throat less than 1 cm long, narrow, all lobes hairy inside.
   2. Leaves somewhat spatulate, the base tapering, usually 0.7–1 cm long, sometimes longer; corolla lavender-violet, lower lobes more hairy inside than upper lobes; terminal branchlets usually blackish   **2. L. minus.**

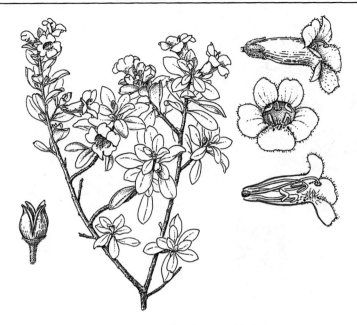

Fig. 318. *Leucophyllum frutescens* (Ceniza)

2. Leaves obovate to nearly round, 0.5–1.8 cm long; corolla deep violet, all lobes hairy inside; terminal branchlets usually gray-pubescent

3. *L. candidum.*

1. Leucophyllum frutescens (Berl.) I. M. Johnst. CENIZA, PURPLE SAGE, TEXAS SILVERLEAF. Fig. 318. [*Leucophyllum texanum* Benth.]. Mostly limestone habitats, frequently in brushlands. South-central part of Brewster Co., low areas vicinity of Chisos Mts. especially toward Boquillas, also N toward Marathon, and SE becoming more abundant through Terrell Co. and Val Verde Co. where most common. 1000–4500 ft.; flowering much of the year. S throughout the Rio Grande Plains; and into NE Mex.

This is the most commonly cultivated species of the genus. White-flowered forms occur infrequently throughout the range. Flyr (1970) recognized two varieties of *Leucophyllum frutescens*, the widespread var. **frutescens** of our area and Mexico, and the var. *johnstoniorum* Flyr of the Sierra Madre Oriental, Tamaulipas, Mexico. The Mexican common name Ceniza refers to the "ash-like" leaves as does the genus name.

2. Leucophyllum minus Gray. BIG BEND SILVERLEAF. Fig. 319. Limestone habitats, rocky flats, foothills, and mountains. Hudspeth Co., Sierra Diablo; Quitman Mts., E end. Culberson Co., Sierra Diablo; Apache Mts.; Salt Flat Station; 2 mi S Kent. Jeff Davis Co., W part of county. Presidio Co., Chinati

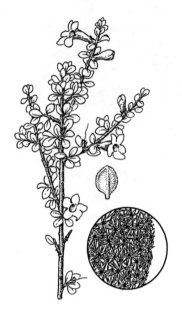

Fig. 319. *Leucophyllum minus*
(Big Bend Silverleaf)

Fig. 320. *Leucophyllum candidum*
(Boquillas Silverleaf)

Mts.; Pinto Canyon; 4 mi W Shafter. Brewster Co., throughout in limestone.
Pecos Co., between Balmorhea and Ft. Stockton; Univ. Mesa; 20–30 mi S Ft.
Stockton. 2000–6500 ft.; Jun–Nov. S NM; also NE Mex.

White-flowered forms of this species occur sporadically throughout most
of the range.

3. Leucophyllum candidum I. M Johnst. BOQUILLAS SILVERLEAF.
Fig. 320. [*Leucophyllum violaceum* Penn.]. Mostly limestone habitats, rocks
or gravel, frequently brushlands. Brewster Co., generally between the Chisos
Mts. and Boquillas Canyon, E to Black Gap refuge; road to Hot Springs, 2 mi
off Park road; Dead Man's Cut; flats near Lone Mt. to Nugent Mt.; Dead Horse
Mts., head of Boquillas Canyon; E slopes Stairstep Mt.; Heath Canyon. 2200–
4000 ft.; Sep–Oct. Extreme E Chih.; W Coah.; N Dgo., Mex.

When in full bloom with their deep violet flowers, these dense, gray shrubs
are the most attractive of all the Texas leucophyllums.

2. PENSTEMON SCHMID. BEARDTONGUE.

Shrubs or herbs. Leaves opposite, often the lower ones with petioles, upper
ones without. Flowers usually in terminal clusters, often with glandular hairs;
sepals 5; corolla bellshaped to tubular, 2-lipped, upper one 2-lobed, lower one

Fig. 321. *Penstemon ambiguus*
(Gilia Penstemon)

3-lobed, inner floor of throat often with colored ridges; fertile stamens 4, with one sterile stamen often bearded apically. Fruit a dehiscent capsule, 4-valved; seeds numerous, angular, with rough surfaces.

A genus of about 300 species distributed from Alaska to Guat. Twenty-three species occur in Texas, all but two of them herbaceous. About 11 species are represented in the Trans-Pecos.

KEY TO THE SPECIES

1. Leaves linear, the margins smooth; flowers glabrous, pinkish to whitish, the throat tubular; usually in sandy soils   **1. *P. ambiguus.***
1. Leaves obovate to oblanceolate, the margins toothed; flowers with glandular hairs, red, throat expanded, crevices of limestone bluffs and rocks
                                                                     2. *P. baccharifolius.*

1. Penstemon ambiguus Torr. GILIA PENSTEMON. Fig. 321. Mostly sandy soil, rarely alluvium, locally common throughout much of the Trans-Pecos. El Paso Co., 17 mi E El Paso; 5 mi W Hueco Mts. Hudspeth Co., 14 mi E Dell City; 4 mi E Hueco Inn. Culberson Co., 12 mi E Van Horn; 21 mi W Kent. Presidio Co., Pinto Canyon road S Marfa. 2600–5000 ft.; May–Aug. Ward, Crane, Winkler, Ector counties; Llano Estacado and Rolling Plains in TX Panhandle; N to KS and CO, W to UT and CA; Chih., Mex.

Fig. 322. *Penstemon baccharifolius*
(Baccharisleaf Penstemon)

2. Penstemon baccharifolius Hook. BACCHARISLEAF PENSTEMON. Fig. 322. Crevices of limestone bluffs, boulders, rocks. Presidio Co., Solitario, N rim; 2.8 mi from Sauceda, road to Solitario. Brewster Co., Doubtful Canyon; Dead Horse Mts., Big Brushy Canyon, upper Heath Canyon; Maravillas Creek. Pecos Co., 25–45 mi SE Ft. Stockton. Terrell Co., canyon of the Rio Grande; mouth of San Francisco Canyon; 2–10 mi N Sanderson; just S of Independence Creek. Val Verde Co., canyons of Pecos River, Devils River, and Rio Grande; Mile Canyon, Langtry. 1100–4400 ft.; Jun–Sep. Edwards Plateau; also adjacent Mex. S to S.L.P.

66. BIGNONIACEAE JUSS. CATALPA FAMILY

Trees, shrubs (in our species), or vines, rarely herbaceous. Leaves opposite, perhaps alternate above, simple to compound, blades or leaflets entire, toothed or lobed; stipules absent. Flowers in clusters or pairs, rather large and showy, perfect, irregular; calyx short, with 4–5 usually unequal teeth; corolla 5-lobed, 2-lipped to nearly regular; stamens usually 4, perhaps 2; pistil 1, ovary superior, style 1, stigma 2-lobed. Fruit a slender capsule, usually opening longitudinally; seeds numerous, flattened, winged, often with tufts of hair; endosperm lacking.

A family of about 100 genera and 800 species distributed primarily in tropical regions of both hemispheres where most species are woody vines. Lumber and fence posts are obtained respectively from *Tabebuia* Gomes *ex* DC. (Boxwood) and *Catalpa* Scop. (Catalpa). Numerous trees, vines, and shrubs are grown as ornamentals, *Catalpa* and *Chilopsis* D. Don being popular in the Trans-Pecos. Only six genera of the family occur in Texas.

KEY TO THE GENERA

1. Small trees to 10 m high or large shrubs; leaves simple, sessile or nearly so; flowers whitish or pinkish, or purplish, or striped, usually tinged with purple or purplish red   **1. *Chilopsis.***
1. Shrubs to 1 m or more high; leaves compound, with petioles; flowers yellow   **2. *Tecoma.***

1. CHILOPSIS D. DON   DESERTWILLOW, MIMBRE

Small trees to 10 m high or spreading shrubs; deciduous. Leaves opposite or alternate, blades glabrous, often sticky, linear to linear-lanceolate, to 30 cm long to 1 cm wide, margins smooth; sessile or very short-petioled. Flowers showy, fragrant in elongated terminal clusters to 30 cm long; calyx 2-lipped, hairy, 1–1.5 cm long; corolla broadly funnelform, 2–3.5 cm long, 2-lipped, whitish and usually purple-tinged, or purplish or pinkish with darker stripes; fertile stamens 4, sterile stamen 1. Fruit a capsule, slender, to 30 cm long, ca 6 mm wide, 2-valved; seeds numerous oval, flat, with wings and a fringe of white hair at each end.

A genus of one species widely distributed in arid North America.

1. **Chilopsis linearis** (Cav.) Sweet.   DESERTWILLOW.   Fig. 323.   [*Chilopsis saligna* D. Don; *C. glutinosa* Engelm.; *C. linearis* var. *glutinosa* (Engelm.) Fosb.]. Common along ephemeral streams, and other drainages. Throughout much of the Trans-Pecos. 2000–5000 ft.; Apr–Sep; also W-cen. TX; W to CA; N Mex.

Two subspecies of Desertwillow are recognized by Henrickson (1985), the subsp. **linearis** and subsp. **arcuata** (Fosb.) Henrickson (Western Desertwillow). The subsp. *linearis* with leaves straight and erect-ascending occurs from west-central New Mexico, across Trans-Pecos Texas where it is abundant, to the upper south Texas plains near the Rio Grande, and is widespread in northeastern Mexico from Chihuahua to Coahuila, Nuevo Leon, Zacatecas, and San Luis Potosi. The subsp. *arcuata* has leaves arching and drooping, and occurs mostly in the Sonoran and Mojave deserts, although it intergrades with subsp. *linearis* in southwestern New Mexico. Glandular and glutinous forms occur in both subspecies (the former var. *glutinosa*). Henrickson (1985) also recog-

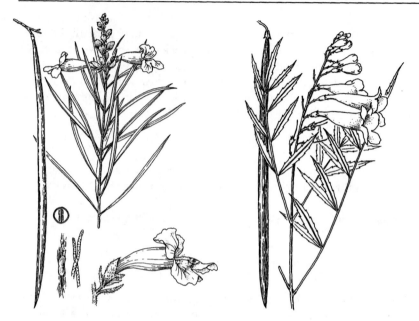

Fig. 323. *Chilopsis linearis* (Desertwillow)   Fig. 324. *Tecoma stans* (Trumpetflower)

nized two varieties of subsp. *linearis*, the typical and widespread var. **linearis** with young stems mostly sparsely pubescent to glabrous, and var. *tomenticaulis* Henrickson, rather restricted in Nuevo Leon and Tamaulipas, Mexico, with young stems canescent-tomentose. A white-flowered form occurs rarely and sporadically throughout the range. The wood of Desertwillow is used as posts and firewood.

2. TECOMA JUSS. TRUMPETFLOWER

Shrubs, ca. 1 m high; deciduous. Leaves opposite, odd-pinnate; leaflets 5–13, mostly glabrous, usually lanceolate or linear-lanceolate, to 10 cm long. Flowers showy, in elongated terminal clusters; calyx broadly tubular, 5-toothed; corolla yellow, broadly funnelform, 3.5–6 cm long, 5-lobed and somewhat 2-lipped; stamens 4. Fruit a capsule to 20 cm long, linear, roundish to slightly flattened, opening into valves; seeds nearly oval, flattened, with two thin wings. A genus of about 16 species distributed in the Western Hemisphere.

1. **Tecoma stans** (L.) Juss. *ex* Kunth. TRUMPETFLOWER, ESPERANZA. Fig. 324. [*Bignonia stans* L.; *Tecoma stans* var. *angustatum* Rehd.]. Rocky bluffs, slopes, and canyons, particularly in desertic mountains, throughout much of

the S Trans-Pecos, El Paso Co., E to Terrell Co. 2000–5200 ft.; Apr–Nov. Also in FL, NM, AZ; S through Mex., C.A., into S.A.; W.I.

In Texas, *Tecoma stans* is reported to occur near San Antonio, but otherwise the Texas populations are restricted to the Trans-Pecos. Reportedly Indians used the wood of Trumpetflower to make bows. Extracts from various parts of the plants including roots have been used medicinally in several ways, such as remedies for diabetes, stomach cramps, intestinal worms, and syphilis. The plants characteristically produce numerous bright yellow blooms and are desirable for ornamental use. The Trans-Pecos plants are considered to be cold hardy.

67. ACANTHACEAE JUSS. ACANTHUS FAMILY

Herbs or small shrubs; usually with cystoliths (mineral concretions), apparent as tiny lines on vegetative parts. Leaves usually opposite, simple, margins usually smooth. Flowers clustered or solitary, usually irregular, or nearly regular, perfect; calyx lobes usually 5(4); corolla tubular, 5-lobed, usually 2-lipped; stamens 4 (or 2), unequal, 2 stamens perhaps functionless; ovary superior, 2-celled, ovules 2–10 in each cell; style slender; stigmas 1–2. Fruit a capsule, often opening elastically with 2 valves recurving from a central column; seeds usually flat and attached by curved stalks, often sticky when wet.

A family of about 250 genera and 2500 species, with pantropical distribution. The Acanthaceae are of little economic importance, although species of several genera, including *Ruellia* L., are grown as ornamentals. Thirteen genera occur in Texas, at least nine in the Trans-Pecos. *Tetramerium nervosum* Nees is a relatively rare Texas species with woody basal parts and characteristic 4-angled flower spikes. It occurs on canyon walls.

KEY TO THE GENERA

1. Stems slender, crowded, broomlike; leaves slender, grasslike   1. *Justicia.*
1. Stems otherwise; leaves otherwise.
  2. Shrubs slender, 1–2.5 m high; flowers red, orange, salmon, pinkish to white; stamens 2   2. *Anisacanthus.*
  2. Shrubs or subshrubs, usually less than 0.5 m high, except *Carlowrightia linearifolia* to 1 m or more high; flowers usually purplish or lavender, rarely white to cream; stamens 2 or 4.
    3. Stamens 4; corolla lobes in bud rolled up longitudinally; corolla throat expanded to 1.5–2.5 cm wide   3. *Ruellia.*
    3. Stamens 2; corolla lobes in bud overlapping; corolla throat not much expanded   4. *Carlowrightia.*

Fig. 325. *Justicia warnockii* (Warnock Justicia)

1. JUSTICIA L.

Shrubs or herbs. Leaves opposite, margins smooth. Flowers purplish to white, solitary or in clusters; calyx parts 5 or 4, slender; corolla tube narrow, the throat 2-lipped, often with purple or white splotches inside, lower lip 3-lobed, upper lip 2-lobed; stamens 2; anther cells 2. Fruit a capsule, club-shaped; seeds 4.

A mostly tropical genus of about 300 species. Five species occur in Texas, two of these in the Trans-Pecos.

1. Justicia warnockii B. L. Turner. WARNOCK JUSTICIA. Fig. 325. Mostly limestone habitats, rocky slopes, mountains, and canyons, endemic to the Trans-Pecos, and adjacent Coah., Mex. Hudspeth Co., Quitman Mts. Presidio Co., Chinati Mts.; Fresno Creek, W of the Solitario. Brewster Co., many localities from Glass Mts. and N foothills S to Chisos Mts. and Dead Horse Mts., and SE along and near the Rio Grande. Terrell Co., Lower Canyons of Rio Grande; 7 mi E Sanderson. Pecos Co., Sierra Madera. 1800–4500 ft.; May–Oct.

This species is most easily recognized by its grasslike habit, leaves usually less than 1 mm wide, and lavender flowers with purple marks in two rows in the throats. Another species, *Justicia wrightii* Gray, mostly endemic on the western edge of the Edwards Plateau but extending into Val Verde and Pecos counties of the Trans-Pecos, is a low, much-branched perennial often with a woody base, and leaves usually 3 mm wide or more.

2. ANISACANTHUS NEES. ANISACANTH

Shrubs to 2.5 m high, branches slender; bark peeling. Leaves opposite broadly lanceolate to linear. Flowers red, orange, salmon, pinkish to white or yellowish, usually arranged in loose clusters; calyx of 5 nearly equal lobes; corolla tubular to funnelform, usually curved, slightly enlarged basally, 2-lipped, these usually long and recurved, lower lip usually entire, upper lip 3-lobed; stamens 2. Fruit a capsule, 1.5–2 cm long somewhat pearshaped, beaked, shiny, borne on a stalk; seeds 2–4, ca. 5 mm in diameter, discoid, somewhat tuberculate.

A genus of about 15 species of the southwestern United States and Mexico. Three species are reported to occur in Texas. *Anisacanthus quadrifidus* (Vahl) Nees var. *wrightii* (Torr.) Henrickson (Henrickson, 1986b), with broadly lanceolate lower leaves and red-orange flowers, occurs on the Edwards Plateau and in northern Mexico.

KEY TO THE SPECIES

1. Leaves linear, usually 2–4 cm long, 1.5–3 mm wide; corollas orange-red, red, to yellowish   **1. *A. linearis.***
1. Leaves broadly lanceolate to lance-ovate, 2.5–8 cm long, corollas pinkish to nearly white   **2. *A. puberulus.***

1. **Anisacanthus linearis** (Hagen) Henrickson & Lott. DWARF ANISACANTH. Fig. 326. [*Anisacanthus insignis* Gray var. *linearis* Hagen]. Along arroyos, dry stream beds, canyons, usually in dense brush. Hudspeth Co., Quitman Mts. Brewster Co., numerous localities in Big Bend Park and Chisos Mts., Paint Gap Hills, Oak and Willow creek canyons, 4 mi W of Government Springs, Basin, W of Lone Mt., Grapevine Hills; also near Marathon. 3000–5000 ft.; Jun–Nov. Also N Mex.

In Correll and Johnston (1970) the Trans-Pecos collections were referred to as *Anisacanthus insignis* var. *linearis* Hagen. Although localized in distribution, this is the most common anisacanth in the Trans-Pecos, easily recognized by its leaves and flower color. The flowers are produced mostly in summer and fall when plants are in leaf.

2. **Anisacanthus puberulus** (Torr.) Henrickson & Lott. PINKY ANISACANTH. Fig. 326. [*Drejera puberula* Torr.; *Anisacanthus insignis* Gray]. Canyons, arroyos, alluvial fans or flats, usually among other shrubs. Brewster Co., near Marathon; Chisos Mts., Oak Creek near Cattail Falls trailhead. Presidio Co., Chinati Mts., Menzies ranch, San Antonio Canyon, Tinaja Prieta Canyon,

Fig. 326. A) *Anisacanthus puberulus* (Pinky Anisacanth); B) *A. linearis* (Dwarf Anisacanth)

Fig. 327. *Ruellia parryi* (Parry Ruellia)

Pinto Canyon, 1 mi W of Ross Mine; near the Rio Grande, 10 mi below Redford. 2800–6300 ft.; Apr–Oct. Also adjacent Chih., and near Parras, Coah., Mex. This recently described species is easily distinguished by its broadly lanceolate leaves and pinkish flowers which are usually produced in the spring, before the leaves. The plants are scattered and not common, mostly in the Chinati Mts.

3. RUELLIA L.   RUELLIA

Shrubs or herbs. Leaves in *Ruellia parryi* obovate to lanceolate, 1–2 cm wide, hairy; petioles present. Flowers red, yellow, white or (*R. parryi*) purplish, rather showy, solitary or in clusters; calyx 5-lobed; corolla tubular or funnelform below usually expanded above, the 5 lobes usually spreading and wheellike; stamens 4, in 2 pairs. Fruit a capsule, clubshaped or oblong.

A genus of more than 200 species, mostly of tropical and subtropical regions. Many species are found in Mexico and Central America. Seventeen species are reported to occur in Texas. Only one species, the shrubby *Ruellia parryi*, is common in the Trans-Pecos, although perhaps one or two herbaceous species extend across the Pecos River in Val Verde and Terrell counties.

1. Ruellia parryi Gray.   PARRY RUELLIA.   Fig. 327.   Usually limestone habitats, also igneous, rocky slopes, hills, canyons, widespread in the Trans-

Pecos. Hudspeth Co., 1 mi N Indian Hot Springs. Culberson Co., 3–4 mi N Kent. Presidio Co., near Shafter; above Capote Falls; between Redford and Lajitas. Brewster Co., Glass Mts. and Doubtful Canyon near Mt. Ord, S through Big Bend Park and Black Gap Refuge. Pecos Co., Sierra Madera. Terrell Co., vicinity of Sanderson and Dryden. Val Verde Co., Pecos River Canyon; Mile Canyon; Pumpville turn-off. 1200–4700 ft.; Mar–Jul. Also SE NM; adjacent Mex.

Parry Ruellia is a low, spreading shrub less than 0.5 m high, with numerous spreading branches that are conspicuously whitish with age, and showy lavender flowers. In limestone areas especially the plants are often common and attractive elements of desert scrub, frequently occurring with *Agave* and *Larrea*.

4. CARLOWRIGHTIA GRAY

Shrubs, subshrubs, or herbs with slender branches; nearly glabrous or pubescent, with or without glandular hairs. Leaves usually smallish and narrow, margins smooth. Flowers blue to cream or white, often with a yellow eye, usually small, in loose elongate clusters; calyx 5-lobed; corolla with a slender tube, with 4 subequal lobes; stamens 2, anther cells equal, inserted equally. Fruit a capsule, stalked; seeds 4.

This is a genus of about 24 species, occurring mainly in Mexico and the southwestern United States. Eight species are reported for Texas, with seven of these occurring in the Trans-Pecos. Henrickson and Daniel (1979) described three new species for the Chihuahuan Desert Region, adding two members to the Trans-Pecos flora. All seven Trans-Pecos species are treated below even though some of them are low, herbaceous perennials with woody bases. The key to the species is modified after Daniel (1980).

KEY TO THE SPECIES

1. Leaves 4–35 times longer than wide; corollas blue, nearly regular, the lower-middle lobe not folded lengthwise; anthers yellow.
  2. Hairs on young stems short and straight, less than 0.2 mm long; corollas 9–11 mm long; capsules 10.5–12.2 mm long; seed margins smooth
    1. *C. linearifolia.*
  2. Hairs on young stems recurved, 0.2–0.6 mm long; corollas 6.5–9 mm long; capsules 7–9 mm long; seed margins toothed   2. *C. parvifolia.*
1. Leaves 0.8–8 times longer than wide; corollas blue or white, 2-lobed, the lower-middle lobe folded lengthwise; anthers maroon.
  3. Glandular hairs present on shoots; corollas 9–15 mm long.
    4. Corollas white; glandular hairs very small, to 0.1 mm long; non-glandular hairs evenly disposed along stems; leaves lanceolate to narrowly ovate   3. *C. arizonica.*

Fig. 328. *Carlowrightia linearifolia*
(Heath Carlowrightia)

4. Corollas blue; glandular hairs larger, 0.1–0.7 mm long; non-glandular hairs disposed in 2 narrow lines along stems; leaves ovate to round   **5. C. serpyllifolia.**
3. Glandular hairs absent (or with glandular flower stalks in *Carlowrightia torreyana* only); corollas 6–9 mm long.
    5. Corollas blue; leaves elliptical-lanceolate to obovate, to 9 mm wide; stem hairs 0.1–0.2 mm long   **4. C. mexicana.**
    5. Corollas white; leaves ovate to round, to 3 mm wide; stem hairs 0.2–1.5 mm long.
        6. Stem hairs recurved; inner bractlets ovate to lanceolate; corolla white with distinct maroon veins on each petal lobe; seed margins smooth   **6. C. texana.**
        6. Stem hairs straight; inner bractlets awlshaped; corolla white with a yellow eye fringed with maroon on upper lip; seed margins minutely toothed   **7. C. torreyana.**

1. **Carlowrightia linearifolia** (Torr.) Gray. HEATH CARLOWRIGHTIA. Fig. 328. Mostly sandy-gravel, alluvial soils, often among rocks, slopes, mountains, and canyons, one of the most widespread carlowrightias in the Trans-Pecos. El Paso Co., Franklin Mts. Hudspeth Co., N slopes, Quitman Mts.

Fig. 329. *Carlowrightia arizonica* (Arizona Carlowrightia)

Culberson Co., E slopes, Van Horn Mts.; Van Horn Wells. Jeff Davis Co., 5 mi W Bloys Encampment. Presidio Co., Sierra Vieja, Musgrave Canyon; Vieja Pass; above Capote Falls; 25 mi S Marfa; Ross Mine, S Chinati Mts. Brewster Co., widespread, from N of Alpine at Leoncita Springs (Kokernot Ranch), S to the Rio Grande, including the Chisos Mts. and Reagan Canyon. 1900–5000 ft.; May–Oct. W to AZ; also N Mex.

2. **Carlowrightia parvifolia** Brandeg.   Limestone slopes and ridges, localized, reported in the Trans-Pecos from two localities, Brewster Co., E slopes of Sierra Madera, 22 mi S of Fort Stockton, 4500 ft.; Blue Creek Canyon, BBNP. Localized but common subshrub in W and Cen. Coah., Mex.

3. **Carlowrightia arizonica** Gray.   ARIZONA CARLOWRIGHTIA.   Fig. 329. Rocky habitats, mostly in S Brewster Co. Chisos Mts., Blue Creek; head of Boquillas Canyon; Hot Springs; 5 mi W Study Butte; W of Wildhorse Mt. Presidio Co., 10 mi below Redford. 1800–5800 ft.; Mar–Sep. W to AZ; also N Mex.

This uncommon species has been confused with the newly described and more common *Carlowrightia mexicana* from which it is distinguished by its white corollas, 1.2–1.7 mm long, with a yellow eye on the upper lobe, seed margins minutely toothed, and other characters (Henrickson and Daniel, 1979; Daniel, 1980). The plant is often browsed by deer.

Fig. 330. *Carlowrightia mexicana*
(Mexican Carlowrightia)

Fig. 331. *Carlowrightia serpyllifolia*

4. Carlowrightia mexicana Henrickson & Daniel. MEXICAN CARLO-
WRIGHTIA. Fig. 330. Mostly limestone canyons, rocky slopes, flats, and
gravel. Presidio Co., N. Chinati Mts., Wildhorse Canyon; 4 mi W Shafter.
Brewster Co., 17 mi E Marathon; Glass Mts., Old Blue; Sibley Ranch. Pecos
Co., 25 mi SW Ft. Stockton. 3500–4700 ft.; Apr–Oct. S to cen. Coah., Mex.
The blue corollas of *C. mexicana* are 0.6–1.1 cm long and its seeds have
smooth margins.

5. Carlowrightia serpyllifolia Gray. Fig. 331. Rocky habitats, bluffs,
canyon walls, boulders, slopes. Brewster Co., Chisos Mts., Ward Spring, base
of Bailey Peak, Pinnacle Mts., Oak Creek Canyon; Aqua Fria; W rim of Maravillas Canyon. Presidio Co., S Chinati Mts., Ross Mine; 2 mi above Shafter;
4 mi W Shafter; Solitario, W of Fresno Peak. 3500–5200 ft.; Jul–Sep. Also
adjacent Mex.
Many specimens of this species have slender, woody basal stems, while others are nearly herbaceous. The flowers of this plant are purplish.

6. Carlowrightia texana Henrickson & Daniel. TEXAS CARLOWRIGHTIA.
Fig. 332. Rocky or gravel slopes, flats, and arroyos, often disturbed habitats.
Culberson Co., Gypsum hills, Pecos-Carlsbad Hwy., 10 mi N of Mentone road.
Jeff Davis Co., 13 mi N Alpine. Presidio Co., Chinati Mts., mid-Pinto Canyon.
Brewster Co., Alpine, golf course; SR Hill; 10 mi NE Alpine; Glass Mts., Iron

Fig. 332. A) *Carlowrightia texana* (Texas Carlowrightia); B) *C. torreyana* (Torrey Carlowrightia)

Mt.; Horse Mt., 20 mi SE Marathon; Nine-Point Mesa; Black Gap, Dell Tank. Pecos Co., 3 mi N of Ft. Stockton; 30 mi E Ft. Stockton; 4 mi W Longfellow. Terrell Co., 3 mi E Sanderson; 14 mi W Sanderson; ca. 30 mi N Sanderson. Val Verde Co., 5 mi E Pandale; near Devils River; between Del Rio and Loma Alta; 6 mi N Juno; 5 mi E Pandale. 1100–4700 ft.; Apr–Nov. Edwards Plateau to Rio Grande Plains; SE NM; Coah., Chih., N.L., S.L.P., Mex.

This is the most widespread and common carlowrightia of the Trans-Pecos. The rather low, compact, suffrutescent plants are distinguished from the related species, *Carlowrightia torreyana*, by the key characters listed above.

7. Carlowrightia torreyana Wasshausen.   TORREY CARLOWRIGHTIA.   Fig. 332.   Mostly rocky limestone habitats. Val Verde Co., near mouth of Pecos

River; just below Seminole Canyon; hills near Devils River. 1200–1700 ft.; May–Sep. Edwards Plateau, to South Plains; Coah., N.L., Mex.

68. RUBIACEAE JUSS. MADDER FAMILY

Trees, shrubs, or herbs, rarely vines. Leaves opposite or whorled, simple, margins usually smooth; stipules present, often fused to form a sheath, rarely leaflike. Flowers in loose or headlike clusters or solitary, perfect or unisexual, regular, calyx tubular with 4–8 parts, often fused with ovary and persistent; corolla tubular, slender, 3–5 lobed, often expanded at apex; stamens 3–5, attached to corolla tube; ovary 1 to several-celled, inferior or mostly so, crowned by a disc sometimes poorly formed; style slender, often forked. Fruit a capsule, berry, drupe, or splitting into two 1-seeded parts.

A family of about 450 genera and 6500 species of world-wide distribution but most common in tropical and subtropical regions. The Rubiaceae are of economic importance perhaps most notably for coffee (*Coffea* L.). The famous antimalarial drug quinine (from *Cinchona* L.) and the medicinal alkaloid ipecac (from *Cephaelis* Sw.) are products of the family. Several members are grown as ornamentals. Members of 15 genera are found in Texas, and about five of these occur in the Trans-Pecos.

KEY TO THE GENERA

1. Flowers red, corolla (tubular) to ca. 3 cm long   **1. *Bouvardia.***
1. Flowers white (corolla basically tubular), less than 1 cm long.
  2. Shrubs or small trees to 10 m high, usually much less, rarely more; flowers arranged in dense, round heads, these 2.5 cm or more in diameter   **2. *Cephalanthus.***
  2. Shrub usually much less than 0.5 m high; flowers in small terminal clusters   **3. *Hedyotis.***

1. BOUVARDIA SALISB.

Shrub, to ca. 1 m high; much-branched. Leaves usually 3–4 in a whorl, lanceolate to ovate; petioles short or absent. Flowers bright red, arranged in terminal clusters; calyx 4-lobed; corolla 1.5–3.3 cm long, with a whitish ring of hairs at the base, otherwise with short scattered hairs, lobes 4, 2–3 mm long. Fruit a capsule, of twin round parts, 5–8 mm wide; seeds many, flattened, winged, brown, ca. 3 mm wide.

A genus of about 50 species mostly distributed from Mexico to South America. One species occurs in Texas.

Fig. 333. *Bouvardia ternifolia*
(Scarlet Bouvardia)

1. Bouvardia ternifolia (Cav.) Schlecht.   SCARLET BOUVARDIA, TROMPE-
TILLA.   Fig. 333.   [*Bouvardia glaberrima* Engelm.]. Rocky habitats, usually in
mountains and canyons. Hudspeth Co., W slopes, Eagle Mts. Jeff Davis Co.,
throughout the Davis Mts. and outliers. Brewster Co., throughout, S to the
Chisos Mts. Presidio Co., Sierra Vieja; Chinati Mts. 3500–7300 ft.; May–Nov.
W to AZ; also throughout much of Mex.

Plants of this common species are easily recognized by the clusters of bright
red, tubular flowers, and leaves usually three at each node. Root extracts have
several medicinal uses in Mexico, including treatments for bleeding, dysentery,
and heat prostration. Scarlet Bouvardia is often grown as an ornamental.

2. CEPHALANTHUS L.   BUTTONBUSH

Shrubs or trees. Leaves opposite or whorled (3), in our species ovate or
lanceolate, to 20 cm long, 8.5 cm wide; petioles to 3 cm long. Flowers white,
arranged in dense round clusters (heads), 1.5 cm or more wide; calyx 4–5
toothed; corolla tubular-funnelform, 5–9 mm long, 4–5-toothed; stamens 4;
ovary 2-celled; style slender, extending prominently; stigma roundish. Fruit a
capsule, 4–8 mm long, splitting basally to form 2–4 segments; seeds 1 in each
segment, with a white aril.

A genus of 18 species distributed in Asia and America. Some taxonomists

Fig. 334. *Cephalanthus occidentalis*
(Common Buttonbush)

place *Cephalanthus* in the segregate family Naucleaceae (DC.) Wernh. Two species occur in Texas.

1. **Cephalanthus occidentalis** L. COMMON BUTTONBUSH, HONEYBALLS, GLOBEFLOWERS. Fig. 334. Almost permanently wet habitats, particularly streams, springs, and seeps. Presidio Co., Chinati Mts., Tinaja Prieta Canyon, and elsewhere; Cibolo Creek, 2 mi above Shafter; Fresno Creek, Charro Canyon. Jeff Davis Co., Musquiz Canyon between Ft. Davis and Alpine; Limpia Canyon, above Ft. Davis. Brewster Co., Leoncita Springs, Kokernot Ranch; Pena Colorado, 5 mi SW Marathon; Gano Spring, W of Chisos Mts.; Rio Grande near Mariscal Canyon. Val Verde Co., Pecos and Devils rivers. 1200–5000 ft.; Jun–Sep. Swamps, ponds, and other water sources throughout TX; N to Can. and NY, W to CA, E to FL; also Mex.

This hydrophilic species forms fairly large, spreading shrubs or small trees, and is perhaps most easily recognized by its white flowerballs (with exserted styles) produced at stem apexes all over the bush. Bark of the Common Buttonbush contains "cephalanthin," a toxic substance that causes convulsions, vomiting, and paralysis. Extracts of the bark are used medicinally to treat venereal diseases, skin ailments, bronchial disorders, as a laxative, and to help fevers. The plants are often cultivated, being easily propagated by cuttings in moist sand. Numerous birds eat the seeds, and bees gather the pollen.

Two varieties are recognized for the species (Correll and Johnston, 1970); var. **californicus** Benth. with more lanceolate leaves, arranged in threes, and with short petioles; and var. **pubescens** Raf. with hairy twigs and hairy lower leaf surfaces.

3. HEDYOTIS L. BLUETS

Herbs or low shrubs. Leaves opposite, often 3–4 whorled, usually linear. Flowers white in our species, purplish or pink in others, small, with styles of different lengths or similar lengths, calyx 4-lobed; corolla tubular with 4 lobes recurved; style slender; stigmas 2. Fruit a capsule of twin parts, or topshaped, opening at top, 2.5 mm wide in our species. [*Houstonia* L.; *Oldenlandia* L.].

A genus of about 300 species mostly in the Old World tropics. Relatively few species occur in temperate regions of Asia and the Western Hemisphere. At least 19 species occur in Texas, eight of these in the Trans-Pecos. The dwarf, prostrate shrublet, *Hedyotis mullerae* Fosb., of Coahuila, Mexico, recently has been located in the Dead Horse Mountains of southern Brewster County (Johnston, 1990).

1. Hedyotis intricata Fosb. FASCICLED BLUET. Fig. 335. [*Houstonia fasciculata* Gray]. Rocky slopes, canyons, ledges, limestone and igneous habitats, usually at higher altitudes. Presidio Co., Sierra Vieja, 5 mi above Hot Springs; Burnt Camp Canyon, Solitario; Chinati Mts. Brewster Co., rather common in the Chisos Mts., Basin to the higher peaks; Dead Horse Mts., above Roy's Peak. 3500–6800 ft.; Jun–Nov. S NM; also N Mex.

The plants are smallish shrubs to 0.5 m or more high, with crowded, fascicled (whorled) leaves, these linear, to 1 cm long and 1 mm or less wide, and smallish, white, 4-lobed flowers.

69. CAPRIFOLIACEAE JUSS. HONEYSUCKLE FAMILY

Shrubs or vines, rarely herbs. Leaves opposite, sometimes the bases fused around the stem (connate-perfoliate), usually simple, compound in *Sambucus*; usually without stipules (except in *Sambucus*), stipules reduced to nectar glands in *Viburnum*. Flowers usually clustered in showy arrangements, perfect, regular or irregular; calyx tubular, fused to ovary; corolla tubular or funnelform usually 5-lobed, often expanded at apex; ovary inferior, 2–5 celled; stamens usually 5 and opposite corolla lobes, attached to tube; stigmas usually as many as ovary cells, perhaps fused. Fruit a berry, drupe, or capsule; seeds 1 to several.

Fig. 335. *Hedyotis intricata* (Fascicled Bluet)

A family of 15 genera and about 400 species distributed widely in temperate regions of the Northern Hemisphere. Many members of the family are of some ornamental value, including *Lonicera* L. (honeysuckles), *Sambucus* L. (Elderberry), *Symphoricarpos* Duham. (Snowberry), and *Viburnum* L. Elderberry wine is made from the fruit of *Sambucus canadensis* L. Only five genera are represented in Texas.

KEY TO THE GENERA

1. Flowers with elongate, more or less tubular corollas; flowers arranged in lateral axils, or terminal, not in large showy clusters; stigma 1; bark peeling.
   2. Viny shrubs, the stems often trailing, sometimes twining; mature fruit a red or blue-green berry with many seeds   **1. Lonicera.**
   2. Sprawling shrubs; stems sometimes trailing, mature fruit a white berrylike drupe with only 2 stones   **2. Symphoricarpos.**
1. Flowers with wheellike or at least broadly and open bellshaped corollas; flowers arranged in showy, flattopped, terminal clusters; stigmas 1–5; bark not peeling.
   3. Leaves pinnately compound; fruit a berry with 3 seeds   **3. Sambucus.**
   3. Leaves simple; fruit a drupe with 1 seed   **4. Viburnum.**

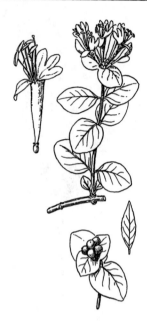

Fig. 336. *Lonicera albiflora*
(White Honeysuckle)

1. LONICERA L. HONEYSUCKLE

Shrubs; stems usually viny, clambering, trailing or twining on other plants (in our species), or erect; bark peeling. Leaves opposite, the margins usually smooth. Flowers reddish or whitish, in small, showy clusters; fragrant; calyx tube roundish or oval, the teeth small; corolla slender-tubular to funnelform, sometimes broadly so, often swollen basally, lobes 5, irregular or nearly regular; ovary 2–3 celled. Fruit a berry; seeds several.

A genus of about 200 species, in North America south to Mexico, and in eastern Asia. Four species occur in Texas, two of these in the Trans-Pecos.

1. Lonicera albiflora T. & G.   WHITE HONEYSUCKLE.   Fig. 336.   Rocky, usually shaded and protected slopes and canyons. Culberson Co., Guadalupe Mts., South McKittrick Canyon, Smith Canyon, Pine Spring Canyon; Sierra Diablo, Victorio Canyon; Apache Mts., Panther Canyon. Jeff Davis Co., Davis Mts., Mt. Livermore, Goat Canyon, Limpia Canyon, Timber Mt., Musquiz Canyon. Brewster Co., Chisos Mts.; Del Norte Mts., Doubtful Canyon; Glass Mts.; Cathedral Mt.; Cienega Mts.; Paisano Mt.; Ranger Canyon. Presidio Co., Chinati Mts., Tigner Canyon; Sierra Vieja, 2–3 mi NW Bunton ranch house. Pecos Co., 30 mi E Ft. Stockton; Sierra Madera; Glass Mts. 3400–6500 ft.; May–Nov. Also N to OK; W to AZ; N Mex.

Two varieties of White Honeysuckle are recognized for the Trans-Pecos: The most common taxon is *Lonicera albiflora* var. *albiflora*, with the distribution noted above; and the rare *L. albiflora* var. **dumosa** Gray, which occurs in pine forests of the Guadalupe Mountains (South McKittrick Canyon, Hunter's Lodge; top of the Guadalupes; 6500–8000 ft.; extending into New Mexico, Arizona, and Utah). The var. *albiflora* has corollas white or cream, 2 cm long or less, lower leaves essentially without petioles, and leaf blades glabrous or with soft hairs. The var. *dumosa* is characterized by its corollas reddish tinged outside, orange inside, 2.5 cm or more long, lower leaves with prominent petioles, and leaf blades with strong spreading hairs underneath. The fruit of *Lonicera albiflora* supposedly contains a substance used in medicine to induce vomiting or catharsis. The common honeysuckle of commerce and ornament is *L. japonica* Thunb., often a troublesome weed when escaping cultivation.

2. SYMPHORICARPOS DUHAM. SNOWBERRY

Shrubs; stems erect or sprawling; bark peeling. Leaves opposite, simple, the margins smooth or toothed. Flowers pink to reddish or white, solitary or in small clusters; corolla tubular to funnelform, sometimes broadly so, 4–5 lobes, regular, usually hairy inside, with 1–5 basal nectaries; ovary 4-celled. Fruit a berrylike drupe, white (in our species), oval to elliptic; stones usually 2, somewhat flattened, others abortive.

A genus of about 20 species, mostly in North America; one species in China. Six species are reported to occur in Texas, five of these in mountains of the Trans-Pecos. Snowberrys are considered good browse plants for livestock and deer, and good cover for wildlife. The berries and stones are eaten by many bird and mammal species, although the berries reportedly are toxic if ingested in quantity. The plants can be propagated by cuttings and from seed.

KEY TO THE SPECIES

1. Leaves usually narrow, oblanceolate to obovate, 0.6–1.5 cm long, 2–5 mm wide; corolla slender-tubular (salverform), 1.1–1.3 cm long

1. *S. longiflorus.*

1. Leaves broader, oval, ovate to broadly elliptic, usually 1.5–3 cm long, 0.8–1.8 cm wide; corolla funnelform to broadly so, 1.2–1.3 cm long.
    2. Corolla 2–3 mm long, nearly campanulate; plants glabrous; twigs reddish   **2. *S. guadalupensis.***
    2. Corolla 6–13 mm long, funnelform; plants with short hairs or glabrous; twigs various.
        3. Twigs glabrous; corolla slightly hairy to glabrous inside

3. *S. oreophilus.*

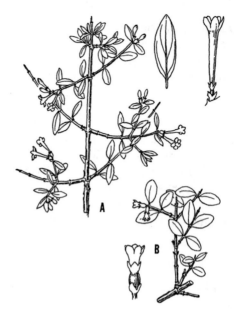

Fig. 337. A) *Symphoricarpos longiflorus*
(Longflower Snowberry); B) *S. guadalupensis*
(Correll Snowberry)

3. Twigs short-hairy; corolla densely hairy inside.
    4. Hairs of twigs dense, straight, spreading; anthers reaching to base of corolla lobes; leaf apexes obtuse-rounded   **4. S. rotundifolius.**
    4. Hairs of twigs short and curved; anthers reaching to middle of corolla lobes; leaf apexes usually with a tiny sharp point   **5. S. palmeri.**

1. Symphoricarpos longiflorus Gray. LONGFLOWER SNOWBERRY. Fig. 337. Higher slopes and canyons, often near streams. Culberson Co., Guadalupe Mts., North and South McKittrick canyons. Brewster Co., Glass Mts., Honeysuckle Canyon. 5000–6500 ft.; Jun–Aug. NW to CO and SE OR, W to SE CA.

This is perhaps the most distinct snowberry of the Trans-Pecos with its smaller leaves having the aspect of Littleleaf Sumac, and rather long, slender, tubular corollas. The leaves are glabrous and glaucous. The shrubs are usually to 1 m high and with spreading, somewhat declining branches to 2 m long.

2. Symphoricarpos guadalupensis Correll. CORRELL SNOWBERRY. Fig. 337. Pine woods. Culberson Co., Guadalupe Mts., head of South McKittrick Canyon, 8100 ft.; Aug–Sep; possible endemic.

This completely glabrous shrub is characterized by its short corollas, 2–4 mm long. I have seen one specimen from Coahuila, Mexico, Del Carmen

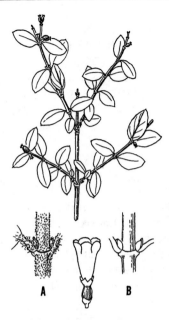

Fig. 338. A) *Symphoricarpos palmeri*
(Palmer Snowberry); B) *S. oreophilus*
(Mountain Snowberry)

Mountains, Picacho del Centinela, 6000 ft., that resembles the Correll Snowberry. The Correll Snowberry is poorly known and requires further study to determine its relationship to other snowberries. It is possibly close to *Symphoricarpos oreophilus*, or conspecific with the latter (also discussed by Burgess and Northington, 1981).

3. Symphoricarpos oreophilus Gray. MOUNTAIN SNOWBERRY. Fig. 338.
Mountains and high canyons. Culberson Co., Guadalupe Mts. Jeff Davis Co., Mt. Livermore. 7500 ft.; spring–summer. Also NM, AZ, NV, UT, CO; N Mex.
The taxonomic distinctions of *Symphoricarpos oreophilus*, *S. rotundifolius* (Dempster, 1992), and *S. palmeri* are not clear, at least as far as the Trans-Pecos populations are concerned. The three taxa appear to be closely related and may represent but one specific entity in the Trans-Pecos. Mountain Snowberry is reported to be an erect shrub to 1.5 m high with slender, spreading branches.

4. Symphoricarpos rotundifolius Gray. ROUNDLEAF SNOWBERRY.
Mountains and high canyons. El Paso Co., Franklin Mts.; Hueco Tanks. Culberson Co., Guadalupe Mts., upper South McKittrick Canyon. 6500–8100 ft.; spring–summer. W to AZ and CO.
The Roundleaf Snowberry is reported to be a low sprawling shrub with slender arching branches.

5. **Symphoricarpos palmeri** G. N. Jones. PALMER SNOWBERRY. Fig. 338. Limestone and igneous-rock habitats, mountains and canyons. Culberson Co., head of South McKittrick Canyon, top of Guadalupe Mts. Jeff Davis Co., Davis Mts., upper Madera Canyon of Mt. Livermore, N slopes of Black Mt. (Eppenauer Ranch), Wild Rose Pass of Limpia Canyon. Brewster Co., Mt. Ord, W slopes (igneous), NE slopes (limestone). Presidio Co., Chinati Mts., NW slopes, upper Indian Cave Canyon. 4600–8000 ft.; spring–summer. Also W to AZ and CO.

3. SAMBUCUS L. ELDERBERRY

Shrubs or small trees, rarely herbs; lenticels prominent in bark; bruised tissue malodorous. Leaves pinnate; leaflets 3–9 (in our species), toothed, apexes pointed. Flowers white to pale yellow, small, arranged in conspicuous, terminal flattopped clusters; calyx teeth minute; corolla wheellike, spreading lobes 5; stamens 5, attached to corolla base; stigmas 3. Fruit a berrylike drupe, edible, juicy, dark blue or blackish, covered with a whitish bloom when ripe; seedlike stones 3.

A genus of about 40 species distributed mostly in temperate and subtropical regions. Three species occur in Texas, two of these in the Trans-Pecos. *Sambucus canadensis* L. is the Common Elderberry of widespread distribution in eastern North America from which most elderberry jellies and wine are made. It is cultivated in Alpine and other areas of the Trans-Pecos. The fruit of most elderberries, including the Trans-Pecos species, is edible and can be used for wine, jelly, candy, and pies. In general elderberries are considered to be important food plants for many wildlife species. The bark, flowers, and fruit have a number of medicinal uses (Vines, 1960). The bark also has been used to make a dye. Dried leaves have been used to make an insecticide. The plants are easily propagated from seeds, cuttings, and root suckers.

KEY TO THE SPECIES

1. Leaflets ovate to ovate-lanceolate, 2.5–3.5 times as long as wide, abruptly acuminate, in our area usually pubescent beneath   **1. S. mexicana.**
1. Leaflets lanceolate, 3.5–5 times as long as wide, long acuminate, in our area glabrous or weakly scabrous along margins and at base   **2. S. cerulea.**

1. Sambucus mexicana Presl. *ex* DC. MEXICAN ELDER. Fig. 339. [*Sambucus cerulea* var. *mexicana* (Presl. *ex* DC.) L. Benson; *S. rehderana* Schwerin]. At lower elevations, usually on slopes, along streams, or in old fields. El Paso Co., below Ysleta. Presidio Co., Alamo, ca. 10 mi SW Casa Piedra; R. White ranch house, Chinati Mts. 1000–4000 ft.; summer. W to CA; N Mex.

Fig. 339. *Sambucus mexicana* (Mexican Elder)   Fig. 340. *Sambucus cerulea* (Blue Elderberry)

The usually treelike or shrubby Mexican Elder has flattopped flower clusters that are usually less than 15 cm wide. This species has numerous medicinal uses, especially in Mexico. Most parts of the plant reportedly are toxic, although ripe or cooked fruits in small amounts and possibly the flowers are harmless.

2. Sambucus cerulea Raf. BLUE ELDERBERRY. Fig. 340. [*Sambucus mexicana* Presl. *ex* DC. subsp. *cerulea* (Raf.) Murr.; *S. mexicana* var. *cerulea* (Raf.) Murr.]. At higher elevations, moist places, canyons, streams, talus slopes, base of cliffs. Brewster Co., Davis Mts., Madera Canyon, Mt. Livermore; Chisos Mts., N slopes Casa Grande. 5000–7000 ft.; Apr–Jun. N to Can., Alta. and B.C.; W to CA; N Mex.

The Blue Elderberry is usually a shrub with many erect stems to 7 m high; its flattopped flower clusters reach 30 cm in width. The Trans-Pecos entity is var. **cerulea.**

4. VIBURNUM L.   VIBURNUM, ARROWWOOD

Shrubs or small trees. Leaves simple; petioles often with stipulelike structures. Flowers usually white, rarely pink, in flattopped clusters of numerous flowers; calyx 5-toothed; corolla essentially wheellike, with 5 spreading lobes; stamens 5, extending from corolla; style none; stigmas 1–3, sessile on ovary. Fruit a drupe, 1-celled, pulpy, often edible; one flattened stone, 1 seed.

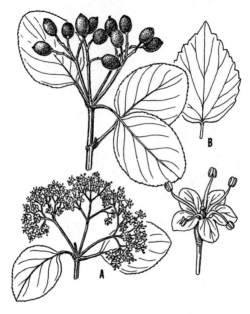

Fig. 341. A) *Viburnum rufidulum* (Southern Blackhaw);
B) *V. rafinesquianum* (Downy Arrowwood), leaf only.

A genus of about 200 species distributed in northern temperate regions. Seven species are reported for Texas.

KEY TO THE SPECIES

1. Leaf margins coarsely toothed, straggling shrubs to ca. 1.5 m high
　　　　　　　　　　　　　　　　1. *V. rafinesquianum* var. *affine.*
1. Leaf margins finely toothed; shrubs or small trees to 10 m high
　　　　　　　　　　　　　　　　　　　　　　2. *V. rufidulum.*

1. Viburnum rafinesquianum Schultes var. **affine** (Bush *ex* Schneid.) House. DOWNY ARROWWOOD. Fig. 341. [*Viburnum affine* Bush *ex* Schneid.; *V. pubescens* (Ait.) Pursh. var. *affine; V. australe* Morton; *V. affine* var. *australe* (Morton) McAtee]. Igneous soil, base of bluffs in mountains. Jeff Davis Co., N slopes of Timber Mt., above Madera Springs. 6000 ft.; Apr–May. Que. to Man., S to GA, KY, AR, and OK; also N.L. and Coah., Mex.

This is an exceedingly rare species with a glandular inflorescence evidently known in the Trans-Pecos only from the locality cited above.

2. Viburnum rufidulum Raf. SOUTHERN BLACKHAW, RUSTY BLACKHAW.
Fig. 341. [*Viburnum rufotomentosum* Small; *V. prunifolium* var. *ferrugineum*
T. & G.; *V. ferrugineum* Small] In the Trans-Pecos known only from one site,
and about 50 shrubs, in a header canyon, Dude Sproul Ranch, Davis Mts., Jeff
Davis Co., NE of McDonald Observatory (Warnock, 1977; color photograph),
Mar–Oct. Nearest populations ca. 250 mi, Edwards Plateau; a widespread
species of bottomlands, streams, and thickets, to E TX; E to FL, N to VA, IL,
OH, MO.

This shrub, to about 3 m (in our population) with checkered blackish bark,
has dense flattopped clusters of white flowers and small, edible blue-black fruit.

70. ASTERACEAE DUM. SUNFLOWER FAMILY

Herbs, subshrubs, shrubs, less often vines or trees; sap in some milky.
Leaves alternate or opposite, rarely whorled, various in shape; stipules absent.
Flowers small, called florets, tightly clustered in heads, surrounded by an involucre of bracts or phyllaries in 1 to several series; flowers borne on an enlarged often flattened area of the peduncle known as the receptacle, the receptacle various in shape; modified bracts (pales) often present on receptacle
subtending or enclosing florets; flowers uni- or bisexual, fertile, ovary inferior; calyx absent or appearing as a pappus of scales and/or awns or bristles
at top of achene near corolla base; corolla of 4–5 fused petals, rarely absent,
usually conforming to one of the following forms: 1) basal tube, somewhat
enlarged throat, topped by 4–5 teeth, these of *disk flowers*, usually bisexual;
2) basal tube and straplike ligule, often 3-toothed apically, these of *ray flowers*,
usually unisexual (pistillate), often occurring peripherally in same head with
disk flowers; 3) bisexual, essentially 2-lipped flowers exclusively of the Mutisieae; 4) usually bisexual, tube-ligule flowers (5-toothed ligules) exclusively of
the Lactuceae; anthers of stamens fused in a ring, and threadlike filaments
usually attached to corolla; pistil 1; ovary inferior, 1-celled; style slender, extending through the tube, often exserted at maturity, usually 2-branched, the
branches often flattened, hairy or glabrous, with stigmatic lines along upper
edges, some appendaged apically. Fruit an achene (or cypsela), cylindrical or
flattened, various in shape, pubescent or glabrous.

The Asteraceae (or Compositae Giseke, the conserved family name) is said
to be the largest family of vascular plants, with more than 1500 genera and
about 23,000 species of worldwide distribution. Only about two percent of
the species are trees and shrubs, but many could be called subshrubby. Modern taxonomic treatments (Bremer, 1994) of Asteraceae recognize three subfamilies and 17 tribes (listed in parentheses): Barnadesioideae (Barnadesieae);
Cichorioideae (Mutisieae, Cardueae, Lactuceae, Vernonieae, Liabeae, and Arc-

toteae); Asteroideae (Inuleae, Plucheeae, Gnaphalieae, Calenduleae, Astereae, Anthemideae, Senecioneae, Helenieae, Heliantheae, and Eupatorieae). The present tribal and subtribal treatment involving woody Asteraceae of the Trans-Pecos is in some respects unconventional by contemporary taxonomic group-ings (Bremer, 1994). It is maintained here only for convenience, and it follows in part the tribal arrangement in Correll and Johnston (1970) or to some extent the taxonomic format suggested by some earlier workers (Carlquist, 1976; Cronquist, 1977; Robinson, 1977; Heywood et al., 1977). Some members of the family are sources of food, e.g., lettuce (*Lactuca* L.), Jerusalem Artichoke (*Helianthus tuberosus* L.), Globe Artichoke (*Cynara* L.), Salsify (*Tragopogon* L.), and Chicory (*Cichorium* L.). Texas is a stronghold for the Compositae, it being the largest family in the state with about 160 genera. A majority of the genera are represented in the Trans-Pecos. Some Compositae species of the Trans-Pecos are strong shrubs 0.5–2.5 m high, while others might be considered weak shrubs or herbaceous. There are no tree-Compositae represented in the Trans-Pecos.

KEY TO THE TRIBES WITH WOODY SPECIES IN THE TRANS-PECOS

1. Corollas, some or all of them, 2-lipped, one lip with 2 teeth, other lip with 3 teeth   **8. *Mutisieae.***
1. Corollas otherwise.
  2. The shrubby species in our area with straight, slender stems, purplish disc corollas, and occurring along watercourses; anthers with slender taillike appendages extending down from the base, these hanging between the filaments; ray flowers absent   **3. *Inuleae.***
  2. Plants otherwise; anthers without taillike appendages; ray flowers present or absent.
    3. Style branches clubshaped or thickened toward the blunt or rounded end, nearly glabrous or minutely and evenly hairy; leaves mostly op-posite, sometimes whorled or alternate; corollas bluish or white, per-haps appearing greenish-yellow, never truly yellow; ray flowers absent
      1. *Eupatorieae.*
    3. Style branches otherwise; leaves mostly alternate, or opposite; corollas often yellow; ray flowers present or absent.
      4. Style branches of disk flowers flattened, marginal stigmatic lines, evi-dent, with a slender or triangular hairy appendage at the tips.
        5. Involucral bracts herbaceous; pappus of bristles or scales; plants not generally aromatic   **2. *Astereae.***
        5. Involucral bracts rather thin, dry and papery; pappus absent; plants with characteristic aromatic smell   **6. *Anthemideae.***
      4. Style branches of disk flowers otherwise, without apical appendages or with only very short appendages.

6. Leaves and usually phyllaries with conspicuous, transparent glands filled with strongly aromatic essential oils   **5. Tageteae.**
6. Leaves and phyllaries without the characteristic glands.
   7. Involucral bracts usually in 2 or more series (rarely 1); pappus of rather stout bristles, or scales, or both (or absent); receptacle chaffy, naked in some; at least lower leaves often opposite   **4. Heliantheae.**
   7. Involucral bracts of equal length in one series; pappus of fine, soft, slender bristles; receptacle naked; leaves alternate
                                                                         7. Senecioneae.

TRIBE 1. EUPATORIEAE CASS.   EUPATORY TRIBE

Shrubs, subshrubs, or herbs. Leaves opposite or alternate. Phyllaries of involucre usually 2 series or more, of nearly equal length or of graduated lengths, often ribbed; receptacle without scales (chaff). Ray flowers absent; disk flowers whitish or greenish, rarely rose; corollas regular; often tubular; pappus of bristles or scales; style branches clubshaped.

A tribe of more than 2000 species and more than 150 genera primarily of the New World (Robinson and King, 1977). About 15 genera and 70 species occur in Texas, most of these in the Trans-Pecos. King and Robinson (1987) have completed a sweeping taxonomic reorganization of the Eupatorieae in which many new genera were recognized. The treatment of Eupatorieae in Correll and Johnston (1970) is classical. The current work incorporates some of the modern views of Robinson and King.

KEY TO THE GENERA

1. Leaves linear or nearly so, 1–3 cm long, resin-dotted; involucre cylindrical, 1.3–2 cm long, phyllaries resin-dotted; pappus persistent, of 10 pointed scales ca. 1.5 cm long, extending from the involucre   **1. Carphochaete.**
1. Leaves, involucre, and pappus otherwise.
   2. Achenes 10-ribbed   **2. Brickellia.**
   2. Achenes 5-ribbed.
      3. Leaves broadly lanceolate, 2.5–9 cm long; heads usually with 3–5 whitish or pinkish-white flowers   **3. Koanophyllon.**
      3. Leaves ovate-deltoid, 1–2 cm long; heads usually with 10–12 whitish flowers   **4. Ageratina.**

1. CARPHOCHAETE GRAY   BRISTLEHEAD

Subshrubs to 0.5 m high, usually shorter. Leaves opposite (or fascicled), linear to linear-oblanceolate, to 3 cm long, resin-dotted, margins smooth.

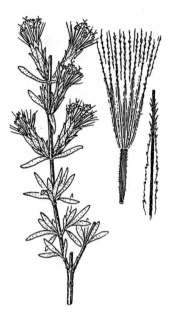

Fig. 342. *Carphochaete bigelovii*
(Bigelow Bristlehead)

Heads solitary, terminal; involucre cylindrical, to 2 cm long; phyllaries linear, resin-dotted, prominently graduate; receptacle flat, naked. Ray flowers absent; disc flowers 4–6, whitish to purple-tinged, 5-lobed, exserted. Achenes ca. 1 cm long, 10-ribbed, with minute hairs; pappus persistent, of ca. 10 pointed scales, these ca. 1.5 cm long and exserted prominently above involucre. Base chromosome number, $x = 11$.

A genus of about three species in the southwestern United States and Mexico. The genus name was inspired by the bristly pappus.

1. Carphochaete bigelovii Gray. BIGELOW BRISTLEHEAD. Fig. 342. Mountain slopes and canyons, grasslands or in shade of trees. El Paso Co., Franklin Mts. Jeff Davis Co., Davis Mts., Mt. Livermore; Davis Mt. State Park; Musquiz Canyon. Presidio Co., Chinati Mts., Chinati Peak, Horse Creek Canyon. Brewster Co., Sunny Glenn near Alpine; Cathedral Mt.; Chisos Mts., Pine Canyon, Green Gulch, near Boot Springs; also reported from limestone hills at Dead Man's Cut (2200 ft.) in Big Bend Park. 4000–6500 ft.; Mar–Jun. Also NM, AZ; Chih., Mex.

This species is easily recognized by its long, cylindrical involucre, long-exserted corollas, and prominently exserted pappus. Bristlehead is browsed by Mule Deer.

2. BRICKELLIA ELL. BRICKELLIA

Shrubs, subshrubs, or perennial herbs (two species annual). Leaves opposite or alternate. Heads solitary or in loose clusters. Ray flowers absent; disc flowers white, greenish, or pinkish; involucre of many phyllaries, these strongly graduated, ribbed on the back; corollas tubular, 5-lobed; style base expanded and hairy. Achenes 10-ribbed, cylindrical, with minute hairs; pappus of bristles, these flattened on the back usually short-plumose or scabrous on lateral margins. Base chromosome number, $x = 9$.

A genus of ca. 100 species, mostly in the western United States and Mexico. About 13 species are found in Texas, and all but one or two of these occur in the Trans-Pecos. Most species of *Brickellia* are either true shrubs or herbaceous perennials with woody bases. Only the most shrubby species are included below. *Brickelliastrum fendleri* (Gray) King and Robins., classically known as *Brickellia fendleri* Gray or *Eupatorium fendleri* (Gray) Gray, is reported in some descriptions to be a small shrub, but in the Trans-Pecos I have found it to be a strong herbaceous perennial.

KEY TO THE SPECIES

1. Petioles exceeding one-fifth as long as the leaf blades.
  2. Leaf blades usually less than 1.5 cm long; heads on very short stalks
                                                            1. *B. veronicaefolia.*
  2. Leaf blades more than 1.5 cm long, or if shorter then heads on stalks 1 cm long.
    3. Branches opposite, outer bark not peeling   2. *B. coulteri.*
    3. Branches alternate; outer bark peeling.
      4. Leaf blades rather thick, leathery, and resin-coated, rather diamond-shaped in outline; leaf bases wedgeshaped   3. *B. baccharidea.*
      4. Leaf blades rather thin, triangular to broadly ovate in outline; leaf bases straight or notched   4. *B. californica.*
1. Petioles less than one-fifth as long as the leaf blades.
    5. Leaf blades irregularly and usually deeply toothed; stems densely leafy   5. *B. laciniata.*
    5. Leaf blades short-toothed or entire.
      6. Leaf blades oblong-lanceolate, usually more than 1.5 cm long, the margins somewhat revolute   6. *V. venosa.*
      6. Leaf blades ovate, usually less than 1.5 cm long, the margins toothed   7. *B. parvula.*

1. **Brickellia veronicaefolia** (Kunth) Gray var. **petrophila** (Robins.) Robins.   Fig. 343.   Known only from slopes and canyons at moderate to high elevations in the Chisos Mts. (Brewster Co.), including Lost Mine Peak, Green

Fig. 343. *Brickellia veronicaefolia*   Fig. 344. *Brickellia coulteri* (Coulter Brickellia)

Gulch, the Chinese Wall, Laguna Trail, and upper Cattail Canyon. 5500–6500 ft. Common over much of the Mexican Plateau. Other varieties of *Brickellia veronicaefolia* occur on the Mexican Plateau.

This species is a low shrub with ovate to kidneyshaped leaves. It is abundant in the Chisos Mountains, especially along the trail to Lost Mine Peak.

2. Brickellia coulteri Gray. COULTER BRICKELLIA. Fig. 344. Usually among rocks or at the base of bluffs in canyons or arroyos, desertic mountain areas. El Paso Co., Franklin Mts., Hudspeth Co., Quitman Mts. Presidio Co., Sierra Vieja, Capote Canyon; Chinati Mts., Pinto Canyon, Tinaja Prieta Canyon, near the Old Ross Mine; 10 mi below Redford. Brewster Co., 02 Ranch; Nine-Point Mesa; 2 mi W Study Butte; Chisos Mts., Crown Mt.; Dead Horse Mts., near McKinney Springs. 2200–4600 ft.; spring–fall. Also NM, AZ, Baja CA; NW Mex.

Coulter Brickellia is a diffuse, sometimes sprawling shrub with slender, brittle branches and leaves that are somewhat triangular in outline. More than one variety may be present in Texas and in Mexico.

3. Brickellia baccharidea Gray. RESINLEAF BRICKELLIA. Fig. 345. In the Trans-Pecos known only from limestone substrates in the Franklin Mts., El Paso Co. Also Oregon Mts., NM; S AZ; N Mex.

Plants of this species are erect shrubs with somewhat diamondshaped leaves

Fig. 345. *Brickellia baccharidea*
(Resinleaf Brickellia)

Fig. 346. *Brickellia californica*
(California Brickellia)

with microscopic glands (overall a resinlike coating) and toothed margins. Probably it is related to *Brickellia laciniata.*

4. Brickellia californica (T. & G.) Gray.   CALIFORNIA BRICKELLIA.   Fig. 346. [*Bulbostylis californica* T. & G.]. A common species, mostly in rocky habitats of mountains. El Paso Co., Franklin Mts. Hudspeth Co., Hueco Mts. Culberson Co., Guadalupe Mts., Apache Mts.; Chispa Mt. Jeff Davis Co., Davis Mts. and outliers. Presidio Co., Chinati Mts. Brewster Co., vicinity of Alpine S to Chisos Mts. 3800–7500 ft.; Aug–Nov. One of the most wide ranging species of the genus; Texas Panhandle near caprock; OK Panhandle; W to CO, UT, ID; S to N Mex., including Baja CA.

Brickellia californica is a shrub to 1 m or more high, with rather thin, ovate to deltoid leaves that are flat or notched at the base, and margins with rounded teeth. The flowering heads are arranged in elongate terminal clusters, and in clusters along the stems as well. Flyr (see Correll and Johnston, 1970) believed that *B. californica* and *B. laciniata* were hybridizing in the Davis Mountains, based upon seemingly intermediate characters of some brickellias growing there. Three varieties of this species are listed by Kartesz (1994); ours is var. **californica.**

5. Brickellia laciniata Gray.   SPLITLEAF BRICKELLIA.   Fig. 347.   A widespread weedy shrub, especially common at roadside, in streambeds, and in

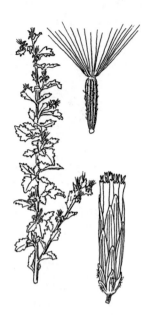

Fig. 347. *Brickellia laciniata*   Fig. 348. *Brickellia venosa* (Veiny Brickellia)
(Splitleaf Brickellia)

various rocky habitats, probably in every county of the Trans-Pecos. 2000–6000 ft.; Aug–Nov. Also E to Kimble Co., TX; one of the most widespread species of the genus, S NM; N to cen. Mex.

This species name refers to the characteristic laciniate leaves that are somewhat sticky and crowded on the stems. The shrubs often exceed 1.5 m and may spread even wider. Splitleaf Brickellia tends to increase in disturbed habitats, and is regionally sympatric with *Brickellia californica* which is characteristically restricted to native habitats. These two species possibly hybridize where they grow together in the Davis Mountains.

6. **Brickellia venosa** (Woot. & Standl.) Robins. VEINY BRICKELLIA. Fig. 348. [*Coleosanthus venosus* Woot. & Standl.]. In the Trans-Pecos known only from slopes, canyons, and arroyos of the Franklin Mts., El Paso Co.; usually limestone substrates. 4600–4800 ft.; Aug–Oct. Also W in S NM, S AZ; Son., Chih., Mex.

The species can be identified by its grayish aspect, narrow oblong leaves that are veiny in appearance, and heads borne in spreading clusters (panicles). The plant is an herbaceous perennial or subshrub, woody mostly at the base.

7. **Brickellia parvula** Gray. SMALL BRICKELLIA. Fig. 349. Limestone habitats, slopes and canyons. El Paso Co., Franklin Mts. Reported from Guadalupe Mts., Culberson Co. 4000–4600 ft.; Sep–Oct. Also S AZ.

Fig. 349. *Brickellia parvula* (Small Brickellia)   Fig. 350. *Koanophyllon solidaginifolia*

The plants are low, much branched shrubs to about 30 cm high, with smallish, dark green ovate leaves. The species is related to *Brickellia brachyphylla*, an herbaceous perennial common in the Guadalupe Mts.

3. KOANOPHYLLON ARRUDA

Shrubs or subshrubs, usually less than 1 cm high. Leaves opposite, in our species blades broadly lanceolate, to 9 cm long, rounded or straight at the base, apex attenuate, essentially glabrous; petioles to 6 mm long; upper leaves much smaller. Heads loosely arranged in rounded masses; heads with 3–6 flowers; involucre ca. 5 mm long, obconic; phyllaries basically in one series; corollas whitish, greenish-white, or pinkish-white. Achenes 5-ribbed with short hairs; pappus of numerous bristles with minute barbs. Base chromosome number, $x = 10$.

A genus of about 114 species in South, Central, and North America (King and Robinson, 1975). In the broad, traditional sense, most of the species were placed with *Eupatorium*.

1. **Koanophyllon solidaginifolia** (Gray) King & Robins. Fig. 350. [*Eupatorium solidaginifolium* Gray]. Usually among rocks in protected can-

yons. Jeff Davis Co., Limpia Canyon, Wildrose Pass; Musquiz Canyon; Fern Canyon. Presidio Co., Sierra Vieja, Knox Canyon, Musgrave Canyon, Capote Canyon; Chinati Mts., Tigner Canyon; near Old Ross Mine; Panther Canyon near Big Hill along the Rio Grande. Brewster Co., Steamboat Mesa and Whirlwind Spring area, 02 Ranch; Chisos Mts., Basin. 2400–5400 ft.; Aug–Nov. W to AZ; Chih., Coah., Dgo., Mex.

This subshrubby species is easily recognized by its broadly lanceolate, goldenrodlike leaves and small heads. It always has a goatlike aroma.

4. AGERATINA SPACH.

Shrubs to 0.5 m high (in our species), intricately branched. Leaves opposite or nearly so, blades ovate-deltoid, 1–2 cm long, glandular; petioles short, often bordered by decurrent blade. Heads in terminal, rounded masses; heads 10–12-flowered; involucre obconic, ca. 4 mm high; flowers whitish, corolla narrow basally, expanded distally. Achenes 5-ribbed, pubescent or glandular or both; pappus of numerous bristles, these easily deciduous. Base chromosome number, $x = 17$. [Batschia Moench.; Ageratiopsis Schultz-Bip.; Mallinoa Coult.; Kyrstenia Neck. ex E. L. Greene].

A genus of about 200 species ranging from the eastern United States through Mexico and Central America into South America and the West Indies.

1. **Ageratina wrightii** (Gray) King & Robins. WRIGHT AGERATINA. Fig. 351. [Eupatorium wrightii Gray]. Mostly limestone substrates in mountains, desertic and mesic. El Paso Co., Franklin Mts., McKelligan Canyon, E slopes. Hudspeth Co., Sierra Diablo. Culberson Co., Guadalupe Mts., Delaware Mts.; Sierra Diablo; 10 mi W Kent. Jeff Davis Co., Davis Mts., above old Ft. Davis. Presidio Co., Chinati Mts., N slopes; near Shafter; the Solitario; Elephant Mt. Brewster Co., Mt. Ord; Glass Mts.; near Santiago Peak, Del Nortes; N slopes, Packsaddle Mt.; Chisos Mts., Basin to Laguna. 3500–7000 ft.; Oct–Nov. Chih., Coah., S.L.P., Mex.

This low rounded shrub is recognized by its smallish, ovate-deltoid leaves, 1–2 cm long.

TRIBE 2. ASTEREAE   ASTER TRIBE

Herbs or shrubs, herbage often resinous. Leaves various. Heads solitary or in clusters; involucre usually in several series, phyllaries mostly green; heads with both ray flowers and disc flowers, or ray flowers absent, ligules cyanic, yellow, or white, disc corollas usually yellow; flowers usually bisexual, unisexual in Baccharis; style branches (except in Baccharis) with marginal stig-

Fig. 351. *Ageratina wrightii* (Wright Ageratina)

matic lines, the apexes not stigmatic, usually hairy and linear to somewhat triangular. Achenes various, often hairy; pappus of very slender bristles or scales, or absent.

A tribe of about 135 genera and 2500 species, of world-wide distribution but largely centered in western North America, South America, and Southern Africa. About 30 genera and 152 species occur in Texas, most of these also in the Trans-Pecos. Much current systematic work and taxonomic reorganization is in progress, particularly regarding *Aster* L. (Nesom, 1994) and the classical polyphyletic genus *Haplopappus* Cass. (Hall, 1928; Lane and Hartman, 1996). Species of several genera are strong herbaceous perennials with woody caudexes or basal stems. These include *Heterotheca villosa* (Pursh) Shinners and related species, *Machaeranthera pinnatifida* (Hook.) Shinners, *M. gypsophila* B. L. Turner, *Xylorhiza wrightii* (Gray) Greene, and others.

KEY TO THE GENERA

1. Flowers unisexual; male and female flowering heads on separate plants
   1. *Baccharis.*
1. Flowers, at least the disc flowers, perfect.
   2. Ligules of ray corollas white.
      3. Leaves linear to oblong, 1–2 cm long at midstem; thorns absent; branches erect, arching, or reclining   2. *Symphyotrichum.*

3. Leaves absent or very small; usually thorns present; branches stiffly erect   **3. Chloracantha.**
2. Ligules of ray corollas yellow, or rays absent.
    4. Pappus essentially absent in both ray and disc flowers, or reduced to a microscopic ring   **4. Gymnosperma.**
    4. Pappus scales or slender bristles present.
        5. Pappus of short scales; ray flowers 1–5 (or more)   **5. Gutierrezia.**
        5. Pappus of slender bristles; ray flowers usually absent, perhaps present in *Chrysothamnus spathulatus* and *Ericameria laricifolia.*
            6. Throat of disc corolla markedly expanded from a short basal tube   **9. Isocoma.**
            6. Throat of disc corolla gradually expanded, the basal tube poorly delimited.
                7. Broad shrubs usually 1 m or more high; phyllaries strongly graduated in 4–5 series in distinct vertical files
                                    6. Chrysothamnus.
                7. Low shrubs usually less than 1 m high; phyllaries not strongly graduated in 4–5 series in distinct vertical files (perhaps appearing so in *Xylothamia*).
                    8. Dense evergreen shrubs; leaves copiously dotted with small, clear glands or leaves white woolly; heads radiate or not, usually with 8–20 disc flowers; disc corollas regular
                                    7. Ericameria.
                    8. Open evergreen shrubs; leaves without copious glands or woolly hairs; heads discoid, with 2–7 (usually 3) disc flowers; disc corollas strongly zygomorphic   **8. Xylothamia.**

1. BACCHARIS L.   GROUNDSELTREE

Shrubs or subshrubs, unisexual. Leaves alternate, sparse to crowded, pointed to rounded, the margins toothed or smooth. Male and female heads on separate plants, usually numerous in slender or broad aggregations; involucres hemispheric to narrowly cylindric; ray flowers absent; female flowers yellowish-white to brown, corolla slender throughout with 5 minute lobes; style forked, glabrous; achenes 4–10-ribbed, yellow to reddish, hairy or smooth; pappus of very numerous slender bristles, in 1 or several series equaling or exceeding the style in length; male flowers white to yellowish-brown, corolla gradually expanded and funnelform, with 5 lanceolate lobes; style club-like or forked; pappus usually in 1 series, not exceeding the style, the bristles rigid, often curled, somewhat plumose-tipped; ovary abortive.

A large genus of about 400 species distributed in North and South America. The unisexual flowers and plants allow distinction of the genus, although the species of *Baccharis* are similar to other genera of the tribe in superficial appearance. Eleven species occur in Texas, 10 of these in the Trans-Pecos. The treatment of *Baccharis* herein closely follows that of Mahler and Waterfall (1964). Worthington (1990) noted the occurrence of *B. sarothroides* Gray in El Paso County, where it apparently has been seeded into the area along roadways.

KEY TO THE SPECIES

1. Plants with short, stiff hairs; leaves sparse, linear, usually less than 1 cm long, 2 mm wide   **1. B. brachyphylla.**
1. Plants glabrous or nearly so; leaves otherwise.
  2. Branchlets round, only slightly striate, rough with short glandular-stalks; heads tightly arranged along the stems (racemose) on short lateral branchlets   **2. B. pteronioides.**
  2. Branchlets striate-angled, essentially not rough with glandular-stalks; heads arranged otherwise.
    3. Pappus of female flowers reddish-brown, arranged in many series; achenes 3–5 mm long, sparsely or prominently rough with glandular-stalks.
      4. Leaves mostly less than 1 cm long, the margins smooth or with colorless teeth; female involucre 9–12 mm long; phyllaries flat to partly keeled   **3. B. wrightii.**
      4. Leaves mostly more than 1 cm long, the margins undulate; female involucre usually 9 mm or less long; phyllaries keeled, midribs swollen   **4. B. texana.**
    3. Pappus of female flowers white to dirty-colored, arranged in 1 or 2 series; achenes usually less than 3 mm long, glabrous.
      5. Achenes 8–10-ribbed; pappus longer than corollas by 5 mm or more.
        6. Leaves oblanceolate; female involucre 6 mm or more long   **5. B. salicina.**
        6. Leaves narrowly linear to narrowly elliptic; female involucre 5 mm or less long   **6. B. neglecta.**
      5. Achenes 4–5-ribbed; pappus longer than corollas by 4 mm or less.
        7. Leaves oblong-elliptic, irregularly cut or coarsely toothed   **8. B. bigelovii.**
        7. Leaves lanceolate to elliptic, linear, or spatulate, not irregularly cut or toothed.
          8. Leaves linear or spatulate, the margins toothed, cut, or smooth   **9. B. havardii.**
          8. Leaves lanceolate or narrowly elliptic; the margins minutely toothed or smooth   **7. B. salicifolia.**

Fig. 352. *Baccharis brachyphylla*

Fig. 353. *Baccharis pteronioides* (Yerba de Pasmo Baccharis); M) male; F) female

1. Baccharis brachyphylla Gray.   Fig. 352.   Infrequent, usually in sand. El Paso Co., along Newman highway, 6 mi NE El Paso; 1 mi N Ft. Bliss; Indian Spring Canyon, Franklin Mts. 3700 ft.; Jul–Aug. Also NM, W to CA; Son., Mex.

This species is characterized by its small, linear leaves, pubescent herbage, and slender, erect, subshrubby habit less than 1 m high.

2. Baccharis pteronioides DC.   YERBA DE PASMO BACCHARIS.   Fig. 353. Mostly mountain areas. El Paso Co., Franklin Mts., Fusselman Canyon, Culberson Co., Guadalupe Mts., McKittrick Canyon, lower Pine Canyon and vicinity; Sierra Diablo, Refuge area. Hudspeth Co., Sierra Blanca. Jeff Davis Co., Mt. Livermore, Goat Canyon; 12 mi NE Ft. Davis, Davis Mts. State Park, 6 mi S Ft. Davis. Presidio Co., 30 mi SE Marfa; San Estaban Lake; N slope Elephant Mt. Brewster Co., Cienega Mt.; Chisos Mts., Pulliam Mt., Basin. 4500–6500 ft.; Apr–Jun. Also NM, and AZ; S to Pue., Mex.

Plants of this species are usually less than 1 m high, with glandular-scabrous branches, clustered and sessile leaves usually about 1 cm long, and heads racemosely arranged on short leafy branches. The plants are poisonous to cattle and sheep. The common name Yerba de Pasmo (chill weed) refers to the use of the leaves in a tonic to treat chills. Dried leaves have been used to treat sores in Coahuila, Mexico.

3. Baccharis wrightii Gray.   WRIGHT BACCHARIS.   Fig. 354.   Localized in distribution, sand, clay-gypsum, limestone, gravel, and saline soils. Hud-

 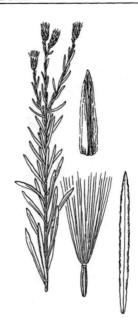

Fig. 354. *Baccharis wrightii* (Wright Baccharis)   Fig. 355. *Baccharis texana* (Prairie Baccharis)

speth Co., Grayton Flats between the Eagle Mts. and Sierra Blanca. Culberson Co., 2 mi E Van Horn. Brewster Co., 4 mi N Agua Fria; Tornillo Flats, Big Bend Park; W of Rosillos Mts.; Lower Canyons of the Rio Grande. 1700–4000 ft.; May–Jun. Also Plains Country; OK, KS, NM, AZ; Chih., Dgo., Mex.

4. Baccharis texana (T. & G.) Gray. PRAIRIE BACCHARIS. Fig. 355. [*Linosyris texana* T. & G.]. Localized in distribution. Reported from Val Verde Co., Del Rio (Mahler and Waterfall, 1964). In TX mostly on the Rio Grande Plains, Edwards Plateau, Plains Country, N-cen., and SE TX; Aug-Nov; also OK; Coah., N.L., Tam., Mex.

5. Baccharis salicina T. & G. WILLOW BACCHARIS. Fig. 356. Rather widespread in various soil types including alluvium, sand, gypsum, frequently in saline habitats, often along natural watercourses and irrigation canals. El Paso Co., El Paso; 5 mi NW Tornillo. Culberson Co., 29 mi N Van Horn; along Delaware Creek. Reeves Co., 4 mi E Pecos; canals at Balmorhea. Presidio Co., Marfa; 12 mi S Marfa. Brewster Co., Kokernot Ranch, Leoncita Springs. Pecos Co., Ft. Stockton golf course; 30 mi E Ft. Stockton; 10 mi N Ft. Stockton; Imperial; also Ward Co. and Winkler Co. 2400–4400 ft.; summer-fall. Also Plains Country; NM, OK.

Baccharis salicina is closely related to *B. neglecta* and perhaps the two should be recognized as one species. in our area the Willow Baccharis has often been known erroneously as *B. emoryi* Gray, a species of more western distribution.

Fig. 356. *Baccharis salicina* (Willow Baccharis)   Fig. 357. *Baccharis neglecta* (Roosevelt Weed)

The leaves of *B. salicina* are nearly sessile, oblanceolate-oblong, prominently toothed, 3–6 cm long, and 0.4–1.5 cm wide.

6. **Baccharis neglecta** Britt.   ROOSEVELT WEED, NEW DEAL WEED, JARA DULCE.   Fig. 357.   Disturbed habitats, roadsides, along watercourses. El Paso Co., Franklin Mts. Reeves Co., Toyah Creek, 3 mi W Balmorhea. Pecos Co., near Sheffield. Presidio Co., 12 mi SE Marfa; Alamito Creek, 8 mi E Presidio; Rio Grande at Lajitas. Brewster Co., near Rio Grande, Castolon area. Val Verde Co., Devils River. 1200–4400 ft.; summer–fall. Throughout much of TX except higher elevations of the Plains Country and deep E TX; widespread AZ to NC; S to Coah. and Dgo., Mex.

In Texas *Baccharis neglecta* has been confused with *B. angustifolia* Michx., a closely related species of the eastern United States. The leaves of *B. neglecta* are narrowly linear to narrowly elliptic, entire or somewhat toothed, 3–8 cm long, and 2–5 mm wide.

7. **Baccharis salicifolia** (R. & P.) Pers.   SEEPWILLOW, JARA, WATERWALLY.   Fig. 358.   [*Baccharis glutinosa* Pers.; *B. viminea* DC.]. The most widespread and common species of the Trans-Pecos, especially along sandy watercourses and dry arroyos; numerous localities in perhaps every county of the Trans-Pecos. 2000–4000 ft.; summer–fall. Widespread in the Americas, N to CO, W to CA; S to Chile, S.A.

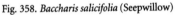

Fig. 358. *Baccharis salicifolia* (Seepwillow)

Fig. 359. *Baccharis bigelovii*
(Bigelow Baccharis)

The leaves of *Baccharis salicifolia* are basically lanceolate and prominently toothed to nearly entire, 3–10 cm long, and 1–2 cm wide. The common Seepwillow (long known erroneously as *B. glutinosa*) evidently has no forage value, but it is important for erosion control along watercourses.

8. Baccharis bigelovii Gray. BIGELOW BACCHARIS. Fig. 359. Mountain slopes and canyons. Jeff Davis Co., Mt. Livermore, Pine Canyon, Madera Canyon; Limpia Canyon near Ft. Davis; Davis Mts. State Park; Musquiz Canyon, 12–18 mi N Alpine; Little Aguja Canyon. Presidio Co., Chinati Mts., Tigna Canyon. Brewster Co., Sunny Glenn W of Alpine; Green Valley, Wilson Range. 3600–7200 ft.; Aug–Nov. Chih. and Coah., Mex.

Plants of *B. bigelovii* are less than 1 m high, with leaves oblong, ovate, or elliptic, coarsely toothed, usually irregularly so, 2–3.5 cm long, and 0.3–1.5 cm wide.

9. Baccharis havardii Gray. HAVARD BACCHARIS. Mountain slopes and canyons. Culberson Co., Guadalupe Mts., North McKittrick Canyon, South McKittrick Canyon to top of Guadalupes, Pine Top Mt., upper Pine Springs Canyon. Jeff Davis Co., Davis Mts. (collected by Young in 1916). Brewster Co., Glass Mts., upper Jail Canyon, W slopes of Gilliland Peak, W slopes of Old Blue; Chisos Mts., S slope Mt. Emory, above the Laguna, Boot Spring, Basin,

Fig. 360. *Symphyotrichum ericoides*
(Heath Aster)

upper Pine Canyon, upper Cattail Canyon. 4500–8200 ft.; Jul–Aug. Also Coah., Mex.

Havard Baccharis is a glutinous subshrub to about 70 cm high, with spatulate to narrowly linear leaves to 4 cm long and 3 mm wide. The plants are reportedly toxic to livestock.

2. SYMPHYOTRICHUM NEES. ASTER

Shrublike perennial herb, rhizomatous; much-branched, the primary branches erect, arching or reclining, bearing numerous branchlets. Leaves alternate, mostly linear or oblong, those of midstem 1–2 cm long, those of branchlets much smaller. Heads clustered; phyllaries graduated in several series; ray flowers several, ligules white; disc flowers numerous, corollas yellow. Achenes slightly compressed, ribbed; pappus of bristles.

A genus of about 97 species distributed in the Americas, as circumscribed by Nesom (1994).

1. **Symphyotrichum ericoides** (L.) Nesom. HEATH ASTER. Fig. 360. [*Aster ericoides* L.; *Lasallea ericoides* (L.) Semple & Brouillet; *Virgulus ericoides* (L.) Reveal & Keener]. Usually in moist places, creeks, arroyos, marshes. Culberson Co., Guadalupe Mts., Choisya Creek. Jeff Davis Co., Musquiz swamp,

7 mi S Ft. Davis. Brewster Co., vicinity of Alpine, golf course, Sul Ross Hill, 1 mi S Alpine; Pena Blanca Springs, 3.5 mi S Marathon. 4400–6000 ft.; fall. Common species much of TX; N to Can.; W to AZ; Coah., Chih., Mex.

This species, long known in our area as *Aster ericoides*, is essentially a rhizomatous, herbaceous perennial. Older plants become woody at the base, and when the branches are supported by fences or other vegetation the plants have the aspect of a shrub. When in full flower Heath Aster is exceedingly showy because of its numerous white-rayed heads. Nesom (1994) lists three varieties of the species.

3. CHLORACANTHA NESOM. DEVILWEED

Shrublike perennial herbs, with stout rhizomes. Stems erect, 0.5–2.3 m tall, glabrous, woody at base, with or without thorns. Leaves mostly basal, alternate, oblanceolate to spatulate, 1-nerved, 1–4 cm long, entire or rarely with 1–2 pairs of teeth, mostly without hairs except the margins. Heads solitary or in groups; phyllaries strongly graduated in (3–)4–5 series; ray flowers 10–30, ligules white; disc flowers numerous, corollas yellow, 3.5–6 mm long. Achenes glabrous, usually 5-nerved, slightly compressed, 1.5–3.5 mm long; pappus of 30–60 bristles in ca. 2 series, about as long as disc corollas.

A monotypic genus, distributed from the southwestern United States across Mexico to Guatemala and Panama (Nesom et al., 1991).

1. **Chloracantha spinosa** (Benth.) Nesom. DEVILWEED Fig. 361. [*Aster spinosus* Benth.; *Erigeron ortegae* Blake; *Leucosyris spinosa* (Benth.) Greene]. Locally common, usually in colonies, usually in sand and beside canals, springs, streams, and other water sources. El Paso Co., near the Rio Grande, and near canals. Hudspeth Co., 12 mi E Hueco Inn. Culberson Co., Guadalupe Mts., Choisya Spring; along Delaware Creek; 2 mi E Van Horn. Reeves Co., along canals at Balmorhea. Loving Co., 1 mi W Mentone. Presidio Co., Capote Canyon; Presidio; 5 mi below Presidio. Brewster Co., Neville Ranch; 02 Ranch headquarters and at Steamboat Springs; Rio Grande below Hot Springs, Big Bend Park. 2600–5800 ft.; summer–fall; widely distributed, S and W TX; W to CA and UT; S to S Mex.

This stiffly erect rhizomatous perennial becomes woody at the base. This essentially leafless, often thorny, asterlike species is easily identified along watercourses. Four varieties are recognized by Sundberg (1991), only one of them, var. **spinosa**, in the United States.

4. GYMNOSPERMA LESS.

Shrub, usually stiffly erect, 0.5–2 m high. Leaves alternate, sessile, linear or linear-lanceolate, entire, sticky, 2–5 cm long, 2–6 mm wide. Heads in dense

Fig. 361. *Chloracantha spinosa*
(Devilweed Aster)

Fig. 362. *Gymnosperma glutinosum*
(Nakedseed Weed)

terminal masses; involucres 3–5 mm high, sticky; phyllaries in about 3 series, overlapping; receptacle glabrous; ray flowers few, corolla yellow, tube longer than ligule; disk flowers few, corolla yellow. Achene hairy; pappus of disks and rays reduced to microscopic ring or absent.

A monotypic genus, closely related to *Gutierrezia* Lag.

1. **Gymnosperma glutinosum** (Spreng.) Less.   NAKEDSEED WEED, TATA-LENCHO, XONOQUILITL.   Fig. 362.   [*Selloa glutinosa* Spreng.; *Xanthocephalum glutinosum* (Spreng.) Shinners]. Rocky slopes of mountains, grasslands, and brushlands, widespread and often common in the Trans-Pecos. El Paso Co., Culberson Co., Guadalupe Mts. Reeves Co., Balmorhea. Presidio Co., near Marfa; Elephant Mt. Jeff Davis Co., near Ft. Davis. Brewster Co., Glass Mts.; Del Norte Mts., Altuda; 8 mi W Alpine; Goat Mt.; Elephant Mt.; Cathedral Mt.; Cienega Mt.; Packsaddle Mt.; 20 mi NE Alpine; 02 Ranch. Pecos Co., near Ft. Stockton. Terrell Co., near Dryden. 2500–8000 ft.; summer–fall. Also Rio Grande Plains, Edwards Plateau; NM, AZ; S to Guat.

The leaves and flowering heads of *Gymnosperma glutinosum* are covered with a glutinous exudate. In Mexico a decoction of the plants is used to treat diarrhea, rheumatism, and ulcers. The species is not often browsed but has been reported to be toxic to livestock.

5. GUTIERREZIA LAG. BROOMWEED, SNAKEWEED

Low shrubs or herbaceous annuals with tap roots. Leaves alternate, simple, or fascicled, usually resinous, margins entire. Heads small, in clusters or solitary; phyllaries in about 3 series, strongly overlapping, tightly appressed, usually resinous; receptacle with hook-tipped, glandular based trichomes; ray flowers pistillate and fertile, ligules yellow (or white, but not in our species) longer than corolla tube; disc flowers staminate or perfect, corollas yellow, gradually expanding, lobes 5; pappus of 1–2 series reduced scales, or a notched cup, or rarely absent in ray florets. Achenes covered with stiff hairs or nearly glabrous. Previously recognized in some works as synonymous with *Xanthocephalum* Willd. and *Amphiachyris* (DC.) Nutt., but these are presently treated as distinct genera (Meredith Lane, pers. comm.).

A genus of possibly 30 species, distributed in North and South America. In common jargon the annual species are called Broomweed and the shrubby species are known as Snakeweed. Some ranchers in the Trans-Pecos refer to the plants as turpentine or kerosene weeds. About four species occur in Texas and all of these are known in the Trans-Pecos. Two of these species are stout annuals. In the Trans-Pecos and elsewhere certain weedy species, particularly *Gutierrezia microcephala*, and *G. sarothrae*, and the related annual *Amphiachyris dracunuloides* (DC.) Nutt. (Lane, 1979) are abundant on rangelands, these weedy invasions evidently being promoted by excessive grazing. The species of *Gutierrezia* and related genera are reported to be toxic to livestock.

KEY TO THE SPECIES

1. Heads with 3–5 ray flowers, disc flowers 3–5, perfect; heads topshaped to cylindrical, in loose clusters **1. G. sarothrae.**
1. Heads with 1 (rarely 2) ray flowers, disc flowers 1 (rarely 2), staminate; heads narrowly cylindrical, in tight clusters **2. G. microcephala.**

1. Gutierrezia sarothrae (Pursh) Britt. & Rusby. BROOM SNAKEWEED. Fig. 363. [*Xanthocephalum sarothrae* (Pursh) Shinners; *Gutierrezia tenuis* Greene; *G. longipappa* Blake]. Widespread and locally abundant, especially in disturbed areas or abused rangelands, found in every county of the Trans-Pecos. 1500–6000 ft.; Jun–Nov. Throughout much of TX; N to Can.; S to Tam., Chih., N.L., Mex.

Plants of the Broom Snakeweed are low shrubs to nearly 1 m high, but usually less than 0.6 m high, with many slender branches below and above. As the common name implies, the plants have been used for brooms. Broom Snakeweed, an indicator of overgrazed conditions, apparently is seldom browsed by livestock, but it is believed to be toxic when eaten in sufficient amounts. A tonic of the plant is reported to be useful as a powerful diuretic and in treating gastric problems.

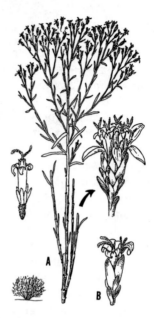

Fig. 363. A) *Gutierrezia sarothrae* (Broom
Snakeweed); B) *G. microcephala* (Threadleaf
Snakeweed), head only.

2. Gutierrezia microcephala (DC.) Gray. THREADLEAF SNAKEWEED.
Fig. 363. [*Xanthocephalum microcephalum* (DC.) Shinners; *Gutierrezia sarothrae* var. *microcephala* (DC.) L. Benson]. Widespread and locally abundant, especially in disturbed areas or abused rangelands, found perhaps in every
county in the Trans-Pecos. 2500–6000 ft.; Jun–Oct. Also E to W parts of the
Edwards Plateau, and N to the Plains Country; W to CA; N to CO; Son., Chih.,
Coah., Mex.

Plants of the Threadleaf Snakeweed are low shrubs to 1 m high, with many
slender branches at the base and above. The Threadleaf Snakeweed is best distinguished from the closely related Broom Snakeweed by its nearly globose
habit, its smaller heads with nearly cylindrical involucres, and usually two florets per head. Threadleaf Snakeweed is an indicator of overgrazed range conditions. The plants are seldom browsed, but are toxic to livestock, especially in
early growth stages.

6. CHRYSOTHAMNUS NUTT. RABBITBRUSH

Shrubs 0.5–1.5 m high, much branched. Leaves alternate, simple, narrow,
1–6 cm long, 1–5 mm wide, glabrous to woolly pubescent, margins entire.

Fig. 364. *Chrysothamnus pulchellus*
(Southwest Rabbitbush)

Heads borne in dense clusters; involucres 0.5–1.5 cm long, cylindric; phyllaries in 4–5 series, strongly graduated and in distinct vertical files; ray flowers usually absent, present only in *Chrysothamnus spathulatus*, then yellow, 1 per head, small; disk flowers 4–5, yellow corolla 0.6–1.2 cm long, with a basal tube and gradually expanded throat, lobes 5. Achenes cylindric, smooth or angled, glabrous or hairy; pappus of slender bristles, these dull-white and several in number.

A genus of perhaps 10 species, distributed in western North America. The genus is closely related to *Ericameria* Nutt. (Nesom, 1990). Two species are represented in Texas and in the Trans-Pecos.

KEY TO THE SPECIES

1. Involucre 1 cm or more long   **1. *C. pulchellus.***
1. Involucre 5–6 mm long   **2. *C. spathulatus.***

1. Chrysothamnus pulchellus (Gray) Greene. SOUTHWEST RABBITBUSH. Fig. 364. [*Chrysothamnus baileyi* Woot. & Standl.]. Mostly in sandy soil. Hudspeth Co., 30 mi E of El Paso, 1 mi E of Hueco; Sierra Diablo, N of McAdoo Ranch hdq. Culberson Co., quartz sand near Guadalupe Mts.; 15 mi

Fig. 365. *Chrysothamnus spathulatus*

E Van Horn. Presidio Co., 1 mi E Love Ranch hdq.; 7 mi S Marfa. Brewster Co., Chisos Mts., Cattail Canyon; trail from Basin to Laguna. Ward, Andrews, Winkler counties. 2600–6500 ft.; Aug–Oct. Also NM, AZ, KS; Chih., Mex.

According to R. Worthington another taxon of this species, *Chrysothamnus pulchellus* subsp. **baileyi** (Woot. & Standl.) Hall & Clements, should be recognized in the Trans-Pecos. The subsp. *baileyi* differs in its scabrous-ciliate leaf margins, shorter leaves, branching habits, and other traits (Hudspeth Co., Hueco Mts., 4.6 mi N Hwy. U.S. 62–180, 5300 ft., low limestone hill).

Chrysothamnus pulchellus is perhaps the most common species of rabbit-bush in the Trans-Pecos, but it is most abundant in adjacent counties to the northeast where deep sandy soils dominate. The leaf margins of the more common form are smooth or finely scabrous-ciliate. Indians reportedly extracted a dye from the inner bark of rabbitbush, and they used the branches for wicker work.

2. **Chrysothamnus spathulatus** L. C. Anders.   Fig. 365.   [*Chrysothamnus viscidiflorus* (Hook.) Nutt. var. *ludens* Shinners]. Usually mountain slopes and canyons. Culberson Co., Guadalupe Mts., McKittrick, Smith, upper Guadalupe, and Pine Spring canyons. Brewster Co., Goat Mt.; Chisos Mts., Laguna trail to Cattail Canyon. 4400–7000 ft.; Aug–Sep. Also in adjacent S NM.

7. ERICAMERIA NUTT.

Shrubs, rounded, evergreen, to 1 m high but usually smaller, glutinous, somewhat aromatic, younger branches in some species white tomentose. Leaves linear, 0.5–2(–4) cm long, 1–2 mm wide, dotted with glands or densely tomentose. Heads discoid or radiate; phyllaries subulate, not in distinct rows and not strongly overlapping, each with a dark midvein extending almost the full length, expanded at the tip or not; ray flowers yellow, if present, 1–5 and small, to 5 mm long; disc flowers 8–20; corollas yellow, ca. 5.6–8 mm long, the throat expanded and with 5 equal lobes. Achenes densely hairy; pappus of numerous slender, unequal bristles, these dirty white.

A genus of 27 species distributed mostly in arid regions of western North America. Nesom (1990) and Nesom and Baird (1993) have produced recent taxonomic studies of *Ericameria*. *Ericameria* is closely related to *Chrysothamnus*.

KEY TO THE SPECIES

1. Younger branches not covered with a whitish mat of hairs; midvein of phyllaries not expanded at tip   **1. E. laricifolia.**
1. Younger branches covered with a whitish mat of hairs; midvein of phyllaries expanded at tip to form dark patch   **2. E. nauseosa.**

1. **Ericameria laricifolia** (Gray) Shinners. LARCHLEAF GOLDENWEED. Fig. 366. [*Haplopappus laricifolius* Gray]. Canyons and slopes of desertic mountains. El Paso Co., Franklin Mts., McKelligan Canyon; E slopes; Hueco Mts. Presidio Co., Chinati Mts., E branch of San Antonio Canyon; S Chinati Mts., flats above Oso Creek; N Chinati Mts.; old Woods Ranch, 18 mi NW Shafter. Reported from Guadalupe Mts. (Vines, 1960). 4200–5100 ft.; Oct–Nov. NM, AZ, CA; Son., Chih., Mex.

This resinous-aromatic shrub is much branched, with numerous small leaves, to nearly 1 m high but usually smaller, and very attractive when the clustered yellow flowers are in bloom. The sap of these plants is reported to contain a small amount of rubber.

2. **Ericameria nauseosa** (Pallas *ex* Pursh) Nesom & Baird. GUADALUPE GOLDENWEED. Fig. 367. [*Chrysothamnus nauseosus* Pallas *ex* Pursh]. Anderson (1980) reported that two varieties of goldenweed occur in or near the Guadalupe Mts.: *Ericameria nauseosa* var. **texensis** (L. Anders.) Nesom & Baird [*Chrysothamnus nauseosus* (Pallas *ex* Pursh) Britt. subsp. *texensis* L. Anders.] with glabrous achenes is localized, usually in or near canyons, Culberson Co., Guadalupe Mts., South and North McKittrick canyons; Smith Canyon; Pine Springs. 5000–6500 ft.; Sep–Oct; also NM, in the Guadalupe Mts. *Eri-*

Fig. 366. *Ericameria laricifolia*
(Larchleaf Goldenweed)

Fig. 367. *Ericameria nauseosa*
(Guadalupe Goldenweed)

cameria nauseosa var. **glabrata** (Gray) Nesom & Baird [*Chrysothamnus nauseosus* subsp. *graveolens* (Nutt.) Hall & Clements] with hairy achenes was reported by Anderson (1980) to occur in Hudspeth Co. bordering the salt lake a few miles W of the Guadalupe Mts. The species *E. nauseosa* is widespread in the western U.S.

8. XYLOTHAMIA NESOM, SUH, MORGAN & SIMPSON

Shrubs, evergreen, 2–10 dm tall; stems minutely papillate, glutinous. Leaves more or less terete, involuted, 5–15(–20) mm long, 0.3–0.5 mm wide. Heads discoid, turbinate, 3–4 mm wide, aggregated in loose cymes; phyllaries strongly graduated, perhaps in near vertical files, with white-indurated, enervate bases, and with an apical, strongly viscid-glandular herbaceous patch; ray flowers absent; disc flowers (2–)3–7; corollas yellow, glabrous, 4–5 mm long, the lobes strongly zygomorphic. Achenes subcylindric to turbinate, densely hairy, with 5–8 weak nerves; pappus of numerous bristles, contorted near the base.

A genus of eight species of northern Mexico and South Texas, with one Chihuahuan and Coahuilan species extending into southern Brewster County of Trans-Pecos Texas. This taxon was recently circumscribed by Nesom et al. (1990). *Xylothamia* is related to *Euthamia*.

Fig. 368. *Xylothamia triantha*
(Threeflower Goldenweed)

1. **Xylothamia triantha** (Blake) Nesom. THREEFLOWER GOLDENWEED. Fig. 368. [*Haplopappus trianthus* Blake; *Ericameria triantha* (Blake) Shinners]. Localized in rocky limestone, gravel, or gypseous-clay habitats of the desert. Brewster Co., N side Packsaddle Mt.; near Terlingua; 1 mi E Lajitas; junction Study Butte–Terlingua; between St. Elena and Castolon; Big Bend Park, 1 mi beyond Tornillo Flats toward the Chisos Mts. and near Hot Springs. 2500–3500 ft.; Aug–Oct. Coah., Chih., N.L., Dgo., Mex.

The species name and common name indicate that this plant has three flowers in each head. Actually the number may vary from 2–7, but usually there are three.

9. ISOCOMA NUTT.

Subshrub to 1 m high, usually smaller, taproots woody, herbage glutinous, glabrous. Leaves linear to nearly oblanceolate or obovate in outline, the margins entire, toothed, or cut, blades with small, depressed, usually dark "glands." Heads in tight clusters of 2–6, rarely solitary, the clusters often numerous and "topping" the plant; involucre 0.4–1.2 cm high, in 3–4 series, strongly overlapping but not in vertical files, phyllaries very glutinous, light-colored except the tips herbaceous; ray flowers absent; disc flowers 10–40 per head; corollas yellow, 4–9.5 mm long, with a prominent basal tube and

Fig. 369. *Isocoma plurifolia* (Jimmyweed)

abruptly expanded throat, the lobes equal. Achenes 2–3 mm long, 4-angled, covered with short whitish hairs; pappus of numerous stiffish, dirty-white bristles, somewhat unequal in length.

An American genus of about 25 species, three of these found in Texas. Only one species occurs in the Trans-Pecos. *Isocoma* is closely related to *Machaeranthera* Nees (*Haplopappus*).

1. **Isocoma plurifolia** (T. & G.) Greene. JIMMYWEED. Fig. 369. [*Isocoma wrightii* (Gray) Rydb.; *Haplopappus heterophyllus* (Gray) Blake]. Locally common, usually in saline, alkaline, or gypseous habitats, often roadside, in irrigated areas, and in overgrazed ranges. Found locally throughout the Trans-Pecos, in all counties except perhaps Val Verde Co. 2600–4600 ft.; Jul–Sep. Crockett Co., N to the Plains Country; NM, AZ; Son., Chih., Mex.

This species is not often eaten by livestock but is poisonous to them. The toxin reportedly can be transferred through milk to humans.

TRIBE 3. INULEAE CASS. EVERLASTING TRIBE

Herbs mostly, rarely shrubs; herbage usually white-woolly but not in our shrub species. Leaves usually alternate, entire or toothed. Heads usually in clusters; phyllaries various, usually mostly membraneous, often specialized and enclosing flowers; receptacle naked or chaffy; ray flowers absent; (rarely present); disc flowers perfect or unisexual, corollas white, yellowish, or purplish (in our species), 4–5-lobed; anthers usually with accessory tails (caudate) at the bases; style branches flattened with marginal stigmatic lines, the apexes blunt or rounded. Achenes small, cylindrical or flattened; pappus of slender bristles.

A tribe of about 180 genera and 2100 species, distributed mainly in South Africa and Australia, to a lesser extent in South America and the Mediterranean, with relatively few species in North America, Eurasia, and Indomalaysia. Eight genera and 21 species represent the Inuleae in Texas, members of five genera and 10 species occur in the Trans-Pecos. Reference here is to the classic Inuleae before *Pluchea* was recognized (Bremer, 1994) as belonging to the tribe Plucheeae Anderb.

1. PLUCHEA CASS. ARROWWEED

Shrubs, 1–2 m high or more, branches erect, rather straight, willowlike, gray-green, malodorous. Leaves alternate, mostly sessile, linear-lanceolate, 1–6 cm long, 2–6 mm wide, the margins entire. Heads in clusters; phyllaries in 2 or more series, 4–5 mm long outer ones ovate, inner ones linear, falling with the flowers; receptacle naked; ray flowers absent; disk flowers numerous, a few central ones perfect but infertile, with purplish, flared corollas that are 5-lobed, the more numerous outer ones pistillate and fertile, the corollas very slender, 4-lobed. Achenes (of fertile flowers) brownish, ca. 0.5 mm long, nearly cylindrical to somewhat flattened, 5-ribbed; pappus of (central staminate) infertile flowers persistent, flattened, bristlelike, whitish at the base, brownish and broadened apically; pappus of (outer) fertile flowers bristlelike, persistent, whitish, not thickened or bicolored.

A mostly American genus of about 40 species, with some in Africa, Asia, and Australia. The genus was reviewed by Nesom (1989).

1. **Pluchea sericea** (Nutt.) Cav. ARROWWEED. Fig. 370. [*Tessaria sericea* (Nutt.) Shinners *T. borealis* T. & G.; *Pluchea borealis* (T. & G.); *Polypappus sericeus* Nutt.; *Bertholetia sericea* (Nutt.) Rydb.]. Locally common along and near desert streams, canals, and springs. Hudspeth Co., 5 mi W Ft. Hancock; Red Bull Springs, Quitman Mts. Presidio Co., irrigation canal, Rio Grande above mouth of Capote Creek; lower Pinto Creek, 4 mi N Ruidosa. Brewster Co., Chisos Mts. area, Tornillo Creek; Chisos Pens. 2800–4300 ft.; summer. Also Crane Co.; NM, W to CA; Son., Chih., Mex.

As the common name implies, Indians used the straight, slender stems for arrow shafts. The twigs were also used for baskets, bird cages, and other structures. The Pima Indians used leaf infusions to treat sore eyes. Arrowweed is correctly placed in *Pluchea* and not *Tessaria* (Nesom, 1989).

Fig. 370. *Pluchea sericea* (Arrowweed)

TRIBE 4. HELIANTHEAE CASS.   SUNFLOWER TRIBE

Herbs mostly, or shrubs. Leaves opposite or alternate, veins pinnate, the margins entire to lobed, pubescence various. Heads solitary or in clusters; phyllaries in 2 to many series, overlapping or subequal, leaflike in texture; receptacle with membranous chaff (scales) subtending and partially enveloping florets; ray flowers usually present, usually pistillate and fertile, ligules yellow or white; disc flowers usually perfect; corollas usually yellow, 5-lobed; style branches blunt, rounded, or tapered apically. Achenes various, cylindrical or flattened; pappus of scales or awns, or rarely absent.

One of the largest and most diverse tribes of Asteraceae, with over 200 genera and several thousand species, distributed primarily in the New World. About 55 genera and over 200 species occur in Texas, with many of these, mostly herbaceous types, represented in the Trans-Pecos. Several members of the tribe are robust herbaceous perennials, some developing woody basal stems with age. Trans-Pecos examples include *Iva dealbata* Gray and *Bebbia juncea* (Benth.) Greene (near El Paso). *Borrichia frutescens* (L.) DC., a subshrub of saline habitats in southern Texas, Mexico, and elsewhere, has been recorded from northwest Crockett Co., just north of the Pecos River.

KEY TO THE GENERA

1. Shrubs 1–2 m high; densely leafy, leaves varnished, with a smell of tar, basically elliptic, to 2.5 cm long   **1. Flourensia.**
1. Shrubs or subshrubs otherwise.
   2. Shrubs commonly 1–2 m high; leaves usually threadlike or linear; male and female heads in same clusters   **2. Hymenoclea.**
   2. Shrubs or subshrubs otherwise.
      3. Disc flowers sterile, but appearing perfect; rays whitish, very small (to 1.5 mm long)   **3. Parthenium.**
      3. Disc flowers fertile; rays (if present; absent in *T. longipes, Pericome,* and some *Perityle*) longer, yellow or white.
         4. Rays persistent on achenes; receptacles conic   **4. Zinnia.**
         4. Rays falling from achenes; receptacles flattish or convex.
            5. Main phyllaries at least partially fused.
               6. Low subshrubs, with leaves basal and slender   **5. Thelesperma.**
               6. Shrubs, with leaves triangular and attenuate at apexes
                                                                  6. Pericome.
            5. Main phyllaries essentially separate.
               7. Disc achenes flattened, with prominent or weak callous margins   **7. Perityle.**
               7. Disc achenes somewhat flattened, but without callous margins.
                  8. Disc achene margins not sharp or winged   **11. Viguiera.**
                  8. Disc achene margins sharp or winged.
                     9. Subshrubs only, usually scapose perennial herbs; achenes not winged, margins pubescent   **10. Encelia.**
                     9. Low shrubs with herbaceous upper stems; achenes winged, the wing margins slightly pubescent or not.
                        10. Leaves ovate to broadly elliptic-ovate, entire, usually 1–3 cm long, often longer; outer phyllaries ovate, loose and enlarged, usually spreading at right angles; pappus not raised on a neck   **8. Jefea.**
                        10. Leaves somewhat broadly lanceolate, toothed or lobed, 5 cm or more long; outer phyllaries lanceolate; pappus raised on a neck at achene apex
                                                                  9. Wedelia.

1. FLOURENSIA DC.

In our species shrubs 1–2 m high, densely leafy, these resinous, varnished, with a smell of tar. Leaves alternate, dark green, glabrous, elliptic, pointed, 1.7–2.5 cm long, more or less 1 cm wide. Heads ca. 1 cm long, nodding, sessile or on short stalks, usually clustered among leaves; involucre bellshaped; phyl-

Fig. 371. *Flourensia cernua* (Tarbush)

laries strongly overlapping, in basically 3 series, herbaceous glutinous, the tips spreading; receptacle chaffy, the pales partially enclosing flowers; ray flowers absent; disc flowers perfect, fertile, corollas yellow. Achenes flattened, hairy, ca. 6 mm long, 2 mm wide; pappus of 2 unequal awns, these fringed, 2.5–3.3 mm long.

1. **Flourensia cernua** DC. TARBUSH, HOJASE. Fig. 371. Common throughout much of the Trans-Pecos, often dominating in desertic flats. El Paso Co., Franklin Mts., and Hudspeth Co., near Sierra Blanca, to Terrell Co., near Dryden. 2300–6500 ft.; Sep–Dec; usually flowering in Oct. Rare in W Plains Country; Winkler, Crockett, and Crane counties; W to AZ; N Mex. S to Dgo. and Zac.

A treatment for indigestion and other ailments is obtained from a decoction of the leaves and heads. Tarbush dominates many valuable acres of potential rangeland but the plants are not palatable to livestock.

2. HYMENOCLEA T. & G. *ex* GRAY

Shrub to 2 m high, branches dense, ascending, broomlike. Leaves alternate usually threadlike, less often linear. Heads numerous, in clusters, ca. 5 mm high, male and female heads in same cluster, male heads most numerous;

Fig. 372. *Hymenoclea monogyra* (Burrobrush)

male heads with 5–10 flowers; phyllaries papery; corollas whitish, tubular, 5-toothed; female heads with 1 flower; involucre whitish, papery, 9–12 spreading outer phyllaries, 2 mm long, forming a saucershaped structure, inner phyllaries united in middle of "saucer," forming a corollalike structure, the 1 female flower of only an ovary and style located inside the tubular-conic structure and basal cup, style tips extending from the cone. Achene falling as a unit with the airborne female head; pappus absent.

A genus of about four species distributed in western America. Only one species occurs in Texas.

1. Hymenoclea monogyra T. & G. *ex* Gray. BURROBRUSH. Fig. 372. Locally common, dry washes and streams of the desert and lower mountains. Culberson Co., Delaware Creek; near Van Horn. Presidio Co., Sierra Vieja. Jeff Davis Co., lower Davis Mts.; Haystack Mt. Brewster Co., vicinity of Alpine S to the lower Chisos Mts. and Rio Grande. Terrell Co., mouth of San Francisco Creek; Independence Creek. 2000–5700 ft.; Sep–Oct. W through NM, AZ, to S CA; Baja CA, Son., Chih., Mex.

Burrobrush is easily recognized by its upright branches, threadlike leaves, male and female heads. This plant is not often collected and thus is perhaps more widely distributed in the Trans-Pecos than indicated. Burrobrush is not usually browsed by livestock. The genus name was taken after the membrane-like phyllaries and the specific epithet refers to the solitary female flowers.

3. PARTHENIUM L.

Shrubs or herbs, usually aromatic and bitter. Leaves alternate, entire to deeply lobed. Heads small, solitary or in clusters; ligules inconspicuous; phyllaries green, broad, inner ones subtending ray achenes; receptacle chaffy; ray flowers 5, pistillate and fertile, white corollas and styles persistent; disc flowers infertile, of normal structure, corollas whitish; central disc florets separating and falling as a unit, the peripheral 10 florets remaining with the ray florets. Achenes of ray florets flattened, round in outline, the margins thickened and attached to the contiguous pair of disc flowers and the subtending phyllary, these separating together at maturity; pappus of 2–3 awns, 2 scales, or absent.

A genus of about 16 species, distributed in the Americas. One species, *Parthenium argentatum* (Guayule), is noted for its production of high quality rubber. Various biological aspects of Guayule are presently under extensive study.

KEY TO THE SPECIES

1. Leaves pinnate-lobed, grayish-pubescent, the hairs long and simple; heads clustered on relatively short peduncles at ends of branches   **1. *P. incanum.***
1. Leaves spatulate to narrowly oblanceolate, entire to toothed, silvery-pubescent, the hairs with flattened, shieldshaped segments on stalks; heads tightly clustered at tips of relatively long, naked peduncles, usually 10–20 cm long, arising from below ends of branches   **2. *P. argentatum.***

1. **Parthenium incanum** Kunth. MARIOLA. Fig. 373. Common throughout the Trans-Pecos, various soil types, especially in desert areas but extending into arid mountains. El Paso Co. to Val Verde Co. 2200–6500 ft.; summer–fall. E to Plains Country, Edwards Plateau, SE to the Rio Grande Plains; W to AZ; to Jal., Mich., and D.F., Mex.

The distribution of Mariola is much more extensive than that of Guayule and it can be found at most sites where Guayule is found. Reportedly the two species form hybrid swarms throughout much of their ranges. Mariola produces only 2–3% rubber and so this hybridization is thought to reduce the rubber-producing capacity of Guayule (8–20% in "pure" stands).

2. **Parthenium argentatum** Gray. GUAYULE. Fig. 374. Locally common, usually in rather stable, rocky limestone habitats in the desert, reported at one locality in igneous soil. Presidio Co., Chinati Mts., 3–5 mi W Shafter; Bandera Mesa, South Canyon, north rim. Brewster Co., 20 mi NE Alpine; Glass Mts., W slopes Baldy Peak; 02 Ranch; near Buckhill Mt.; 51 mi S Alpine; 65 mi S Alpine; Packsaddle Mt.; Dead Horse Mts., head of Heath Canyon, Big Brushy Canyon; Pope Ranch; Bailey Ranch; Julian Tank (igneous soil), 101 Ranch.

Fig. 373. *Parthenium incanum* (Mariola)   Fig. 374. *Parthenium argentatum* (Guayule)

Pecos Co., Seven-Mile Mesa; University Mesa; 25 mi E Ft. Stockton; E and NE slopes and canyons of Sierra Madera. 2600–4500 ft.; flowering spring, summer, or fall after rains. Chih., Coah., N.L., Dgo., Zac., Hgo., and S.L.P., Mex. Guayule is a strong shrub usually less than 1 m high. The rubber produced by these plants is of high quality, approaching or equaling that of the tropical rubber tree *Hevea*. The rubber is produced in tissues of the stems and roots, and unfortunately must be extracted by complex mechanical and chemical processes after grinding the plants.

Most of the natural stands of Guayule are in Mexico, with the species entering the United States only in Trans-Pecos Texas. Commercial production of Guayule rubber is being reinvestigated at a plant near Saltillo, Mexico and by various groups in the United States. The first commercial efforts began in Zacatecas, Mexico in 1892 (Vines, 1960). Guayule rubber could not compete with *Hevea* rubber and commercial exploitation of *Parthenium argentatum* was suspended until East Indian rubber supplies were threatened during World War II. At this time Guayule was cultivated extensively in southern California and to some extent in Arizona, but the fields were destroyed when *Hevea brasiliensis* (Willd.) Muell.-Arg. rubber supplies were once again abundant. The prospect of commercially significant production of Guayule was revived in Mexico during the mid 1960's, and this effort has caught the attention of businesspersons and biologists interested in developing arid land resources.

4. ZINNIA L.   ZINNIA

Low shrublets, ca. 10–20 cm high; taproots woody; much-branched from the base. Leaves opposite, linear, entire, sessile, the bases partially fused. Heads terminal on short peduncles; involucre nearly cylindric to slightly expanded above; phyllaries strongly graduated and overlapping, the apexes rounded and minutely irregular-toothed; ray flowers pistillate and fertile, ligules yellow, or white, persistent on achenes; disc flowers perfect; fertile, corollas yellow, red, to white, 5-toothed, 1 tooth longer than others; style branches velvety. Achenes (of disc) flattened or angular, glabrous or hairy; pappus of awns. [*Diplothrix* DC.].

A genus of 17 species, distributed in the Americas. Three species occur in Texas and in the Trans-Pecos.

KEY TO THE SPECIES

1. Rays white; leaves needlelike to linear, bases with 1 nerve   **1. Z. acerosa.**
1. Rays yellow; leaves linear to lanceolate, basal halves with 3 nerves.
   2. Ligules of ray florets to 1.8 cm long, heads 5–8 mm long
                                                                 2. Z. grandiflora.
   2. Ligules to 0.6 cm long or shorter, or rays absent; heads 8–10 mm long
                                                                 3. Z. anomala.

1. Zinnia acerosa (DC.) Gray.   SPINYLEAF ZINNIA.   Fig. 375.   Mostly limestone habitats, desert flats, grasslands, and slopes. El Paso Co., Franklin Mts. Hudspeth Co., Eagle Mts. Culberson Co., 2–10 mi W Kent; Van Horn Mts. Presidio Co., Sierra Vieja; 20 mi S Marfa. Reeves Co., 18 mi E Balmorhea. Brewster Co., Glass Mts., vicinity of Marathon, 35 mi S Alpine S to Dead Horse Mts.; Julian Tank, 101 Ranch. Pecos Co., vicinity of Ft. Stockton to 30 mi E. Terrell Co., near Dryden; 30 mi N Sanderson. 2500–5200 ft.; summer–fall. NE to Loving and Crane counties; W to AZ; Son., Chih., Coah., N.L., Mex.

Along with its white rays, this species is characterized by its needlelike leaves, an attribute from which the genus name *Zinnia* is derived.

2. Zinnia grandiflora Nutt.   PLAINS ZINNIA.   Fig. 376.   Widespread and abundant, various soil types including limestone, igneous, and sand. El Paso Co. to Pecos Co. 2600–6000 ft.; summer–fall. NE to Plains Country; N to KS and CO, W to AZ; Chih., Coah., Dgo., Zac., Mex.

This species is most easily distinguished by its showy yellow ligules.

3. Zinnia anomala Gray.   SHORTRAY ZINNIA.   Fig. 377.   Localized and infrequent to rare, usually in limestone habitats, less often in disturbed habitats. Brewster Co., flats near Leonard Mt.; 2–6 mi, 15–16 mi N Marathon; Pena Colorado, 5 mi S Marathon. Pecos Co., 30 mi E of Ft. Stockton; 45 mi

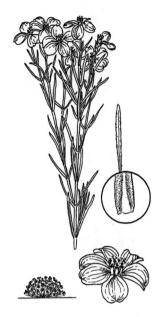

Fig. 375. *Zinnia acerosa* (Spinyleaf Zinnia)   Fig. 376. *Zinnia grandiflora* (Plains Zinnia)

S of Ft. Stockton; 20 mi W Sanderson. Terrell Co., 2–10 mi N Sanderson. 2800–4400 ft.; summer–fall. Rare E in the Edwards Plateau; Coah., N.L., Zac., Mex.

This species is easily distinguished from the other Trans-Pecos zinnias by its larger heads, short (or absent) ligules that are usually dull orange-yellow, and striking rich orange corollas.

5. THELESPERMA LESS. GREENTHREAD

Herbaceous annuals, perennials, or subshrubs, mostly glabrous. Leaves opposite pinnatifid or simple, the segments threadlike, linear, or narrowly oblanceolate. Heads usually solitary on naked peduncles; phyllaries of two sizes, the outer herbaceous, linear, spreading or appressed, often with membranous margins, the inner phyllaries longer, membranous, basally fused; ray florets present or absent, ligules yellow, often with red or brown pigments; disc flowers perfect, fertile, corollas yellow, veins red-brown, 5-lobed, the lobes equal or one longer. Achenes linear-oblong, somewhat cylindrical, curved, and flattened, warty or smooth, usually enclosed by a subtending pale; pappus of 2–3 awns, or absent.

A genus of about 12 species, distributed in warmer parts of the Americas. Nine species occur in Texas, five of which are represented in the Trans-Pecos.

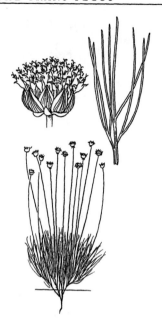

Fig. 377. *Zinnia anomala* (Shortray Zinnia)

Fig. 378. *Thelesperma longipes*
(Longstalk Greenthread)

1. Thelesperma longipes Gray. LONGSTALK GREENTHREAD. Fig. 378. Plants scattered but rather abundant in certain areas, often in calcareous soils and rocky habitats, less often in igneous soil or clay. El Paso Co., Franklin Mts. Culberson Co., Guadalupe Mts.; Apache Mts. Presidio Co., Chinati Mts.; near Casa Piedra; Solitario; Bofecillos Mts., Arroyo Segundo. Brewster Co., Sul Ross Hill in Alpine; Cathedral Mt.; Cienega Mt.; Dead Horse Mts., Heath Canyon; near Lajitas. Reeves Co. Terrell Co., vicinity of Dryden and Sanderson; Lower Canyons of the Rio Grande. 2150–6500 ft.; summer–fall; W Edwards Plateau, Plains Country; W to AZ; S to S.L.P., Mex.

Thelesperma longipes is mostly an herbaceous perennial with woody basal stems and caudex. The leaves are primarily basal and very slender, and the yellow, discoid heads are extended on rather long, naked peduncles, the latter trait accounting for the specific epithet. In Mexico the plants are boiled to make a tea.

6. PERICOME GRAY

Subshrubs or herbaceous perennials, stems spreading 1 m or more long, minutely hairy. Leaves mostly opposite, sticky, bitter-tasting, minutely hairy,

Fig. 379. *Pericome caudata* (Tailleaf Pericome)

dot-glandular, 5–16 cm long, basically triangular, apexes long-attenuated, tail-like, margins lobed or toothed. Heads clustered; phyllaries in one series, fused at least halfway, minutely pubescent; ray flowers absent; disc flowers perfect, fertile; corollas yellow, 3–10 mm long, 4-lobed. Achenes black, 3.5–5 mm long, flattened, slender, margins hairy; pappus a crown of scales, ca. 1 mm long, bristles 1–2, 1–4.5 mm long, or bristles absent.

A genus of two species of the southwestern United States and northern Mexico south to Durango. One species occurs in Texas.

1. Pericome caudata Gray. TAILLEAF PERICOME. Fig. 379. [*Pericome glandulosa* Goodman; *P. caudata* var. *glandulosa* (Goodman) Harrington]. Among rocks or boulders, talus slopes, sides of protected canyons, also in sand or gravel, often in disturbed sites at roadside. Presidio Co., NE side Chinati Peak. Jeff Davis Co., Sawtooth Mt.; Madera Canyon, Mt. Livermore; roadside NW Sawtooth Mt. Brewster Co., Chisos Mts., upper Green Gulch. 4300–7000 ft. OK panhandle, CO, NM, AZ, NV, S CA; Chih., Mex.

In the Trans-Pecos these plants may spread to 2 m wide and are most commonly found on talus slopes. In the western states *Pericome caudata* may be found up to 9000 ft. in elevation. The species name was taken after the taillike leaf apexes.

7. PERITYLE BENTH. ROCKDAISY

Subshrubs or herbs, most species growing in rock crevices. Leaves opposite or alternate, glabrous to white-hairy, sticky, bitter-tasting, variable in shape and size. Heads solitary or in clusters, on very short or relatively long peduncles; phyllaries in 2 equal or subequal series; ray flowers present or absent, pistillate and fertile; ligules yellow or white; disc flowers perfect, fertile; corollas yellow or white, sometimes purple-tinged, 4-lobed. Achenes black, usually flattened, with prominent or weak callous margins, the margins with few hairs, or densely hairy; pappus absent or of 1, 2, or numerous (10–30) bristles, or of a short crown of scales with 1–2 (rarely 0) bristles. [*Closia* Remy; *Laphamia* Gray; *Monothrix* Torr.; *Galinsogeopsis* Sch. Bip.; *Nesothamnus* Rydb.; *Leptopharynx* Rydb.; *Pappothrix* (Gray) Rydb.].

A genus of about 55 species, distributed in the southwestern United States and Mexico. Fifteen species occur in Texas, 14 of these in the Trans-Pecos. These plants are remarkable in that most species grow only in crevices of bare rock bluffs and boulders. The plants are low, often flattened, miniature shrubs, with woody bases and short, woody stems. A few species are herbaceous. Two Trans-Pecos species occur in soil substrates. Three sections of the genus are recognized (Powell, 1969; 1973; 1974). Probably the genus *Perityle* (and all of subtribe Peritylinae) belongs in the tribe Helenieae Benth. (Bremer, 1994).

KEY TO THE SECTIONS

1. Pappus of (2–7–) 10–35 bristles; achenes subcylindric to partially flattened, margins short-hairy   A. Sect. *Pappothrix.*
1. Pappus of 0–2 (–3–6) bristles; achenes flattened, margins short-hairy or profusely hairy.
    2. Pappus of bristles only (rarely none) or with very small, vestigial scales; achene margins sparsely short-hairy   B. Sect. *Laphamia.*
    2. Pappus of bristles (rarely none) and a crown of scales; achene margins profusely hairy   C. Sect. *Perityle.*

A. SECTION PAPPOTHRIX Gray

A group of six species, all of them distributed in the Trans-Pecos except for *Perityle cernua* (Greene) Shinners, a large-headed species with about 150 florets per head, endemic to the Organ Mts., Doña Ana Co., New Mexico. All species of this group have discoid heads (rays absent).

KEY TO THE SPECIES

1. Flowers usually 5–6; leaves somewhat lustrous, olive-green, thick, usually somewhat kidneyshaped, glabrous to sparsely short-pubescent
                                                                    1. *P. quinqueflora.*

Fig. 380. *Perityle quinqueflora*
(Fiveflower Rockdaisy)

1. Flowers usually 8–16; leaves lighter green, rather thin, variously ovate, triangular, or heartshaped, notably pubescent.
  2. Corollas yellow or white; pappus of 20–30 well-developed bristles.
    3. Leaves basically 3-parted, or deeply 3-lobed; Apache Mts. **2. *P. fosteri.***
    3. Leaves basically ovate or triangular in outline, the margins prominently toothed but not 3-parted; Davis Mts. S to Chisos Mts. **3. *P. rupestris.***
  2. Corollas white; pappus reduced or well-developed.
    4. Pappus reduced to 2–3(6) main bristles, less often 10–20, including vestigial nubs; leaves with soft, straight hairs; Glass Mts.
                                               4. *P. vitreomontana.*
    4. Pappus of 14–20 well-developed bristles; leaves covered with matted, white hairs (tomentose); Pecos, Upton, S Brewster counties
                                                    5. *P. cinerea.*

  1. **Perityle quinqueflora** (Steyerm.) Shinners. FIVEFLOWER ROCKDAISY. Fig. 380. [*Laphamia quinqueflora* Steyerm.; *Pappothrix quinqueflora* (Steyerm.) Everly]. Crevices of limestone bluffs (rarely igneous in the Sierra Vieja and Eagle Mts.), high canyons and caprock. Hudspeth Co., Quitman Mts., Quitman Canyon; Sierra Diablo, Victorio Canyon and elsewhere; Eagle Mts., old Love Ranch. Culberson Co., Guadalupe Mts., McKittrick Canyon and else-

where; Beach Mts.; Jeff Davis Co., San Carlos Tunnel. Presidio Co., Sierra Vieja, Bracks Canyon and elsewhere. 4000–7500 ft.; spring–fall. NM, Eddy Co., Guadalupe Mts.; near Carlsbad Caverns; Dark Canyon.

A discussion of this species and its relationship to *Perityle rupestris* can be found in Powell (1969).

2. Perityle fosteri Powell.   FOSTER ROCKDAISY.   Known only from Panther Canyon, Apache Mts., Culberson Co., ca. 4500–5000 ft.; bluffs of the canyon walls, near the floor to near the top.

This species is closely related to *Perityle rupestris* but differs significantly in its triparted, lobed leaves.

3. Perityle rupestris (Gray) Shinners.   LEAFY ROCKDAISY.   [*Laphamia rupestris* Gray; *Pappothrix rupestris* (Gray) Rydb.]. Two varieties of this species are recognized.

3a. Perityle rupestris var. **rupestris.**   Common in crevices of igneous bluffs and boulders, from about 10 mi N of Alpine throughout the Davis Mts. of Jeff Davis Co.; possibly N Presidio Co. also; endemic. 4400–7000 ft.; spring–fall.

This plant is variable in leaf shape, pubescence, head size, and chromosome number, but the taxon is easily identified by its yellow flowers.

3b. Perityle rupestris var. **albiflora** Powell.   Common in crevices of igneous and limestone bluffs and boulders, from about 10 mi N of Alpine S throughout Brewster Co. to the Chisos Mts. Jeff Davis Co., extreme S portion. Presidio Co., extreme E portion. This plant is easily distinguished by its white disc flowers. Like var. *rupestris,* the var. *albiflora* is variable in vegetative and floral traits and in chromosome number.

4. Perityle vitreomontana Warnock.   GLASSMOUNTAIN ROCKDAISY. Known only from the Glass Mts., Brewster Co., N and NW sides, and limestone walls of the major canyons; about 4400–6000 ft.; spring–fall.

This plant is related to *Perityle rupestris* var. *albiflora* and is characterized by its reduced pappus of 2–3 main bristles.

5. Perityle cinerea (Gray) Powell.   GRAYLEAF ROCKDAISY.   [*Laphamia cinerea* Gray; *Pappothrix cinerea* (Gray) Rydb.]. Crevices of Cretaceous limestone caprock of mesas. Pecos Co., Seven-Mile Mesa near Fort Stockton; 6 mi E Bakersfield; near Escondido Creek, 30 mi E Fort Stockton. Upton Co., 10 mi S Rankin. Brewster Co. reported from Bullis Gap range, near the Rio Grande.

This species is easily recognized by its gray (tomentose-canescent) leaves. Protected individuals of this species may reach nearly 0.5 m high as rather sturdy shrubs.

B. SECTION LAPHAMIA (Gray) Powell

A group of 23 species ranging from western Texas throughout the southwestern United States to southern California and northern Mexico. Six species occur in Texas, all but one of these in the Trans-Pecos.

KEY TO THE SPECIES

1. Flowers white; plants 2–12 cm high; pappus absent or typically of 2 rather flattened bristles.
    2. Pappus absent; leaves rough-pubescent   **1. *P. warnockii.***
    2. Pappus usually of 2 bristles; leaves essentially glabrous except in var. scalaris   **2. *P. bisetosa.***
1. Flowers yellow; plants usually more than 12 cm high; pappus absent or of 1–3 (–6) rounded bristles.
    3. Heads with ray flowers.
        4. Leaves broadly ovate to broadly lanceolate, blades 2–5 cm long; heads usually tightly clustered; Edwards Plateau   **3. *P. lindheimeri.***
        4. Leaves ovate to triangular in outline, prominently toothed, blades less than 2 cm long; heads solitary or loosely clustered; Hueco Mts.   **4. *P. huecoensis.***
    3. Heads without ray flowers.
        5. Leaves irregularly dissected, relatively long-pubescent; pappus of 1, rarely 0–4, bristles to 3 mm long   **6. *P. dissecta.***
        5. Leaves linear to lanceolate, 3–5-toothed or lobed, essentially glabrous; pappus usually absent, rarely with 1–2 bristles to 2 mm long, and perhaps a vestigiate crown of scales   **5. *P. angustifolia.***

1. Perityle warnockii Powell. WARNOCK ROCKDAISY. Known only from Val Verde Co., NW part of county, 1 mi E of Pecos River, crevices and small pockets of solid Cretaceous limestone exposures. Flowering in the fall. This species is related to *Perityle bisetosa* but is easily distinguished by the key characters listed above.

2. Perityle bisetosa (Torr. *ex* Gray) Shinners. TWOBRISTLE ROCKDAISY. [*Laphamia bisetosa* Torr. *ex* Gray]. Four varieties of this species are recognized (Powell, 1969), each of them geographically isolated and differing in relatively minor traits. Three of the varieties occur in Trans-Pecos Texas and one of them, var. *spathulata* Powell, in Coah., Mexico.

2a. Perityle bisetosa var. **bisetosa.** Crevices and pockets of limestone exposures. Brewster Co., Cox Ranch, near Longfellow, McRae Canyon, and 7.1 mi SW of Hwy. 90; spring–fall. This plant is delimited by its sessile or nearly sessile leaves, usually opposite, essentially glabrous, with margins entire to minutely toothed.

2b. Perityle bisetosa var. **scalaris** Powell.   Known only from Brewster Co., Black Gap Game Preserve, Cave Hill, along E side of Stairstep Mt., ca. 4 mi S of headquarters, crevices of lower limestone bluffs; and bluffs along Big Brushy Canyon above Black Gap boundary; spring–fall. The plant is recognized by its rough-pubescent leaves that are distinctly petiolate and alternate with toothed margins.

2c. Perityle bisetosa var. **appressa** Powell.   Limestone caprock, small peak of N rim of San Francisco Creek Canyon, Brewster Co.; also reported from bluffs along the Lower Canyons of the Rio Grande; spring–fall. Coah., Mex., Colorado Canyon, Serranias del Burro. This plant is distinguished by its essentially glabrous (ovate) leaves that are petioled and alternate with toothed margins.

3. Perityle lindheimeri (Gray) Shinners.   LINDHEIMER ROCKDAISY.   Two varieties of this species are recognized (Powell, 1973).

3a. Perityle lindheimeri var. **lindheimeri.**   [*Laphamia lindheimeri* Gray; *L. rotundata* Rydb.]. Common in crevices of Cretaceous limestone exposures, particularly beside streams and springs in canyons of the Edwards Plateau; spring–fall. This plant is delimited by its distribution and one pappus bristle.

3b. Perityle lindheimeri var. **halimifolia** (Gray) Powell.   DWARF ROCK-DAISY.   [*Laphamia halimifolia* Gray; *Perityle halimifolia* (Gray) Shinners]. Rare on Cretaceous limestone exposures in SW Val Verde Co., 8–12 mi S Loma Alta; Fawcett Lodge, Devils River; spring. This variety, of doubtful distinction from var. *lindheimeri*, is delimited mainly by its restricted distribution and usually the pappus bristle absent, or at least reduced.

4. Perityle huecoensis Powell.   HUECOMOUNTAIN ROCKDAISY.   Known only from the Southern Hueco Mountains, Hudspeth Co. Navar Ranch, vicinity of a fossil packrat midden. The species appears related to *Perityle staurophylla* (Barneby) Shinners of S-cen. NM. The leaves of *P. huecoensis* are eggshaped or somewhat triangular in outline and prominently toothed, while the leaves of *P. staurophylla* are in the shape of a cross.

5. Perityle angustifolia (Gray) Shinners.   RAYLESS ROCKDAISY.   Fig. 381. [*Laphamia angustifolia* Gray; *L. angustifolia* var. *laciniata* Torr.; *L. laciniata* (Torr.) Rydb.]. Common in crevices of Cretaceous limestone exposures, eroded W edge of the Edwards Plateau, along and near the Rio Grande from Devils River to near Sanderson. Pecos, Terrell, Crockett, Val Verde counties; spring–fall.

Perityle angustifolia is closely related to *P. lindheimeri*. Its distinguishing features include narrow leaf shape, discoid heads, and epappose achenes.

6. Perityle dissecta (Torr.) Gray.   SLIMLOBE ROCKDAISY.   Fig. 382.   [*Laphamia dissecta* Torr.; *Leptopharynx dissecta* (Torr.) Rydb.]. Locally common

Fig. 381. *Perityle angustifolia*   Fig. 382. A) *Perityle dissecta* (Slimlobe
(Rayless Rockdaisy)   Rockdaisy); B) *P. aglossa* (Rayless Perityle)

on limestone walls of canyons in desertic mountain areas. Brewster Co., Santa Elena Canyon, Presidio Co., 5 mi W Shafter, near old Ross Mine; Santa Cruz Mt., near Presidio. Spring–fall. Chih., Mex.

This is the only Rockdaisy of the Trans-Pecos with finely dissected, pilose leaves. The species is related to *Perityle castillonii* of adjacent Coahuila and Chihuahua, Mexico and *P. lemmoni* of southeastern Arizona.

C. SECTION PERITYLE Benth.

A group of 27 species distributed mainly in northwestern Mexico and Baja California, with species also in the southwestern United States. One species occurs in Chile and Peru of South America. Four species occur in Texas, three of these in the Trans-Pecos.

KEY TO THE SPECIES

1. Ray flowers present, yellow.
  2. Leaves typically palmately divided into 3 lobes or subcruciform (cross-shaped); taprooted perennials, herbaceous or subshrubby, in soil

  1. P. vaseyi.

  2. Leaves typically 3-lobed but not deeply so, heartshaped to nearly kidney-

shaped in outline; woody-based subshrubs in rock crevices or taprooted
in soil   **2. P. parryi.**
1. Ray flowers absent; disc flowers yellow   **3. P. aglossa.**

1. Perityle vaseyi Coult. MARGINED PERITYLE. Common in desert soils, especially gypsiferous clay and disturbed roadside, SW Trans-Pecos and adjacent Mex. Brewster Co., Big Bend Park near Hot Springs to near Castolon, Terlingua, and Lajitas; Packsaddle Mt.; flowering essentially year-round. Chih., Coah., Mex.

Perityle vaseyi, typically a soil-dwelling herbaceous perennial, less often suffruticose, is closely related to *P. parryi,* typically a rock-dwelling subshrub that occasionally occurs in the soil as herbaceous or suffruticose perennial. *Perityle vaseyi* usually can be distinguished by its soil-dwelling habit, deeply trisected leaves, and shorter pappus bristles with retrorse barbs at the tips (Powell, 1974).

2. Perityle parryi Gray. HEARTLEAF PERITYLE. [*Laphamia parryi* (Gray) Benth.; *Leptopharynx trisecta* Rydb.]. Common in rock crevices and among rocks, less frequent in gravel soils, W Trans-Pecos and adjacent Mex. Brewster Co., Chisos Mts. and vicinity, including Santa Elena Canyon, N to Rosillos Mts.; 02 Ranch. Presidio Co., Sierra Vieja, S to near Lajitas, common 12–14 mi S Redford. Flowering essentially year around; Chih., Mex.

In addition to traits already listed, *Perityle parryi* is delimited from *P. vaseyi* by long-tapering pappus bristles (one per achene) that are antrorsely barbed, and disc corollas with narrowly tubular throats (Powell, 1974).

3. Perityle aglossa Gray. RAYLESS PERITYLE. Fig. 382. [*Laphamia aglossa* (Gray) Benth.; *Leptopharynx aglossa* (Gray) Rydb.]. Locally infrequent, crevices of limestone boulders and bluffs, often in canyons along and near the Rio Grande. Brewster Co., mouth of Reagan Canyon; Heath Canyon, Black Gap; near Big Bend tunnel; 4 mi W Hot Springs; San Vicente Canyon. Terrell Co., Lower Canyons of the Rio Grande; mouth of San Francisco Canyon; 9 mi E Sanderson.

This species is most closely related to *Perityle parryi,* but is delimited by its discoid, yellow-flowered heads, and pink- or purple-tinged corollas.

8. JEFEA STROTHER

Small shrubs. Leaves usually opposite, entire or few-toothed, sessile or with peduncles; involucre hemispheric or bellshaped; phyllaries herbaceous, in 3–4 series, graduate; ray flowers usually (5–)11–13, fertile, ligules yellow to orange; disc flowers perfect, fertile, corollas yellow or orange. Achenes (disc) somewhat flattened, oblong or obovate, the flattened edges with corky wings; pappus of 2–3 unequal awns and several somewhat fused scales.

A genus of about five species, distributed from southern New Mexico south

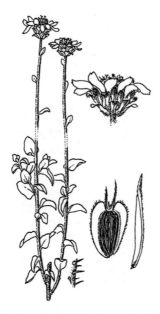

Fig. 383. *Jefea brevifolia* (Shorthorn Jefea)

through Mexico into Guatemala. One species occurs in Texas. *Jefea* is of Spanish derivation and is meant to honor Prof. B. L. Turner as acknowledged by his students (Strother, 1991). *Jefea* may be related to *Verbesina*.

1. **Jefea brevifolia** (Gray) Strother. SHORTHORN JEFEA. Fig. 383. [*Zexmenia brevifolia* Gray]. Various habitats in desertic areas, usually in limestone but also present in other substrates, often among desert scrub. Hudspeth Co., Eagle Mts., W slopes; Sierra Diablo, Victorio Canyon. Culberson Co., Apache Mts. Presidio Co., vicinity of Shafter; Chinati Mts., Pinto Canyon; 1 mi W of Presidio. Brewster Co., from Marathon and 02 Ranch south to the Rio Grande, common in Chisos Mts., Dead Horse Mts., Pecos Co., Sierra Madera. Terrell Co., 5–10 mi E Dryden. 1800–5700 ft.; summer–fall. S NM; Chih., Coah., Dgo., N.L., S.L.P., Tam., Zac., Mex.

Plants of this species are low, rounded shrubs usually about 0.5 m high but to 1 m high. The plant is quickly recognized by its smallish ovate leaves that are covered with short, stiff hairs and very rough to the touch. The species was long known in Texas as *Zexmenia brevifolia* (Shorthorn Zexmenia).

9. WEDELIA JAC.

Shrubs 2–5(-10) dm high, branching mostly at the base. Leaves opposite, rhombic-lanceolate or ovate-lanceolate, margins toothed, both surfaces scab-

Fig. 384. *Wedelia acapulcensis* var. *hispida*
(Orange Wedelia)

rous to hispid. Heads usually solitary; involucre cylindric-campanulate, 5–12 mm high, larger in fruit; phyllaries 12–16, subequal, the outer ones lanceolate, subfoliaceous; ray florets 5–8, corollas yellow to orange. Achenes (peripheral) narrowly cuneate, 4–5 mm long, 3-angled, 2–3-winged, glabrous, inner achenes slightly longer, 2-winged, hispid; pappus borne on a neck 0.3–0.5 mm high, pappus a crown of scales 0.5–1 mm high, plus 0–3 unequal awns to 4 mm long.

Wedelia is a genus of about 20 species distributed mostly from central Texas throughout most of Mexico and Central America. One species occurs in Texas.

1. **Wedelia acapulcensis** Kunth var. **hispida** (Kunth) Strother. ORANGE WEDELIA. Fig. 384. [*Zexmenia hispida* (Kunth) Gray *ex* Small]. Common in limestone habitats in the E Trans-Pecos. Terrell Co., near Sanderson and Dryden; 25 mi SW Sheffield; Independence Creek; mouth of San Francisco Creek. Val Verde Co., Pumpville turnoff; 1 mi W of the Pecos River; near Devils River. 1500–2800 ft.; summer–fall. Common on Edwards Plateau, S to Rio Grande Plains, into SE and cen. TX; NE Mex., to Ver., Hgo., Mich., Mex.

This species was long known in Texas as *Zexmenia hispida* (Orange Zexmenia). *Zexmenia*, according to Strother (1991), does not occur in Texas, but is a genus of two species in southern Mexico and Central America. The broadly lanceolate leaves of *Wedelia acapulcensis* var. *hispida* are rough pubescent as

Fig. 385. *Encelia scaposa* (Onehead Encelia)

indicated by the specific epithet. Swellings found near the bases of the achenes contain oils and supposedly are functional in the dispersal of fruits by ants (Strother, 1991).

10. ENCELIA ADANS.

Herbaceous perennial (in our species) with a strong woody rootstock. Leaves crowded at the base, the blades narrow, sublinear, 3–10 cm long, 0.1– 0.8 cm wide. Heads solitary on long, naked peduncles; involucre broadly hemispheric; phyllaries in 2–3 series, linear; ray flowers 20–40, pistillate and sterile; ligules yellow, ca. 1.5 cm long; disc flowers perfect, fertile, corollas yellow, 5-toothed. Achenes flattened, edges sharp and very hairy; pappus of 2 hairs or awns, easily falling from achene shoulders and often absent from mature achenes.

A genus of about 15 species, mostly in the western Americas. One species occurs in Texas.

1. Encelia scaposa (Gray) Gray. ONEHEAD ENCELIA. Fig. 385. [*Encelia scaposa* var. *stenophylla* Shinners]. Restricted and spotty distribution but locally abundant at known localities during "good years," mostly rocky limestone hills in the desert. Hudspeth Co., Eagle Mts., Panther Peak; W slopes, Quitman Mts., 3 mi NE of Indian Hot Springs. Presidio Co., from Shafter to

Fig. 386. *Viguiera stenoloba*
(Skeletonleaf Goldeneye)

1–3 mi S. Terrell Co. 3500–5000 ft.; spring–summer–fall. NM; Chih., Mex. This somewhat rare species is best recognized by its scapose habit and heads with showy figures. The species may correctly belong with *Enceliopsis* (Gray) A. Nels.

11. VIGUIERA KUNTH   GOLDENEYE

Herbs or shrubs. Leaves usually opposite at least below, sessile or with short petioles. Heads solitary; involucres hemispheric or bellshaped; phyllaries in 2– 5 series, graduated or nearly equal, somewhat herbaceous especially the apexes; receptacle chaffy throughout, pales persistent around achenes; ray flowers pistillate and sterile, ligules yellow; disc flowers numerous, perfect, fertile; corolla yellow. Achenes (disc) somewhat flattened, with short, appressed hairs, without ribs or margins; pappus absent, or of 2 awns and several shorter scales, these free or fused. *Heliomeris* Nutt.; *Hymenostephium* Benth.].

A genus of about 200 species distributed in North and South America. Six species occur in Texas and all of these are represented in the Trans-Pecos.

1. **Viguiera stenoloba** Blake. SKELETONLEAF GOLDENEYE. Fig. 386. Widespread and abundant in various habitats throughout the Trans-Pecos. El Paso Co. to Val Verde Co. 2000–6200 ft.; summer. Also to W Edwards Plateau and Rio Grande Plains; NM; N Mex., S to Dgo.

This plant is a much-branched shrub that often exceeds 1 m high, and is one of the largest woody composites in the Trans-Pecos. The Trans-Pecos entity is *Viguiera stenoloba* var. **chihuahuensis** Butterwick (in edit.; Johnston, 1990). The plants are exceedingly attractive when in full bloom with numerous yellow-flowered heads against a dark green background of dense linear-lobed leaves, and might be considered for ornamental use. This species is lightly browsed by cattle and deer especially during stress periods.

TRIBE 5. TAGETEAE CASS.

Annual or perennial, herbs, subshrubs or shrubs. Leaves opposite or alternate, simple or pinnate, glabrous or hairy, usually bearing prominent glands or cavities with strong smelling essential oils. Heads solitary or in clusters; phyllaries separate or fused, in 1–2 series, usually bearing glands; receptacle naked or hairy; ray flowers present or absent, pistillate and fertile, ligules yellow to orange; disc flowers perfect, corollas yellow to orange, 5-lobed; style branches blunt or pointed. Achenes narrow, usually ribbed or lined, glabrous or hairy; pappus of scales, bristles, or awns, or absent.

A tribe of 16–18 genera and about 237 species of New World distribution, with a few species adventive in the Old World (Strother, 1977). The center of geographic diversity is in the highlands of Mexico. The Tageteae are a natural group related to and commonly treated as subtribe of the Heliantheae (Robinson, 1981). About six genera and 23 species occur in Texas, most of these in the Trans-Pecos. The plants of many species are used to make a medicinal tea. Bremer (1994) does not recognize the tribe Tageteae, instead placing most taxa (including *Thymophylla*, *Chrysactinia*, and *Porophyllum*) assigned there by earlier authors in the subtribe Pectidinae of the tribe Helenieae.

KEY TO THE SPECIES

1. Pappus of ca. 20 scales, each dissected into 3–5 bristles   **1. Thymophylla.**
1. Pappus of numerous distinct, slender bristles.
  2. Ray flowers present   **2. Chrysactinia.**
  2. Ray flowers absent   **3. Porophyllum.**

1. THYMOPHYLLA LAG.   DOGWEED, FETID MARIGOLD

Herbs or shrubs, strongly aromatic glabrous to densely hairy. Leaves (and phyllaries) dotted with orange or brown oil glands. Heads solitary or in clusters; involucre hemispheric to cylindric; phyllaries in 2 series, free or at least partially united; ray flowers present (in *Thymophylla acerosa*), pistillate, ligules yellow to orange; disc florets perfect and fertile, corollas yellow. Achenes various, broad and hairy to slender and glabrous; pappus of 5–22 scales, awned or dissected into several bristles.

Fig. 387. *Thymophylla acerosa*
(Prickleaf Dogweed)

A genus of about 11 species (Strother, 1986), distributed in the Americas, most common in the southwestern United States and northern Mexico. Nine species are found in Texas, with about six of these occurring in the Trans-Pecos.

1. Thymophylla acerosa (DC.) Strother.   PRICKLEAF DOGWEED.   Fig. 387.   [*Dyssodia acerosa* DC.]. Widespread and common in desert habitats throughout much of the Trans-Pecos. El Paso Co. to Loving Co. and Val Verde Co. 1900–6000 ft.; summer–fall E to cen. TX; W to UT and NV; S to Hgo. and Zac., Mex.

The genus name *Thymophylla* is after the Greek *thymos*, gland, and Greek *phyllon*, leaf, a reference to glands on the foliage, and *Dyssodia* is rooted in the Greek *dysodia*, which means "ill smell," a trait that applies to all members of the tribe Tageteae. The species name is taken after the needlelike leaves of *T. acerosa*.

2. CHRYSACTINIA GRAY

Shrub, low and spreading, 10–40 cm high, aromatic, essentially glabrous, densely leafy. Leaves opposite or alternate, linear, ca. 1 cm long, dark green, somewhat fleshy, oil glands minute. Heads numerous, solitary on naked pe-

Fig. 388. *Chrysactinia mexicana* (Damianita)

duncles rising above crowded leaves; phyllaries ca. 12 in one series, linear; ray flowers usually 12, pistillate and fertile, ligules bright yellow; disc flowers ca. 20–25, perfect and fertile, corollas yellow. Achenes slender, 3–4 mm long, black, ribbed, minutely hairy; pappus of numerous whitish, unequal bristles.

A genus of four species, mostly Mexican in distribution. One species occurs in Texas.

1. Chrysactinia mexicana Gray. DAMIANITA. Fig. 388. Mostly on rocky limestone outcrops of ridges, hills, and mountains, also on igneous substrates, widespread throughout most of the Trans-Pecos. El Paso Co., Franklin Mts. (rare). Hudspeth Co., Quitman Mts. to Val Verde Co., 3 mi E of Shumla. 1800–7000 ft.; spring–summer–fall. Also Edwards Plateau; NM; N Mex. S to Ver.

Plants of this low, spreading shrub are very attractive when in full bloom and are of potential ornamental value. The genus name, *Chrysactinia*, is taken after the golden-yellow flowers. Extracts from the plant are used medicinally to treat various ailments.

3. POROPHYLLUM ADANS. PORELEAF

Herbs, subshrubs, or shrubs, glabrous, aromatic. Leaves alternate or opposite, simple, often threadlike to linear, usually with oil glands. Heads discoid,

Fig. 389. *Porophyllum scoparium*
(Shrubby Poreleaf)

solitary or in small clusters; phyllaries 5–9, in one series, oil glands in 2 rows; disc flowers perfect, fertile, corolla yellow, whitish or purplish. Achenes slender, ribbed, minutely hairy; pappus of numerous free bristles, these with minute barbs or hairs.

A genus of about 30 species distributed in the Americas. In Mexico and other countries some species are used for medicinal purposes or eaten as greens. Four species occur in Texas, all of these in the Trans-Pecos.

KEY TO THE SPECIES

1. Erect, stiff, much-branched shrub or subshrub; flowers yellow; phyllaries 7–9   1. *P. scoparium.*
1. Weakly erect, little-branched shrub or subshrub; flowers white to purplish; phyllaries   2. *P. gracile.*

1. **Porophyllum scoparium** Gray. SHRUBBY PORELEAF. Fig. 389. Widespread and locally abundant in various desert habitats. El Paso Co. to Val Verde Co., mostly in S regions, often in dense stands, especially in desert foothills of the Chisos Mts., Brewster Co. 1800–5200 ft.; flowering throughout much of the year. NM; Chih., Coah., N.L., Mex.

The stiffly erect, broomlike stems of this species with few threadlike leaves

Fig. 390. *Porophyllum gracile*
(Slender Poreleaf)

bear some resemblance to *Ephedra*. The stems are at first green then become brown with age. In Mexico the plants are used medicinally for intestinal disorders, fever, and rheumatism.

2. Porophyllum gracile Benth. SLENDER PORELEAF. Fig. 390. [*Porophyllum junciforme* Greene]. Evidently a rare species of desertic slopes and grasslands. El Paso Co., Franklin Mts., E slopes N of McKelligan Canyon. 4800 ft.; summer–fall. NV, AZ, S CA; Baja CA, N Mex.

According to Johnson (1969) *Porophyllum gracile* is known to occur in Texas only in the Franklin Mountains. The threadlike leaves of these slender plants are used by natives of the southwest and Mexico to make a decoction for treating intestinal disorders.

TRIBE 6. ANTHEMIDEAE CASS.

Perennial or annual, herbs, subshrubs, or shrubs, foliage strongly scented. Leaves usually alternate, usually pinnate. Heads usually clustered; phyllaries in 1–4 overlapping series, wholly membranous or herbaceous with membranous margins and apex; receptacle naked, hairy, or scaly; ray flowers present or absent, if present in one or more rows, usually pistillate and fertile, ligules white, yellow, or reddish, often bicolored or multicolored; disc flowers usually perfect, 4–5-lobed, the lobes equal or unequal, corollas usually yellow, rarely red; style branches blunt and hairy at apexes, with marginal stigmatic lines. Achenes variable, cylindrical, angled, or flattened, ribbed or winged; pappus usually a scalelike rim or cap, or absent.

A tribe of 102 genera and about 1400 species, essentially palaearctic in distribution, but also centered in South Africa, Australia, and South America (Heywood and Humphries, 1977). Only four genera and about 11 species occur in Texas.

1. ARTEMISIA L. WORMWOOD, SAGEBRUSH

Herbs, subshrubs, or shrubs, usually aromatic, leaves and stems glabrous or short-woolly and gray, much branched, to 1 m high. Leaves alternate. Heads small, usually nodding and crowded in clusters; involucre 3–6 mm long; phyllaries in 3 series, 2 size classes, with broad membranous margins, often densely hairy; ray flowers present, 1 to few, pistillate, fertile or sterile; corolla yellowish-white, ca. 1 mm long, somewhat cylindrical, V-gapped on the inside; disc flowers 3–20, perfect, fertile or sterile, corollas very small, yellowish-white. Achenes brown, oblong to obovate in outline, ca. 1 mm long, weakly 10 ribbed; pappus absent.

A genus of several hundred species distributed in cool and dry regions of the world. The dominant "sagebrush" of the western United States is *Artemisia tridentata* Nutt., although several other species occur in the broad region. Seven species occur in Texas, all of these in the Trans-Pecos. Pollen from the sagebrush species is highly allergenic and is responsible for hayfever in many people. The plants are generally good browse for cattle and wildlife. The green alcoholic liquor, absinthe, is made from leaves of the common "wormwood," *A. absinthium* L. The cooking herb, tarragon, comes from *A. dracunculus* L.

KEY TO THE SPECIES

1. Leaves or their lobes threadlike   **1. A. filifolia.**
1. Leaves otherwise.
    2. Leaves 1.5–2.5 cm long, 0.2–0.4 cm wide, tips expanded, blunt, 3-toothed, the teeth 1–2 mm long   **2. A. bigelovii.**
    2. Leaves 1–6 cm long, 0.3–1 cm wide, entire or lobed, variable in shape but the main axis often lanceolate, upper surfaces often darker green than gray lower surfaces   **3. A. ludoviciana.**

1. Artemisia filifolia Torr. SAND SAGEBRUSH. Fig. 391. Locally common in areas of dunes and deep sand, less common in gypseous or calcareous soils. El Paso Co., between Ysleta and Hueco Tanks; Hueco Mts. Hudspeth Co.,

Fig. 391. *Artemisia filifolia* (Sand Sagebrush)   Fig. 392. *Artemisia bigelovii*
(Bigelow Sagebrush)

5 mi E of Hueco. Culberson Co., between Orla and Texline; 5 mi E Salt Flats. Loving Co., 3 mi W Mentone. Ward Co., near Monahans. Winkler Co., near Kermit. 2500–5000 ft.; spring–fall. Also Crane and Andrews counties; Plains Country; to NE, WY, AZ, NV; Chih., Mex.

This species with woody basal stems is most commonly found in deep sandy soils and can be recognized by its threadlike (filiform) leaves. A decoction of the leaves has been used to treat stomach disorders and intestinal worms.

2. **Artemisia bigelovii** Gray. BIGELOW SAGEBRUSH. Fig. 392. Reported to be rare in the Trans-Pecos and Plains Country (near the Canadian River); Sep–Oct. NM, AZ, CO, UT.

This species, a true shrub to 0.5 m high, is very closely related to the more northwestern Big Sagebrush, *Artemisia tridentata*, differing mainly in the presence of one or two ray flowers per head in Bigelow Sagebrush. The plant could be valuable for browse if it were more abundant.

3. **Artemisia ludoviciana** Nutt. LOUISIANA SAGEWORT, WESTERN MUG-WORT, WHITE SAGE. Fig. 393. [*Artemisia mexicana* Willd. *ex* Spreng.; *A. gnaphalodes* Nutt.; *A. vulgaris* var. *americana* Bess.; *A. redolens* Gray; *A. albula* Woot.]. The most widespread species of *Artemisia* in the Trans-Pecos; to be expected from 4000–8100 ft. in all of the major mountains or ranges in the region, also locally common at 2500–4000 ft.; El Paso Co., SE and E to Pecos,

Fig. 393. *Artemisia ludoviciana* (White Sage)

Crockett, Crane, and Ward counties; summer–fall; found over much of TX except extreme S areas. Widespread in temperate N.A.

Artemisia ludoviciana is extremely variable in leaf morphology, an aspect that has contributed to the considerable synonymy listed above, and the recognition of at least eight subspecies (Kartesz, 1994). The species is mostly herbaceous, being sometimes woody at the base.

TRIBE 7. SENECIONEAE CASS. GROUNDSEL TRIBE

Perennial or annual, herbs, shrubs, vines, or trees, glabrous or hairy. Leaves usually opposite, usually lobed, toothed, or pinnate. Heads solitary or in clusters; phyllaries in 1–2 series, usually equal or nearly so, separate or fused; receptacle naked; ray flowers present or absent, usually pistillate and fertile; ligules yellow or orange, white, or reddish, purple, or pink; disc flowers usually perfect, corollas yellow, white, or cyanic, usually 5-lobed; style branches usually flattened, apexes blunt or pointed and hairy. Achenes cylindrical, angled, or flattened, smooth or ribbed, glabrous or pubescent; pappus usually of 1–many series of slender bristles, these usually smooth, whitish or straw-colored.

A tribe of about 100 genera and 3000 species of worldwide distribution, as treated by Nordenstam (1977), but other authors (Turner and Powell, 1977) include additional species (e.g., *Perityle, Pericome*) in a broader concept of the Senecioneae. Robinson (1981) includes *Perityle, Pericome, Haploesthes,* and *Pseudoclappia* in the Heliantheae. Bremer (1994) places *Haploesthes* and *Pseudoclappia* in subtribe Flaveriinae of Helenieae, while retaining *Lepidospartum* in Senecioneae. *Senecio,* with 1500–2000 species of cosmopolitan distribution, is the largest genus of the tribe and of the entire family. About eight genera and 25 species occur in Texas, many of them in the Trans-Pecos.

KEY TO THE GENERA

1. Florets 3; prominent phyllaries 3, each subtending a floret; silvery-white shrub to 1 m high **1. Lepidospartum.**
1. Florets, phyllaries, and plants otherwise.
    2. Phyllaries in 3–4 crude series, uneven in length and unorganized
    2. Pseudoclappia.
    2. Phyllaries in 1–2 series, these rather even and organized.
        3. Phyllaries 5, in 1 series, broad, overlapping **3. Haploesthes.**
        3. Phyllaries 15–25, in 2 series **4. Senecio.**

1. LEPIDOSPARTUM (GRAY) GRAY SCALEBROOM

Shrubs to 0.7 m high, silvery-white from matted hairs on broomlike branches, stems with oil glands. Leaves alternate, needlelike to 1.2 cm long. Heads 1–4; phyllaries 10, outer 6–7 much reduced and overlapping in 3 irregular series, inner 3 much longer, rounded apically; ray flowers absent; disc flowers perfect, 3, each subtended by a phyllary; corolla 1 cm long, lobes 5. Achenes densely white-hairy; pappus of 30–40 bristles 8–9 mm long.

A genus of three species, distributed in the southwestern United States and northwestern Mexico. One species occurs in Texas.

1. **Lepidospartum burgessii** B. L. Turner. Fig. 394. A rare species known only from the gypsum dunes and low, stable, gypsum crust, Hudspeth Co., 10–13 mi E of Dell City and on the E margin of the dry lake bed in the area.

This whitish shrub is easily recognized by its pustulate (oil glands) stems, 3-flowered heads with each floret embraced by a phyllary, and achenes covered with white hairs (Turner, 1977).

2. PSEUDOCLAPPIA RYDB.

Shrubs or subshrubs, 0.2–0.8 m high, much-branched. Leaves opposite or alternate, often crowded, fleshy, nearly cylindrical, 1–2 cm long, glabrous. Heads solitary on erect peduncles; phyllaries in 3–4 unequal series, basically

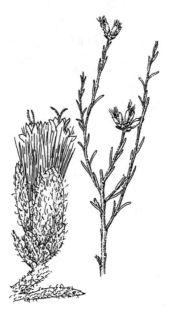

Fig. 394. *Lepidospartum burgessii*

linear, somewhat fleshy, glabrous; ray flowers 2–4 per head, pistillate, fertile, ligules linear, yellow; disc flowers 20–30, perfect, fertile, corollas yellow. Achenes darkish, 3–4 mm long, 10-ribbed, intermediate ribs weak, prominent ribs with short stiff hairs; pappus of numerous unequal bristles, these somewhat flattened, to 10 mm long, with minute barbs.

A genus of two species, distributed in southern New Mexico south to northern Mexico. Both species occur in Texas, one of them perhaps endemic.

KEY TO THE SPECIES

1. Strong, intricately branched, low shrub; dry, gypseous-clay soils
   1. *P. watsonii.*
1. Weak, fewer branched, low shrub; more mesic, saline-gypsum habitats
   2. *P. arenaria.*

1. **Pseudoclappia watsonii** Powell & B. L. Turner.   Somewhat barren clay hills, flats, and arroyos, moderately rocky and gypseous soils, known only from two localities. Hudspeth Co., 1 mi E of Tommy's Town, 14 mi E of McNary. Presidio Co., 53.8 mi N of Candelaria, road to Chispa, Sierra Vieja foothills. Spring–fall.

The two species of *Pseudoclappia* are similar. In addition to the habit and habitat differences listed above, *P. watsonii* has larger floral features than *P. arenaria*.

Fig. 395. *Pseudoclappia arenaria*

2. **Pseudoclappia arenaria** Rydb. Fig. 395. Relatively mesic saline-gypsum habitats in flats and along playa lakes in the desert. Culberson Co., lower bajada W of Patterson Hills. Reeves Co., 1 mi N Pecos. 3500 ft.; summer–fall. NM, Otero Co., White Sands Nat'l Mon.; reported from Coah., Mex.

3. HAPLOESTHES GRAY

Subshrubs, to 0.3–1.5 m high, basal stems herbaceous or woody, taproots woody, stems erect, essentially glabrous. Leaves opposite, linear to nearly threadlike, to 5 cm long. Heads in clusters; phyllaries 4–6 in 1 series, 3–5 mm long, drying dusky, to bluish or green, subequal, overlapping; ray flowers 5–8, pistillate, fertile; ligules yellow, 1–2 mm long; disc flowers perfect, fertile; corollas yellow, 5-toothed. Achenes blackish, 9–10 ribbed, cylindric; pappus of numerous bristles, buffy, unequal.

A genus of three species distributed from Oklahoma and southcentral New Mexico, south through parts of Texas, into Coahuila and Nuevo Leon, Mexico (Turner, 1975).

1. **Haploesthes greggii** Gray var. **texana** (Coult.) I. M. Johnst. FALSE-BROOMWEED. Fig. 396. [*Haplopappus texanus* Coult.] Locally common on gypsum outcrops, also present in saline-gypsum habitats, seemingly also in

Fig. 396. *Haploesthes greggii* (Falsebroomweed)

calcareous soils, but localized, and these also possibly gypseous. Reeves Co., near Pecos. Brewster Co., Chisos Mts. area, Grapevine Hills; Alamo Springs; 15 mi SE Castolon; Black Gap; near Terlingua Creek and elsewhere between Study Butte and Lajitas; 4 mi N Agua Fria; Packsaddle Mt.; lower slopes, Nine-Point Mesa; localized 35–65 mi S Alpine. Terrell Co., 4–10 mi E Sanderson; 30 mi NE Sanderson; S of Dryden. Val Verde Co., Pumpville turnoff; 20 mi W Langtry; near Devils River. 2000–4000 ft.; flowering most of the year; gypsum outcrops Ward, Winkler, Crane, and Ector counties. Isolated populations from near OK-KS border S through Plains Country, TX, to NE Trans-Pecos, Rio Grande Plains.

Two other varieties of this species are distributed in gypsum habitats in Coahuila and Nuevo Leon, Mexico, as are the other two species of the genus (Turner, 1975). Populations of *Haploethes greggii* var. *texana* in south Brewster Co., vicinity of Terlingua, have a larger, more upright habit and larger heads with more florets than do other populations of this widespread variety, and possibly deserve at least varietal status.

4. SENECIO L.   GROUNDSEL, RAGWORT, SQUAWWEED

Herbs or subshrubs. Leaves alternate, usually lobed or pinnatifid. Heads solitary or in clusters; phyllaries usually in 2 sizes, inner (longer) 12–25, linear equal, in 2 series; outer phyllaries (bracteoles) shorter needlelike or absent; ray

Fig. 397. *Senecio flaccidus* var. *flaccidus*
(Threadleaf Groundsel)

flowers pistillate, fertile; ligules yellow; disc flowers perfect, fertile; corolla yellow, 5-toothed. Achene cylindric, ribbed; pappus of numerous slender bristles.

A huge genus of 1500–2000 species, worldwide in distribution, perhaps the largest angiosperm genus. About 18 species occur in Texas, 10 of these in the Trans-Pecos. Only two species are treated here, but several regional species of *Senecio* are vigorous herbaceous perennials with woody caudexes, including *S. riddellii* T. & G., which in larger plants may have woody stems.

KEY TO THE SPECIES

1. Plants whitish, especially the upper parts covered with matted white hairs, in some the mats rather thin; heads 1 cm wide or less; other phyllaries (bracteoles) absent, or few, less than one-half as long as inner phyllaries
1. *S. flaccidus* var. *flaccidus.*

1. Plants greenish, mostly glabrous, or with thin mats of white hairs, rarely the herbage white (tomentose); heads usually more than 1 cm side; outer phyllaries prominent, some about one-half as long as inner phyllaries
2. *S. warnockii.*

1. **Senecio flaccidus** Less. var. **flaccidus** THREADLEAF GROUNDSEL. Fig. 397. [*Senecio douglasii* DC. var. *jamesii* (Torr. & Gray) Ediger; *S. doug-*

lasii DC. var. *longilobus* (Benth.) L. Benson; *S. filifolius* Nutt.]. Widespread and locally common especially in disturbed habitats and overgrazed rangelands, throughout most of the Trans-Pecos. El Paso Co. to Pecos Co. and S Brewster Co. 2500–6500 ft. E to Scurry and Crockett counties, rarely to Rio Grande Plains; widespread in W U.S.; extreme N Mex.

The Threadleaf Groundsel of the Trans-Pecos region has long been recognized by some authors as a distinct species, *Senecio longilobus*. The present treatment follows that of Turner and Barkley (1990) and Barkley (1978). This species is considered poisonous to livestock and is considered by some Trans-Pecos ranchers to be one of the most toxic and destructive rangeland weeds, along with locoweeds, in the area. Supposedly the plants are not usually eaten by livestock except in times of stress when the animals acquire a taste for the poisonous weeds. Natives along the United States-Mexican border are reported to use Threadleaf Groundsel (also called Gordolobos) medicinally, but this practice is extremely dangerous and should be discouraged because extracts of the plant are liver-toxic. The plants often form strong subshrubs or shrubs more than 1 m high, and when in full bloom with numerous yellow heads and whitish herbage are attractive plants with ornamental potential.

2. **Senecio warnockii** Shinners.   [*Senecio douglasii* DC. var. *douglasii*]. Locally abundant in gypseous soils. Culberson Co., 40 mi N Van Horn; between Orla and Texline. Hudspeth Co., perhaps elsewhere in the Trans-Pecos. 4000 ft.; Sep–Oct.

The above localities are recorded for the gypsum endemic populations of *Senecio warnockii* which Ediger (1970) regarded as an ecological phase of a widespread and variable *S. douglasii* DC. After studying the *S. flaccidus* complex (including *S. douglasii*), B. L. Turner (pers. comm.) has concluded that *S. warnockii* should be maintained as a distinct gypsum endemic species.

TRIBE 8. MUTISIEAE CASS.   MUTISIA TRIBE

Perennial or annual, herbs, subshrubs, shrubs, vines, or trees. Leaves usually alternate, simple, lobed, or divided. Heads solitary or in clusters; phyllaries usually multiseriate; receptacle mostly naked; ray flowers present or absent, when present pistillate or perfect, corollas typically 2-lipped; disc flowers usually perfect, typically 2-lipped with external lip 3-lobed and internal lip deeply 2-lobed; anthers typically sagittate; styles undivided or branched, apexes various. Achenes topshaped or obconic, glabrous or hairy; pappus usually of bristles, rough or feathery, in 1 or more series.

A tribe of 89 genera and about 974 species, distributed in tropical and subtropical regions in the Americas, Africa, Asia, Australia, and Hawaii (Cabrera, 1977). Only four genera and eight species occur in Texas, half of these in the

Fig. 398. *Trixis californica* (American Trixis)

Trans-Pecos, including members of *Acourtia* D. Don., *Perezia* Thunb., and *Chaptalia* Vent.

1. TRIXIS P. BR.

Shrubs, weak-stemmed, 0.5–2 m high. Leaves alternate, sessile, lanceolate or nearly so, the margins smooth or toothed, in our species short-hairy beneath and densely gland-dotted. Heads in clusters; phyllaries 8, linear-lanceolate; flowers perfect, fertile; corolla yellow, 2-lipped, ligulelike part 3-toothed, the 2 shorter parts pointed; anther cells with white appendage. Achenes 4–7 mm long, linear, minutely glandular-hairy, expanded apically; pappus of numerous stiff bristles, 1 cm long or more, persistent, off-white buffy.

A genus of about 35 species distributed in warmer regions of the New World. Only two species occur in Texas, one in the Trans-Pecos.

1. Trixis californica Kell. AMERICAN TRIXIS. Fig. 398. Common on slopes and in canyons, desertic mountains and foothills, less frequent at high elevations. El Paso Co., Franklin Mts. Culberson Co., Guadalupe Mts. Jeff Davis Co., Davis Mts. and foothills; Haystack Mt.; Musquiz Canyon. Presidio

Co., Chinati Mts., near Shafter, Pinto Canyon; 20 mi SW Alpine. Brewster Co., vicinity of Alpine S to Chisos Mts., Dead Horse Mts. 2700–6000 ft.; spring–fall. W to CA; N Mex.

American Trixis is easily recognized by its broad-lanceolate leaves with gland-dotted lower surfaces, yellow flowers, and conspicuous pappus. The generic name *Trixis* means "threefold" in reference to the 3-toothed, lower (ray-like) lip of the corolla. The plant is only occasionally browsed.

Selected Glossary

Achene (Akene). A small, dry, indehiscent, one-seeded, usually hard fruit in which the ovary wall is free from the seed.

Actinomorphic. Exhibiting radial symmetry, as a regular flower.

Acuminate. Gradually tapering to a diminishing point and with the margin bowing inward; long-pointed. Cf. *Acute, Attenuate.*

Acute. Sharp-pointed, but less tapering than acuminate.

Adhere. To stick fast or cleave. *Adherent:* Attached or joined, though naturally or normally separate.

Adnate. Grown together entirely or partially with an unlike part, as the calyx tube with an inferior ovary, or an anther by its whole length with the filament.

Adventitious. Out of the usual place, as a bud produced from the stem instead of in the axils of leaves.

Adventive. Applied to an introduced plant, not definitely established or naturalized.

Aerial. Epiphytic plants; plants or part of plants living above the surface of the ground or water.

Aggregate. Collected into dense clusters or tufts. *Aggregate Fruit:* one formed by the clustering together of pistils that were distinct in the flower, as blackberry.

Alkaline. Of, pertaining to, or having the properties of an alkali (a soluble mineral salt present in some soils of arid regions).

Allergenic. Having the substance to cause allergy or to cause it to become manifest.

Alluvial. Soils deposited by running water.

Alternate. Any arrangement of parts along the axis other than opposite or whorled; situated regularly between other organs, as stamens alternate with petals.

Ament. Catkin; a spike of flowers usually bracteate and frequently deciduous, as the male flowers of willow, beech, oak, etc.

Amorphous.   Shapeless, the form not regular or definite.

Angular, Angulate.   Angled. Used when an organ shows a determinate number of angles.

Annual.   Of one year's or season's duration from seed to maturity and death. *Winter Annual:* a plant from autumn-germinating seeds that fruits in the following spring.

Annular.   Circular; in the form of a ring or marked transversely by rings. *Annulate:* ringshaped.

Anther.   The pollen-bearing part of the stamen.

Anthesis.   Strictly, the time of expansion of the flower, but also used for the period during which the flower is open and functional.

Anthocarp.   A structure in which the fruit proper is united with the perianth or receptacle, as in Nyctaginaceae.

Antrorse (-ly).   Directed upward or forward.

Apetalous.   Without petals.

Apex.   Situated at the tip (pl. *Apexes*).

Apophysis.   An enlargement or swelling of the surface of an organ; the part of a cone scale that is exposed when the cone is closed.

Appendage.   Any attached supplementary or secondary part. *Appendiculate:* furnished with an appendage.

Appressed.   Pressed flat against another organ.

Arborescent.   Treelike in tendency.

Aril.   A process of the placenta adhering about the hilum of a seed. *Arillate:* with an aril.

Aromatic.   Fragrant, pungent, spicy to smell or taste.

Arroyo.   A water course, or channel or gully, often dry, carved by water.

Articulate.   Jointed; having a place for natural separation with a clean-cut scar.

Ascendent, Ascending.   Rising obliquely or curving upward.

Asepalous.   Without sepals.

Asexual.   Sexless; without sex; arising without the phenomenon of sex.

Attenuate.   Slenderly tapering or prolonged; more gradual than acuminate.

Auricle.   An earshaped appendage. *Auricular, Auriculate:* auricled.

Awlshaped.   Tapering from the base to a slender or stiff point.

Awn.   A terminal slender bristle on an organ.

Axial.   Relating to the morphological axis, as distinct from its appendages.

Axil.   Upper angle formed by a leaf or branch with the stem. *Axillary:* situated in the axil.

Axile.   Belonging to, or situated in, the axis.

Banner.   Upper petal of a papilionaceous flower.

Barbate.   Bearded with long stiff hairs.

Barbed.   Bearing sharp rigid reflexed points like barbs of a fish-hook. *Barbellate:* finely barbed, usually with short stiff hairs. *Barbule:* a small barb.

Basal. Relating to, or situated at, the base.

Basifixed. Attached by the base.

Beak. A prolonged firm tip, particularly of a seed or fruit. *Beaked:* ending in a beak.

Bearded. Bearing long stiff hairs.

Berry. A pulpy indehiscent fruit with no true stone, as the tomato.

Biennial. Of two years' duration from seed to maturity and death.

Bifid. Two-cleft to about the middle.

Bifurcate. Two-forked or -pronged.

Bilabiate. Two-lipped (calyx or corolla).

Bilobed. Divided into two lobes. *Bilobulate:* the diminutive.

Bilocular. Two-celled.

Bipartite. Divided into two parts almost to the base; two-parted.

Bipinnate. Doubly or twice pinnate; when both primary and secondary divisions of a leaf are pinnate. *Bipinnatifid:* twice pinnately cleft; with the divisions extending deeply but not to the rachis or midvein.

Bisexual. Having both sexes on the same individual; a hermaphrodite.

Blade. The expanded part of a leaf or petal.

Bloom. (Cf. *Glaucous.*) The waxy or powderlike covering of many fruits and leaves.

Bract. A reduced leaf subtending a flower, usually associated with an inflorescence. *Bracteate:* provided with bracts.

Bractlet. A secondary bract borne on a pedicel instead of subtending it; sepaloid subtending the sepals in many Rosaceae. *Bracteolate:* with bractlets.

Bristle. A stiff hair. *Bristly:* bearing stiff strong hair or bristles.

Bud. An underdeveloped stem, leaf, or flower. Buds are often enclosed by reduced or specialized leaves termed bud scales.

Bulb. An underground leaf bud with thickened scales or coats like the onion.

Bundle Sheaths. In pines the sheath at the base of leaf bundles (fascicles).

Bush. See *Shrub.*

Caducous. Falling off very early or prematurely.

Calcareous. Containing an excess of available calcium, usually in the form of the compound calcium carbonate; "Limy."

Caliche. A crust of calcium carbonate formed on stony soils in arid regions.

Calyculate. Bearing bracts around the calyx imitating an outer involucre in some Asteraceae. *Calyculum:* the involucre simulating an additional calyx; a whorl of bracts outside the true calyx.

Calyx (pl. *Calyxes* or *Calyces*). The external, usually green, whorl of a flower, contrasted with the inner showy corolla.

Calyx Lobe. In a gamosepalous calyx, the free projecting parts.

Campanulate. Bellshaped.

Canescent. Covered with grayish-white or hoary fine hairs.

Capitate.   Headshaped; aggregated into very dense clusters or heads. *Capitulum* (-*a*): See *Head.*

Capsule.   A dry dehiscent fruit composed of more than one carpel. *Capsular:* pertaining to a capsule; formed like a capsule.

Carpel.   A simple pistil, or one of the modified leaves forming a compound pistil. *Carpellate:* possessing carpels.

Catkin.   A scaly deciduous spike; ament.

Caudate.   Bearing a tail or slender taillike appendage. ·

Caudex. (pl. *Caudices*).   The woody base of an otherwise herbaceous perennial.

Caulescent.   With an obvious leafy stem; plants with radical leaves and flowers on a scape are called acaulescent.

Cauline.   Belonging to the stem.

Cell.   A cavity of an anther containing the pollen, or of an ovary containing the ovules.

Chartaceous.   With the texture of stiffish writing paper.

Cinereous.   Ash-colored; light-gray. *Cinereo-:* used in combination to denote gray-.

Circumscissile.   Dehiscing by a transverse line around the fruit or anther, the top falling as a lid.

Clavate.   Clubshaped; gradually thickened toward the apex from a slender base. *Claviform:* clubshaped.

Claw.   The narrow petiolelike base of some petals and sepals. *Clawed:* with a claw.

Cleft.   Cut about halfway to the midrib.

Cleistogamous, Cleistogamic.   Small flowers self-fertilizing without opening; usually additional to the ordinary flower and inconspicuous, as in some violets. *Cleistogamy:* the condition described.

Coalescent.   Said of organs of one kind that have grown together. *Coalesce:* to form union by growth.

Coccus (pl. *Cocci*).   A berry; in particular one of the parts of a lobed fruit with one-seeded cells; part of a schizocarp or lobed fruit.

Coherent.   Congenitally united with another organ of the same kind (*Coalescent*), or of another kind (*Adnate*). *Cohere:* to become coherent.

Columella.   The persistent axis of certain capsules.

Column.   Body formed by union of stamens in mallows and milkweeds. *Columnar:* having the form of a column.

Coma.   A tuft of hairs, particularly at the end of some seeds. *Comose:* furnished with a coma.

Complete.   Having all the parts belonging to it, as a flower with sepals, petals, stamens, and pistils.

Complicate.   Folded together.

Compound.   Having two or more similar parts in one organ. *Compound Leaf:*

one with two or more separate leaflets. *Compound Pistil:* having two or more carpels united or at least coalescent.

Compressed.   Flattened laterally.

Concave.   Hollow, as the bowl of a spoon. *Concavity:* an existing hollow.

Cone.   The "fruit" of a pine or fir-tree with scales forming a strobile; an inflorescence of "fruit" with overlapping scales. *Conoid:* conelike.

Conic, Conical.   Coneshaped, with the point of attachment at the broad base.

Connate.   Congenitally united, as similar organs joined as one.

Connective.   Portion of the filament connecting the two cells of an anther.

Constricted.   Tightened or drawn together.

Contracted.   Narrowed in a particular place, or shortened; the opposite of open or spreading (inflorescence).

Convex.   Rounded on the surface.

Convolute.   Rolled up longitudinally. Said of blades or floral envelopes in the bud when one edge is outside and the other inside.

Cordate.   Heartshaped with the notch at the base and ovate in general outline. *Cordiform:* shaped like a heart.

Coriaceous.   Leathery in texture; tough.

Corm.   A short, bulblike, underground stem, as the "bulb" of a gladiolus.

Corneous.   Of the texture of horn.

Corolla.   The inner perianth of a flower, composed of colored petals, which may be almost wholly united. *Corolline, Corolloid:* belonging to a corolla, corollalike, or seated on a corolla.

Corona.   A crown. *Coroniform:* crownshaped. *Coronate:* crowned; having a crown.

Corymb.   An indeterminate flat-topped or convex racemose flower cluster, the lower or outer pedicels longer, their flowers opening first. *Corymbiform:* shaped like a corymb. *Corymbose:* arranged in corymbs.

Crenate.   Having the margin cut with rounded teeth; scalloped. *Crenulate:* the diminutive.

Cuneate, Cuneiform.   Wedgeshaped; triangular, with the narrow part at point of attachment.

Cupule.   The cup of such fruits as the acorn; an involucre composed of bracts adherent by their base at least. *Cupulate, Cupular:* cupshaped, as the cup (involucre) of the acorn.

Cusp.   A sharp, rigid point. *Cuspidate:* tipped with a cusp, or short, rigid point.

Cyathium (pl. *Cyathia*).   The ultimate inflorescence of *Euphorbia*, consisting of a cuplike involucre bearing the flowers from its base.

Cylindraceous, cylindric.   Somewhat or nearly cylindrical. *Cylindroid:* of a cylindric shape. *Cylindro-*. Used in various combinations to denote cylindric.

Cyme.   A determinate flower cluster in which the first flower is terminal on the main axis, the next flower(s) terminal on axes arising from the axils of bracts subtending the first flower, and so on; often cymes are flat-topped or convex.

Cymose.   Arranged in cymes.

Deciduous.   Falling off, as petals fall after flowering, or leaves of nonevergreen trees in autumn or said of plants whose leaves fall, as in "deciduous tree."

Dehiscent, Dehisce, Dehiscence.   Opening spontaneously when ripe to discharge the contents, as an anther or seed vessel.

Deltoid, Deltate.   Equilaterally triangular.

Dentate: Having the margin cut with sharp salient teeth not directed forward. *Denticulate:* slightly and finely toothed.

Diadelphous.   Stamens united by their filaments into two sets.

Didynamous.   With four stamens in two pairs of unequal length as in most Lamiaceae.

Dioecious.   Having staminate and pistillate flowers in different plants.

Discoid.   Disklike, in the Asteraceae, a head without ray florets. *Disciform:* flat and circular like a disk.

Disk, Disc.   A fleshy development of the receptacle about the base of the ovary; in Asteraceae, the tubular flowers (disk florets) of the head as distinct from the ray.

Dissected.   Deeply divided into numerous usually fine segments.

Distinct.   Separate; not united with parts in the same cycle. Cf. *Free.*

Dorsifixed.   Attached by or to the back.

Drupe.   A fleshy one-seeded indehiscent fruit containing a stone with a kernel; a stone-fruit such as a plum. *Drupelet:* a diminutive drupe. *Drupaceous:* resembling a drupe, possessing its character, or producing similar fruit.

Ebracteate.   Without bracts.

Edaphic.   Pertaining to, influenced by, soil conditions.

Elliptic.   In the form of a flattened circle usually more than twice as long as broad. *Ellipsoid:* an elliptic solid.

Elongate.   Drawn out in length.

Emarginate.   With a small notch at the apex.

Embryo.   The incipient plantlet in the seed.

Endemic.   Confined to a given region, as a country or island. *Endemism:* the condition of endemic plants.

Endosperm.   The nutritive tissue surrounding the embryo of a seed and formed within the embryo sac.

Entire.   Undivided; the margin continuous, not incised or toothed.

Envelope.   The surrounding part. *Enveloping:* involucrate; to enclose.

Epappose.   Without pappus.

Epetiolate.   Without petals.

Ephemeral.   Lasting for a day or less.

Epidermis. The true cellular skin or covering of a plant below the cuticle. *Epidermal:* relating to the epidermis.

Epigynous. Borne on the ovary; said of floral parts when the ovary is wholly inferior. *Epigyny:* the state of having epigynous flowers.

Epipetalous. Borne upon the petals.

Epiphyte, Epiphytic. Characterized by growing on other plants or objects but not parasitically, such as orchids, bromeliads, and ferns.

Erose. Irregularly toothed as if gnawed.

Escape. A cultivated plant found growing as though wild, dispersed by some agency.

Evergreen. Remaining green through the winter.

Excrescence. Small warty outgrowth.

Excurrent. Projecting beyond the edge, as the midrib of a mucronate leaf or nerve of a floral segment.

Falcate. Sickleshaped. *Falciform:* sicklelike.

Farina. Starch or starchy matter. *Farinaceous:* containing starch; mealy in texture. *Farinose:* covered with a mealiness.

Fascicle. A close cluster or bundle of flowers, leaves, stems or roots. *Fasciculate:* in a fascicle.

Fibrous. Having numerous woody fibers, as the scales of some bulbous plants.

Filament. A thread, especially the stalk of an anther. *Filamentous:* formed of filaments or fibers.

Filiform. Threadlike.

Fimbriate. Fringed (with longer or coarser hairs as compared with ciliate). *Fimbrillate:* the diminutive.

Fissured. To be cracked or fractured, as the bark of a tree.

Flabelliate, Flabelliform. Fanshaped, broadly wedgeshaped.

Flaccid. Weak, limp, soft or flabby.

Fleshy. Thick and juicy; succulent.

Flexuous, Flexuose. Zigzag, bending alternately in opposite directions. *Flexed:* to be alternately bent.

Flora. The aggregate of plants of a country or district, or a work which contains the enumeration of them.

Floral. Of or pertaining to flowers. *Floral Tube* (or *Cup*): a more or less elongate tube consisting of perianth or other floral parts.

Floret. The individual flower of the Asteraceae; a small flower of a dense cluster.

Foliaceous. Leaflike; said especially of sepals or bracts that in texture or appearance resemble leaves. *Foliar:* leafy or leaflike. *Foliose:* having numerous leaves.

Foliage. The leafy covering, especially of trees.

Follicetum.   A whorl or glomerule of follicles sometimes more or less coalescent at base.

Follicle.   A dry fruit with one carpel, opening only on the ventral suture. *Follicular:* shaped like a follicle.

Free.   Not joined to other organs; the reverse of adnate.

Fruit.   The ripened pistil with all its accessory parts.

Frutescent, Fruticose.   Shrubby or bushy in the sense of being woody. *Fruticulose:* applied to a little shrub.

Fulvous.   Dull yellow.

Funnelform.   Gradually widening upwards, like a funnel.

Furrowed.   With longitudinal channels or grooves; striate on a large scale; sulcate.

Fusiform.   Spindleshaped; thickest near the middle and tapering toward each end.

Gamopetalous.   Corolla with petals united. Same as sympetalous and monopetalous.

Gamophyllous.   Composed of coalescent leaves or leaflike organs.

Gamosepalous.   Calyx with sepals united.

Glabrous.   Without hairs. *Glabrate:* almost glabrous; tending to be glabrous. *Glabrescent:* becoming glabrous.

Glaucous.   Covered or whitened with a bloom, as a cabbage leaf; bluish-white or bluish-gray. *Glaucescent:* becoming glaucous.

Globose.   Spherical or rounded. *Globular:* somewhat or nearly globose. *Globule:* a little globe; a small spherical particle.

Glochid.   A barbed hair or bristle. *Glochidiate:* barbed at the tip, as a bristle.

Glomerate.   Densely compacted in clusters or heads. *Glomerule:* a compact capitate cymme. *Glomerulate:* arranged in small clusters.

Glutinous.   With a gluey exudation.

Gynobasic.   Applied to a style which adheres by its base to a prolongation upwards of the receptacle between carpels.

Habit.   General appearance of a plant.

Habitat.   The normal situation in which a plant lives.

Halophyte.   A plant of salty or alkaline soils. *Halophytic* (adj.).

Hastate.   Halberdshaped; of the shape of an arrowhead but with the basal lobes turned outward.

Head.   A dense globular cluster of sessile or subsessile flowers arising essentially from the same point on the peduncle; capitulum.

Helicoid, Helical.   Curved or spiraled like a snail shell.

Hemi-.   In composition means half.

Hemispheric, Hemispheroidal.   Shaped like half of sphere.

Herb.   A plant without persistent woody stem, at least above ground.

Herbaceous.   Pertaining to a herb; opposed to woody; having the texture or color of a foliage leaf; dying to the ground each year.

Herbage.   Collectively, the green parts of a plant.

Herbarium.   A collection of dried and pressed plants, usually mounted on strong sheets of rag paper or otherwise prepared for permanent preservation, and usually systematically arranged.

Hesperidium.   A superior, polycarpellary, syncarpous berry, pulpy within, and externally covered with a tough rind, as an orange.

Hilum.   The scar at the point of attachment of an ovule or seed. *Hilar:* relating to the hilum.

Hip.   The fruit of the rose; technically a cynarrhodium.

Hirsute.   Rough with coarse or shaggy hairs. *Hirsutulous* (-ose): the diminutive. *Hirtellous:* minutely hirsute.

Hispid.   Rough with stiff or bristly hairs. *Hispidulous* (-ose): the diminutive. *Hispidulo-:* used in combination to denote stiff or bristly hairs.

Horny.   Hard or dense in texture.

Husk.   The outer covering of certain fruits or seeds, as in the Juglandaceae.

Hyaline.   Colorless or translucent, rarely transparent.

Hypanthium.   A cupshaped enlargement of the receptacle on which the calyx, corolla, and often the stamens are inserted; in perigyny the "calyx tube."

Igneous.   Resulting from the action of intense heat, as igneous rock.

Imbricate.   Overlapping as shingles on a roof.

Incised.   Cut rather deeply and sharply.

Inferior.   Lower or beneath. *Inferior Ovary:* one that is abnate to the hypanthium and situated below the calyx lobes.

Inflated.   Blown up; bladdery.

Inflorescence.   The flower cluster of a plant, or, more correctly, the disposition of the flowers on an axis.

Inrolled.   Rolled inward.

Inserted.   Attached to or growing upon.

Insertion.   The place or mode of attachment of an organ to its support.

Internode.   The portion of stem between two nodes. *Internodal* (adj.).

Intra-.   A prefix used to denote within.

Introduced.   Brought from another region.

Introrse.   Turned inward, towards the axis.

Invaginate.   To enclose in a sheath. *Invagination:* enclosing in a sheath.

Involucel.   A secondary involucre.

Involucre.   A whorl of bracts (phyllaries) subtending a flower cluster, as in the heads of Asteraceae. *Involucral:* pertaining to an involucre. *Involucrate:* having an involucre.

Irregular.   Showing a lack of uniformity; asymmetric, as a zygomorphic flower.

Keel.   A prominent longitudinal ridge, analogous to the keel of a boat; the two lower and united petals of a papilionaceous corolla.

Lacerate.   Appearing irregularly torn or cleft.

Lanceolate, Lance.   Lanceshaped; much longer than broad, tapering from below the middle to the apex and (more abruptly) to the base.

Leaflet.   A segment of a compound leaf.

Legume.   The seed vessel of Fabaceae, one-celled and two-valved, but various in form; a superior one-celled fruit of a simple pistil usually dehiscent into two valves, having the seeds attached along the ventral suture; a leguminous plant.

Leguminous.   Pertaining to a legume or the family Fabaceae.

Lenticular.   Lensshaped. *Lenticulate* (adj.).

Lepidote.   Covered with small scurfy scales; scurfy; furfuraceous.

Ligneous.   Woody. *Lignescent:* somewhat woody or becoming woody.

Linear.   Resembling a line; long and narrow, of uniform width, as the leaf blade of grasses.

Lip.   One of the two divisions of a bilabiate corolla or calyx, hence an upper lip and a lower lip, although one lip may be wanting.

Lobe.   A division or segment of an organ, usually rounded or obtuse; cut less than halfway to the midrib (of a leaf). *Lobed:* bearing lobes.

Locule. Loculus.   Compartment of cell or pistil or anther.

Loculicidal.   Dehiscent longitudinally through the middle of the back of a pericarp, between the partitions into the cavity.

Lustrous.   Shining, having a sheen.

Male (plant or flowers).   Having stamens but no pistils.

Malpighiaceous Hairs.   Straight appressed hairs attached by the middle and tapering to the free tips.

Marginal.   Of, pertaining to, or attached to the edge.

Membrane, Membranaceous, Membranous.   Of the nature of a membrane; thin, soft and pliable.

-merous.   Greek suffix, having parts, as pentamerous or 5-merous, having 5 parts.

Mesa.   A flattopped hill with abrupt or steeply sloping side or sides.

Mesic.   Characterized by or pertaining to conditions of medium moisture supply.

Micropyle.   The minute orifice in the integuments of an ovule through which the pollen enters the seed cavity. *Micropylar:* relating to the micropyle.

Midrib.   The central rib of a leaf or other organ.

Monadelphous.   Stamens united by their filaments into a tube surrounding the gynoecium, as in malvaceous flowers.

Monoecious. Having staminate and pistillate flowers on the same plant but not perfect ones.

Mucro, Mucronation. A small and short abrupt tip of an organ, as the projection of the midrib of a leaf. *Mucronate:* with a mucro. *Mucronulate:* minutely mucronate.

Muricate, Murication. Rough with short and firm sharp excrescences. *Muriculate:* the diminutive.

Naked. With a usual covering wanting, as a flower destitute of a perianth.

Naturalized. Of foreign origin, but established and reproducing itself as though a native.

Nectary. The organ in which nectar is secreted, formerly applied to any anomalous part of a flower, as its spurred petal. *Nectariferous:* nectar bearing; having a nectary, or an organ which secretes nectar.

Needle(s). Stiff, linear leaves as in Pinaceae.

Node. The joint of a stem; the point of insertion of a leaf or leaves.

Nut. A hard-shelled and one-seeded indehiscent fruit derived from a simple or compound ovary.

Nutlet. Diminutive of nut; applied to any small and dry nutlike fruit or seed. Thicker walled than an achene.

Ob-. Latin prefix signifying the reverse or contrariwise.

Obcordate. Inversely cordate, the notch at the apex.

Obdeltoid. Inversely deltoid.

Oblanceolate. Inversely lanceolate.

Oblate. Flattened at the poles.

Oblique. Of unequal sides (as in leaves), slanting.

Oblong. Much longer than broad with nearly parallel sides.

Obovate. Inversely ovate.

Obovoid. Inversely ovoid.

Obsolete. Rudimentary or not evident; applied to an organ that is almost entirely suppressed; vestigial. *Obsolescent:* becoming rudimentary or extinct.

Obtuse. Blunt or rounded at the end.

Odd-pinnatifid. Pinnately cleft, with an unpaired terminal leaflet and the lateral leaflets without a distinct petiolule and the rachis winged between them.

Opposite. Set against, as leaves when two at a node; one part before another, as a stamen in front of a petal.

Orbicular, Orbiculate. Approximately circular in outline.

Oval. Broadly elliptic.

Ovary. The part of the pistil that contains the ovules.

Ovate. With the outline of an hen's egg in longitudinal section, the broader end downward.

Ovoid.   Solid ovate or solid oval.

Ovule.   The megasporangium of a seed plant; the body in the ovary which becomes a seed. *Ovulate, Ovuliferous:* bearing ovules.

Palmate.   Handshaped with the fingers spread; in a leaf, having the lobes or divisions radiating from a common point.

Panicle.   A compound racemose inflorescence. *Paniculate:* borne in a panicle. *Paniculiform:* panicleshaped.

Papilionaceous.   Applied to the butterflylike corolla of the pea, with banner, wings, and keel.

Papilla (-ae).   A minute nippleshaped projection. *Papillate, Papillose:* bearing minute conical processes, or papillae. *Papillary:* resembling papilla. *Papilliform:* shaped like a papilla.

Pappus.   The modified calyx limb in Asteraceae, consisting of a crown of bristles or scales on the summit of the achene.

Parasite.   An organism subsisting on another, the host. *Parasitic:* deriving nourishment from another organism.

Pectinate.   With narrow closely set divisions like the teeth of a comb.

Pedicel.   The stalk of a single flower in a flower cluster or of a spikelet in grasses. *Pedicelled, Pedicellary, Pedicellate:* having a pedicel, as opposed to sessile.

Peduncle.   The general term for the stalk of a flower or a cluster of flowers. *Pedunculate, Peduncular:* having a peduncle. *Pedunculiform:* in the form of a peduncle.

Pendant, Pendulous.   Suspended or hanging, as an ovule that hangs from the side of the locule; nodding.

Peltate.   Shieldshaped, with stalk attachment in middle of the flat body.

Perfect.   A flower having both stamens and pistils.

Perianth.   The floral envelopes collectively; usually used when calyx and corolla are not clearly differentiated.

Pericarp.   The ripened walls of the ovary, referring to a fruit. *Pericarpial:* in reference to, or like, a pericarp.

Perigynous.   Borne around the ovary in contrast to beneath it, as the stamens and corolla are inserted on the floral tube.

Persistent.   Remaining attached, as a calyx on the fruit.

Petal.   One of the leaves of a corolla, usually colored. *Petaline:* pertaining to a petal; attached to, or resembling a petal. *Petaloid:* having the aspect of or colored as petals. *Petaliferous:* bearing petals.

Petiole.   A leaf stalk. *Petiolate:* having a petiole. *Petiolar:* borne on or pertaining to a petiole.

Pilose.   Bearing soft and straight spreading hairs. *Pilosulous (-ose):* the diminutive. *Pilosity:* Hairiness.

Pinna (-ae).   A leaflet or primary division of a pinnate leaf.

Pinnate. A compound leaf, having the leaflets arranged on each side of a common petiole; featherlike. *Odd-pinnate:* pinnate with a single terminal leaflet (imparipinnate). *Abruptly Pinnate:* pinnate without an odd terminal leaflet (paripinnate).

Pinnatifid. Pinnately cleft into narrow lobes not reaching to the midrib.

Pistil. The ovule-bearing organ of a flower, consisting of stigma and ovary, usually with a style between.

Pistillate. Provided with pistils and without stamens; female.

Placenta (-ae). The ovule-bearing surface in the ovary. *Placentary:* a placenta that is long and narrow and bears many ovules. *Placentation:* the arrangement or orientation of the placentas.

Plumose. Feathery; having fine hairs on each side as a plume.

Pod. Any dry dehiscent fruit; specifically a legume.

Pome. An applelike fruit.

Prickle. Sharp outgrowth of the bark or epidermis. *Prickly:* armed with prickles, as the rose.

Puberulent. Minutely pubescent. *Puberulous:* slightly hairy.

Pubescent, Pubescence. Covered with short soft hairs; downy.

Punctate. Dotted with punctures or with translucent pitted glands or with colored dots. *Puncticulate (-ose):* the diminutive.

Pungent. Ending in a rigid, sharp point or prickle; acrid (to the taste or smell).

Pyriform. Pearshaped.

Raceme. A simple, elongated, indeterminate inflorescence with each flower subequally pedicelled. *Racemiform, Racemose:* of the nature or shape of a raceme or in racemes.

Rachis. The axis of a spike or raceme, or of a compound leaf.

Radial. Belong to the ray, as in the flowers of Asteraceae.

Ray. A primary branch of an umbel; the ligule of a ray floret in Asteraceae, the ray florets being marginal and differentiated from the disk florets.

Receptacle. That portion of the floral axis upon which the flower parts are borne, or, in Asteraceae, that which bears the florets in the head. *Receptacular:* pertaining to the receptacle or attached to the receptacle.

Regular. Said of a flower having a radial symmetry, with the parts in each series alike.

Remote. Distantly spaced.

Reniform. Kidneyshaped.

Repand. Weakly sinuate.

Resin Duct. A definitive space or canal, e.g., as seen in cross-sections of pine needles, in which resin is secreted.

Reticulate. With a network; net-veined.

Retrorse. Bent backward or downward.

Revolute.   Rolled backward from both margins, i.e., toward the underside.

Rhizome.   An underground stem or rootstock, with scales at the nodes and producing leafy shoots on the upper side and roots on the lower side. *Rhizomatous:* having a rhizome.

Rhombic.   Somewhat diamondshaped. *Rhombiform:* rhombshaped. *Rhomboidal:* a solid with a rhombic outline.

Rib.   The primary vein of a leaf, or a ridge on a fruit. *Ribbed:* with prominent ribs.

Rosette.   A crowded cluster of radiating leaves appearing to rise from the ground.

Rostrate.   Beaked. *Rostellate:* the diminutive.

Rotate.   Wheelshaped; said of a sympetalous corolla with obsolete tube and with a flat and circular limb.

Sac.   The cavity of an anther; a pouch or bag. *Saccate:* furnished with a sac or pouch.

Sagitate.   Shaped as an arrowhead, with the basal lobes turned downward. Cf. *Hastate. Sagittiform:* arrowshaped.

Saline.   Of, or pertaining to salt; growing in salt marshes.

Salverform.   A corolla with slender tube abruptly expanding into a flat limb.

Samara.   An indehiscent winged fruit.

Saponaceous.   Soapy, slippery to the touch. *Saponifying:* to convert into soapiness.

Scabrous.   Rough to the touch, owing to the structure of the epidermis or to the presence of short stiff hairs. *Scabrid:* somewhat rough. *Scabridulous:* slightly rough. *Scabrate:* made rough or roughened.

Scale.   Any thin scarious bract; usually a vestigial leaf. *Scaly:* squamose; scarious.

Scape.   A leafless peduncle rising from the ground in acaulescent plants. *Scapiform, Scapose:* resembling or bearing a scape.

Scarious.   Thin, dry, and membranaceous, not green.

Schizocarp.   A pericarp that splits into 1-seeded portions, mericarps.

Scorpioid.   Said of a unilateral inflorescence circinately coiled in the bud.

Scrub.   Stunted or densely packed bushes; stunted due to want of water, with strong transpiration.

Scurfy.   Clothed with small branlike scales; furfuraceous.

Seed.   The ripened ovule.

Sepal.   A leaf or segment of the calyx. *Sepaline:* relating to or resembling sepals. *Sepaloid:* sepallike.

Septicidal.   Dehiscence of a capsule through the septa and between the locules.

Septum (-a).   A partition between cavities. *Septate:* divided by partitions or septa.

Serrate. Saw-toothed, the sharp teeth pointing forward. *Serrulate:* finely serrate.

Sessile. Attached directly by the base; not stalked, as a leaf without petiole.

Seta (-ae). A bristle, or a rigid, sharp-pointed, bristlelike organ. *Setaceous, Setose:* clothed with bristles. *Setiform:* in the shape of a bristle. *Setulose:* bearing minute bristles.

Shrub. A woody plant of smaller proportions than a tree, which usually produces several branches from the base.

Silique. A narrow many-seeded capsule of the Brassicaceae, with 2 valves splitting from the bottom and leaving the placentae with the false partition (replum) between them. *Silicle:* a short silique, not much longer than wide.

Simple. Unbranched, as a stem or hair; uncompounded, as a leaf; single, as a pistil of one carpel.

Sinuate, Sinuous. With a strongly wavy margin. Cf. *Repand.*

Smooth. Not rough to the touch; Cf. *Glabrous,* without hairs, which may be either smooth or scabrous.

Solitary. Borne singly.

Spatulate. Like a spatula, a knife rounded above and gradually narrowed to the base.

Spike. An elongated rachis of sessile flowers or spikelets. *Spikelet:* a secondary spike. *Spicule:* a diminutive or secondary spike.

Spine. A sharp-pointed, stiff, woody body, arising from below the epidermis; commonly the counterpart of a leaf or stipule. Cf. *Prickle. Spinescent:* more or less spiny, spine-tipped. *Spiniferous:* bearing spines. *Spinous, Spinose:* bearing spines. *Spinulose:* bearing diminutive spines.

Squarrose. Spreading rigidly at right angles or more, as the tips of bracts.

Stalk. The stem of any organ, as the petiole, peduncle, pedicel, filament, culm, or stipe.

Stamen. The male organ of the flower, which bears the pollen.

Staminate, Staminal. Having stamens but not pistils; said of a flower or plant that is male, hence is not seed-bearing.

Staminode (-ia, -ium). A sterile stamen (not producing viable pollen) or what corresponds to a stamen.

Standard. The upper petal of a papilionaceous flower.

Stellate. Starshaped. *Stellular, Stellulate:* resembling a little star or stars.

Stigma. The receptive part of the pistil on which the pollen germinates. *Stigmatal, Stigmatic:* pertaining to the stigma.

Stipule. One of the pair of usually foliaceous appendages found at the base of the petiole in many plants. *Stipulate, Stipular:* possessing stipules.

Stomate. A breathing pore or aperture in the epidermis.

Stone. The bony endocarp of a drupe. *Stone Cells:* the individual cells that have become hardened by secondary deposit, the components of sclerogen.

Style. The contracted portion of the pistil between the ovary and the stigma. *Style Branches* may be only in part stigmatic, the remainder then being appendage. *Stylar:* relating to the style. *Styliferous:* bearing a style.

Subulate. Awlshaped. *Subuliferous:* bearing sharp points.

Succulent. Juicy; fleshy and soft.

Suffrutescent. Obscurely shrubby; very little woody, but not necessarily low. *Suffruticose, Suffruticulose.* With only the lower parts of the stems woody, the upper stems herbaceous and annual. Cf. *Fruticulose.*

Sulcate. Longitudinally grooved, furrowed or channeled.

Superior. Growing above, as an ovary that is free from the other floral organs.

Symmetrical. Possessing one or more planes of symmetry (i.e., planes which divide the object into mirrow-image halves).

Sympetalous. With petals united in a one-piece corolla; gamopetalous.

Syncarp. A multiple or fleshy aggregate fruit, as the mulberry or magnolia.

Tendril. A slender, coiling or twining organ by which a climbing plant grasps its support.

Tepal. Used in the plural for sepals and petals of similar form and not readily differentiated, as in Agavaceae.

Terete. Cylindrical; round in cross section.

Terminal. Proceeding from, or belonging to, the end or apex.

Thorn. Cf. *Spine,* but technically a sharp-pointed stiff woody body derived from a modified branch.

Throat. The orifice of a gamopetalous corolla; the expanded portion.

Tomentose. With tomentum; covered with a rather short, densely matted, soft white wool. *Tomentulose:* the diminutive. *Tomentum:* a covering of such densely matted woolly hairs.

Tooth. Any small marginal lobe. *Toothed:* dentate.

Tree. A woody plant with one main stem, and at least four or five meters tall.

Trichome. Any hairlike outgrowth of the epidermis, as a hair or bristle.

Trifid. Three-cleft to about the middle.

Trifoliate. Having three leaves, as in *Trillium. Trifoliolate:* with three leaflets.

Truncate. As if cut off squarely at the end.

Trunk. The main stem of a tree.

Tube. The narrow basal portion of a gamopetalous corolla or a gamosepalous calyx. *Tubiform:* tubular or trumpetshaped.

Tuber. A thickened, solid, and short underground stem with many buds. *Tuberous, Tuberiferous:* bearing a tuber; resembling a tuber. *Tuberiform:* shaped like a tuber. *Tuberoid:* said of a fleshy-thickened root, resembling a tuber.

Tubercle. A small tuberlike prominence or nodule; the persistent base of the style in some Cyperaceae. *Tubercled, Tuberculate:* beset with tubercles or warty excrescences; verrucose. *Tuberculose:* consisting of or having tubercles.

Tuft, Tufted. Cespitose, clustered or clumped.
Turbinate. Topshaped; inversely conical.
Turgid. Swollen; inflated.

Umbel. A flat or convex flower cluster in which the pedicels arise from a common point, like rays of an umbrella.
Umbo, Umbone. A boss or protuberance. *Umbonate:* bearing an umbo or boss or conical projection in the center, as the scale of a pine cone.
Undulate. Wavy; repand; with less pronounced "waves" than sinuate.
Unilocular. Having one locule or cell.
Unisexual. Flowers having only stamens or pistils; of one sex.
Urceolate. Urnshaped or pitcherlike, contracted at the mouth.
Utricle. A small, bladdery one-seeded fruit. *Utricular:* having little bladders; inflated.

Valve. One of the segments into which a dehiscent capsule or legume separates. *Valvate, Valvular:* opening as if by valves, as most capsules and some anthers; in flower buds, meeting at the edges without overlapping.
Venation. The arrangement of the veins of a leaf; nervation; veining. *Venose:* veiny, abounding in veins. *Venulose:* abounding in veinlets.
Versatile. An anther attached near the middle and capable of swinging freely on the filament.
Vesicle. A little bladder or air cavity. *Vesicular:* pertaining to, or having the form of, a vesicle. *Vesiculate: Vesiculous:* as if composed of little bladders.
Vestigial. Reduced to a vestige or trace of a part or organ originally more perfectly developed.
Villous (-ose). Bearing long and soft and not matted hairs; shaggy. *Villosity:* shagginess, a coating of long weak hairs.
Viscid, Viscous. Sticky; glutinous. *Viscidulous:* slightly viscid.

Whip Leaves. Leaves of distal branches, whips, as in junipers.
Whorl. A ring of similar organs radiating from a node; verticil.
Woolly. Having long, soft, entangled hairs; lanate. Cf. *Tomentose.*

Xeric. Characterized by or pertaining to conditions of scanty moisture supply.
Xerophyte. A drought-resistant or desert plant. *Xerophytic* (adj.).

Zygomorphic, Zygomorphous. Bilaterally symmetrical as an irregular flower; that which can be bisected by only one plane into similar halves. *Zygomorphy:* state of being zygomorphic.

Literature Cited

Adams, R. P. 1973. Reevaluation of the biological status of *Juniperus deppeana* var. *sperryi* Correll. Brittonia 25:284–289.

Adams, R. P. 1975. Numerical-chemosystematic studies of infraspecific variation in *Juniperus pinchotii*. Biochem. Syst. and Ecology 3:71–74.

Adams, R. P. 1977. Chemosystematics—analyses of populational differentiation and variability of ancestral and recent populations of *Juniperus ashei*. Ann. Missouri Bot. Gard. 64:184–209.

Adams, R. P. 1993. Nomenclatural note: *Juniperus coahuilensis* (Martinez) Gaussen *ex* R. P. Adams. Phytologia 74:413

Adams, R. P. 1994. Geographic variation and systematics of monospermous *Juniperus* (Cupressaceae) from the Chihuahua Desert based on RAPDs and terpenes. Biochem. Syst. and Ecol. 22:699–710.

Adams, R. P. and J. R. Kistler. 1991. Hybridization between *Juniperus erythrocarpa* Cory and *Juniperus pinchotii* Sudworth in the Chisos Mountains, Texas. Southwest. Nat. 36:295–301.

Adams, R. P. and T. A. Zanoni. 1979. The distribution, synonymy, and taxonomy of three Junipers of southwestern United States and northern Mexico. Southwest. Nat. 24:323–329.

Anderson, L. C. 1980. Morphology and biogeography of *Chrysothamnus nauseous* ssp. *texensis* (Asteraceae): A new Guadalupe Mountains endemic. Southwest. Nat. 25: 197–206.

Argus, G. W. and C. L. McJannet. 1992. A taxonomic reconsideration of *Salix taxifolia* sensu lato (Salicaceae). Brittonia 44:461–474.

Bailey, D. K. and F. G. Hawksworth. 1979. Pinyons of the Chihuahuan Desert Region. Phytologia 44:129–133.

Barkley, T. M. 1978. *Senecio*. *In* North American Flora Series II, part 10. 50–139. New York Botanical Garden.

Barneby, R. C. 1977. *Dalea Imagines*. Mem. N.Y. Bot. Gard. 27:1–892.

Barneby, R. C. 1986. Notes on some Mimosae (Leguminosae: Mimosoideae) of the Chihuahuan Desert akin to *M. zygophylla*. Brittonia 38:4–8.

Barneby, R. C. 1991. Sensitivae Censitae. Mem. N. Y. Bot. Gard., vol. 65. N. Y. Bot. Gard., Bronx.

Barneby, R. C. and D. Isely. 1986. Reevaluation of *Mimosa biuncifera* and *M. texana* (Leguminosae: Mimosoideae). Brittonia 38:119–122.

Baum, B. R. 1967. Introduced and naturalized Tamarisks in the United States and Canada (Tamaricaceae). Baileya 15:19–25.

Benson, L. 1982. The Cacti of the United States and Canada. Stanford Univ. Press, Stanford, California.

Benson, L. and R. A. Darrow. 1954. Trees and Shrubs of the Southwestern Deserts. 3rd ed., Univ. of Arizona Press, Tucson.

Benson, L. and R. A. Darrow. 1981. Trees and Shrubs of the Southwestern Deserts. 3rd ed., Univ. of Arizona Press, Tucson.

Bremer, K. 1994. Asteraceae Cladistics and Classification. Timber Press, Portland, Oregon.

Burgess, T. L. 1979. *Agave*—Complex of the Guadalupe Mountains National Park; Putative hybridization between members of different subgenera. *In* Genoways, H. H. and R. J. Baker, Biological Investigations in the Guadalupe Mountains National Park. National Park Service, Proceedings Series Number Four.

Burgess, T. L. and D. K. Northington. 1981. Plants of the Guadalupe Mountains and Carlsbad Caverns National Parks. An annotated checklist. Chihuahuan Desert Research Institute, Contrib. No. 107.

Burt-Utley, K. and J. F. Utley. 1987. Contributions toward a revision of *Hechtia* (Bromeliaceae). Brittonia 39:37–43.

Cabrera, A. L. 1977. Mutisieae—systematic review. V. H. Heywood, J. B. Harborne, and B. L. Turner (eds.). *In* The Biology and Chemistry of the Compositae. Vol. 2:1039–1066.

Chiang, C. F. 1981. A taxonomic study of the North American species of *Lycium* (Solanaceae). Ph.D. Dissertation, Univ. of Texas, Austin.

Carlquist, S. 1976. Tribal interrelationships and phylogeny of the Asteraceae. Aliso 8:465–492.

Castetter, E. F., W. H. Bell, and A. R. Grove. 1938. The early utilization and distribution of *Agave* in the American southwest. Univ. N. Mex. Bull. 335, 92 pp.

Clarke, H. D., D. S. Seigler, and J. E. Ebinger. 1989. *Acacia farnesiana* (Fabaceae: Mimosoideae) and related species from Mexico, the southwestern U. S., and the Caribbean. Syst. Bot. 14:549–564.

Correll, D. S. and M. C. Johnston. 1970. Manual of the Vascular Plants of Texas. Texas Research Foundation, Renner, Texas.

Cronquist, A. 1964. *Salix. In* C. L. Hitchcock and A. Cronquist, Vascular Plants of the Pacific Northwest. 2:37–70.

Cronquist, A. 1977. The Compositae revisited. Brittonia 29:137–153.

Cronquist, A. 1981. An Integrated System of Classification of Flowering Plants. Columbia University Press, New York.

Dahling, G. V. 1978. Systematics of *Garrya*. Contrib. Gray Herb. 209:1–104.

Daniel, T. F. 1980. Range extensions of *Carlowrightia* (Acanthaceae) and a key to the species of the United States. Southwest. Nat. 25:425–26.

Dempster, L. T. 1992. A nomenclatural change in *Symphoricarpos* (Caprifoliaceae). Madroño 39:77–78.

Dodd, R. J. and Y. B. Linhart. 1994. Reproductive consequences of interactions between

Yucca glauca (Agavaceae) and *Tegiticula yuccasella* in Colorado. Amer. J. Bot. 81: 815–825.

Ferguson, D. J. 1986. *Opuntia chisosensis* (Anthony) comb. nov. Cactus and Succulent J. 58:124–127.

Ferguson, D. J. 1988. *Opuntia macrocentra* Eng. and *Opuntia chlorotica* Eng. & Big. Cactus and Succulent J. 60:155–160.

Eckenwalder, J. E. 1977. North American cottonwoods (*Populus*, Salicaceae) of sections *Abaso* and *Aigeiros*. J. Arnold Arb. 58:193–208.

Ediger, R. I. 1970. Revision of section *suffruticosi* of the genus *Senecio* (Compositae). Sida 3:504–524.

Flyr, D. L. 1970. A systematic study of the tribe Leucophylleae (Scrophulariaceae). Ph.D. dissertation, Univ. of Texas, Austin.

Fryxell, P. A. 1975. *Batesimalva y Meximalva*, dos generos nuevos de Malvaceas Mexicanas. Bol. Soc. Bot. Mex. 35:23–36.

Gehlbach, F. R. and R. C. Gardner. 1983. Relationships of sugarmaples (*Acer saccharum* and *A. grandidentatum*) in Texas and Oklahoma with special reference to relict populations. Tex. J. Sci. 35:231–237.

Gentry, H. S. 1972. The Agave Family in Sonora. Agriculture Handbook No. 399. USDA, U. S. Gov. Printing Office, Washington, DC.

Gentry, H. S. 1982. Agaves of Continental North America. Univ. of Ariz. Press, Tucson.

Gibson, A. C. 1979. Anatomy of *Koeberlinia* and *Canotia* revisited. Madroño 26:1–12.

Gillis, W. T. 1971. The systematics and ecology of poison-ivy and the poison-oaks (*Toxicodendron*, Anacardiaceae). Rhodora 73:72–159; 161–237; 371–443; 465–540.

Gonsoulin, G. J. 1974. A revision of *Styrax* (Styracaceae) in North America, Central America, and the Caribbean. Sida 5:191–258.

Gould, F. W. 1962. Texas Plants—A Checklist and Ecological Summary. Texas Agricultural Experiment Station, Texas A&M University.

Hall, H. M. 1928. The genus *Haplopappus*. Carnegie Institution of Washington, Pub. No. 389.

Heil, K. D. and S. Brack. 1988. The cacti of Big Bend National Park. Cactus and Succulent J. 60:17–34.

Heisey, R. M. 1996. Identification of an allelopathic compound from *Ailanthus altissima* (Simaroubaceae) and characterization of its herbicidal activity. Amer. J. Bot. 83: 192–200.

Henrickson, J. 1972. A Taxonomic revision of the Fouquieriaceae. Aliso 7:439–537.

Henrickson, J. 1977. Saline habitats and halophytic vegetation of the Chihuahuan Desert Region. *In* Wauer and Riskind, Transactions of the Symposium on the Biological Resources of Chihuahuan Desert. U.S. Dept. Interior, NPS, No. 3.

Henrickson, J. 1985. A taxonomic revision of *Chilopsis* (Bignoniaceae). Aliso 11: 179–197.

Henrickson, J. 1986a. Notes on Rosaceae. Phytologia 60:468.

Henrickson, J. 1986b. *Anisacanthus quadrifidus sensu lato* (Acanthaceae). Sida 11: 286–299.

Henrickson, J. 1988. A revision of the *Atriplex acanthocarpa* complex (Chenopodiaceae). Southwest. Nat. 33:451–463.

Henrickson, J. 1996. Studies in *Macrosiphonia* (Apocynaceae): Generic recognition of *Telosiphonia*. Aliso 14:179–195.

Henrickson, J. and T. F. Daniel. 1979. Three new species of *Carlowrightia* (Acanthaceae) from the Chihuahuan Desert region. Madroño 26:26–36.

Henrickson, J. and S. Sundbeg. 1986. On the submersion of *Dicraurus* into *Iresine* (Amaranthaceae). Aliso 11:355–364.

Hess, W. J. and J. Henrickson. 1987. A taxonomic revision of *Vauquelinia* (Rosaceae). Sida 12:101–163.

Heywood, V. H., J. B. Harborne, and B. L. Turner (eds.). 1977. The Biology and Chemistry of the Compositae. Vols. I and II. Academic Press, London.

Heywood, V. H. and C. J. Humphries. 1977. Anthemideae—systematic review. *In* V. H. Heywood, J. B. Harborne, and B. L. Turner (eds.), The Biology and Chemistry of the Compositae. Vol. 2:851–898. Academic Press, New York.

Holmgren, N. H. 1988. *Glossopetalon* (Crossosomataceae) and a new variety of *G. spinescens* from the Great Basin, U.S.A. Brittonia 40:269–274.

Hopkins, C. O. and W. H. Blackwell. 1977. Synopsis of *Suaeda* (Chenopodiaceae) in North America. Sida 7:147–173.

Horton, J. S. 1977. The development and perpetuation of the permanent Tamarisk type in the phreatophyte zone of the Southwest. *In* Importance, Preservation, and Management of Riparian Habitat: A Symposium. USDA Forest Service, Report RM-43.

Hu, S. Y. 1954–56. A monograph of the genus *Philadelphus*. Journal of the Arnold Arboretum 35:275–333; 36:52–109, 325–368; 37:15–90.

Hutchinson, J. 1934. The Families of Flowering Plants. Vol. II. Monocotyledons. Macmillan, London.

Isely, D. 1972. Legumes of the U.S. VI. *Calliandra, Pithecellobium, Prosopis*. Madroño 21:273–298.

Isely, D. 1973. Leguminosae of the United States: I. Subfamily Mimosoidae. Mem. N. Y. Bot. Gard. 25:1–152.

Johnson, R. R. 1969. Monograph of the plant genus *Porophyllum* (Compositae: Helenieae). Univ. of Kansas Sci. Bull. 48:225–267.

Johnston, M. C. 1969. Rhamnaceae. *In* Flora of Texas II:357–392.

Johnston, M. C. 1974. *Acacia emoryana* in Texas and Mexico and its relationship to *A. berlandieri* and *A. greggii*. Southwest. Nat. 19:331–333.

Johnston, M. C. 1975. Synopsis of *Canotia* (Celastraceae) including a new species from the Chihuahuan Desert. Brittonia 27:119–122.

Johnston, M. C. 1990. The Vascular Plants of Texas, an update. Second Edition. 3905 Ave. G., Austin, Texas 78751.

Jones, G. N. 1945. *Malacomeles*, a genus of Mexican and Guatemalan shrubs. Madroño 8:33–64.

Kartesz, J. T. 1994. A Synonymized Checklist of the Vascular Flora of the United States, Canada, and Greenland. Second edition, vol. 1. Timber Press, Portland, Oregon.

Kearney, T. H. and R. H. Peebles. 1951. Arizona Flora. Univ. Calif. Press, Berkeley.

Key, L. 1980. Where rainbows wait for rain. *In* The Chihuahuan Desert Discovery, March, No. 7, Chihuahuan Desert Research Institute, Alpine, TX.

King, R. M. and H. Robinson. 1975. II. Eupatorieae, *In* Flora of Panama. Ann. Missouri Bot. Gard. 62:888–1004.

King, R. M. and H. Robinson. 1987. The Genera of the Eupatorieae (Asteraceae). Monographs in Systematic Botany, vol. 22. Missouri Botanical Garden, St. Louis.

Kral, R. 1993. *Pinus*, pp. 373–398. *In* Flora of North America, North of Mexico, vol. 2. Oxford University Press, New York.

Lane, M. A. 1979. Taxonomy of the genus *Amphiachyris* (Asteraceae: Astereae). Systematic Botany 4:178–189.

Lane, M. A. and R. L. Hartman. 1996. Reclassification of North American *Haplopappus* (Compositae: Astereae) completed: *Rayjacksonia* gen. nov. Amer. J. Bot. 83:356–370.

Lawrence, J. G., A. Colwell, and O. J. Sexton. 1991. The ecological impact of allelopathy in *Ailanthus altissima* (Simaroubaceae). Amer. J. Bot. 78:948–958.

Lee, Y. S., D. S. Seigler, and J. E. Ebinger. 1989. *Acacia rigidula* (Fabaceae) and related species in Mexico and Texas. Syst. Bot. 14:91–100.

Lersten, N. R. and J. D. Curtis. 1995. Two foliar idioblasts of taxonomic significance in *Cercidium* and *Parkinsonia* (Leguminosae: Caesalpinioideae. Amer. J. Bot. 82:565–570.

Luckow, M. 1993. Monograph of *Desmanthus* (Leguminosae-Mimosoideae). Syst. Bot. Monographs 38:1–166.

Mahler, W. F. and U. T. Waterfall. 1964. *Baccharis* (Compositae) in Oklahoma, Texas, and New Mexico. Southwest. Nat. 9:189–202.

Miller, G. N. 1955. The genus *Fraxinus*, the Ashes, in North America, north of Mexico. Cornell Experiment Station Memoir 335. Cornell Univ., Ithaca, N.Y.

Muller, C. H. 1941. The Holacanthoid plants of North America. Madroño 6:128–132.

Nesom, G. 1989. New species, new sections, and a taxonomic overview of American *Pluchea* (Compositae: Inulae). Phytologia 67:158–167.

Nesom, G. L. 1990. Taxonomic summary of *Ericameria* (Asteraceae: Astereae), with the inclusion of *Haplopappus* sects. *Macronema* and *Asiris*. Phytologia 68:144–155.

Nesom, G. L. 1994. Review of the taxonomy of *Aster* sensu lato (Asteraceae: Astereae), emphasizing the New World species. Phytologia 77:141–297.

Nesom, G. L. and G. I. Baird. 1993. Completion of *Ericameria* (Asteraceae: Astereae), diminution of *Chrysothamnus*. Phytologia 75:74–93.

Nesom, G. L., Y. Suh, D. R. Morgan, and B. B. Simpson. 1990. *Xylothamia* (Asteraceae: Astereae), a new genus related to *Euthamia*. Sida 14:101–116.

Nesom, G. L., Y. Suh, D. R. Morgan, S. D. Sundberg, and B. B. Simpson. 1991. *Chloracantha*, a new genus of North American Astereae (Asteraceae). Phytologia 70:371–381.

Nixon, K. C. and C. H. Muller. 1992. The taxonomic resurrection of *Quercus laceyi* Small (Fagaceae). Sida 15:57–69.

Nixon, K. C. and C. H. Muller. 1993. The *Quercus hypoxantha* complex (Fagaceae) in northeastern Mexico. Brittonia 45:146–153.

Nordenstam, B. 1977. Senecionae and Liabeae—systematic review. *In* V. H. Heywood, J. B. Harborne, and B. L. Turner (eds.), The Biology and Chemistry of the Compositae. Vol. 2:799–830.

Northington, D. K. and T. L. Burgess. 1979. Status of rare and endangered plant species of the Guadalupe Mountains National Park, Texas. *In* Genoways, H. H. and R. J. Baker, Biological Investigations in the Guadalupe Mountains National Park, Texas. National Park Service Proceedings Series Four.

Parfitt, B. D. 1991. Biosystematics of the *Opuntia polyacantha* complex (Cactaceae) of western North America. Ph. D. dissertation, Arizona State University, Tempe.

Parfitt, B. D. and D. J. Pinkava. 1988. Nomenclatural and systematic reassessment of *Opuntia engelmannia* and *O. lindheimeri* (Cactaceae). Madroño 35:342–349.

Pinkava, D. J. and B. D. Parfitt. 1988. Nomenclatural changes in Chihuahuan Desert *Opuntia* (Cactaceae). Sida 13:125–130.

Porter, D. M. 1974. Disjunct distributions in the New World Zygophyllaceae. Taxon 23: 339–346.

Powell, A. M. 1969. Taxonomy of *Perityle* section *Pappothrix* (Compositae—Peritylanae). Rhodora 71:58–93.

Powell, A. M. 1973. Taxonomy of *Perityle* section *Laphamia* (Compositae—Helenieae—Peritylinae). Sida 5:61–128.

Powell, A. M. 1974. Taxonomy of *Perityle* section *Perityle*. Rhodora 76:229–306.

Powell, A. M. 1988. Trees and shrubs of Trans-Pecos Texas. Big Bend Natural History Association, Big Bend National Park, TX.

Powell, A. M., S. A. Powell, and A. S. Tomb. 1977. Cytotypes in *Cevallia sinuata* (Loasaceae). Southwest. Nat. 21:433–441.

Powell A. M., and B. L. Turner. 1977. Aspects of the plant biology of the gypsum outcrops of the Chihuahuan Desert. *In* Wauer, R. H. and D. H. Riskind, Transactions of the Symposium on the Biological Resources of the Chihuahuan Desert. U.S. Dept. of Interior, NPS No. 3.

Ralston, B. E. and R. A. Hilsenbeck. 1989. Taxonomy of the *Opuntia schottii* complex (Cactaceae) in Texas. Madroño 36:221–231.

Ralston, B. E. and R. A. Hilsenbeck. 1992. *Opuntia densispina* (Cactaceae): A new club cholla from the Big Bend region of Texas. Madroño 39:281–284.

Richardson, A. 1976. Reinstatement of the genus *Tiquilia* (Boraginaceae: Ehretioideae) and descriptions of four new species. Sida 6:235–240.

Robinson, H. 1977. An analysis of the characters and relationships of the tribes Eupatorieae and Vernonieae (Asteraceae). Systematic Botany 2:199–208.

Robinson, H. 1981. A revision of the tribal and subtribal limits of the Heliantheae (Asteraceae). Smithsonian Contrib. to Botany, No. 51, 1–102 pp.

Robinson, H. and R. M. King. 1977. Eupatorieae—systematic review. *In* V. H. Heywood, J. B. Harborne, and B. L. Turner (eds.), The Biology and Chemistry of the Compositae. Vol. 1:437–485. Academic Press, New York.

Sanderson, S. C. and H. C. Stutz. 1994. High chromosome numbers in Mojavean and Sonoran Desert *Atriplex canescens* (Chenopodiaceae). Amer. J. Bot. 81:1045–1053.

Schmidly, D. J. 1977. The Mammals of Trans-Pecos Texas. Texas A&M University Press, College Station.

Schmidt, R. H. 1979. A climatic delineation of the "real" Chihuahuan Desert. J. Arid Environments 2:243–250.

Schmidt, R. H. 1985. Where is the Chihuahuan Desert? Chihuahuan Desert Discovery, CDRI, No. 17, Spring 1985.

Simpson, B. J. 1988. A Field Guide to Texas Trees. Texas Monthly Press, Austin.

Simpson, B. B. 1989. Krameriaceae. Flora Neotropica, monograph 49. New York Bot. Gard., N.Y.

Smith, S. D. and J. A. Ludwig. 1976. Reproductive and vegetative growth patterns in *Yucca elata* Engelm. Southwest. Nat. 21:177–184.

Spellenberg, R. 1995. On the hybrid nature of *Quercus basaseachicensis* (Fagaceae, sect. *Quercus*). Sida 16:427–437.

Strother, J. L. 1977. Tageteae—systematic review. *In* V. H. Heywood, J. B. Harborne, and B. L. Turner (eds.), The Biology and Chemistry of the Compositae. Vol. 2:769–783. Academic Press, New York.

Strother, J. L. 1986. Renovation of *Dyssodia* (Compositae: Tageteae). Sida 11:371–378.

Strother, J. L. 1991. Taxonomy of *Complaya, Elaphandra, Iogeton, Jefea, Wamalchitamia, Wedelia, Zexmenia,* and *Zyzyxia* (Compositae—Heliantheae—Ecliptinae). System. Bot. Monographs, vol. 33, pp. 1–111. American Society of Plant Taxonomists, University of Michigan Herbarium, Ann Arbor.

Sundberg, S. D. 1991. Infraspecific classification of *Chloracantha spinosa* (Benth.) Nesom (Asteraceae) Astereae. Phytologia 70:382–391.

Throne, R. F. and R. Scogin. 1978. *Forsellesia* Greene (*Glossopetalon* Gray), a third genus in the Crossosomataceae, Rosineae, Rosales. Aliso 9:71–178.

Tunnell, C. 1981. Wax, Men, and Money: A Historical and Archeological Study of Candelilla Wax Camps along the Rio Grande Border of Texas. Office of the State Archeologist Report 32, Texas Historical Commission, Austin.

Turner, B. L. 1959. The Legumes of Texas. Univ. of Texas Press, Austin.

Turner, B. L. 1975. Taxonomy of *Haploesthes* (Asteraceae-Senecioneae). Wrightia 5:108–115.

Turner, B. L. 1977. *Lepidospartum burgessii* (Asteraceae, Senecioneae), a remarkable new gypsophilic species from Trans-Pecos Texas. Wrightia 5:354–355.

Turner, B. L. 1991. An overview of the North American species of *Menodora* (Oleaceae). Phytologia 71:340–356.

Turner, B. L. and T. M. Barkley. 1990. Taxonomic overview of the *Senecio flaccidus* complex in North America, including *S. douglasii*. Phytologia 68:51–55.

Turner, B. L. and A. M. Powell. 1977. Helenieae—systematic review. *In* V. H. Heywood, J. B. Harborne, and B. L. Turner (eds.), The Biology and Chemistry of the Compositae. Vol. 2:669–737. Academic Press, New York.

Ullrich, B. 1992. On the history of *Agave asperrima* and *A. scabra* (Agavaceae) as well as some taxa of the *Parryanae*. Sida 15:241–261.

Urbatsch, L. E. 1978. The Chihuahuan Desert species of *Ericameria* (Compositae: Astereae). Sida 7:298–303.

Van Devender, T., C. E. Freeman, and R. D. Worthington. 1978. Full-glacial and recent vegetation of Livingston Hills, Presidio County, Texas. Southwest. Nat. 23:289–302.

Van Devender, T. R. and D. H. Riskind. 1979. Late Pleistocene and early Holocene plant remains from Hueco Tanks Historical Park: The development of a refugium. Southwest. Nat. 24:127–140.

Van Devender, T. R. and W. G. Spaulding. 1979. Development of vegetation and climate in the Southwestern United States. Science 204:701–710.

Vasek, F. C. 1980. Creosote bush: long-lived clones in the Mojave Desert. Amer. J. Bot. 67:246–255.

Vines, R. A. 1960. Trees, Shrubs, and Woody Vines of the Southwest. Univ. of Texas Press, Austin.

Warnock, B. H. 1970. Wildflowers of the Big Bend Country Texas. Sul Ross State University Press, Alpine, Texas.

Warnock, B. H. 1974. Wildflowers of the Guadalupe Mountains and the Sand Dune Country, Texas. Sul Ross State University Press, Alpine, Texas.

Warnock, B. H. 1977. Wildflowers of the Davis Mountains and Marathon Basin, Texas. Sul Ross State University Press, Alpine, Texas.

Weedin, J. F. and A. M. Powell. 1978. Chromosome numbers in Chihuahuan Desert Cactaceae. Trans-Pecos Texas. Amer. J. Bot. 65:531–537.

Wells, P. V. 1966. Late Pleistocene vegetation and degree of pluvial climatic change in the Chihuahuan Desert. Science 153:970–975.

Wendt, T. 1979. Notes on the genus *Polygala* in the United States and Mexico. J. Arnold Arb. 60:504–514.

Wendt, T. 1993. A new variety of *Ephedra torreyana* (Ephedraceae) from west Texas and Chihuahua, with notes on hybridization in the *E. torreyana* complex. Phytologia 74: 141–150.

Weniger, D. 1984. Cacti of Texas and Neighboring States. University of Texas Press, Austin.

Williams, J. K. 1995. Miscellaneous notes on *Haplophyton* (Apocynaceae: Plumerieae: Haplophytinae). Sida 16:469–475.

Worthington, R. D. 1989. An annotated checklist of the native and naturalized flora of El Paso County, TX. El Paso Southwest Miscellany No. 1, El Paso, TX.

Worthington, R. D. 1990. Additions to the flora of Texas from El Paso County. Sida 14: 135–137.

Worthington, R. D. 1995. Biota of the Franklin Mountains. Part II. Flora. Report to Texas Parks and Wildlife Department, Austin.

Index

CPSIA information can be obtained
at www.ICGtesting.com
Printed in the USA
FSOW02n1620130115
4504FS

9 780292 765733